中国孔子基金会
泰山学者工程专项经费资助

周易英译

Illuminating the Book of Changes and Its Intentionality

温海明 著

［英］寇哲明
何　圆　译

山东友谊出版社·济南

图书在版编目（CIP）数据

周易英译 / 温海明著；（英）寇哲明，何圆译. -- 济南：山东友谊出版社，2024.12. -- ISBN 978-7-5516-3325-3

Ⅰ.B221

中国国家版本馆 CIP 数据核字第2024DG5047号

周易英译
ZHOUYI YING YI

责任编辑：孙　锋　肖　杉
装帧设计：刘一凡

主管单位：山东出版传媒股份有限公司
出版发行：山东友谊出版社
　　　　　地址：济南市英雄山路189号　邮政编码：250002
　　　　　电话：出版管理部（0531）82098756
　　　　　　　　发行综合部（0531）82705187
　　　　　网址：www.sdyouyi.com.cn
印　　刷：济南乾丰云印刷科技有限公司

开本：710mm×1000 mm　1/16
印张：42.25　　　　　　　　　字数：1261千字
版次：2024年12月第1版　印次：2024年12月第1次印刷
定价：158.00元

《周易英译》编委会

学术顾问：安乐哲　陈　来
主　　任：国承彦
副 主 任：周　静　郭思克　刘　皓　朱瑞显
　　　　　米怀勇　温海明　孔德立
委　　员：张国强　王　丽　丁加军　彭彦华　张　旻
　　　　　李　青　于素月　路则权　常　强　袁　春

主　　编：国承彦
副 主 编：刘　皓　温海明
译　　者：寇哲明（Benjamin Michael Coles）　何　圆
编　　辑：孟　贞　王盛宇　李祉炜　曲怡盈　张小宇童
　　　　　刘科迪　胡继月　邹紫玲　唐　军　庞子文
　　　　　郝梦起　王　硕　陈建军　高小慧

目 录
contents

第一章　导论——《周易》哲学的人天之意 ················ 1
Chapter I Introduction: Humanity-Heaven Intentionality in the Philosophy of the *Book of Changes* ················ 1

一、《周易》是中国哲学与文化的总源头 ················ 3
I. The *Book of Changes* as the Source of Chinese Philosophy and Culture ················ 3

二、《周易》的原理与基础 ················ 8
II. The Principles and Foundation of the *Book of Changes* ················ 8

三、《周易》的内在结构 ················ 15
III. The Internal Structure of the *Book of Changes* ················ 15

四、《周易》的卦爻符号系统 ················ 23
IV. The Symbolic System of Hexagrams and Lines in the *Book of Changes* ················ 23

五、《周易》的经与传 ················ 35
V. The Classic and Commentaries of the *Book of Changes* ················ 35

六、明解《周易》的方法 ················ 43
VI. Methods for Elucidating the *Book of Changes* ················ 43

七、《周易》的哲学——人天之意 ················ 53
Ⅶ. The Philosophy of the *Book of Changes*: Human-Cosmological Intentionality ················ 53

第二章　易经明意——爻意分说（上经） ········· 71
Chapter Ⅱ Illuminating the *Classic of Changes* and Its Intentionality: Exposition of the Intentionality of the Lines（Part Ⅰ）······················ 71

乾为天（卦一）（乾下乾上）···························· 73
Qian (Creativity), Heaven (Hexagram 1)　(Qian below, Qian above) ········· 73

坤为地（卦二）（坤下坤上）···························· 88
Kun (Support), Earth (Hexagram 2)　(Kun below, Kun above)············· 88

水雷屯（卦三）（震下坎上）··························· 101
Zhun (Emergence), Water and Thunder (Hexagram 3)　(Zhen below, Kan above)········ 101

山水蒙（卦四）（坎下艮上）··························· 109
Meng (Youthful Ignorance), Mountain and Water (Hexagram 4)　(Kan below, Gen above) ··· 109

水天需（卦五）（乾下坎上）··························· 119
Xu (Waiting), Water and Heaven (Hexagram 5)　(Qian below, Kan above) ········ 119

天水讼（卦六）（坎下乾上）··························· 129
Song (Disputation), Heaven and Water (Hexagram 6)　(Kan below, Qian above) ········ 129

地水师（卦七）（坎下坤上）··························· 139
Shi (Leading), Earth and Water (Hexagram 7)　(Kan below, Kun above) ········· 139

水地比（卦八）（坤下坎上）··························· 148
Bi (Affinity), Water and Earth (Hexagram 8)　(Kun below, Kan above) ········· 148

风天小畜（卦九）（乾下巽上）·························· 157
Xiaoxu (Small Savings), Wind and Heaven (Hexagram 9)　(Qian below, Xun above) ········· 157

天泽履（卦十）（兑下乾上）··························· 168
Lü (Tracking), Heaven and Lake (Hexagram 10)　(Dui below, Qian above) ········· 168

地天泰（卦十一）（乾下坤上）·························· 178
Tai (Communication), Earth and Heaven (Hexagram 11)　(Qian below, Kun above) ········ 178

天地否（卦十二）（坤下乾上）·· 188
Pi (Non-Communication), Heaven and Earth (Hexagram 12)　(Kun below, Qian above) ······ 188

天火同人（卦十三）（离下乾上）·· 198
Tongren (Comradeship), Heaven and Fire (Hexagram 13)　(Li below, Qian above) ········· 198

火天大有（卦十四）（乾下离上）·· 207
Dayou (Great Wealth), Fire and Heaven (Hexagram 14)　(Qian below, Li above) ········· 207

地山谦（卦十五）（艮下坤上）·· 215
Qian (Humility), Earth and Mountain (Hexagram 15)　(Gen below, Kun above) ·········· 215

雷地豫（卦十六）（坤下震上）·· 223
Yu (Enjoyment), Thunder and Earth (Hexagram 16)　(Kun below, Zhen above) ·········· 223

泽雷随（卦十七）（震下兑上）·· 231
Sui (Following), Lake and Thunder (Hexagram 17)　(Zhen below, Dui above) ············ 231

山风蛊（卦十八）（巽下艮上）·· 239
Gu (Corruption), Mountain and Wind (Hexagram 18)　(Xun below, Gen above) ·········· 239

地泽临（卦十九）（兑下坤上）·· 248
Lin (Presence), Earth and Lake (Hexagram 19)　(Dui below, Kun above)················ 248

风地观（卦二十）　坤下巽上）·· 256
Guan (Observation), Wind and Earth (Hexagram 20)　(Kun below, Xun above) ·········· 256

火雷噬嗑（卦二十一）（震下离上）·· 265
Shihe (Punishment), Fire and Thunder (Hexagram 21)　(Zhen below, Li above) ········· 265

山火贲（卦二十二）（离下艮上）·· 274
Bi (Decoration), Mountain and Fire (Hexagram 22)　(Li below, Gen above)············· 274

山地剥（卦二十三）（坤下艮上）·· 284
Bo (Peeling), Mountain and Earth (Hexagram 23)　(Kun below, Gen above) ············ 284

地雷复（卦二十四）（震下坤上）·· 292
Fu (Returning), Earth and Thunder (Hexagram 24)　(Zhen below, Kun above) ········· 292

天雷无妄（卦二十五）（震下乾上） ················· 301
Wuwang (Non-Delusion), Heaven and Thunder (Hexagram 25)
(Zhen below, Qian above) ················· 301

山天大畜（卦二十六）（乾下艮上） ················· 311
Daxu (Accumulation), Mountain and Heaven (Hexagram 26)　(Qian below, Gen above) ······ 311

山雷颐（卦二十七）（震下艮上） ················· 319
Yi (Nourishment), Mountain and Thunder (Hexagram 27)　(Zhen below, Gen above) ······ 319

泽风大过（卦二十八）（巽下兑上） ················· 329
Daguo (Great Excess), Lake and Wind (Hexagram 28)　(Xun below, Dui above) ······ 329

坎为水（卦二十九）（坎下坎上） ················· 337
Kan (In Danger), Water (Hexagram 29)　(Kan below, Kan above) ················· 337

离为火（卦三十）（离下离上） ················· 348
Li (Illumination), Fire (Hexagram 30)　(Li below, Li above) ················· 348

第三章　易经明意——爻意分说（下经） ················· 359

Chapter Ⅲ　Illuminating the *Classic of Changes* and Its Intentionality: Exposition of the Intentionality of the Lines (Part II) ················· 359

泽山咸（卦三十一）　（艮下兑上） ················· 361
Xian (Resonance), Lake and Mountain (Hexagram 31)　(Gen below, Dui above) ······ 361

雷风恒（卦三十二）（巽下震上） ················· 369
Heng (Constancy), Thunder and Wind (Hexagram 32)　(Xun below, Zhen above) ······ 369

天山遁（卦三十三）（艮下乾上） ················· 378
Dun (Retreat), Heaven and Mountain (Hexagram 33)　(Gen below, Qian above) ······ 378

雷天大壮（卦三十四）（乾下震上）·················· 386
Dazhuang (Exuberance), Thunder and Heaven (Hexagram 34) (Qian below, Zhen above) ··· 386

火地晋（卦三十五）（坤下离上）·················· 395
Jin (Promotion), Fire and Earth (Hexagram 35) (Kun below, Li above) ·················· 395

地火明夷（卦三十六）（离下坤上）·················· 405
Mingyi (Fading Light), Earth and Fire (Hexagram 36) (Li below, Kun above)·················· 405

风火家人（卦三十七）（离下巽上）·················· 414
Jiaren (Family), Wind and Fire (Hexagram 37) (Li below, Xun above) ·················· 414

火泽睽（卦三十八）（兑下离上）·················· 424
Kui (Separation), Fire and Lake (Hexagram 38) (Dui below, Li above) ·················· 424

水山蹇（卦三十九）（艮下坎上）·················· 433
Jian (Dragging), Water and Mountain (Hexagram 39) (Gen below, Kan above) ·················· 433

雷水解（卦四十）（坎下震上）·················· 442
Jie (Relaxation), Thunder and Water (Hexagram 40) (Kan below, Zhen above) ·················· 442

山泽损（卦四十一）（兑下艮上）·················· 451
Sun (Diminishing), Mountain and Lake (Hexagram 41) (Dui below, Gen above)·················· 451

风雷益（卦四十二）（震下巽上）·················· 459
Yi (Increase), Wind and Thunder (Hexagram 42) (Zhen below, Xun above) ·················· 459

泽天夬（卦四十三）（乾下兑上）·················· 467
Guai (Determination), Lake and Heaven (Hexagram 43) (Qian below, Dui above) ·················· 467

天风姤（卦四十四）（巽下乾上）·················· 477
Gou (Encounter), Heaven and Wind (Hexagram 44) (Xun below, Qian above) ·················· 477

泽地萃（卦四十五）（坤下兑上）·················· 485
Cui (Gathering), Lake and Earth (Hexagram 45) (Kun below, Dui above) ·················· 485

地风升（卦四十六）（巽下坤上）······494
Sheng (Ascent), Earth and Wind (Hexagram 46)　(Xun below, Kun above) ······ 494

泽水困（卦四十七）（坎下兑上）······501
Kun (Entanglement), Lake and Water (Hexagram 47)　(Kan below, Dui above) ······ 501

水风井（卦四十八）（巽下坎上）······511
Jing (The Well), Water and Wind (Hexagram 48)　(Xun below, Kan above) ······ 511

泽火革（卦四十九）（离下兑上）······521
Ge (Revolution), Lake and Fire (Hexagram 49)　(Li below, Dui above) ······ 521

火风鼎（卦五十）（巽下离上）······530
Ding (Establishment), Fire and Wind (Hexagram 50)　(Xun below, Li above) ······ 530

震为雷（卦五十一）（震下震上）······540
Zhen (Shaking), Thunder (Hexagram 51)　(Zhen below, Zhen above) ······ 540

艮为山（卦五十二）（艮下艮上）······549
Gen (Stopping), Mountain (Hexagram 52)　(Gen below, Gen above) ······ 549

风山渐（卦五十三）（艮下巽上）······558
Jian (Engagement), Wind and Mountain (Hexagram 53)　(Gen below, Xun above) ······ 558

雷泽归妹（卦五十四）（兑下震上）······568
Guimei (Marriage), Thunder and Lake (Hexagram 54)　(Dui below, Zhen above) ······ 568

雷火丰（卦五十五）（离下震上）······577
Feng (Abundance), Thunder and Fire (Hexagram 55)　(Li below, Zhen above) ······ 577

火山旅（卦五十六）（艮下离上）······586
Lü (Traveling), Fire and Mountain (Hexagram 56)　(Gen below, Li above) ······ 586

巽为风（卦五十七）（巽下巽上）······596
Xun (Submission), Wind (Hexagram 57)　(Xun below, Xun above) ······ 596

兑为泽（卦五十八）（兑下兑上） ·· 604
Dui (Sharing), Lake (Hexagram 58)　(Dui below, Dui above) ································· 604

风水涣（卦五十九）（坎下巽上） ·· 612
Huan (Melting), Wind and Water (Hexagram 59)　(Kan below, Xun above) ············ 612

水泽节（卦六十）（兑下坎上） ·· 621
Jie (Regulation), Water and Lake (Hexagram 60)　(Dui below, Kan above) ············ 621

风泽中孚（卦六十一）（兑下巽上） ·· 630
Zhongfu (Trust), Wind and Lake (Hexagram 61)　(Dui below, Xun above) ············· 630

雷山小过（卦六十二）（艮下震上） ·· 639
Xiaoguo (Slight Overreaching), Thunder and Mountain (Hexagram 62)
(Gen below, Zhen above) ·· 639

水火既济（卦六十三）（离下坎上） ·· 648
Jiji (Success), Water and Fire (Hexagram 63)　(Li below, Kan above) ···················· 648

火水未济（卦六十四）（坎下离上） ·· 655
Weiji (Unfinished), Fire and Water (Hexagram 64)　(Kan below, Li above) ············· 655

第一章　导论
——《周易》哲学的人天之意

Chapter I Introduction: Humanity-Heaven Intentionality in the Philosophy of the *Book of Changes*

第一章　导论
——《周易》哲学的人天之意

一、《周易》是中国哲学与文化的总源头

I.The *Book of Changes* as the Source of Chinese Philosophy and Culture

易本心易，心通于物，心物一元。《周易明意》以意为本，建构人天之意论。

易之为书，导人意通于天道，理顺天地之变化，通达阴阳不测、显幽无间之意，而明实意为创生世界之源，生生不息之本。本书从建构"意本论"的根本点出发，通过以传解经，尤其是通过《说卦传》解释卦爻辞，在了解每卦每爻精义的基础上，建构以"人天之意"为核心的"意本论"。

Ultimately, the *Book of Changes* is a book that is related to the movement of intentionality. This intentionality is always in continuity with things-events, and these two (mind-heart/things-events, or subject/object) should be perceived as a continuous unity. This book is an attempt to construct a new Chinese philosophical "theory of foundational intentionality" by arguing that human intentionality should be always continuous with the cosmos, and thus, a new Chinese philosophical concept of "*yi* 意 (intentionality)" and a new philosophy are simultaneously under construction.

The *Book of Changes* directs human intentionality to the heavenly *dao* by clarifying how things change between heaven and earth, explaining this through the unpredictable interaction between *yin*/soft lines and *yang*/strong lines, which illustrates the intentional movements between the obvious and the obscure. The purpose of this book is to show how intentionality should be regarded as the source of cosmological creation and the foundation of the endless changes in the world. Rooted in this new philosophy of intentionality, this book constructs a "theory of foundational intentionality" using continuous argument through one hexagram after another, constructing the "unified intentionality of humanity and heaven" at its core by interpreting the changing lines in each hexagram and thus interpreting the text of the *Book of Changes,* especially based on the *Commentary Explaining Trigrams* (*Shuo gua zhuan* 说卦传).

《周易》是"群经之首，大道之源"，是中国哲学与文化的总源头。中国历史上，《周易》是在经学、哲学与文化史上影响极为深远和广泛的经典。《周易》的核心是易道，

《周易》是一部揭示天地变化之道的书，为的是济物利民。《周易》作者在长期仰观俯察的基础上，运用卦画的形式，对宇宙万物的变化进行模拟。《周易》的基础和原理跟日月运行、阴阳变化、占卜实践有关系。《周易》内在结构的成型过程是从数到象，从象到卦，从卦到辞。数和象是《周易》最明显的特色，也是研读《周易》一开始就要打下的基础，如果单纯从文辞入手，是很难理解《周易》独特的成书方式和内在义理的。在《周易》的卦爻符号系统中，无论从太极到阴阳，还是从先后天八卦到六十四卦，整个体系及其各部分都为表达宇宙变化之"道"。通过对符号体系的推演，模拟天道的运行，在此基础上阐明人事运作的道理。

Renowned as "the foremost of the ancient classics and the source of the great *dao*", the *Book of Changes* is the source of Chinese philosophy and culture with an extensive and far-reaching impact on the history of philosophy and culture in general as one of the most important Confucian classics. At the core of the *Changes* is the *dao* of changes, which reveals the mechanism of changes between heaven and earth with the aim of facilitating people to live harmoniously with their surrounding cosmological existence. Based on long-term observation, the ancient authors of the *Changes* used hexagrams to model the changing things in the cosmos. The foundation and patterns of the *Changes* are based on the movement of the sun and the moon, from which came the interaction of *yin*/soft lines and *yang*/strong lines, which in turn set the foundation for the practice of divination.

The internal structure of the *Book of Changes* is formed from numbers to images, then to the eight trigrams and 64 hexagrams, and finally to verbal explanations. As the most distinct characteristics of the *Changes*, numbers and images are one of the basic foundations for understanding this unique book. If we attempted to approach it with only verbal explanations, it would be nearly impossible to understand the unique way of composition and internal intentionality of the *Changes*. In the line symbol system of the *Changes*, whether *Taiji* changes into *yin* and *yang*, or the eight trigrams change into the 64 hexagrams, the entire system and its various parts are designed to express the *dao* of changes, which represents unchanging cosmological patterns. Based on the deduction of the symbolic system and its simulation of the operation of the heavenly *dao*, the patterns of human activities are thus elucidated through hermeneutical unpacking processes.

关于《周易》的学问——易学包括《周易》的起源、演变、成书、诠释和传播等各个方面。除了作为哲理著作之外，《周易》的特色是通过卜筮文化体现出与其他经典不同的实践智慧，能够给予不同境遇中的人从易理到现实策略的指导。卦爻符号系统是《周易》表达数和象最为特殊的部分，也是解读全书，理解《周易》的根基。《周易》作为流传几千年的著作，主要是由《经》和《传》两部分构成的。易学包罗万象，涵盖天地万物的运行。易学史是综罗百代，涉及中国传统文化方方面面的"百科全书"。

第一章　导论
——《周易》哲学的人天之意

The study of the *Book of Changes* includes various aspects such as its origin, evolution, wording, interpretation, and historical dissemination. Apart from being a philosophical work, the *Changes* is characterized by its practical wisdom accumulated through ancient divination culture, which can provide both philosophical intentionality and practical guidance or strategies for people to deal with changing situations. The trigrams, hexagrams and line symbol system are the most unique part of the *Changes* based on its expression of numbers and images, and also the foundation for interpreting and understanding the entire book. As a work that has been passed down for thousands of years, the book is mainly composed of two parts: the *Classic* (*jing* 经) and the *Commentaries* (*zhuan* 传). Yixue 易学, the study of the *Book of Changes,* is an all-inclusive endeavor covering the operation of existence between heaven and earth, and its history is an encyclopedia that involves every aspect of traditional Chinese culture over hundreds of generations.

《周易明意》认为，人天之意哲学思维方式塑造了中国哲学独特的"哲学意识"，中国哲学意识的根本缘发点是人天之意——即接通人的心意与天道来推演哲学运思的独特方式。换言之，《周易》哲学的基本点是"推天道以明人事"，即通过卦爻体系来推演天道的运行，进而启发人用"意"去运世之化的一整套精深哲理。《周易》哲学作为人天之意的系统，从根本上说是"心易"，即心灵意识通于天道之易；换言之，《周易》哲理的核心是人意合于天意，这就是《周易明意》的核心思想。

This book argues that the unique "philosophical sensibility" of Chinese philosophy is shaped by the mindset of "unifying the intentionality of humanity with that of the cosmos", which means connecting human intentionality with the *dao* of nature or the cosmos. In other words, the philosophy of the *Book of Changes* is based on "extending the heavenly *dao* to illuminate human affairs", a whole set of profound philosophical principles that involves deducing the operation of the cosmos through the systematic construction of hexagrams and lines, in order to inspire people to transform the world with their "intentionality." The philosophy of the *Changes*, as a system of human-cosmological intentionality, argues that the unified changing of human intentions/minds corresponds with their fluctuating cosmological existence, which means that human intentions/consciousness should change harmoniously with the heavenly *dao*. In other words, the core idea of the *Changes* is that human intentionality should conform to heavenly or cosmological intentionality, and therefore a special concept of intentionality (*yi* 意) which comprises an intentionality of human and cosmological significance is constructed line by line throughout this book.

本书致力于揭示人天之意作为沟通人与天、人与自然、人与世界的核心，提出"意本论"，认为"意"既是世界之本，也是哲学宇宙论的基础。人类通过"意"结合成为一个命运共同体，可以说，"意"是内在于世界，并高于世界的存在，并且是贯通世界万物本相的本体性存在。由此出发，《周易明意》哲学体系阐发六十四卦三百八十四爻和《易传》的哲学内涵。

This book aims to reveal the continuity of human intentionality and cosmological intentionality as the core of communication between humanity and heaven, between humanity and nature, and between humanity and the world. A new philosophical theory based on intentionality (*yibenlun* 意本论) is thus proposed to show that intentionality is not only the foundation of human and worldly existence, but also the basis for a new understanding of philosophical cosmology. A human community with a shared future is formed through a unified intentions. It can be said that intentionality is an ontological existence that lies within and together with the world, and connects all things in the world in one union. This is a starting point for this book to elucidate the philosophical connotations of the *Classic of Changes* (*Yijing* 易经), i.e. the 64 hexagrams and their 384 lines, based on the ten traditional Confucian *Commentaries on the Changes* (*Yizhuan* 易传), also named *Ten Wings* (*Shiyi* 十翼).

意本论认为，"意"为天地万物之本，从"意"本原上可以开发出人类存在和生存的哲学系统，把人理解为"意"念实化的存在，人生是"意"念实化流行的过程，人可以通过提升反思意念的认知力、增强意念运化的力量来改变自己的命运。《周易明意》一书通过对《周易》卦爻辞每卦每爻的详尽解析，致力于阐发贯通宇宙间一切存在的"意"的哲学共性，建构能为各哲学提供彼此融通的"意本论"哲学基石。总之，《周易明意》致力于以"意"为本解释《周易》卦爻辞，立足于把"意本论"建构为人之为"意"念实化的哲学原点，对《周易》相关的事变做出哲学体系性解释和建构。

The theory of intentionality holds that "intentionality" is the foundation of all existence between heaven and earth. From the origin of "intentionality", a philosophical system for human life and existence can be developed which comprehends lived human experience as a materialized existence or concretizing process of "intentionality." Life is a process of the substantialization and circulation of "intentionality". People can change their destiny by improving their cognitive ability to reflect on their minds and enhancing their power of intentional operation. This book is dedicated to elucidating the philosophical commonality that connects all existence in the cosmos and constructing a philosophical cornerstone of a "theory of intentionality" which enables mutual integration among various philosophies. In short, this book is committed to interpreting the 64 hexagrams and 384 lines in the *Book of Changes* based on a new philosophical understanding of "intentionality", which is the philosophical origin of the substantialization of human beings, thus providing a new systematic explanation and philosophical construction of the *Book of Changes*.

《周易明意》分导论、易经明意、易传明意三部分。其中"导论"说明解读《周易》的基础知识，以及《周易明意》的哲学意义，可以说是"意本论"的总纲。"易经明意"是对六十四卦三百八十四爻每卦每爻的精准解释和哲学建构。"易传明意"基于《易传》

对卦的总说来建立"意本论"诠释,是理解"意本论"的基本理论系统。《周易明意》致力于说明,《周易》的哲学系统可以通过以"意"为本的角度,对每卦每爻加以精细诠释,并重构成为一个浑然天成的思想体系。

This book is composed of three parts: an introduction, a sub-discussion of the 64 hexagrams and 384 lines, and a general discussion of the theory of foundational intentionality based on my new explanation of the *Commentaries on the Changes*. The Introduction, as the overall outline of the new theory of foundational intentionality, explains the basic knowledge concerning how to interpret the *Book of Changes*, as well as the philosophical significance of the *Book of Changes*. The sub-discussion part is a precise interpretation and philosophical construction of the 64 hexagrams and 384 lines. The third part establishes an interpretation of the "theory of foundational intentionality" based on a new hermeneutical explanation of the *Commentaries on the Changes*, and therefore sets a basic theoretical system for understanding the "theory of foundational intentionality." This book aims to illustrate that the philosophical system of the *Book of Changes* can be meticulously interpreted from a perspective based on intentionality and thus, that it is possible to reconstruct a complete and self-sustained new philosophical system of intentionality.

本导论是对《周易明意》提纲挈领的说明,将从《周易》基础知识、明解《周易》的方法、《周易》哲学基本思想等角度建构意本论,其中的哲学含义主要是要说明宇宙创生的根源,再从意物一元的角度来讨论宇宙与存在,并为全书的引申阐释做铺垫。

As an overarching explanation of the entire book, this introductory part will build the philosophy of intentionality from the perspectives of the basic knowledge of the *Book of Changes*, the methods for interpreting it, and the basic philosophical intentionality within it, with the aim of explaining the fundamental source of cosmological creativity, and then discuss the cosmos and existence from the perspective of the continuity of intention/intentionality and physical things, to lay a foundation for the hermeneutical interpretation and philosophical construction of the entire book.

二、《周易》的原理与基础
II. The Principles and Foundation of the *Book of Changes*

1. 原理
1. Principles

《周易》是古人"仰观天文、俯察地理"之后，形成的一部"与天地准"而且能够"弥纶大地之道"的伟大著作。所以《周易》最原始、最根本的原理是天文学原理，是古人对于天上的日月星辰长期观察之后，形成一套模拟星体运转之道的象征符号系统之上的哲理体系。这套体系最根本的原理是对阴阳的区分和体察，而阴阳的基础是贯通宇宙万物的气一元论。古人认为，宇宙之间的一切事物都是气构成的，气是日月星辰和天地之间一切变化的物质基础，也是人身与心意变化的根本基础，所以气不是单纯的物质，而且是物质与心灵贯通的一体性存在。

The *Book of Changes* is a great work created by ancient sages based on their observation of astronomical and geographical phenomena, so it is in line with the *dao* of heaven and earth and can model the *dao* of heaven and earth. The most primitive and fundamental principles in the *Book of Changes* were astronomical ones, which were turned into a significant philosophical system when ancient sages used symbols to model the movement of the stars. The foundation of this system was the distinction and observation of changing *yin* and *yang qi* 气 or cosmological *yin/yang* powers, whose theoretical basis was a monism of *qi* as a substance that penetrates through all things/events in the cosmos. Ancient Chinese people perceived the whole cosmos as composed of *qi*, which was regarded as the material basis for the changes both in celestial bodies and between heaven and earth, as well as the fundamental basis for changes in the human body and mind. Therefore, *qi* is not simply concrete matter, but a oneness psycho-material existence that connects matter and mind.

第一章　导论
——《周易》哲学的人天之意

气永远在运动变化，人所理解的阴阳观念，也随着时间时刻变化，体现在每天从早晨到中午阳气生长，阴气消退；从中午到夜里阴气生长，阳气消退周而复始的过程之中。同理，从冬天到夏天，阳气生长，阴气消退；从夏天到冬天，阴气生长，阳气消退，阴阳之气体现在天时和天地之间气息时刻不停地变化流转当中。在这个意义上说，气一元论和变动的阴阳观分分秒秒影响着人们的生活。在古代农业社会当中，人们按照天时流逝的特点，如春生夏长秋收冬藏来播种和收割，进而安排相应的社会生活，实现人与自然之间和谐相处。从地理空间上，古人选择合适的地点埋葬先祖，建设合适的阳宅来居住，都是因为要选择生气汇聚之处以利于生养自己的生命，促进事业的发展。因此，历代阴阳宅建筑基本遵从《周易》当中的八卦数理与方位等来修建。

Cosmological *qi* always moves and changes with time, as does people's concept of *yin* and *yang*, reflected in the daily wax and wane of *yangqi* and *yinqi*. From morning to noon, *yangqi* grows and *yinqi* fades, and from noon to night, *yinqi* grows and *yangqi* fades, forming a continuous cycle repeating again and again. Similarly, from winter to summer, *yangqi* grows while *yinqi* subsides; from summer to winter, *yinqi* grows and *yangqi* subsides. The changes of *yinqi* and *yangqi* are reflected in their constant circulation between heaven and earth. In this sense, the monism of *qi* and the interchanging view of *yin* and *yang* affect people's lives every minute. In ancient agricultural societies, people sowed and harvested in accordance with seasonal climate changes and correspondingly arranged their social life to achieve a harmonious coexistence between humanity and nature. From a geographical perspective, ancient people chose suitable places to bury their ancestors and build houses to live in, places where vital *qi* could continuously gather to benefit their offspring's health and careers. Therefore, throughout history, residential buildings and tombs were theoretically built in accordance with the mathematical principles and directions of the Eight Trigrams in the *Book of Changes*.

要理解易学，首先就要理解《周易》的阴阳爻符号和《易传》"一阴一阳之谓道"的阴阳观念。其实，阴阳观念体现在生活的很多方面，比如在从日月、天地、男女到上下、左右、前后等等耳熟能详的生活情境当中，都有阴阳对应统一观念的显现，可谓无处没有阴阳。换言之，一切对待的观念，都是阴阳，而人的意识跟世界接触，最诡异的特点，就是没有办法直接把握一元性的整体，如理解道必须通过阴阳对待的思维方式。

To understand the studies of the *Book of Changes*, one must first understand the *yin* and *yang* line symbols in the *Book of Changes* and the idea that "the movement of one *yin* and one *yang* is the *dao*" in the *Commentaries* (*Yizhuan*). In fact, the concept of *yin* and *yang* is reflected in many aspects of our daily life, such as the comings and goings of the sun and the moon, the heavens and the earth, male and female, up and down, left and right, front and back, etc., and it can be said *yin* and *yang* are in an omnipresent union with one another. In other words, all such concepts of equivalence can be regarded as embodiments of *yin-yang* movements and changes, yet the most bizarre feature of human consciousness is that it cannot directly grasp the unitary whole, but has to take such a correlative *yin-yang* approach to understand the *dao* as philosophical monism.

《周易》的气一元论和阴阳观念，渗透在中国古代天文、地理、风水、建筑、中医，甚至传统的音乐、数学、军事等等实践智慧之中，在西方文明领先世界之前，人类文明的主要历史时期里面，中华文明领先于世界上大多数文明体系，从最深刻的根源上说，跟基于《周易》的气一元论和阴阳观原理基础上的整个思想和运用体系密切相关。

The monism of *qi* and the concepts of *yin* and *yang* in the *Book of Changes* have penetrated the practical wisdom of ancient Chinese astronomy, geography, *fengshui*, architecture, medicine, and even traditional music, mathematics, military theory, etc. Before Western civilization took its leading historical position, Chinese civilization was more advanced than most others during the major part of human history, the deepest reason for which was closely connected to this thought and practice system based on the *qi* monism of the *Book of Changes*.

2. 占卜

《周易》可以用于预测，帮助人们了解事情发展的方向，也可以作为人行动的指南和成事的参考。不了解《周易》的人，容易把《周易》跟迷信联系起来，而《周易》其实从成书开始，就是一部破除迷信的著作，是中国上古文化脱离巫术和鬼神崇拜，走向人文理性的伟大著作。无论是卦爻的推演，还是卦爻辞的书写和诠释过程，都体现出人的精神和意志是世间变化之主宰的主导思想。所以可以说，《周易》基本没有迷信的成分，没有对超越世间之天神的执迷不悟和盲目信仰，也否定被外在力量迷惑和轻易信从超自然力的倾向。

2.Divination

The *Book of Changes* can help people to predict and understand the moving trends of events, or can be used as a guide of action and reference to achieve success. Many people who do not understand the philosophy of the *Book of Changes* are prone to associate it with superstition. However, since its formation, the *Book of Changes* has been against superstition, a great work to show the transition in ancient Chinese culture from witchcraft and worship of ghosts and gods toward humanistic rationality. Both the deduction and the writing and interpretation of hexagrams and lines reflected the dominant idea that the human spirit and will are the masters of changes in the human world. Therefore, the *Book of Changes* should be regarded as a book almost entirely free of superstition, without obsession with blind faith in transcendent gods and external or supernatural forces.

当然,《周易》的起源与占卜有关,如朱熹曾说:"易本卜筮之书",但占卜本身并不就是迷信,从孔子开始,历朝历代的大儒都了解、研究占卜,很多还精通占卜,认为占卜有助于解决人生的疑难,理解《周易》的大道。应该说,占卜不等于迷信,在人们碰到无法解释,或者无法解决的疑难和问题之时,占卜一直是一种寻找答案的方式,接近于今天心理辅导和决策咨询。

Of course, the origin of the *Book of Changes* is related to divination, as Zhu Xi once noted: "The *Changes* was originally a book of divination." However, divination itself is not inherently superstitious. Since Confucius' time, great scholars through history tended to study, comprehend and use divination, some even to the degree of proficiency, and many believed that divination could help solve problems in life and illuminate the great *dao* of the *Book of Changes*. It should be said that divination is not synonymous with superstition, but rather a way to help people when they encounter inexplicable or unsolvable problems. The role of divination is similar to modern-day psychological counseling or decision-making consultation.

不能因为占卜的结果有一定的准确性,就认为占卜是非常正确的,所以应该完全按照占卜的结果去行动,这就是一种宿命论或者被决定论的态度。宿命论认为,一切都预先注定,人类的努力不可能改变事情的发展,于是放弃一切努力。被决定论认为,一切发展变化都是预先决定了的,人类的意志很难改变事情的发展变化,不过,如果要事情按照决定的结果发生,还是应该顺其自然去努力,因为人顺其自然去努力本身也是一种被决定的过程,非人力本身可以更改的。如果用宿命论和被决定论的方式来理解占卜,就不算正确理解占卜的态度,因为这样容易对占卜的结果执迷不悟,严重的时候,认为应该放弃人的主观努力,那就走向了《周易》之教的反面。

We should not base our actions blindly on divination, and should not assume the results are completely correct based on their certain degree of accuracy. That is a fatalistic or deterministic attitude. Fatalism believes that everything is predetermined, and human efforts cannot change the development of events, so humans should give up all effort. Determinists hold that all development and changes are predetermined, and it is difficult for people to make any change, but one should still make efforts as this is part of the natural occurrence which is also predetermined and cannot be changed by human will. If we understand divination from the perspective of fatalism and determinism, we adopt a wrong attitude, because this can easily lead to obsession with definite results. In severe cases, we might believe that we should give up trying, which leads to the opposite of the teachings of the *Book of Changes*.

《周易明意》的建构顺从《易传》的教导，帮助人们领略心意的几微，从人心与人意发动之处反省体察，格物致知，为善去恶，进而改变人生，提振人心与人之"意"念对于改变人生命运的力量。从这个意义上说，"意本论"是一种自由意志论，是相信人的"意"可以领略和通达宇宙之道，可以通过修行"意"来接续宇宙的天机，从而改变作为实意过程的人生。也就是说，人生的轨迹之变化在于如何实化意念，甚至主要在于如何把握和驾驭意念发动的瞬间。

This book is structured in compliance with the teachings of the *Commentaries on Book of Changes*, hoping to help people understand the subtleties of their minds, reflect on and observe their motives from the very start, investigate things and extend their knowledge, try to maintain good and eliminate evil in their intentions, and boost the power of their intentions to improve their life and destiny. In this sense, the philosophy of intentionality is a form of free will theory which believes that human intentions can comprehend and connect to the cosmological *dao* through the cultivation of one's mind, thereby changing one's life as a process of realizing one's intentions. That is to say, the changes in the trajectory of one's life lie in how one concretizes one's intentions, especially in how to grasp and control the moment when intentions are initiated.

3. 易的含义

《周易》的"易"有三个意思：变易、不易、简易。"变易"指事物恒变，《周易》是一本关于变化的书。"不易"指事物虽然变动不居，但变化的现象之中有相对不变的"道"存在，自然与人事之道都有不变的性质，也可以说是做事的法则和事物运动的规律。"易"的另一个含义是"简易"，即《周易》虽难，但易道理解起来、用起来却容易简单。

3. The meanings of *Yi*

The character *Yi* in the title of the *Book of Changes* (*Zhouyi*) has three meanings: change, invariability, and simplicity. "Change" refers to the constant changing process of things, and the *Book of Changes* is a book just talking about all kinds of changes. "Invariability" refers to the fact that although everything is in a process of constant change, there is a relatively unchanging *dao* in the phenomena of changes, and hence both nature and human affairs have unchanging properties. There is invariability in both the laws of action and the laws of movement of things. The other meaning of *yi* is "simplicity," which means that although the *Changes* seems very difficult, the *dao* of changes is easy to understand and use.

东汉许慎《说文解字》说易是"日"与"月"这两种天地之间最根本的阴阳物象组合而成，代表天地之间阴气与阳气永恒的交流与变化，所以"易"最根本的意思就是变易，即阴阳的交互变化。从"变易"引申出变化的世界有永恒不变的道，所以有不易之义；还有简易之义。东汉郑玄说："易，一名而含三义：易简，一也；变易，二也；不易，三也。"《系辞传》以天地之间的生机为易之变化的本质，这是《易传》儒家倾向的标志。

An Explication of Written Characters (Shuowen Jiezi 说文解字) by Xu Shen 许慎 of the Eastern Han Dynasty (25 AD-220 AD) states that the Chinese character yi 易 is a combination of the characters for the sun and the moon, the two most fundamental phenomena of yang and yin between heaven and earth, thus it represents the eternal exchange and change of cosmological yin and yang powers between heaven and earth. Therefore, the most fundamental meaning of yi is change, that is, the interaction and change of yin and yang cosmological powers. Everything is unceasingly changing, but this changing world has an eternal and unchanging dao, hence there is the meaning of "not changing" or "unchanging". There is also the meaning of simplicity. According to Zheng Xuan 郑玄 of the Eastern Han Dynasty, yi is a term with three meanings: the first is simplicity, the second is change and the third is invariability. The Attached Words (Xici 系辞) or Great Appendix (Dazhuan 大传) regards the living and generative vitality (shengsheng 生生) between heaven and earth as the essence of change, which indicates a Confucian tendency in the Commentaries on the Changes (Yizhuan) or Ten Wings (Shiyi 十翼).

《周易》的"周"通常有两个意思，一是指周代成书的著作，二是指"周普""周备""普遍"（郑玄、陆德明和贾公彦）的意思。人们通常说的《周易》包括《易经》和《易传》两部分。《易经》指经文部分，相传是殷周之际，由周文王姬昌推演作出。司马迁《史记·太史公自序》说周文王被拘禁时，推演出后天八卦，并写下了卦爻辞。《易传》是解释《易经》的文字，相传是孔子对传下来的解易内容加以整理和发挥而完成的，是解释《易经》最为可靠的根据。关于《经》与《传》之间问题的讨论，会在后面涉及。

The character Zhou 周 in the title of the Book of Changes (Zhouyi) usually has two meanings, one referring to a book written during the Zhou Dynasty (1046 BC-256 BC), and the other referring to the meanings of "commonplace", "complete" and "universal", according to scholars such as Zheng Xuan 郑玄, Lu Deming 陆德明, and Jia Gongyan 贾公彦. The Book of Changes, as people usually refer to it, includes two parts: the Classic of Changes (Yijing) and the Commentaries on the Changes (Yizhuan). The Classic refers to the ancient scripture said to have been written by King Wen of Zhou (1152 BC-1056 BC), whose name was Ji Chang, during the transitional period between the Shang and Zhou dynasties. In Sima Qian's Preface by the Grand Historian Himself in his Records of the Grand Historian (Shiji: Taishigong Zixu 史记·太史公自序), it states that when the old King Wen was detained, he re-organized the Eight Trigrams and wrote down interpretations for all 384 lines of the 64 hexagrams. The *Commentaries* is a collection of ten texts to explain the *Classic*, and it has been regarded as the most reliable basis for interpretation as it was said to have been compiled by Confucius himself based on the ancient interpretations before him. The relationship between the *Classic* and the *Commentaries* will be discussed in detail below.

三、《周易》的内在结构
III. The Internal Structure of the *Book of Changes*

《周易》包括数、象、卦、辞几个部分。读懂《周易》必须要有象数基础。朱熹曾说:"读《易》亦佳,但经书难读,而此经为尤难。盖未开卷时,已有一重象数大概功夫。"如果不了解象数基础知识,《周易》就难以入门。朱熹完成《周易本义》后又写《易学启蒙》,就是为了要求初学《周易》者必须有坚实的象数基础,是河图洛书、卦画、蓍策、筮仪、占变等基础知识构筑了《周易》全书的内在架构,也就是说,数与象是构成八卦六十四卦还有卦爻辞系统的基础,渗透在整个体系的方方面面,所以是《周易》的内在结构。

The *Book of Changes* consists of several parts: numbers, images, hexagrams, and words. A mathematical foundation is required to understand the *Book of Changes*, as Zhu Xi once said, "It is also good to read the *Book of Changes*, but all classics are difficult to read, with this classic being particularly difficult. Before opening the book, a foundation of basic knowledge about images and numbers (*xiang-shu* 象数) should be laid." It is difficult to get started with the *Book of Changes* without basic knowledge of images and numbers. After completing his *Original Meaning of the Book of Changes* (*Zhouyi Benyi* 周易本义), Zhu Xi wrote *Enlightening the Book of Changes* (*Yixue Qimeng* 易学启蒙) in order to prepare beginner readers with a solid foundation in image-number knowledge, which includes basic knowledge of the River Diagram and Luo Chart, the diagrams of the eight trigrams and 64 hexagrams, divination rituals and processes, hexagram-changes patterns (*guabian tu* 卦变图), etc. that constructs the internal structure of the entire book. In other words, numbers and images are the foundation for the formation of the 64 hexagrams, and they permeate the whole system, so they compose the internal structure of the *Book of Changes*.

1. 数理:河图洛书

《周易》的基础是数。根据《易传》,传说古时有龙马背负"河图"跃出黄河,神龟背负"洛书"浮出洛水。伏羲看到河图和洛书之后，依其数理发明了八卦。河图和洛书是在天地自然之数的基础上，由于阴数静、阳数动的自然交流而形成的。河图由一到十这十个数字组成，洛书由一到九这九个数字组成。

1.Mathematical Principles: The River Diagram and Luo Chart

The foundation of the *Book of Changes* is numbers. According to the *Commentaries* (*Yizhuan*), once upon a time a dragon horse carrying the "River Diagram" (*He-tu* 河图) jumped out of the Yellow River, while a turtle carrying the "Luo Chart" (*Luo-shu* 洛书) emerged to the surface of the Luo River. By observing the heavenly River Diagram and Luo Chart, the Chinese forefather Fu Xi invented the Eight Trigrams based on their mathematical patterns, as the River Diagram and Luo Chart are based on the natural numbers and formed through natural exchange of the *yin*/still numbers and the *yang*/moving numbers. The River Diagram consists of ten numbers from one to ten, while the Luo Chart consists of nine numbers from one to nine.

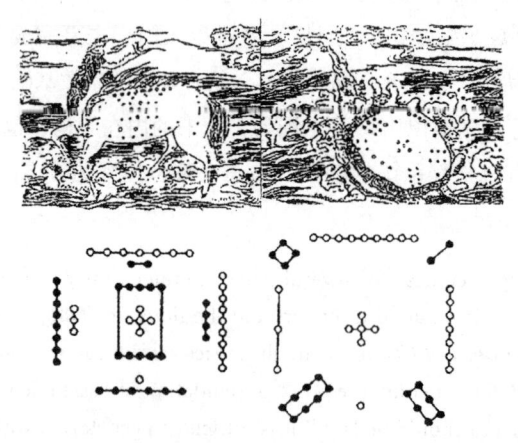

河图、洛书启发人们由数的奇偶分出阴阳，认识到自然数有阴阳属性。《周易》的数、卦体系是平衡的，其数理基础可以通过洛书来理解。洛书揭示了数与卦之间的关系，虽然不是西方哲学意义上严格的逻辑关系，但体现出中国古人严密而有效的独特哲学思维方式。

The River Diagram and Luo Chart inspired people to distinguish cosmological *yin* and *yang* powers by comprehending the odd and even aspect of numbers as representations and to recognize that natural numbers could be regarded with *yin* and *yang* attributes. The system of numbers and hexagrams in the *Book of Changes* is balanced, and its mathematical basis can be understood with the help of the Luo Chart as it reveals the relationship between numbers and hexagrams, reflecting the unique and rigorous philosophical reasoning of the ancient Chinese people, although not strictly logical in the Western philosophical sense.

河图洛书自古以来有大量记载，《尚书·顾命》篇和《系辞传》有提及，《论语·子罕》里孔子说："河不出图，洛不出书，吾已矣夫"，说明上古之时确有其物，不可轻易否定。至于历史上关于河图洛书到底是什么样子，世传不一，但其确实法乎天象，本乎天地自然之数，自成系统，有其内在的逻辑和条理，能够不断启发人们对于易道的领悟和认识。

There have been a large number of records about River Diagram and Luo Chart since ancient times. For example, they are mentioned in the "Testamentary Charge" Chapter of the *Book of Documents* (*Shangshu Guming* 尚书·顾命) and the *Great Appendix* (*Dazhuan* 大传 or *Xici zhuan* 系辞传). In the "Zihan" chapter of the *Analects* (*Lunyu Zihan* 论语·子罕), Confucius says, "If the Diagram no longer appears in the Yellow River, and the Chart is not seen again in the Luo River, I would have no hope [because they imply that the continual effort of promoting ancient culture would have come to an end]." These are historical and textual proofs of the existence of the River Diagram and Luo Chart that cannot be denied. As for what the River Diagram and Luo Chart were really like in history, there have been various legendary versions, but it is certain that they were based on celestial phenomena and the natural numbers of heaven and earth, forming their own system with an inherent logic that continuously inspired Chinese people's understanding of the cosmological *dao*.

2. 筮法

数作为宇宙万物存在的基本方式，在《周易》体系中的运用主要是筮法，就是算卦的演算方法。用揲蓍求卦的过程是：推演天地运化之数的蓍草总共需五十根，其中实际运用的共有四十九根（其中一根象征天地未分之前的太极，取出之后一直虚置不用）。用两只手将剩余的四十九根蓍草任意一分为二，左边的一部分象征"天"，右边的一部分象征"地"，这就是"分二"。从右边部分，也就是从"地"上取一根蓍草，放在左手小拇指与无名指之间，此为"挂一"。这根蓍草象征人，至此形成天、地、人"三才"的格局。

2. Divination Methods

Natural numbers are a basic form of existence in the cosmos, and their application in the system of the *Book of Changes* is mainly as the calculation method of divination. The process of using yarrow to calculate hexagrams is as follows: The number of yarrows needed to model the movements between heaven and earth is fifty, but only forty-nine are actually used (the odd one symbolizes the *Taiji* before the division of heaven and earth, and therefore is left unused throughout). The remaining forty-nine yarrows are divided randomly into two by hand, with the left part symbolizing "heaven" and the right part symbolizing "earth", a process called "dividing into two" (*fen'er* 分二). A yarrow is taken from the right part, that is, from the "earth," and placed between the left pinkie and ring finger, which is called "hanging one" (*guayi* 挂一). This yarrow symbolizes human beings, forming a pattern of the "three talents" of heaven, earth, and human beings.

以四根为一组，先用右手去分左边的蓍草，然后用左手分右边的蓍草，此即"揲四"。将左边剩余的蓍草（等于或少于四根）夹在左手的中指与无名指之间（此时你的左手小指和无名指之间还有一根象征"人"的蓍草）以象征闰月，每五年有两次闰月，所以再将右边剩余的蓍草（等于或少于四根）夹在左手食指与中指中间，即是"归奇"。至此完成蓍草演变的四道程序，称为"四营"，经过四营的第一步，古称"第一变"。要再经过重复两次同样的操作，完成三变才可以得出一爻之数。

Take out four yarrows from the left with the right hand and four yarrows from the right with the left hand, a process called "taking four" (*shesi* 揲四). Place the remaining yarrows on the left (equal to or less than four) between the middle and ring fingers of the left hand (at this point, there is still a yarrow symbolizing "human beings" between the little and ring fingers) to symbolize leap months. There are two leap months every five years. Next, place the remaining yarrows on the right (equal to or less than four) between the index and middle fingers of the left hand, an action called "returning the odd" (*guiji* 归奇). At this point, the four steps of yarrow calculation, known as the "four steps" (*siying* 四营), have been completed. After the first of the four steps, the "first change" (*di yi bian* 第一变) is completed. To obtain the numerical value of one line, it is necessary to repeat the same process twice, so it takes three changes (*sanbian* 三变) to complete one number, which will be one among 6, 7, 8 or 9.

经过这四次经营才能完成一爻的一变，每个爻需要经过三变才能完成，因每个卦有六爻，所以演算出一个卦需要十八变。朱熹在《周易本义》卷首记载了揲蓍成卦的筮仪，主要说明古代演卦的过程是要找洁净精微之所，让心思安宁纯净，去除杂念，在静定之中接续天机。朱熹在《易学启蒙》中还记载了卦演算成了之后，如何断卦的不同方法。

Since each hexagram is composed of six *yin* or *yang* lines, it takes eighteen changes to calculate the numerical values of the six lines of any particular hexagram. At the beginning of his *Original Meaning of the Book of Changes* (*Zhouyi Benyi* 周易本义), Zhu Xi recorded the divination ritual and process of how to create a hexagram, mainly explaining that ancient people would find a clean and refined place before the process of divination, in order to remove distractions from their intentionality and make it peaceful and pure, ready to receive the celestial communion in stillness. In his *Enlightening the Book of Changes* (*Yixue Qimeng* 易学启蒙), Zhu Xi also recorded the different methods of divination judgement after the completion of a hexagram.

3. 象
3. Images

象是《周易》成书的依据。"象"字有模仿、象征的意义。每个卦都象征天地之间某一类事物。古人认为,天地之间最基本的事物有八类,分别以天、地、雷、风、水、火、山、泽为代表,可分别用乾、坤、震、巽、坎、离、艮、兑八卦来表示。

Images are the foundation for completing the *Book of Changes*. The Chinese character *xiang* 象 (image) has the meaning of imitation and symbolizing. Each hexagram symbolizes a certain type of thing between heaven and earth. Ancient Chinese people believed that there were eight basic types of things between heaven and earth, represented by heaven, earth, thunder, wind, water, fire, mountains, and lakes, which could be expressed by the Eight Trigrams of Qian, Kun, Zhen, Xun, Kan, Li, Gen, and Dui.

要了解八卦所具体代表的象,必须以《说卦传》为基础,因为《说卦传》是专门为说明卦象而写的。《说卦传》对先天八卦、后天八卦的卦象和方位做了说明,并分别解释每一卦象征的一类事物。除《说卦传》之外,解读六爻卦还需要一些看象的方法,如互卦、覆卦、整体象等。

To understand the specific images represented by the Eight Trigrams, it is necessary to refer to the *Commentary Explaining Trigrams* (*Shuogua Zhuan* 说卦传), which was specifically written to explain the images of trigrams with explanations of the specific orientations of the Pre-Celestial Eight Trigrams and the Post-Celestial Eight Trigrams as well as the different types of things symbolized by each trigram. In addition to the *Commentary Explaining Trigrams*, interpreting the six lines of a hexagram also requires some visual methods, such as reading the trigrams inside a hexagram, reading images by inverting a hexagram, and reading images from a hexagram as a whole, etc.

4. 卦
4.Trigrams and Hexagrams

《周易》是由居住在中原黄河流域一带的古人在长期历史发展进程中发明的哲学体系。《周易》的基本符号是连线"——",即阳爻或刚爻,和断线"- -",即阴爻或柔爻。阳爻代表阳气,阴爻代表阴气,阴阳二气的交感流通化生万物。三爻交错组成八卦,八卦象征自然界当中最基本的八类事物。八卦两两重叠成六十四卦,如六十四卦第一卦是乾卦,由六个阳爻组成;第二卦是坤卦,由六个阴爻组成。

The *Book of Changes* is a philosophical system invented by ancient Chinese people who lived in the central Yellow River area over a long historical period. The basic symbols of the *Book of Changes* are the solid line "——", which is a positive line or a *yang* line, and the broken line "- -", which is a soft line or a *yin* line. The *yang* line represents *yangqi*, while the *yin* line represents *yinqi*. The interaction and circulation of *yinqi* and *yangqi* generates all things. Three *yin* or *yang* lines combine to form one of the Eight Trigrams, which symbolize the most basic eight types of things in nature. The eight trigrams overlap in pairs to form the 64 hexagrams. For example, the first of the 64 hexagrams is Hexagram Qian (Creativity), which is composed of six *yang* lines, and the second is Hexagram Kun (Support), consisting of six *yin* lines.

六十四卦之间的排列"非覆即变",另外,每一爻改变,一个卦就变成另一个卦,这就是变卦,变之前的叫本卦或遇卦,变出来的叫之卦。变卦是占筮当中因为动爻的变化而引起的,如乾卦初爻动变姤卦。占筮的时候,六个爻出来形成一个卦,中间某个爻动形成一个新卦,这叫之卦。占筮时的用语叫变卦。《左传》《国语》里面有很多事例可以做证。《周易》体系里变卦确实存在,没有争议。

The sequence of arranging the 64 hexagrams is obtained by "either inverting or changing." Also, when any line of a hexagram changes, the hexagram changes into another one, which is then called the Changed Hexagram (*Zhi Gua* 之卦), while the hexagram before changing is called an Original Hexagram (*Ben Gua* 本卦) or Meeting Hexagram (*Yu Gua* 遇卦). The change of a hexagram is caused by a change of a mobile line in a hexagram. For example, Hexagram Qian (Creativity) changes into Hexagram Gou (Encounter) by changing the first *yang* line in the former to the first *yin* line in the latter. During divination, six lines are produced to form a hexagram, but when any one of these lines changes, a new hexagram is formed, which is called a Changed Hexagram (*Zhi Gua*), a process termed Changing Hexagrams (*biangua* 变卦). There is much evidence in the historical books *Zuozhuan* and *Guoyu* to prove the undisputable existence of Changing Hexagrams.

卦变是推演《周易》、给卦爻系辞时,发现爻在卦中间推移而形成的推移运动规律。也就是说,卦变是在解释卦爻辞的时候,为了说明爻辞的来源和根据而进行解释的体系。但因为历史上传述纷乱,卦变一直有争议。《说卦》说古代是先有爻的阴阳才确立卦形或卦体,而卦里面的阴阳爻会发生变化,阴变阳,或阳变阴,而卦就变成另一个卦。《系辞》说爻在卦里推荡会产生卦的变化。还说阴阳爻的变化象征着阴阳之力的进与退。这些都明确提到爻的变化,而且把爻变当做易的根本特征。可以说,因为爻的变化必然会引起卦的变化。这些都是说如何理解卦的变化。

Hexagram-changes (*guabian* 卦变) refers to the patterns of line movements in hexagrams that were found to develop when words were being attached to hexagrams and lines. Put another way, hexagram-changes is a system of changing lines in any hexagram used when interpreting where the wording of any hexagram and line comes from. However, there have been many different and often contradictory views on how hexagram-changes exist throughout history. In *Commentary Explaining Trigrams* (*Shuogua Zhuan* 说卦传), it is said that in ancient times, the hexagrams came into being only after *yin* lines and *yang* lines were established. Inside any particular hexagram, *yin* lines could change to be *yang* lines so that one hexagram could be changed into another one. In the *Attached Words* (*Xici* 系辞), it is said that lines will move their places so that a hexagram can be changed into another one, and that the *yin* and *yang* changes in the hexagrams represent the waxing and waning movement of the soft/weak and hard/strong cosmological powers. All these mean that lines will change in any hexagram, and this is the most important characteristic of the *Book of Changes*. In short, it is because of the change of lines that all hexagrams keep changing.

5. 辞
5. Words

《周易》全书的文辞主要有两部分：经文和传文。传说经文经历了伏羲、文王两个圣人的创制而成。经文古奥，简洁，全文不到五千字，是对六十四卦三百八十四爻每卦每爻的解释。历代对经文的注释很多。古时把代表卦的木片挂起来，从中看出卦里的象，比如乾卦代表天、君、父等，再通过卦象去想象，而后形成断语。卦辞和爻辞是这样写下来的。

The text of the *Book of Changes* mainly consists of two parts: the *Classic* and the *Commentaries*. Reputedly, the *Classic* was created by two ancient sages, Fu Xi and King Wen. The *Classic* is abstruse and concise, with less than 5,000 words in total explaining the 64 hexagrams and 384 lines one by one. Throughout history, there have been many annotations on the *Classic*. In ancient times, wooden pieces representing the hexagrams were hung up for people to figure out the images in the hexagrams, such as Trigram Qian representing heaven, monarch, father, etc., and then judgements were written down based on imagination whenever Trigram Qian appears in any hexagram.

《系辞下》说伏羲氏"作结绳而为网罟，以佃以渔，盖取诸离。"这里的离卦是六画卦，说明伏羲时代就有八卦两两重叠为六十四卦之象，只是当时以观象为主，卦爻辞应该是到文王时代才确定下来的，也有说武王或周公作爻辞的，总的来说是商末周初的时候。解读卦爻辞必须以对卦象的理解为基础，抛弃卦象解读卦爻辞就是建构空中楼阁，不可能触及卦爻辞的本来面目。

According to the second half of *Attached Words* (*Xici* 系辞), Fu Xi made rope knots to weave nets for hunting and fishing, which gave inspiration to the birth of Hexagram Li (Illumination). Hexagram Li (Illumination) is comprised of six lines, indicating that during Fu Xi's era, there was already the practice of overlapping the eight trigrams in pairs to form 64 hexagrams. However, at that time, observing images in any hexagram was most important, while verbal explanations were not determined until the reign of King Wen in the Zhou Dynasty. It is also said that verbal explanations were made by King Wu or the Duke of Zhou, roughly during the late Shang and early Zhou Dynasties. The interpretation of hexagrams and lines must be based on the comprehension of images, without which the interpretation of line statements would be like building castles in the air or on sand, and it would be thus impossible to catch the original intentions behind them.

四、《周易》的卦爻符号系统

IV. The Symbolic System of Hexagrams and Lines in the *Book of Changes*

《周易》的重要特点之一，是以阴阳两爻来象征天地间阴阳之气的变化，并以阴阳爻分化推演构成八卦和六十四卦。所以了解《周易》的第一步是读懂八卦和六十四卦的卦画，如果看不懂卦画，那就会觉得《周易》无法理解，深不可测。所以我们学习《周易》，首先要破解基于阴阳的卦爻符号系统，理解《周易》卦爻辞文字系统和卦画系统之间存在天衣无缝的象征和比合关系，也就是说，必须先有坚实的卦爻符号系统的知识，以及培养出对于卦爻之变的悟性和形象思维之后，才能够去解读卦爻辞。否则，就字论字来解读卦爻辞，很容易犯望文生义的毛病。《周易》如果只是用历史主义、文献学和文字学的方法来解读，基本上就跟读天书一般，得出的结论基本都是隔靴搔痒的谬见，可能惊世骇俗，但对于希望连贯系统地理解卦爻辞的愿望多无益处。

An important characteristic of the *Book of Changes* is that it uses *yin* lines and *yang* lines to symbolize the changes of cosmological *yinqi* and *yangqi* between heaven and earth, and to formulate the Eight Trigrams and 64 hexagrams based on the differentiation of *yin* lines and *yang* lines. So, the first step is to understand the images of the Eight Trigrams and 64 hexagrams. If one cannot understand the images in the trigrams or hexagrams, one will feel that the *Book of Changes* is full of mystery and incomprehensible. So when we study the *Book of Changes*, we first need to decipher the *yin-yang* symbolic system, to understand the close symbolic and comparative relationship between the textual and pictorial systems of the hexagrams and lines in the *Book of Changes*. In other words, we must first have a solid knowledge of the symbolic system of the hexagrams and lines, as well as cultivate an understanding and visual thinking of the changes in the hexagrams and lines, before we can interpret their meanings. Otherwise, if we only base our interpretation on literal words, we might easily make the mistake of taking the words too superficially. If the *Book of Changes* is interpreted only using the approaches of historicism, paleography and philology, it will be almost like reading an incomprehensible book from the heavens, and the conclusions drawn will mostly be fallacies that may sound sensational but will not be beneficial to achieving a coherent and systematic understanding of the hexagrams and lines.

1. 太极
1. *Taiji*

在《周易》卦爻系统当中，从存在论的角度看，世界上每一事物都有太极，而天地万物总体也是太极。从生成论上说，太极是宇宙的起点。《系辞上》说："易有太极，是生两仪，两仪生四象，四象生八卦。"这既可以说明宇宙的起源过程，也可以说明事物的存在是不断可分、一多统一的。

Taking an ontological perspective to look at the hexagram and line system of the *Book of Changes*, everything in the world has a *Taiji* 太极 (Ultimate Polarity) and the world and myriad things as a whole is also a *Taiji*. From a generative perspective, *Taiji* is the starting point of the cosmos. The first part of the *At-tached Words* (*Xici* 系辞) says: "In the great Change there is a *Taiji*, which produces the Two Forms. The Two Forms produce the Four Images, and the Four Images produce the Eight Trigrams." This can not only explain the generation process of the cosmos, but also indicate that the existence of things is divisible in a both holistic and individualized way.

太极用图表示出来，就是太极图，一条流动的曲线中分一圆，一半为白（阳），一半为黑（阴），有若鱼形，又称阴阳鱼。可以说宇宙起源于浑沌未分的元气，元气蕴含生机，化为阴阳二气，阳气轻清上升为天，阴气重浊下降为地，此谓天地开辟；也可以说，任何事物都是一整体的太极，可由总体而分阴阳。

If we illustrate *Taiji* in a form of a picture, we get the *Taiji* diagram, which consists of a circle divided in the middle by a curved line, with half being white (*yang*) and half being black (*yin*), each half resembling a fish, also known as the *yin-yang* fishes. It can be said that the cosmos originated from chaotic and undivided primordial *qi* with its vital impetus, which then transformed into *yinqi* and *yangqi*. The *yangqi*, light and clear, rose to the sky, and the *yinqi*, heavy and turbid, descended to the earth, a process called the separation of heaven and earth. It can also be said that everything is a holistic entity like *Taiji*, one which can be divided into *yin* and *yang*.

"两仪生四象"是说阴阳两仪再分阴分阳,或各生一阴一阳而成四象:太阳、少阴、少阳、太阴。四象的基础上再各分阴阳,或生一阴一阳,形成八卦。

"The Two Forms Produce the Four Images" refers to the division of *yin* and *yang* into *yin* and *yang* again,to form the four Images: Greater *yang*, Lesser *yin*, Lesser *yang*, and Greater *yin*. Each of these four is again divided into *yin* and *yang*, thus forming the Eight Trigrams.

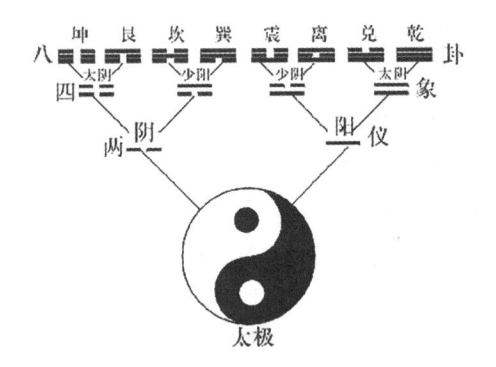

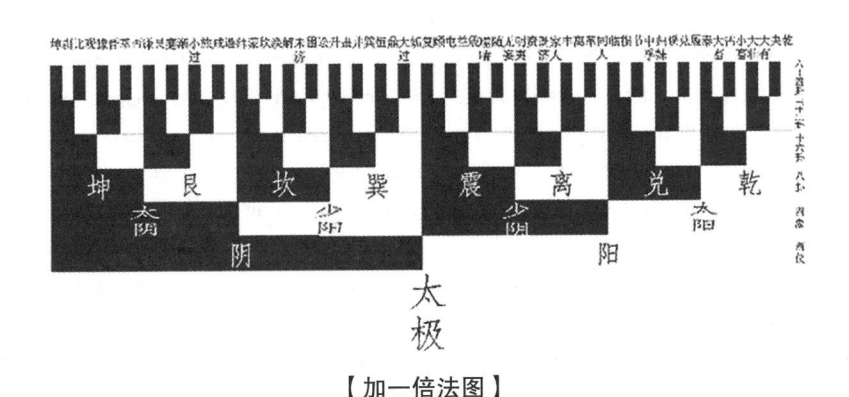

【加一倍法图】

周敦颐《太极图说》整合了阴阳、三才与五行学说。需要注意的是,朱熹认为,太极与无极无时间先后,无极是状语修饰太极,表明太极无有形迹。《太极图说》继承了先秦到汉代的阴阳五行解释宇宙生成和发展的哲学系统,再次阐发了圣人能够继天立极,以其人意接续天意的圣人之道。

Zhou Dunyi's (1017-1073) *Explanation of the Taiji Diagram* (*Taiji Tushuo* 太极图说) integrates theories of *yin* and *yang*, the Three Talents (*Sancai* 三才), and the Five Phases (*Wuxing* 五行). It should be noted that Zhu Xi believed that *Taiji* and *Wuji* (the Non-Ultimate, Non-Polar) did not appear one after the other, but rather that *Wuji* was used as an adverbial modifier to indicate that *Taiji* has no form or trace. Zhou's *Explanation of the Taiji Diagram* inherited the *yin-yang* and Five Phases philosophical system used from the Pre-Qin period to the Han Dynasty to explain the generation and development of the cosmos, and once again elucidated the *dao* of the sages, those who could inherit heaven's intentionality to establish the spiritual ultimate and connect their human intentions with the sages' *dao* of heavenly intentionality.

2. 先天八卦
2. The Pre-Celestial Eight Trigrams

八卦有先天八卦、后天八卦之分。先天八卦次序是乾、兑、离、震、巽、坎、艮、坤，分别对应天地之间最基本的八种物象：天、泽、火、雷、风、水、山、地。为了方便记忆，朱熹《周易本义》中有"八卦取象歌"："乾三连☰，坤六断☷，震仰盂☳，艮覆碗☶，兑上缺☱，巽下断☴，离中虚☲，坎中满☵。"先天八卦表达天地自然本来的面貌。古人认为，先天八卦是为了揭示世界的原初形态，但太极元气分化之后，其性质并不发生变化，如太极生两仪、四象、八卦，即使分成六十四卦之后，太极元气仍然存在，一分为多，但性质未变。

There are two versions of the Eight Trigrams: the Pre-Celestial Eight Trigrams and the Post-Celestial Eight Trigrams. The sequence of the Pre-Celestial Eight Trigrams is Qian, Dui, Li, Zhen, Xun, Kan, Gen, and Kun, corresponding to the eight most basic phenomena between heaven and earth: heaven, lake, fire, thunder, wind, water, mountain, and earth. For the convenience of memory, in Zhu Xi's *Original Meaning of the Book of Changes*, there is a song based on the forms of the Eight Trigrams:

Qian is three unbroken long lines, while Kun is six broken short lines; Zhen resembles a bowl facing up (with upper and middle broken lines), while Gen resembles a bowl facing down (with middle and bottom broken lines); Dui's upper line is broken, while Xun's bottom line is broken; Li's middle line is broken, while Kan's middle line is unbroken.

The Pre-Celestial Eight Trigrams express the original appearance of the natural world, as ancient people believed that the Pre-Celestial Eight Trigrams were meant to reveal the embryonic prototype of the cosmos, yet even after the primordial *qi* of *Taiji* divided, its nature did not change. For example, even after *Taiji* divides into the Two Forms, then the Four Images, and then the Eight Trigrams and 64 Hexagrams, it still exists as itself and its nature remains unchanged.

第一章　导论
——《周易》哲学的人天之意

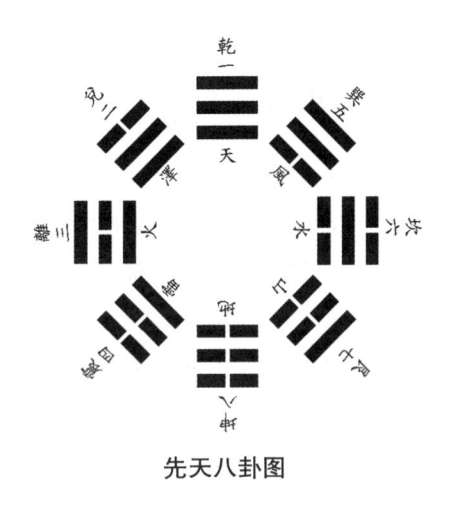

先天八卦图

先天八卦一般说是邵雍从陈抟那里得来，至于其历史性的确切起源无从得知。但最为重要的是，先天八卦不能简单看作一个历史性的图形，而必须从其宇宙起源和自然本相的意义上去认识和理解。

Reputedly, the Pre-Celestial Eight Trigrams were obtained by Shao Yong from Chen Tuan in the Northern Song Dynasty (960-1127), although the exact historical origin remains unclear. Most importantly, the Pre-Celestial Eight Trigrams cannot simply be seen as a historical patterns of lines, but must be recognized and understood in the significance of their cosmic origin and natural appearance.

太极图配先天八卦方位图

3. 后天八卦
3. The Post-Celestial Eight Trigrams

后天八卦是把先天八卦位置调整之后形成的八卦方位图。按照司马迁的说法，周文王姬昌原是商末周族首领，封西伯，被殷纣王囚禁在羑里城（汤阴城北）七年。纣王把姬昌的长子伯邑考杀害，剁成肉酱，烙成肉饼，强令姬昌咽下。八十二岁高龄的姬昌含悲忍痛啖子肉，躲过一劫，之后他在狱中发愤治学，潜心钻研，将伏羲八卦方位按照五行生克原理重新排列之后成后天八卦。因为相传是文王发明的，所以后天八卦又称"文王后天八卦"。

The Post-Celestial Eight Trigrams form an orientation map acquired after adjustment of the orientation of the Pre-Celestial Eight Trigrams. According to Sima Qian, Ji Chang, King Wen of the Zhou Dynasty, was a former chief of the Zhou clan in the late Shang Dynasty. He was granted the title of Marquis Xibo, and was imprisoned in the city of Youli (north of Tangyin city) for seven years. King Zhou killed his eldest son Yikao, and forced Ji Chang to swallow a meat pie made from his own son's dismembered body. Ji Chang, at the age of 82, endured the pain of swallowing his own son to escape death. After that he devoted himself to the study of the Eight Trigrams and rearranged them to form the Post-Celestial Eight Trigrams, which were also known as King Wen's Post-Celestial Eight Trigrams.

后天八卦从东方开始，顺时针方向排列而成。后天八卦与方位、时令相配，并与斗柄旋转的天文现象一致。因此，《周易》的运用主要是以后天八卦为基础，涉及古代天文、地理、乐律、兵法、音韵、算术、医学、风水、炼丹等各个方面。周文王在监狱里殚精竭虑所重排的后天八卦，可以说是中国古代实用文化的理论根基。

The Post-Celestial Eight Trigrams are arranged clockwise starting from the east and keep in line with natural directions and seasons, as well as with the revolving direction of the Big Dipper constellation. Therefore, the use of the *Book of Changes* is based on the Post-Celestial Eight Trigrams and takes into consideration ancient astronomy, geography, music and rhythm, military technique, phonetics, arithmetic, medicine, *fengshui*, alchemy, and so on. The Post-Celestial Eight Trigrams rearranged by King Wen of Zhou in prison can be said to be the theoretical foundation of ancient Chinese practical culture.

后天八卦方位图

通常来说，先天八卦代表天地未分之前的先天状态，也就是元气的本然状态，是一个全体，只是不得不通过阴阳分判，加一倍法分裂成为八卦来理解宇宙元气的全体而已。所以先天八卦次序应该理解为元气本然的次序。

Generally speaking, the Pre-Celestial Eight Trigrams represent the pre-celestial state before the division of heaven and earth, the original state of primordial *qi*. This is a whole, but has to be split into the Eight Trigrams through the divisions of *yin* and *yang* in order to understand the moving patterns of the cosmos. Thus the pre-celestial order of the Pre-Celestial Eight Trigrams should be understood as the original order of primordial *qi*.

后天八卦是按照八卦的方位和五行属性重新排列之后而成的，其与东南西北方位的对应，以及相应的五行方位和特点的对应关系，是把八卦带入后天现实的状态当中，也就是天地之道运行和变化的实际情境当中，或者是先天意念的后天实化与运用当中。

The Post-Celestial Eight Trigrams were rearranged according to their orientation and Five Phases attributes. Their correspondence with the four directions and the Five Phases orientations is a reflection of bringing the Eight Trigrams into an actual state of reality, that is, the actual situation of the movement and changes of the *dao* of heaven and earth, or the realization and application of pre-heavenly intentionality.

先后天八卦代表古代圣人以人意接续天意的八种基本模式："生—能—向—缘—识—行—量—境"，也可以称为人天之意的八种原型，对应于"意"作为心物一元的宇宙本体发动而展开成为"缘—识—向—境—能—生—行—量"八种不同推演的模式。这八种模式发动合乎阴阳五行运动的内在规律，再通过六十四卦的推演，八种实意模式可以演化为三百八十四种意念实化的样态。

The Pre-Celestial and Post-Celestial Eight Trigrams represent the eight basic patterns of communion between ancient sages' intentions and heavenly intentionality: creating—energizing—orientating—depending—awaking—moving—situating—contexting, which can also be referred to as the eight prototypes of human-cosmological intentionality. Correspondingly, intentionality as the cosmic substance of the unity of mind and things and things/events/matters is concretized and developed into eight derived post-celestial patterns: depending—awaking—orientating—contexting—energizing—creating—moving—situating. These eight modes are in line with the internal laws of *yin-yang* and Five Phases movement, and through the deduction of the 64 hexagrams, the eight realization modes of intentionality can evolve into 384 specific and intentional situations.

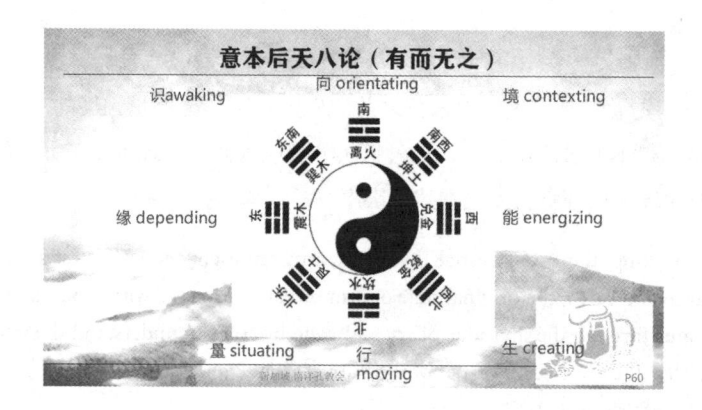

4. 五行
4. Five Phases

《周易》产生于黄河领域。中原地带的古人长期观测天地历象的变化，基于其生活环境和经验发明了五行生克理论。木、火、土、金、水五行与方位相配，木在东，东方木旺，木可燃烧，也可自燃，故木生火；南方热，故火在南，火烧完之后化为灰烬，回归泥土，故火生土；土居中央，土旺四季，土中含金，聚土成山，山必长石，故土生金；西方多山、多金石，故金在西，山上金石出泉，西山多为江河之源，故金生水；北方为水，木由水滋养，故水生木。木火土金水"比相生，间相克"：木生火、火生土、土生金、金生水、水生木，这是五行相生；木克土、土克水、水克火、火克金、金克木，这是五行相克。树木克土生长，土能挡水，水能灭火，火能熔金，金能伐木。五行配方位有利于解释文王后天八卦的由来。

The *Book of Changes* was produced in the Yellow River area of central China where ancient people invented the generation and restriction theory of the Five Phases, namely, Wood, Fire, Earth, Metal and Water, and matched it to the natural directions. Wood belongs to the east, as it flourishes in the eastern part of China, especially in the season of Spring. Wood can be burned by fire, so wood generates fire. Fire belongs to the south as it is hot in southern China. After the burning of fire, ashes are left which return to the earth, so fire generates earth. Earth belongs to central China as it brings prosperity in all four seasons. Earth contains metal and piles up to form mountains of stone, so soil generates metal. In western China there are many high mountains which are rich in metal and stone, so metal belongs to the west. Out of the metal and stone often comes springs, and the western Chinese mountains are usually sources of great rivers. Therefore, metal generates water. Water belongs to the north, and water nourishes wood, so water generates wood.

Generally speaking, Wood, Fire, Earth, Metal and Water are mutually generated and mutually restrained: Wood generates Fire, Fire generates Earth, Earth generates Metal, Metal generates Water, and Water generates Wood. This is the mutual generation of the Five Phases. Wood conquers Earth, Earth conquers Water, Water conquers Fire, Fire conquers Metal, and Metal conquers Wood. This is the mutual restriction of the Five Phases. Trees grow against earth; earth can block water; water can extinguish fire; fire can melt metal; and metal can cut wood. The correlation and correspondence of the Five Phases and the directions can help explain the origin of King Wen's Post-Celestial Eight Trigrams.

5. 六十四卦方图和圆图
5. The Square and Circle Diagrams of the 64 Hexagrams

八卦两两相重，成为六十四卦。六十四卦有多种排列顺序，但基本上都按照"阳长阴消，阴长阳消"的规则来排列。六十四卦方图以坤卦和乾卦为对角线，以泰卦和否卦为另一个对角线，顺序变动阴阳爻排列而成。

The Eight Trigrams overlap in pairs to form the 64 hexagrams, which have various arrangements, but all based on the rule of "When *yang* increases, *yin* decreases; and when *yin* increases, *yang* decreases." The square diagram of the 64 hexagrams is composed by changing the *yin* and *yang* lines in a certain sequence, with Hexagram Kun (Support) and Hexagram Qian (Creativity) at the two ends of one diagonal line, and Hexagram Tai (Communication) and Hexagram Pi (Non-Communication) at the two ends of the other diagonal line. The circle diagram of the 64 hexagrams starts from Hexagram Qian (Creativity) and follows the generation order of the Pre-Celestial Eight Trigrams.

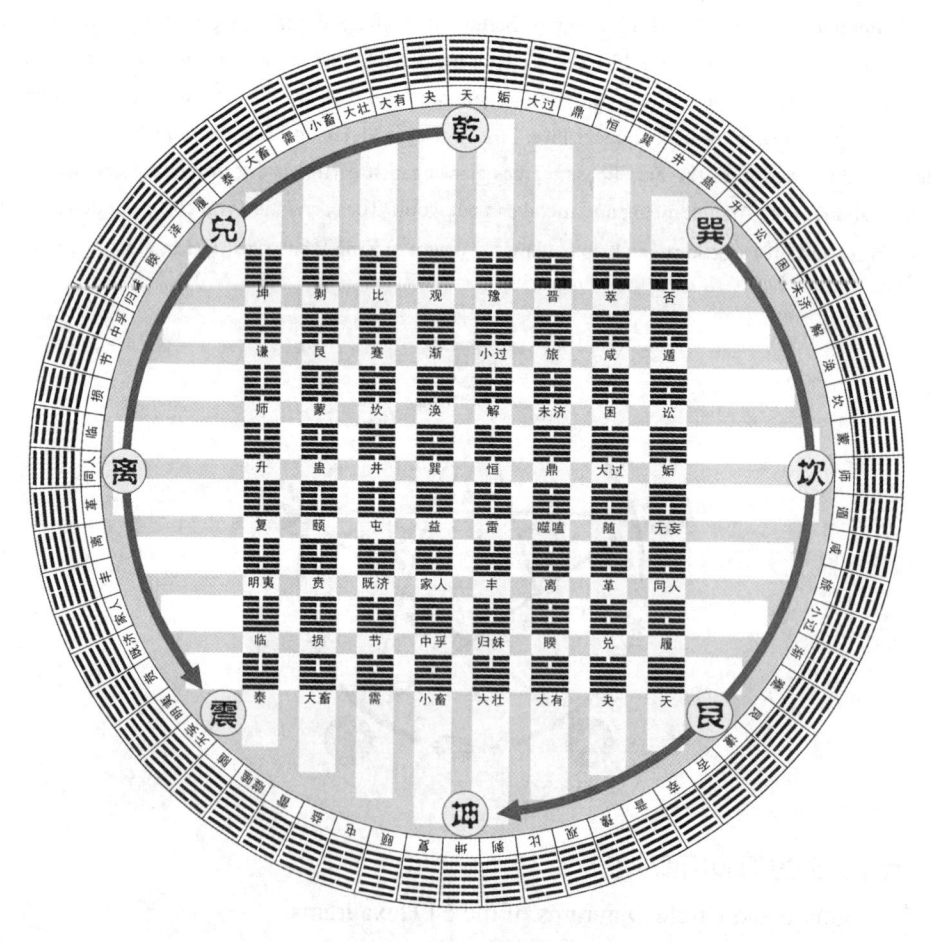

六十四卦方圆图

六十四卦方图和圆图排列有精准的次序，仿佛来自天然，非人力所能安排。邵雍认为，这是伏羲发明的图式，包涵天地万物所有的道理。朱熹认为圆图的重点是讲阴阳流行，方图则强调阴阳定位，圆图配时间过程，方图配空间方位。后来此图被莱布尼茨看成是二进制的体现，用于论证他发明的二进制，由此可以反证，中国古人已经发现二进制相关的数理模型和符号体系。

The arrangements of the square and circle diagrams of the 64 hexagrams have a precise order, as if they come from nature and are beyond artificial design. Shao Yong believed that this was a schema invented by Fu Xi that encompasses all the patterns of heaven and earth. Zhu Xi believed that the circle diagram emphasized the circulation of *yin* and *yang*, while the square diagram emphasized the positioning of *yin* and *yang*, with the circle diagram matching the temporal process and the square diagram matching the spatial orientation. Later, this diagram was viewed by Leibniz as an example of a binary system, and he used it to demonstrate his invention of the binary system. This proves that ancient Chinese had already discovered a mathematical model and symbolic system related to the binary system.

6. 六十四卦次序
6. Order of the 64 Hexagrams

今本《周易》六十四卦有固定的排列顺序，具体见于《序卦传》，仔细说明并分析为什么要如此排列。《杂卦传》打乱了卦序，但对卦的特性做了进一步的说明。

The extant version of the *Book of Changes* has a fixed order of arrangement for the 64 hexagrams, and a detailed explanation and analysis can be found in the *Commentary on the Sequence of the Hexagrams* (*Xugua Zhuan* 序卦传). The *Commentary on Miscellaneous Characteristics of the Hexagrams* (*Zagua Zhuan* 杂卦传) disrupts this sequence but further explains the characteristics of the 64 hexagrams.

7. 八宫卦
7. The Eight Palace Hexagrams

西汉京房（前77–前37）根据八卦设立八宫，把八经卦自身的重卦称为"八纯上世卦"与其宫相对应。每一纯卦根据一定的变易规律又分别统帅七个"子宫卦"。从一世卦到五世卦是依次由初爻向五爻逐渐爻变的过程，而游魂卦与归魂卦则是至极而逆变的过程。这是《八宫卦次图》在纵向上的一种变化规律。

Jing Fang (77 BC-37 BC) of the Western Han Dynasty (202 BC-8 AD) invented a theory of Eight

Palace Hexagrams (*ba gong gua* 八宫卦), eight pure hexagrams based on duplications of the Eight Trigrams. These eight pure hexagrams based on the Eight Trigrams are also referred to as the Eight Classical Hexagrams (*ba jing gua* 八经卦), which are regarded as Eight Pure Hexagrams in which the top line could be referred to the subject who reads the hexagram. Each Pure Hexagram leads another seven son-palace hexagrams (*zi gong gua* 子宫卦) according to a certain variation pattern: changing from the bottom line to the fifth line, each of which could be referred to as the subject itself. Wandering-soul hexagrams (*you hun gua* 游魂卦) and coming-back-soul hexagrams (*gui hun gua* 归魂卦) refer to the pattern of returning back after things reach their peak. This is a vertical variation pattern inside each hexagram in the pattern of the Eight Palace Hexagrams.

八宫的顺序是按照后天八卦图的顺序排列的。按后天八卦图的顺序，顺时针方向，从乾在西北开始，之后坎在正北，艮在东北，震在正东，巽在东南，离在正南，坤在西南，兑在正西排列。八卦图的南北东西方位，与现代地图上北下南相反，而是上南下北，这是跟中国古人发明八卦的时候处于中原地带的方位感有关。

The sequence of the Eight Palace Hexagrams is arranged according to the diagram of the Post-Celestial Eight Trigrams, which is in a clockwise direction, starting from Trigram Qian in the northwest, then Trigram Kan in the north, Trigram Gen in the northeast, Trigram Zhen in the east, Trigram Xun in the southeast, Trigram Li in the south, Trigram Kun in the southwest, and Trigram Dui in the west. The south-north orientation of the Post-Celestial Eight Trigrams diagram is opposite to modern maps, with south above and north below. This is related to the sense of orientation in the central plains region when ancient Chinese invented the Eight Trigrams.

《周易明意》先天八论和后天八论基于八宫卦象次序。先天八论为：生–能–向–缘–识–行–量–境，分论作为宇宙起源和存在本体的"意"基于先天的八个维度；并对应于后天八论：缘–识–向–境–能–生–行–量，分造八维度之意而能运世之化。

The Pre-celestial Eight philosophical theories and Post-celestial Eight philosophical theories in this book are based on the sequence of the Eight Palace Hexagrams. The pre-celestial eight philosophical theories are: creating—energizing—orienting—depending—awaking—moving—situating—contexting. Intentionality as the source and ontological substance of the cosmos is based on these eight dimensions, and corresponds to the post-celestial eight theories: depending—awaking—orienting—contexting—energizing—creating—moving—situating, thus producing the eight dimensions of intentionality, transformations that can be applied in worldly practice.

五、《周易》的经与传

V. The Classic and Commentaries of the *Book of Changes*

1.《周易》的经
1. The Classic of the *Book of Changes*

传统几千家注释《周易》的作者，基本上都把卦爻辞看成一个体系，认为是有意义的创作，可以通过《易传》加以理解。但是，因为其中有一些卦爻辞很难解，加上运用爻辞占断在实践当中可行，所以也有一些学者认为，卦爻辞就是古代占卜的记录，因而是无序的，无规律的，也就可以任意解释，任意发挥。这就导致近代以来"古史辨派"的学者们，根据新近的出土文物和文献证据，推翻传统上对于卦爻辞的系统解释，在抛弃《易传》的基础上，运用自己的想象力加以发挥，虽然形成了很多有学术见地的成果，但总的来说还是无助于解释卦爻辞的意义系统。

Traditionally, thousands of authors who have annotated the *Book of Changes* have viewed the hexagrams and lines as a holistic system of meaningful creation that can be understood through the *Commentaries on the Changes*. However, because some of the explanations of hexagrams and lines are difficult to interpret, and it is feasible to apply these words in divination practice, some scholars believe that these explanations are merely records of ancient divination, that they are disorderly and irregular, and that they, therefore, can be interpreted and elaborated freely. This led many modern scholars of the "Discriminating Ancient History School (*gu shi bian pai* 古史辨派)" to overturn traditional systematic interpretations with the help of recently unearthed cultural relics and documentary evidence that were not traditionally available in ancient history. Having abandoned the *Commentaries*, they used their imagination together with what they called new evidence to produce many new academic achievements, but little real progress has been made in explaining the meaningful system of the 64 hexagrams and 384 lines.

近现代以来，一方面质疑传统易学的成果层出不穷，似乎花样翻新，异见迭出；另一方面，一些系统解释卦爻辞的学者，坚持传统经传不分的路子，虽然也参考新的考古证据和带有新见的著作，但这些证据和新见对解释流传了两千多年的卦爻辞系统的帮助有限。吊诡的是，偏离传统经传不分路子的新派易学，由于其提出新见的前提就是否定《易传》对《易经》的解释力，只能在抛弃以传解经的传统正路上越走越远。

In modern and contemporary times, while endless new doubts and opinions have emerged about the achievements of traditional *Changes* Studies, there have also been scholars who stick to the practice of systematically explaining the hexagrams and lines and hold the traditional viewpoint that the *Classic* and its *Commentaries* should be studied together as a unity. Although they also refer to recent archaeological evidence and research, these provide limited help in understanding the more than 2000-year-old system of hexagrams and lines. Paradoxically, scholars of the new schools of *Changes* Studies, basing their new theories on denying that the *Commentaries* are able to interpret the *Classic*, have gone further and further in abandoning the traditionally orthodox methodology of using commentaries to explain classics.

2.《周易》的传
2. The Commentaries on the *Book of Changes*

自汉代有经学开始，解释《周易》卦爻辞就不能够离开《易传》的辅助，或许在春秋战国时代，《周易》传承还没有公开的时候，与今本《易传》相关的内容对经文的解释力度应该也是不容置疑的，所以《易经》和《易传》才会代代相传，同时列为五经之首，成为不可分割的大道之源。

Since the Han Dynasty (202 BC-220 AD), the interpretation of the hexagrams and lines of the *Book of Changes* cannot be separated from the assistance of the *Commentaries*. Perhaps during the Spring and Autumn Period (770 BC-476 BC) and the Warring States Period (476 BC-221 BC), even when the inheritance of the *Book of Changes* was not yet publicly available, the explanatory power of the *Commentaries*, particularly that which remains consistent with the current extant version, should be undeniable. Therefore, the *Classic of Changes* and its *Commentaries* were passed down from generation to generation, and were listed together as first among the Five Classics, becoming the inseparable source of the great *dao*.

《易传》有十篇，简称"十翼"。《易传》是解释经文的，可以说是经文的附录。我们今天要想读懂《周易》，必须借助《易传》十篇。按传统的说法，《易传》是孔子写的或者是他整理的。

The *Commentaries* has ten chapters, abbreviated as the *Ten Wings* (*shiyi* 十翼). It is an explanatory text and can be considered an appendix to the *Classic*. To understand the *Book of Changes* today, we have to rely on the ten chapters of the *Commentaries*, which were reputedly written or compiled by Confucius himself.

3.《易传》的成书
3. The composition of the *Commentaries on the Changes*

关于《易传》的成书年代的讨论很复杂，很多学者把"十翼"分篇拆开，从单篇文字与不同时代的文献之间的文字之出入来比对，说明不同篇章跟不同时代的文字有关系，从而判断不同的篇章形成于不同的年代，不过总体来说，纷繁杂乱，莫衷一是。基本上近代以来大部分关于《易传》成书年代的讨论，都要否定孔子与《易传》的关系，当然也有部分学者坚持传统的说法。

There are many different views on how the *Commentaries* came into being, and it has become a complicated issue. Many scholars have broken the *Ten Wings* down into segments and compared the individual texts with other historical documents to determine that different chapters were formed in different eras. However, these researches include many different views and conclusions, and the question turns out to be more and more complicated. Basically, most discussions since modern times have denied the relationship between Confucius and the *Commentaries*, as opposed to a small number of scholars who stick to the traditional view.

按照传统的看法，孔子是《周易》成书"人更三圣"的"三圣"之一，《易传》成书经过孔子之手。近现代说法非常杂乱，大部分的说法，包括结合出土文献的说法，都不可以作为推翻传统说法的权威观点。

Traditionally, Confucius was believed to be one of the "Three Sages (*sansheng* 三圣)" who had contributed to the historical formation of the *Classic of Changes*, and its *Commentaries* were thought to have passed through his hands. Modern theories regarding this are miscellaneous and most of them, including those based on newly unearthed literature, have no authority or power to overturn the traditional view.

4.《易传》与孔子
4. The *Commentaries on the Changes* and Confucius

孔子与《周易》的关系，在明清以前的传统社会当中不是太大的问题，虽有人提出疑问，但基本上公认孔子是《易传》的作者或者整理者，这与《周易》为六经之首的地位也是相匹配的。只是近代以来，因为知识分子们把国家一连串的失败归结到文化的根源上，认为需要推翻孔子的权威性，第一要务就是要撇清孔子与《易传》的关系，这影响到现当代很多学者，他们不再认为孔子是《易传》的作者或整理者，《易传》也就成为很多人一起完成，而且成书年代相对较晚的书。

The relationship between Confucius and the *Book of Changes* was not a major issue in traditional society before the Ming (1368-1644) and Qing (1644-1911) dynasties. Despite various doubts, it was widely recognized that Confucius was the author or compiler of the *Commentaries*, which also matched the position of the *Book of Changes* as first among the Six Classics. Since modern times, the intellectual community has attributed a series of Chinese national failures to her cultural roots, believing that the authority of Confucius should be overthrown and that the top priority was to disassociate Confucius from the *Commentaries*. This has influenced a large number of contemporary scholars to believe that Confucius was not the author or compiler of the *Commentaries* and that it was a production of later generations by collective authorship.

确实可以说，没有孔子（与其弟子）整理和创作的《易传》，后人基本上不可能读懂《易经》，而近现代人脱离《易传》试图解释《易经》的努力，对于解释说明《周易》卦爻辞体系的连贯性这一段千古难题来说，基本上都是盲人摸象。毕竟脱离《易传》之后的所有解释，可以说都跟《周易》本来的卦爻辞体系没有多少关系，甚至可以说，对出土文献和新材料的解读，如果不是建立在对传统周易卦爻辞体系的扎实理解的基础上，那么研究得越深入，就离开探索《周易》卦爻辞连贯性的母题越远，更偏离了《周易》卦爻辞本身所包含的"推天道以明人事"的根本宗旨。

Indeed, it was almost impossible for later generations to understand the *Classic* without the *Commentaries* compiled and composed by Confucius (and his disciples). However, the attempt of modern people to break away from the *Commentaries* to explain the coherence of the hexagram and line system are basically blind and full of failure. It can even be said that the interpretation of unearthed texts and new materials, if not based on a solid understanding of the traditional system of hexagrams and lines, is a deviation from the fundamental purpose of "extending the heavenly *dao* to illuminate human affairs" contained in the 64 hexagrams and 384 lines of the *Book of Changes*. The deeper such modern research goes, the further it goes astray from exploring the coherence of the hexagrams and lines in the *Book of Changes*, and thus the fundamental purpose of promoting the heavenly way to clarify human affairs.

5.《易传》与儒家思想
5. The Commentaries on the Changes and Confucian Thought

《周易》与孔子创立的儒家思想关系直接而且密切。首先孔子晚年读易非常勤奋，"韦编三绝"就是描述他读易读到连接竹简的牛皮绳都断了很多次。其次，他晚年不但熟读《易经》，整理写作《易传》，而且可能还有比较丰富的占卜实践经验，这又促进了他对卦爻辞的理解和诠释。

The relationship between the *Book of Changes* and the Confucian thoughts founded by Confucius is direct and close. Firstly, Confucius was very diligent in reading the *Classic of Changes* in his later years. A story describes how he read the book until the cowhide rope binding the bamboo slips broke many times. Secondly, he not only read the *Classic of Changes* proficiently, and compiled and wrote the *Commentaries*, but also may well have had relatively rich practical experience in divination, which promoted his understanding and interpretation of the hexagrams and lines.

再说，《易传》有非常典型的儒家气象，比如《系辞上》说："一阴一阳之谓道，继之者善也，成之者性也。"一阴一阳的继续状态就是善，这是从生生不息的根本出发点来说善，而天地自然之善是儒家形上学的根本出发点，能够把天地的生生领悟成善，就是一种典型的儒家气象。再次，《系辞》里多次提到："富有之谓大业""崇高莫大乎富贵"等等说法，都是认可"富有""富贵"这样的现实价值的，并认为值得人们在了解易道的基础上去不断努力，这都有明确的儒家气象，与道家和佛家的气象可以明确区别开来。有些《大象》和《小象》的言辞也有很明显的儒家色彩，这在本书的翻译和解释中也可以看出来。

Furthermore, the *Commentaries* has a very typical Confucian atmosphere, as is said in the first part of the *Attached Words* (*Xici* 系辞)："One *yin* and one *yang* compose the *dao*; that which continues this is good; and that which accomplishes this is inherent nature." The continuing state of one *yin* and one *yang* is the good, which is viewed as the fundamental starting point of endless generation. The natural goodness of heaven and earth is the fundamental starting point of Confucian metaphysics, and the comprehension of the endless generation of heaven and earth into goodness is a typical Confucian thought. Thirdly, the *Attached Words* (*Xici*) repeatedly mentions that "wealth is a great achievement" and "the sublime knows nothing greater than wealth and nobility", all of which recognize the practical value of being wealthy and noble, which encourage people's continuous efforts on the basis of understanding the *dao* of changes. This Confucian thinking in the *Commentaries* can be clearly distinguished from the views of Daoism and Buddhism on this question. Some of the words in the *Great Images* (*Daxiang* 大象) and *Small Images* (*Xiaoxiang* 小象) also have a clear Confucian flavor, which can be seen in the translation and interpretation of this book.

《易传》当中体现出来的本末终始说、迁善说、性命说、继善成性说等等，这都是有明显儒家思想的说法。《易传》解释的这种儒家色彩，在中国哲学史、思想史、文化史上有深远的影响和重大的意义，后世儒者基本上都受到《易传》儒家风格的影响，进而融会道家道教和佛教的思想资源，对中华民族文化的定型和发展有巨大的奠基性和范式意义。

Doctrines reflected in the *Commentaries*, such as the doctrine of beginning and end, the doctrine of moving towards goodness, the doctrine of life and inherent nature, and the doctrine of inheriting goodness to accomplish inherent nature, are all obvious Confucian thoughts that have had a profound influence and significant impact on the history of Chinese philosophy, thought, and culture. Later generations of Confucians were basically influenced by the Confucian mindset in the *Commentaries* before they further integrated the ideological resources of Daoism and Buddhism. This has had a huge foundational and paradigmatic significance for the shaping and development of Chinese culture.

6. 经传关系
6. The Relationship Between the Classic and its Commentaries

《经》与《传》的关系，最根本的是要确认用《易传》解《易经》不仅在过去的历史上是合理的，而且将来也必然是合理的。《易经》的作者传统上说人更三圣，圣圣相传，后来有《易传》以后，《易传》就一直是解释《易经》的。只是近代以来，很多学者倾向于把经传分开，认为经是经，传是传。一种理由是《周易》的经和传形成于不同的历史时代，既然《易传》成书一定比《易经》更晚，所以必须分开，这样的理由其实是靠不住的，既然《易传》是解释《易经》的，成书必然晚，不能说因为成书晚了，就不具备解释力了。如果因为《易传》成书更晚，就认为《易传》不再具备解释《易经》的合理性，就非得分开成为两部不相干的著作，这是站不住脚的。成书年代绝不是分开经与传的充足理由。另外一种说法认为，既然《易经》是占卜书，《易传》是哲学书，那就不能够用哲学的内容来解释占卜的内容，这种说法听起来很有道理，但这样一来，就强调《易经》和《易传》完全是两部性质不同的书，占卜的书跟哲学的书本来就没有关系，不可以强扯在一起。这样说的学者，既不了解《易经》的内容，也没有读懂《易传》，可以说是凭空猜测，想当然论断。所以这两种说法都似是而非，导致不少近代易学家的解易作品引经据典，看起来言之凿凿，但其实望文生义，不知所云，越解释越糊涂。很多读者，读了很多近代的易学著作，完全如坠五里雾中，以致丧失了辨别力，以为《易经》可以抛开《易传》胡乱解释，只要强调《易传》跟《易经》没关系，《易经》的卦爻辞就可以随意解读，这就造成了《周易》解释史上的一大谬误——"经传分观的谬误"。

On the issue of the relationship between the *Classic* and the *Commentaries*, it is fundamental to confirm that using the *Commentaries* to interpret the *Classic* is not only reasonable in past history, but also inevitable in the future. The authors of the *Classic* have traditionally been said to be the three sages throughout history. Since their completion, the Confucian *Commentaries* have been used to explain the *Classic*. Since modern times, many scholars have tended to separate the Confucian *Commentaries* from the *Classic*, believing that they are independent from each other. One reason is that the two were formed in different historical periods. Since the *Commentaries* must have been written later than the *Classic*, they should be separated accordingly. This reason is very questionable, as the ability of the *Commentaries* to explain the *Classic* cannot be denied just due to their later appearance. Another view which sounds reasonable is that, since the *Classic* is a divination book and the *Commentaries* is much more philosophical, it is not possible to explain the content of divination with philosophical content. However, scholars who hold this view do not understand the content of the *Book of Changes* properly, nor do they understand the Confucian *Commentaries* appropriately, but in fact only take them for granted based on their literal meanings.

Both of these arguments are skeptical, and, as a result, many modern scholars seem to be eloquent and convincing when citing the *Classic* in their works, but actually their arguments are generally vague and unclear, and the more explanations they make, the more confusion is caused. Many readers who have read much modern research on the *Classic* have lost their discernment and believe that the *Classic* can be interpreted indiscriminately without the *Commentaries*, resulting in a major fallacy in the history of the interpretation of the *Book of Changes*—the fallacy of separating the *Classic* from its *Commentaries*.

This fallacy has a wide and serious impact, not only causing confusion in the academic community, but, more importantly, as a byproduct of the campaign to overthrow the authority of Confucianism, leading to a lack of reverence or sanctity towards traditional classics and Confucius who had been revered as the "most holy teacher of ten-thousand generations." Since Confucius' works no longer have authority, people today can explain them as they wish, even to the degree of explaining the hexagrams and lines in ignorance of the significance of *yin* and *yang*, or the Eight Trigrams, thus casually creating alternative directions and styles of interpretation. There are also practices of elucidating by ignoring the inherent rationality of the *Classic* system and resulting in chaos in the academic community. The source of all of these modern confusion can be attributed to this fallacy.

今天的中国易学界应该抛弃"经传分观"的谬误，不少拆分经传的易学著作，于道不通，却随意曲解经文，看起来似乎人人可懂，其实是谬种流传。今天可以用现代科学方法如考古学或文献学方法来研究《周易》古经和相关材料，但经文与传文一并传世已经两三千年，现有的研究并不能够推翻传统的解法，所以今天应该不再继续"经传分观"的谬误。

Today's academic community should abandon the fallacy of separating the *Commentaries* from the *Classic*. Many researchers on *Changes* Studies arbitrarily distort the *Classic* and are not sensible about the basic knowledge of systematic understanding. Of course, modern scientific methods such as archaeology and philology should be applied to study the ancient *Classic* and related materials, but such modern research cannot overturn traditional explications completely, especially if they have been passed down for two to three thousand years. Today, it is time that we put an end to this modern fallacy of separating the *Classic* from its *Commentaries*.

六、明解《周易》的方法
VI. Methods for Elucidating the *Book of Changes*

当代的《周易》研究，在经文方面是否能够做到"明解《周易》"，就要经传互证、辨象证义，以精准解释卦爻辞和合理阐发义理为基准；而《周易》哲学在今天的推进，要以易学哲学思想的当代创造和转化为标准。

Whether contemporary research on the *Book of Changes* can achieve an illluminating explication depends on the mutual verification of the Classic and its Commentaries, the identification of images and their correlated meanings, and the accurate interpretation of hexagrams, lines, and words, as well as the reasonable interpretation of the patterns of intention. The advancement of *Changes* Studies today should be based on the modern creation and transformation of the traditional *Book of Changes* philosophy.

1. 抛弃"象数与义理分开的谬误"
1. Abandon the "fallacy of separating image-number from meaning-principle"

历代易学家为了明解《周易》，有所谓"两派六宗"之说。"两派"是指象数派和义理派，象数派认为，数为象本，象因数生，象为卦爻的根本，而数为象根之本源，所以要把卦爻辞解释清楚，必须首先把象数的根据说明清楚，认为一切离开象数的义理，都是没有根据的随意发挥；义理派认为，义为理本，理因义生，卦爻是说明义理的工具，理解了义理可以摆脱卦爻的束缚，所以主要的目标是把义理讲透，至于象数的基础，最多作为辅助。象数和义理两派都有道理，不应该相互排斥。在本书中，是通过卦变体系将两者贯通起来的。

In the history of elucidating the *Book of Changes*, the many approaches have been generally divided into "two schools and six sects." The two schools are the image-number school and the meaning-principle school. The image-number school holds that numbers are the foundation of images and that images are generated from numbers, so it is necessary to clarify the foundation of images-numbers before clarifying line statements; otherwise there is only arbitrary elaboration without any systematic pattern. However, the meaning-principle school holds that meaning is the root of principle and the goal of *Changes* hermeneutics, and that line statements are just tools to explain meaning and principle, so after meaning and principle are understood, one can cast aside the lines, images and statements. Therefore, the primary goal is to explicate meaning and principle clearly. As for the basis of images and numbers, they are just auxiliary to illuminating meaning and principle. Actually, both the image-number school and the meaning-principle school are reasonable, and they should not be regarded as mutually exclusive. In this book, the two traditional schools are connected together through a hexagram-changes (*guabian* 卦变) system.

2. 抛弃"经传分开的谬误"
2. Abandon the "fallacy of separating the classic and its commentaries"

明解《周易》的第一步是抛弃"经传分开的谬误",重新把《易传》作为解易的核心文献,不否认《易传》解易传统的合理性。以古史辨派为代表的,致力于推翻传统易学、打击古代中国学问作为世界中心的学术倾向,今天被越来越多研究认为并不可取,很多研究甚至怀着破坏民族自信、毁灭民族文化等历史虚无主义倾向,甚至与摧毁民族自信等不可告人的计划与目的相配合的。

The first step in elucidating the *Book of Changes* is to abandon the fallacy of separating the Classic from its Commentaries and once again establish the *Commentaries* as the core text for explaining the changes, without denying the reasonableness of this tradition. The academic tendency represented by the Discriminating Ancient History School, which has tried to overturn traditional *Changes* Studies and attacked the world-center position of ancient Chinese scholarship, has been regarded as unreasonable by more and more research today. Some studies even display a historical nihilist tendency with the goal and objective of destroying national confidence and culture.

要想明解《周易》卦爻辞,就必须坚持《系辞》的哲学大旨不可违背,不应该把《系辞》作非哲学的解释,否则,《系辞》作为最具备传统哲学意味的文献,如果都被否定,其实是一种中国哲学虚无主义的倾向。否认传统中国哲学思想的深度和力度在中国哲学史研究中长期存在。如果因为对《周易》和其象数体系不熟悉就连带否定《系辞》的哲学意义,不认可《系辞》是代表早期中国哲学的文献,否定系辞当中对于天地之道,对于人生哲学的深刻探讨,更不要说否定对《系辞》当中,解析卦爻辞的部分体现出的上古人文历史和哲学思想发展的深刻理解,是非常不可取的。

To fully understand the line statements of the *Book of Changes*, it is necessary to adhere to the philosophical essence of the *Attached Words* (*Xici* 系辞) commentary and not give it a non-philosophical interpretation. Otherwise, if *Attached Words* as the most traditional philosophical document is denied, this represents a nihilistic tendency against Chinese philosophy, one that has long existed in the study of the history of Chinese philosophy. If one is not familiar with *Changes* and its image-number system, and, therefore, negates the philosophical significance of the *Attached Words*, not recognizing it as a representative work of early Chinese philosophy, if one negates the profound exploration of the *dao* of heaven and earth and the philosophy of life in the *Attached Words*, as well as the profound understanding of ancient human history and philosophical development reflected in the analysis of the hexagrams and lines in the *Attached Words*, this is totally untenable.

3. 抛弃"离象释义的谬误"
3. Abandon the "fallacy of explaining meanings without reference to images"

《说卦》是解读《周易》卦爻辞的密码本,《说卦》的取象原则在解易的过程当中应该严格遵守。不讲象却试图解释《周易》卦爻辞的方法偏离了《周易》传统。《说卦》对卦爻辞的解释力度,甚至超过《系辞》,因为它渗透到卦爻辞字字句句当中。

Explaining the Hexagrams (*shuogua* 说卦) is a codebook to decipher the *Book of Changes*, and its principles for deriving images should be strictly observed. Any attempt to explain the line statements without taking images into consideration goes against the tradition of the *Book of Changes*. Actually the power of *Explaining the Hexagrams* to explain the *Classic* even exceeds the *Attached Words* (*Xici*), because the explanation penetrates each word and sentence of the 64 hexagrams and 384 lines statements.

如何解读六十四卦和卦爻辞,是古往今来研究《周易》的核心课题。"辨象证义"是解读卦爻辞的根本方法,即辨别卦爻象,理解爻的推移带来的爻象变化,进而体会和理解卦爻辞的来源和根据,在此基础上推演运作心意的分寸,和实化意念进而行动的哲学系统。

How to interpret the 64 hexagrams and 384 line statements has been the core issue of *Changes Studies* since ancient times. "Demonstrating meaning by distinguishing images (*bianxiang zhengyi* 辨象证义)" is the fundamental way to explain the line statements, and means it is important to distinguish the images inside a hexagram and their changes in order to illuminate the basis for the movement of lines and thus for the hexagram and line statements. Humans illuminate the movement of lines in the hexagrams so that this will shed light on how to handle to the proper degree the change in the *yin* and *yang* movements of their minds and realize the intentions to put them into action in their changing cosmological environment.

4. 抛弃"否定卦变的谬误"
4. Abandon the "fallacy of denying hexagram-changes"

在易学史上,关于卦变的争议很大,总的来说可以分成两派,一派认为卦变存在,一派否定卦变存在。承认和否定卦变最大的区别在于对待《象传》的态度,即《象传》是否具有解释卦爻辞的权威性。如果认为解释卦爻辞不能离开《象传》的提示,那么,不承认卦变就完全站不住脚。因为《象传》里面有很多关于卦变的提示,除了用爻的上下推移来解释,很难做其他更好的理解。

In the history of *Changes* Studies, there has been much controversy about hexagram-changes (*guabian* 卦变). Generally speaking, views can be divided into two schools. One school claims that hexagram-changes do exist and are needed for explaining the text, while the other school denies the existence of hexagram-changes, and argues that they are not necessary for clarifying the meaning of the text. The biggest difference between acknowledging and denying hexagram-changes lies in the attitude towards the *Judgment Commentary* (*Tuan Zhuan* 彖传), that is, whether the *Judgment Commentary* is authoritative in interpreting the hexagrams and lines. If we think that the explanation of hexagrams and lines cannot be separated from the hints in the *Judgment Commentary*, then it is totally untenable to not admit hexagram-changes, because there are many hints concerning hexagram-changes in the text of the *Judgment Commentary*. It is difficult to find any better understanding than using the rising and falling movement of the lines in a particular hexagram, and this implies the reasonableness of the hexagram-changes theory.

几乎每一卦的《象传》都交待刚柔爻位置的推移,这就是卦变的方式。如果不承认卦变,就无法把《象传》中与爻变有关的内容解释清楚。纵观历代《易》注,不承认卦变者对这些文字几乎都注得模棱两可,甚至作者自己都不知所云。并且,不承认卦变的存在,就不符合《周易》卦爻辞成书的实际过程,因为只有通过卦变引发的象的变化,才能把卦爻辞每个字的来源讲明确。

In almost every hexagram, the *Judgment Commentary* explains the change in position of hard and soft lines, and this is the mode of hexagram-changes. If we do not acknowledge hexagram-changes, we cannot clearly explain the content related to how lines change in the *Judgment Commentary*. Looking back at the annotations to the *Changes* in past dynasties, those who did not admit hexagram-changes almost all annotated these words in ambiguous ways, and sometimes even the authors themselves did not seem to know what they really meant. Moreover, not recognizing the existence of hexagram-changes is inconsistent with the actual process of composition for the hexagram and line statements in the *Changes*, because only through the changes in images caused by hexagram-changes can the origin of each word in the hexagram and line statements be made clear.

易学史上，王弼、孔颖达、程颐这些义理派易学家，都在一定程度上继承了卦变说，都承认卦变说有其合理性。后来一些易学家反对卦变，其实是认为乘承比应可以完美地解释卦爻辞，于是走上了否定卦变的道路。

In the history of *Changes* Studies, most scholars of the meaning-principle school, including Wang Bi, Kong Yingda, and Cheng Yi among others, in fact took up the hexagram-changes (*guabian* 卦变) theory to a certain extent, and most of them admitted that the hexagram-changes theory was not completely unreasonable. Later, when some *Changes* scholars opposed the existence of hexagram-changes, they in fact believed that "accommodating, overriding, neighboring, and corresponding (*chengcheng biying* 乘承比应)" could be sufficient to explain the hexagram and line statements, and thus embarked on the path of denying hexagram-changes.

卦变说本来是解《易》的常例，当然，其中存在是否取用和解释力度的问题。可发展到今天，使用卦变解《易》是否合理，都成了需要讨论的问题。我们认为，否定卦变的易学研究者是被义理派的方法给误导了，走向了易学传统的反面。我们有必要认真研究王弼、孔颖达、程颐等人对汉易卦变说的继承和肯定，而不应该继续否定卦变说。

The theory of hexagram-changes was originally a common hermeneutical way to interpret the *Changes*. Of course, there are issues concerning whether or not it should be used in particular cases and how convincing its explanations are. However, in today's academia, whether or not it is reasonable to use hexagram-changes to interpret the *Changes* has become a problem that needs to be discussed. We believe that *Changes* Studies researchers who deny hexagram-changes have been misled by the methods of the meaning-principle school and have in fact gone against the *Changes* Studies tradition. It is necessary for us to carefully study the inheritance and affirmation of the Han Dynasty hexagram-changes theory by Wang Bi, Kong Yingda, Cheng Yi and others, and we should not continue to deny the hexagram-changes theory.

4.1. 马恒君《周易正宗》的卦变系统
4.1 The hexagram-changes system in Ma Hengjun's *Orthodox Interpretation of the Book of Changes* (*Zhouyi Zhengzong* 周易正宗)

马恒君在《周易正宗》中对历史上的各种卦变说进行了总结，认为卦变是构成《易经》的三大序列之一，可以通过《象传》中的大量文句获得证实。《周易正宗》的卦变体系回归汉易卦变，在荀爽、虞翻卦变说的基础上梳理出了更具体系性的卦变系统。

Ma Hengjun (1944-) summarized various theories of hexagram-changes in his *Orthodox Interpretation of the Book of Changes* (*Zhouyi Zhengzong* 周易正宗) and believed that hexagram-changes are one of the three major sequences that make up the *Book of Changes*, as can be confirmed by a large amount of textual evidence in the *Judgment Commentary*. The hexagram-changes system of *Orthodox Interpretation of the Book of Changes* returns to the hexagram-changes system of the Han Dynasty (206 BC – 220 A D), and a more systematic hexagram-changes system is sorted out based on the hexagram-changes theories of Xun Shuang (128-190) and Yu Fan (164-233).

卦变体系在易学研究中居于特殊地位，类似于数学研究中的哥德巴赫猜想，历代易学家前赴后继，力图将卦变系统贯穿全经，但几乎没有完备且成功者，可谓"四圣之易千载长夜"的核心部分。迄今为止，只有马恒君《周易正宗》里建构起一个完备的卦变系统，并成功地贯穿全经六十四卦三百八十四爻。

The hexagram-changes system occupies a special position in the history of *Changes* Studies, one that can be compared to Goldbach's conjecture in mathematical research. Nearly all *Changes* scholars through the generations have tried hard to integrate the hexagram-changes system throughout the entire classic, but very few have been complete and successful. This can be said to be the core part of what Lai Zhide (1525-1604) of the Ming Dynasty called "the millennia-long dark night of the Four Sages' *Changes* tradition." So far, only Ma Hengjun's *Orthodox Interpretation of the Book of Changes* has constructed a complete new system of hexagram-changes, one that successfully runs through the 64 hexagrams and the 384 lines of the whole classic.

本书在继承马恒君卦变说的基础上有所修正，从而使得卦变系统更加"尽广大而尽精微"，卦变解易从未有达到如此完备精密的程度，正所谓"四圣千古不传之秘，尽泄于此"。本书的"明意"部分，多发扬卦变解易的精妙义理，并据此建构"意本论"哲学系统。

This book has made some modifications on the basis of inheriting Ma Hengjun's theory of hexagram-changes, so that the hexagram-changes system can be "more broad and subtle." Historically, the interpretation of hexagram-changes has never reached such a complete and precise level. This can be said to be "the ancient secret of the Four Sages untold through the millennia, revealed in this book." The *Illuminating Intentionality* (*Ming Yi*) part of this book mostly develops the subtle meanings and principles of the hexagram-changes interpretation of the *Changes*, and constructs the philosophical system of the "theory of foundational intentionality" based on this.

4.2. 文王卦变方圆图
4.2 The Square and Circular Diagram of King Wen's Hexagram-Changes System

根据《周易明意》的卦变体系，可以画出文王卦变圆图：

According to the hexagram-changes system of this work *Illuminating the Book of Changes and Its Intentionality*, the circular diagram of King Wen's hexagram-changes system can be drawn as follows:

乾

同人-履=夬 姤=小畜-大有

睽-大畜-中孚-大过-革-兑 需=大壮　遯=讼-巽-鼎-无妄-家人-离

蛊-井-恒-贲-既济-丰-损-节-归妹=泰 否=渐-旅-咸-涣-未济-困-益-噬嗑-随

坎-解-升-屯-震-明夷=临 观=晋-艮-蒙-颐-小过-萃-蹇

比-豫=复 剥=谦-师

坤

文王卦变圆图（卦名版）

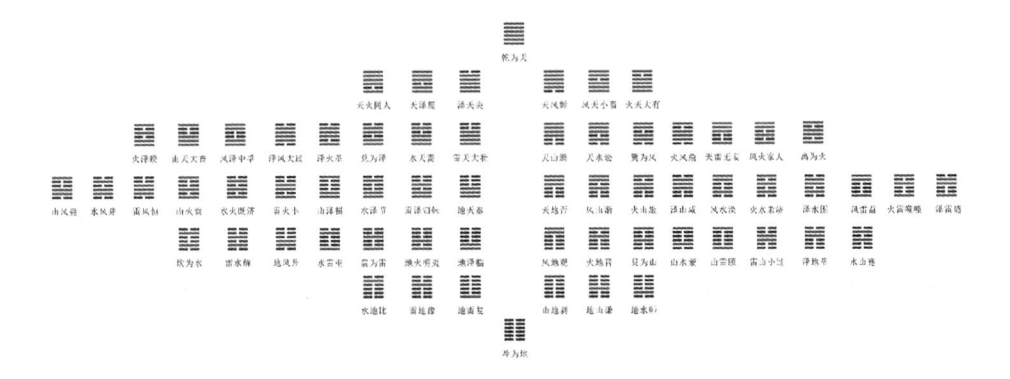

文王卦变圆图（卦画版）

《周易明意》文王卦变方圆图乃文王作卦爻辞所参考的重要卦变图。由文王卦变方图可知，中孚卦和小过卦作为卦变的中间环节非常合理。周文王依据卦变体系创作卦爻辞的系统，至此牢不可破，无懈可击。

The square and circle diagram of King Wen's hexagram-changes in the *Book of Changes* is an important hexagram diagram that King Wen used as a reference for his elucidations of the 64 hexagrams and 384 lines. From King Wen's diagram of hexagram-changes, it can be seen that it is very reasonable to regard Hexagram Zhongfu (Trust) and Hexagram Xiaoguo (Slight Overreaching) as the intermediate links of hexagram-changes. That King Wen of Zhou created the system of hexagrams and lines based on the system of hexagram-changes is now undeniable and unassailable.

由此可见，周文王创作卦爻辞的时候，是在十二消息卦生六十四卦的体系基础之上，参照六十四卦之间彼此相错相综卦的体系来"观象系辞"，可以说，周文王创作卦爻辞时写下的每一个字，都是严格按照这个卦变体系写下来的。

It can be seen that when King Wen of Zhou created the hexagrams and lines, he based them on the system of twelve waxing and waning hexagrams (*shier xiaoxi gua* 十二消息卦) giving rise to 64 hexagrams. The 64 hexagrams were intertwined with each other by "observing the changing images and attaching words" (*guanxiang jici* 观象系辞). It can be said that every word of King Wen of Zhou when he created the statements for the 64 hexagrams and 384 lines was written strictly in accordance with this system of hexagram-changes.

文王卦变方圆图可能一直是秘传，孔子可能见过文王卦变方圆图，所以才能整理传述于世的《易传》系统，使之与卦爻辞对应得天衣无缝。文王卦变图春秋战国时代已经失传，到汉代荀爽、虞翻之时，已经无缘得见此二图，只能根据十二消息卦和错综卦来解释卦爻辞，不过至少失之未远。

The square and circle diagrams of King Wen's hexagram-changes were likely passed down in secret before Confucius' time. Confucius may well have seen the square and circle diagrams of King Wen's hexagram-changes, enabling him to organize the system of *Commentaries on the Changes* transmitted to the world so that it corresponds seamlessly with the 64 hexagrams and 384 lines. The diagrams of King Wen's hexagram-changes were very likely lost during the Spring and Autumn Period and the Warring States Period. By the time of Xun Shuang and Yu Fan in the Han Dynasty, these two diagrams were no longer available, so the hexagrams and lines could only be explained based on the twelve waxing and waning hexagrams and the upside down or interlocking (*cuo zong gua* 错综卦) hexagrams, but these at least were not too far away from the appropriate diagrams.

到魏晋时代王弼扫荡象数，不仅仅"开了几百年的倒车"[1]，可以说是开了上千年的倒车。到唐代孔颖达《周易正义》之后，文王卦变图可谓湮没无踪，幸好李鼎祚《周易集

---

[1] 马恒君：《周易正宗》，北京：华夏出版社，2014年，第264页。

解》保留了汉易的重要线索。宋代陈抟邵雍传出图书之学，朱震、朱熹重提卦变说，使得卦变说的合理性得到证实，但争议和否定之声不断，甚至很多重要的易学家都视卦变为畏途，直接加以否定。

By the time of the Wei and Jin Dynasties (220-420), Wang Bi's (227-249) campaign against the image-number school not only "reversed progress for hundreds of years" (Ma Hengjun), it can be said to have reversed progress for thousands of years. After Kong Yingda's (574-648) *Correct Meaning of the Book of Changes* (*Zhouyi Zhengyi* 周易正义) in the Tang Dynasty, the diagram of King Wen's hexagram-changes can be said to have been completely lost. Fortunately, Li Dingzuo's *Collected Interpretations of the Book of Changes* (*Zhouyi Jijie* 周易集解) retained important clues to the achievements in the Han Dynasty. In the Song Dynasty, Chen Tuan and Shao Yong spread the learning of the River Diagram and Luo Chart, and Zhu Zhen and Zhu Xi mentioned the hexagram-changes theory again, confirming the rationality of the hexagram-changes theory. However, after them there were constant disputes and denials, and even many important *Changes* scholars regarded the hexagram-changes theory as a fearful path, and denied it directly and completely.

卦变说经历明清到近现代众多易学家前赴后继的不懈努力，顶住了巨大的否定之声，得以蹒跚而行至今日。马恒君《周易正宗》立足传世的卦变说，梳理并建立一个全新的卦变体系，这是《周易明意》文王卦变图的坚实基础。文王卦变图既遵循了《周易正宗》的卦变原则，又弥补和完善了其卦变体系的不足。今日文王卦变图得以在三千年之后重现于世，想必文王卦变图自有其天命乎！

The theory of hexagram-changes received unremitting effort from countless *Changes* scholars from the Ming and Qing dynasties to modern times, withstood the huge voice of negation, and was able to stumble forward to this day. Ma Hengjun's *Orthodox Interpretation of the Book of Changes* was based on the hexagram-changes system handed down from ancient times, sorted out and established a new hexagram-changes system, and is regarded as the solid foundation for King Wen's hexagram-changes diagram in this work *Illuminating the Book of Changes and Its Intentionality*. King Wen's hexagram-changes diagram not only follows the hexagram-changes patterns of *Orthodox Interpretation of the Book of Changes*, but also makes up for and improves the shortcomings of its hexagram-changes system. For King Wen's hexagram-changes diagrams have reappeared in the world today after three thousand years, it must be that the diagram of King Wen's hexagram-changes theory has its own heavenly destiny!

研究《周易》卦爻辞，如果不从文王卦变图这个卦变体系入手，就无法知道卦爻辞这幢精美的大厦是如何构造起来的。这就是两千年来的易学家难以彻底破解其中密码的原因所在。《周易明意》继承《周易正宗》卦变系统并有所推进，确定解释卦爻辞只有从卦变和爻象上梳理清楚，才能明白经文没有一个字没有出处，"观象系辞"的说法绝非虚言。文王卦变圆图和方图可以说是一个被拆除而后世难以发现的脚手架，如今这个脚手架得以系统连贯地重新构架起来，支撑起卦爻辞的肌体，使之纲举目张。从今往后，羲文诸圣所传易之深意至此而明。

In studying the hexagrams and lines of the *Book of Changes*, if we do not start with the hexagram-changes system of King Wen's diagram, we would be unable to understand how this exquisite edifice of hexagrams and lines was constructed. This is why *Changes* scholars over the past two thousand years have found it difficult to completely crack the code. This work *Illuminating the Book of Changes and Its Intentionality* inherits and advances the hexagram-changes system of Ma Hengjun's *Orthodox Interpretation of the Book of Changes*, and determines the explanation of the 64 hexagrams and 384 lines as accurately as possible. Only by sorting out the hexagram-changes and line images can we understand that not a single word in the *Classic* is without origin. "Observing the changing images and attaching words" is not an empty claim. The circle and square hexagram-changes diagrams of King Wen can be said to be a scaffolding that was dismantled in ancient times and became very difficult to be rediscovered by later generations. Now, this scaffolding has been re-constructed systematically and coherently, supporting the body of the 64 hexagrams and 384 lines, making it clear and visible. From now on, the profound intentionality of the *Changes* passed down by sages such as Fu Xi and King Wen will be clear.

七、《周易》的哲学——人天之意

Ⅶ. The Philosophy of the *Book of Changes*: Human-Cosmological Intentionality

《周易》本是融汇宇宙生命的哲学著作,《周易明意》基于天人之间的人天之意,从而建构人意如何通于天道。《周易明意》认为,每一卦都是通过刚柔爻的组合和推移表达易道显现的状态,向人们昭示天道的运行状态和如何以人意合天意的指南。人在每一卦都应该意会到刚爻代表的刚强之力当如何主导事变,而阴爻代表的阴柔之力又当如何顺从时势,并因此体会精神与意念之力合乎天道运行的合理方式。

The *Book of Changes* is originally a philosophical work that integrates the living things in the cosmos. This work *Illuminating the Book of Changes and Its Intentionality* is based on the human-cosmological intentionality between heaven and humanity, thereby constructing how human intentionality should be harmoniously connected with the *dao* of heaven. This book argues that each hexagram expresses a state of the *dao* through the combination and progression of strong/*yang* and soft/*yin* lines, showing people the operational status of the heavenly *dao* and providing a guide on how to align human intentionality with that of the cosmos. In each hexagram, people should grasp how the strong force represented by *yang* lines should dominate events, and how the soft force represented by *yin* lines tends to obey or follow current trends, and, therefore, understand the reasonable way in which the power of spirit and thought is in line with the operation of the *dao* of heaven.

每一卦既有其宏观的形势,又可以延伸出无数的细枝末节,都是圆融贯通的,既不可以舍本逐末,也不可以顾此失彼,要把宏观情境与卦爻辞的文字细节精准对应,反复参验,不断修正考订,才能确定每卦每爻的内涵,以及每个字的来源和出处。既要力透纸背地发明其内在的实理,又要兼顾其与其他爻之间和整个卦,甚至其他卦之间变动不居的情境之流。

Each hexagram contains both a macro situational propensity and countless derivative details, all of which are integrated and connected, warning us against going to extremes with the details, or placing too much emphasis on some aspects while neglecting others. It is necessary to accurately correlate the macro situational propensity with the textual details of the hexagram and line words, repeatedly refer to them, and continuously revise and verify them, in order to determine the connotations of each hexagram and line, as well as the source of each word. It is necessary not only to illuminate the inner truth between the lines, but also to take into account the ever-changing flow of context between one line and other lines and even the entire hexagram and other hexagrams.

1. 人天之意的宗教感
1. The Religious Sense of Human-Cosmological Intentionality

《周易》最重要的问题是天人关系问题——"推天道以明人事",即如何打通天道人事,人如何推演、了解、配合天道。《周易》中的天道主要通过阴阳来表达,人能够领会阴阳之气的推移形成天地之变化,然后从卦的刚柔爻相推去体会天地和人事变化的道理,琢磨人在不同的时势和位置要如何领会其生存情境,进而去面对生活当中的问题,寻找合适的解决策略,趋吉避凶。圣人能够看清楚天地形势,利用卦爻象来看明白天地人道,从而进德修业,安身立命。总之,学《周易》是为了通达天人。

The most important issue in the *Book of Changes* is the relationship between heaven and humanity—"Extending the heavenly *dao* to illuminate human affairs," that is, how to connect the heavenly *dao* with human affairs, and how people can deduce, understand, and cooperate with the heavenly *dao*. The heavenly *dao* in the *Book of Changes* is mainly expressed through *yin* and *yang qi*, the shifting of which to form the changes of heaven and earth can be understood by humans, who can then deduce the patterns in the change of heaven and earth and human affairs from the strong *yang* and soft/*yin* lines of the hexagrams. People can thus understand their existential situations in different times and positions, and then face problems in life, find suitable solutions, seek good fortune and avoid bad fortune. Sages can see the situational propensity of heaven and earth clearly, use hexagrams and symbols to understand the *dao* of heaven, earth and humanity, and thus cultivate virtue and rest settled in their own position. In short, studying the *Book of Changes* is for the purpose of connecting the cosmos and humanity.

中国的宗教意识从一开始就是圣人代天立极,人的意识境遇可以达到人天之意,不仅理论上可能,而且实践当中完全可以做到。《周易》就是这样一部修炼著作,让我们提升自己的意识水平,达到如神如天一般的境界,却不离开每天的日常生活。

From the very beginning, Chinese religious consciousness was characterized by the sages establishing the spiritual ultimate as a representative of heaven. That the situation of human consciousness can reach a human-cosmological intentionality is not only theoretically possible, but also fully achievable in practice. The *Book of Changes* is just this kind of cultivational work that allows us to elevate our conscious situation and reach a spiritual plane like that of a heavenly god, without leaving one's daily life.

从人的心念是贯通天道的家的角度上说，儒学是有家的哲学。心念可以跟宇宙，跟家庭和他人，与所有存在物的生机永远不息连通。这跟西方存在主义哲学，如海德格尔"向死而生"，萨特说"存在先于本质"，加缪对人生荒诞感的描绘等说法表现出人无家可归的意识很不一样。海德格尔说"语言是存在的家"，体现出无家可归的无奈。西方哲学家的语言体系所演绎的是孤独个体在自由世界当中无家可归的形式主义体系，和中国的哲学家不断地去领会生生不息的宇宙大化、充满元气淋漓的生机系统完全不可同日而语。

From the perspective of the family that connects the human mind with the heavenly *dao*, Confucianism is a philosophy based on family. The mind can be continually connected to the cosmos, to family and to others, and indeed to the vital energy of all beings. This is very different from Western existentialist philosophy, such as Heidegger's "living towards death", Sartre's statement that "existence precedes essence", and Camus' depiction of the absurdity of life, which demonstrate a sense of people's homelessness. Heidegger's saying that "Language is the house of Being" reflects the helplessness of homelessness. The linguistic systems of Western philosophers portray the formalistic systems of lonely individuals homeless in a free world, which are completely different from Chinese philosophers' continuous understanding of the continuous productivity of the transforming cosmos and its vital system filled with the vibrancy of primordial *qi*.

2. 意本形上学
2. The Metaphysics of Foundational Intentionality

宇宙以元气的生意为第一义，元气即万物存在之根基，在意念领会的状态下展现其生机。意本论认为，人可在后天的有形世界里，运化先天乾阳之力，从而转化世间阴阳，通过观察体悟天道，让心意接续元气不断运行的生机和活力，让乾阳之力为己所运化，从而让心意接续道意，犹如接续天机一般，接通宇宙的创生之力。宇宙万物流转必须进入意念的境域才能被领会。

The Chinese sensibility of the cosmos takes as primary the vital and generative intentionality of primordial *qi*, which is the foundation of the existence of all things, displaying its vitality through the understanding state of intentionality. According to the theory of foundational intentionality, humans can utilize the power of pre-celestial Qian-*yang* in the post-celestial tangible world, thereby transforming the world's *yin* and *yang* powers. By observing and experiencing the heavenly *dao*, the mind's intentionality can inherit the vitality and energy of the continuous movement of primordial *qi*, allowing the power of Qian-*yang* to be utilized by oneself, and thus uniting the mind's intentionality with that of the *dao*, just like inheriting the vitality of nature to connect with the creative power of the cosmos. The circulation of the myriad things/events in the cosmos must enter the realm of intentional thought in order to be understood.

意本论认为意在道先，万物的创生之力需要人的意识领会之后，生机方能开显。如万物之性需要为意念领会之后，性的能动性和绵延性才能够表达和展现出来。意念的领会能够唤醒生命之力，使得生命的存在超越行尸走肉的自然存在层次。意力是对性力（原生本性之力）的领会和主动驱动，人通过意力转化其生存状态，化被动为主动。意本论认为，人可以通过意念的修持，转化生命的被动状态为主动状态。

The theory of foundational intentionality suggests that intentionality is prior to the *dao*, and that the creative power of the myriad things/events must be understood by human consciousness in order that productive vitality manifest itself. Similarly, the inherent nature of things needs to be comprehended by intentionality before its motility and persistence can be expressed and developed. The power of life can be awakened through the understanding of intentional thought, allowing the existence of life to transcend the natural existence level of a mere physical body. The power of intentionality is the understanding and active driving of the power of inherent nature (original vital power), through which people transform their state of existence and turn passivity into activity. According to the theory of foundational intentionality, people can transform their passive state of life into an active state through the practice of intentional thought.

3. 意本创生论
3. The Creativity Theory of Foundational Intentionality

道存在论或者气本体论的核心其实是创生论。《周易》本体论是充满生机的本体论。宇宙本体性的创造自有其创生力，因为宇宙没有创生力就无法存续。《周易》本体论不是简单说事物如何存在，而是在事物存在的动态过程当中，显现出生生不息的生机，而且这种生机是跟当下的生命力量和宇宙大化流行的所有一切存在融贯起来。

The core of any *dao* ontology or *qi* ontology is actually a theory of creativity. The ontology of the *Changes* is full of vitality. The ontological creation of the cosmos has its inherent creative power without which it is impossible for the cosmos to be sustained. The ontology of the *Changes* is not simply about how everything exists, but about how things display ceaseless vitality in the dynamic process of their existence, and how this vitality is fused with the living power and transformative circulation of the whole cosmos at every moment.

宇宙创生过程接近于化生的过程,"化"是物的迁延转化。宇宙最根本的全体不断转化出太极、两仪、四象等,对转化过程的理解其实又与人之意向和视角相连。因为如果没有人的参与,世界只是一个自在的本体,独立于人的意志自然而然存在,换言之,道存在的方式不因为人而变化,但因为人的视角参与而导致了万物的流变和分化。

The creation process of the cosmos is similar to a transformation process, in which "transformation" (*hua* 化) means the transition and conversion of things. The most fundamental whole of the cosmos constantly transforms into the Ultimate Polarity (*Taiji* 太极), the Two Forms (*liangyi* 两仪) and the Four Images (*sixiang* 四象). The understanding of this transformation is associated with human intentions and perspectives, because without human engagement, the world is simply an in-itself noumenon, the existence of which is independent from human will. In other words, how the *dao* exists is not dependent on human observation, but human observation leads to the flowing transformation and differentiation of all things.

物的分化就是人的视角参与并加以意会的结果,人来看这个世界,就一定要分出阴阳、前后、东西、上下等,因为人的意识就是有这种特点,人只能意会到对待双方的一方;从某一个角度观察事物,意识只能朝向某一个方向,而难以意识到宇宙全体,至少表面上意识刚开始的时候只能是倾向于某一方的,至于之后的反思和反身意识到的全体,是反思之后的意识收摄状态。一般人通常不能够看到世界全体,只能用自己的视角去面对混沌的太极,所以自然而然就会有两仪等的分化,而八卦和六十四卦即是分化和转化。

The differentiation of things is the result of human perspectival participation and intentional understanding. In human eyes there must be a difference between *yin* and *yang*, front and back, east and west, up and down and so forth, because these are attributes of human consciousness or intentionality. Human intentionality can only understand one side of things when there are actually two sides, and the human perspective makes consciousness operate in a one-way direction and fail to realize the whole picture. At least this is true at the initial moment of consciousness, although it can realize the whole picture after reflection. Most people cannot see the whole picture of the world, but have to face the chaotic *Taiji* with their limited perspective, leading to a natural differentiation into the Two Forms, etc., hence the Eight Trigrams and 64 hexagrams represent differentiation and transformation.

4. 意本认识论
4. The Epistemology of Foundational Intentionality

　　《周易明意》认为，几微是意物同源的核心。意本论体现出中国传统意物关系的特殊性。从理解意物交汇之原点开始，中国哲人就不运用西方哲学家对认识论问题采用的分析方法，因他们认为逻辑推理无助于全体性地理解认识对象，所以主张直接面对事物，从意物同源出发，让心用直觉领悟的方式认识物的全体。

This work *Illuminating the Book of Changes and Its Intentionality* holds that subtle changes are the core of the common source of intentions and things/events. The theory of foundational intentionality embodies the particularity of the traditional Chinese intention-things/events relationship. Starting from understanding the origin of the intersection of intentionality and things/events, Chinese philosophers have not used the analytical methods used by Western philosophers to analyze epistemological issues. Because they believe that logical reasoning is not conducive to a comprehensive understanding of cognitive objects, they advocate facing things directly and, starting from the common source of intentions and things/events, letting the mind understand things holistically through intuitive understanding.

　　意物关系的问题即意念如何把握认识对象的问题。从本体上说，我们和宇宙融为一体，就像我们在游泳池或大海里游泳，跟自然的水融为一体，但因为人可以反身意识到自己是人，在参与对象化存在的变化、当人有自我意识的时候，人跟物相分，然后人又用意去理解把握对象化的物。从本体论上说人与物不分，心跟物是通的，这是从本体论出发的第一层意思。

The problem of the relationship between intentions and objects is the problem of how intentionality grasps an object of cognition. Ontologically speaking, we are integrated with the cosmos, just like when we swim in a swimming pool or the ocean, we are integrated with the water of nature. However, because people can reflexively realize that they are human beings and participate in the changes of objectified existence, when people have self-awareness, they are separated from objects, and they then use their intentionality to understand and grasp objectified objects. From an ontological point of view, there is no separation between people and things, and the mind and things are connected. This is the first level of meaning starting from ontology.

　　第二层意思是，人通过体悟，即身体感知整体性了解来理解事物，"体知"与物融贯，虽跟西方哲学家们谈论对意物的理解不同，但是意物关系还是最根本的，也就是说，我们之所以能够体悟世界作为整体性存在，而不仅把它作为一种对象化的存在，是因为人与世界本来就是通的，这个通只能通过我们整体性的感知来体悟。认识是各种感官维度都参与的，意识是整体性的综合，心物感通的状态。人跟万物交接感通才有意识，意是整体性通于存在，又通于认识的。

The second meaning is that people understand things through body-understanding, that is, bodily perception with an overall understanding, a "bodily knowledge" that is always integrated with things/events. Although it is different from the understanding of intentionality and things/events discussed by Western philosophers, the relationship between intentionality and things/events is still most fundamental. In other words, the reason why we can understand the world as a holistic existence, not just as an objectified existence, is that people and the world are inherently connected, and this connection can only be understood through our holistic perception. Cognition and comprehension involve the participation of various sensory dimensions, and intentional consciousness is a holistic synthesis, a state of mind-matter or intention-object connection. Only when people have a sense of affective connection with things can they become conscious, thus intentionality implies that wholeness is connected to both existence and knowledge.

5. 意本相容论
5. The Compatibilism Theory of Foundational Intentionality

从意本论的本体论和认识论出发，可以谈论命定论与自由意志问题。《周易》的命定论主要通过术数派体现出来，如占卜通过数的推演来达到对天下各种事物的把握，相信命是注定的说法。术数派体现出来的精神就是决定论，认为生命是一个被决定的过程，我们每个人做自由选择的空间都比较小。我们与生俱来的命和运的格局，从生活的环境如父母、家庭状况等在相当大程度上影响了人的命运走向。当然，即使是命定论的视角也不认为命运完全不能改变，比如一个人愿意调整风水，积德行善，努力读书，改变姓名，都可能在不同程度上改变命运的发展。虽有改命之说，但是从命定论角度来说，大部分情况很难改变。

Starting from the ontology and epistemology of the theory of foundational intentionality, we can talk about issues of determinism and free will. The determinism of the *Book of Changes* is mainly reflected through the technique-number school. For example, divination uses the deduction of numbers to grasp various things in the world, and believes that human destiny is fixed. The spirit embodied by the technique-number school is determinism, which believes that life is a determined process, and each of us has relatively little room for free choice. The pattern of fate and fortune we are born with, including our living environment such as parents and family status, affects our destiny to a considerable extent. Of course, even the perspective of determinism does not believe that destiny cannot be changed at all. For example, if a person is willing to adjust their *fengshui*, accumulate virtue and do good, study hard, or change their name, this may change the development of their destiny to varying degrees. Although there is talk of changing destiny, from the perspective of determinism, most situations are difficult to change.

命定论的另一面是非决定论，或者是自由意志论。《周易》可以"穷理尽性以至于命"，通过对理和性的理解而通达命运。当然这种说法既可以做命定论的理解，也可以做自由意志论的理解。意本论主要是自由意志论的，通过理解变化的世界来把握命运。意本论认为，对变的认识本身是个变化过程，这个变化的过程可以有两种态度：一种是被动的，一种是主动的。被动的叫"变通"，比如"船到桥头自然直"，调整自己，顺应形势。另一种叫"通变"，即通达变化，是一种在领悟变化的基础上，对变化的趋势做出判断，这种对变化趋势的领悟让人有一种视野或愿景（vision），看到未来会有怎么样的发展，再随之产生一种见识力（insight），也就是能够看穿这个事情的发展趋势。

The other side of determinism is indeterminism, or free will. The *Book of Changes* can "fathom principles and exhaust the inherent nature of all living things, and thereby attain destiny." Of course, this statement can be understood in both deterministic and indeterministic terms. The theory of foundational intentionality is primarily indeterministic, grasping destiny by understanding the changing world, and argues that the understanding of change is itself a process of change. This process of change can have two attitudes: one is passive and the other is active. The passive is called "flexible" (*biantong* 变通), such as how a boat will naturally straighten itself when it reaches a bridge by adjusting itself and adapting to the situation. The other is called "transformative" (*tongbian* 通变), which means understanding change and leading the tendency of changes. It is a judgment concerning the trend of change based on understanding change, and understanding of the trend of change gives people a vision about the future. Seeing what kind of development there will be in the future produces a kind of insight, that is, the ability to see through the development trends of changing events.

因为有vision和insight，你的意向比别人远大，你能看出事情的发展方向，而且能够让人认可你看到的发展方向，那么你就能通达变化，你才能够反过来影响别人。能够通达变化以后，就可以领导变化，这就是所谓的领导力（leadership）。

Once one has vision and insight, one's intentions are broader and deeper than others, one might foretell the direction of development of things, and one might make others move toward the direction of development that one sees. This means that if one understands the changes, one can influence others to move toward a certain direction. Once one is able to understand tendencies of change, one can lead change. This is what leadership means: that once leaders have vision and insight, they can have the power to lead.

领导力实际上是要领导事情的发展变化,领导力是人有能力去领导情境的变化。领导者是那些能够预先看到事情发展变化的人,他要比一般人看得远一点。按照郭象"独化于玄冥之境"的说法,可以说我们每个人虽然都睁着眼睛,但在看不清未来的意义上,大家都生活在黑暗当中,世界本无所谓黑暗还是光明,也可以是无善无恶,整个世界本体的状态是一种玄冥之境。所有的人和物都在变,但是这个光明的世界从另一个角度看其实是黑暗的。我们在黑暗当中,几乎没有人能够看见未来。郭象的说法一定程度上排除了领导的必要性和可能性,因为领导也在黑暗中,也看不见。但有些人能够看见事情的发展方向,所谓领导力就是这么来的。领导力是说有些人有一种前瞻性的眼光,能够引发周围人的认可,然后带领周围人一起去参与这个世界的变化,实际上在某种意义上说,领导者的意识境遇,连同他带动的意识情境,一起改变世界变化的进程。

Leadership is actually about leading the development and change of things, the ability of people to lead change in situations. Leaders are those who can foresee the development and change of things in advance. They can see further than ordinary people. According to Guo Xiang's statement that things "transform alone in a realm of dark and remote (*xuanming* 玄冥) situations," it can be said that although each of us has our eyes open, we still cannot see the future clearly because we all live in darkness. The world does not originally know anything of darkness or light, just as there is originally no good or evil, as the state of the entire world is a plane of mysterious obscurity. All people and things are changing, but this bright world is actually dark from another perspective. People live in darkness and few can see the future. Guo Xiang's statement excludes the necessity and possibility of leadership to a certain extent, because leaders are also in the dark and cannot be seen. But some people can see where things are going, and that is where leadership comes from. Leadership means that some people have a forward-looking vision that can arouse recognition in people around them, and then lead people around them to participate in changes in the world. In fact, in a sense, the leader's conscious state, along with the conscious situation he leads, together change the process of worldly transformation.

6. 意本感通论
6. The Holistic Affectivity Theory of Foundational Intentionality

相对来说,西方哲学没有中国哲学那么强调领悟和感通,西方哲学更强调人要用理性、逻辑去分析推理,看看论证是不是和我们所理解的对象化存在吻合,是否可以为真。比如柏拉图讲知识是"可以论证的真实信仰"(justified true belief)。意本论认为,知识是可以感通、可以领悟的,不完全可用信念的方式清楚表达出来,它需要人通过象的方式去领悟。意本论讲全体性的把握,而柏拉图讲如何让一个陈述成为真的陈述,然后去论证它为真。这种陈述就是命题与判断，但只能表达事物的某种属性，属性通过逻辑的关系要表达对象的真，然后我们认为它是真的，这就是知识，也就是哲学的真理。柏拉图意义上的认识论得把主体抽离出来，变成观察物的对象，这种表达方式说明，陈述本身不再有感悟的成分，全体性和感通这两个部分是意本论哲学的特殊之处。

Relatively speaking, Western philosophy does not emphasize enlightenment as much as Chinese philosophy, which places more emphasis on realization and holistic affectivity. Western philosophy places more emphasis on people using rationality and logic to analyze and deduce, to see if an argument is consistent with our understanding of objectified existence, and thus whether it can be true. For example, Plato talked about knowledge as "justified true belief." The theory of foundational intentionality argues that knowledge can be holistically affective and realized, and as such cannot be completely expressed in the form of beliefs, requiring people to understand through images. The theory of foundational intentionality talks about grasping the whole, while Plato talks about how to make a statement become a true statement and then prove that it is true. Such statements are propositions and judgments, but they can only express certain attributes of things. These attributes express the truth of the object through logical relationships, and then we think it is true. This is knowledge, and the truth of philosophy. Epistemology in the Platonic sense requires the subject to be freed and turned into a counterpart of the object of observation. This way of expression shows that the statement itself no longer has the component of affective realization. The affectivity of holistic understanding and perception are special features of the philosophy of foundational intentionality.

人生是一个与物互动的过程，而与物互动也可以理解为一个修道过程，也就是修行自己的心灵意识状态的过程。人的心意与世界运动合拍，与宇宙的能量运动合拍，才能够形成有力的道，心之道落实为物之道，成为意物关联相通之道。人应努力应对各种意识境遇变化，调整其意识境遇跟集体的意识境遇之间的关系，不能够让情不自禁的冲动继续随意地表现出来，不能够让原初的、已经得到满足的需求再自然而然地成为意识的基本状态，也就是人对于自己的意识境遇应该随着时势的改变不断调适。人有时候需要他人，也需要根据他人的需要来校正自己的意识境遇，在意识发动的瞬间，调整意识生成的机制。

Life is a process of interacting with living things, and interacting with things can also be understood as a process of spiritual cultivation, that is, the process of cultivating one's own state of spiritual consciousness. Only when human intentionality is in harmony with the movement of the world and the energetic movement of the cosmos can a powerful *dao* be formed. The *dao* of the mind can thus be implemented as the *dao* of things/events, and become the *dao* of interconnection between intentionality and things/events. When people strive to cope with various changes in conscious situations and adjust the relationship between their consciousness and the collective consciousness, they cannot allow uncontrollable impulses to continue to express themselves at will, and cannot allow original and already satisfied needs to naturally manifest themselves again. The basic state of consciousness should be that people constantly adjust their own conscious situation as situational propensities change. People sometimes need others, and they also need to correct their own intentional situation according to the needs of others, and adjust the mechanism of conscious generation at the moment when intentionality is initiated.

"缸中之脑"的讲法一定是主客两分的，而《周易明意》哲学主要是基于感通性的，我们跟这个世界本来就是不分的，我们在讲世界生生不息的状态，人是要感通才可能认识到的。人跟世界所有的认识，包括我们的行动力，它都是感通的。这个感通的主体，比较被切换到另一种状态去，再用虚假的东西重新切掉它，替换它。假如说我们看到授课老师现在只是一个"缸中之脑"，他不过是电脑的一个延伸物件，那么学生们很自然地意识到这个电脑讲的东西尽管跟老师讲的每个字都一样，但是主体跟电脑之间是没有感通的。比如说有台电脑，它打在屏幕上的每一个字，每一种说法都跟授课老师讲出来的话一样，那大家可能不会有什么感觉，不会有什么样的理解，至少说跟老师这个人在讲的同样内容的理解是不一样的。

The "brain in a vat" metaphor must be based on the division of subject and object, and the philosophy of this work *Illuminating the Book of Changes and Its Intentionality* is mainly based on the affective continuity of intentions and things/events in perception, which means that humans are inseparable from the world. When we speak of the state of the world as ceaseless production and reproduction, people need holistic affectivity to be able to realize this. All human understanding of the world, including our ability to act, are connected to holistic affectivity. The subject of this holistic affectivity is comparatively switched to another state, then cut off and replaced with something false. If we see that a teacher is merely a "brain in a vat" or just an extension of a computer, then students will naturally realize that, even if every word the computer says is the same as what the teacher said, there is no holistic affectivity between the subject and the computer. For example, if there is a computer and every word and statement displayed on its screen is the same as what the teacher said, then people may not have any feeling or understanding like that with the teacher. The understanding of the same content that the teacher as a person talked about would be different.

7. 意本心通物论
7. The Foundational Intentionality Theory of Mind-Things Continuity

意本论从本体论到伦理学、心物关系、动机与行为等都和当代哲学不同。意本论以感通为中心，与笛卡尔二元论、休谟怀疑论等不以感通为中心的西方哲学传统判然有别。

笛卡尔怀疑到最后说只有"我在怀疑"不能怀疑。休谟认为运动是观念之间的连接。这样的怀疑论传统影响到今天的心灵哲学和以机器为基础研究人的认知科学。行为主义或物理主义认为，人对世界的认知可以还原为纯粹物理性的神经活动。这种物理主义还原显然消解了感通。从西方唯物主义、物理主义到行为主义，再到认知科学、心灵哲学，直到现在人工智能，都是基于主客两分，把主体看作与对象化客体相对的存在物。正是在感通这点上，意本论哲学跟西方哲学的风格有巨大差别。意本论基于感悟感通，他心也是能够感通的。

From ontology to ethics, the mind-matter relationship, motivation and behavior, the philosophy of foundational intentionality is different from contemporary philosophies. The theory of foundational intentionality is centered on a holistic affectivity, which is completely different from Western philosophical traditions such as Descartes' dualism and Hume's skepticism that do not focus on holistic affectivity. Descartes doubted everything and in the end claimed that only the fact that I am doubting cannot be doubted. Hume believed that motion is a connection between ideas. This skeptical tradition has influenced today's philosophy of mind and cognitive science which study humans based on machines. Behaviorism and physicalism believe that people's cognition of the world can be reduced to purely physical neural activities. This physicalist reduction obviously dissolves any holistic affectivity. From Western materialism and physicalism to behaviorism, cognitive science, philosophy of mind, and now artificial intelligence, all are based on the subject-object division, and the subject is regarded as an existent relative to an objectified object. It is on this point of understanding concerning holistic affectivity that there is a huge difference between the styles of the Chinese philosophy of intentionality and mainstream modern Western philosophy. The theory of foundational intentionality is based on an affective understanding of things as a whole, one in which other minds can also be understood.

人的精神力量有可能去理解和吸纳情境的变化，这种同一性因为人的精神包容度而有所不同。但意本论希望人们能够在经历过事情变化以后扩展自己的心灵，延展自己的心灵到各种各样的方面去。所以人的同一性，一方面是相对稳定的，一方面又有能力去吸纳情境变化。意本论帮助人们通过自己的意识参与宇宙变化，在参与的过程中让自己的意识融贯在整个宇宙变化当中，全体性地去把握融通变化，从而变成一个心意通天状态的人，即通过格物致知而能够通物通天，融贯世界全体的"大人"。意本论认为，人在跟具体物打交道的过程当中，能够转化物、理解物，从而进入一种感通天地和整个宇宙的状态。人的心念可以从小人状态发展成为跟宇宙意识相通的大人状态——"与天地合其德，与日月合其明，与四时合其序，与鬼神合其吉凶"，大人的起心动念都能跟天地变化相贯通，其精神意识的力量可以吸纳整个情境的变化。

It is possible for people's spiritual power to understand and absorb changes in situations, a unity that varies depending on people's degree of spiritual tolerance. The theory of foundational intentionality however hopes that people can expand and extend their minds to various aspects after experiencing changes in affairs. Therefore, human identity is relatively stable on the one hand, yet it has the ability to absorb changes in situations on the other. The theory of foundational intentionality helps people to participate in the changes of the cosmos through their own intentional consciousness, and in the process of participation, let their consciousness be integrated into the changes of the entire cosmos, and grasp and integrate these changes holistically, so as to become a person with a cosmological sensibility of intentionality.

That is, by becoming an adult who is able to investigate things and extend their knowledge, and thereby connecting with things and the cosmos as a whole, the theory of foundational intentionality argues that in the process of dealing with specific objects, people can transform and comprehend objects, thereby entering a state of holistic affectivity with heaven and earth and the entire cosmos. A person's thought can develop from a state of petty humanity to a state of great humanity that is connected with the consciousness of the cosmos—"in harmony with the virtues of heaven and earth, in harmony with the brightness of the sun and moon, in harmony with the order of the four seasons, and in harmony with the good and bad fortune of ghosts and spirits." The active, initiative thought of great people can be connected holistically with the changes and transformations of heaven and earth, and their power of spiritual consciousness can absorb the changes and transformations of the entire situation.

8. 意本伦理学
8. The Ethics of Foundational Intentionality

意本论以修养为本，其伦理倾向是期待人们去扩展自己的心灵，成就自己。扩展心灵实际上就是努力厚德载物，让德行越来越厚，能够承载的物也就越多。不断加深加大深厚的德，就可能容纳宽度和广度像大地一样的事物。《周易》讲的虽然是趋利避害的哲学，带有朴素功利主义倾向，但同时教导人们去增进道德，提升修养，加大心灵的力量，让心灵广阔无边，与天地相通，如果人的心灵意识修养深厚，就可以承担更大的事物，也就是载更多的物。

The theory of foundational intentionality is founded upon self-cultivation and adopts an ethical attitude of encouraging people to expand their mind and accomplish a perfect self. Expanding the mind actually means to endeavor to "make their virtue deep enough to bear and support things." The deeper the virtue is, the greater its capacity is to accommodate and support others. By increasing the breadth and depth of virtue, one will be able to encompass things as broad as heaven and earth. Although the philosophy of the *Book of Changes* is concerned with drawing on benefit and avoiding harm, with its tendency toward simple utilitarianism, it also teaches people to promote morality, elevate their cultivation, and expand the capacity of their intentionality to connect with heaven and earth. If people's spiritual consciousness is deeply cultivated, they can take on greater causes, that is, bear more responsibilities.

《周易》强调人在天地之间模仿天地之道的变化成就自我。道有天道、地道、人道，人把天道领会出来变成人道来运用。《周易》教人如何将天之道与天地、日月之道融会贯通，让道在人世间显现出来。人要能够运用天地阴阳相推之道，形成对自己所在时势的判断，进而把握好自己的进退。如果把"一阴一阳之谓道"理解为天道，那么"继之者善，成之者性"可以理解为人道，人道能够继承天道阴阳的变化，把它不断创生发展起来，一切都好，这是"继之者善"所谓的天道自然之善。天道自然之善灌注在世间，成就各种各样的事物，成为事物的本性，这说明宇宙生命内在统一性是相通的，人性跟物性、跟天地之性完全相通，这是从天道灌注到人道的融贯系统。

The *Book of Changes* emphasizes that people become themselves by imitating the changes and transformations in the *dao* of heaven and earth. Dao includes the heavenly *dao*, the earthly *dao*, and the human *dao*. People understand the heavenly *dao* and turn it into the human *dao* for use. The *Book of Changes* teaches people how to integrate with the heavenly *dao*, with the *dao* of heaven and earth, and sun and moon, so that the *dao* can appear in the human world. People must be able to use the *yin* and *yang* of heaven and earth to form judgments on their current situation, and then grasp their own advance and retreat.

If the moving pattern between "one *yin* and one *yang* is called the *dao*," which is understood as the heavenly *dao*, then "that which continues this is good, and that which completes this is inherent nature" can be understood as the unfolding process of the human *dao*. The human *dao* can inherit the changes and transformations of *yin* and *yang* in the heavenly *dao*, and continuously create and develop these, so that everything can flourish, and this is the so-called natural goodness of the heavenly *dao*. The natural goodness of heaven is poured into the world, achieving various things and becoming the original nature of things. This shows that the inner unity of life in the cosmos is connected. Human nature is completely connected with the nature of things and the nature of heaven and earth. This is infusion from the heavenly *dao* to the human *dao*.

9. 意本动机论
9. The Motivation Theory of Foundational Intentionality

意本论的核心是动机论为主，目的是修养人的心意状态，有明显的动机论色彩。为人处事的核心是动机，认为动机比结果重要。关键是发心要正，才能正心诚意，至于是否实现功利目的并不是最重要的，所以不是后果论。意本论作为一种动机论的重要特点之一,是以动机的善为核心,意识要从天道自然之善出发,进而建立自我反省、自我关照、自我澄明的先天自然之善,把它发掘、理解出来,再把它推出去。天地自然之善即从孟子到王阳明所讲的良知,是天机生生之善的自然呈现。良知之本体性的状态是连贯的,良知在宇宙当中自然呈现。人参与宇宙的变化就是良知自然呈现的过程。这个意义上,良知就是人天之意在人参与宇宙过程当中显现的意识状态。

The core of the theory of foundational intentionality is motivationism and its purpose is to cultivate humans' intentional states. The core of human action and treatment of others is motivation, so motivation is considered to be more important than consequences. The point is that human motivations should be upright in order to make intentions sincere. It does not matter whether or not a utilitarian goal is fulfilled, so this is not a theory based on the consequences of action. The theory of foundational intentionality is a form of motivationism characterized by the emphasis on goodness of motivation. Human consciousness should be developed from the inherent natural goodness of the heavenly *dao* and be established on the basis of self-reflection, self-care and self-clarification, which should excavate, explicate and then extend it. The natural goodness of heaven and earth is the "intuitive moral knowing (*liangzhi* 良知)" spoken of by Confucians from Mencius to Wang Yangming. It is a natural presentation of the heavenly goodness of ceaseless production and reproduction. The ontological state of intuitive moral knowing is interconnected in its natural presentation in the cosmos. The process of humanity's participation in the change and transformation of the cosmos is that of the natural presentation of man's intuitive moral knowing. In this sense, intuitive moral knowing is the state of consciousness manifested in the process of participating in the cosmos through human-cosmological intentionality.

意本论的行事原则是动机论,是先天自然之善的推致和自然呈现,不按照任何外在原则来行事。如果康德的说法是义务论的,那么意本论基本没有义务论色彩,我们不必按照某种绝对纯善的道德原则来行事。人领悟先天自然之善,自然而然就能够把它呈现出来,与"非礼勿视,非礼勿听,非礼勿言,非礼勿动"那种把礼作为外在规则不同。孔子的伦理学一方面把礼作为外在的行为规范,要求人的心意和思想、视听言动都要合于礼;但另一方面,他也讲"吾欲仁斯仁至矣",这更接近于良知现成自然存在的状态,不一定需要某种外在原则作为行动准则。

The principle of action of the theory of foundational intentionality is motivationism, a natural deduction and presentation of a priori spontaneous goodness that does not follow any external rules. If Kant's theory is deontological, then there is practically no element of this in the theory of foundational intentionality, as we do not need to act according to a certain moral rule of absolute goodness. Humanity realizes the a priori goodness of nature and can, therefore, manifest it in a natural way which is different from regarding ritual propriety as an external requirement like "Do not see, listen, speak or act in any way that goes against ritual propriety." Confucius' ethics takes ritual propriety as an external norm of behavior that calls for obedience in one's mind, intentions, thoughts and perceptions. However, on the other hand, he also claims that "If one desires to be benevolent, then this benevolence arrives [in one intention]." This is closer to the natural, pre-formed existential state of intuitive moral knowing without the necessity of external restrictions on action.

10. 意本政治哲学
10. The Political Philosophy of Foundational Intentionality

《易传》讲"富有之谓大业",提倡积极用事,公平本来是天道的公平,人间的公平应该是天道的公平的推演,从终极意义上说,人间本来就是天地自然的一种存在方式,只是人私心用智而离天道的分配越来越远,但最终还是会有天道的公平显现出来,天道在人间社会当会起作用。善恶斗争过程当中的正义不是善的势力把恶的势力全部清除干净才叫正义。阴阳永远共存,所以正义的存续其实恰恰因为恶势力的存在,善的力量对恶势力的一种分寸感才是正义的显现。如果一个社会当中全部都是善的,那就无所谓正义与不正义的问题。正义是对于弱势群体,对恶的群体保持某种分寸感,是分配的尺度和状态。在阴阳的消长过程当中,要让阴阳处于一种合理的平衡,当阳的力量快要灭阴的状态发生,需要保持一种合理的分寸感,在社会分配当中也是如此,这是社会性的正义。

The *Commentaries* emphasizes that "wealth and nobility is the great enterprise" of human achievement, encouraging an active, pragmatic spirit. The fairness in the human world is derived from that of the heavenly *dao*, because, ultimately, the human world is a form of existence of heaven and earth and nature. Although in their selfish and clever pursuits, people move further and further away from the distribution of the heavenly *dao*, cosmological fairness will eventually exert itself and play its due role. Justice does not mean eradication of any forces of evil in a battle of good against evil, since, just as *yin* and *yang* coexist forever, so justice depends on evil forces to exist, and the manifestation of justice lies in the proportion of goodness and evil. If a society were purely good, there would be no question of justice or injustice. Justice is a matter of degree and proportion in distribution regarding the protection of underprivileged groups. A balance should be maintained in the waxing and waning process of *yin* and *yang* powers, so when *yang* grows to the degree of nearly extinguishing *yin*, there is the need for a reasonable sense of measure, as should also be the case in social distribution. This is the Confucian sense of social justice.

意本论主张人以人天之意的状态来适应天地自然的运行。当人能够领会人天之意的状态,说话做事都可以跟天地运行的节律相合拍。"与天地相似,故不违",起心动念与天地的运动相似，所以行动当然能够跟天地之道一致；"先天而天弗违，后天而奉天时"，人领悟易道，进入人天之意的状态，做事的方式能够合乎天地运行的大道而不会有偏差。具备人天之意的"大人"行动能够与自然的运作相合拍，其心意之发，皆通于宇宙大道，进而在瞬间把个体的人提升到"宇宙意识"层次的"大人"。理解意本论，就具备人天之意的哲学意识，心意发动之处，即通于宇宙万物，当下的"意"就有充沛的宇宙意识，人也就转化成为能与天地变化相和谐的"大人"，心意发动之间，就能够改造阴阳之气的运行，进而运世之化。

The theory of foundational intentionality advocates that people should adapt to the natural operation of heaven and earth by unifying their intentions with that of the cosmos. When people understand the state of human-cosmological intentionality, their action and speech will keep in line with the tempo of the operation of heaven and earth: "In likeness to heaven and earth, there is no violation." As human intentionality moves in accordance with that of heaven and earth, so human action can confirm to the *dao* of nature: "If it is ahead of the heaven, heaven will not go against it; if it follows heaven, it will abide by its natural pace." In true comprehension of the *dao* of the *Changes*, one enters into a state of unified human-cosmological intentionality and one's behaviour never strays from the great *dao* of heaven and earth. The "Great Person" (*da ren* 大人), with such enlightenment, will keep his action in pace with the operation of nature. Since all his intentions are connected to the cosmological *dao*, his individual consciousness can be all of a sudden upgraded to the level of cosmological consciousness. Grasping the philosophy of foundational intentionality, one possesses a philosophical awareness of cosmological intentionality, one's "intention" at the moment is full of cosmological awareness, and one's personality expands into that of the "Great Person" who can change the operation of *yinqi* and *yangqi*, thereby transforming the operation of the world with the initiation of his intentionality.

第二章　易经明意
——爻意分说（上经）

Chapter Ⅱ Illuminating the *Classic of Changes* and Its Intentionality: Exposition of the Intentionality of the Lines (Part I)

乾为天（卦一）　（乾下乾上）

Qian (Creativity), Heaven (Hexagram 1)　(Qian below, Qian above)

　　古代中国宇宙创始论是纯粹自然主义的哲学思想，也就是宇宙本于道，是道的自然之意发动，进入人的意识世界，而道因意识的生生而开显。没有固定的宇宙存在之始基，而事物自然创始，如此这般，自然而然。但没有意念与物交关的创始或缘发之点，就不会有被领悟的世界，而时间和空间也无从开始，更无所谓价值建构如仁义道德。人间的仁德之类，其实都是意念与万物沟通之后才开始发动的，人的价值判断有其自然力绵延的一面，也有其进入意念而被意念判断的一面，是意念领会了世界创始，心意与物交之后，自然力的绵延在人间心与事的互动中表现为各种价值的判断，如吉凶悔吝、仁义道德等等。

Ancient Chinese cosmogony is a purely naturalistic philosophical thought, that is, the cosmos is based on *dao* and is the natural intentionality of *dao* as it enters the world of human consciousness, hence *dao* is revealed due to the creativity of intentional consciousness. There is no fixed foundation for the existence of the cosmos, and things are created naturally, just as naturally as could be. But without the origin of the relationship between intentions and things, there would be no world to be understood, and time and space would not have a beginning, let alone the construction of values such as benevolence, justice and morality. In fact, benevolence and virtue in the world are initiated only after intentionality communicates with the myriad things. Human value judgments have an aspect that extends natural forces, but this also enters into intentionality and is judged by the mind. It is intentionality that understands the creation of the world. After the mind interacts with things, the persistence of natural forces manifests itself in the interaction between human intentions and things in various value judgments, such as good or bad fortune, regret, difficulties, benevolence, righteousness, morality, etc.

乾，元亨利贞。

《彖》曰：大哉乾元，万物资始，乃统天。云行雨施，品物流形。大明终始，六位时成。时乘六龙以御天。乾道变化，各正性命。保合太和，乃利贞。首出庶物，万国咸宁。

《象》曰：天行健。君子以自强不息。

【明译】

乾卦象征阳天之意，元始创生，亨通顺畅，和谐有利，强健贞正。

《彖传》说：乾阳的创生之力真伟大啊！万物依赖它创生，而得到自己的生命和适宜的本性，它统帅着天道和天体的运行过程。云气流行，雨泽施布，生机充沛，阳气流变化生成为有形的万物。太阳东升西落，循环往复，意念根据太阳运动过程区分出六个时空状态，对应乾卦六爻的不同时位，好像阳气按时乘着六条巨龙驾驭大自然的运化。乾阳之道运行流转，化生万物，成就万物各自相宜的性和命，聚合乾阳元气并保持在最和谐的状态，以利于强健正固，（万物生生不息）。（乾阳的创生之力贯通在天道与人世之间），创生出各种事物，让天下万邦都安宁昌顺。

《象传》说：乾阳的创生之道周而复始，永无止息，刚健强劲，君子应效法乾阳创生之道，坚志强意，奋发进取，绝不停歇。

Hexagram Qian (Creativity) symbolizes the intentionality of *yang* and heavenly power, so it represents the beginning of creation, prosperity and smoothness, harmony and benefit, strength and integrity.

The *Judgment Commentary* (*Tuan Zhuan* 彖传) says: Qian-*yang*'s power of creation is so great! All things rely on it in creation and thus obtain their own life and appropriate natures. It directs the movement of the heavenly *dao* and celestial bodies. The clouds flow, rain falls, vitality is abundant, and *yangqi* changes and transforms to form tangible things. The sun rises in the east and sets in the west, repeating the cycle. Intentionality distinguishes six states of time and space based on the movement of the sun, corresponding to the different time positions of the six lines of Hexagram Qian (Creativity), as if *yangqi* rides on six giant dragons to control the movements of nature in time. The *dao* of Qian-*yang* moves and flows, transforming and producing the myriad things, achieving their appropriate natures and destinies, gathering Qian-*yang* energy and maintaining it in the most harmonious state, so as to be strong and solid (the myriad things produce and reproduce endlessly). (The creative power of Qian-*yang* runs between heaven and the human world), creating all kinds of things, making all nations in the world peaceful and prosperous.

第二章　易经明意
——爻意分说（上经）

The *Image Commentary* (*Xiang Zhuan* 象传) says: The *dao* of Qian-*yang*'s creativity begins over and over again, strong and powerful without end. An exemplary person should imitate the *dao* of Qian-*yang*'s creativity, be strong-minded, forge ahead, and never stop.

【明意】

乾阳元气是宇宙创生不止、大道不息的动力，表现为万物之始生、存续、发展之力，此力显现于意念之中，表现得创生不止，巨大无穷，所以意念对于道生元气唯有赞叹，表现出无限的崇高感和无法企及之感。万物皆自此道意之力而始，元气通于万物，如意通于道，犹如六龙腾布。只要心思意念每时每刻贯通于宇宙创生之根源，就可以与乾阳同体，接收到乾阳元气的巨大能量。没有乾阳元气，宇宙可以被假设存在，但无法存亡续绝，永动不止；而对于乾阳元气的领悟，就是道意。

[Illuminating Intentionality]

Qian-*yang*'s primordial *qi* is the driving force for the endless creativity of the cosmos and the ceaseless *dao*. It is manifested as the birth, survival, and development of the myriad things. This power appears in the mind, showing that creation is endless and infinite, and thus intentionality generates only admiration for the vital primordial *qi* produced by *dao*, expressing its infinite sublimity and feeling of unattainability. As all things originate from the power of *dao*, its primordial *qi* flows through the myriad things, and intentionality is connected to *dao*, just like six dragons flying across the sky. As long as one's intentionality is connected to the source of creation of the cosmos at all times, one can form one continuous body with Qian-*yang* and receive great energy from its cosmological vitality. Without Qian-*yang*'s primordial *qi*, the cosmos can be assumed to exist, but it cannot continue to exist and move continuously. The understanding of Qian-*yang*'s primordial *qi* is the intentionality of *dao*.

对于所有存在的事物来说，从无始以来的乾阳元气的获得与保持，是其存续在宇宙和世界之中的根本，也是世间万物生命力量存亡续绝的根基所在。因为物的生机，皆依赖于无始以来的乾阳的创造性力量，这是万物本始内在的生命之力，此力在身体和世间发动，构成了性渊意海，生生不息，流转不止。心意之力乃元气所保有的内在活力，保持此内在活力对生命的维系至关重要，因为这是元气发动可以感天动地、同于大道的根本所在。

For the myriad things in existence, the acquisition and maintenance of Qian-*yang* vitality from beginningless time is the foundation for its existence in the cosmos and the world, and it is also the foundation for the continued existence of the life force of the myriad things in the world. Because the vitality of things depends on the creative power of Qian-*yang* since time immemorial, this is the inherent life force of the myriad things which is initiated in the body and the world, forming a pool of inherent nature and ocean of intentionality (*xingyuan yihai* 性渊意海), which endlessly circulates. The power of this intentionality is the inner vitality maintained by all primordial *qi*. Maintaining this inner vitality is crucial to the maintenance of life, since this is the fundamental reason why primordial *qi* can move heaven and earth and be in harmony with the great *dao*.

龙其实就是无形运行的乾阳之力的形象化。乾阳之力的变化，通过龙的时位而比喻化地展现出来，对乾阳之力量的领会当中，宇宙无始以来乾阳的正面创生的力量，好像时间本身一样，就在那个地方，必须通过形象化的图形，之后用卦图才能把构成万物性命变化的各种力量和状态加以想象和表达出来。

The "dragon" here actually represents a visualization of the invisible power of Qian-*yang*. The changes in the power of Qian-*yang* are metaphorically displayed through the temporal position of the dragon. In understanding the power of Qian-*yang*, the positive creative power of Qian-*yang* since the non-beginning of the cosmos is like time itself, which is always naturally there as it is. It is necessary to use visual images and then hexagrams to imagine and express the various forces and states that constitute the changes in the lives of the myriad things.

宇宙万物当中都有乾阳之力贯注下来，形成各自的本性。本性在世间的存续需要维系保有宇宙的阳力，作为过程性延续的时间状态——生命的表现才能够维系和延续下去。如果天下万物都保持自己的乾阳之力处于和谐的状态，那么万国才可以得到安宁。这实指万物都通过自我意识的涵养，保持元气不失而得其性命之正。所以，保持宇宙无始以来的乾阳元气，是成就事业，也是安身立命的核心所在。这种乾阳元力不是简单外在的有形之物，而是通过生命力、性能量等表现出来的创造力和生机，是世间万物生生不息的核心力量，也是从性到命的根源和支撑之力。

The power of Qian-*yang* is imbued in the myriad things in the cosmos, forming their respective natures. The survival of this inherent nature in the world requires maintaining the *yang* force of the cosmos as a processual and continuous temporal state—the expression of life can then be maintained and continued. All things in the world can maintain their Qian-*yang* power in a harmonious state, and only then can all nations be at peace. This actually means that through the cultivation of self-awareness, the myriad things can maintain their vitality and keep their lives in rectitude. Therefore, maintaining the vitality of Qian-*yang* since the non-beginning of the cosmos is the core of achievement in affairs and settling oneself so that one can continue to live in the world. This kind of Qian-*yang* primordial power is not a simple external tangible thing, but the creativity and vitality expressed through vital forces like life, sexual energy, etc. It is the core force for the endless growth of the myriad things in the world, and it is also the source and supporting power from an individual's nature to their life.

初九：潜龙，勿用。

《象》曰："潜龙勿用"，阳在下也。

【明译】

初九：龙潜于水中或藏于地下，不可急于施展才用，当潜藏意念以待时。

第二章　易经明意
——爻意分说（上经）

《象传》说：蛰伏在地下的龙，意念宜保持不发动的状态，等待意念发动的时机。潜藏的意念好比初九阳爻处于全卦的最下位，不应当发动是因为即使发动了也发挥不了什么作用。

Nine (*yang*/strong line) in the first place: A dragon is lurking in the water or hiding underground. Don't rush to use it. Hide your thoughts and wait for an appropriate time.

The *Image Commentary* (*Xiang Zhuan*) says: For a dragon dormant underground, it is better to keep its intentions inactive and wait for the opportunity to initiate them. These hidden intentions are like the *yang* line in the first place, which is at the lowest position of the whole hexagram. It should not be initiated because even if it is initiated, it will not have any effect.

【明意】

潜龙喻意念深藏的状态，意会之力聚久而通，当其展现于世后能因时势而转化以通达，通畅于存在之物。潜为元气深藏之态，是元力通于未知未见之所，而后因时因势才能够与他心他意之力感通，最后才能通达于世。心意潜藏不宜展示，即无力或时势不允许显现心意的实化。

[Illuminating Intentionality]

The hidden dragon is a metaphor for the state of deep intentions. The power of understanding is gathered over time and can be accessed. When it is revealed to the world, it can be transformed and accessed according to the current situation, and it can be accessed by existing things. Latent is the state in which vital power is deeply hidden, which is when vitality reaches unknown and unseen places. Then, depending on the time and circumstances, it can communicate with the power of other people's intentions and minds, and only then can it reach the world. It is not suitable to show hidden intentions, that is, there is no power or the current situation does not allow the realization of the thoughts to be revealed.

要沉潜如水中之龙，在心意沉潜不为人知的时候，就要涵养心意使之具有龙的品德。龙为物之精者，其心意必有其特殊品性，这里强调的更多是龙内在的、即使其心意未显也本来具有的深厚道德。潜龙时势未通，但潜龙的心意状态（即心境）其实相当通畅。不为外物所动，不为俗见所改，不追名逐利，没有丝毫抱怨。随缘行事，也能够造缘行事。因有独立的见识，故不为外物所动。心心念念让善缘继续，这样就不会让邪意有实化成邪行的机会。这里强调的是即使时势未通，人也要有强大的控制心念的力量，意通世间的变化。这种"意通"的状态是潜龙的核心。

To dive like a dragon in the water, when intentionality is hidden and unknown, it is necessary to cultivate intentionality so that it has the character of a dragon. The dragon represents the essence of things, and its intentionality must have its own special character. What is emphasized here is the deep morality inherent in the dragon, even if its intentionality is not revealed. A hiding dragon's current situation is not clear, but a hiding dragon's state of intentionality (i.e. his state of mind) is actually quite smooth. Don't be moved by external things, don't be changed by common opinions, don't pursue fame and fortune, and don't complain at all. Acting according to dependent co-arising can also create dependent co-arising. Because one has independent knowledge, one is not moved by external things. Ensure your good intentions and intentionality continue, so that evil intentions will not have the opportunity to turn into evil deeds. What is emphasized here is that even if the times are not clear, people must have strong power to control their minds and understand the changes of the world. This state of "communicative intentionality" is the core of the hidden dragon.

九二：见龙在田，利见大人。

《象》曰："见龙在田"，德施普也。

【明译】

九二：龙出现在田地之上，象征有利于见到大人物的时机。

《象传》说：龙已出现在地面上，其心意开始为世所知，好像人的意念实化之德行施布普遍，并得到广泛认可。

Nine (*yang*/strong line) in the second place: The dragon appears on the field, symbolizing a favorable time to meet an important person.

The *Image Commentary* (*Xiang Zhuan*) says: The dragon has appeared on the ground, and its thoughts have begun to be known to the world, just like the virtues of people's intentions realized are spread universally and widely recognized.

【明意】

想象人的心意达到九二具备龙德之境，也就是持守心意的状态要修养到中正的状态，相当于时刻保持正念，而不给邪念实化的可能性和空间。在日常意念的发动之时即可唤起广博深远的意念之境，这种意念之境无所不通。而人的意念是否通达，与人的"龙意"的感应之力和感应机缘有关，即和是否能够得到"大人之意"的感应有关。九二限于其位与形势，但其意境仍有大人之龙德，能够具有通达通畅的力量，实现感应而通达，即其意境如有通天之力，而能够与他意相应和，并内敛而不夸耀，不断伸展其仁人之意。丝毫不间断地持守而不偏，不让意念偏向阴力去感应而出偏，所以是否出偏皆在意念的感应。

[Illuminating Intentionality]

Imagine that a person's intentionality has reached a state of intentionality with the dragon's virtue, that is, one's state of intentionality must be cultivated to an appropriate state, which is equivalent to maintaining right intentions at all times and not giving the possibility and space for evil intentions to materialize. When daily intentions are initiated, a broad and far-reaching realm of intentionality can be evoked, and this realm of intentionality is all-encompassing. Whether a person's intentions are accessible or not is related to the power and chance of sensing the "dragon's will", that is, whether one can get a sense of the "will of a person of great virtue (or a great person)". The Nine (*yang*/strong line) in the second place is limited to its position and situation, but its intentional context still has the dragon virtue of a person, and it can have the power of access and smoothness, and can achieve resonance and understanding. That is, its intentional context has the power to reach a cosmological existence, and should be consistent with other people's intentions, and restrained and not flaunted, but rather constantly extend one's benevolent intentions. Persevere without any interruption and do not deviate, and do not let intentionality be deflected to the *yin* force to induce it, so whether it goes astray depends on the resonance of intentions.

九三：君子终日乾乾，夕惕若厉，无咎。

《象》曰："终日乾乾"，反复道也。

【明译】

九三：君子一天到晚勤勉健行，直到深夜时意念都保持警惕，好像戒慎的状态危险如影随形，心天之意保持这样的忧患意识，就能够免遭过失和祸患。

《象传》说：君子白天夜晚都精进不休，自强不息，这是说君子按照乾阳之道反复修炼之的人天之意。

Nine (*yang*/strong line) in the third place: An exemplary person walks diligently all day long, and keeps one's intentionality alert until late at night, as if the state of alertness and danger are always with him. If one maintains such a sense of worry in one's mind, one will be able to avoid mistakes and disasters.

The *Image Commentary* (*Xiang Zhuan*) says: An exemplary person works hard day and night and strives for self-improvement. This means that an exemplary person cultivates repeatedly according to the moving patterns of Qian-*yang*, which is the cosmological intentionality connecting humanity with the heavens.

【明意】

知至至之，人天之意通于天，即人能够感应时势的几微变化。修辞与修道近似，言为心声，让人了解你的诚意，还是要靠语言，所以要通过锤炼自己的语言来修正自己意念的实化过程。

实化自己意念的过程如一个聚气的过程，是一个努力学习，反复修养自己，淬炼自己心意的进程。意念进退的分寸在反复实化自己意念和反身状态的反思过程中，这个过程里，人在意念的修为当中，要培养直觉和先见之明，让意念顺时而动，领悟到先机之所在，甚至可以于未发之中控制意念的实化进程，于意念发动之前不让邪念得以实化。

[Illuminating Intentionality]

Once known, human-cosmological intentionality connects humanity with heaven, that is, humans have the ability to sense the slightest changes in their current situation. Rhetoric is similar to cultivating oneself. Words are the voice of the heart, and people still need to rely on language to understand one's sincerity of intention. Therefore, one must refine one's language to correct the realization process of one's intentions.

The process of realizing one's intentions is like a process of gathering energy. It is a process of studying hard, cultivating oneself repeatedly, and tempering one's mind. The propriety of the advance and retreat of intentions is a reflexive process of repeatedly realizing and reflecting on one's own intentions. In this process, in the cultivation of intentions, people must cultivate intuition and foresight, let their intentions move in time, understand where opportunities lie, and can even control the actualization process of intentions before they occur, and prevent evil intentions from materializing before they are initiated.

德与业皆意所生，进德修业、崇德广业而成盛德大业，皆意念修为生生而成。意念之"进"与"修"决定君子成德立业之规模与魄力。忠信就是诚心实意，诚心实意是在意念发动处真诚实在。人的心意发动之处，虽从一窈冥之境生起，却需意念时刻保持真诚实在方可。心意之要与言辞相符，实化心意之发若合符节，以最恰当的言辞来表达心意发动的分寸。在这个意义上，对言辞的控制力就是对意念控制力的直接表现，人要在意念发动与言辞的修饰之间找到最完美的分寸。

Virtue and karma are both born from intentions. Advancing virtue and cultivating karma, upholding virtue and spreading karma to achieve a great virtuous career are all born from the cultivation of one's intentions. The "advancing" and "cultivation" of intentions determine the scale and courage of an exemplary person's virtue and career. Loyalty means sincerity, and sincerity means being sincere and authentic in the place where intentions are initiated. Where a person's intentionality is initiated, although it arises from a state of darkness, it needs to remain sincere and authentic at all times. The utterances of intentionality should be consistent with one's words. If the utterances of one's actual intentions are in line with cosmological rhythms, the most appropriate words should be used to express the propriety of one's intentions. In this sense, the control of words is a direct expression of the control of intention. People must find the perfect balance between the initiation of intention and the embellishment of words.

九四：或跃在渊，无咎。

《象》曰："或跃在渊"，进无咎也。

【明译】

九四：或腾跃上进，或退居深渊，都没有过错和祸患。

《象传》说：龙在此位，或者向上一跃登天，上天行云布雨，施展自己的本事；或者向下潜回深渊之中，回到本来的安居之所，前进没有过错和祸患，可以尝试进取。

Nine (*yang*/strong line) in the fourth place: Whether you leap forward or retreat into the abyss, there is no fault or disaster.

The *Image Commentary* (*Xiang Zhuan*) says: When the dragon is in this position, it can either leap upward to the sky, moving clouds and dispersing rain from the sky, and displaying its own abilities, or it can dive back into the abyss and return to its original home, and there will be no mistakes or missteps in its progress. Since there is no disaster, one can try to make progress at this time.

【明意】

九四为风云激荡变化时刻的意向，气魄恢宏，准备巨大的跌宕起伏。在身行之试前，心要有足够的气魄与力量来运思进退的可能性。心境在可进可退的时候，要通于跃成之境，也要通于跃不成而入于渊之境，不可因为可进可退而大意不加深思。

未来如何在意向性中存在，心意对于未来的期待和想象是如何可能的？九四要想跃上九五之尊的五位，虽然近在咫尺，但还是难乎其难，确实需要有豁得出去的勇气、随时准备从头来过的气魄才可以。历史记住很多伟大的灵魂，他们其实是失败的英雄，其人生可能就是一连串挫折甚至大溃败的记录。他们跃了，但没有跃上去，或者跃上去后来还是入于渊，很多人再也没有起来，但他们跃的时候体现出来的气魄后人却永远铭记。

[Illuminating Intentionality]

Nine (*yang*/strong line) in the fourth place is intention at a moment of turmoil and change. It is magnificent and prepared for huge ups and downs. Before making an attempt in person, the mind must have enough courage and strength to think about the possibilities of advance and retreat. When the state of intentionality can be advanced or retreated, it must be in a state of leaping into success, and it must also be in a state of failing and leaping into the abyss. Do not be careless and fail to think deeply just because you can either advance or retreat.

How does the future exist in intentionality, and how is the mind's expectation and imagination of the future possible? If the Nine (*yang*/strong line) in the fourth place wants to jump ahead to the honored position of Nine (*yang*/strong line) in the fifth place, although it is very close, it is still very difficult. It really requires the courage to be brave and ready to start all over again at this time. History remembers many great souls who were actually failed heroes, and their lives may be a record of a series of setbacks or even great defeats. They jumped, but did not reach their goals, or fell into the abyss after jumping ahead. Many people never had the chance to come back again, but the courage they showed when they jumped will be remembered forever by future generations.

国家命运往往在于主事者的一念之间，如果风险太高，就要按兵不动，不可轻举妄动。所以九四虽然可以一试身手，可能开始改革或者变革，但还是要慎之又慎才行。审慎揣度就是因为跃不上去的代价很高，回到深渊里潜龙未必从头来过，还不知道何时能够东山再起，也可能永远就起不来了，所以要非常审慎，三思而后跃。当然，就具备龙德的君子来说，已磨炼到一定程度，就可以尝试变革，可能会成功，即使不能一步到位，也不会有太大风险。所以当进则进，哪怕重回深渊从头来过也要进，可以说是有点悲壮的、不成功便成仁的气象。但成就伟大的功勋事业需要有英雄史诗般的气魄才有可能。

The destiny of a country often lies in the whims of those in charge. If the risk is too high, we must stand still and not act rashly. Therefore, although the Nine (*yang*/strong line) in the fourth place can move, trying to initiate reform or change, this still needs to be carried out with serious caution. Careful speculation is needed because the price of not jumping up is very high. If one goes back to the abyss and hides, then one might not have the chance to start all over again. One cannot tell when one will be able to make a comeback, and one may never get up, so one must be very cautious and think twice before jumping. Of course, for an exemplary person with the virtue of a dragon, if one has been tempered to a certain extent, one can try to change, and one may succeed. Even if one cannot get it right in one step, there will not be too much risk. Therefore, when the time is right to advance, one should try to advance, and even if one returns to the abyss and has to start all over again, one must still make the advance. The outcome might be said to be a little tragic, and even a scene of failure, but achieving great meritorious deeds requires heroic and epic courage.

九五：飞龙在天，利见大人。
《象》曰："飞龙在天"，大人造也。

【明译】

九五：龙在天空中高飞，出现有德有位人人的有利时机到了。

《象传》说：龙飞上了高位，处在一个十分有利的时势地位，这是能够实化人天之意的大人的造化，风云际会，可以一展身手，建功立业。

Nine (*yang*/strong line) in the fifth place: The dragon is flying high in the sky, and it is a favorable time for a virtuous and powerful person to appear.

The *Image Commentary* (*Xiang Zhuan*) says: The dragon has reached a high position and is in a very favorable situation. This is the blessing of a great person who can realize the cosmological intentionality of humanity and heaven. In an event of great change, one can show one's skills and make achievements.

【明意】

大人能"造"，在顺应阴阳的基础上转化阴阳，也就能"化"。圣人心动，时势配合，能够主动转化阴阳，令天地间的阴阳之气的运行发生变化。圣人是靠心意感通于天地之动，不是靠身体或者其他部分来感通。大人心念广大，能够实化其心意，居于其位，能够吸引同类大人，彼此心意相通而共同成就大事业。他们善于心意感通以转化阴阳，大人是"大心之人"，也就是时时刻刻有"人天之意"的人。同时，他们是善于"实意"，也就是把意念实化的人。他们通过感应，各从其类来体现人的阴阳主动性，主体意识跃入天地阴阳的客体，犹如一个人跃入泳池、拨开水面一般分开天地的阴阳。

学习《周易》，先理解阴阳，其次顺从阴阳，最后转化阴阳。天地阴阳本身每时每刻都在转化，乾卦的卦爻辞在于说服人们，只要心意修行到位，人就可以主动转化外物，从时势造英雄英雄造时势来看，只要条件允许，心是随时随地能够改变阴阳的。

[Illuminating Intentionality]

Great people can "create" and transform *yin* and *yang* powers on the basis of adapting and responding to *yin* and *yang* situations. The sage's heart is moved, and the current situation cooperates, so one can actively transform *yin* and *yang* powers, causing changes in the movement of *yin* and *yang* between heaven and earth. Sages rely on their minds to sense the movements of heaven and earth, not their bodies or other parts. Great people have broad intentions, can realize their intentions, occupy their positions, and can attract great people of the same kind. They can connect with each other and achieve great things together. They are good at communicating with intentionality to transform *yin* and *yang* situations. Great people are "people with a great mind," that is, people who always have the cosmological intentionality of humanity and heaven. At the same time, they are good at "realizing intentionality," that is, they are people who concretize their intentions. Through resonance, they embody the *yin* and *yang* initiative of human beings according to their kind. The subject's consciousness leaps into the *yin* and *yang* of heaven and earth, just as a person jumps into a swimming pool and separates the *yin* and *yang* situation of the water.

To study the *Book of Changes*, one must first understand *yin* and *yang*, then obey *yin* and *yang*, and finally transform *yin* and *yang*. The *yin* and *yang* of heaven and earth themselves are transforming all the time. The hexagrams and lines of Hexagram Qian (Creativity) aim to convince people that as long as intentionality is cultivated in place, people can actively transform external objects. Judging from the fact that times create their heroes and heroes can create their times, as long as conditions permit, the heart-mind can change *yin* and *yang* anytime and anywhere.

圣人时时刻刻感天动地，心意发动通于天地阴阳。于是天地分化，万物各从其类，可见圣人心意一动，世间阴阳就会发生分化和转化。意念拨动阴阳，转化阴阳，大人通于天地、日月、四时、鬼神，心动与自然节奏完全合拍，也就是大人的心行即天行的自然流动。心意发动，本是天地阴阳运行的自然流行，所以对心意的有意控制，本身就是拨动阴阳。类似于通常说的聚集人气、造声势，但需要时势合宜，而且从心底里打动大家才可以达到天下响应的状态。圣人心意感天动地，天地阴阳为之变化。圣人起心动念都带着不同寻常的能量。圣人心意有巨大的气场，一旦时势造英雄，就能改天换地。而所谓英雄造时势，就是大人在语默动静之间就可以营造一个顺应其心意的气场。位居九五的至尊者借助其九五之尊的时位，每时每刻起心动念都可以改天换地，所以必须慎之又慎。从初爻开始德就修得基本到位，而等到九五之尊时，是时势造英雄，此时人心发动就能改变世界，此时德时位配合，也就是时势允许。

The sage is always aware of the movement of heaven and earth, and one's intentionality is initiated to connect the *yin* and *yang* of heaven and earth. When heaven and earth divide, and the myriad things move according to their own categories, it can be seen that when the sage's intentionality moves, the *yin* and *yang* in the world will differentiate and transform. Intentions move the *yin* and *yang* powers to transform *yin* and *yang* situations. The great person is connected to heaven and earth, the sun and moon, the four seasons, and ghosts and spirits, and their intentions are in perfect harmony with natural rhythms. That is to say, the great person's intentional movement follows the natural flow of heavenly movement. The initiation of intentionality is the natural flow of the movement of *yin* and *yang* powers between heaven and earth, so the intentional control of intentionality itself is the movement of *yin* and *yang* powers. This is similar to what is usually said about gathering popularity and building momentum, but it needs to be done at the right time and move everyone from the bottom of their hearts to achieve a state of response from the world. The sage's intentions move heaven and earth, and the *yin* and *yang* of heaven and earth change accordingly. Every intention of a sage carries unusual energy, and the sage's intentionality has a huge aura. Once the times are right to create a hero, one can change the world. The so-called hero creates the situation, that is, great people can create an aura that conforms to their wishes in silence and movement. The supreme leader of the Nine (*yang*/strong line) in the fifth place takes advantage of one's temporal position as the Nine-Fifth Master (*jiuwu zhizun* 九五之尊), and can change the world every time one's intentions move, so one must be cautious. From the beginning of the first line, virtue has been basically cultivated in place, and when one reaches the fifth level, the times help create heroes. At this time, a person's intentions can easily change the world, so we say that the times and virtue can cooperate to work out because temporal propensity allows for this.

上九：亢龙，有悔。

《象》曰："亢龙有悔"，盈不可久也。

【明译】

上九：龙飞到穷极高亢之处，必有悔恨。

《象传》说：龙飞到极高之处，必然会出错而后悔，因为盈满完美的状态不可能持续长久。

Nine (*yang*/strong line) in the top place: When the dragon flies to an extremely lofty place, there will be regret.

The *Image Commentary* (*Xiang Zhuan*) says: When a dragon flies to a very high place, it will inevitably make mistakes and have regrets, because states of fullness and perfection never last long.

【明意】

亢龙代表气息高扬的末端，盈满过度则无法保持。外在的聚合之意缘需要生机维系，而已经完满的状态想要继续保持下去非常之难，所有意念在进取有所得的时候，总要保持退亡有所失的准备，也就是说，一念升起的生意之间，要随时看空放下意念所聚的意缘，如果真的能够一念放空，反而能够更好地保有和持续意缘的聚合。

第二章　易经明意
——爻意分说（上经）

[Illuminating Intentionality]

The dragon in the highest position represents the end of lofty *qi*, which cannot be maintained if it is too full. The external aggregation of intentionality requires vitality to be maintained, and it is very difficult to maintain an already perfect state. All intentions must always be prepared to retreat and lose in the process of advancing, progressing and gaining, that is to say, when an intention arises, one should always let go of the confluence of undetermined intentions. If one can really let go of these intentions, one will be able to better maintain and sustain the gathering of intentions.

意念聚合的规律是：所有正向凝聚的意向，都要以负向散开的意向作为情境，意念之生意才能维系，意念之发动方能进退裕如。意念里单维地进和退都是不存在的，因为进的意念要以退的意境为基础，得的意念要以失的意境为根基。人知道这个道理就可以主动时刻提醒警示自己：意念实化之处，即是事情的转而虚化，需要无中生有的关键所在。心意如何适时因应事变是《周易》之教，也就是心意之变当通于《易》道之转化。即使如亢龙之时位也有转机，而转机都在起心动念之间。要顺应阴阳之力的变化来调整自己的心意与行动。如果人能够提前预知事情的发展方向，努力控制自己的意念转化及与之相关的阴阳之力，也就可以有所预备，提前准备好意念生机之方向，和发动意能的状态。

The law of intentional aggregation is: all positive condensed intentions must be contextualized by negative divergent intentions. Only then can the mechanism of intentionality be maintained, and only when the intentions are initiated can they advance and retreat smoothly. Unidimensional advance and retreat do not exist in the mind, because the intention of advancement must be based on the intentional context of retreat, and the intention of gain must be based on the intentional context of loss. If people know this truth, they can take the initiative in intentionality and warn themselves at all times: where intentions are realized, this is where things-events turn and become virtual, and the key point is to create something out of nothing. How intentionality can respond to events in a timely manner is taught by the *Book of Changes*, that is, changes in intentionality should be connected to the transformation of the *dao* in the *Book of Changes*. Even if one is in the position of a powerful dragon, there will be a turning point, and these turning points are all found in the moment of intention. One must adapt to the changes in the power of *yin* and *yang* to adjust one's intentions and actions. If people can predict the developmental direction of things in advance and strive to control their intentions to transform the related *yin* and *yang* power, they can be prepared in advance, foretelling the direction of the vitality of intention and the state of intentional energy in initiating the intentions.

用九：见群龙无首，吉。

《象》曰："用九"，天德不可为首也。

【明译】

用九：用老阳之数"九"，它在乾卦六爻随时都可能出现，犹如出现群龙，无首无尾，都不以首领自居，所以吉祥。

《象传》说：用老阳之数"九"，六个阳爻都不以首领自居，这是效法乾阳之大德，创生万物，功成而不居首，不居功。

Using the Nine: Using the Nine of old *yang*, (which may appear at any time in the sixth line of Hexagram Qian (Creativity),) it is like a group of dragons appearing, without a head or tail, none of which considers itself the leader, so it is auspicious.

The *Image Commentary* (*Xiang Zhuan*) says: Using the Nine of old *yang*, the six *yang* lines do not take themselves as the leader. This imitates the great virtue of Qian-*yang*, creates the myriad things, and achieves success without ranking first or taking credit.

【明意】

群龙无首无尾，乃生意顺应天道回环之象。意念之气通达，不受一时一地时空条件的约束，则意念实化可以转化天地不通之状态，这是《周易》教人实化意念以改换阴阳之术。"乾元用九，乃见天则"，是通过运用乾阳创生变化之刚爻（九）来体现出天道运行的法则。也就是占卜的时候，运用老阳之数九，能够体现天道变化的根本法则。九为老阳，代表阳气之极，自然变阴，这是天道自然运行变化的规律。

群龙无首通常被当作贬义来理解，而用九此处说吉，那就要颇费思量。此处的天人之道，就在于六爻一体，都是群龙，都刚健进取，都奋发有为，但都不强为首，众志成城，精诚团结，不吉利都不可能。"群龙"也可以理解为君子群居，"无首"是说君子们彼此谦让互不为首，各自负责，各自维系群体的和谐和共生共存。这样的说法，都是君子心意相通，互不居首，能够集体顺应天道变化的原则。

[Illuminating Intentionality]

The dragons have no head or tail, which is a symbol of intentionality's creation following the heavenly *dao*. If the energy of intentions is accessible and is not constrained by the temporal and spatial conditions of one time and place, then the realization of intentions can transform a state of blockage between heaven and earth. This is the art of the *Book of Changes* teaching people to concretize intentions to exchange *yin* and *yang* powers. "Using the Nine in Qian-*yang* to see the laws of heaven" embodies the law of heavenly operation by using the strong line (Nine) of Qian-*yang* to create changes. That is, when doing divination, using the number nine of old *yang* can reflect the moving pattern of heaven, the fundamental law of change. Nine is old *yang*, representing the extreme of *yang* energy, which naturally changes into *yin*. This is the pattern of natural movement and the change of heaven.

"Without a head or tail" (leaderless) is usually understood as derogatory, and it takes a lot of thought to comprehend the nine places as auspicious. The *dao* of heaven and humanity here lies in the fact that the six lines are as one, they are all dragons, they are all strong and enterprising, they are all hard-working and promising, but none of them takes themselves as a leader. If they are united sincerely, it is impossible for them to meet with misfortune. "Group of dragons" can also be understood as exemplary people living in a group. "Leaderless" means that exemplary people are humble to each other and do not take the lead. They are responsible for each other and maintain the harmony and symbiosis of the group. Such statements are based on the principle that exemplary people have the same mind, do not take precedence over each other, and can collectively adapt to changes in the heavenly *dao*.

坤为地（卦二） （坤下坤上）

Kun (Support), Earth (Hexagram 2)   (Kun below, Kun above)

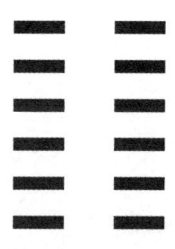

☷
☷

意境为心意发动之基础，意境与外物关联共在，物都在意境之中，意动指向外物，境中意动即物依意境而生。自我作为心识的主体，是物在意境之中生生不息的反身式存在，是在反身的过程当中逐渐建立起来的，是意识发动生成之时，在乾动与坤顺之间的反身存在状态。坤阴之意总是必须随顺阳意才能依境而生，才能于意境中表现出阴意的力量。阴意发展之极致即化成阳意，但不能脱离具体的境域来实现这一点。

The intentional context is the basis for the initiation of intention. The intentional context and external objects are related and co-exist. Objects are all in an intentional context, and the intentions move and point to external objects. The intentional context means that objects are born according to a context full of intentionality. As the subject of consciousness, the self is the reflexive existence of objects in an intentional context, which is gradually established in the process of reflexivity, and it is thus in the reflexive existence between the initiative of Qian and the following of Kun when consciousness is generated. The intentionality of Kun-*yin* must always follow the intentionality of Qian-*yang* in order to be produced according to the situation and to express the power of *yin* in the intentional context. The ultimate development of *yin* power will turn into *yang*, but this cannot be achieved in isolation from its specific context.

坤，元亨。利牝马之贞。君子有攸往，先迷，后得主，利西南得朋，东北丧朋。安贞吉。

《彖》曰：至哉坤元，万物资生，乃顺承天。坤厚载物，德合无疆。含弘光大，品物咸亨。牝马地类，行地无疆，柔顺利贞。君子攸行，先迷失道，后顺得常。"西南得朋"，乃与类行。"东北丧朋"，乃终有庆。"安贞"之"吉"，应地无疆。

《象》曰：地势坤。君子以厚德载物。

【明译】

坤卦象征地，元始化生，亨通顺畅。如果像雌马那样持柔守正，就会有利。君子有所前往，如果抢先居首就会迷失方向，如果随后顺从，就会得到有乾阳之意的主人。在西、南的阴方，与同类相伴，会找到朋友，有利；在东、北的阳方，失去同类朋友，却可以找到阳为主人，也有利。安于柔顺，持守正道，吉祥。

Hexagram Kun (Support) symbolizes the earth, the beginning of transformation, prosperity and smoothness. It will be beneficial if you stay as gentle and upright as a female horse. An exemplary person has a destination, but if one strives to take the lead, one will lose his way. If one obeys later, one will get a master who has the intention of Qian-*yang*. In the *yin* side of the west and south, it is beneficial to find friends who are of the same kind; in the *yang* side of the east and north, one may lose friends of the same kind, but one may find a *yang* power as one's master, which is also beneficial. Be at peace with meekness, adhere to the right *dao*, and all will be auspicious.

《彖传》说：广大至极的坤阴元气的化生之力啊！万物都依赖它才能化生，它顺从秉承乾阳之意才能形成阴阳合体，成就事物。坤阴之意是大地深厚载万物的象征，它的柔顺德性与乾天刚健相合，万物生生，久远无边。内涵弘博，光明远大，博施厚济，万物遍受滋养，亨顺通畅。雌马与坤地都有着同样类型的德性，在无边无际的大地上驰骋，它温柔和顺，利于持守正固。

君子有所前往，如果抢先居首就会迷失方向，这违背阳主阴顺的常道；如果随后顺从，就会得到有乾阳之力的主人，这符合阳主阴顺的常道。在西方（坤兑）和南方（巽离）的阴方，会找到朋友，这是与同类相伴，在东方（艮震）、北方（乾坎）的阳方，失去同类朋友，却可以找到乾阳主人，最终得到喜乐吉庆。安于持守顺承乾阳正道的吉祥，这应和大地无边无际、无穷无尽的化生之力。

The *Judgment Commentary* (*Tuan Zhuan*) says: The transformative power of the vast vital *qi* of Kun-*yin*! All things rely on it to transform into life, and it obeys and upholds the intentionality of Qian-*yang* to form the combination of *yin* and *yang* and accomplish things and events. The intentionality of Kun-*yin* is a symbol of the deepness of the earth that supports the myriad things. Its suppleness and virtue are in harmony with the strength of the cosmos, in which the myriad things are produced and reproduce without end in space or time. Its content is grand, its light far-reaching, its blessings are generous, and the myriad things are nourished and prosper. The female horse has the same type of virtue as earth with its Kun virtue. It gallops on boundless land in a gentle and tender manner, which is conducive to maintaining integrity.

An exemplary person is advancing, but if one takes the lead, one will lose his way, going against the normal way of *yang* being dominated by *yin* and being submissive. If one then obeys, one will get a master with the power of Qian-*yang*, which is in line with the normal way of *yang* being dominant and *yin* being submissive. In the *yin* side of the west (Trigrams Kun, Dui) and south (Trigrams Xun, Li), you will find friends who are companions of the same kind. In the *yang* side of the east (Trigrams Gen, Zhen) and north (Trigrams Qian, Kan), though you may lose the same kind of friends, you can find Qian-*yang*, and thus finally attain happiness and good fortune. Being content with the auspiciousness of adhering to the righteous *dao* of Qian-*yang* should be in harmony with the boundless and endless power of transformation and rebirth of the earth.

《象传》说：坤阴之意象征大地的气势，顺承乾阳之意，化生并包容万物。君子修行人天之意要效法大地的气势，不断增厚德性，承载万事万物。

The *Image Commentary* (*Xiang Zhuan*) says: The intentionality of Kun-*yin* symbolizes the momentum of the earth, follows the intentionality of Qian-*yang*, and transforms and embraces the myriad things. An exemplary person who practices the cosmological intention of humanity and heaven must imitate the momentum of the earth, constantly strengthen their virtue, and support the myriad things.

【明意】

坤阴之意如同天地不断散发出来的玄妙之母性温情与爱意，犹如《道德经》中提及的"玄牝"那般极度有力，爱意无穷，好像母性之意，具有驰骋、包容、笼罩大地的气魄和力量。

[Illuminating Intentionality]

The intentionality of Kun-*yin* is like the mysterious maternal warmth and love that constantly emanates from heaven and earth. It is as extremely powerful and infinitely loving as the "mysterious femininity" (*xuanpin* 玄牝) mentioned in Chapter 6 of the *Daodejing* (道德经). It seems that the intentionality of motherhood has the characteristics of galloping, tolerating, and covering. This is the spirit and power of the earth.

坤阴之意随顺乾阳之意而成意境，因其能够随顺而让坤阴之意表现有力。可是如果坤阴之意一旦先行，则容易随顺无力，意识之境域则无法展开。所以坤阴之力离开乾阳之意就难以表现出其力量。坤阴之意以其深厚内在的才能方能承受起强力的乾阳之意。坤阴之意如果倡先可能不知何为其所主，因其对自身领导力与情境之间的互动了解有限。如果明白自身的领导力有比较强的坤性特点，就应该主动随顺乾阳之力，跟随和帮助乾阳之意成事而毫不居功。因坤阴之意的本性就是一个跟随乾天之阳意，从而乾坤并健而能成就有力之意境。所以强调坤阴之意有强大的包容和容纳力，能够承载一切，这样随顺乾阳之意，就能构筑意境。

The intentionality of Kun-*yin* follows the intentionality of Qian-*yang* and forms an intentional context. Because it can follow the intentionality of Qian-*yang*, this enables the intentionality of Kun-*yin* to express itself powerfully. However, if the intention of Kun-*yin* comes first, it will easily become powerless, and the realm of consciousness will not be able to expand. Therefore, it is difficult for the power of Kun-*yin* to express its power without the intention of Qian-*yang*. The intentionality of Kun-*yin* can only withstand the strong intentionality of Qian-*yang* because of its profound inner capability. Kun-*yin*'s intentionality, if initiated, may not know its master, because the understanding of the interaction between one's own leadership and the situation may be limited. If one understands that one's leadership has relatively strong Kun-nature characteristics, one should take the initiative to follow the power of Qian-*yang*, and follow and help Qian-*yang*'s will to achieve things without taking any credit. Because the nature of the intentionality of Kun-*yin* is to follow the *yang* intention of heavenly Qian-*yang*, Qian and Kun are in harmony and can achieve a powerful intentional context. Therefore, it is emphasized that the intentionality of Kun-*yin* has a strong tolerance and can support everything. In this way, following the intentionality of Qian-*yang*, an intentional context can be constructed.

坤阴之柔顺因其随顺刚健的阳意而有力量，柔顺而有力因坤阴之意能够跟随乾阳之意运动。坤阴之意跟随顺应乾阳之意，于静之极致的意境中透显出无穷的力量，所以坤阴之意境包容涵纳着巨大的智慧和力量。

The suppleness of Kun-*yin* is powerful because it follows a strong Qian-*yang* intention, hence the suppleness and strength of Kun-*yin* can reveal itself because it can follow the movement of Qian-*yang*. The intentionality of Kun-*yin* follows the intentionality of Qian-*yang*, revealing infinite power in an intentional context of ultimate tranquility. Therefore, the intentional context of Kun-*yin* contains great wisdom and power.

初六：履霜，坚冰至。

《象》曰："履霜、坚冰"，阴始凝也，驯致其道，至"坚冰"也。

【明译】

初六：脚上踩到了霜，说明凝结成坚冰的严寒时节就要来到。

《象传》说："脚上踩到了霜，凝结成坚冰的严寒时节就要来到"，是因为初六为阴爻，霜的出现说明阴气已经开始凝结，顺着这个趋势发展下去，阴气凝聚成为坚冰的严寒时节就会自然来到。

Six (*yin*/soft line) in the first place: If you step on frost, the cold season will soon come and condense it into solid ice.

The *Image Commentary* (*Xiang Zhuan*) says: "If you step on frost, the cold season will condense it into solid ice." This is because the Six (*yin*/soft line) in the first place is a *yin* line, and the appearance of frost indicates that *yin* energy has begun to condense, so this trend will continue to develop, and the severe cold season when *yinqi* condenses into solid ice will come naturally.

【明意】

防微杜渐不仅为了说明一个道理，更重要的是要强调，要想成就善业，在特定的时与境当中，不可一念离却善心善意，不能一刻中断善行。反之亦然，恶意不断，则恶业积累，最后恶贯满盈，万劫不复。意念的力量有累积的效应，心灵意念长期累积可能会表现出相当巨大的能量。分辨心意的阴阳是一种对他心之动的判断能力，但人们如果不能摒除主观成见，就可能因为主观过度强烈的倾向，导致难以分辨情境当中他人心意的变化，甚至忽视长期累积的心意变化。

[Illuminating Intentionality]

Preventing the subtle and putting a stop to the gradual is not only to illustrate a truth, but more importantly, to emphasize that in order to achieve good deeds, in a specific time and situation, one must not lose one's good intention and will, and must not interrupt one's good deeds for a moment. On the contrary, if bad intentions continue, bad *karma* will accumulate, and eventually evil will be fulfilled and there can be no recovery. The power of intention has a cumulative effect, and the long-term accumulation of mental intentionality may show considerable energy. Distinguishing the *yin* and *yang* of intentionality is an ability to judge the movements of other people's minds. However, if people cannot get rid of subjective prejudices, it may be difficult to distinguish the changes in other people's minds in a situation due to an overly strong subjective tendency, or even ignore long-term accumulated changes in intention.

防微杜渐的意识运作功夫说明意念事件与物理事件发生之间有着对应或联通的关系，对意识事件的控制，可能改变长远的物理事件生成与发展的状态。意念事件并不单独发生在心意之间，但也不是物理事件的简单对应，意念事件时刻与物理事件处于融通和谐的状态当中，不是一种主客、内外那样的单纯反映模式。否则对于同一个物理事件，不同的人应该有相同的意念事件，但事实并不如此。本爻希望人们在当下意念的反思中预见意念实化的结果，进而通过控制意念的生发状态，来掌控意念实化的结果，这是典型的心意能够拨动和改变世间阴阳的教导。

The operation of consciousness to prevent subtle events shows that there is a correspondence or connection between the occurrence of intentional events and physical beings. The control of consciousness may change the long-term formation and development of physical events. Intentional events do not occur alone between intentions, but they equally do not simply correspond to physical existences. Intentional events are always in a harmonious state with physical events, and not a simple reflection mode like subject and object, internal and external. Otherwise, for the same physical event, different people should have the same mental event, but this is not the case. This line hopes that people can foresee the result of the realization of intention in reflection on the current situation, and then control the result of the realization of intention by controlling the generative state of the mind. This is a typical teaching that intentionality can stir and change the *yin* and *yang* powers of the world.

六二：直、方、大，不习，无不利。

《象》曰：六二之动，直以方也。"不习无不利"，地道光也。

【明译】

六二：大地生物正直，地体端方，包容广大，从无刻意修习营为，万物自然化生，无所不利。

《象传》说：六二的变动，正直而端方。从无刻意修习营为，万物自然化生，无所不利，这就是大地广阔无尽的柔顺之道。

Six (*yin*/soft line) in the second place: The creatures on earth are upright, the body of the earth is regular, and it is tolerant and vast. There is no deliberate practice of cultivation. All things are born naturally, and nothing is disadvantageous.

The *Image Commentary* (*Xiang Zhuan*) says: The changes in the Six (*yin*/soft line) in the second place are upright and regular. Without any deliberate practice, the myriad things will be born naturally, without any disadvantage. This is the vast, endless and gentle way of the earth.

【明意】

坤阴之意发动的状态，应是顺着坤阴深藏含纳之厚意而自然而然生发至理想状态。坤阴之意的正直，是指意对应的事件的发生合乎意原初发动的意愿。坤阴之意的端方表现为力量型的心意实化过程展开之意境有端方之形制，而不仅如小石头投入湖里的那种自然而然同心圆式的展开，因为心意借助坤阴之意如同在大地上展开的力度和广度可以自我把握，予以端方之制。所以，内心保持一种从大地之厚德而生成的诚敬心意，心意实化之时坤阴表现得方正不阿，美成万物，恰如借助大地之力一般。通过心天之意长期持久借助坤阴之意的内在操练，不断重复，试判评估心意发动的结果来形成良性的预判机制之后，形成良好的大地之意那样"习"成天然，此为性与"习"成。意念长期操习有度形成习惯，可以形成对于可能事件的有效评估和调控，这种评估是主客一体的，阴意与阳意交融改变天地之间的阴阳，通达牵引着事物的变化。

[Illuminating Intentionality]

The state in which the intention of Kun-*yin* is initiated should follow the deep intentionality of Kun-*yin* and naturally develop into an ideal state. The integrity of the intentionality of Kun-*yin* means that the events corresponding to the intentionality occur in accordance with the original intention of the intentionality. The uprightness of the intentionality of Kun-*yin* is manifested as the powerful realization process of intention. The intentional context has a regular shape, not just the natural concentric unfolding of a small stone thrown into a lake, because its intentionality relies on the intentionality of Kun-*yin*. Just like the strength and breadth unfolding on the earth, one can control it oneself and regulate it, provided that one keeps a sincere and respectful intentionality in one's heart that is generated from the kindness of the earth. When its intentionality is realized, Kun-*yin* will appear upright and beautiful, and the myriad things will be harmonious, just as if they are relying on the power of the earth. Through the long-term inner practice of the intentionality of the heart-mind and heaven with the assistance of Kun-*yin* intentionality, through continuous repetition, judgment and evaluation of the results of the initiation of intentionality to form a benign prejudgment mechanism, and then forming a beneficial earth intentionality through habituation, it becomes second nature. The long-term practice of intentions to form a habit can develop an effective evaluation and control of possible events. This kind of evaluation is an integration of subject and object. The fusion of *yin* and *yang* intentions will change the *yin* and *yang* powers between heaven and earth, and thus understanding leads to the change of things.

六三：含章可贞，或从王事，无成有终。
《象》曰："含章可贞"，以时发也。"或从王事"，知（zhì）光大也。
【明译】
六三：蕴含章美心意，足以持守正道。如果跟从君王做事，即使不建功立业，也能够得到善终。
《象传》说：蕴含章美心意，足以持守正道，说明六三应该等待合适的时机再展现其心意。如果时机适宜，可以跟从君王做事，但即使成事也不认为是自己心意实化所致，不过是顺乾阳之意而成事，这才是智慧广大恢弘的表现。

Six (*yin*/soft line) in the third place: Containing beautiful intention, it is enough to uphold the right *dao*. If one follows the king in affairs, one can get a good death even if one does not make any achievements.

The *Image Commentary* (*Xiang Zhuan*) says: It contains beautiful intention, which is enough to uphold the right *dao*, indicating that the Six (*yin*/soft line) in the third place should wait for the right time to show one's intention. If the time is right, one can follow the king in one's affairs things, but even if one succeeds, one should not think this is due to the realization of one's own intention, but rather to following the intentions of Qian-*yang*. This is a manifestation of the vastness and magnificence of wisdom.

【明意】
坤阴之意不显，因为代乾阳之意成事而自择不显，或不敢彰显，以期有好的结果。既然坤阴之意本来就要借助乾阳之意才能够表现出内在的章美才华，所以坤阴之意在实化过程中，要主动择"无成"以把握好分寸，不可以表现出好像是坤阴之意无待乾阳之意而自然实化，这样居功是不合适的。

坤阴之意发动需要借助对自己时位的正确判断，知道合适地辅助乾阳之意以成就功业且不居功，这需要很大的智慧。而在功业将成之时，能够控制自己的意念，需要更大的智慧和更强的意志力，所以非内在"光大（广大）"的意识之境不能说明人对自己欲望和意志的控制之艰难。坤阴之意虽然顺从乾阳之意，但其意的深沉内涵待时而发，也就意味着意识主体需要修养出非常深刻的意念控制的智慧。

[Illuminating Intentionality]

That the intention of Kun-*yin* is not manifested is because, although the intention of Qian-*yang* is realized, it chooses not to manifest it, or dare not manifest it, in the hope of good results. Since the intentionality of Kun-*yin* originally relies on the intentionality of Qian-*yang* to express its inner beauty and talent, so in the process of realizing the intentionality of Kun-*yin*, one must actively choose "no achievement" to grasp the sense of proportion and not express it. Though it seems that the intentionality of Kun-*yin* is realized naturally without waiting for the intentionality of Qian-*yang*, it is inappropriate to take credit in this way.

To initiate Kun-*yin* intention, one needs to rely on the correct judgment of one's own time and position, and to know how to properly assist the Qian-*yang* intention to make achievements without taking credit, which requires a lot of wisdom. When one's achievements are about to be completed, being able to control one's own intentions requires greater wisdom and stronger willpower. Therefore, only a state of consciousness that is intrinsically "bright (broad)" can explain the difficulty of controlling one's own desires and will. Although the intentionality of Kun-*yin* obeys the intentionality of Qian-*yang*, the deep content of its intentionality will be revealed in time, which means that the conscious subject needs to cultivate very profound wisdom of intentionality control.

六四：括囊，无咎无誉。

《象》曰："括囊无咎"，慎不害也。

【明译】

六四：扎紧袋口，虽然得不到赞誉，但也不会有危害。

《象传》说：扎紧袋口，不会有危害，是因为六四之时位应该谨言慎行，不显心露意，不与人争功，以避免危害。

Six (*yin*/soft line) in the fourth place: Tie the mouth of the bag tightly. Although you will not receive praise, there will be no harm.

The *Image Commentary* (*Xiang Zhuan*) says: There will be no harm if the bag is tied tightly, because, to avoid harm as the Six (*yin*/soft line) in the fourth place, one should be cautious in words and deeds, not reveal one's intentions, and not compete for credit with others.

【明意】

坤意之境到六四暗藏危险，故当谨慎操持，念起即有功业，却不可一点一滴自居有功，因身位力量皆不能自主，稍有不慎就会满盘皆输。这种谨慎小心来自与六五的接近，所谓伴君如伴虎，一刻不得疏忽大意，加上与六五都为阴爻，同性气息不畅，只能自守意念，闭合不出。此爻以阴爻居阴位，性柔善守，故可慎密不动，守得意念如收藏行囊，闭门不出。此爻之意虽不出，但心境仍通于全境，明白畅达。可见对意念的坚实控制为本，而事功彰显在心念一动，谨慎操持意念，控制心境以避免灾祸。

[Illuminating Intentionality]

There are hidden dangers in the realm of Kun intentionality, so one should be cautious in handling it. One will have merit as soon as one thinks about it, but one cannot claim to have merit bit by bit, because one cannot control one's body and strength, and one will lose everything if one is not careful. This kind of caution comes from being close to the Six (*yin*/soft line) in the fifth place. It is said that accompanying the king is like accompanying a tiger, and one must not be careless for a moment. In addition, both the Six (*yin*/soft line) in the fourth place and the Six (*yin*/soft line) in the fifth place are *yin* lines, and two *qi* of the same nature are not free to flow, so they can only keep their intentions to themselves and cannot reveal them. This line is a *yin* line located in a *yin* position. It has a soft nature and is good at guarding, and as such can be kept close and immobile. Guarding intentionality is like storing up in a travel bag and keeping one's door closed. Although the intention of this line cannot be expressed, the state of intentionality is still clear. It can be seen that solid control of intentions is the basis, and achievements can be manifested in a single intention, so carefully controlling intentions and the state of intentionality can avoid disaster.

身居"多惧"的六四之位，意念发动之时，即可感受到灾祸如影随形，所以要尽可能持守心意不出，宁可谨言慎行，闭言闭意，毁誉置之度外，不求赞誉，也要避免祸患。此爻为阴爻阴位，形势险难之时，更见控制意念的修为与力量。

If one is in the "fearful" position of Six (*yin*/soft line) in the fourth place, when one's intentions are initiated, one can feel that disasters are following, so one should try one's best to hold on to one's intentions. One would be best to be careful with one's words and deeds, keep one's words and intentions to oneself, ignore reputation and evaluation, and not seek any praise, while also avoiding disaster. This line is a *yin* line in a *yin* position, so when the situation is dangerous, the cultivation and power of controlling intentions can be seen.

六五：黄裳（cháng），元吉。

《象》曰："黄裳元吉"，文在中也。

【明译】

六五：身着黄色裙裳，大吉大利。

《象传》说：穿着黄色衣裳，跟各种颜色都能和谐配合，大吉大利，说明六五居于上卦中位，不但外表中正和美，而且内涵文彩之美。

Six (*yin*/soft line) in the fifth place: Wearing a yellow dress brings good fortune.

The *Image Commentary* (*Xiang Zhuan*) says: Wearing yellow clothes can harmoniously match with various colors, and it will bring good fortune and great benefit. This means that the Six (*yin*/soft line) in the fifth place is in the middle of the upper Trigram, and is not only upright and beautiful in appearance, but also has the beauty of literary color.

【明意】

坤阴之意美极可谓臻于和谐之极致，由内而外，和乐美顺，此谓意念发动的美学，意念之动即有美感。美非对象、非外在。意念所发皆中极至美，阴意之境皆是天境的人化，也是人境的天化，一种天人完全融汇不二的状态。

[Illuminating Intentionality]

The beauty of Kun-*yin* can be said to attain the perfection of harmony, as from the inside out, it is harmonious and smooth. This is called the aesthetics of intentional initiation, in which the movement of intentions creates a sense of beauty. Beauty is not an object, and not external. All intentional initiation is of the utmost beauty, and all the realms of *yin* intentionality are a humanization of the heavenly realm, and also a naturalization of the human realm, a state in which heaven and humanity are completely integrated.

君子的念头发动之处即有光辉，也就是说，坤阴之意的展开，有一种圣洁的美感，好像内里有光辉灿烂的色彩。而君子善于收摄和控制自己的心念，使之随时随地与时势相应。于是心意一动，皆能与事物之动相和谐，自然有所成就，这就好像事功来自心灵的发动，举手投足之间如行云流水一般完美。于是心灵的意识带起的人生境遇就好比打开一幅美丽的画卷，成就一道优美的风景线。

There is brilliance wherever an exemplary person's intentions are initiated. In other words, the unfolding of Kun-*yin*'s intentionality has a sacred beauty, as if it has brilliant colors inside. The exemplary person is good at gathering and controlling their intentionality so that it can respond to the current situation anytime and anywhere. Therefore, every movement of his intentionality can be in harmony with the movements of things, and achievements will be achieved naturally. It is as if his achievements come from the initiative of the heart-mind, and the movements of one's hands and feet are as perfect as flowing clouds and flowing water. Therefore, the life situation brought about by the consciousness of the heart-mind is like opening a beautiful scroll painting and creating a beautiful scene.

心念发动处就带出圣洁的光辉，因为君子之意念接于天机，天人、物心之通皆在境中升起，依境而生，依境不二。

The radiance of sanctity is brought out wherever intentionality is initiated, because the intentionality of an exemplary person is connected to heaven, and the connections between heaven, man, matter and mind all arise in a situational environment, are produced according to their context, and are consistent with cosmological existence.

上六：龙战于野，其血（xuè）玄黄。

《象》曰："龙战于野"，其道穷也。

【明译】

上六：龙在郊野交战，两败俱伤，流出的血青黄混杂。

《象传》说：地龙与天龙在郊野交战，是因为纯阴之道发展到了穷途末路（上六），非战不可。

Six (*yin*/soft line) in the top place: Dragons fighting in the countryside, both sides injured, their blood flowing out mixed in black and yellow.

The *Image Commentary* (*Xiang Zhuan*) says: The earthly dragon and the heavenly dragon fight in the countryside because the way of pure *yin* has developed to the end, the Six (*yin*/soft line) in the top place, and must fight.

【明意】

乾阳之意不愿意退出。阴柔之坤道本来应该顺应乾道来发动，如果阴意上升到一定程度，怀疑阳意，把阳意排斥在先，让阳意感到危机四伏，则必激发阳意的反击，以致发生争斗和决战。

[Illuminating Intentionality]

Qian-*yang*'s intention is not willing to quit. The *yin*-soft Kun *dao* should originally be initiated in accordance with the *dao* of Qian. If *yin* intention rises to a certain level, it doubts *yang* intention, excludes *yang* intention first, and makes *yang* intention feel that it is surrounded by danger, inevitably triggering a counterattack by *yang* intention, leading to fights and decisive battles.

坤阴之意到了不明了事物客观状态的地步，就可能因心意持守失去分寸而滑向危险的境地。阴意上升到了一个极点，就以为可以除去阳意，自己掌控整个世界。但易理认为，阴主阳从，阴阳颠倒的状态不可能长久，因为坤阴之意取代乾阳之意主事，必然导致矛盾激化。何况这样的想法最多只是一时所想，不可能实化为真实事件。

When Kun-*yin*'s intention is unclear as to the objective state of things, it may lead to a dangerous situation due to the loss of sense of proportion and persistence of intention. When *yin* intentionality reaches an extreme level, one thinks that one can get rid of *yang* intention and control the whole world by oneself. However, the principles of the *Book of Changes* argue that, when *yin* dominates and *yang* follows, such an inverted state of *yin* and *yang* cannot last long, because the intentionality of Kun-*yin* replaces the intentionality of Qian-*yang* in managing affairs, which inevitably leads to intensification of conflict. Furthermore, such an intention is only a momentary spiritual movement at best, and cannot be transformed into a real event.

因为阳意从不可能彻底消退，而且一旦阴意以为可以完全排斥阳意，自己主宰，那么阴阳之意会因嫌疑而交战，导致激化矛盾，甚至天地变色。这还是因为易理认为，坤阴之意不具备独立主事的力量，如果意图取代阳意主事，就必然导致阳意的反击，最后还是会迫使阴意退却，这是天道自然运行本然如此。

Because *yang* never completely subsides, once *yin* intention believes it can completely reject *yang* and dominate it, then *yin* and *yang* will fight due to suspicion, leading to intensified conflict and even the changing colors of heaven and earth. This is because the principle of the *Book of Changes* holds that Kun-*yin*'s intentionality does not have the power to take charge independently. If it intends to replace *yang*'s intention, it will inevitably lead to *yang*'s counterattack and eventually force *yin*'s intentionality to retreat. The functioning of the natural and heavenly *dao* is originally like this.

可见，阴柔之心意若没有阳力的辅助，就一定要离开主导的位置。否则，自以为是一定跟阳意引发生死决战，最后通常都是阴意失败。坤阴之意应当明白领会和处理好自己所在的心意境遇与心意角色，不要随意放任心意的状态，在影响心物交通的过程中产生决定性的作用，在不适合挑战阳意的时候，就应该固守阴柔的姿态，否则就是自取灭亡。

It can be seen that if *solf/yin* intentionality is not assisted by *yang* force, it must leave the dominant position, otherwise self-righteousness will definitely lead to a life-and-death battle with *yang* intentionality, and in the end *yin* intention usually fails. The intentionality of Kun-*yin* should clearly understand and handle the psychological situation and role of its intentions, not letting the state of intentionality play a decisive role in affecting the communication of intentionality and things/events. When it is not suitable to challenge *yang* intentionality, one should stick to a *yin* posture, or one will perish.

用六：利永贞。

《象》曰：用六"永贞"，以大终也。

【明译】

用老阴之数六：利于永远持守正道。

《象传》说：用老阴之数六，有利于永久保持贞正的操守，这样才能最终成就坤阴广大的化生之功。

Using old *yin*'s Six: It will help you always maintain the right *dao*.

The *Image Commentary* (*Xiang Zhuan*) says: Using old *yin*'s Six is conducive to permanently maintaining steadfastness and integrity, and in this way the ultimate achievement of Kun-*yin*'s transformation and rebirth can be achieved.

【明意】

坤卦用六是坤道阴柔之静正不动以应付变化的世界，以不变应万变，以辅助乾阳之意成就事业。坤阴之意不动的智慧高于动，因为不动反而能够全面判断事物的发展变化，等待时机让事情向有利于自己的方向转化。坤阴之意顺静之道既深且广，因为静顺方能成就大势，方能厚德载物，才能"永贞"，即永远保持意念的静顺正道。

[Illuminating Intentionality]

The use of Six in Hexagram Kun (Support) is using the quietness, uprightness, and immobility of the Kun *dao* to cope with the changing world, to cope with the ever-changing world with immutability, and to assist Qian-*yang* intentionality to achieve success. Kun-*yin* means that the wisdom of immobility is higher than that of movement, because immobility can comprehensively judge the development and changes of things, and wait for the opportunity to turn things in a direction that is beneficial to oneself. The intentionality of Kun-*yin* is that the way of calmness and tranquility is both deep and broad, because only by being calm and obedient can we achieve great things, be virtuous, and be eternally upright and correct, that is, always maintain the right *dao* of tranquility and obedience in our intentions.

水雷屯（卦三）　（震下坎上）

Zhun (Emergence), Water and Thunder (Hexagram 3)　(Zhen below, Kan above)

屯继承乾坤之交而来，说明天地阴阳交流开始之时，其情境充满艰辛，也说明开始的意念成长之艰难，所以刚开始要有极强的心力。世间一切从无中生有，从来不是容易的事情。生长带有集中心力的意思，否则心力不足就无法具备成长的力量。雷雨发动，草木舒张，象征心力背景的开启就是一场心与世界的战争，这战争心初始的力量越大，心意才越有萌生和艰难成长的可能。

Hexagram Zhun (Emergence) inherits the connection between Hexagram Qian (Creativity) as heaven and Hexagram Kun (Support) as earth, which shows that, when the exchange of *yin* and *yang* powers between heaven and earth begins, the situation is full of hardships, and that the initial growth of intentions is always difficult, so you must have strong mental fortitude in the beginning. It is never easy to create anything in the world from nothing. Growth means concentrating intentionality, since the power of growth will not be possible if intentionality is insufficient. A thunderstorm starts and vegetation expands, which symbolizes the opening of the background of mental fortitude, a war between the heart-mind and the world. The greater the initial strength of the mind in this war, the more likely it is that intentionality will sprout and grow through the difficulties.

屯，元亨，利贞。勿用有攸往，利建侯。

《彖》曰：屯，刚柔始交而难生。动乎险中，大亨贞。雷雨之动满盈，天造草昧。宜

"建侯"而不宁。

《象》曰：云雷，屯。君子以经纶。

【明译】

屯卦象征阳意初生，初始亨通，有利于持守正道。阳意初创之期，不利于有所前往，利于像立君建国那样建立秩序。

《彖传》说：屯卦，阳意与阴意开始交感，刚开始化生出阴阳交感之体的过程充满艰难。下卦震为动，上卦坎为险，阳意萌动于艰险之中，想要亨通有利就必须持守正道。震雷动，坎雨聚，雷雨发动，万物复苏，天地充满而丰盈，恰似天地草创之际，万物处于冥昧之中的情状，象征此时适宜调动阳意封爵建国，努力屯聚力量，才能把不安宁的状态转化为安宁。

《象传》说：上卦坎为云，下卦震为雷，组合成为屯卦。君子在时局初创之际，心意阴阳交接之时，要努力经营筹划，意求有所屯聚。

Hexagram Zhun (Emergence) symbolizes the birth of *yang*/positive intentions, which is initially prosperous and conducive to maintaining the right *dao*. The initial period of *yang*/positive intentions is not conducive to advancing, but it is conducive to establishing order like establishing a king and a country.

The *Judgment Commentary* (*Tuan Zhuan*) says: In Hexagram Zhun (Emergence), *yang* and *yin* begin to interact, and the process of giving birth to a body of *yin* and *yang* that interacts with each other is full of difficulties. The lower Trigram Zhen means shaking, the upper Trigram Kan means danger, and *yang* intentionality is stirred in hardships and dangers. If you want to be prosperous and beneficial, you must stick to the right *dao*. Thunder shakes, rain gathers, thunderstorms start, the myriad things revive, heaven and earth are full and abundant, just like the situation when heaven and earth were created and the myriad things were in darkness, symbolizing that it is appropriate to mobilize *yang*/positive intentions at this time it is appropriate to build a country, and work hard to gather strength and achieve success. People should transform restless situations into tranquility.

The *Image Commentary* (*Xiang Zhuan*) says: The upper Trigram Kan is a cloud, the lower Trigram Zhen is thunder, and the combination becomes Hexagram Zhun (Emergence). At the beginning of the current situation, when the *yin* and *yang* of intentionality are changing, an exemplary person should work hard to plan and gather his intentions.

【明意】

屯卦说明人间的秩序来自于人为自然立法，人的意识理解宇宙的秩序之后为人的世界建立秩序。换言之，秩序是人心建立的，是人的意识领悟天地的秩序之后模仿来建构的，秩序永远是一种意识的秩序，也永远是意识的建构。天地蛮荒的时候，是心力发动源生之态，也是需要对心力梳理出秩序的时候。这时，心力最强者往往能够统合他人的心力以形成合力，而对形势构成影响。所谓社会的组织根本上就是心力的梳理能力，有些人能够与他人的心力形成合力，进而整合更多人的心力，有些人则不具有与他人的心力进行整合的能力，所以基本上就只能够从众。

[Illuminating Intentionality]

Hexagram Zhun (Emergence) explains that the order of the human world comes from humanity legislating for heaven, and that human consciousness establishes order for the human world after understanding the order of the cosmos. In other words, order is established by human intentionality, constructed by imitation after human consciousness understands the order of heaven and earth. Order is always an order of consciousness, and it is always a construction of consciousness. When the world is wild and chaotic, this is the time when mental power is initiated, and also the time when mental fortitude needs to be sorted out to produce order. At this time, the person with the strongest mental fortitude can often integrate the mental assets of others to form a joint force and influence the situation. The so-called social organization is basically the ability to organize intentional energy. Some people can form synergies with other people's mental liveliness and integrate more people's mental vigor. Some people do not have the ability to integrate other people's intentional energy, so basically they can only follow the herd.

初九：盘桓，利居贞。利建侯。

《象》曰：虽"盘桓"，志行正也。以贵下贱，大得民也。

【明译】

初九：盘旋，观望、犹豫，有利于居正稳固，有利于封建诸侯。

《象传》说：虽然盘旋观望，犹豫不定，但前进的心愿合乎正道。初九以高贵的身份谦处卑贱人之下，表示初九心志远大，亲和民众，能够广泛获得民心支持。

Nine (*yang*/strong line) in the first place: Circling, waiting and hesitating, it is good to stay in the right and stable position, and good for noble people to establish their states.

The *Image Commentary* (*Xiang Zhuan*) says: Although one is hovering and watching, hesitant, one's desire to move forward is in line with the right *dao*. With a noble status, the Nine (*yang*/strong line) in the first place humbles oneself under base people, which means that the Nine (*yang*/strong line) in the first place is ambitious, friendly to the people, and can gain widespread support from the people.

【明意】

人之心意本然通天，虽然一来到世界首先是自然人，或者本来就是自然人，但因为总是与他人在一起，所以心意总是与他心相交织，艰难而危险，所以从无序当中梳理出秩序非常必要。这种以心灵的平衡秩序梳理天地阴意与阳意运动秩序的态度带有一种贵族气息，而心灵贵气来自一种心意通天的特殊平静。心转物而不为物转，就是心灵的高贵状态。反之，心灵的贱则是因为心灵随物转动。当心为物转，则心力消散，就进入心灵相对卑贱的状态。也就是说，心灵的高贵状态能够控制和把握心灵的低贱状态，因为心灵的高贵状态转动事物，而心灵的低贱状态为事物所转。心力的持续需要魄力，心意本然通天，心意与宇宙不断交接，但如何梳理心意与宇宙的秩序，需要一个立足点，不断积累心意的能量以寻求突破。刚开始寻求心意与宇宙秩序的状态中，要谦恭居下，才能汇聚心意，而形成合力。

[Illuminating Intentionality]

Human intentionality is inherently connected to the cosmos. However, although it is a natural person when it comes to the world, or is originally natural, because it is always together with others, intentionality is always intertwined with other people's intentions. This is difficult and dangerous, so it is necessary to sort out the disorder and produce order. This attitude of sorting out the movement order of *yin* and *yang* powers in the world with the balanced order of the heart-mind has a kind of nobility, and the nobility of the heart-mind comes from a special kind of tranquility that is continuous with the heavens. When intentionality transforms things but is not transformed by things, it is the noble state of the heart-mind. On the contrary, the ignobility of the heart-mind is due to the fact that the heart-mind is transformed by things. When intentionality is transformed by things, intentional energy dissipates and intentionality enters a relatively ignoble state. That is to say, the noble state of the heart-mind can control and grasp the ignoble state of the heart-mind, because the noble state of the heart-mind transforms things, and the ignoble state of the heart-mind is transformed by things. Sustaining mental strength requires courage. Intentionality is naturally and constantly continuous with the cosmos. However, how to sort out the order of intentionality and the cosmos requires a foothold, and to constantly accumulate the energy of intentionality to seek breakthroughs. When one first starts to seek intentionality and the order of the cosmos, one has to be humble in order to gather one's intentionality and form a synergy.

六二：屯如邅（zhān）如，乘马班如。匪寇，婚媾。女子贞不字，十年乃字。

《象》曰：六二之难，乘刚也。"十年乃字"，反常也。

【明译】

六二：初创坎坷，徘徊难进，骑马打转彷徨不前。对六二来说，初九不是强盗，而是来求婚的。女子贞定，自守正道，不答应嫁人，十年之后才应许。

《象传》说：六二徘徊难进，是因为柔爻乘驾在刚爻（初九）之上，女子（六二）十年之后才答应嫁人（初九），这是从（本意想阻碍初九的）违反常理的状态回复到常道（顺应初九阳意上升）。

Six (*yin*/soft line) in the second place: Bumpy in the beginning, one wanders and it is difficult to advance, thus one hesitates and rides in circles. For the Six (*yin*/soft line) in the second place, the Nine (*yang*/strong line) in the first place is not a robber, but a man who proposes marriage. If a woman is chaste and upright, she will not agree to marry until ten years later.

The *Image Commentary* (*Xiang Zhuan*) says: The Six (*yin*/soft line) in the second place lingers and has difficulties in advancing, because the soft line rides on a *yang*/strong line, the Nine in the first place, and the woman, the Six (*yin*/soft line, in the second place) does not agree to marry until ten years later. This originally intending to hinder the Nine (*yang*/strong line) in the first place, goes against common sense and returns to a normal state, according to the rise of *yang*/positive intentions in the Nine (*yang*/strong line) in the first place.

【明意】

建构心灵与世界的秩序是艰辛困苦的过程，甚至常常要压抑人的自然欲望，因为人的自然欲望与天下动植物的自然意志一样，虽有其自然秩序，但却是混沌不明的，如果人放任自己的自然欲望，就不可能建构一个心灵与宇宙的秩序。所以人要在顺应心意与宇宙的自然秩序的基础上，带着压抑人自然欲望的努力来建构心灵与宇宙的秩序。比如，人能够建构社会文明，就是不断压抑自然欲望的过程。弗洛伊德在其《文明及其缺憾》中揭示了这样一种道理，那就是文明的产生代表心意与宇宙相通并建立秩序的过程，这个过程与压抑人的本性分不开。儒家强调对人性天然发动状态的主动克制和修为，宋明理学的"存天理灭人欲"也可以理解为为了保持人天之意而需要压抑人性。

[Illuminating Intentionality]

Constructing the order of mind and world is an arduous and difficult process, and it often even requires suppressing people's natural desires, because people's natural desires are the same as the natural will of animals and plants in the world. Although they have their own natural order, they are chaotic and unclear. It is impossible to construct an order of mind and cosmos by giving natural desires free reign. Therefore, people should construct the order of mind and cosmos on the basis of complying with the natural order of mind and cosmos, and with effort to suppress people's natural desires. For example, the ability of people to construct a social civilization is a process of constantly suppressing natural desires. As Sigmund Freud revealed in his *Civilization and Its Discontents*, the emergence of civilization represents a process of connecting intentionality with the cosmos and establishing order. This process is inseparable from the suppression of natural human desire. Confucianism emphasizes the active restraint and cultivation of the natural initiative state of human nature. When the Neo-Confucianism of the Song and Ming dynasties spoke of "preserving the patterns of heaven and extinguishing human desires," this can also be understood as the need to suppress human nature in order to maintain cosmological intentionality and harmonize humanity and nature.

六三：即鹿无虞，惟入于林中，君子几不如舍，往吝。

《象》曰："即鹿无虞"，以从禽也。君子舍之，"往吝"穷也。

【明译】

六三：追逐野鹿，已经挨近，没有虞人作向导，只会盲目钻入深山老林中去。君子见机行事，轻率追踪不如舍弃不追，如果一意孤行，前往易有吝难。

《象传》说：追逐野鹿，已经挨近，没有虞人作向导，还紧追不舍，就是贪图猎物的表现。君子见机行事，马上舍弃，是因为知道穷追不舍定然陷入困境。

Six (*yin*/soft line) in the third place: Chasing a wild deer, it is already close by, but without a guide as a leader, one will just blindly dive into deep mountains and old forests. An exemplary person acts when an opportunity rises. It is better to give up and not pursue than to pursue rashly. If one insists on going one's own way, one can easily fall into difficulties.

The *Image Commentary (Xiang Zhuan)* says: Chasing a wild deer, it is already close by, but without a guide as a leader, if one still pursues it, this is a sign of greed for prey. An exemplary person acts when an opportunity arises and gives up immediately when one knows that, if one keeps pursuing something, one will definitely get into trouble.

【明意】

为了领悟阴意与阳意交接的时空之境，我们需要把握几微的变化。领悟与把握几微，就是领悟与预测事物变化的方向。有时心意遇到难以领悟与驾驭的时机化状态，这时不如暂时放弃直面这种情境。所有的几微变化都是时间与空间交融之境。不仅时间每时每刻流动，而且空间也在时刻改变。而时间的改变，通过空间的改变进入感官系统；空间的改变，可能一时觉得与时间改变没有明显关系，但空间的任何一点改变都伴随着时间的流逝。可见，时空是一个能量体，几微是微妙莫测的心意与时空交接的能量复合体，是整个情境的集中体现。

[Illuminating Intentionality]

In order to understand the spatiotemporal context where *yin* and *yang* powers meet, we need to grasp subtle changes. To understand and grasp these subtleties is to understand and predict the direction of changes in things. Sometimes intentionality encounters an opportunistic state that is difficult to understand and control. At this time, it is better to temporarily give up facing the situation head-on. All these subtle changes are the blending of time and space. Not only does time flow at every moment, but space also changes moment by moment. The change of time enters the sensory system through the change of space; the change of space may not be obviously related to the change of time for a while, but any change in space is accompanied by the flow of time. It can be seen that time and space form an energetic body, and minute changes are the subtle and unpredictable energy complex at the intersection of intentionality and time and space, which is the concentrated expression of an entire situation.

六四：乘马班如，求婚媾。往吉，无不利。

《象》曰："求"而"往"，明也。

【明译】

六四：骑着马团团打转，犹豫要不要去求婚。如果坚定不移地前往，结果定然吉祥没有不利。

《象传》说：为求婚而坚定不移地去追求（初九），是明智的选择。

Six (*yin*/soft line) in the fourth place: Riding in circles, hesitating whether to propose or not. If one goes ahead unswervingly, the result will be auspicious and not disadvantageous.

The *Image Commentary* (*Xiang Zhuan*) says: It is a wise choice to pursue the marriage proposal (with the Nine (*yang*/strong line) in the first place) unswervingly.

【明意】

《周易》是强调自由意志的，但自由意志不是简单纯粹的自由而已，而是在对情境有明确理解和把握之后的理性的自由选择。这样的实化意念才是明智的。君子实化自己意念的每一个瞬间都明智地通达于全境，但小人实化意念只为了自己的欲望，所以不明而小。

[Illuminating Intentionality]

The *Book of Changes* emphasizes free will, but free will is not simply pure freedom, but a rational free choice after a clear understanding and grasp of the situation. It is wise to concretize such intentions. When an exemplary person concretizes their intentions, they wisely understand the whole situation at each moment, but when a petty person concretizes their intentions only for their own desires, they are confused and petty.

九五：屯其膏，小贞，吉；大贞，凶。

《象》曰："屯其膏"，施未光也。

【明译】

九五：（屯难之时）屯聚了一点膏泽能量，此时如果心意弱小而持守，做事就吉祥；心意如果强大而正固，就会有凶险。

《象传》说：屯聚了一点膏泽能量，是心意不能施布广泛。

Nine (*yang*/strong line) in the fifth place: (When a situation is difficult,) a little beneficial energy has been gathered. At this time, if one's intentionality is weak but persistent, things will be auspicious; if one's intentionality is strong and upright, there will be danger.

The *Image Commentary* (*Xiang Zhuan*) says: If you gather a little beneficial energy, your intentionality cannot spread it widely.

【明意】

在艰难时势当中，就算身居九五有些能量，但心意不可有一刻舒展，需要大而小之，小心翼翼地持守自己的心意状态，以谦柔弱小的心意面对危机，这样即使不能施布广泛，也尚可转危为安。可见，吸收能量储备的过程，是一个小心地把心意持守而转化的过程，在艰难持守之中，储备一点点能量都不容易，意念之行需要小心地护持这种意识能量，持守住自己的实力。

[Illuminating Intentionality]

In difficult times, even if one has some energy as the Nine (*yang*/strong line) in the fifth place, one's intentionality must not relax for a moment. One needs to be great but intentionally keep small. Carefully maintain your state of intentionality and face the crisis with a humble and soft intention. In this way, even if one cannot give help extensively, it can still turn a crisis into safety. It can be seen that the process of absorbing energy reserves is a process of carefully holding on to intentionality and transforming it. In difficult persistence, it is not easy to reserve a little bit of energy. The journey of intentionality requires careful protection of this kind of conscious energy and holding on to oneself with real strength.

上六：乘马班如，泣血涟如。

《象》曰："泣血涟如"，何可长也？

【明译】

上六：骑在马上，盘旋徘徊，血泪涟涟，十分凄惨。

《象传》说：穷途末路，泪干泣血，凄惨至极，这种惨状怎么可能长久维持呢？

Six (*yin*/soft line) in the top place: Riding on a horse, circling and wandering, full of blood and tears, truly miserable.

The *Image Commentary* (*Xiang Zhuan*) says: At the end of the road, tears dry up and blood is shed, and it is extremely miserable. How can such a miserable situation be maintained for a long time?

【明意】

上六的警示在于，应对艰难形势稍有不慎就可能覆灭初创的雄心壮志，而且心意的持守时时刻刻都要明智而有分寸，不可不知有所聚已达到极致和幸运的状态，一旦过刚过强，艰难的形势马上表现出吞没初创心意的一面，让自己万劫不复。一旦进入这种艰难状态，原先囤聚的能量就会被迅速打散，很难保持长久。

[Illuminating Intentionality]

The warning of the Six (*yin*/soft line) in the top place is that a little carelessness in dealing with difficult situations may destroy the ambitions of a new creation, and the persistence in one's intentionality must be wise and measured at all times. One must know when one has reached an ultimate and fortunate state. If one is too strong or feels too powerful, a difficult situation will immediately show a side that swallows up one's original intention, making it irrecoverable. Once you enter this difficult state, the energy that was originally accumulated will be quickly dispersed, making it difficult to maintain it for a long time.

山水蒙（卦四） （坎下艮上）

Meng (Youthful Ignorance), Mountain and Water (Hexagram 4) (Kan below, Gen above)

  人的意向指向各种各样的意缘，但意向所及之缘可能被蒙住，就不知道何意为正确正当的意向之缘。而受教育者，受启蒙者通过顺应启蒙者，可能找到自己内心本有的潜能所及的意缘之方向。教育让学生们找到合适的意向，也就知道如何控制和驾驭人的缘分。教育的根本在于教会人控制意念的方向，驾驭人生的"缘"分，包括自己与他人、他心的"缘"，以及与他物的"缘"。

  每个人在论及人生未定的"缘"面前，通常都深感困惑，这就是一开始就被蒙住，找不到意向的感觉。但有先知先觉的圣人，能够通达缘分于阴阳未分之前，从而建立教育的系统，以引导常人的意向，让常人得以遵从。

  People's intentions are directed to various conditions, but the conditions to which intention reaches may be obscured, and one does not know what the right and proper intention should be. Those who are educated and enlightened may find the direction of their inner potential by complying with an enlightened person. Education allows students to find the right intention, and learn how to control the fate of dependent co-arising. The foundation of education is to teach people to control the direction of their intentions and control their destiny in life, including the fate between oneself and others, that of other intentions, and that with other things.

  Everyone is usually deeply confused when it comes to undetermined dependent co-arising in life. This is the feeling of being blinded from the beginning and unable to find the direction of intentionality. But sages with foresight can understand dependent co-arising before *yin* and *yang* powers are separated, and thus establish an education system to guide ordinary people's intentions and allow ordinary people to follow them.

蒙，亨。匪我求童蒙，童蒙求我。初筮告，再三渎，渎则不告。利贞。

《彖》曰：蒙，山下有险，险而止，蒙。"蒙亨"，以亨行时中也。"匪我求童蒙，童蒙求我"，志应也。"初筮告"，以刚中也。"再三渎，渎则不告"，渎蒙也。蒙以养正，圣功也。

《象》曰：山下出泉，蒙。君子以果行育德。

【明译】

蒙卦象征因困蒙而启蒙。不是我（施教者）去求被蒙住的儿童（受教者），而是被蒙者来请教启蒙者。师道如同占筮之道，初次占筮，可以有问必答；但被蒙者一而再、再而三地问同样的问题就是亵渎和轻侮启蒙者，就如同再三占筮亵渎神灵一样（表示被蒙者缺乏应有的恭敬之心），既然如此，启蒙者就不必继续回答他了。这样有利于启蒙者和被蒙者都保持贞正的心意状态。

Hexagram Meng (Youthful Ignorance) symbolizes enlightenment through hardships. It is not me (the teacher) who goes to seek ignorant children (the ones who are being taught), but the ignorant who come to ask the enlightener. The way of being a teacher is like the way of divination. For the first time of divination, all questions can be answered, but if a person being enlightened asks the same question again and again, it is disrespectful and insulting to the enlightener, just like disrespecting the spirits by repeatedly divining (which means that the initiate lacks due respect). In this case, the enlightener need not to continue to answer him. It is helpful for both the enlightener and the initiate to maintain an upright state of intentionality.

《彖传》说：蒙卦的组合是上艮下坎，艮为山，坎为险，卦象是山下有险。艮又为止，遇险而止，不知该怎么办，蒙住了。蒙卦说明通过启蒙，能够亨通顺利，是因为施教双方都奉行中正之道，启蒙者适可而止，受教者心怀诚意，都能够顺应时势。不是我去求童蒙而是童蒙来求我，是因为九二与六五是应爻，心意相互呼应。初次占筮可以告诉被蒙者，是因为九二是刚爻又在中位，具备中庸之道又刚毅能断，有施教的能力，故可告。一而再，再而三地占筮，是一种糊涂的做法，既蒙昧又亵渎，当然不能告诉被蒙者。蒙卦揭示出被蒙者从蒙昧状态出发培养正道的可能性，存在能够开发被蒙者使之修养成为圣人的功夫。

The *Judgment Commentary* (*Tuan Zhuan*) says: The assemblage of Hexagram Meng (Youthful Ignorance) is upper Trigram Gen and lower Trigram Kan, in which Gen is mountain, and Kan is danger, thus the hexagram image means danger at the foot of a mountain. Trigram Gen entails that one stops when one is in danger, and does not know what to do because one is blinded. Hexagram Meng (Youthful Ignorance) shows that through enlightenment, success can be achieved because both the teaching party and the taught party adhere to the right *dao*, the enlightener is moderate, and the initiate is sincere and can adapt to the current situation. It is not me who seeks a child to enlighten, but a child who seeks me to be enlightened, because the Nine (*yang*/strong line) in the second place and the Six (*yin*/soft line) in the fifth place are resonating lines, and their intentions echo each other. It is possible to inform a person who is in ignorance in the first divination because the Nine (*yang*/strong line) in the second place is a strong line and in the middle place, possesses the golden mean, is resolute and decisive, and has the ability to learn, so can be informed. Divining over and over again is a foolish practice, which is both ignorant and disrespectful, so of course such a person in ignorance cannot be informed. Hexagram Meng (Youthful Ignorance) reveals the possibility of an ignorant person starting from an ignorant state but cultivating a righteous *dao*, and that there is an effort that can cultivate an ignorant person and make one into a sage.

《象传》说：上卦艮为山，下卦坎为水，卦象是山下流出泉水，这就是蒙卦。山泉清纯不杂，流出后汇为江河，虽然蒙昧不知流向何处，但显示出果敢向前的勇气。君子看这个卦象要反求诸己，培养自己的道德要从真纯清澈开始，以果敢的行为由小而大积累成圣功。

The *Image Commentary* (*Xiang Zhuan*) says: The upper Trigram Gen is mountain, the lower Trigram Kan is water, and the image of the hexagram is spring water flowing out of a mountain. This is Hexagram Meng (Youthful Ignorance). Mountain springs are pure and unmixed. After flowing out, they merge into rivers. Although they do not know where they flow, they show the courage to move forward boldly. When an exemplary person looks at this hexagram, one should turn to oneself, cultivate one's own virtue, start from purity and clarity, and accumulate sagely efforts from small to large with courageous actions.

【明意】

人来到世界上，刚开始都是蒙昧的、易被蒙住的，也是幼稚的，意念的初生都无理由，无原因，但随着人的意念介入周围人的意念之境，启蒙者的意念能够起着塑造蒙昧者意念情境之作用。蒙也意味着人意念境遇的新生。很多时候，人虽然成长了，但总觉得自己还很幼稚，很蒙昧。意识境遇可以每时每刻刷新，通过教育者启蒙找到新的方向，心灵状态可以每时每刻都是新的。

[Illuminating Intentionality]

When people come into the world, they are ignorant, easily deceived, and naive at first. The initial birth of their intentions has no reason or purpose. But as people's intentions intervene in the intentions of the people around them, enlightened intentions can play a role in shaping the intellectual situation of the ignorant. Hexagram Meng (Youthful Ignorance) also means the rebirth of people's intentional situation. Many times, although people have grown up, they feel that they are still naive and ignorant. The state of consciousness can be refreshed every moment, new directions can be found through educators' enlightenment, and the state of intentionality can be new at every moment.

儒释道亦哲学亦宗教，更是教育理论，都教人驾驭人生缘分的意念方向，可以帮助蒙昧中人端正立身处世的思想与行为，引领他们开悟，从而不会在人生复杂的关系和幻起幻灭的缘分当中迷失自我。

Confucianism, Buddhism, and Daoism are both philosophies and religions, as well as educational theories because they all teach people to control the direction of their intentions and change their destiny in life. They can help ignorant people learn how to think and behave in the world, and lead them to enlightenment, so that they will not be disillusioned by the complex relationships and illusions in life, or lose themselves in the process of living experience.

初六：发蒙，利用刑人，用说桎梏，以往吝。

《象》曰："利用刑人"，以正法也。

【明译】

初六：对蒙昧的开发教育，最好的办法是主动树立楷模，用以脱去刑具桎梏。如果放任自流，或者急于求成，就可能遭遇吝难。

《象传》说：用树立模范的办法，对人进行处罚教育，是为了端正法规，以便遵循。

Six (*yin*/soft line) in the first place: The best way to develop and educate ignorant people is to take the initiative to set an example to remove punishing shackles. If you let things slide or rush for success, you may encounter difficulties.

The *Image Commentary* (*Xiang Zhuan*) says: The purpose of punishing and educating people by setting an example is to correct laws and regulations so that they can be followed.

【明意】

启蒙教育之模型是一个对他者的认知与内化过程。父母老师作为被模仿的对象，希望蒙昧的孩童学习模仿。当然，这有明显希望孩童成长为某一类型的人的意思在里面。儒家希望学生能够"止于至善"，将心向集中在最高善的方向上，从而脱离错误的心向，免于灾难。孩子在模仿之中控制自己的心念，这是教育的根基。那种发泄、导引式的教育不能说没有道理，但那是后天功夫，效果并不显著，而且心向一旦发动，就很难停止，除非学会自我控制。

[Illuminating Intentionality]

The model of enlightenment education is a process of recognition and internalization in others. Parents and teachers, as the objects to be imitated, hope that ignorant children will learn to imitate them. Of course, this obviously means hoping that children will grow into a certain type of person.

Confucianism hopes that students can always aspire to stop at the highest good and focus their intentions in the direction of the highest good, so as to escape from wrong intentions and avoid disasters. Children learn to control their own intentions through imitation, which is the foundation of education. That kind of venting and guiding education cannot be said to be unreasonable, but it is an acquired skill and the effect is not obvious. Moreover, once desire has started, it is difficult to stop unless one learns to control oneself.

教会学生于未发之前控制意念，其实是教育的真义。意境的塑造是人格塑造的根本。正法不仅仅是行为合法，更重要的是心意的合理合法。人如果依蒙昧之心而动，缘发而无可控制，就容易走向邪途，邪缘一个接一个，甚至可能万劫不复。此无名之心，或者基督教所谓原罪，也就是人心自然蒙昧，需要启蒙，自我开化，从而在意缘发动之端点，即行有效把握。

从文化的角度来说，启蒙是欧洲文化的核心主题之一，也曾经是中国近代文化转型的重要主题，二者的假设前提是之前的文化处于蒙昧状态，需要借助先进文化来启蒙，从而走出新的意识方向。蒙昧是封闭、闭塞的同义词，而先进文化的启蒙意味着时代开启新文化方向。

Teaching students to control their intentions before they occur is actually the true spirit of education. The shaping of intentional context is the foundation of personality shaping. Positive law is not only the legality of behavior, but more importantly, the reasonableness and legality of intention. If a person acts on an ignorant intention and meets with uncontrollable conditions, he will easily go down a wrong path. Evil conditions will follow one after another, and may even be catastrophic. This nameless heart, or the so-called original sin in Christianity, means that the human heart is naturally ignorant and needs enlightenment and self-edification, so that it can be effectively grasped at the end of the initiation of intentional conditions.

From a cultural perspective, enlightenment is one of the core themes of European culture, and was once an important theme of China's modern cultural transformation. The premise of both is that the previous culture was in a state of ignorance and needed to be enlightened with advanced culture, so as to emerge in a new direction of consciousness. Ignorance is synonymous with isolation, while the enlightenment of advanced culture means that the era has opened up a new cultural direction.

九二：包蒙，吉。纳妇，吉。子克家。

《象》曰："子克家"，刚柔接也。

【明译】

九二：启蒙者能够广泛地包容蒙昧的人，当然是吉祥的。正如家里娶了好媳妇是吉祥的一样，教出来的儿子能持家。

《象传》说：这样包容的老师教出来的儿子将来能持家，说明刚爻（九二）能够胜任领导柔爻（初六、六三、六四、六五）的职责，而且九二在互震（长子）里，故可持家，犹如家长刚柔节制适当。

Nine (*yang*/strong line) in the second place: It is of course auspicious for an enlightened person to be able to widely tolerate ignorant people. Just as it is auspicious for a family to have a good daughter-in-law, since sons who are educated can run the family.

The *Image Commentary* (*Xiang Zhuan*) says: The son taught by such a tolerant teacher will be able to run the family in the future, which shows that the strong/*yang* line (the Nine in the second place) is qualified to lead the soft/*yin* lines (the Sixes in the first, third, fourth and fifth places), while the Nine (*yang*/strong line) in the second place (the eldest son) is also in an inner Trigram Zhen, so he can manage the family, just like parents who are strong, gentle and moderate.

【明意】

教育在于培养开放的心胸，而且是有把握、有控制力的心胸，能够主动、顺利地让心灵的力量与他者发生关系。"克家"说明一个人有持家的心意，能够包容接纳，否则心意不能持家，不能驾驭其他关系，也就不可能持续心与他心的"意缘"，在驾驭中把握好意念的方向。

[Illuminating Intentionality]

Education is about cultivating an open mind, which is an intentionality that is sure and in control, and can actively and smoothly allow the power of the heart-mind to relate to others. "Run the family" shows that a person has the intention to manage a household and is able to be tolerant and accepting, since otherwise, one's intentions cannot manage a household and control other relationships. It would also be impossible to maintain an "intentional coarising" between one's own heart-mind and those of others, and to grasp the direction of intentionality in the process of control.

六三：勿用取女，见金夫，不有躬。无攸利。

《象》曰："勿用取女"，行不顺也。

【明译】

六三：不能娶这样的女子，见到有财势的美男子就会不守妇道，娶她没有好处。

《象传》说：不能娶这样的女子，因为她的行为不顺合礼节（六三阴爻乘刚）。

Six (*yin*/soft line) in the third place: One cannot marry such a woman, since she will be improper when she sees a handsome and wealthy man. There is no benefit in marrying her.

The *Image Commentary* (*Xiang Zhuan*) says: One cannot marry such a woman because her behavior is not in line with ritual propriety (the Six (*yin*/soft line) in the third place is riding above a *yang*/strong line).

【明意】

人与世界的缘分，不仅仅是与人的缘分，也是与人的附属物的缘分。阶层的存在首先是人的物质生活的差异，社会的确依各种身外之物分出阶层，就难免有人看中身外之物重于人心本身发动的力量。但如果一个人看中其他人的附属物重于此人本身，那就没有把人与人的关系建立在人与人心灵的沟通上，而是建立在人与物的附属关系上。如果心灵看重人的附属品而不是人心本身，那就偏离了教育当涵养人心意的初衷。

[Illuminating Intentionality]

Fate between people and the world is not only fate between people, but also fate between people and their attachments to material things. It is true that the existence of classes is first and foremost a difference in people's material lives, and society is indeed divided into classes based on various external things. It is inevitable that some people value external things more than the power of the human heart-mind itself. But if a person values other people's belongings more than the person himself, then the relationship between people is not based on communication between people's heart-minds, but on a subsidiary relationship between people and material things. If the heart-mind values people's accessories rather than the human heart-mind itself, it will deviate from the original intention of education to cultivate human intentionality.

六四：困蒙，吝。

《象》曰："困蒙"之"吝"，独远实也。

【明译】

六四：被困在蒙昧中，犹如陷入困境之中。

《象传》说：六四在蒙卦里，只能是"困蒙"，因为六四是阴爻中唯一与刚爻毫无关系的，只有它远离刚（实）爻，犹如远离良师益友的指教。

Six (*yin*/soft line) in the fourth place: Being trapped in ignorance is like being trapped in a difficult situation.

The *Image Commentary* (*Xiang Zhuan*) says: The Six (*yin*/soft line) in the fourth place in Hexagram Meng (Youthful Ignorance) can only be in a confusing and difficult situation, because the Six (*yin*/soft line) in the fourth place is the only *yin* line that has nothing to do with the *yang*/strong lines. It is the only one that is far away from the *yang*/strong lines, just like a person far away from a good teacher and friend, so no one can provide any advice.

【明意】

人生来在蒙昧之中，处于柔弱的地位，需要刚强的力量来引导，如果没有刚强的力量，一个人就只能长久在蒙昧之中。一个人努力改变蒙昧状态之后仍然无法达到的高度，或者一个人对于某一种状态的限度，就一个人的人生尺度来说就是命。至于是否命定，这并不重要；固然有相当一部分命定的成分，但把自己的限度都归于命定，则可能归于宿命论，这样看来，宿命论不过是一种态度，而积极有为，不相信宿命，也是一种态度。

[Illuminating Intentionality]

Human beings are born in ignorance, in a weak position, and need a strong power to guide them. Without such a strong power, a person can only remain in ignorance for a long time. The heights that a person still cannot reach after trying hard to change his state of ignorance, or the limit that a person has for a certain state, is destiny in terms of a person's life scale. As for whether this is predestined or not, it is not important; although there is a considerable element of fate, attributing all your limitations to fate may be attributed to fatalism. From this point of view, fatalism is just an attitude, and being proactive and not believing in fatalism is also an attitude.

六五：童蒙，吉。

《象》曰："童蒙"之"吉"，顺以巽也。

【明译】

六五：蒙昧之人如儿童一般虚心向老师求教，这是吉祥的。

《象传》说：蒙童虚心向老师求教的这种吉祥状态，是因为柔顺进入中位，犹如受教者虚心学习，如和风顺应循循善诱的施教者。

Six (*yin*/soft line) in the fifth place: It is auspicious for ignorant people to seek advice from teachers humbly like children.

The *Image Commentary* (*Xiang Zhuan*) says: This auspicious state of a child humbly asking for advice from a teacher is because the suppleness enters the middle position, just like a student who learns humbly, and a gentle and obedient teacher.

【明意】

蒙卦是修性之卦，而修性的核心是心意结构的启蒙与建构，对于被启蒙者而言，谦虚顺应启蒙者就能吉祥。谦虚顺应是性之倾向流露的状态，而指向未来的结构就是命。

性命是一个统一的体系，人有其限定性，但人还有超越其既有限定的能力和可能性。儒家认为，"诚身""尽心"是实现本性、让本性得以合理展开的功夫。当然，如果作为一个自然人没有这种功夫的话，人也可以自然地活一辈子，但这是没有意义的一辈子，或者说，是没有自明意义的一辈子：不了解自己是谁，不知道自己为什么活着。所以儒家认为，人从儿童时代就需要启蒙，这样就知道哪些是比较合适的心意状态，并试图保持这种心意状态。早期启蒙如果能够"顺以巽也"，那么后期发展就有良好的基础，给意念发动开启开放而有意义的方向。

[Illuminating Intentionality]

Hexagram Meng (Youthful Ignorance) is a hexagram for cultivating one's nature, and the core of cultivating one's nature is the enlightenment and construction of mental-intentional structure. For those who are being enlightened, being humble and complying with enlightenment will bring good fortune. Humility and compliance are states in which the inclinations of inherent nature are revealed, and the structure that points to the future is destiny.

Inherent nature and destiny form a unified system, and people have their limitations, but they also have the ability and possibility to transcend their existing limitations. Confucianism believes that "being sincere in one's intentions" and "exerting one's heart-mind" are the skills required to realize one's original nature and allow it to develop reasonably. Of course, if a natural person does not have this skill, they can live a natural life, but this is a meaningless life, or in other words, a life without self-evident intentionality: one does not know who one is or why one lives. Therefore, Confucians believe that people need enlightenment from childhood, so that they can know which mental states are more appropriate and try to maintain these mental states. If the early enlightenment can be accommodating, then there will be a good foundation for later development, opening up an open and meaningful direction for the initiation of intentions.

上九：击蒙，不利为寇，利御寇。

《象》曰：利用"御寇"，上下顺也。

【明译】

上九：用打骂责罚的方式启蒙，但不能像作寇盗那种方式来毒打受教者，而应该采取抵御寇盗那种谨慎小心的态度才有利。

《象传》说：采取抵御寇盗那种谨慎小心的态度（如果蒙童没有恰当启蒙将来就可能成为强盗，要防止把蒙童教成未来的强盗）才有利，这样施教者和受教者双方的关系才能够理顺（上九在全卦上位，下有互坤，坤为顺）。

Nine (*yang*/strong line) in the top place: Using beating, scolding and punishments to initiate enlightenment, it is not beneficial to beat an initiate like a bandit. Instead, it is beneficial to adopt a cautious attitude like warding off bandits.

The *Image Commentary* (*Xiang Zhuan*) says: It is advantageous to adopt a cautious attitude to resist bandits (if an ignorant child is not properly educated, one may become a bandit in the future, and it is necessary to prevent an ignorant child from becoming a future bandit), so that teacher and initiate should handle their relationship properly to keep things running smoothly (the upper Nine is in the top position of the whole hexagram, and below there is a inner Trigram Kun, which means running smoothly).

【明意】

经文中虽然多处出现如何应付盗寇，但从来没有让我们真的去打强盗，都是要通过驾驭自己的心灵来驾驭他人。教育过程之中，当一个学生需要老师去打击的时候，最能看出老师驾驭自己心意的功夫，需要合适的意量和意向，因循学生，如引诱强盗一般，此中之道即"击蒙"之道，如"产婆术"一般，教老师把握好击蒙之道：有时需要棒喝，前提是学生有悟性，没悟性就是打了也不能开悟，反而残废了。可见，把握化蒙的度是为师之艺术，而且击蒙需要很高的师技，即合适地惩罚学生需要技巧。

[Illuminating Intentionality]

Although the text of the *Classic* shows how to deal with bandits in many places, it never asks us to actually fight robbers. We must influence others by controlling our own intentions. In the education process, when a student requires a teacher to use physical force, the teacher's ability to control his own intentionality can best be seen. The teacher needs the appropriate degree and and direction of intention to follow the student, just like tempting a robber. The way to do this is to "attack the ignorance." In this method, like the Socratic "art of intellectual midwifery," a teacher should know how to master the method of attacking the ignorance: sometimes it is necessary to give a blow, but the prerequisite is that the student has the ability to understand. If the student has no ability of understanding, they will not be enlightened even if they are beaten, but will rather be disabled. It can be seen that mastering the degree of transformation is the art of being a teacher, and it requires a high level of teaching skill, that is, the skill required to punish students appropriately.

在教育现代化的今天，虽然肉体的打击，如体罚等作为教育的方式被否定了，但心灵的打击作为教育的方式并不容否定，而且也仍然有效。甚至有些时候，心灵的打击比肉体的打击更加残酷，因为其持久并能够烙下阴影，难以除去，有时甚至是终身的。蒙卦在于改变意缘的方向，即意与他意的缘分，说明一个教育者改变他人心意的方向如何可能。首先受教育者要心诚谦虚，否则免谈；其次教育要因材施教，适时施教，也就是有强大的驾驭自己内心意念的能力，才能改变受教育者的他心。可见，教育致力于可以改变他人心意的过程，尤其是养心上正路，其实是一门高超的实践艺术。

In today's modernization of education, although physical blows, such as corporal punishment, have been denied as a method of education, spiritual blows as a method of education cannot be denied and are still effective. Sometimes, a blow to the soul is even more cruel than a physical blow, because it is long-lasting and can leave a shadow that is difficult to remove, sometimes even for life. Hexagram Meng (Youthful Ignorance) is about changing the direction of one's intentionality, that is, the connection between one's intentions and another's intentions. It explains how it is possible for an educator to change the direction of another person's intentionality. First of all, the educated must be sincere and humble, otherwise there will be no need to talk; secondly, education must teach students in accordance with their aptitude and teach at the right time. Only by having a strong ability to control their own inner intentions can the other mind of an educated person be changed. It can be seen that education is dedicated to the process of changing other people's minds, especially cultivating intentions on the right *dao*, which is actually a superb practical art.

水天需（卦五）　（乾下坎上）

Xu (Waiting), Water and Heaven (Hexagram 5)　(Qian below, Kan above)

　　需乃等待之意，前有险而等待，是识时务等待之意境。需是内心刚健有乾天之意，能够渡过困难的阻碍。人生而有需要，也生来就在等待中。人的需要不可能马上实现，而且需要只能在等待中实现。有些人知道如何通过等待实现需要，有些人在等待中错失实现需要的时机。所以，如何思考需要和等待之间的关系就成为一门控制意念的艺术，如何在等待的过程当中实现需要也需要制意有术。有些人在等待中，意识紊乱，精神错乱，因为无法控制等待的过程，即使需要在被实现的过程中，心志也难以控制。应该说，等待之艺术的主旨就是节制和忍耐，也就是知道哪些意识合理地指向自己想要实现的需要，而哪些意识其实有悖于实现自己的需要，因此要节制，要调节忍耐。否则，一旦欲望高涨，迷失心志，人们内心真正的需要反而不可能实现。

　　Hexagram Xu means waiting. Waiting when there is danger ahead is the intentional context of knowing the time to wait. You need to be mentally strong and willing to work hard, and be able to overcome difficult obstacles. A human is born with needs, and also with the mental power of waiting. Human needs cannot be realized immediately, and needs can only be realized through waiting. Some people know how to realize their needs by waiting, and some people miss the opportunity to realize their needs while waiting. Therefore, how to think about the relationship between needs and waiting becomes an art of controlling intentions, and how to realize needs during the waiting process also requires skill in controlling intentions. Some people become confused and insane while waiting, because they cannot control the process of waiting. Even when needs are being realized, it is difficult to control intentions. It should be said that the main theme of the art of waiting is moderation and patience, that is, knowing which consciousness is reasonably directed to the needs that one wants to realize, and which consciousness is actually contrary to realizing one's own needs, so one must exercise moderation and adjust one's patience. Otherwise, once desires are heightened and ambitions are lost, people's true inner needs will not be realized.

人因需要而等待，期待局势朝着有利于自己的方向发展，应同时意识到自己与他人的需要。人应该既意识到自己的需要，又意识到别人的需要，他的意识境域才能是一种相对成熟合理的意识境域，在心念发动的瞬间会顾及他人心意发动的情况，包括可能引起他人的妒忌与憎恨等等。因为小心，因为意识境域的宽广，反而能够保持心念的长久稳固发展。

People wait out of need and expect a situation to develop in a direction that is beneficial to them. They should be aware of their own needs and the needs of others at the same time. A person should be aware of both his own needs and the needs of others, so that his state of consciousness can be a relatively mature and reasonable state of consciousness. At the moment when his intentions are initiated, he will take into account the situation of other people's intentions, including the possible jealousy of others, hate and so on. With caution and a broad realm of consciousness, we can maintain the long-term and stable development of our intentions.

需，有孚，光亨，贞吉。利涉大川。

《彖》曰：需，须也，险在前也。刚健而不陷，其义不困穷矣。"需，有孚，光亨，贞吉"，位乎天位，以正中也。"利涉大川"，往有功也。

《象》曰：云上于天，需。君子以饮食宴乐。

【明译】

需卦象征需要，等待，心怀诚信，光明亨通，持守正道可获吉祥。有利于涉过大川险阻而有所作为。

《彖传》说：需是等待的意思。上（前）卦是坎，坎为险。下卦是乾，乾为刚健，上卦坎为坎陷，因为心意刚健，所以不会陷入险难的情境出不来，从道理上讲不会被困在危险的境地。需要，等待，心怀诚信，光明亨通，持守正道可获吉祥，因为主爻九五在尊贵的天位又有中正之德。有利于涉过大川险阻的难关，能成就功业。

《象传》说：下卦乾为天，上卦坎为云，需卦的卦象是云气上集于天（雨待时而降）。君子从卦象中得到启示，要饮食宴乐，积蓄力量，等待时机。

Hexagram Xu (Waiting) symbolizes need, waiting, integrity, brightness and prosperity, and good fortune can be obtained by adhering to the right *dao*. It is conducive to wading through the dangers of a river and making a difference.

The *Judgment Commentary* (*Tuan Zhuan*) says: Hexagram Xu (Waiting) means waiting. The upper (front) trigram is Kan, which means a dangerous trap. The lower trigram is Qian, which means strong. When intentionality is strong, when facing a perilous river or trap, one will not fall into a hazardous situation and be unable to get out. Logically speaking, a strong intention will not be trapped in treacherous situations. Needs require waiting with integrity in one's mind, being bright and positive, and sticking to the right *dao* to gain good fortune, because the main line, the Nine (*yang*/strong line) in the fifth place, is virtuous and righteous in the noble position of heaven. It is helpful to get through the dangerous difficulties of the river, and you can make great achievements if you advance.

The *Image Commentary* (*Xiang Zhuan*) says: The lower Trigram Qian is sky, the upper Trigram Kan is cloud, so the image of Hexagram Xu (Waiting) is clouds gathering in the sky (rain will fall in due time). An exemplary person is inspired by this hexagram to wait while eating, drinking and enjoying oneself, accumulating strength and waiting for an opportunity.

【明意】

在等待中，人把自己内心的需要意识转化为具有公共意识境域的整体意识，这时人意识的缘发境域就离开原初的私我和小我的境地，进入与人与物共在的大我境地。人意念发动，对于外物所在的情势可以有危险和平易的判断。如果外在的情势可能对自己构成伤害，则应该等待时机，等待情境的改变，在等待中保持内心的刚健，以维持健康的身体和平易的意境之本。因为没有健康的身体，就没有清醒的意境，也就不能够对外物存在与心灵联通的状态有精准的判断。

[Illuminating Intentionality]

While waiting, people transform their inner consciousness into an overall consciousness with a realm of public consciousness. At this time, the realm of human consciousness leaves the original realm of private self and ego and enters the realm of coexistence with other people and things. When people's intentions are initiated, they can make dangerous and easy judgments about the situation of external objects. If the external situation may cause harm to you, you should wait for the opportunity, wait for the situation to change, and keep your inner strength while waiting, so as to maintain a healthy body and an easeful intentional context. Without a healthy body, there can be no clear mental state, and it is impossible to accurately judge the state of the connection between the existence of external objects and the heart-mind.

初九：需于郊，利用恒，无咎。

《象》曰："需于郊"，不犯难行也。"利用恒，无咎"，未失常也。

【明译】

初九：在郊远之地等待，有利于保持恒常的心态，没有咎害。

《象传》说：在郊远之地等待，不冒险去行动。保持恒常的心意状态并持之以恒，等待时机，因为危险还比较远，情况还没到非常时期，有利于初九持守常心。

Nine (*yang*/strong line) in the first place: Waiting in the distant suburbs is conducive to maintaining a constant state of intentionality, and there is no guilt.

The *Image Commentary* (*Xiang Zhuan*) says: Wait in the countryside and do not take risks. Maintain a constant state of intentionality and persevere, waiting for the opportunity, because the danger is still far away and the situation has not reached an emergency yet, which is conducive to maintaining a normal intentionality as the Nine (*yang*/strong line) in the first place.

【明意】

初九相当于意之初生，似乎与坎险之境隔着遥远的距离，好像仅仅就是心意在发动一般，其实心意一动就与坎境一起动起来了，只是从心意的反身状态（reflexive state）来说，好像还没有开始一样。意之萌发，如入无物之境，好像不与物对，但又必须与物相对，即意总是与意缘相关。心动落实于意念的实化，就成为行动，而行动会作用于意缘，所以应该小心，在时机不合适以前，不轻易冒险而动。

恒心是心力的保持，为了维持在郊远之地等待有利于持守恒常的心境，这说明对于等待而言，有一种平常的意境心态可以说最为关键。在等待过程中，时机忽隐忽现，如果人没有平常之心，就会失却本心而追逐外物，在追逐外物当中耗散意缘，消耗意能，导致意行杂乱无章，最后伤害意念发动的状态本身。所以此爻提示人们既然已经在远方等待，要让意缘保持对于外物的超然态度，不为迁变的外物所动，所以要有常心，安心等待而不必着急。

[Illuminating Intentionality]

A Nine (*yang*/strong line) in the first place is equivalent to the birth of intention. It seems to be far away from a dangerous situation, as if it is just intentionality that is moving. In fact, as soon as intentionality moves, it starts to move with the dangerous situation, and it is just that, from the perspective of the reflexive state of intentionality, it seems like it hasn't started yet. The germination of intentionality is like entering a realm of nothingness, one which does not seem to be opposite to things, but must be opposite to things. That is to say, intentionality is always related to situations. The initiative of the heart-mind becomes an action when an intention is realized, and the action will affect the intentional context, so you should be careful not to take risks easily before the time is right.

Perseverance is the maintenance of mental strength. In order to maintain a constant state of intentionality while waiting in the countryside, this shows that having a normal mood is the most critical aspect to waiting. In the process of waiting, opportunities flicker and appear. If people do not have a calm heart-mind, they will lose their original intentionality and chase external objects. In the pursuit of external objects, they will dissipate their mental connections and consume their intentional energy, resulting in disorganized intentions and ultimately harming their thoughts as initiated mental states. Therefore, this line reminds people that since they are already waiting in the distant suburbs, they should maintain a detached attitude towards external objects and not be affected by changing external objects. Therefore, they should have a constant heart-mind and wait with a tranquility of intentionality without being anxious.

九二：需于沙，小有言，终吉。

《象》曰："需于沙"，衍在中也。虽"小有言"，以终吉也。

【明译】

九二：在沙滩上等待，遭到小的闲言碎语，最终吉祥。

《象传》说：在沙滩上等待，九二位置在下卦中位，犹如在水中的沙洲上从容自在。虽有些闲言碎语，只要宽心等待，合理因应，最终结果吉祥。

Nine (*yang*/strong line) in the second place: Waiting on the beach, meeting with a little gossip, there is finally good fortune.

The *Image Commentary* (*Xiang Zhuan*) says: Waiting on the beach, the position of the Nine (*yang*/strong line) in the second place is in the middle of the lower Trigram, just like being at ease on a sandbank in the water. Although there is some gossip, as long as one waits patiently and responds appropriately, the final result will be auspicious.

【明意】

人的经验有其整全性（the wholeness of experience），人通过自己意识到的有限经验和世界融合的整体性来连接自己的心意与世界。经验的整全性与具体的心意如何联通？在本爻中，言语纠葛是断定本爻处境的关键，因能够引发他人言语纠葛，说明此爻的等待与他心之间存在利益冲突甚至竞争关系，或者虽有共同目标，但因为资源有限而关系紧张。可是心意发动并不直接地觉知有限资源的存在，往往需要通过一定时间的等待和判断，这期间可能有言语纠葛，因为对于心之动与追求目标相关性之间存在一种时间性的延迟，而延迟之时，人就好像被搁置在水中的沙洲上，虽然不安全，但是这个延续性的等待还是给了自己一个重新审视世界与自己关系的时间与空间，使得人对自己的需要与事物的流变及周围人的反应能够重新加以得失利弊的审查和判断。

[Illuminating Intentionality]

Human experience has its wholeness (the wholeness of experience), and people connect their intentions and world through the integration of the limited experience they are aware of with the wholeness of the world. In order to connect the integrity of experience with specific intentions, in this line, verbal entanglement is the key to determine its situation. Because it can trigger other people's verbal entanglements, it shows that there is a conflict of interest or even competition between this line's waiting and other people's intentions, or although they have a common goal, the relationship is tense due to limited resources. However, the initiation of intentionality does not directly recognize the existence of limited resources, and often requires a certain period of waiting and judgment. During this period, there may be verbal entanglements, because there is a temporal delay between the movement of intentionality and the relevance of pursuing the goal, and when delayed, people seem to be stranded on a sandbank in the water. Although it is not safe, this continuous waiting still gives them the time and space to re-examine their relationship with the world, allowing people to understand that their own needs, the changes in things and the reactions of people around them can be reviewed and judged again on their pros and cons.

九三：需于泥，致寇至。

《象》曰："需于泥"，灾在外也。自我"致寇"。敬慎不败也。

【明译】

九三：在泥泞中等待，（偏偏此时还）招来寇难。

《象传》说：在泥泞中等待，寸步难行，灾难（坎）就在外边，不时就来。偏偏是自己招惹强盗来，不过只要敬谨审慎，高度警戒，就不会陷于危败（因为还未陷入坎险之中）。

Nine (*yang*/strong line) in the third place: Waiting in the mud will (especially at this time) bring trouble from bandits.

The *Image Commentary* (*Xiang Zhuan*) says: Waiting in the mud, it will be difficult to move even an inch. Disasters (bumps) are just outside and will come from time to time. Although one has provoked the robbers oneself, as long as one is cautious and alert, one will not be in danger (because one has not yet fallen into a trap).

【明意】

人的心念一起就有需要，虽然如行云流水，却如坎陷一般，如影随形，自然就有危险伴随，这就需要学会等待，也就要在意识的绵延中付出时空能量。人对于欲望应该有条件地自我控制，否则就会不断地陷入危险的境地，而且不断付出代价，直到自己付不出为止，那就把原初的心物平衡体系打破了。

[Illuminating Intentionality]

People's intentions arise with certain needs. Although they are like floating clouds and flowing water, needs are like obstacles and shadows. Naturally, needs are accompanied by dangers. This requires learning to wait, and it also requires spending temporal and spatial energy in the continuity of consciousness. People should have conditional self-control over their desires, otherwise they will continue to fall into dangerous situations and continue to pay the price until they can no longer pay more, which will break the original balance system of intentionality and material.

刚强地争取需要的意识必然引起他人警惕、提防甚至污蔑和攻击，人应该知道争取合理需要的意识分寸，但也要意识到他人的利益与自己处于竞争的状况，虽可以争取，但毕竟有危险，因此不求务必得到，所谓"尽人事，听天命"就是一种直面危险的刚强意境。在等待中明白危险无处不在，同时保守恒常平易之心，知道需求的分寸，也就善于把握等待的时机。

A strong awareness of striving for needs will inevitably arouse others' vigilance, wariness, and even slander and attack. People should know the appropriateness of striving for reasonable needs, but they must also realize that the interests of others are in competition with their own. Although they can fight for them, after all, there are dangers, so one ought not demand certain attainment. As is said, "Do your human best and await heaven's destiny" is a strong intentional context of facing danger directly. While waiting, you should understand that dangers are everywhere, and at the same time maintain a calm intentionality and know the proportion of needs, then you will be good at seizing the opportunities that await.

六四：需于血，出自穴。

《象》曰："需于血"，顺以听也。

【明译】

六四：在血泊中等待，从洞穴中爬出来。

《象传》说：在血泊中等待，要随顺听命，冷静地顺从九五，听命于时势而行，最后能化险为夷。

Six (*yin*/soft line) in the fourth place: Waiting in a pool of blood, crawling out of a cave.

The *Image Commentary* (*Xiang Zhuan*) says: Waiting in a pool of blood, one must accept one's destiny, calmly follow the Nine (*yang*/strong line) in the fifth place, obey orders and act according to the current situation, then in the end one can turn danger into safety.

【明意】

此爻之象提及洞里面都是血水，从危险至极的血泊之中逃命，所以有点像海明威《老人与海》里老人与大鱼艰难搏斗的味道，捕鱼捕得浑身是血，血染江河。可见，为外在的物欲和获取世间的利益，人们往往付出太长时间的等待，而这种等待的本身是遮蔽人天之意的，也就是忘记了我们本来就是通于天地自然之意的。

[Illuminating Intentionality]

The image in this line refers to a cave full of blood, and escaping from the extreme danger of the pool of blood, so it is a bit like the old man and the big fish struggling hard in Ernest Hemingway's *The Old Man and the Sea*, the fisherman covered in blood and facing the difficulty with courage. It can be seen that for external material desires and obtaining worldly benefits, people often wait for too long, and this waiting itself obscures the intentionality of humanity and heaven, that is, we forget that we are originally connected to the cosmological intentionality of heaven, earth, and nature.

心为物役是心一直想使役外物，但却常常处于被物驱动的艰难之中。心可能驾驭的外物往往是付出很多心血之后才能够得到的，而付出心血的代价可能远远超过自己的预期。心力使役外物的过程，通常来说是心的负累，需要琢磨心力运作与外物交流的合适分寸，所以往往不是非常轻巧就可以实现的。当然，另外一个矛盾也存在，不去努力使役外物，心就往往为他心甚至他物所使役，被外物拖着走。所以，这里面有一个使役和被使役的分寸问题，归根结底，还是一个人到底需要什么，为了这个需要一个人到底应该如何去等待？这其实是一个人生的难题，也是人生的一大学问。

The heart-mind is subject to external objects, which means that intentionality always wants to use external objects, but is often in the difficult situation of being driven by objects. The external objects that the heart-mind can control are often only obtained after a lot of hard work, and the price of hard work may be far beyond one's expectations. The process of using intentionality to use external objects is usually a burden on the intentions. It requires thinking about the appropriate proportion of an intention's operation to communicate with external objects, so it is often not something that can be achieved very easily. Of course, another contradiction also exists. If we do not make efforts to use external objects, our intentionality will often be used by other minds or even other objects, and be dragged away by external objects. Therefore, there is a question of proportion between servitude and being served. In the final analysis, this is a question of what a person needs, and how a person should wait for this need. This is actually a difficult problem and a great question in life.

九五：需于酒食，贞吉。

《象》曰："酒食贞吉"，以中正也。

【明译】

九五：在美食宴饮中等待，安于守正可获吉祥。

《象传》说：在美食宴饮中安于守正可获吉祥，是因为九五阳刚中正。

Nine (*yang*/strong line) in the fifth place: Waiting with delicious food and wine, staying righteous will bring good fortune.

The *Image Commentary* (*Xiang Zhuan*) says: Staying upright with food and wine can bring good fortune, because the Nine (*yang*/strong line) in the fifth place is strong and upright.

【明意】

一个人付出心血的那种意境如果在他人看来是成功的，就应该跟他人分享，因为个人的成功来自人与他人共存的意境，很多时候他人有意成全，即使是竞争成功，也主要是一时一地的阴阳之力的转化而已，世易时移，时势变化，所以应该遵守阴阳转化的原理，给自己的竞争对手留下地盘。

[Illuminating Intentionality]

If the intentional context of a person's hard work is success in the eyes of others, he should share it with others, because personal success comes from the intentional context of coexistence between people and others. Many times, others intend to achieve success, and even if this is success in competition, it is mainly a transformation of the power of *yin* and *yang* in one place and time. The world changes with time and the current situation changes. Therefore, we should abide by the principle of *yin* and *yang* transformation and leave territory for our competitors.

不能让人的某些需求发展成为盲目的欲望，进而占据人的心灵意识整体，否则就可能迷失自己，不知道自己真正的意识所向。人在需要的过程中，等待是一个修道的过程，也是修行自己心灵意境的过程。人的心意与世界融通，与宇宙能量运动合拍，才能够形成有力的意道，意道实化为物之道，成为心物关联相通之道。人天之意的力量是来自心意与宇宙节律的合拍，知道如何等待而合拍，本身就是有力量的表现。

Certain needs of people cannot be allowed to develop into blind desires which then occupy the entirety of human intentionality and consciousness, since then people may lose themselves and not know where their true consciousness lies. When people are in need, waiting is a process of cultivating the *dao*, and it is also a process of cultivating one's own spiritual conception. Only when human intentionality is integrated with the world and in tune with the movement of the energy of the cosmos can it form a powerful *dao* of intentionality, which can be transformed into the *dao* of things and become the *dao* of interconnection between intentionality and things/events. The power of the cosmological intentionality of humans and heaven comes from the synchronization of intentionality with the rhythms of the cosmos. Knowing how to wait and synchronize is itself a powerful expression.

上六：入于穴，有不速之客三人来，敬之终吉。

《象》曰："不速之客来，敬之终吉"，虽不当位，未大失也。

【明译】

上六：被迫落入洞穴之中，有三位不请自来的客人，对他们恭敬相待，最终获得吉祥。

《象传》说：有几位不请自来的客人，对他们恭敬相待，最终获得吉祥。说明本爻虽然所处位置不当，但敬慎小心，则不至于招致重大损失。

Six (*yin*/soft line) in the top place: Forced to fall into a cave, there are three uninvited guests, and if one treats them respectfully, there will finally be good fortune.

The *Image Commentary* (*Xiang Zhuan*) says: There are several uninvited guests, who if treated respectfully, will finally bring good fortune. This shows that, although this line is in an inappropriate position, if one is careful, one will not incur heavy losses.

【明意】

人需要学会等待，在等待中调适自己的心意与周围情境的关系，修炼特定时空能量场域中的人天之意。一个人对于自己心意控制的能力如果不能够把握好分寸，就可能会招致无端的麻烦。一个人的心意满足自己的需求，但往往违背周围意识境遇之他人的心灵需求，于是就需要学会协调和调整自己的心灵境遇与他人意境的关系。

[Illuminating Intentionality]

People need to learn to wait, adjust the relationship between their own intentionality and the surrounding situation while waiting, and cultivate the intentionality of humanity and heaven within a specific time and space energy field. If a person cannot control his intentionality well, he may cause unwarranted trouble. A person's intentionality meets his or her own needs, but may often go against the spiritual needs of others in the surrounding conscious context. Therefore, one needs to learn to coordinate and adjust the relationship between one's own spiritual state and the intentional context of others.

时势即命运，知道待时就是知道等待命运，知道等待命运就是在把握命运。郭象说"所遇为命"通常做被动的理解，有点接近庄子"知其不可奈何而安之若命"，但也可以做积极等待来理解，阴意与阳意的相遇，如果懂得等待和把握相遇的时机，就是懂得隐忍待命，也知道用敬慎的态度面对生命中众多的变数。

One's current propensity is destiny, knowing to wait for the appropriate time is knowing to wait for destiny, and knowing to wait for destiny is to grasp destiny. When Guo Xiang said, "Everything one encounters is destiny," this is usually understood passively, close to Zhuangzi's "Knowing that which there is nothing one can do about and accepting it as destiny", but it can also be understood as active waiting. In the encounter between *yin* and *yang* intentionality, if one knows how to wait and grasp the opportunity one meets with, one knows how to be patient and wait, and to face the many variables in life with a cautious attitude.

天水讼（卦六） （坎下乾上）

Song (Disputation), Heaven and Water (Hexagram 6)   (Kan below, Qian above)

  需卦的意向是等待之向，一种无方向的意向性状态，因为无方向，所以难以把握，常人易于把意向集中于饮食和享乐之上，自然对于具体享受对象的意向性交叉度不高，而易于产生纷争。讼卦代表的是意向的纷争之状，即意向对象的有限性与意向产生主体对意向对象的无限性占有之间的矛盾，导致纷争和冲突升级。

  讼卦最后希望人要节制，而且即使利益关头也要自我节制，知道如果把利益看得很重，就可能因小失大。意向明确地处理利益的争夺，有时反而会伤害自身的利益，所以要谦让和忍耐，不仅仅要求人们在等待之中自我了解、自我劝慰，而且要求人在利益冲突的时候，能够冷静思考，把握进退。

  The intention of Hexagram Xu (Waiting) is the direction of waiting, a directionless intentional state. Because it has no direction, it is difficult to grasp. Ordinary people tend to focus their intentions on food and enjoyment. Naturally, the degree of intentionality for the specific objects of enjoyment is not high, and prone to giving rise to disputes. Hexagram Song (Disputation) represents the state of disputes among intentions, that is, the contradiction between the finite nature of intentional objects and the unlimited possession of an intentional object by the subject that generates the intention, leading to the escalation of disputes and conflicts.

  Hexagram Song (Disputation) ultimately hopes that people can exercise restraint, even when their interests are at stake, knowing that if they take interests too seriously, they may end up losing a lot for a small amount. Dealing with competition between interests with clear intentionality can sometimes harm one's own interests. Therefore, humility and patience not only require people to understand and comfort themselves while waiting, but also to think calmly and grasp the situation of advance and retreat when interests conflict.

讼卦对人的意识修行的要求其实非常之高，一个人能够自始至终，即使在极端重要的个人利益面前，都冷静分析自己意向的后果，知道他人应对的可能性，如果能够做到如此冷静和清醒，那么人的意识修行状态就达到相当高明的成功状态。

Hexagram Song (Disputation) actually has very high requirements for people's conscious cultivation. A person can calmly analyze the consequences of his own intentions from beginning to end, even in the face of extremely important personal interests, and know the possibility of others' responses. If people can do this, they are able to be calm and sober, and their consciousness can reach a very advanced state of success.

讼，有孚，窒，惕，中吉，终凶。利见大人。不利涉大川。

《彖》曰：讼，上刚下险，险而健，讼。"讼有孚窒惕，中吉"，刚来而得中也。"终凶"，讼不可成也。"利见大人"，尚中正也。"不利涉大川"，入于渊也。

《象》曰：天与水违行，讼。君子以作事谋始。

【明译】

讼卦象征打官司，有证据，但诚信受阻，双方互不信任，就诉诸法庭，如能持中，心有惕戒，适可而止，中途结束官司吉祥，把官司打到底凶险。有利于见到公正的法官，但不利于渡过大川险阻。

《彖传》说：讼卦，上卦乾为刚健，下卦坎为险，内心险恶外表刚健，就容易引发争讼，总想打官司。所以称作讼卦。讼卦象征打官司，有证据，但诚信受阻，双方互不信任，就诉诸法庭，如能持中，心有惕戒，适可而止，中途结束官司吉祥，因为主爻九二（刚爻）由遯卦三位下来得到下卦中位。把官司打到底凶险，因为打官司不宜纠缠不休，否则最终一定两败俱伤。有利于见到公正的法官，因为决讼追求守正持中，所以希望中正的法官（九五）秉公断案。但不利于渡过大川险阻，是说恃刚乘险终将陷入深渊，任何诉讼都充满危险的变数。

Hexagram Song (Disputation) symbolizes a lawsuit. If there is evidence, but integrity is hindered and neither party trusts the other, they will resort to court. If one can hold on to the right, be vigilant and stop when it is appropriate, it will be auspicious to end the lawsuit in the middle, but it will be dangerous to fight the lawsuit to the end. It is good to meet a fair judge, but it is not good to go through the dangers of a great river.

The *Judgment Commentary* (*Tuan Zhuan*) says: In Hexagram Song (Disputation), the upper

Trigram Qian is strong, and the lower Trigram Kan is dangerous. If the inner heart-mind is sinister and the outer appearance is strong, it will easily give rise to lawsuits and to always wanting to file a lawsuit. This is why the hexagram is called Song (Disputation). Hexagram Song (Disputation) symbolizes a lawsuit. If there is evidence, but integrity is hindered and neither party trusts the other, they will resort to court. If one can hold on to the right, be vigilant and stop when it is appropriate, it will be auspicious to end the lawsuit in the middle, because the main line Nine (*yang*/strong line) in the second place is composed of the third line from Hexagram Dun (Retreat) moving down to the middle position of the lower Trigram. It is dangerous to fight the lawsuit to the end, because it is not advisable to get entangled in the lawsuit, otherwise both sides will lose in the end. It is helpful to see a fair judge, because we pursue fairness and impartiality in deciding lawsuits, so we hope that a fair judge (the Nine (*yang*/strong line) in the fifth place) will decide the case impartially. But it is not conducive to overcoming the dangers of a great river, because relying on strength will eventually lead to the abyss. Any lawsuit is full of dangerous variables.

《象传》说：上卦乾为天，下卦坎为水，天向上浮，水向下流，（或者太阳从东向西转动，河流自西向东流），越离越远，不能亲合，相争不息，所以是个讼卦。君子见到这种相互背离的卦象，处事从一开始就要认真谋划，从源头杜绝产生争讼的可能。

The *Image Commentary* (*Xiang Zhuan*) says: The upper Trigram Qian is sky, and the lower Trigram Kan is water. Sky floats upward and water flows downward, (or the sun revolves from east to west, and the river flows from west to east), so the farther they move, the farther they are from each other, and they cannot join together. They are constantly fighting, so this is Hexagram Song (Disputation). When an exemplary person sees such a contradictory hexagram image, one must plan carefully from the beginning to eliminate the possibility of legal fighting from its very source.

【明意】

讼卦认为争讼不是解决社会治理之道，中国虽然需要依法治国，但不可完全照搬西方的法治精神。中国传统上是法理兼治，或者法情兼备的国家，人们的生活一方面需要法律调控，一方面需要情理来把持。孟子说："徒法不足以自行"是有道理的。法家比较简单化，看不到制定和执行法令背后的人情；而儒家其实是儒法兼治的，不完全排除法律的尊严，但强调法律的制定与实施都应以良心为前提，否则以恶法治国，必定乱得一团糟，连情理都无处可讲。

[Illuminating Intentionality]

Hexagram Song (Disputation) believes that litigation is not the solution to social governance. Although China needs to be governed according to law, it cannot completely copy the legal spirit from the West. China has traditionally been a country governed by both law and moral principle, or by both law and feeling/circumstance. People's lives need to be regulated by law on the one hand, and controlled by feeling and moral principle on the other. Mencius claimed that "laws alone are insufficient to implement themselves," and this makes sense. Legalism is relatively simplistic and cannot see the human feelings behind the formulation and execution of laws. Confucianism is actually a combination of Confucian benevolence and law, which does not completely exclude the dignity of law, but emphasizes that the formulation and implementation of laws should be based on humane conscience, otherwise the state may be ruled with evil laws. The rule of law would then end up as a mess, and there would be no feeling or moral principle worth speaking of.

法治精神是希望法律能够约束个人的意识方向，让活泼的人心依从没有血气的条文来行事，但这种机械式的强制命令又往往难以真正化解人心内在的冲突。因为人心之间有彼此感应和沟通的可能，所以法治应该给心灵的流动和对话留下地盘，即应该让良心的发动高于法令条文本身存在和实现的具体化状态。

The spirit of the rule of law hopes that the law can constrain the direction of individual consciousness and allow lively people to act in accordance with bloodless textual provisions. However, this kind of mechanical, coercive order often fails to truly resolve the inner conflicts of people. Since there is the possibility of mutual induction and communication between people's intentions, the rule of law should leave room for flow and dialogue between heart-minds, that is, it should allow the initiation of conscience to be higher than the concrete state of the existence and realization of legal provisions themselves.

初六：不永所事，小有言，终吉。

《象》曰："不永所事"，讼不可长也。虽"小有言"，其辩明也。

【明译】

初六：不要久缠于争讼之中，必要时当稍做辩解，让小的闲言碎语尽快过去，最后才会吉祥。

《象传》说：不要久缠于争讼之中，因为诉讼不是长久之计。即使有一些闲言碎语，做点辩解，是非最后都可以辨别明白。

Six (*yin*/soft line) in the first place: Do not become entangled in disputes for a long time. If necessary, make a small argument and let the petty gossip pass as soon as possible. Only in the end will it be auspicious.

The *Image Commentary* (*Xiang Zhuan*) says: Do not become entangled in disputes for a long time, because litigation is not a long-term solution. Even if there are some excuses and gossip, right and wrong can be distinguished in the end.

【明意】

每个人的生活状态有一部分不易改变，人现实的地位如与生俱来的家庭条件一样，只能面对，难以更改。地位的低下通常不是一个人主观自我选择的结果，如果可能，没有人会甘心选择弱势，受人欺压，而相对的地位又客观存在，所以地位的差异性就是一个人必须面对的时势状态。

官司不能一直打下去，要及时调整意念的方向，该撤回的时候就撤回，说明人的意向性可以根据情境的判断来加以调整。对于无法通达的意缘，可能最后还是需要通过在意向性的发动状态中加以调整，尽量通达，才能化解诉讼生起之后的意境。

[Illuminating Intentionality]

There are parts of everyone's living conditions that are difficult to change. A person's actual status is like his or her inherent family conditions, which can only be dealt with but cannot be changed. Low status is usually not the result of a person's subjective self-selection. If possible, no one would be willing to choose to be weak and bullied by others, and relative status exists objectively, so difference in status is a situation that a person must face.

A lawsuit should not go on forever. It is necessary to adjust the direction of one's intentions in time and withdraw when it is time to withdraw. This shows that people's intentionality can be adjusted according to their judgment of a situation. For unreachable intentional contexts, it may be necessary to adjust them in the active state of intentionality and make them as accessible as possible, in order to resolve the intentional context after the lawsuit arises.

九二：不克讼，归而逋（bū）。其邑人三百户，无眚（shěng）。

《象》曰："不克讼"，归逋窜也。自下讼上，患至掇（duō）也。

【明译】

九二：不能赢得官司，逃回家躲起来，那是只有三百户人家的小村庄，不会遭到迫害。

《象传》说：官司打败了，只好逃窜回归故里。在下位的人（九二）去告在上位的人（九五），这是自己拣来的祸患。

Nine (*yang*/strong line) in the second place: If you cannot win the case, run away and hide in your home. It is a small village with only 300 households and you will not be persecuted.

The *Image Commentary* (*Xiang Zhuan*) says: After losing the lawsuit, he had to flee and return to his hometown. A person in a lower position (the Nine (*yang*/strong line) in the second place) sues a person in a higher position (the Nine (*yang*/strong line) in the fifth place). This is a disaster of his own choosing.

【明意】

时势在意向中开显，为意向所领会。本爻涉及未来在心意中的开显与心意的退守，如未来在意念中升起的状态，心意如何判断未来，心意的退守与形势的关系等；形势不妙之时，当及时调整自己的意向，该退就退，以保全自己的安全为上。

主体所发意向的时势、地位、力量有别。诉讼的产生多是弱者希望通过诉讼讨回公道，通过本爻我们看到弱者如果不善于意会时势，明辨自己的位置，不善于判断事情发展的方向，不但不可能打赢官司，而且有被强势人物迫害甚至追杀的危险。

[Illuminating Intentionality]

The current intentional propensity is revealed in one's mind and understood when one's intentions arise. This line involves the unfolding of the future in intentionality and the retreat of intentionality, such as the state of the future arising in one's awareness, how intentionality judges the future, the relationship between the retreat of intentionality and the situational propensity, etc.; when the situational propensity is not good, one should adjust one's attitude in time. If you have power to control your own intentions, retreat when you need to, to protect your own safety first.

The temporal propensity, status, and power of a subject's intentionality are different. Lawsuits mostly arise because the weak hope to seek justice through litigation. Through this line, we see that if the weak sides are usually not good at understanding the whole picture of a current situation, clearly distinguishing their own position, and judging the direction of development of events, then the weak will not only feel it difficult to win a lawsuit, they will also need to face the danger of being persecuted or even hunted by powerful people.

六三．食旧德，贞厉，终吉。或从王事，无成。

《象》曰："食旧德"，从上吉也。

【明译】

六三：享用祖宗旧日积累的功德，守住正道，提防危险来临，终将获得吉祥。或跟从君王做事，不能以成功自居。

《象传》说：享用祖宗旧日积累的功德，因为六三顺从阳刚尊上（上乾为君王）吉祥。

Six (*yin*/soft line) in the third place: Enjoy the merits accumulated by your ancestors in the past, keep to the right *dao*, beware of dangers, and you will eventually gain good fortune. Or, if you follow the king and gain some achievements, do not think of yourself as successful.

The *Image Commentary* (*Xiang Zhuan*) says: Enjoy the merits accumulated by your ancestors in the past, because the Six (*yin*/soft line) in the third place obeys the *yang*/strong superior (the superior Trigram Qian represents the king) and is auspicious.

【明意】

为什么有些人到了关键时刻可以用得上祖辈的功德，好像祖辈的功德对一个人来说已经预设了某种先行结构一样。可见，祖上的旧缘和过去的意向作为情境之力可以延续比较长的时间，甚至几代人的时间，关键在于一个人把握旧缘和过去意向的尺度如何。这一爻说明，六三在危险的诉讼情境之中，对祖上旧缘要小心维护才能持续，等于关键时刻能够得到祖先阴德的庇护，有利于在危险当中守正。

[Illuminating Intentionality]

Why can some people use the merits of their ancestors at a critical moment? It is as if the merits of their ancestors have preset a certain prior structure for a person. It can be seen that old ties and past intentions from ancestors can last for a relatively long time as situational forces, sometimes even for several generations. The key lies in how well a person grasps old ties and past intentions. This line shows that in a dangerous litigation situation, the Six (*yin*/soft line) in the third place must carefully maintain the old relationship with his ancestors in order to continue. This means that he can get the protection of his ancestors at critical moments, which is conducive to keeping upright in danger.

九四：不克讼，复即命，渝安贞，吉。

《象》曰："复即命，渝安贞"，不失也。

【明译】

九四：无法打赢官司，转念回复命之正道，消除争讼的意念，变得安分守正，吉祥。

《象传》说：转念回复命之正道，消除争讼的意念，变得安分守正，说明九四安顺守正不会有失误。

Nine (*yang*/strong line) in the fourth place: When you cannot win a lawsuit, you should change your intentionality to restore your life to the right *dao*, eliminate the intention of litigation, and become law-abiding; this is then auspicious.

The *Image Commentary* (*Xiang Zhuan*) says: Changing your intentionality to restore the right *dao* of life, eliminating the intention of fighting a lawsuit, and becoming peaceful and upright, means that there will be no mistakes in being safe and upright as the Nine (*yang*/strong line) in the fourth place.

【明意】

本爻说明人调整意向的主要方法是明白事理，明了时势，从而自我控制。人的诉讼意向往往是因为对大势不能明白，如果明白大势则容易调整诉讼的意向。即使不能胜诉，人也可以听从自己内在良心的呼唤，不再继续希望通过官司改变公共意境，回到自己本分的意境中，这样虽败犹荣。承认每个人与生俱来本性不同，如大鹏和麻雀不可比，就容易把争端放下。

[Illuminating Intentionality]

This line explains that the main way for people to adjust their intentions is to understand the truth and the current situation, so as to control themselves. People's intention to litigate is often due to their inability to understand the general situation and trend. If they understand the general trend, it will be easier to adjust their intention to litigate. Even if one cannot win the lawsuit, one can still listen to the call of one's inner conscience, no longer hope to change the public mood through litigation, and return to one's own intentional context. In this way, it is still glorious to lose. It is easier to put aside

135

disputes when we admit that everyone is born with different natures, such as a roc and a sparrow being incomparable.

当意识到自己面对的人生境遇有相当部分不是主观愿望能够改变的，就应该安于"性各有分"的自然"命"定状态。同样，我们不可能知道何时死去，无论如何努力都不可能避免死亡发生，所以应该回到各自命定的分际，从各自的本性出发做最好的自己。

When you realize that a considerable part of the life situations you face cannot be changed by subjective wishes, you should be content with the natural "destined" state in which "every inherent nature has its own share." Similarly, it is impossible for us to know when we will die, and no matter how hard we try, we cannot avoid death. Therefore, we should return to our respective destined moments and be the best version of ourselves based on our respective natures.

从终极意义上说，人在宇宙中似乎不可能做什么真正改变宇宙变化的事情，我们来了又去，好像什么都不可能改变。所以，如果能够明白自己人生命定的分际，其实也是一种宇宙意识的大明，是人心沟通宇宙意识的一种觉悟状态，使人在处理一生的各种缘散缘聚时，会有一种超然的态度。可见，调整自己的意识向度回到自己把握的合适分寸，其实是每时每刻的当下一念控制意向的功夫。

In the ultimate sense, it seems impossible for humans to do anything in the cosmos that truly changes the cosmos. We come and go, and it seems that nothing can change. Therefore, if one can understand the divisions of one's life, it is actually a kind of great enlightenment of cosmic consciousness. It is an awakened state in which the human heart-mind communicates with cosmic consciousness, and can give rise to a transcendent ability to deal with the various dependent co-arisings and gatherings in a person's life. It can be seen that adjusting the dimension of one's consciousness back to the appropriate proportion that one has grasped is actually the effort of controlling intentionality with the current situation at every moment.

九五：讼，元吉。

《象》曰："讼，元吉"，以中正也。

【明译】

九五：明断争讼，至为吉祥。

《象传》说：判案公正，明断合宜，大吉大利，是因为九五在上卦中位，品性光明正大，有中正之德。

Nine (*yang*/strong line) in the fifth place: It is extremely auspicious to resolve disputes clearly.

The *Image Commentary* (*Xiang Zhuan*) says: The judgment of the case is fair and righteous, the judgment is clear and appropriate, and good fortune results. This is because the Nine (*yang*/strong line) in the fifth place is in the middle of the upper Trigram, and its character is upright and bright.

【明意】

此爻要求人们，即使在讼的状态，心思也应该公正廉明，胸怀宽广，不带私心。人天之意展示在公共务实的意向性里。主事者不应简单为了个人私利而兴讼，要尽量化解和减少诉讼之意念，如果主事的人常陷于诉讼陷阱之中，就不可能推进公正的公共意境建设，更不要说建立公平公正的公共意识境域了。

这种上位者可讼亦可止讼的观念是权势者在争讼中拥有优势的体现，真正纯粹人人平等意义上的公义在现实中往往缺乏，下位者讼上位者的情况虽多，但上位者通常有较大的把握胜出，这是争讼的吊诡之处。此爻也说明，改变命运需要有一定条件，尤其是通过诉讼的方式来立命，需要九五之尊这样的权力和权位保障才有可能，因为有权势的在位的大人，碰到不正之风的情形是可以讼的，而且最后有把握止讼。

[Illuminating Intentionality]

This line requires people, even in a state of litigation, to be fair, honest, broad-minded, and unselfish. The will of humanity and heaven is displayed in public and pragmatic intentionality. A person in charge should not simply initiate litigation for personal gain, but should try to resolve and reduce the intention of litigation. If a person in charge is often caught in the trap of litigation, it will be impossible to promote the construction of a fair public mood, let alone the establishment of a fair and just public mood or realm of consciousness.

The concept that a superior person can litigate or stop a lawsuit is a reflection of the advantage that the powerful have in disputes. Justice in the true sense of equality for all is often lacking in reality. Although there are many cases of the lower litigating against the higher, the one with the upper hand is usually more likely to win, which is the paradox of litigation. This line also shows that certain conditions are needed to change one's destiny, especially in the way to establish one's destiny through litigation. This is only possible if the power and position of the Nine (*yang*/strong line) in the fifth place are guaranteed, because authoritative great people in power can easily win a lawsuit with evildoers who have surely committed crimes, and such a lawsuit can finally be ended with certainty.

上九：或锡（cì）之鞶（pán）带，终朝三褫（chǐ）之。

《象》曰：以讼受服，亦不足敬也。

【明译】

上九：诉讼（偶然）获胜，君王赏赐饰有大带的官服，但一天之内会被剥夺三次。

《象传》说：因打官司获胜而得到高官厚禄，不足以为人敬重。

Nine (*yang*/strong line) in the top place: The lawsuit is won (accidentally), and the king rewards an official uniform with a large belt, but it will be expropriated three times in one day.

The *Image Commentary* (*Xiang Zhuan*) says: Receiving a high official position and a generous salary because of winning a lawsuit is not enough to be respected by others.

【明意】

如果能在"讼"时仍保持中正的意向,就可能获得元吉的结果;如果不能秉持中正的意向,把"讼"的手段用到极致,那么就算获胜得利,也只是短时得利,终究会失去。此爻说明不要以侵犯和伤害他人来获得利益,更不可因此沾沾自喜,因为这不能长久,长久的互利一定基于公益和良心。既然诉讼根本就是一种两败俱伤的状态,即使官司打胜得到利益也很难取得他人的尊敬,所以主观上放弃这种争讼的努力才比较合适。

[Illuminating Intentionality]

If one can still maintain central and upright intention during the "litigation", one may obtain a good result; if one cannot uphold central and upright intention and uses the "litigation" method to the extreme, then even if one wins, it will only be a short-term gain, which will eventually be lost. This line illustrates that one should not gain benefits by infringing or harming others, and one should not be complacent because this cannot last long. Long-term mutual benefit must be based on public welfare and conscience. Since litigation is basically a lose-lose situation, even if one wins the lawsuit and gets benefits, it is difficult to gain respect from others, so it is more appropriate to give up the effort of this kind of litigation subjectively.

良心是心念发动之根本,从孟子到王阳明都有类似说法,康德的说法也近似,如你必须如此行事,你的这种行为方式可以作为所有人的行动典范。意即当下意念发动之际,内心所依从的道德律可以成为所有人行事的法则。康德没有以"仁"来定义,但要求在意念动处包容所有人的心念,这就是当下一念能涵纳天下大同的意向境遇。只有以大同的意向境遇才能够终止诉讼,否则一般的诉讼对双方的意向发展来说就是两败俱伤,应该避免。虽然个人的意向转换和努力并不能保证他人也能够如此放弃争讼,但多少能够感应和影响到对方,如果对方继续争讼,而自己着力止讼,争讼的意向可以在一念之间停止下来,这样,化解争讼最后变成制念的艺术。

Conscience is the foundation for the initiation of intentions. From Mencius to Wang Yangming, there are similar sayings, and Kant's statements are also similar. If you must act like this, your principle of behavior should serve as a model for everyone. This means that when intentions are initiated, the moral law obeyed by the heart can become the law for everyone to act. Kant did not define this in terms of "benevolence", but required that everyone's intentions be included in the movement of intentionality. This is the intentional situation in which one intention at one moment can contain the world's unity. Only with intentions in great harmonious situation can a lawsuit be terminated. Otherwise, ordinary litigation will be a lose-lose situation for both parties' intentional development and should be avoided. Although personal change of intention and hard work cannot guarantee that others will give up a lawsuit, it can somehow induce and influence the other party. If the other party continues to litigate, and you work hard to stop the lawsuit, the intention to litigate can be stopped in a moment. In this way, resolving disputes finally becomes the art of controlling thought.

地水师（卦七）　（坎下坤上）

Shi (Leading), Earth and Water (Hexagram 7)　(Kan below, Kun above)

　　师卦在处理矛盾的过程当中，无疑比讼卦更进一步，不仅仅处理个人的意念，为了更大的利益，可以武装他人的思想，进而达到控制和改变他人的肉体力量的目的，形成合力用战争的方式去摧毁另一方的集体利益。但这种利益之争，师卦告诉人们要"贞"，也就是走正道，替天行道，否则，为了个人或者小集体的私利而争，从长远看并不好。

　　《周易》有很多论述心意斗争艺术的内容。人的意向性既有其存在论、宇宙论、伦理学上的各种哲学意义，更有人与天的心意之间的冲突与斗争的意义。而且，心意之间的斗争，成为依于天时而动的开端，坎（水）为天一生水之所，故坎为意念之行动，使得意念带出了世界全体的存在与变化。

In the process of dealing with conflicts, Hexagram Shi (Leading) undoubtedly goes further than Hexagram Yi (Nourishment). It not only deals with personal intentions, but also can wield the intentions of others for greater benefit, thereby achieving the purpose of controlling and changing the physical strength of others, forming a joint force like war to destroy the collective interests of another party. But in this kind of struggle for interests, Hexagram Shi tells people to be steadfast, that is, to follow the right *dao* and do justice for the world. Otherwise, fighting for the selfish interests of individuals or small groups will not be good in the long run.

The *Book of Changes* contains a lot of content discussing the art of mental and intentional struggle. Human intentionality not only has various philosophical meanings in ontology, cosmology, and ethics, but also has the meaning of conflict and struggle between the intentions of humanity and heaven. Moreover, the struggle between intentionality and the heart-mind becomes the beginning of the movement according to the temporality of heaven. Trigram Kan (Water) is the place where the heavenly One creates water, so Kan is the action of intention, which brings out the existence and changes of the entire world.

师，贞。丈人吉，无咎。

《彖》曰：师，众也。贞，正也。能以众正，可以王矣。刚中而应，行险而顺，以此毒天下，而民从之，吉又何咎矣。

《象》曰：地中有水，师。君子以容民畜众。

【明译】

师卦象征领兵打仗，善守正道，有德望、有经验的英明统帅领导军队，就能吉祥而不会有什么灾祸。

《彖传》说：师是部属众多；贞是善守正道。如果善于带领众多的部属行走正道，就是率领正义之师，就可以成为王者施行王道。内心刚健中正（九二）又有人（六五）响应，从事危险之事，行进在险难中，因顺合正道而能顺利。凭借这样的优势去"荼毒"天下，而人民心甘情愿跟随他去干，势必吉祥，又会有什么咎害呢？

《象传》说：上卦坤为地，下卦坎为水，地中有水就是师卦。君子从地中蕴藏大量的水当中得到启示，要像大地蓄水一样蓄聚民力，广容百姓，爱护群众。

Hexagram Shi (Leading) symbolizes leading troops in war, steadfastly adhering to the right *dao*, and leading the army with a wise and experienced commander, which will bring good fortune and no disaster.

The *Judgment Commentary* (*Tuan Zhuan*) says: A leader means having many subordinates; being steadfast means being good at keeping to the right *dao*. If one is good at leading many subordinates to follow the right *dao*, one is a leader leading with justice, and one can become a king and execute the kingly way. The inner heart-mind is strong and upright, the Nine (*yang*/strong line) in the second place, and there are people, the Six (*yin*/soft line) in the fifth place, responding to it. If you engage in dangerous affairs and travel in danger, you will be able to go smoothly because you follow the right *dao*. Even if using such an advantage makes the world suffer, if the people are willing to follow you, it is bound to be auspicious, so what harm will there be?

The *Image Commentary* (*Xiang Zhuan*) says: The upper Trigram Kun is earth, the lower Trigram Kan is water, and water in the earth is Hexagram Shi (Leading). An exemplary person is inspired by the large amount of water contained in the earth, and one must gather the power of the people, tolerate the people, and care for the people just like the earth stores water.

第二章　易经明意
——爻意分说（上经）

【明意】

战争为境的一种，需要认真面对。战争需要走正道（贞），有正当性，是王道的体现，而不是彰显霸权，不为了纯粹的输赢或武力的征服，更不为了两败俱伤的恶性竞争，而必须能够兼顾每个人的尊严，将心比心，才能够没有过失。打仗是带领众人走正道，所以能够成就王侯的功业。战争领导人（丈人）的心念必须绝对端正，不能够有一点偏失，否则对于军队（师）的影响非常巨大，因为师的心念对情境有绝对的塑造作用，所以要非常小心。统帅的心念发动是否出于公义，而不是为了私人和党派的利益，对于战争的结果非常关键。

[Illuminating Intentionality]

War is a situation that needs to be faced seriously. War needs to be on the right *dao* (steadfast), be legitimate, and be a manifestation of kingship rather than hegemony. It is not for sheer victory or defeat or conquest by force, let alone vicious competition that hurts both sides, but must be able to take into account everyone's dignity. Only by comparing one's heart to others' can one avoid making mistakes. Fighting is to lead people on the right *dao*, so one can make the achievements of kings and princes. The intentions of the war leaders (divisions) must be absolutely correct and cannot be a little biased, otherwise it will have a huge impact on the army (troops), because the intentions of the division have an absolute role in shaping the situation, so be very careful. Whether a commander's intentions are motivated by justice, rather than for personal and partisan interests, is very critical to the outcome of a war.

初六：师出以律，否臧凶。

《象》曰："师出以律"，失律凶也。

【明译】

初六：出师打战全凭军律严明，军律不良必然凶险。

《象传》说：出师打战必须纪律严明，如果失去军纪的约束必将招致凶险。

Six (*yin*/soft line) in the first place: Going out to fight depends on strict military discipline. Poor military discipline will inevitably lead to danger.

The *Image Commentary* (*Xiang Zhuan*) says: When going out to fight, you must have strict discipline. If you lose the restraint of military discipline, you will definitely be in danger.

【明意】

集中意向性需要遵守一定规律和法则。就军队而言，没有良好的纪律，出兵打仗凶多吉少。拿孙子操练宫女的例子来说，人之意向性合力决定身位，决定身体运动的方向。就军队的操练来说，士兵必须听从命令，以不同程度的惩罚，甚至肉体消灭来保证个体意向性朝集体意向性（通常也是统帅的意向性）方向发展。

141

[Illuminating Intentionality]

Concentrating intentionality requires observing certain rules and laws. As far as the army is concerned, without good discipline, sending troops to fight will be worse than disaster. Take the example of Sunzi training the palace maids. Human intentionality works together to determine the body's position and the direction of bodily movement. As far as military training is concerned, soldiers must obey orders and varying degrees of punishment or even physical destruction must be used to ensure that individual intentionality develops in the direction of collective intentionality (usually the commander's intentionality).

九二：在师中吉，无咎，王三锡（cì）命。

《象》曰："在师中吉"，承天宠也。"王三锡命"，怀万邦也。

【明译】

九二：在三军中位，吉祥，没有咎害，君王三次赐命嘉奖。

《象传》说：军中统帅持中守正就可以获得吉祥，因为承受了天子的宠信。君王多次通令嘉奖，是因为（君王）志在平定天下万国。

Nine (*yang*/strong line) in the second place: In the middle position among three armies, it is auspicious and without any fault. The king gives orders and rewards three times.

The *Image Commentary* (*Xiang Zhuan*) says: The commander-in-chief of the army can gain good fortune by holding to the center and keeping upright, because he has received the favor of the emperor. The king issues orders and commendations many times, because he (the king) aspires to pacify all nations in the world.

【明意】

为了战争的胜利，领导人需要任命合适的将领，他有能力通过有限的资源整合众人意向的合力，如何使得众心聚合形成战力是一门艺术。领导者将有限的资源分配给重要的将领，让有能力的将领来整合人心，而将领统帅队伍的权力，自然来自领导人的授权。

《周易》哲学帮助人们通过阴阳之意领会到心通物境，也就是心意与物原初未分的境域。从分别甚至斗争的心意状态回复到和谐未分的状态，要在意向性活动当中认识意会到相当不易。

[Illuminating Intentionality]

In order to win a war, leaders need to appoint suitable generals who have the ability to integrate everyone's intentions through limited resources. How to unite everyone's intentions to form military power is an art. Leaders allocate limited resources to important generals, allowing capable generals to integrate people's intentions, and the power of generals to command their team naturally comes from the leader's authorization.

The philosophy of the *Book of Changes* helps people understand the realm of intentionality and material things through the intentionality of *yin* and *yang* powers, that is, the realm where intentionality and things/events are not originally separated. It is quite difficult to realize and actualize in intentional activities a return from a mental state of separation or even struggle to a state of harmony and undividedness.

六三：师或舆尸，凶。
《象》曰："师或舆尸"，大无功也。
【明译】
六三：军队很可能会载运尸体回来，非常凶险。
《象传》说：领兵仗打的结果极有可能是一车一车的尸体从战场上运回来，说明彻底败北，无功而返。

Six (*yin*/soft line) in the third place: One will probably carry corpses back, which is very dangerous.
The *Image Commentary* (*Xiang Zhuan*) says: The result of leading the army into battle is very likely to be carts of corpses brought back from the battlefield, indicating a complete defeat and returning without success.

【明意】
本爻涉及意识存在与肉体的关系（身心问题）。只要意向性介入世界，就必须要面对不同意向性之间的矛盾征战。人的意向性的生成状态决定人无法通过意识的分判来回避矛盾，否则就只有消弭意识，而这对于有生机的机体来说基本上是不可能的，除非等肉体存在的力量彻底消失，意识就不再进入世界，也就从矛盾状态当中退出，不再分别，不再计较。

意向性活动以肉体性的存在为前提，但战争消灭的不仅仅是肉体，而更重要的是打垮集体的精神。只要肉体存在，意识绵延，意向性就在对待之中，也常处于交战状态。战争从来都是凶险无比的，战争是一种将生命都押上的赌博，双方都要随时做好一无所有的准备，是意向性之间针锋相对你死我活的状态。《孙子兵法》提出要"慎战"，即使赢家从来通吃，但付出的巨大代价使得战争的赢家很难说就是真正的赢家。

[Illuminating Intentionality]
This line involves the relationship between conscious existence and the physical body (the mind-body problem). As long as intentionality intervenes in the world, it must face the conflict between different intentionalities. The generative state of human intentionality determines that people cannot avoid contradictions through conscious judgments, otherwise they can only eliminate consciousness, which is basically impossible for a living organism, unless the power of physical existence completely disappears. Consciousness no longer enters the world and withdraws from a contradictory state, no longer distinguishing or caring.

Intentional activities presuppose the existence of physicality, but war destroys not only the physical body, but more importantly, the collective spirit. As long as the body exists and consciousness endures, intentionality is being handled and is constantly in a state of war. War has always been extremely dangerous. It is a gamble in which lives are staked, and both sides must be prepared to lose everything at any time, in a tit-for-tat confrontation between intentionalities and life or death. *The Art of War* (*Sunzi Bingfa* 孙子兵法)proposes to start a war only with caution. Even if the winner always takes all, the huge price paid by the winner makes it difficult to say that the winner of a war is a real winner.

六四：师左次，无咎。

《象》曰："左次无咎"，未失常也。

【明译】

六四：部队退后驻扎，没有灾祸。

《象传》说：率领部队撤退，当退则退，说明六四并没有失去用兵的常道。

【明译】

Six (*yin*/soft line) in the fourth place: The troops retreat and are stationed, and there is no disaster.

The *Image Commentary* (*Xiang Zhuan*) says: Leading the troops to retreat, retreating when necessary, this shows that the Six (*yin*/soft line) in the fourth place did not lose the normal way of using troops.

【明意】

《周易》不回避人与人之间的矛盾，也不回避矛盾无法解决，只能用战争的方式，即消灭意向性从不排斥消灭肉体作为意识存在根基的暴力方式，这是一种现实主义的眼光，是人文主义和理想主义情怀无法改变现实，而不得不使用的最后策略。

人生如棋局，意向的活动如战场，这是师卦揭示的人生境遇之真理。人生意向的修炼，以及意向性的层级与意能量的高低，成为修行的根本要素。意向活动都在矛盾当中，在矛盾中意向方能展开。对于矛盾展开的状态，有些时候需要退却来冷观，以便看清楚矛盾的状态，寻找意向重新介入矛盾的时机。本爻说明，承认在一定条件下对矛盾作出退让也是一种合理的解决方式，当然这是基于对矛盾双方的状态和情境加以领悟，知道退让以等待时机，以备东山再起。

[Illuminating Intentionality]

The *Book of Changes* does not avoid conflicts among groups of people, nor does it avoid conflicts that cannot be resolved except through war. That is, the elimination of intentionality does not exclude the violent method of eliminating the body as the foundation of consciousness. This is a kind of realism. This vision is the last resort strategy that humanism and idealism have to use when they cannot change reality.

Life is like a chess game, and the activities of intentionality are like a battlefield. This is a truth about life situations revealed by Hexagram Shi (Leading). The cultivation of life's intentions, as well as the levels of intentionality and intentional energy, have become the fundamental elements of cultivational practice. Intentional activities are all in contradiction, and it is in contradiction that intentions can unfold. Regarding the unfolding state of conflicts, sometimes it is necessary to retreat and take a cold look, in order to see clearly the state of the conflict and look for opportunities to re-intervene in the conflict. This line explains that it is recognized that making concessions to conflicts under certain conditions is also a reasonable way to resolve conflicts. Of course, this is based on understanding the status and situation of both parties to the conflict, knowing how to give in and waiting for the opportunity to prepare for a comeback.

六五：田有禽。利执言，无咎。长子帅师，弟子舆尸，贞凶。

《象》曰："长子帅师"，以中行也。"弟子舆尸"，使不当也。

【明译】

六五：打猎时在田地当中遇到来祸害的禽兽，可以率军仗义执言地猎获，有利，没有咎害。君王任命长子（德高望重的长者）带兵打仗好，但如果任命弟子（品德不高的人）带兵打仗，就会载尸败归。六五如果正固不动有凶。

《象传》说：任命长子（德高望重的长者）成为军中主帅，是行施中道（六五在上卦中位）。如果任命弟子（品德不高的人）为统帅，就会载尸败归，因为所用非人（六三不是长子）。

Six (*yin*/soft line) in the fifth place: If one encounters a beast that causes harm in the fields while hunting, one can lead one's army to hunt it out righteously and without any harm. It is good for the king to appoint his eldest son (a virtuous and highly respected elder) to lead the army in war, but if he appoints his disciples (people with low moral character) to lead the army in war, he will be defeated with corpses. If the Six (*yin*/soft line) in the fifth place is upright and rigid, there will be misfortune.

The *Image Commentary* (*Xiang Zhuan*) says: Appointing the eldest son (a virtuous and highly respected elder) to be the commander-in-chief of the army is a way of practicing the middle way, (the Six (*yin*/soft line) in the fifth place is in the middle of the upper Trigram). If a disciple (a person with low moral character) is appointed as the commander-in-chief, he will be defeated because he is not the correct person, (the Six (*yin*/soft line) in the third place is not the eldest son).

【明意】

战争发动之后，用什么手段彰显正义，用什么人为将帅，都非常关键。打仗要师出有名，禽兽有害，正好又是田猎的对象，自然可以师出有名。师动的名分包括讨伐行动的名分和帅兵打仗的人的名分，二者都很重要。因为打仗需要名正言顺，领兵也要名正言顺，也就是帅师之人的名分必须正当。

君王有决定是否打仗的自由，更有决定由何人去领兵打仗的自由，明智的君王知道如何运用好这种自由，对于何种人适合于何种场景能够做到知人善任。一场成功的战争，不可能纯粹为了某种兴趣，也不可能仅仅为了参与者的利益，而必然是一种天时地利人和的因缘和合，各种心力的完美聚合。对于拿生命冒险的事业，其实没有多少现实的利益能够鼓动大家，所以必须有超越个人现实利益的崇高目标才能够感动人为之献身，如赶走侵略者，建立一个新国家等等。

[Illuminating Intentionality]

After the war is launched, it is very critical to consider what means to use to demonstrate justice and who to use as the general. In battle, one must have a good reputation. Animals are harmful, and they happen to be the targets of field hunting, so naturally one can have a good reputation for leading against them. The status of a division leader includes the status of a crusader and a person who leads troops in battle, both of which are important. Because fighting requires a good name, and leading troops also requires legitimacy, that is, the person who leads the army must have a good name and reasonable position.

The king has the freedom to decide whether or not to go to war, and he also has the freedom to decide who will lead the troops in the war. A wise king knows how to make good use of this freedom, and can know who is suitable for a certain situation. A successful war cannot be purely for some kind of interest, nor can it be just for the benefit of the participants. It must be a combination of causes and conditions, the right time, the right place and the right people, and the perfect aggregation of various mental efforts. For a cause that risks one's life, there are actually not many realistic interests that can inspire everyone. Therefore, there must be a lofty goal that transcends personal real interests to move people to devote themselves to it, such as driving away invaders, establishing a new country, etc.

上六：大君有命，开国承家，小人勿用。

《象》曰："大君有命"，以正功也。"小人勿用"，必乱邦也。

【明译】

上六：天子得到宗庙祖先的神启和命令，要给功臣封侯，建立家祠，但品德不良的小人绝不可重用。

《象传》说：先王有命令，要论功行赏，正当奖赏有功之臣，但绝对不能重用品德不良的小人，因为分封小人必会危乱邦国。

Six (*yin*/soft line) in the top place: The emperor received a divine revelation and order from the ancestors of the ancestral temple and wanted to grant marquis-ships to meritorious officials and build ancestral halls, but petty people with bad moral character must not be given prominent positions.

The *Image Commentary* (*Xiang Zhuan*) says: The former king had an order to reward meritorious officials and ministers appropriately. However, petty people with bad morals must not be valued, because enfeoffing petty people will certainly endanger the country.

【明意】

在人生当中的某些特殊时刻，如祭祀或者特别成功的状态，可能特别感恩先祖，当时所有意向性似乎都收摄到先人那边，成为在天之灵的意向性，回到意与宇宙不分的原始混沌状态之中，并笼罩在整个家族成员之上。心意完成使命之后，应当有一种宗教性的感恩情怀，知道人在世间的努力皆要天道的庇佑和天时的配合、情境的顺应才可能，都与天时的能量不能分开。《周易》是利用天时，让天时配合意念之行的艺术。

[Illuminating Intentionality]

At certain special moments in life, such as sacrifices or a state of particular success, you may be particularly grateful to your ancestors. At that time, all intentionality seems to be absorbed by the ancestors, becoming the intentionality of the spirits in heaven, and returning to the place where intention is inseparable from the cosmos. In a state of primitive chaos, it enveloped the entire clan of family members. After this intentionality has completed its mission, there should be a religious feeling of gratitude, knowing that human efforts in this world require the blessing of heaven and the cooperation of heaven and earth. Only with adaptation to situations is this possible, and these are inseparable from the energy of heavenly temporality. The *Book of Changes* is the art of making use of heavenly temporality, and making this coordinate with the flow of intentions.

水地比（卦八） （坤下坎上）

Bi (Affinity), Water and Earth (Hexagram 8)　(Kun below, Kan above)

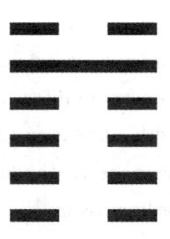

　　主动亲比的人要真心实意地顺从被亲比的人，把自己意境的一部分交出去，顺从被亲比者来调控自己的意境，相信对方的经验和智慧。被亲比的主人也要检验自己的意境是否能够得到民众的回应，"民"是否尊重自己。"主"人的意境能够保持一定的影响力需要通过"民"的意境的回应来判断。权力意识来自亲比的艺术，如果一个人的意识能够与掌权者的意识相通，得到其认可，彼此亲和，则其意识的生发，就超越了个体的存在，具有整体情境的意味，如果亲比有术，个体的意识境域就可能不断增长，这就是权力和优势地位可能帮助个人意识扩张，使其意识境域达到更广大的境地。

　　权力意识来自比附的意识，是因为只有在比附的过程中才会出现强弱贫富的分殊，处在强势的一方必然会产生权力意识。比附也加强了不平等的权势，进而强化分配不均和贫富分化。人的社会化是对其自然差异意义上的不平等的强化，导致权力和制度安排上的不平等。《易》不去追求纯粹理想化的平等，而是从现实意义上不平等的意识出发，寻找和建构可能的、合理的沟通方式和包容亲比的意识融通境域。

　　Those who take the initiative to be friends should sincerely obey the person they want to make friends with, even hand over part of their own intentional context, obey the person and ask for regulation of their own intentional context, and trust the experience and wisdom of the other person. The host who is being befriended also needs to test whether the host's intentional context can be responded to by the people and whether the people really respect the host. Whether the intentional context of a leader can maintain a certain influence needs to be judged by the response of the intentional context of the people. The consciousness of power comes from the art of affinity. If a person's consciousness can communicate with the consciousness of the person in power, be recognized by the person, and gain reciprocal intimacy, then the development of the individual's consciousness will transcend the existence of the individual, and possess the intentionality of the overall situation. If the affinity is skillful, the individual's realm of consciousness may continue to grow. This is how power and dominant position may help an individual's consciousness expand and reach a broader realm.

The consciousness of power comes from the consciousness of making friends, because only in the process of making friends can the distinctions between the strong, weak, rich and poor appear, and the stronger party will inevitably have a sense of power. Being friends also strengthens unequal power, thereby strengthening uneven distribution and polarization between rich and poor. The socialization of people is the reinforcement of inequality in the sense of their natural differences, leading to inequalities in power and institutional arrangements. The *Book of Changes* does not pursue a purely idealized equality, but starts from the awareness of inequality in a practical sense to find and construct possible and reasonable communication methods and an inclusive and compatible realm of consciousness.

比，吉。原筮，元永贞，无咎。不宁方来，后夫凶。

《彖》曰：比，吉也；比，辅也，下顺从也。"原筮，元永贞，无咎"，以刚中也。"不宁方来"，上下应也。"后夫凶"，其道穷也。

《象》曰：地上有水，比。先王以建万国，亲诸侯。

【明译】

比卦象征亲近比辅，团结亲密，自然吉祥。（建国之初用占卜）推原真情，筮占厚意，占决推举一个能够永久持守正道的有德君长作为亲比的对象，帮助大家自始至终持守正道，这样就没有咎害。形势从不安宁状态中刚转过来，那些觉得不安宁者赶紧多方前来亲比，而迟迟不来亲比的就会有凶险了。

《彖传》说：亲比团结自然吉祥。比是在下者心甘情愿归顺辅佐在上者。推原真情，筮占厚意，占决而推举出一个能够永久持守正道的有德君长作为亲比的对象，从而能够让大家都自始至终持守正道，这样就没有咎害，因为主爻九五占据上卦中位，象征着有刚健中正之德的君长。感受不到安宁者多方前来亲比，因为上下（九五与六二上下正应，与初六、六四都亲比）心意相通，彼此响应。迟迟不来亲比的人（上六）有凶险了，因为已处在穷困之中，无路可走。

《象传》说：上卦坎为水，下卦坤为地；卦象显示的是地上有水，这就是比卦。开国的先王从水附大地，地水无间，地纳江河之象中得到启示，要封邦建国，亲合诸侯，继以亲民。

Hexagram Bi (Affinity) symbolizes closeness, friendship, solidarity and intimacy, and is naturally auspicious. (Divination was used in the early days of founding a state) to deduce true feelings, predict good intentions, and choose a virtuous ruler who can permanently uphold the right *dao* as the object of affinity to help everyone keep the right *dao* from beginning to end, so that there will be no blame. The situational propensity has just turned from an uneasy state. Those who feel uneasy quickly come and share their affinity, and those who delay coming to share their affinity with each other will be in danger.

The *Judgment Commentary* (*Tuan Zhuan*) says: "Affinity and solidarity are naturally auspicious." This means that those below are willing to submit and assist those above. Infer the true feelings, take advantage of the kindness, and choose a virtuous monarch who can always uphold the right *dao* as the object of friendship, so that everyone can stick to the right *dao* from beginning to end. In this way, there will be no blame, because the main line Nine (*yang*/strong line) in the fifth place occupies the middle position of the upper Trigram, symbolizing a strong and upright ruler. People who cannot feel peace come to visit in many ways, because the upper and lower parts—the Nine (*yang*/strong line) in the fifth place and Six (*yin*/soft line) in the second place correspond to each other, and share affinities with both Sixes (*yin*/soft lines) in the first and fourth places—are connected in intentionality and respond to each other. Those who delay coming to see each other, the Six (*yin*/soft line) in the top place, are in danger because they are already in poverty and have no way out.

The *Image Commentary* (*Xiang Zhuan*) says: The upper Trigram Kan is water, and the lower Trigram Kun is earth; the hexagram image shows that there is water on the ground, which is Hexagram Bi. The founding kings of the country were inspired by the image of water surrounding the earth, the earth and water being inexhaustible, and the earth being connected to rivers. They wanted to establish a state, ally with the princes, and then with the people.

【明意】

比卦强调亲比的人天之意。儒家王道伦理是一种对等伦理，不讲绝对服从，而强调双向关系。亲比的应该是人与人之间心境与品德，而不是身外之物。人必然要与他人一起生活，那么，人的意境也必然时刻处在与他人意境的沟通和协同过程当中，可谓无时不比。

古代王国建立（草创）靠推举，大家认可某人德行的情况下，推举他作为群体的领导，这跟主动要求他人支持自己的现代选举制很不相同。当一个人意识到自己的意境可以亲比于某个君子，就尽可能地追随和顺从他。被追随者应该做到"元永贞"，就是自始至终要保持正道，有良好的节操，美好的修养，高尚的德行，在自己的意境里包容他人，给予他人足够的尊重，从而得到别人的拥护和爱戴。

[Illuminating Intentionality]

Hexagram Bi (Affinity) emphasizes the intentionality of close friendship between humanity and heaven. Confucian kingly ethics is a reciprocal ethics that does not emphasize absolute obedience but rather two-way relationships. A friendship should be about the state of intentionality and character between people, not things beyond them. People must live with others, so people's intentional context must always be in the process of communication and coordination with other people's intentional context. It can be said that this is always the case.

Ancient kingdoms were established (founded) by recommendation. When everyone recognized someone's virtue, they elected him as the leader of the group. This is very different from the modern electoral system in which people actively ask others to support them. When a person realizes that one's intentional context shares an affinity with that of an exemplary person, one should follow and obey the person as much as possible. Followers should be always be loyal, that is, they must maintain the right *dao* from beginning to end, have good moral integrity, good cultivation and noble virtue, tolerate others in their own intentional context, and give others enough respect, so as to gain the support and affection of others.

初六：有孚，比之，无咎。有孚盈缶，终来有它吉。

《象》曰："比之"初六，"有它吉"也。

【明译】

初六：心怀诚信，心甘情愿地去亲比他，不会有咎害。诚信充满如盈满的水盆，最终来亲比，终会有格外的吉祥。

《象传》说：连初六那么远都来亲比，说明九五领导的邦国已经会有非同一般的吉祥。

Six (*yin*/soft line) in the first place: Be sincere and be friends with him willingly, and there will be no harm. Integrity is like a full water basin. When you finally come to be friends with each other, it will be extraordinarily auspicious.

The *Image Commentary* (*Xiang Zhuan*) says: Even coming from as far away as the Six (*yin*/soft line) in the first place, it shows that the country led by the Nine (*yang*/strong line) in the fifth place already has extraordinary auspiciousness.

【明意】

比卦初六讨论心意的诚信与其时空场域，落脚点在王道和远方。初六说明王道传播很远的强盛邦国之状态。信任是双方顺从天地生机运化而成事，心意与人与物的能量交流互动处于正向的状态，意念必然要发生于一定情境之中，有些时候需要归属或者比附领导。人与人之间意念的感通有选择性，不仅是独立思维和感应而已。最典型的意念比附是主动向着领导者的意向行动，可谓寻找意向的伙伴，而人的意识行动都需要寻找伙伴，通过伙伴的意识境域来放大自身的意境。

[Illuminating Intentionality]

For the Six (*yin*/soft line) in the first place, we discuss the integrity of intentionality and its temporal and spatial fields, focusing on the kingly way and distant places. The Six (*yin*/soft line) in the

151

first place illustrates the state of a strong and prosperous country where the kingly way spreads far and wide. Trust is a result of both parties obeying the vitality of heaven and earth. The energy exchange and interaction between intentionality and people and things are in a positive state. Ideas must be generated in certain situations, and sometimes it is necessary to belong to or follow the leader. The communication of intentions between people is selective and is not just about independent thinking and induction. The most typical form of ideological friendship is to take the initiative to act toward the leader's intentions, which can be said to be looking for a partner of intention. People's conscious actions need to find partners, and to amplify their own intentional context through the consciousness realm of their partners.

六二：比之自内，贞吉。

《象》曰："比之自内"，不自失也。

【明译】

六二：从内而外，真诚亲比，持守正道吉祥。

《象传》说：发自内心地、真诚地亲比九五，说明自己贞守正道，没有失误（六二位中又正）。

Six (*yin*/soft line) in the second place: From the inside out, be sincere and friendly, and uphold the right *dao* in auspiciousness.

The *Image Commentary* (*Xiang Zhuan*) says: Comparing oneself to the Nine (*yang*/strong line) in the fifth place sincerely from the bottom of one's heart shows that one is on the right *dao* and has made no mistakes (the Six (*yin*/soft line) in the second place is also central and upright).

【明意】

本爻关乎心意真诚的分寸与力量。意念行动是一连串对于意念发动的决断和决定，其中最为重要的是分寸，分寸是意念发动和把握的关键所在。从内部向九五表达内心的忠诚，即使当位也要讲究方式和时机。意境的扩大来自内心对事件把握的分寸感。越有分寸感，把握得越到位，就越有力量。

[Illuminating Intentionality]

This line is about the sense of proportion and strength of sincerity. Thoughtful action is a series of decisions about initiating intentions, the most important of which is sense of proportion. Sense of proportion is the key to initiating and grasping intentions. Express your inner loyalty to the Nine (*yang*/strong line) in the fifth place from within, and pay attention to method and timing even when in the right position. The expansion of intentional context comes from the inner sense of proportion in grasping events. The more sense of proportion one has and the better one's grasp is, the more powerful one will be.

六三：比之匪人。

《象》曰："比之匪人"，不亦伤乎？

【明译】

六三：亲比的不是该亲比的而是行为失正的人。

《象传》说：亲比于不仁不义，行为不端的人，是找错亲比的对象，怎么不是令人伤叹的事呢！

Six (*yin*/soft line) in the third place: Those who are being befriended are not those who should be befriended, but those who behave inappropriately.

The *Image Commentary* (*Xiang Zhuan*) says: The affinities built are with inhumane and unjust reople, and people are looking for the wrong person to find affinities with. How can this not be sad?

【明意】

亲比是要把自己的意识境遇跟自己意境中的领导人沟通，如果不跟领导沟通，而仅跟周围人沟通，就容易出问题。因为情境的领导人对被领导者的意境有相当大的影响和决定作用。对于情境中的个人来说，要慎重选择亲比的对象，在大家都亲比九五的形势下，如果去亲比附近的人，就是不理解形势，会给自己带来伤害。

[Illuminating Intentionality]

The purpose of affinities is to communicate your own conscious situation with the leaders in your own intentional context. If you do not communicate with the leaders, but only communicate with the people around you, problems will easily arise. Because the situational leader has a considerable influence and determination on the intentional context of the led, for individuals in the situation, you should carefully choose the person you want to find affinities with. In a situation where everyone is befriending the most superior, if one befriends people nearby, one will not understand the situation and will cause harm to oneself.

六四：外比之，贞吉。

《象》曰："外比"于贤，以从上也。

【明译】

六四：向外亲比团结外面的人，守正吉祥。

《象传》说：向外亲比是亲比到贤人身上，是主动亲随上面贤明领导（九五）的心志。

Six (*yin*/soft line) in the fourth place: Be friendly and unite with people outside, and all will be upright and auspicious.

The *Image Commentary* (*Xiang Zhuan*) says: Befriend those in the outside world is to come close to wise people, and to take the initiative to follow a wise leader above (the Nine *yang*/strong line) in the fifth place).

【明意】

就本爻的状态来说，阴爻当位而承刚，基本吉祥，表示弱势者处于相对合适的地位和采用柔性的意向策略，可能得到合适的亲比对象和状态，有扩展自身的意识境遇，增强意向行为的能力。在一定的时空能量场域当中，如果时空行为受到比较明显的外在条件限制，或者因为这些条件，使得意向行为看起来似乎被先行决定。

[Illuminating Intentionality]

As far as the state of the original line is concerned, the *yin* line is in position and supports the strong, which is basically auspicious, since it means that the weak are in a relatively suitable position and adopt flexible intentional strategies. They may obtain suitable objects and states of friendship and expand their own consciousness, enhancing their ability of intentional behavior. In a certain space-time energy field, if the spatio-temporal behavior is restricted by relatively obvious external conditions, or because of these conditions, intentional behavior seems to be determined in advance.

九五：显比。王用三驱，失前禽，邑人不诫，吉。

《象》曰："显比"之"吉"，位正中也。舍逆取顺，"失前禽"也。"邑人不诫"，上使中也。

【明译】

九五：九五象征光明无私而最明显地得到大家拥护的亲比对象。君王用三驱之礼狩猎，网开一面，让前面跑得快的禽兽逃走。国邑里的人看到君王如此仁慈，不惊怕，不警戒，这样自然吉祥。

《象传》说：九五刚爻居刚位位正，在上卦中位，德行中正，以身作则让大家诚心拥护。对愿意归顺的留下，不愿归顺的任他自去，不强迫他们，好像网开一面，舍去逆我而来的猎物，猎取顺我而逃的猎物。百姓看到君王的心意如此中正仁慈，便不心存警戒，也可以说是下面的阴爻愿意拥戴九五上去居于中位，作为大家归附的核心。

Nine (*yang*/strong line) in the fifth place: The Nine (*yang*/strong line) in the fifth place symbolizes the bright and selfless person who is most obviously supported by everyone. The king hunts with the gift of three drives, opening the net to one side to let the fast animals in front escape. When people in the country see that the king is so kind, they are not frightened or watchful, which is naturally auspicious.

The *Image Commentary* (*Xiang Zhuan*) says: The Nine (*yang*/strong line) in the fifth place is in the right position, in the middle of the upper Trigram Kan, has upright virtues, and leads by example so that everyone can sincerely support it. Keeping those who are willing to submit, and letting go those who are unwilling to submit, without forcing them, is like opening a net to let go of the prey that goes against me, while hunting the prey that escape in my way. When the people see that the king's intentions are so upright and benevolent, they do not feel wary. It can also be said that those below were willing to support the Nine (*yang*/strong line) in the fifth place to occupy the middle position as the core of everyone's allegiance.

【明意】

心意的分寸后来成为礼制的起源。当然不是平常人的心意分寸都可以成为礼制的起源，《易》认为，领导人（九五）的心意分寸能成为礼制的起源。领导人的意向性对情境领悟的分寸与尺度可以实化为规范性的条理，从而成为礼制的发源点，如将"显比"理解为众人来朝贡的显赫之比，当比的意境达到最顶峰的状态，周围自然生成一种约束思想意识与行为的礼制与分寸。

一个人从学习他人到被他人学习，这种意识境遇的转换是很明显的。被亲比的人需要有很好的修养才能够成为他人的典范，如果被亲比的人没有明确的自我意识，不能够调整自己的意识境遇，那就不能很好地引导周围的意境形成合力。

[Illuminating Intentionality]

Sense of proportion of intentionality later became the origin of ritual propriety. Of course, not ordinary people's will and proportion can be the origin of ritual propriety. The *Book of Changes* believes that leaders' (the Nine (*yang*/strong line) in the fifth place) intentions and proportion can be the origin of ritual propriety. The leader's intentionality and scale of situational understanding can be transformed into normative order, thus becoming the origin of ritual propriety. For example, manifesting affinity can be understood as the ratio of prominence when people come to pay tribute. When the intentional context of affinity reaches a peak state, there is a natural ritual propriety and proportion around you that restricts your intentions and behaviors.

The transformation of a person's consciousness from learning from others to being learned from by others is obvious. The person being befriended needs to be well-educated to become a role model for others. If the person being befriended does not have a clear self-awareness and cannot adjust his or her own conscious situation, then he or she cannot guide the surrounding intentional context well to form a synergy.

上六：比之无首，凶。

《象》曰："比之无首"，无所终也。

【明译】

上六：想亲比依靠但找不到首领，这样就会有凶祸。

《象传》说：上六想亲比依靠，但如果不能真心以领导的心意为首来配合领导，就不会有什么好结果。

Six (*yin*/soft line) in the top place: If you want to rely on someone but cannot find the leader, there will be disaster.

The *Image Commentary* (*Xiang Zhuan*) says: The Six (*yin*/soft line) in the top place wants to find affinities with others and rely on them, but if you can't really cooperate with the leader based on the leader's intentions, there will not be any good results.

【明意】

人的心意因时势的逼迫有时不得不作出唯一的选择。虚情假意可能得一时的现实利益，但最后肯定不好。上六自己的时位不合适，在比卦的大势之中要亲比，可是亲比九五却得不到。可谓虽然作了亲比的姿态，但得不到亲比的效果，反而可能有凶祸。

人对自己和领导人的意识境遇之间关系的判断，不完全受自己理性分析和选择的支配。当然，通常不能真心地以领导的心意为首，并配合领导的带领，就难以有好结果。

[Illuminating Intentionality]

People's intentions are sometimes forced to make the only choice due to the propensities of the times. Hypocrisy may gain temporary practical benefits, but it will definitely not be good in the end. The time of the Six (*yin*/soft line) in the top place is not suitable. In the general propensity of Hexagram Bi, it wants to be friends with another, but cannot get it with the Nine (*yang*/strong line) in the fifth place. It can be said that although the gesture of friendship is made, the effect of affinity is not achieved, and it may be harmful.

People's judgments about the relationship between themselves and their leaders' conscious situations are not entirely governed by their own rational analysis and choices. Of course, if you cannot truly put the leader's intentions first and cooperate with the leader's leadership, it will be difficult to achieve good results.

第二章　易经明意
——爻意分说（上经）

风天小畜（卦九）　（乾下巽上）

Xiaoxu (Small Savings), Wind and Heaven (Hexagram 9)   (Qian below, Xun above)

　　通过亲比，人必然可以有所积蓄，扩大意识之境与他人结盟，意识扩大之后收获的是权力的影响和利益的扩大，也就是都有所积蓄。人与动物的根本区别就在意识的积蓄和沉淀增长。人有记忆，能够从经验当中反思积累，通过反思和梳理意识的秩序，可以让人的人天之意的意识流逐渐清晰有序。当意识流经过梳理，进入记忆，即可成为积蓄的意能，因为意识存在于天地之间，如果意识能够从天地之间梳理出一个有序状态，那么梳理意识的过程本身，其实就是梳理天地秩序，即给天地建立秩序的过程。

　　天行而风起，世间之物生长发育，意识如巽风，风过物长而有所积蓄。天意行于天地之间，有如风行大地，百物复苏，自然成长，自然物生生不息相当于天的心意不断积累，万物皆因意而有阴阳之化，文明之教。人用人天之意转化理解天地自然之意，而后有人天之意逐步累积。文明的起源、生成和创造来自人天之意小有积蓄的状态。

　　Through affinity, people are inevitably able to accumulate something, expand their consciousness and form alliances with others. What they gain after the expansion of consciousness is the influence of power and the expansion of interests, that is, everyone has accumulated something. The fundamental difference between humans and animals lies in the accumulation and growth of consciousness. People have memories and can reflect and accumulate from their experiences. Through reflection and sorting out the order of consciousness, people's stream of consciousness of human-heavenly intentionality can

157

gradually become clearer and more orderly. Once the stream of consciousness is sorted out and entered into memory, it can become accumulated intentional energy, because consciousness exists between heaven and earth. If consciousness can sort out an orderly state between heaven and earth, then the process of sorting out consciousness itself is actually sorting out the order of heaven and earth, the process of establishing order for heaven and earth.

As the sky moves and the wind rises, things in the world grow and develop. Consciousness is like the wind, which passes by and things grow and accumulate. Cosmological intentionality moves between heaven and earth, just like the wind moves on the earth, and all things revive and grow naturally. The endless generation of natural creatures is equivalent to a continuous accumulation of cosmological intentionality. Because of intentionality, all things are ordered into *yin* and *yang* transformations and the teachings of civilization. Humans use the cosmological intentionality of humanity and heaven to transform and understand the intentionality of heaven, earth and nature, and then the intentionality of humanity and heaven gradually accumulates. The origin, generation and creation of civilization all come from a state of small savings of the intentionality of humanity and heaven.

小畜，亨。密云不雨。自我西郊。

《彖》曰：小畜，柔得位而上下应之，曰"小畜"。健而巽，刚中而志行，乃亨。"密云不雨"，尚往也。"自我西郊"，施未行也。

《象》曰：风行天上，小畜。君子以懿文德。

【明译】

小畜卦象征小有积蓄，亨通。天空密布浓云，却不降雨，乌云从我西边的郊外升起来。

《彖传》说：小畜卦，柔爻六四取得合适位置，上下五个刚爻都来跟它应合，好像把它们蓄积在一起，所以称"小有积蓄"。下卦乾为健，上卦巽为顺风，不但刚健而且有顺风相助，而且上下卦中位都是刚爻，意味着内心刚健，心志能够得到推行。因此可以亨通。"天空密布浓云，却不降雨"，因为柔爻没有力量蓄积足够的阳气，聚拢了一点却没有下雨的实效，好像风把云吹往天上去了，还得继续往上吹。"乌云从我西边的郊外升起来"是说天上飘来密布的浓云，但雨却降不下来，犹如蓄聚了一点恩泽，想要施布，却没有到真正付诸行动的时候。

《象传》说：上卦巽为风，下卦乾为天，小畜卦就是和风在天上飘行的卦象。君子看到乌云密布、等待下雨这样的卦象，就要效法天象，不断美化文彩，修养品德，以待时机。

Hexagram Xiaoxu (Small Savings) symbolizes small accumulation and prosperity. The sky is densely clouded, but there is no rain. Dark clouds are rising from my western suburbs.

The *Judgment Commentary* (*Tuan Zhuan*) says: In Hexagram Xiaoxu (Small Savings), the Six (*yin*/soft line) in the fourth place is in the right position, and the five *yang* lines above and below all come to respond to and join with it, as if they are accumulated together, so it is called "small savings." The lower Trigram Qian is strength, and the upper Trigram Xun is wind, so it is not only strong but also supported by a favorable wind. Moreover, the middle positions of the upper and lower Trigrams are both strong lines, which means that the heart is strong and the intentions can be carried out, and, therefore, one can prosper. "The sky is densely covered with clouds, but there is no rain." This is because the soft line does not have the power to accumulate enough *yangqi*. It gathers a little but has no actual effect of rain, like the wind has blown the clouds to the sky but has to continue to blow upwards. "Dark clouds are rising from my western suburbs" means that there are dense clouds in the sky, but the rain cannot fall, like accumulating a little kindness and wanting to give it out, but it being not yet time to take action.

The *Image Commentary* (*Xiang Zhuan*) says: The upper Trigram Xun is wind, the lower Trigram Qian is sky, so Hexagram Xiaoxu (Small Savings) is the image of a gentle wind floating in the sky. When an exemplary person sees a hexagram such as dark clouds and waiting for rain, one must imitate the celestial phenomena, constantly improve one's cultural background, cultivate his character, and wait for an opportunity.

【明意】

人之异于动物的地方，就在于知道心意通于天地的几微意识的变幻，能够领悟、理解并积累记忆。人类文明的创始之初，就是心意的沉淀和积累，比身外之物的积累重要得多。在乎身外之物，人的意识就可能成为外物的奴隶，人羡慕财富，贪恋外物，甚至展开侵占他人的行动，人难以抵制物欲的诱惑，是人性之恶的发展，所以征服物欲当是修行的开始。能够征服物欲、惩恶扬善的君子，如果有合适的时位就可以做圣人。可见，心意对事物的控制，是否有能力择善固执，不断积累善言善行，是一个修养之善恶的重要分界线，也是文明是否可以正常生长发育的重要分节点。

[Illuminating Intentionality]

What makes humans different from animals is that they know the subtle changes in consciousness that connect intentionality to heaven and earth, and are able to comprehend, understand and accumulate memories. The founding of human civilization is an accumulation of intentionality, which is much more important than the accumulation of things outside the body. If people care about external things, their consciousness may become a slave to external things. People envy wealth and covet external things, which may even lead to actions that encroach on others. It is difficult for people to resist the temptation of material desires, which are a development of the evil in human nature, hence conquering material desires should be a spiritual practice. An exemplary person who can conquer material desires, punish evil and promote the good can become a sage if the time is right. It can be seen that the intentions' control over things, the ability to choose the good and persist in it, and the continuous accumulation of good words and good deeds are important dividing lines between good and evil in cultivation, and also an important node in whether or not a civilization can grow and develop normally.

初九：复自道，何其咎？吉。

《象》曰："复自道"，其义吉也。

【明译】

初九：（心念发动出错了）赶快返回自身阳刚之道，哪里会有什么咎害？这样做必定吉祥。

《象传》说：初九意识到心念发动出了偏差，赶快调整过来，复返自身阳刚正道，从道理上讲初九这样做是合适的，肯定会吉祥。

Nine (*yang*/strong line) in the first place: (When the act of initiating intentionality goes wrong) Quickly return to your own *yang*/strong way, then where can there be any harm? Doing so is bound to be auspicious.

The *Image Commentary* (*Xiang Zhuan*) says: As the Nine (*yang*/strong line) is in the first place, when you realize that your intentionality has gone awry, you should adjust it quickly and return to your own *yang*/strong and righteous *dao*. Logically speaking, doing this as the Nine (*yang*/strong line) is in the first place is appropriate and will definitely bring good fortune.

【明意】

意识的调适，最后都要反求诸己，通过自己对意识的反身判断来调整，来评判意识的方向是否合理。人是否能够参与文明社会，根子上来自于对正道意识发动状态的锤炼。

君子面对几微未起的状态，对其所在的情境不能够有明显的把握和领会，这时应该蓄养意识之力，如果急于发动意识，可能往往不在合理的道中，需要自己重新找到合理的自道，多做自我反省和修炼的功夫。

[Illuminating Intentionality]

The adjustment of consciousness must ultimately turn to oneself and adjust through one's own reflexive judgment of consciousness to judge whether or not the direction of consciousness is reasonable. Whether a person can participate in civilized society fundamentally comes from tempering the initiative state of righteous consciousness.

An exemplary person faced with a subtle state that has barely risen cannot have a clear grasp and understanding of the situation. At this time, one should cultivate the power of consciousness. If one is eager to initiate the consciousness, it often may not arise in a reasonable way and one may need to find a reasonable *dao* again by doing more self-reflection and cultivational practice.

九二：牵复，吉。

《象》曰："牵复"在中，亦不自失也。

【明译】

九二：受到牵引，能返回正道，吉祥。

《象传》说：九二受到六四的引诱和牵引，但因为在中位，受到牵引而反思，觉得还是要走中道为好，所以没有大失误。九二在下卦中位，行为中正，自己没有过失。

Nine (*yang*/strong line) in the second place: Being pulled and able to return to the right *dao*, auspicious.

The *Image Commentary* (*Xiang Zhuan*) says: The Nine (*yang*/strong line) in the second place was tempted and pulled by the Six (*yin*/soft line) in the fourth place, but because one was in the middle, one was pulled and reflected, feeling that it was better to take the middle *dao*, so one did not make a big mistake. The Nine (*yang*/strong line) in the second place is in the middle position of the lower Trigram, and one's behavior is upright, so one has no fault.

【明意】

被牵引离开正道，和被牵引返回正道，理解虽然不同，但道理可通，即人的心思意念离开正道，往往受到外物牵引，被诱惑而迷失自己的本心，离开本来之道。初九自己可以返回，而九二可以理解为被牵引返回，被师长、朋友或者其他的意念牵引返回，回到自己本来正常发展的意识境遇和道路之中。文明的教化无非就是被动教化和主动学习，但被动教化需要意识的内化机制加以转化，而主动学习是自己作出努力接受牵引以改变原有的意识境域。

海德格尔在《存在与时间》当中，提到人在时间之中要面对的"上手"状态，也就是人必然与他人与他物打交道的状态，是人不可能逃避的、与他人他物共在的状态，心念无法不与他人他物发生关系而独立存在，人的心思意念必然在"上手"状态当中，也就必然在牵引和牵绊当中。人都希望自我决定自己的心思意识，但却无时无刻不在各种关联与缠绕当中，不可能逃避，而只有面对，这时候选择非常重要，接受牵引还是反对牵引，成为关键性选择。如果能够在中道状态去面对，就不会自我迷失太远，而如果被牵引而迷失，就有点可惜。可见，意识发动和存在之延续可谓步步艰险、难乎其难。

[Illuminating Intentionality]

Although there are different understandings of being led away from the right *dao* and being led back to the right *dao*, the truth is common. That is, when people's thoughts and intentions leave the right *dao*, they are often pulled by external objects, and they are tempted to lose their original intention and leave their original way. The Nine (*yang*/strong line) in the first place can return by itself, and the Nine (*yang*/strong line) in the second place can understand that it is being led back by teachers, friends, or other intentions, back to its own normally developing conscious context and path.

161

Civilizing education is nothing more than passive education and active learning, but passive education requires the internalization mechanism of consciousness to be transformed, while active learning requires one's own effort to accept being led to change the original realm of consciousness.

In *Being and Time*, Heidegger mentioned the state of being "ready-to-hand" that people have to face in time, that is, a state in which people must deal with other people and other things, in which it is impossible for people to escape from other people and things. In a state of coexistence with things, intentions cannot exist independently without being related to other people and other things. People's intentions and minds must be in a "ready-to-hand" state, and they must be pulled and tied. Everyone hopes to self-determine their own intentionality and consciousness, but they are always involved in various relationships and entanglements which are impossible to escape, but can only be faced. At this time, one's choice is very important, and accepting or opposing the pull becomes a key choice. If one can face it in the middle *dao*, one will not lose oneself too far. However, it would be a pity if one is led and lost. It can be seen that the initiation of consciousness and the continuation of existence are both difficult and dangerous steps.

九三：舆说（tuō）辐。夫妻反目。

《象》曰："夫妻反目"，不能正室也。

【明译】

九三：大车辐条脱落解体，犹如夫妻反目失和。

《象传》说：夫妻反目失和，说明丈夫（九三）不能规正妻室，把家庭关系理顺。

Nine (*yang*/strong line) in the third place: The spokes of the cart fall off and disintegrate, just like a husband and wife turning against each other.

The *Image Commentary* (*Xiang Zhuan*) says: A husband and wife are at odds with each other, which means that the husband (the Nine (*yang*/strong line) in the third place) cannot regulate his wife in the family and straighten out the family relationships.

【明意】

人与人之间心意的开闭分合，阴意与阳意的交流虽是常态，但也有不通的时候。意识发动的力量受到自己内在力量的把握，有些人很刚强，导致意识发动比较强悍，但如果遇到对方也很强悍，就往往不愿妥协，导致二者分离背向。意识境域相反可以说是因为对自我意识境遇的过度坚持而导致的，往往在一方坚持的时候，另一方也可能因此更加不愿妥协，于是彼此的意识境域越离越远。

人要超越自己所在的历史时势以及各种外在的条件谈何容易。心念无论如何坚实坚强，也在各种外在条件的约束之中，难以真正有所超越。文明的发展都是在心意不合的竞争和斗争过程当中展开的，是在斗争的历程上不断发展进步的，而有所积蓄需要通过不同的意识之争才能够继续丰富和发展。

[Illuminating Intentionality]

Although the opening and closing of intentions between people and the exchange of *yin* and *yang* powers are normal, there are also times when things fail to connect. The power of consciousness initiation is controlled by one's own inner strength. Some people are very strong, which leads to stronger consciousness initiation. However, if they meet another party who is also very strong, they are often unwilling to compromise, causing the two to separate and turn away. Contrary states of consciousness can be said to be caused by excessive insistence on a state of self-awareness. Often when one party insists, the other party may be more unwilling to compromise, so the two parties' states of consciousness become further and further apart.

It is not easy for people to transcend their own historical situation and various external conditions. No matter how solid and strong their intentionality is, it is still constrained by various external conditions and cannot truly transcend it. The development of civilization is carried out in the process of competition and struggle between minds. It is constantly developing and progressing in the process of struggle, and accumulation requires the struggle of different consciousnesses to continue to enrich and develop.

六四：有孚，血去，惕出，无咎。

《象》曰："有孚惕出"，上合志也。

【明译】

六四：有阳刚真诚相助，得以离开流血之灾，从遗留下来的忧惧中走出，没有太大的影响。

《象传》说：上天（九五）以诚信感化助人（六四），帮人（六四）离开了流血之灾，走出了恐惧的阴影，说明向上与九五（天子）心志相合。

Six (*yin*/soft line) in the fourth place: With *yang*/strong line's sincere help, one is able to escape the bloody disaster and walk away from the remaining worries without much impact.

The *Image Commentary* (*Xiang Zhuan*) says: Heaven (the Nine (*yang*/strong line) in the fifth place) influences people (the Six (*yin*/soft line) in the fourth place) with integrity and helps people (the Six (*yin*/soft line) in the fourth place) escape the disaster of bloodshed and walk out of the shadow of fear, which shows that the Six (*yin*/soft line) in the fourth place and the Nine (*yang*/strong line) in the fifth place (the emperor) have the same aspirations.

【明意】

意识之间的应和，与互助、本性、时势、利益等有关，不同时空状态中有不同的沟通状态。六四阴爻当家做主，得天下男人之钟情于一身，是文德教化、柔顺中正的贵妇之象，其意识境遇性的展开，能够容蓄天下人心而有万种风情。

六四在众阳之中，犹如四两拨千斤，从小而柔弱的意识出发，力图思考进而拨动大的形势，其比较合理的方式是顺应外在阳意的合力，结合成柔顺但有力量的形势，这样可能拨动全局。这与抽象思考时间与空间的西方哲学家的思路很不一样，因为《周易》中时空的相互转化是能量的互动，而且可以越来越有力量。

[Illuminating Intentionality]

The correspondence between consciousnesses is related to mutual assistance, original nature, temporal propensity, interests, etc. There are different communication states in different temporal and spatial states. The Six (*yin*/soft line) in the fourth place is the mistress of the house and is loved by men the world over. She is the image of a noble lady who is enlightened by literature and virtue, and is tender and upright. The development of her consciousness and context can accommodate the intentions of all people in the world and have countless styles.

Among all the *yang*/strong lines, the Six (*yin*/soft line) in the fourth place is like four ounces pulling a thousand pounds. Starting from a small and weak consciousness, we try to think and move a big situation. The more reasonable way is to comply with the combined force of the external *yang* and combine with it into a supple but powerful situation, one which may change the overall situation. This is very different from the thinking of Western philosophers who think abstractly about time and space, because the mutual transformation of time and space in the *Book of Changes* is an interaction of energy, and it can become more and more powerful.

九五：有孚挛如，富以其邻。

《象》曰："有孚挛如"，不独富也。

【明译】

九五：自己心怀诚信，跟群阳携手，一起拳拳系恋一阴，与近邻共同分享阳刚之富实。

《象传》说：自己心怀诚信，跟群阳携手，一起拳拳系恋一阴，说明九五不独自享受阳刚之富实。

Nine (*yang*/strong line) in the fifth place: With integrity in your heart, join hands with the *yang* group, love the *yin* sincerely together, and share the wealth of masculine strength with your neighbors.

The *Image Commentary* (*Xiang Zhuan*) says: With sincerity in one's heart, one joins hands with the group of *yang* lines and together they sincerely love the *yin*, which shows that the Nine (*yang*/strong line) in the fifth place does not enjoy the wealth of one's strength alone.

【明意】

"富以其邻"是财富分配的艺术，让邻居们（阳爻）享受到财富的好处和分配的正义，更重要的是，在分配的过程中，感受到"有孚挛如"，好像如一家人见面之后要紧紧握住家人的手，体会到那种深情厚谊。这是把国家、社会财富的分配归结到家庭情感的中心上面，也就是全社会应该要像一家人那样分配和共享财富，也要让被分配的人觉得自己受到了家人的待遇，感受到分配者的深厚情谊。

　　社会当中富有的人愿意主动分配财富，对于道德系统的建立和完善有风向标的作用。罗尔斯在《正义论》中设定了无知之幕，但这种理想化的设定，虽然近似科学和几何的公理起点，有某种超越的原则的意味，但离开现实的状态很远。《周易》说明社会财富的合理分配，最后还要回到人的良心原点，无论是分配者还是被分配者，都不可能离开良心意识来单独讨论社会正义的问题。这一爻象征文明的成就性状态，首先是富有，其次是领导人富而有礼，乐善好施，促进全社会的礼乐教化，形成互助友爱、公平公正的文明社会氛围。

　　[Illuminating Intentionality]

　　"Sharing richness with one's neighbors" is the art of wealth distribution, so that one's neighbors (*yang* lines) can enjoy the benefits of wealth and the justice of distribution. More importantly, in the process of distribution, they can feel close feelings, as if after a family meeting, one holds the hands of one's family members tightly and experiences deep friendship. This is to attribute the distribution of national and social wealth to the emotional center of the family. That is to say, the whole society should distribute and share wealth like a family, and the people who are distributed to should feel that they are being treated by their family and feel the deep affection of those who distribute.

　　Wealthy people in society are willing to actively distribute wealth and play a role as a bellwether for the establishment and improvement of the moral system. Rawls set up a veil of ignorance in *A Theory of Justice*, but this ideal setting, although it is close to the axiomatic starting point of science and geometry, and has some intentionality of transcendent principles, is far from reality. The *Book of Changes* explains that the reasonable distribution of social wealth must ultimately return to the origin of human conscience. Neither the distributor nor the recipient can discuss the issue of social justice alone without conscience. This line symbolizes an achieved state of civilization: first of all, wealth, and secondly, leaders who are wealthy and polite, willing to do good, promote the ritual propriety and education of the whole society, and form a civilized social atmosphere of mutual aid, friendship, fairness and justice.

　　上九：既雨既处，尚德载，妇贞厉。月几（jī）望，君子征凶。

　　《象》曰："既雨既处"，德积载也。"君子征凶"有所疑也。

　　【明译】

　　上九：密云已经降了雨，也停了（阳刚被释放，阴阳已经安然相处）。（得到物质滋养之后），是应该崇尚积累道德的时候了。妇女（在阳卦上位置不正）需要持守正道以防危险，要像月亮将圆而不盈满，君子此时如果还盲目进取和追求（物质财富），会（像月满则亏一样）有凶险。

　　《象传》说：密云已经降了雨，也停了（阳刚被释放，阴阳已经安然相处）。（物质满足之后），现在是积累道德的时候了。君子此时如果还盲目地进取和追求（物质财富），就会被其周遭的情境所质疑。

Nine (*yang*/strong line) in the top place: The dense clouds have rained and stopped (masculine strength has been released, and *yin* and *yang* now coexist peacefully). (After receiving material nourishment,) it is time to advocate accumulation of morality. Women (who are not in the right position on the *yang* trigram) need to stay on the right *dao* to avoid danger, just like the moon when it is about to be round but not yet full. If an exemplary person is still blindly enterprising and pursuing (material wealth) at this time, he will meet with danger (like the moon when it is full and begins to wane).

The *Image Commentary* (*Xiang Zhuan*) says: The dense clouds have rained and stopped (the masculine strength has been released, and *yin* and *yang* now peacefully coexist). (After material satisfaction,) now is the time to accumulate morality. If an exemplary person is still blindly enterprising and pursuing (material wealth) at this time, he will be questioned by the situation around him.

【明意】

一个人有挑战世俗标准的心念，有可能成就大事，也可能铸成大错。一个安分守己的人，不能够有多少成就，一个独辟蹊径的人，既可能成就大事，但也可能越走越窄。所以，对于心思意念之动，需要谨慎小心，应该既能够让它升起，也能够让它消灭，要掌控自己做心动和意识的主人，让心意做欲望和物质的主人，才是心灵之动的合理方向。

事情皆起自心灵之几微之动。心念几微之成事，在于心灵之动能够运作外物，形成形势。风在天上，几微难测，风云变幻，心力能够运作风雨，有些时候，可以要风得风，要雨得雨，时间之转换，时势之万变，迅捷异常，令人吃惊。心灵之力量，时势之变化，起于几微，发于毫末，却不可不察。《孙子兵法》谈及时势，其实时势来自心念之动，而营造形势，也来自心念之力。物质力量不断流转，忽然出现又忽然消失，精神力量长远而巨大。心力的修为是心灵改天换地的艺术，是真正的力量之源。

[Illuminating Intentionality]

A person who has the intention to challenge worldly standards may achieve great things or make big mistakes, while a person who keeps to oneself will not be able to achieve much. A person who takes a unique path may achieve great things, but one may also take a narrower path. Therefore, we need to be cautious about the movements of our intentions and minds. We should be able to let them rise and disappear. We must control ourselves to be the masters of our intentional movements and consciousness, and let our minds be the masters of desires and matter. This is the reasonable direction for movement of the heart-mind.

Everything starts from the slightest movement of the heart-mind. The success of a few intentions in intentionality lies in the fact that the movement of intentionality can manipulate external objects to form a situation. Wind is in the sky, and wind is unpredictable. The wind and clouds are changing, and intentionality can control the wind and rain. Sometimes, one can get wind when you wants wind, and rain when one wants rain. The changes of time and situational propensity are fast and surprising. The power of the heart-mind and the changes in temporal propensity arise from a few moments and occur at the smallest moment, but they cannot be ignored. *The Art of War* talks about temporal propensity. In fact, temporal propensity comes from the movement of intention, and the creation of a situation also comes from the power of the mind. Material power is constantly flowing, appearing and disappearing suddenly, while spiritual power is long-lasting and huge. The cultivation of mental power is the art of changing intentions, and it is the real source of power.

天泽履（卦十）　（兑下乾上）

Lü (Tracking), Heaven and Lake (Hexagram 10)　(Dui below, Qian above)

　　人稍微有积蓄，开始崭露头角，反而犹如随时会踩到老虎尾巴一样危机四伏，必须小心谨慎。因为走向文明、保持成功，和刚想成功的开始状态有所不同。履卦希望人们知道要履危而安，也要富而有礼，这其实有"伴君如伴虎"的延伸意味，也就是他人作为自己的心灵意识对象，并不非常了解自己作为意识发动的主体，因此要对他心他意心存尊敬与感念，意念发动之后，当时刻做好退回自己分限的准备，承认自己身体的有限性和精神意识境域的有限性，因为逾越边界可能非礼或无礼，意量可能减弱，导向意识发动的反面。

　　礼的存在是对天地自然本来秩序的模仿，礼其实是人的意量的外化。认识与理解世界的意愿要落实在建构人自身与宇宙关系的秩序上。正如康德在《纯粹理性批判》当中所论证的：时间是一种先验结构，帮助人们整合感性杂多，知性在此基础上才能通过范畴和判断等来理解世界。这种认识世界的过程需要建构一个与世界先验结构对应的内在时空范畴判断结构，并认为它与我们认识的世界有着一致性的先天结构。

　　People who have small savings and start to stand out are faced with dangers like stepping on the tail of a tiger at any time, so they must be cautious, because becoming civilized and maintaining success are different from the initial state of wanting to succeed. Hexagram Lü (Tracking) hopes that people will know that they should be secure in danger, but also rich and polite. This actually has an extended meaning of "accompanying a ruler is like accompanying a tiger," that is, others are the objects of their own spiritual consciousness, and do not fully understand themselves as subjects of consciousness. Therefore, we must respect and be grateful for other people's wills and intentions. After initiating our intentions, we should always be prepared to return to our own limits and acknowledge the limitations of our bodies and spiritual consciousness, because crossing the boundaries may be disrespectful or improper. Intentional power may weaken, leading to the opposite of conscious initiation.

The existence of ritual propriety is an imitation of the original natural order of heaven and earth, but in fact, ritual propriety is an externalization of human intentionality. The intention to know and understand the world must be implemented in the order of constructing a relationship between humanity and the cosmos. As Kant argued in the *Critique of Pure Reason*: Time is a transcendental structure that helps people integrate perceptual complexity, and on this basis, intelligence can understand the world through categories and judgments. This process of understanding the world requires the construction of an internal space-time category judgment structure that corresponds to the a priori structure of the world, and believing that it is consistent with the transcendental structure of the world we know.

履虎尾，不咥（dié）人，亨。

《彖》曰：履，柔履刚也。说而应乎乾，是以"履虎尾，不咥人，亨"。刚中正，履帝位而不疚，光明也。

《象》曰：上天下泽，履。君子以辨上下，定民志。

【明译】

履卦象征小心行事，踩到了老虎的尾巴，老虎却没有回头咬人，亨通。

《彖传》说："小心行事"，柔爻礼遇刚爻（犹如应对刚猛之虎，需以阴柔之道来小心行事）。下卦兑为悦，上卦乾为天，内心和悦顺应刚健，所以才能"踩到了老虎的尾巴，老虎却没有回头咬人，亨通"。帝位上的九五是刚爻，居上卦乾的中位，阳爻居阳位位正。九五登上皇帝之位问心无愧，因为心地和行为都正大光明（上卦乾为白昼，故光明）。

《象传》说：上卦乾为天，下卦兑为泽，天在上，泽在下，履卦象征着这种自然的秩序。君子学习履卦乾天刚健在上，兑泽柔顺承之而有礼的卦象，要深明大义，分辨上下名分，安定民心，守礼有序。

Hexagram Lü (Tracking) symbolizes acting with caution, stepping on a tiger's tail, but the tiger does not turn around and bite, so all is prosperous.

The *Judgment Commentary* (*Tuan Zhuan*) says: "Be careful when proceeding" means the soft line is polite in meeting a strong line (just like dealing with a fierce tiger, you need to be careful and gentle). The lower Trigram Dui is joy, the upper Trigram Qian is heaven, so the heart is harmonious and strorg, and it is possible to "step on a tiger's tail, but the tiger does not turn around to bite, and all is prosperous." The Nine (*yang*/strong) line in the fifth place represents the emperor's throne, occupying the middle position of the upper Trigram Qian, and the *yang* line is proper in a *yang*/upright position. When he ascends to the position of emperor, he has a clear conscience, because his heart and behavior are upright and bright (the upper Trigram Qian is day, so it is bright).

The *Image Commentary* (*Xiang Zhuan*) says: The upper Trigram Qian is sky, and the lower Trigram Dui is lake, the sky above and the lake below. Hexagram Lü (Tracking) symbolizes this natural order. An exemplary person learns from the upper Trigram Qian in Hexagram Lü (Tracking) meaning Tian, which is strong and bright above, and Trigram Dui being gentle and polite, inferring from this that one must have a deep understanding of righteousness, distinguish the status of superiors and inferiors, stabilize the people's intentions, and observe ritual propriety and order.

【明意】

人有所积蓄，有一定的社会地位，就可以践行、实化、扩展自己的心意，而心意的开端，很多人误以为是自我，其实当是天道，是天地阴阳之动。如果把个人心意都当作自己小我的发动，最后把周围存在都当作自己欲望和利益的实现过程，则最后成就的只是小我，无论小我多大，最后都会被天地的形势所淹没，因为一个人心意发动，天网恢恢，不出天道，应该在反身意识当中，能够洞若观火，明明白白，体会到私心发动不可能逃脱天道整体的范围。

[Illuminating Intentionality]

Once people have some savings and a certain social status, they can practice, realize, and expand their intentions. However, many people mistakenly think that the beginning of their intentions is the self, while it should in fact be the heavenly *dao*, the movement of *yin* and *yang* in heaven and earth. If one regard one's personal intentions as the motivation of one's own ego, and finally regard the surrounding existence as the realization process of your own desires and interests, then only one's limited ego will be achieved in the end. No matter how big this ego is, it will eventually be overwhelmed by the situation of heaven and earth, because when a person's intentionality is initiated, the heavenly net is wide and does not go beyond the heavenly *dao*. In reflexive consciousness, one should be able to see the fire clearly and understand clearly that it is impossible for selfishness to escape the scope of the heavenly *dao* as a whole.

初九：素履，往无咎。

《象》曰："素履"之"往"，独行愿也。

【明译】

初九：按平素的做法小心行事，独来独往，没有咎害。

《象传》说：保持自己纯朴的本性，不失本色地谨慎行动，专心努力想去实现自己的意愿。

Nine (*yang*/strong line) in the first place: Act cautiously as usual, go alone, and there is no harm.

The *Image Commentary* (*Xiang Zhuan*) says: Keep your simple nature, act cautiously without losing your true character, and work hard to concretize your intentions.

【明意】

心志合于天道，我行我素，安心专注，纯朴地顺性而为，则意量自然通于自然之节度，也通于人间之礼仪。所以这种心意并非没有全境意识，更有通天的意识境遇在其中。心意合于天道有利于努力认识和理解存在的生机。如果人一开始的意向就真诚纯粹，意向活动不夹杂私欲污浊之意，那么，人意的本质就是天意，人行的本质就是天行。

[Illuminating Intentionality]

If my intentionality and will are in line with the heavenly *dao*, I will go my own way, be at ease and focused, and simply act according to my inherent nature, then my intentions will naturally be connected to the restraints of nature and the ritual propriety of the human world. Therefore, this kind of intentionality does not lack consciousness of the whole world, but also has the consciousness of continuity with heaven within it. The alignment of intentionality with the heavenly *dao* is conducive to striving to recognize and understand the vitality of existence. If people's intentions from the beginning are sincere and pure, and their intentional activities are not mixed with selfish desires and corrupt intentions, then the essence of human intentionality is heavenly intentionality, and the essence of human action is cosmological action.

九二：履道坦坦，幽人贞吉。

《象》曰："幽人贞吉"，中不自乱也。

【明译】

九二：履进的道路平坦宽阔，即使如盲人在幽暗之中，只要持守正道前行也能吉祥。

《象传》说：即使如盲人在幽暗之中，只要持守正道前行也能吉祥，因为九二能够坚守中位不自乱阵脚。

Nine (*yang*/strong line) in the second place: The road ahead is smooth and wide. Even if one is like a blind man in the dark, you will be fortunate as long as you keep the right *dao*.

The *Image Commentary* (*Xiang Zhuan*) says: Even if one is like a blind man in the dark, as long as you stick to the right *dao*, you will be fortunate, because the Nine (*yang*/strong line) in the second place can stick to the middle position and not cause your own downfall.

【明意】

认识世界的核心是人的心意可与外在世界的秩序同构。安宁平和的意量可以实化为和谐有序的礼仪制度。潜幽的状态当中，心意从纷乱的杂事之中分离出来，从而形成对于世界秩序的本然意向性，这是心意之静能够如镜子一般映射出通于天地之结构的道理。

换言之，内心意念的平和中正是认识世界的核心状态。人世秩序有意建构在对天然秩序的先行了悟之基础上。一个人的意识了悟了先行结构，即使眼力不好、环境杂乱，也会自寻清幽之境，守住意识的中道，让世界的本相自然显现，这是事物变化通于人心先天自然结构在意向性活动中的显现。

[Illuminating Intentionality]

The core of understanding the world is that human intentionality can be isomorphic with the order of the external world. The intentionality of tranquility and peace can be realized in a harmonious and orderly system of ritual propriety. In a state of seclusion, intentionality is separated from chaotic affairs, and thus forms its original intentionality for the order of the world. This is the reason why the tranquility of intentionality can reflect the structure of heaven and earth like a mirror. In other words, inner peace is the core state for understanding the world. The order of the human world is intentionally constructed on the basis of a prior understanding of the natural order. When a person's consciousness understands this prior structure, even if one's eyesight is poor and one's environment is chaotic, one will still find a quiet place, keep the middle *dao* of consciousness, and let the true nature of the world appear naturally. This represents the continuity of the changes of things with the transcendental natural structure of human intentionality becoming actualized in intentional activity.

六三：眇（miǎo）能视，跛能履，履虎尾，咥人，凶。武人为于大君。

《象》曰："眇能视"，不足以有明也。"跛能履"，不足以与行也。"咥人之凶"，位不当也。"武人为于大君"，志刚也。

【明译】

六三：一只眼不好，还能看得见。拐子还能走路。在这种情况下，走路不利索，如果还踩在老虎尾巴上，就迟早会被老虎咬到，凶祸。有武力但缺乏仁德的军人（六三），自不量力，还要向帝位履进。

《象传》说：一只眼睛快瞎了，不能看得很清楚，没法辨明事物。脚跛了，不能像常人那样走路。踩在老虎尾巴上，有被咬到的危险，六三阴爻居阳位，位置很不妥当。有武力但缺乏仁德的军人，自不量力，想登上大君的宝位，虽为柔爻，但心志比刚爻还刚强。

Six (*yin*/soft line) in the third place: One eye is bad, but I can still see. The lame can still walk, but only with difficulty. If you still step on a tiger's tail, you will be bitten by the tiger sooner or later, which is a disaster. A soldier who has force but lacks benevolence (the Six (*yin*/soft line) in the third place) does not know his own capabilities, but still strives for the throne.

The *Image Commentary* (*Xiang Zhuan*) says: One eye is almost blind and cannot see clearly or distinguish things. My feet are lame and I cannot walk like normal people. If you step on a tiger's tail, there is a risk of being bitten. The Six (*yin*/soft line) in the third place is in a *yang* position, which is very inappropriate. Soldiers who have force but lack benevolence do not know their own capabilities and want to ascend to the throne of the king. Although they are soft lines, their ambitions are stronger than those of strong lines.

【明意】

认识世界是在秩序基础上的有意识领会和强化。礼仪政治制度与人的心意秩序之间存在同构性，秩序的背后是力量，要有心力才能整合人生的秩序，使生活有序，而有序则必有心力；否则，无心力则必无序。但这种用意有力整治的分寸不易把握。在认识世界的开始时期，心意的量不足以认识世界存在的量，或者至少不匹配也无法应和天道的结构，所以要在每一念起念灭中尽力顺从天道，其中最重要的是放下对外物的执着，让意识与世界运行的本相自然感通，就可能洞见天道的本然结构。牟宗三认为，通过"智的直觉"可能认识康德所谓理性无法认识的"自在之物"。《易》也认为，人意通于天意的直觉性智慧说明意识可以在"幽"寂之中通达世界本来的自在状态。

[Illuminating Intentionality]

Understanding the world is conscious understanding and strengthening based on order. There is an isomorphism between the political system of ritual propriety and the order of people's intentions. Behind any order is power, as only with mental strength can we integrate the order of life and make life orderly. To be orderly, there must be mental strength, as without mental strength, there will be no sequence. However, it is difficult to grasp the appropriateness of this kind of effective regulation. At the beginning of understanding the world, the capacity of intentionality is not enough to understand the existence of the world, or at least it does not match or cope with the structure of the heavenly *dao*. Therefore, we must try our best to obey the heavenly *dao* in the rise and fall of every intention, in which the most important thing is to let go of external desires. The persistence of things allows consciousness to naturally connect with the true nature of the world's operation, and it is possible to gain insight into the natural structure of the heavenly *dao*. Mu Zongsan believed that through "intellectual intuition" it is possible to understand what Kant calls "things-in-themselves" that cannot be understood by reason. The *Book of Changes* also believes that the intuitive wisdom of human intentionality connecting with heaven's intentionality shows that consciousness can access the original free state of the world in "quiet" silence.

九四：履虎尾，愬愬（shuò），终吉。

《象》曰："愬愬，终吉"，志行也。

【明译】

九四：踩在老虎尾巴上，戒慎恐惧，终归能够吉祥。

《象传》说：戒慎恐惧，终归能够吉祥，说明处事小心谨慎，能够逐步推行自己的心志。

Nine (*yang*/strong line) in the fourth place: If you step on the tiger's tail, be careful and fearful, and you will be fortunate in the end.

The *Image Commentary* (*Xiang Zhuan*) says: Be careful and fearful, and it will eventually bring good fortune. This means that one can be careful and cautious in dealing with affairs, and one can gradually implement one's own aspirations.

【明意】

伦理学前提之一是人格平等，是把人当人的平等，不是人与人之间事实上的平等，因为事实平等客观上并不存在，事实上也难以实现。在不断面对和处理不平等的人世身份关系当中，需要知道自己心意所发，自然会穿越到自己耳目之外的远方，感应到那些眼不见耳不闻的，所以需要极度谨慎小心。

此爻说明在实践当中建立礼制要非常小心。礼顺人情，达时变，不是罗尔斯意义上"无知之幕"那样的理论假设，而是可在实践当中检验和修正的体系。而礼制背后是人意通达天意的结构，这个结构古往今来为儒家圣哲一再重复，如孟子的"万物皆备于我"，程颢的"仁者浑然与物同体"，王阳明的"心外无物"等，都说明人的意量能够感通于天下万物。既然人的意识所及之量度可能通达所有存在物，那么人在意识当中所建立的秩序和制度，确实可以通达天地本然的先行结构。

[Illuminating Intentionality]

One of the prerequisites of ethics is equality of personality, which is the equality of people as human beings, not a *de facto* equality between people, because *de facto* equality does not exist objectively and is difficult to achieve in fact. In the midst of constantly facing and dealing with unequal status relationships in the world, one needs to know that anything arising from one's intentions will naturally travel far beyond one's own ears and eyes, resonating with things that cannot be seen or heard, so one must be extremely cautious.

This line shows that great care must be taken in establishing ritual systems in practice. Ritual propriety obeys human feelings and adapts to the changing times. It is not a theoretical assumption like the "veil of ignorance" in Rawls' sense, but a system that can be tested and modified in practice. Behind any ritual propriety system is the structure of human and cosmological intentionality, a structure that has existed throughout the ages. As has been constantly repeated by Confucian sages, including Mencius' "all things are prepared in me," Cheng Hao's "the benevolent fuse to form one body with things," and Wang Yangming's "there is nothing outside the mind," human intentionality can be affectively continuous with the myriad things in the world under heaven. Since the capacity of human consciousness can reach all existing things, the order and systems established by human consciousness can indeed reach the original prior structure of heaven and earth.

九五：夬履，贞厉。

《象》曰："夬履，贞厉"，位正当也。

【明译】

九五：果断刚决，小心行事，守正能防危厉。

《象传》说：独断专行，刚愎自用，不能灵活应对会有危险，说明九五位置中正，处尊得位，恃正可以决刚。

Nine (*yang*/strong line) in the fifth place: Be decisive, act with caution, and be upright to guard against danger.

The *Image Commentary* (*Xiang Zhuan*) says: Being arbitrary and self-willed, not being able to respond flexibly will be dangerous. This shows that the Nine (*yang*/strong line) in the fifth place is in the middle and upright, and the position is respected, and relying on uprightness can determine one's strength.

【明意】

领导人对于文明的成果如礼仪制度有信心，作为意量的实化已经在实践当中检验合格，就要果决地推广出去，才能扭转整个意识境域和社会风气。此刻的领导力所表现的文明系统，其实就是对天道的开发和解悟。引导人心认识世界要诉诸人心发动之前的结构，这是一种静寂之中心物融通、物我不二、心意与天地未分之前的先验结构。领导人意识到人心结构秩序可以融通于世界秩序之本相，在引导众人建构社会和文明秩序的过程中，除了顺应形势之外，还要小心引导众人意量整体性的流变。

[Illuminating Intentionality]

Leaders have confidence in the achievements of civilization such as systems of ritual propriety. As realizations of intentionality, these have been tested and qualified in practice, and must be promoted decisively in order to change the entire conscious realm and social atmosphere. The civilized system represented by leadership at this moment is actually the development and understanding of the heavenly *dao*. To guide human intentionality to understand the world, we must appeal to a structure before human intentionality is initiated. This is a transcendental structure in the center of silence in which mind and things are integrated, things and the self are not dual, and intentionality has not yet separated from heaven and earth. Leaders realize that the structural order of people's intentions can be integrated into the true structure of world order. In the process of guiding everyone to construct a social and civilized order, in addition to adapting to situational propensities, they must also carefully guide the overall change of everyone's intentionality.

上九：视履考祥，其旋元吉。

《象》曰："元吉"在上，大有庆也。

【明译】

上九：审视一路小心走来的行为，思索考察其间得失。回头看看（六三），大吉大利。

《象传》说：大吉大利在上位，一路小心走来实在不易，真是修来值得大喜庆祝的福气。

Nine (*yang*/strong line) in the top place: Examine the actions you have taken along the way carefully, and think about the gains and losses during the process. Looking back (at the Six (*yin*/soft line) in the third place), there is good fortune.

The *Image Commentary* (*Xiang Zhuan*) says: Good fortune and great benefit are found in the upper position. It is not easy to walk carefully all the way. It is really a blessing worthy of great joy and celebration.

【明意】

人所建立的文明世界和礼仪制度经历千难万险，终于通过实践检验，认真回顾起来，真是很了不起的成就，值得庆贺。如果人在世间建立的礼仪体系和文明系统，符合意念对生生不息的世界本相的领会，那真是非常不容易的事情。人间制度的建立者，在制度经历过血与火的考验，穿越时空延续下去的时候，都会有一种自己的意识量度合于世界本来量度的自我实现感。

《周易》认为，世界本相是生生之动态，不存在静止的、对象化世界作为意识之对象，这与西方把世界当作静物来分析其属性，而后试图把握全体的认识过程很不一样。天道可以体现在每时每刻的意念发动之间，即天道的生机表现在人仁爱之心的生成和保持上面。人顺着生生的仁心建构相对合理的接近世界本相的秩序。天道生生不息，仁心也生生不息，一刻不曾止息。只有内心的仁意自然而然地流露出来，才能够让心意通于天道。《周易》力图将人世的先行结构与天地的结构在心意发动处同构，而不刻意遵循某种超越的自然法原则。

[Illuminating Intentionality]

The civilized world and ritual propriety systems established by humanity have gone through many difficulties and dangers, and finally passed the test of practice. Looking back carefully, it is an amazing achievement that is worthy of celebration. If the ritual propriety and civilizational systems established by people in the world are to be in line with the mind's understanding of the true nature of the world as endless production and reproduction, this is truly not an easy matter. The founders of human systems will have a sense of self-realization when a system has experienced the test of blood and fire and continues through time and space.

The *Book of Changes* believes that the true nature of the world is dynamic, and there is no static, objectified world as the object of consciousness. This is very different from the Western cognitive process of analyzing the world as a still life and then trying to grasp it as a whole. The heavenly *dao* can be reflected in the initiation of intention at every moment, that is, the vitality of the heavenly *dao* is expressed in the generation and maintenance of human kindness and love. People follow their benevolence to construct a relatively reasonable order that is close to the true nature of the world. The heavenly *dao* is endless, and benevolence is also endless, never ending for a moment. Only when the benevolence in the heart is revealed naturally can intentionality be connected to the heavenly *dao*. The *Book of Changes* strives to make the prior structure of the human world isomorphic with the structure of heaven and earth at the point of initiation of intention, without deliberately following any transcendent natural law principles.

地天泰（卦十一）　（乾下坤上）

Tai (Communication), Earth and Heaven (Hexagram 11)　(Qian below, Kun above)

　　阴意与阳意和谐平衡之境，天地交泰。世间事情的泰与否都离不开意念的参与，是人的意志介入世间变化而分出存在物的泰与否，如果人的心意不参与世间的变化，事情自然变化，则无所谓泰否。

　　泰卦之境是君子之意境，君子来、小人去的意境。君子小人对待而存在，因为有小人，君子才显得是君子，所以君子不应该起把小人消灭干净的念头，因为消灭所有小人之一念起，就是小人境界了。但君子可以感化小人，让小人自己改变，参与共同建构一个太平的世界。

A state of harmony and balance between *yin* and *yang* powers, where heaven and earth are at peace. Whether things in the world are good or bad cannot be separated from the participation of intentionality. It is human will that intervenes in the changes of the world to determine whether things are good or bad. If people's intentions do not participate in the changes of the world and things change naturally, it does not matter whether they are good or bad.

The realm of Hexagram Tai (Communication) is the intentional context of the exemplary person, in which, when an exemplary person comes, a petty person goes. Exemplary people exist correlatively with petty people, since it is only because there are petty people that an exemplary person appears as an exemplary person. Therefore, an exemplary person should not have the intention of annihilating all petty people, because the intention of eliminating all petty people itself belongs to the realm of petty people. However, an exemplary person can influence petty people, let petty people change themselves, and jointly build a peaceful world with them.

泰，小往大来，吉，亨。

《彖》曰："泰，小往大来，吉，亨"，则是天地交而万物通也，上下交而其志同也。内阳而外阴，内健而外顺，内君子而外小人，君子道长，小人道消也。

《象》曰：天地交，泰。后以财成天地之道，辅相天地之宜，以左右民。

【明译】

泰卦象征安泰通顺，小的去往，大的到来，吉祥，亨通。

《彖传》说：泰卦，小的去往，大的到来，吉祥，亨通。天地阴阳交感，万物亨通畅达。上下交互感应交流，心意协同，志愿相通。阳气内葆，阴气外发。内卦（心）刚健，外卦（表）柔顺。内近君子（阳爻）外远小人（阴爻）。君子之（力）道在昌盛生长，小人之（力）道在减弱消退。

《象传》说：下卦乾为天，上卦坤为地，天地阴阳二气交接感应，这就是泰卦。君王学习天地之间阴阳交流就通达，不交流就闭塞的道理，制定出社会的合理制度，助成天地化生万物的合宜运行，以此来指导佑助民众。

Hexagram Tai (Communication) symbolizes peace and smoothness, small things leaving, great things coming, good fortune and prosperity.

The *Judgment Commentary* (*Tuan Zhuan*) says: In Hexagram Tai (Communication), the small leaves and the great comes, so it is auspicious and prosperous. The *yin* and *yang* of heaven and earth interact with each other, and the myriad things are prosperous and smooth. The upper and lower interaction resonates and communicates, intentions and minds are coordinated, and aspirations are interconnected. *Yangqi* is maintained internally and *yinqi* is released externally. The inner hexagram (heart) is strong, and the outer hexagram (surface) is supple. An exemplary person is close inside (*yang* lines) and a petty person is far outside (*yin* lines). The power of the exemplary person is prospering and growing, while the power of the petty person is weakening and fading.

The *Image Commentary* (*Xiang Zhuan*) says: The lower Trigram Qian is sky, and the upper Trigram Kun is earth. The *yin* and *yang* of heaven and earth interact and resonate; this is Hexagram Tai (Communication). The sovereign learns from the principle that communication of *yin* and *yang* between heaven and earth leads to interconnection, and that absence of communication leads to blockage. One, therefore, formulates a reasonable social system to help heaven and earth transform and operate appropriately, and in this way guides and helps the people.

【明意】

君子只能自己团结，让君子之道长，让君子的意识境遇的存在感压过小人的意识境遇，那样小人之道消，所以君子要结盟，形成君子的意境就可以抗击小人的意境。所以君子要建构一个和谐太平的世界，离不开如何处理与小人共在的艺术。君子必须选择与小人共同建构一个不完美的世界，在不完美的世界当中力求建构出完美来。

"天下太平"是君子小人共同的责任，而不能仅仅是君子的理想。君子的意识境遇在天下，每时每刻意念都合乎天道，如果指向自己的小家，则不再是君子了。君子不可以独善其身，不能因为自己有君子的品德就看不起他人，也不与小人打交道。三阳开泰就是君子要发动阳意，调动阳气，通过阴阳合力来开创出一个和谐的局面，而君子之胸襟，当以天之高，下于地之下，以大事小，方能开创和平安泰的境遇出来。

[Illuminating Intentionality]

Exemplary people can only unite among themselves, let the exemplary person's way grow, and let the exemplary person's sense of existence prevail over the petty person's consciousness. Then the petty person's way will disappear, so the exemplary person must form an alliance to form the exemplary person's intentional context, which can resist the petty person's intentional context. Therefore, the exemplary person's construction of a harmonious and peaceful world cannot be separated from how to deal with the art of coexisting with petty people. An exemplary person must choose to build an imperfect world with petty people, and strive to create perfection in an imperfect world.

"Peace in the world under heaven" is the common responsibility of exemplary and petty people, and cannot be just the ideal of exemplary people. An exemplary person's consciousness is in the world, and one's intentions are in line with the heavenly *dao* at all times. If one is directed to one's own small family, one is no longer an exemplary person. An exemplary person cannot keep to oneself or look down on others just because one has the character of an exemplary person, nor can one associate with petty people. Three *yang* lines open a peaceful scenario (*san yang kai tai* 三阳开泰) means that an exemplary person should initiate *yang* intention, mobilize *yangqi*, and create a harmonious situation through the combined forces of *yin* and *yang*. An exemplary person's intentionality should be as high as the sky to serve as low as the earth, and by applying a grand mindset to serve small minds one can create a peaceful and harmonious situation.

初九：拔茅，茹以其汇。征吉。

《象》曰："拔茅征吉"，志在外也。

【明译】

初九：拔茅草的时候，连根带泥拔出，因为根系牵连带着同类，说明跟志同道合的人一起征进吉祥。

《象传》说：拔起茅草，跟志同道合的人一起征进吉祥，说明初九的心志是向外发展。

Nine (*yang*/strong line) in the first place: When pulling up couchgrass, pull out the roots and mud too, because the roots involve the same kind, which means it is auspicious to march together with like-minded people.

The *Image Commentary* (*Xiang Zhuan*) says: Pulling up couchgrass and marching together with like-minded people to achieve auspiciousness shows that the ambition of the Nine (*yang*/strong line) in the first place is to develop outward.

【明意】

要实现通泰的境界，就要从初九开始调动阳意，进而改变阳气的运行。一往无前地实化阳意可能开创新的局面，意识可以调控情境的气息。领导人的意念可以带动一个团队，开创新局面需要有人做急先锋、打头阵，如统帅身先士卒可以改变战场上的阴阳之意的平衡。因此，要改变意境，往往需要强有力的阳意带领，在特定的时势中，敢于突破既有的意识状态，从而改变意境。

[Illuminating Intentionality]

To achieve a situational state of continuous communication, it is necessary to mobilize *yang*/positive intentions from the Nine (*yang*/strong line) in the first place and thereby change the movement of *yangqi*. The unremitting realization of *yang*/positive intentions can create new situations, and consciousness can regulate the atmosphere of the situation. A leader's intentions can drive a team, as to create a new situation, someone needs to be the vanguard and take the lead. If a commander leads by example, it can change the balance of *yin* and *yang* on the battlefield. Therefore, to change an intentional context, one often needs the guidance of strong *yang*/positive intentionality, one who, in a specific situation, has the courage to break through the existing state of consciousness, thus changing the intentional context.

九二：包荒，用冯（píng）河，不遐遗。朋亡，得尚于中行。

《象》曰："包荒……得尚于中行"，以光大也。

【明译】

九二：心胸宽广，能够包容广远，连徒步过河这类人都起用，再远的人也不遗弃，同时没有朋党以结党营私，能够保持中正之道而行，于是就能受到推崇。

《象传》说：胸怀宽广，保持中道，正道而行，受到推崇，是因为心念光明磊落，仁德高尚。

Nine (*yang*/strong line) in the second place: One who is broad-minded, able to tolerate far-reaching people, even those who wade the river on foot, and does not abandon people no matter how far away they are. At the same time, such people have no cliques to form for personal gain, and can maintain the right *dao*, so they can be respected.

The *Image Commentary* (*Xiang Zhuan*) says: Be broad-minded, keep to the middle way, and walk on the right *dao*. One is respected because one's intentionality is open and aboveboard, and one is benevolent and noble.

【明意】

成就君子之境，不排斥各种心意和各种力量。此爻说明，调动和聚拢阳意需要心胸开阔，志向远大，才能一往无前。要高瞻远瞩，阴阳融通，意向远方。意念实现包容与通达是可能的，意念之境广大有力，能够通达小人之心，意念涵盖的境遇非常宽容远大，什么人都可以包容。君子齐心协力，与大家一起精进，不结党营私搞朋党内斗。能够这样做的才是君子团队的骨干。君子广结善缘，其意念发动的瞬间，就跟各种气息沟通来往，从而能够调动社会力量，使其意念展开之境清明旷达，包容广远，富于力量，足以通达小人之心。

[Illuminating Intentionality]

To achieve the state of an exemplary person, one does not exclude any kind of intentions or power. This line shows that mobilizing and gathering *yang*/positive intentions requires an open intentionality and high ambitions in order to move forward in an indomitable way. We need to be far-sighted, integrate *yin* and *yang*, and aim for the future. It is possible to achieve tolerance and access with intentions, as the realm of intentionality is vast and powerful, and can reach the intentions of petty people. The situations covered by intentionality are very tolerant and far-reaching, and can tolerate everyone. An exemplary person works and makes progress together with everyone, and does not form cliques for personal gain or engage in intra-party fighting. Those who can do this are the backbone of an exemplary person's team. An exemplary person builds good relationships, and the moment his intentions are initiated, one communicates with various attitudes, thereby mobilizing social forces and making one's intentions clear, broad, inclusive, and powerful enough to reach the intentions of even petty people.

九三：无平不陂（pō），无往不复。艰贞无咎。勿恤其孚，于食有福。

《象》曰："无往不复"，天地际也。

【明译】

九三：没有只平坦而不起伏的，也没有只前往而不复返的。在艰难的境遇中保持合理的操守就可以免于灾害。不必忧虑自己内心通天的诚信无法让别人相信，只要在艰困之中保持衣食无忧就是很大的福报。

《象传》说：有去就有回，这是天地交际之处转化而然。

Nine (*yang*/strong line) in the third place: There is nothing that is flat with no ups and downs, and there is nothing that just goes forward and never comes back. Maintaining reasonable conduct in difficult situations can prevent disaster. One need not worry about one's inner integrity not being believed by others. As long as one can maintain adequate food and clothing amidst hardships, it is a great blessing.

The *Image Commentary* (*Xiang Zhuan*) says: Once something goes, it will come back. This is transformation in the communication between heaven and earth.

【明意】

天地之交也是形势变革之际，既是困境也是转机，要努力化危为机。对君子个人来说，面对变局当不改其志，自食其力谨守正道；君子群体应该齐心协力，维系住好不容易开创的三阳开泰局面，力图在天地之变中度过艰难时世，以期能够鼎立新局。此时，君子的意识要从天地之际吸取能量，让意能实化进而转化人生境遇。

三阳开泰，君子当齐心协力，如果不能压过小人，就会前功尽弃。政治是君子结盟以对付小人抱团力量的艺术。如果君子不结盟，可能被小人各个击破，那样泰的局面就不可能开创，更无法保持，其实也是很可怜的。在艰难的困境之中，仅仅自己保持正念，不为恶念所扰乱是不够的，还需要与他人共同创造合适的境遇。人在得意的时候，往往忘记自己可能要面对的艰难局面，也容易忘乎所以，不保持正念，那么马上形势就会急转直下。君子既要有善的动机，做善事，做好人，还要团结一致对付小人，否则，仅仅自得其乐，跟小人也没有什么区别。不敢担当责任的，不对自己的君子伙伴负责的，其实称不上君子，反而近乎小人。

[Illuminating Intentionality]

The interaction between heaven and earth is also a time when a situation is changing, both a dilemma and a turning point in which one must work hard to turn crises into opportunities. An individual exemplary person should not change one's ambitions in the face of changes,and should make one's own efforts and stick to the right *dao*; a group of exemplary people should work together to maintain the situation of three *yang* lines opening a great scenario (*san yang kai tai*) that was finally created, and strive to survive the difficult times amidst the changes in heaven and earth, in order to establish a new situation. At this time, the exemplary person's consciousness must absorb energy from the boundary between heaven and earth, allowing intentionality to materialize and transform life situations.

When the three *yang* lines prosper, exemplary people should work together. If they cannot defeat or overcome people, all their previous efforts will be in vain. Politics is the art of forming alliances between exemplary people to deal with the power of petty people. If exemplary people do not form an alliance, they may be defeated by petty people one by one. In that case, a communicating situation will be impossible to create, let alone maintain, which is actually very pitiful. In difficult situations, it is not enough to just maintain righteous intentions and not be disturbed by evil intentions. One also needs to work with others to create a suitable situation. When people are proud, they often forget about the difficult situations they may have to face, and they tend to get carried away. If they don't maintain righteous intentions, the situation will soon take a turn for the worse. An exemplary person must not only have good motives, do good deeds, and be a good person, but must also unite to deal with petty people. Otherwise, one just enjoys oneself and is no different from petty people. Those who dare not take responsibility and are not responsible for their fellow exemplary people cannot actually be called exemplary people, but are closer to petty people.

六四：翩翩，不富以其邻，不戒以孚。

《象》曰："翩翩不富"，皆失实也。"不戒以孚"，中心愿也。

【明译】

六四：轻飘飘地下降，与邻居一样都不富余，对近邻不加戒备，还心存孚信。

《象传》说：轻飘飘地下降，与邻居一样都不富余，因为六四与六五、上六都是柔爻，柔爻为虚，都不实，所以都不富。对近邻不加戒备，还心存孚信，因为六四愿意亲近九三，是从内心深处愿意无所戒备地真诚相处。

Six (yin/soft line) in the fourth place: Descending lightly, no more wealthy than one's neighbors, not wary of one's neighbors, but still trusting.

The *Image Commentary* (*Xiang Zhuan*) says: Descending lightly, like their neighbors, they are not rich, because the Six (yin/soft line) in the fourth place, the Six (yin/soft line) in the fifth place, and the Six (yin/soft line) in the top place are all soft lines, and the soft lines are empty, they are not solid, so they are not rich. They are not wary of their neighbors, but still have good faith, because the Six (yin/soft line) in the fourth place is willing to get close to the Nine (yang/strong line) in the third place, as deep down in their intentions they are willing to get along with each other sincerely and without guarding.

【明意】

如果君子时刻运化阳意以调动阳气，小人（阴气）也会主动改变自己的状态来投奔配合，从而一通百通。六四的意愿随境而迁，作出了战略性的转移，不能说六四没有自由意志，但这种意志首先受到阴阳相吸的影响。看到阳意上升，乐观其成，自己愿意包容接纳。本来应该下降的姿态，也变成顺应阳意上升，翩翩上浮了。这不是因为小人有良心，而是因为小人不能抵抗本性的内驱力，即阴阳相吸的内驱之力超过了情境的压力，甚至甘于把情境的压力放下来，宁可配合阳意的上升。所以一方面，阴意的改变受到整体意境的影响，但另一方面，也有内驱本性欲望使然。这样解释，就不涉及情欲与良心之间的选择问题了。

[Illuminating Intentionality]

If an exemplary person always transforms his *yang*/positive intentionality to mobilize his *yang* energy, a petty person with *yin* energy will also take the initiative to change his state to join in and cooperate, thus when one connects all are connected. The intentions of the Six (yin/soft line) in the fourth place change with the circumstances and make strategic shifts. It cannot be said that the Six (yin/soft line) in the fourth place does not have free will, but rather that this will was first affected by the attraction of *yin* and *yang*. Seeing the rising *yang* lines, be optimistic about their success, and be willing to tolerate and accept it. The attitude that should have been falling has become rising in accordance with the *yang*/positive intentionality, and floats gracefully. This is not because a petty person has a conscience, but because a petty person cannot resist the inner driving force of his nature, that is, the internal driving force of the attraction of *yin* and *yang* exceeds the pressure of the situation, and he is even willing to let go of the pressure of the situation and would rather cooperate with the rise of *yang* intentionality. Therefore, on the one hand, changes in *yin*/soft intention are affected by the overall intentional context, but on the other hand, they are also caused by intrinsic desires. Thus explained, the issue of a choice between passion and conscience is not involved.

六五：帝乙归妹，以祉（zhǐ）元吉。

《象》曰："以祉元吉"，中以行愿也。

【明译】

六五：帝乙嫁出自己的妹妹，妹妹因下嫁而收获幸福，这是十分吉利的事情。

《象传》说：妹妹因下嫁而收获幸福，这是十分吉利的事情，是因为六五居中应阳，代表妹妹（柔爻）能够保持中正之德，从而实现长期以来的美好愿望。

Six (*yin*/soft line) in the fifth place: Emperor Yi sends his younger sister to get married, and the sister gains happiness because of her marriage (with King Wen of Zhou). This is a very auspicious event.

The *Image Commentary* (*Xiang Zhuan*) says: It is very auspicious for a younger sister to gain happiness because of her marriage. This is because the Six (*yin*/soft line) in the fifth place is in the middle and resonates with the *yang* line in the second place, which means that the sister (the soft line) can maintain integrity and realize her long-existing hopes for a good future.

【明意】

六五阴意索性推行三阳的意志，跟君子们合谋，把女儿都嫁掉了。或者六五把九二提拔起来，让君子掌权，把女儿的命运也交给君子，等于不仅把自己，而且把一家人的身家性命都交给上升期间的君子们了。

阴意能够主动顺应阳意，阴气被上升的阳气给理顺了，圆融无碍。阴意主动配合阳意大升的境遇，不惜赌上自己的身家性命，把前程命运都交出去，这是看到阳意大升势不可挡。换言之，天地变化虽不过一时之交融，但天地之间本来就是阴意与阳意之交融过程，当看到形势大变，阴意连身家性命都要主动交出，这样的意念转换才能在必然改变其境遇的大势当中尽量掌握主动。

[Illuminating Intentionality]

The Six (*yin*/soft line) in the fifth place simply carries out the will of the three *yang* lines and conspires with exemplary people to marry off their daughters. Or, the Six (*yin*/soft line) in the fifth place promotes the Nine (*yang*/strong line) in the second place and puts an exemplary person in power, entrusting the fate of his daughter to him. This is tantamount to handing over not only himself, but also his family's wealth and life to an exemplary person in a rising period.

Yin power can actively adapt to *yang* power, and *yin* power is straightened out by rising *yang* power, making it harmonious and smooth. *Yin*/negative intentionality takes the initiative to cooperate with the situation of *yang*/positive intentionality, risking its own wealth and life, and handing over its future and destiny. This is because one sees that the rise of *yang*/positive intentionality is unstoppable. In other words, although the change of heaven and earth is only a temporary blending, the relationship between heaven and earth is originally a blending process of *yin* and *yang*. Upon seeing a great change in the situation, *yin* intentionality takes the initiative to hand over even its family and life. Only such a transformation of intentionality can do its utmost to take the initiative in the general trend of an inevitably changing situation.

上六：城复于隍，勿用师。自邑告命。贞吝。

《象》曰："城复于隍"，其命乱也。

【明译】

上六：城墙倒塌在城外壕沟里，自己的兵力没有用了，也不需要麻烦他国出兵。只能够在自己的采邑里传递告急的命令，危难之时还继续顽固不化必有吝难。

《象传》说：城墙倒塌在护城河里，因为天命都已经变了。

Six (*yin*/soft line) in the top place: The city wall collapses in a trench outside the city. One's own troops are useless, but there is no need to trouble other countries to send troops. One can only deliver urgent orders in one's own fief. If one continues to be stubborn in times of crisis, one will inevitably have difficulties.

The *Image Commentary* (*Xiang Zhuan*) says: The city wall collapses in the moat, because the mandate of heaven has already changed.

【明意】

本爻上六完全挡不住形势的变化，城墙坍塌，小人势力分崩离析，君子们连军队都可以不出动，这种情况下动武其实就是君子的失败。小人四散奔逃，阵脚紊乱，他们想保护的旧朝廷的天命已经没有了。君子不但要团结，还需要未雨绸缪，不能连城墙都推倒，那样反而乱套了。君子结盟到此刻可以看出是否真正精诚团结，动机是否自始至终不变，能否继续分享对形势的判断，共同推动形势向前发展。

命有形势超出个人控制的意味，所以命与决定论有关。人的意识境遇无疑可以影响其所在形势，也就构成其命运。《周易》的命运观不是决定论，更不是预成论，或预先决定论，但也说不上是自由意志论，或许可以说是有限的自由意志论，即人的自由意志受到时空条件的限制，人的自由意志的动机与效果应该同时考虑。在意念实化为行动前，人应该多考察与修正自己的意识状态于未发之前，不然就只有在行动发出后，通过不断修正意识境域来调适自己的行为。当然，随时势调整自己的心意和行为是《周易》之教的基本内容。

[Illuminating Intentionality]

This line is completely unable to stop the changes in the situation. The city wall collapses, petty people's power falls apart, and exemplary people could not even send out the army. In this case, the use of force is actually the failure of exemplary people. Petty people are running away in all directions, their positions are in disarray, and the mandate of the old court they wanted to protect is gone. Exemplary people not only need to unite, but also to prepare for a rainy day. They cannot even tear down the city walls, which will lead to chaos. At this point in the alliance among exemplary people, we can see whether they are truly united sincerely, whether their motivations remain unchanged from beginning to end, and whether they can continue to share their judgment on the situation and jointly push the situation forward.

Fate means that a situation is beyond personal control, so fate is related to determinism. A person's conscious state can undoubtedly affect his situational propensity, which also constitutes his fate. The view of fate in the *Book of Changes* is not determinism, let alone preformation, or predeterminism, but it cannot be said to be a theory of free will. It may be said to be a theory of limited free will, that is, human free will is limited by spatio-temporal conditions. The motivations and effects of free will should be considered simultaneously. Before intentions are turned into actions, people should examine and correct their conscious state significantly, before anything is initiated. Otherwise, they can only adjust their behavior by constantly revising their consciousness after an action is initiated. Of course, adjusting one's intentionality and behavior according to a situation is the basic content of the teachings of the *Book of Changes*.

天地否（卦十二） （坤下乾上）

Pi (Non-Communication), Heaven and Earth (Hexagram 12)　(Kun below, Qian above)

世界之生机全在困顿与艰难中生发成长。即使在天地闭塞，心意与行为难以中正，自觉可耻而且会招致羞辱的状态中，也还要竭尽全力维系意念之生机。此卦由心气不通讨论心生问题，心生与自然之生的关系。此卦论艰难时世当中，维持心生何以可能。内心纯正立志走正道的人，不是总是生得通的，因为形势可能非常否塞，天下无道，小人当道，这时君子最好退隐，小人得志，君子有志难伸。君子不能跟小人斗，因为斗的话，修养就跟他们一样了，但君子既不能同流合污，又不能独善其身，要在跟小人缠而不破中维系意识的生机。

The vitality of the world all grows and develops amidst adversity and difficulty. Even if heaven and earth are closed up, if it is difficult to rectify one's intentions and actions, and one feels shameful and incurs humiliation, one must still do one's best to maintain the vitality of one's intentions. This hexagram discusses the problem of intentional life and the relationship between intentional life and natural life based on blocked intentional *qi*. This hexagram discusses how it is possible to maintain an intentional life in difficult times. People who are pure in heart and determined to follow the right *dao* are not always successful, because sometimes situations are very difficult, the world lacks order, and petty people are in charge. At such times, it is best for an exemplary person to retreat, because petty people will succeed, and it is difficult for an exemplary person to achieve one's aspirations. An exemplary person cannot fight with petty people, because if one fights, one's cultivation will be the same as theirs. However, an exemplary person can neither join with others in corruption, nor maintain one's integrity alone. One must maintain the vitality of one's consciousness while entangled with petty people without breaking up.

否之匪人，不利君子贞，大往小来。

《彖》曰："否之匪人，不利君子贞，大往小来"，则是天地不交而万物不通也，上下不交而天下无邦也；内阴而外阳，内柔而外刚，内小人而外君子，小人道长，君子道消也。

《象》曰：天地不交，否。君子以俭德辟（bì）难，不可荣以禄。

【明译】

否卦象征闭塞不通。在否闭无道的世道当中，不该被否塞的君子也会被折磨地失去人样，不利于君子迂腐不加变通，因为正大的阳气还在消往离去，卑小的阴气正在生长到来。

《彖传》说：在否闭无道的世道当中，不该被否塞的君子也会被折磨地失去人样，不利于君子迂腐不加变通，因为正大的阳气还在消往离去，卑小的阴气正在生长到来。上卦乾为天，下卦坤为地，天的阳气上行，地的阴气下行，天地悬隔，不能交感流通，导致万物无法生长，上下不再沟通。在上位的人不亲下，在下位的人不爱上，互不交往，天下就没有安定的邦国。内部阴（爻）暗，外表阳（爻）明；内里柔弱，外表刚强；小人受宠于内，君子排挤在外；这是小人之邪道在生长，君子之正道在消退。

《象传》说：乾天之卦在上，坤地之卦在下，阳气上升，阴气下降，天地之气上下不交流，这就是否卦。君子从阴阳不交的形势当中得到启示，要暂时退隐，收敛才华，自我约束，俭损德行，躲避时灾，不可去追求利禄，谋取荣华富贵。

Hexagram Pi (Non-Communication) symbolizes blockage. In a world of denial and ignorance, an exemplary person who should not be denied will be tortured and lose one's human appearance, which is not conducive to an exemplary person's stubbornness and inflexibility, because the upright *yangqi* is still disappearing and the growth of lowly *yinqi* is still coming.

The *Judgment Commentary* (*Tuan Zhuan*) says: In a world of denial and ignorance, an exemplary person who should not be denied will be tortured and lose one's human appearance, which is not conducive to an exemplary person's stubbornness and lack of flexibility, because upright *yangqi* is still disappearing and leaving, and lowly *yinqi* is growing and coming. The upper Trigram Qian is sky, and the lower Trigram Kun is earth. The *yang* power of the sky ascends, and the *yin* power of the earth descends. The sky and the earth are separated and cannot interact with each other. As a result, the myriad things cannot grow, and the upper and lower parts no longer communicate. If those in higher positions do not feel affection for their subordinates, those in lower positions do not feel affection for their superiors, and the two do not interact with each other, there will be no stable country under heaven. The inner *yin* lines are dark, and the outer *yang* lines are bright; the inside is weak, and the outside is strong; petty people are favored inside, while exemplary people are excluded outside; this is the evil ways of petty people growing, and the righteousness of exemplary people fading.

The *Image Commentary* (*Xiang Zhuan*) says: The Trigram Qian (Heaven) is on top, and the Trigram Kun(Earth) is on the bottom. *Yangqi* rises and *yinqi* falls. If the *qi* of heaven and earth above and below do not communicate, this is a negative hexagram. Exemplary people are inspired by the situation where *yin* and *yang* are not in harmony, and learn that they should retreat temporarily, curb their talents, exercise self-restraint, be frugal in their virtues, and avoid disasters. They should not pursue honor or wealth.

【明意】

否卦是小人乱生，心意不通，有口难言，有意念无法表达，换言之，心意难生，即使生也不得畅通。人对意会之境判断心意发生的必要性，如果感到很难，就宁可放弃，所以否是在不通的境遇当中，既是心意客观上难生，也是意念发动自我控制，使得心意难于生发。君子在闭塞无道的形势之下，正确的处理方法是选择退隐和收摄意念。阴阳不交、天地不通之时，讲话会无法沟通，讲了也没有效果，那么意念宁可少发动或者不发动。

这样说来，心意生与不生不仅仅是主观把握，也相当程度上取决于情境中是否有生机。有时意念判断为否塞不通的情境，仍然可能会有生机，而且生机可能最终会转变否塞的形势。

[Illuminating Intentionality]

Hexagram Pi (Non-Communication) means that petty people live in disorder, their intentionality is blocked, their words are hard to express, and their intentions cannot be expressed. In other words, it is difficult for their intentionality to be produced, and even if it is produced, it will not go smoothly. People judge the necessity of the expression of intentions in their state of understanding, and if they find it difficult, they would rather give up. Therefore, Hexagram Pi (Non-Communication) represents how, in an unreasonable situation, it is not only objectively difficult for intentions to arise, but also common for the intentions to initiate self-control, making it difficult for intentions to be expressed. When an exemplary person is in a situation where one is blocked and has no way forward, the correct way to deal with it is to choose to retreat and gather one's intentionality. When *yin* and *yang* are not in harmony and heaven and earth are blocked, communication will be impossible and speech will have no effect, so it is better to initiate less or even no intentions.

In this way, whether intentionality is produced or not is not only matter of subjective grasping, but also depends to a considerable extent on whether there is vitality in a situation. Sometimes a situation that is judged as blocked by intentionality may still have vitality, and this vitality may eventually change the propensity of a blocked situation.

初六：拔茅，茹以其汇。贞吉，亨。

《象》曰："拔茅贞吉"，志在君也。

【明译】

初六：拔茅草的时候，连根带泥拔出，因为根系牵连带着同类，说明跟志同道合的人一起安定地持守正道吉祥，亨通。

《象传》说：拔茅草的时候，同类相连，象征大家一起共同进取，心里都念着君王，愿意顺应君王（初六正应九四在上卦乾，为君王，阴爻柔顺与九四正应）。

Six (*yin*/soft line) in the first place: When pulling out couchgrass, pull out the roots and the mud, because the roots involve the same kind, so staying on the right *dao* with like-minded people will be auspicious and prosperous.

The *Image Commentary* (*Xiang Zhuan*) says: When pulling up couchgrass, like people are connected, which symbolizes that everyone is making progress together, thinking about the monarch in their hearts, and willing to obey the monarch (the Six (*yin*/soft line) in the first place corresponds to the Nine (*yang*/strong line) in the fourth place in the upper Trigram Qian, which is the monarch, and the *yin* line is supple and responds to the Nine (*yang*/strong line) in the fourth place.

【明意】

心意之生，首先是同类相保相生，互相支撑，彼此相应。所谓在否塞的形势之下，最为关键的需要点在于寻找同类相通之人，一起安守正道而同志征进，力求转化否塞不通的形势为通。心念的志同还要同于一主为好，由于大家有共同的心志，心意皆往一处使，所以在困境当中，更要力求变通，改变使自己心力分散的形势。如果没有心智的方向，没有共通的升力，就难以改变艰难的形势。

[Illuminating Intentionality]

The birth of intentionality, first of all, is mutual preservation, mutual support, and mutual correspondence between entities of the same kind. In a situation where there is a blockage, the most critical need is to find people of the same kind who can stick to the right *dao* and march forward together, and strive to transform the situation where there is a blockage and no communication into a communicating solution. It is better for like-minded people to be unified under one ruler. Since everyone has the same ambition and all their intentions are directed towards the same place, in difficult situations, they must strive to be flexible and change the situational propensities that disperse their intentionality. If there is no mental direction and no common elevating force, it will be hard to change a difficult situation.

六二：包承，小人吉，大人否。亨。

《象》曰："大人否亨"，不乱群也。

【明译】

六二：能够包容并且顺承大人（九五），对于小人来说是吉祥的。大人能够拒绝否定小人（六二），就会亨通。

《象传》说：大人能够拒绝否定小人，就会亨通，是因为大人不会与小人一起同流合污，成为害群之马。

Six (*yin*/soft line) in the second place: Being able to tolerate and obey great people (the Nine (*yang*/strong line) in the fifth place) is auspicious for petty people. If a great person can resist denying petty people (the Six (*yin*/soft line) in the second place), one will prosper.

The *Image Commentary* (*Xiang Zhuan*) says: If a great person can resist denying petty people, one will prosper, because a great person will not collaborate with petty people and become a rotten apple.

【明意】

阳意之生，处于否闭的时势是正常的，不必主动丧失阳意的生意，而去顺应阴意生长的形势。所以要静守待时，不与小人同流合污。大人遭遇否塞的时势，不可与小人一样，没有见识，没有胸怀，急于用世，急于求成，最后反而乱了分寸。也就是说，大人倒霉的时候，固穷才能通，加入小人的阵营对自己有害无益。

艰难时势之下，阳意的生机需要自我持守，大人君子即使困顿不顺，也要坚守自己的中正贞固，静候时机变化，等事态局面改变之后，再去行动。虽然他心不是此心的创造，但人与他心交流时，他心他意会受到此心此意的影响。世界始于感应，成于交流，但形势不合的时候，要能够静守己意，等待时势转化。

[Illuminating Intentionality]

It is normal for the vitality of *yang* intentionality to be in negative situations. There is no need to actively give up *yang* intentionality's vitality and adapt to the growing propensity of *yin* intentionality. Therefore, one must wait patiently and not join in the bad deeds of petty people. When a great person encounters an adverse situation, one should not be like the petty person, who has no knowledge, no ambition, is eager to use the world, and is eager for success, and in the end loses one's sense of proportion. In other words, when a great person is in misfortune, one must stay in poverty to get ahead. Joining the petty people's camp is harmful to oneself.

In difficult times, the vitality of *yang*/positive intentions needs to be maintained by oneself. Even if a situation is difficult, an exemplary person should stick to one's integrity, await an opportunity for transformation, and wait until the situation changes before taking action. Although other minds are not creations of one's mind, when one communicates with other minds, their minds and intentions will be affected by one's own mind. The world begins with affective response and ends with communication, but when the situational propensity is compatible, one must be able to remain silent and wait for the situation to change.

六三：包羞。

《象》曰："包羞"，位不当也。

【明译】

六三：被包容而为非作歹，招致羞辱。

《象传》说：被包容而为非作歹，招致羞辱，因为六三居于不正当之位。

Six (*yin*/soft line) in the third place: Being tolerated and doing evil will lead to humiliation.

The *Image Commentary* (*Xiang Zhuan*) says: Being tolerated and doing evil will lead to humiliation, because the Six (*yin*/soft line) in the third place occupies an improper position.

【明意】

羞耻感的产生既与他心的感应有关，又与自我评估有关，让自己体会到羞辱，进而产生羞耻心，其实带有明显的反思意味。"耻"涉及精神慰藉，正如佛教有忏悔业障，基督教对人生而有罪的界定。耻的意义在于，为人类从内心深处接纳自己提供了机会，从而安放人的精神。人的迷茫与困惑一部分源于自我认知的矛盾，而"耻"的出现一方面是对过去错误行为的承认，从心理上承担错误行为的后果，觉得不应该给他人带去伤害，从而接纳自己成为一个不完美的人的过程；"耻"感也往往是个人人格重建的开始。"耻"可以说是个人的自我道德审判。耻感不仅是内在的，有时也是外在的，即公共的耻，集体客观外在的耻，以外在的、反对的形式加予自己。

[Illuminating Intentionality]

The production of shame is not only related to affective responses to other people's intentions, but also to one's own self-evaluation. Allowing oneself to experience shame then produces a sense of shame, hence it in fact has an obvious sense of self-reflection. Shame involves spiritual comfort, just as Buddhism involves the repentance of karma, and Christianity defines people as born with original sin. The significance of shame is that it provides an opportunity for human beings to accept themselves from the depths of their intentionality, thereby settling the human spirit. Part of people's confusion and misperception stems from contradictions in self-perception, and the emergence of shame on the one hand is a process of the recognition of past wrongdoing, psychologically bearing the consequences of misconduct, feeling that one should not bring harm to others, and thus accepting oneself becoming an imperfect person; a sense of shame is often the beginning of an individual's personality reconstruction. Shame can be said to be an individual's self-moral judgment. Shame is not only internal, but sometimes also external, that is, public shame, collective objective external shame, imposed on oneself in an external and oppositional form.

九四：有命，无咎，畴（chóu）离祉。

《象》曰："有命无咎"，志行也。

【明译】

九四：接受命令扭转否道，不犯过失，同类（上三爻）依附，共享福祉。

《象传》说：按照命令去做事，不会有咎害，因为上面的心志能推行（九四奉九五君命行事，同时也把自己的心愿推行下去）。

Nine (*yang*/strong line) in the fourth place: Accept the order to change the *dao*, do not make mistakes, keep attached to the same kind (the three upper lines), and share the blessings.

The *Image Commentary* (*Xiang Zhuan*) says: There will be no harm if one does things according to orders, because the will of one's superiors can be carried out (the Nine (*yang*/strong line) in the fourth place acts under the orders of the leading Nine (*yang*/strong line) in the fifth place, and at the same time carries out his own wishes.

【明意】

九四的阳意既与同类团结，又首当其冲，表现出有气魄和担当，而且还要顺君命，通晓大势，其心意发动与君意相通共生。人需要依从形势而控制心意，有时要延缓必须发动的意念，需要按照形势来控制自己的意识，等待发动意念的合适时机。为了转化小人上升的形势，君子要努力控制自己意念发动的过程，尤其需要延缓自己觉得必须发动的意念，要学会通过意识来调控和转化阴阳。

[Illuminating Intentionality]

The *yang*/positive intentionality of the Nine (*yang*/strong line) in the fourth place not only unites with the same kind, but also bears the brunt of the impact, showing courage and responsibility. It must also obey the ruler's orders and understand the general trend, and its intentions and purposes are interlinked and symbiotic with the ruler's intentions. People need to accommodate their intentions according to their situation. Sometimes they have to delay intentions that must be initiated. They need to control their consciousness according to the situation and wait for the right time to initiate their intentions. In order to transform the situation of petty people rising, an exemplary person must work hard to control the process of initiating one's own intentions. In particular, one must delay intentions that one feels must be initiated, and must learn to regulate and transform *yin* and *yang* through consciousness.

九五：休否，大人吉。其亡其亡，系于苞桑。

《象》曰："大人"之"吉"，位正当也。

【明译】

九五：否闭的局势休止住了，大人将获得吉祥。（但意念仍然时刻居安思危：）可能会灭亡啊，可能会灭亡啊，这样才能好像被拴在丛生的大桑树上一样安然无恙。

《象传》说：大人能够吉祥，是因为九五居于中位，合适得当。

Nine (*yang*/strong line) in the fifth place: The negative situation has stopped, and great people will be blessed. (But intentionality is still always prepared for danger:) It may perish; it may perish! Thus it can be safe and sound as if tied to a large mulberry tree.

The *Image Commentary* (*Xiang Zhuan*) says: The reason why great people can be auspicious is because the Nine (*yang*/strong line) in the fifth place is in the middle, which is appropriate.

【明意】

卦象不吉的卦也存在着转机。在逆境中，人的意念仍然有转变情境的可能。意识有对事物把握、控制和转化的力量，并受潜意识的影响。起心动念是九五之运势得以转化的原因。《周易》不仅告诫我们要转化心念，同时也要知道绝处逢生的道理，如上爻提到，君子要认识到自己的信念，对自己本心有把握，充分意会到意念发动的先天结构，让意念适时即是大人境界，即能将内心的光明适时彰显出来。因此，只要时时刻刻本着自己内心的光明，即便环境艰险，也可尽量减损对个人的伤害。

位高权重者的一个念头就可能改变事情的发展方向。意念与权位的生克关系非常微妙，有权之人一念之间对情境的影响比无权之人要大。但即使如此，意念最后还是自我决定，而且要学会克服时位情境的限制，在危机当中，也要善于自我决定。

[Illuminating Intentionality]

Unfortunate hexagrams also contain opportunities for change. In adversity, human intentions still have the possibility to change a situation. Consciousness has the power to grasp, control and transform things, and is influenced by subconscious intentionality. Aroused intentionality is the reason why the fortune of the Nine (*yang*/strong line) in the fifth place can be transformed. The *Book of Changes* not only warns us to transform our intentions, but also to know how to survive in desperate situations. As mentioned in the above line, an exemplary person must understand one's own beliefs, be sure of one's own heart, and fully realize the transcendental structure of intentionality. This allows intentions to attain the state of a great person at the right time, which reveals the light in the heart at the right time. Therefore, as long as one acts on one's inner light at all times, even if the environment is difficult and dangerous, one can minimize the harm to individuals.

A single intention from a powerful decision-maker can change the direction of events. The relationship between intentions and power is very subtle. A powerful person's intentions have a greater impact on a situation than a person without power. But even so, intentions ultimately determine themselves, and one must learn to overcome the limitations of time and situation, and be good at self-determination in times of crisis.

上九：倾否，先否后喜。

《象》曰：否终则倾，何可长也。

【明译】

上九：困顿不通的局面将发生天翻地覆的改变，改变开始的时候还会有点闭塞不顺，最后通达顺畅，皆大欢喜。

《象传》说：否塞到了极点就必然要发生倾覆，闭塞的局面怎么能够继续长久保持下去！

Nine (*yang*/strong line) in the top place: A difficult and blocked situation undergoes earth-shaking changes. At the beginning of the change, things are a little blocked and unsmooth, but in the end all is successful and smooth, and everyone is happy.

The *Image Commentary* (*Xiang Zhuan*) says: If congestion reaches its extreme, it will inevitably begin to overturn. How can a blocked situation be maintained for a long time?

【明意】

人的每一个念头都与外境共同作用，不存在离却外境而生的念头，而念头的方向往往决定念头的生灭。意念如火之生生，生成万物的同时，也毁灭万物；所以可谓一念生机，亦一念火机，生火无常，却又存乎一心。所以如何领悟念头生机的决死之境，是掌控意念的力量及修行的核心所在。知道意念流转之间，可以瞬间天翻地覆，则对于意念的生生灭灭，无不要慎之又慎。就念头的本质生灭之境、相对于权位而言，生机与敬畏密切相关。生机需要面对否塞不通的情境才有生的力量。意念之生是存在之生的根本，故可谓生意为世界之本。天地之大德曰生，而生意乃大德之根，意生而事生，进而世存。念头之生即世界之生，故于念起念灭之间，要掌控生机之发，所以，意念生发之几，当为宇宙之大本根。

[Illuminating Intentionality]

Every intention of a person interacts with their external environment. There is no intention that arises in isolation from an external environment, and the direction of intention often determines the birth and death of intention. Intentions are like the vitality of fire, which creates and destroys the myriad things at the same time. Therefore, it can be said that one intention both brings life and annihilates, the impermanence of birth and death existing in a single intention. Therefore, how to understand the life-and-death state of the vitality of intentions is the core of controlling the power of intentions and cultivating practice. Knowing that the flow of intentionality can turn everything upside down in an instant, we should be extremely cautious about the birth and death of intentions. In terms of the nature of intentionality as a state of birth and death, relative to power and position, vitality and awe are closely related. Vitality needs to face overwhelming situations to have the power to survive. The production of intention is the foundation of the production of existence, so it can be said that productive intentionality is the foundation of the world. The great virtue of heaven and earth is production, and productive intentionality is the root of great virtue. When intentions arise, things arise, and then exist in the world. The production of intentionality is the production of the world. Therefore, between the rise and fall of intentions, we must control the growth of vitality. Therefore, the subtlety of intentions that arise should be the fundamental root of the cosmos.

天火同人（卦十三）　（离下乾上）
Tongren (Comradeship), Heaven and Fire (Hexagram 13)　(Li below, Qian above)

　　同人的同心同德之意向，经历争讼之后才会珍惜。从争讼意向的分崩离析到同人的众心聚合，有一个过程。领导者在争讼之后，如何重新沟通和聚合天下人心？虽然，天下大同一直是中国古人的善良政治理想，希望君主对所有人一视同仁，"家—国"的领导人都能够做到天下为公，没有私心私利，但是，人与人之间其实不太可能实现事实上的平等，最多能够做到的是人格上、人之为人以及心灵修养上的平等，而这种平等显然不是客观存在的。

　　古代中国没有现代国家观念，但有世界大同的观念，这与汉民族生存的环境有关，一方面汉民族有其自身独立的文化源头，源远流长，绵延不绝，所以有独立的民族和家国认同；但另一方面，汉民族本身的生存困境以及与异族的互动，都让这个民族觉得天下大同理想之可贵，并落实在领导人能否与百姓"同人"这一点上。在近代史上，中国被迫进入西方民族国家的体系，不得不建立所谓的现代民族国家，而传统天下观念被挤压一两百年。直到中国对世界的影响重新恢复，人们才意识到中国古典天下观对于世界政治有正面意义。可见，某种意义上说，没有实力，世界大同对本国和世界都没有意义。换言之，没有国家性的强大意向做基础，"王"道作为一种价值理念的实际作用可能非常有限。

The shared intentions and virtues of comrades can be cherished only after going through disputes.

There is a process from the disintegration of the intention to litigate to the convergence of people's intentions. How do leaders reconnect and gather the intentions of the world after a dispute? Although the great harmony of the world was always a good political ideal of the ancient Chinese, hoping that the monarch would treat everyone equally and that the leaders of the family and the country could serve the world for the common good and have no selfish interests, in fact, between people it is impossible to achieve de facto equality. The most that can be achieved is equality in personality, for people as human beings, and in terms of spiritual cultivation, and this equality obviously does not exist objectively.

Ancient China did not have the modern concept of a nation-state, but it did have a concept of world unity. This is related to the environment in which the Han people lived. On the one hand, the Han people has its own independent cultural origin, which has a long and continuous history, so it has an independent national and family-state identity. But on the other hand, the Han people's own survival difficulties and interactions with other ethnic groups made this people feel that the ideal of world unity is valuable, and it was implemented in terms of whether leaders could be "of the same people" as the common people. In modern history, China was forced to enter the Western nation-state system and had to establish a so-called modern nation-state, while the traditional concept of "all under heaven" (*tianxia* 天下) was squeezed for a couple of hundred years. It was not until China's influence on the world resumed that people realized that China's classical view of the world had positive implications for world politics. It can be seen that, in a sense, without strength, world unity is meaningless to the country and the world. In other words, without strong national intentions as a foundation, the actual role of the kingship as a value concept may be very limited.

同人于野，亨。利涉大川，利君子贞。

《彖》曰：同人，柔得位、得中，而应乎乾，曰同人。同人曰："同人于野，亨。利涉大川"，乾行也。文明以健，中正而应，君子正也。唯君子为能通天下之志。

《象》曰：天与火，同人。君子以类族辨物。

【明译】

同人卦象征与人同心，与在野的人同心同德就会获得亨通。有利于涉越大河，有利于君子持守正道。

《彖传》说：同人卦，柔爻六二取得柔位，处下卦之中，又与上卦乾的九五相应，所以称作同人。与在野的人同心同德就会获得亨通。有利于涉越大河，这是乾阳之力与人同心的志意刚健运行的结果。内卦离为文明，外卦乾为刚健，象征秉性文明而刚健有为。主爻六二与上乾九五皆居中当位，而且阴阳正应，象征着君子持守正道，求同存异，和同于人。只有君子才能沟通和同天下人的心志。

《象传》说：上卦乾为天，下卦离为火，天在高处，火熊熊燃烧向上跟天相互亲和，火光冲天，一片光明之象。离为依附，太阳依附在天上，人心和同于天光，这就是同人卦。君子要判断事物的类别，分辨事物的本质特性。

Hexagram Tongren (Comradeship) symbolizes being of the same intentionality as others. If one is of one heart and one intention with those who are not in power, you will achieve prosperity. It is beneficial for one to cross a great river and for an exemplary person to keep to the right *dao*.

The *Judgment Commentary* (*Tuan Zhuan*) says: In Hexagram Tongren (Comradeship), the Six (*yin*/soft line) in the second place obtains the soft position, is in the lower Trigram, and corresponds to the Nine (*yang*/strong line) in the fifth place in the upper Trigram Qian, so it is called Tongren (Comradeship). If you work with those who are not in power, you will prosper. It is conducive to crossing a large river, which is the result of the strong operation of the power of Qian-*yang* and people's concentric will. The lower Trigram Li signifies civilization, and the outer Trigram Qian is strength, symbolizing a civilized and vigorous nature. The main Six (*yin*/soft line) in the second place and the upper Nine (*yang*/strong line) in the fifth place are both in the middle position, and their *yin* and *yang* correspond to each other, symbolizing that an exemplary person adheres to the right *dao*, seeks common ground while reserving differences, and works in harmony with others. Only an exemplary person can communicate and share the aspirations of the people in the world.

The *Image Commentary* (*Xiang Zhuan*) says: The upper Trigram Qian is sky, and the lower Trigram Li is fire. The sky is a high place, and the fire is burning upwards and close to the sky. The fire soaring into the sky makes it a bright image. Trigram Li is attached, indicating that the sun is attached to the sky, and the human heart is in harmony with the light of the sky, which is Hexagram Tongren (Comradeship). An exemplary person must judge the categories of things and discern their essential characteristics.

【明意】

沟通天下人心，方能成就事业，所以人需要结缘，而缘力来自意缘发动的力道。生命之道因"意能"而改变，进而自然阴阳之道。或者说，通过"意缘"的理解和把握来改变"意能"，即意的能动性，从而实化和创造。同人即意向"能""缘"，即主动选择"意缘"是心力"意能"的现实化。主动选择意缘是自由，但这种选择又受一定时空和外在条件的限制，带有命定论、宿命论和决定论的意味，不过，尽管人生不可能纯粹自由，但同人卦就代表着对意缘的决定和选择，是自由意志的体现和追求。

[Illuminating Intentionality]

Only by connecting people's intentions in the world can one achieve success, so people need to form connections, and the power of dependent co-arising comes from the power of cosmological intentionality. The *dao* of life changes due to "intentional energy", and thus forms the natural *dao* of *yin* and *yang*. In other words, through the understanding and grasp of "intentional dependent co-arising", this changes "intentional energy", that is, the initiative of intention, which is thereby concretized and creates. Hexagram Tongren (Comradeship) means that intentionality can communicate and connect with others, that is, actively choosing "intentional dependent co-arising" is

200

the actualization of the mental power of intention. It is the freedom to actively choose one's destiny, but this choice is limited by certain spatio-temporal and external conditions, and carries senses of fatalism, passivity and determinism. However, although life cannot be purely free, Hexagram Tongren (Comradeship) represents the relationship between the two. Decisions and choices about dependent co-arising are the embodiment and pursuit of free will.

初九：同人于门，无咎。

《象》曰：出"门""同人"，又谁咎也？

【明译】

初九：出门就能够和同于人，这没有什么问题。

《象传》说：出门就能够和同于人，又会有谁来责怪呢（大家欢迎这样）？

Nine (*yang*/strong line) in the first place: Being able to get along with others when one first goes out, there is no problem.

The *Image Commentary* (*Xiang Zhuan*) says: If you can be harmonious with others as soon as you head out, who will blame you (since everyone welcomes this)?

【明意】

主动与人同心同德，缘分发动，涉及意志的方向与场域。出门就是离开私人场域，进入公共场域，但有些人进入公共场域之后缺乏公义之心，结果还是私人一个。此爻希望人们心存公义之心，进入公共场域跟人同心同德。公共场域是意向交汇之处，人到公共场域寻找意向沟通的共在状态，并在意念与公共场域交流的过程中把意念实化。但每个人对于公共场域的理解不同，有些人的心念能够尽可能广大，而有些人则相对狭隘，也就是说，不同的人与人同心同德的范围和边界有所不同。

[Illuminating Intentionality]

Taking the initiative to be of one intentionality and mind with others, and initiating connections between people involves the direction and field of the will. Going out means leaving the private sphere and entering the public sphere. However, some people lack justice after entering the public sphere, and end up remaining simply a private person. This line hopes that people will have a righteous heart and enter the public square to be of one heart-mind and one intentionality with others. Public fields are places where intentions meet, and people go to public fields to find a state of co-presence in which intentions are communicated, realizing their intentions in the process of communicating with them. Nonetheless, everyone has a different understanding of the public sphere, and some people's intentions can be as broad as possible, while others are relatively narrow. In other words, the scope and boundaries of different people's senses of unity are different.

六二：同人于宗，吝。

《象》曰："同人于宗"，吝道也。

【明译】

六二：只与同宗同室的亲戚、朋友同胞同心同德，鄙吝。

《象传》说：六二与初九不同，不能大同，只跟同宗同室的亲戚、朋友同胞打交道，走的是鄙吝之道，太可惜了。

Six (*yin*/soft line) in the second place: Only sharing one heart-mind and intention with relatives, friends and compatriots of the same clan and house, this is stingy.

The *Image Commentary* (*Xiang Zhuan*) says: The Six (*yin*/soft line) in the second place is different from the Nine (*yang*/strong line) in the first place, and they cannot be unified. It is a pity to only deal with relatives, friends and compatriots of the same clan and house.

【明意】

意向集中在同宗人身上，虽然较为自然，好像无可厚非，但不够宽广。换言之，如果人把意向的关注点只集中于小集团，其意向显然不够开明。意向发动，即使不能够顾念天下苍生，也不应该仅仅集中在自己同宗人有限的小集体上面。虽然修养自己的意向当从亲戚朋友同胞开始，但如果自己的意向界限太明，则不利于拓展自己的意念到天下的人。

《周易》是人天之学，教人修习人意通天的艺术，所以对于将心思意念仅仅落实到家族的倾向，是持批判态度的。可见，在《周易》作者看来，随顺情感之自然，心念发动通于人情，不是心念格局小的借口和理由。

[Illuminating Intentionality]

If intentionality is focused on people of the same clan, although this is quite natural and understandable, it is not broad enough. In other words, if people focus their intentionality only on small groups, their intentions are obviously not enlightened enough. When intention is initiated, even if one cannot care about all the people in the world, one should not just focus on a small group with a limited number of members of one's own clan. Although cultivating one's own intentions should start with relatives, friends and compatriots, if the boundaries of one's own intentions are too clear, it is not conducive to expanding one's own intentions to the people under heaven.

The *Book of Changes* is a study of humanity and celestial nature, teaching people to practice the art of connecting human intentionality with heaven, so it is critical of the tendency to only implement intentions and purposes in the family. It can be seen that in the opinion of the authors of the *Book of Changes*, following the natural flow of emotion and initiating intentionality to connect with human feelings is not an excuse or reason for having a small framework of intentions.

九三：伏戎于莽，升其高陵，三岁不兴。

《象》曰："伏戎于莽"，敌刚也。"三岁不兴"，安行也。

【明译】

九三：一会儿埋伏兵甲在林莽之中，一会儿登上高陵侦察情况，折腾了三年，都不敢兴兵交仗。

《象传》说：埋伏兵甲在林莽之中，因为跟对手势均力敌。折腾了三年，都不敢兴兵交仗，说明九三安稳健行。

Nine (*yang*/strong line) in the third place: One time one was hiding ambush soldiers in the forest, and another one was on high land to reconnoiter the situation. After three years of torment, one still dared not raise troops to fight.

The *Image Commentary* (*Xiang Zhuan*) says: The ambush soldiers are in the forest, because they are evenly matched with their opponents. After three years of torment, they still dare not raise troops to fight, which shows that the Nine (*yang*/strong line) in the third place remains safe and sound.

【明意】

此爻涉及意向互动的复杂基础。意向的发动与争斗有一个力图均衡、最后失衡以及相应的时机问题。换言之，意向从不确定到确定性的实化有一个博弈过程。对危险要充分了解，才敢发动攻击的意向。关于自己与对方实力的评估需要不断调整，毕竟安稳健行最重要，最后没有发动攻击的意向，也是合情合理的，并且是可行的。

意向的发动和联系存在某种特殊的机制，毕竟，意向的发动规律与事物之间遵守的物理定律不同。人与人之间的意向联系一方面有某种规律性，一方面又几乎完全没有规律可言。《周易》说明人们意向互动的规律既涉及人的本性，又涉及时机、时势等，这些都是人的意向互动应该考虑的内容。

[Illuminating Intentionality]

This line deals with the complex basis of intentional interaction. The initiation and struggle of intentions involve a matter of striving for balance, final imbalance, and corresponding timing. In other words, the realization of intention from uncertainty to certainty involves a game-like process. One must fully understand the danger before one dares to initiate an intentional attack. The assessment of one's own and the opponent's strength needs to be constantly adjusted. After all, safe operation is the most important. In the end, it is reasonable and feasible to have no intention of launching an attack.

There is a special mechanism for the initiation and connection of intentions. After all, the rules for initiating intentions are different from the physical laws observed between things. On the one hand, there is a certain regularity in the intentional connections between people, but on the other hand, there is almost no regularity at all. The *Book of Changes* explains that the laws of people's intentional interactions involve not only human nature, but also timing, situational propensities, etc. These are the contents that should be considered in people's intentional interaction.

九四：乘其墉，弗克攻，吉。

《象》曰："乘其墉"，义弗克也。其"吉"，则困而反则也。

【明译】

九四：登上城墙，放弃攻打对手，这是吉祥的。

《象传》说：登上城墙，从道理上说，九四没有必要去攻击对手初九，这一爻吉祥的程度不高，不过平安而已，因为九四被推上城墙，遇到不得不打仗的窘困境遇，但知道应该返回到同人的正当原则上来。

Nine (*yang*/strong line) in the fourth place: It is auspicious to climb the city wall and give up attacking the opponent.

The *Image Commentary* (*Xiang Zhuan*) says: Climbing the city wall, logically speaking, there is no need for the Nine (*yang*/strong line) in the fourth place to attack his opponent, the Nine (*yang*/strong line) in the first place. The degree of auspiciousness of this line is not high, but it is just about safe, because the Nine (*yang*/strong line) in the fourth place has been pushed up to the city wall and encounters a troubling situation of having to fight, but knows that one should return to the legitimate pattern of one's colleagues.

【明意】

九四经过评估形势，自己消解了战斗的意志，放弃了战斗的意向，也因主动改变意向的方向，冲突就从自己这里避免了。可见，人的意念的方向和力量都由自己把控和注入，主动调节也就改变了相关情境，当坏的恶念不得实化，就不会有坏结果。因为没有人敢发兵，所以是和平的。九三不敢打，九四不当位，也不敢打。可见，和平不是抽象的概念，很多时候是因为战争双方的战争欲念被暂时压制住了，也就是战争恶念被压抑，并且有机制来维持压抑恶念的状态，这样和平状态才能持续。

[Illuminating Intentionality]

After assessing the situation, the Nine (*yang*/strong line) in the fourth place dispells the will to fight and gives up the intention to fight. One also takes the initiative to change the direction of one's intention, thus avoiding conflicts starting from oneself. It can be seen that the direction and power of people's intentions are controlled and infused by themselves, and that active adjustment also changes relevant situations. When bad evil intentions are not concretized, there are no bad results. Because no one dares to send troops, all is peaceful. If one does not dare to fight as the Nine (*yang*/strong line) in the third place, one will not dare to fight if one is not in the right position as the Nine (*yang*/strong line) in the fourth place. It can be seen that peace is not an abstract concept. In many cases, the desire for war on both sides of a war is temporarily suppressed, that is, the evil intentions of war are suppressed, and there are mechanisms to maintain the state of suppressing evil intentions, so that the state of peace can continue.

九五：同人，先号咷而后笑，大师克相遇。

《象》曰："同人"之"先"，以中直也。"大师相遇"，言相克也。

【明译】

九五：把群众聚合起来，先号咷大哭，后破涕为笑，好像大部队胜利会师。

《象传》说：把群众聚合起来，先号咷而后笑，是因为居于中位，而行为正直。大部队能够会师，是因为已经战胜了敌人。

Nine (*yang*/strong line) in the fifth place: Gathering the masses together, first howling and crying, then bursting into laughter, as if a large army joins forces in victory.

The *Image Commentary* (*Xiang Zhuan*) says: When the masses are gathered together, they shout first and then laugh, because they are in the middle position and behave uprightly. The large army is able to join forces because they have defeated the enemy.

【明意】

善恶之念构筑的意境，是于心念未发之间控制意念之形势，这种意境实化出来，犹如和平来自军事力量的相互制衡，双方都尽力克制发动战争的念头。集体意向的发动是可以通过情境的力量来调节的。彼此都自制约束可能获得和平，而一念出偏，就可能和平尽失。作为同人卦的九五爻，可谓永久和平之望，但《周易》作者非常清醒地意识到，非暴力的和平观念很难存续，这也可以说明，为什么非暴力很难在中国生根发芽，因为中国的非暴力来自武力的平衡，而不存在纯粹的非暴力，或把暴力虚无化的理论渊源。

在《周易》传统当中，非暴力是一种假设的理想情境，犹如罗尔斯的"无知之幕"，大家都是理想的好人，而且人足以被感化，但《周易》不是基于某些假设基础上开始的理论，《周易》的卦爻象都有明确的现实指涉。《周易》作者的思路其实是：如果坏人不能够收回自己的恶念，不能自控自己邪恶的意向的生发，那就只有兴正义之师去讨伐他，直到把他战胜为止。

[Illuminating Intentionality]

The intentional context constructed by intentions of good and evil is a situational propensity of controlling intentions before they are expressed. The concretization of this intentional context is like peace coming from the mutual checks and balances of military power, in which both sides try their best to restrain the intention of starting a war. The initiation of collective intentions can be mediated by situational forces. Peace can be achieved by restraining each other, but if one goes astray, peace can be lost. As the Nine (*yang*/strong line) in the fifth place of Hexagram Tongren (Comradeship), it can be said that this is the hope of lasting peace. However, the author of the *Book of Changes* is very clearly aware that it is difficult for the idea of non-violent peace to survive. This can also explain why it was difficult for non-violence to take root in China, because Chinese non-violence comes from the balance of force, and there was no theoretical origin of pure non-violence or nihilization of violence.

In the tradition of the *Book of Changes*, non-violence is a hypothetically ideal situation, just like Rawls' "veil of ignorance". Everyone is ideally a good person, and people can be influenced, but the *Book of Changes* is not a theory based on certain foundational assumptions, and the hexagrams and lines in the *Book of Changes* all have clear realistic references. The authors' intention behind the *Book of Changes* was actually: If a bad person cannot take back his evil intentions and cannot control the initiation of his evil intentions, then only a righteous army can attack him until he is defeated.

上九：同人于郊，无悔。

《象》曰："同人于郊"，志未得也。

【明译】

上九：到郊野之外跟人同心同德，不必忧悔。

《象传》说：与荒郊野外的人和睦相处，说明上九天下大同的志向没有实现。

Nine (*yang*/strong line) in the top place: Going out into the suburbs and being of one intentionality and mind with others, there is no need to worry.

The *Image Commentary* (*Xiang Zhuan*) says: Living in harmony with people in the wilds shows that the Nine (*yang*/strong line) in the fifth place's ambition of great unity under heaven has not been realized.

【明意】

意向的整合不可过度，过度了就离开现实的权力场域，同心同德也就只能得到郊野之人的认可。虽然努力了一个阶段，但也是努力在"域"外之"郊"而已，达不到"野"的状态。即使无位无应，不能感通天下，也可以努力与人同心同德，在与人和同的沟通中，随着意向性的融合，意识的境遇会越来越重合，生物基因和文化基因都在整合且越来越趋同，虽然直到最后也不可能完全消除差异，但通过心意的交流而实现某种共同的意识境域是可能的。

[Illuminating Intentionality]

The integration of intentions should not be excessive, since if it is excessive, it will leave the real power field, and the unity of one heart-minds and one intentionality will only be recognized by people in the suburbs. Although one has worked hard for a period of time, one has only tried hard to stay in the suburbs outside the territory, and cannot reach a wild state. Even if one has no position, no response, and cannot connect with the world, one can still work hard to be of one intentionality and heart with others. In communicating with others, with the integration of intentionality, the situation of consciousness will become more and more overlapping, and biological and cultural genes will become more and more overlapping, all integrating and becoming more and more similar. Although it is impossible to completely eliminate differences even at the end, it is possible to achieve a certain common realm of consciousness through communication of intentions.

火天大有（卦十四）　（乾下离上）

Dayou (Great Wealth), Fire and Heaven (Hexagram 14)　(Qian below, Li above)

　　《周易》的意念之生，遵守五行的因果律，只是这种自然因果规律不是物理世界严格的因果定律。如木生火后化成灰（土），不是严格意义上绝对必然的，但又不仅只是可能的，而更多是在现实和经验意义上终极性的，可以理解的。当然，因果律本身带有强烈的必然性意味，相信一个事物是另一个事物存在的原因，而另一个事物是前一个事物的结果。因果律帮助人们解释世界，也帮助人们预知世界，但基于自然科学的数理模型却未必能够揭示事物的必然走向。《周易》看世界上的事物从一种状态过渡到另一种状态，之间也基本存在某些必然的规律，并希望通过揭示这些规律来预知未来。应该说，因果关系的基础是共同经验，而五行生克关系的基础也是人类共同经验的意识境域。

　　"顺天休命"是人要在意念的生机当中，去实现上天赋予的美好使命，在意生的瞬间，人需要不断克制恶念，发扬善念，这是宋儒强调的"存天理，灭人欲"功夫。从此意念生机所归之论出发，不难理解佛儒一理。大有的根本境界，是在意念生发之处，生发而能够接续天机，则意念生发通于天机，犹如接续了意念缘生之源泉，则意念可以生生不灭而终至于大有之境界。

The creation of intentions in the *Book of Changes* abides by the law of cause and effect of the Five Phases, but this natural law of cause and effect is not the strict law of cause and effect in the physical world. For example, wood turning into ashes (earth) after producing fire is not absolutely inevitable in a strict sense, but it is not merely possible, but more ultimate and understandable in a realistic and experiential sense. Of course, the law of cause and effect itself has a strong sense of necessity, believing that one thing is the cause of the existence of another thing, and that another thing is the result of a previous thing. The law of cause and effect helps people explain and predict the world, but mathematical models based on natural science may not be able to reveal the inevitable direction of things. The *Book of Changes* looks at the transition of things in the world from one state to another, and how there are basically certain inevitable laws between them, and hopes to predict the future by revealing these laws. It should be said that the basis of causality is common experience, and the basis of the relationship between the Five Phases is also the conscious realm of human common experience.

"Submitting one's life to follow heaven" means that people should realize the beautiful mission given by heaven in the vitality of their intentions. At the moment when their intentions are born, people need to constantly restrain their evil intentions and carry forward their good intentions. This is what Song Confucianism emphasized: "Preserve heavenly principle and eliminate human desire." Starting from this theory of the destination of the vitality of intentions, it is not difficult to understand the common principle shared by Buddhism and Confucianism. The fundamental state of great existence is where the intentions arise. If intentions arise and can continue the heavenly patterns, then the intentions arise and connect with the heavenly patterns, like connecting with the origin of codependently-arising intentions. Then the intentions can arise and perish, and finally reach a state of great wealth.

大有，元亨。

《彖》曰：大有，柔得尊位，大中而上下应之，曰"大有"。其德刚健而文明，应乎天而时行，是以"元亨"。

《象》曰：火在天上，大有。君子以遏恶扬善，顺天休命。

【明译】

大有卦象征光大富有，非常亨通。

《彖传》说：大有卦，柔爻六五取得尊贵的位置，最中正而且上下的刚爻都跟它应合，故称大有。下卦乾为刚健，上卦离为文明，所以大有卦有刚健而文明的卦德，顺应天道按四季的顺序而运行，因此大亨通。

《象传》说：下卦乾为天，上卦离为火，组合在一起是火在天上，这就是大有卦。君子看到光明普照的现象，要遏止恶念，发扬善念，顺应天道赋予人的美好使命。

Hexagram Dayou (Great Wealth) symbolizes great wealth and prosperity.

The *Judgment Commentary* (*Tuan Zhuan*) says: In Hexagram Dayou (Great Wealth), the soft line Six (*yin*/soft line) in the fifth place acquires a distinguished position, and is the most central and upright, and the *yang*/strong lines above and below it all correspond to it, so it is called Hexagram Dayou (Great Wealth). The lower Trigram Qian is strong, and the upper Trigram Li is civilized.

Therefore, the hexagram has strong and civilized virtues. It follows the heavenly *dao* and runs in the order of the four seasons, so it is prosperous.

The *Image Commentary* (*Xiang Zhuan*) says: The lower Trigram Qian is sky, and the upper Trigram Li is fire. When combined together, fire is in the sky; this is Hexagram Dayou (Great Wealth). When an exemplary person sees the phenomenon of blazing light, he should curb evil intentions, promote good intentions, and comply with the beautiful mission given to humanity by the *dao* of heaven.

【明意】

一个人公共意念之境越广大，意念能够含摄他人他物的力量也越大，与他人志同道合，让他人归附的力量也越来越大，逐渐达到大有的状态。单纯的物质聚集不可能长久，只有道德和意念的长期聚集，才能够产生巨大的影响。天底下最有聚集力的是思想和愿力，可能在人的肉身消失之后继续发挥效力。

常人把意念的生机附着在对外在事物的执念上，这其实是对建立事业之人最大的考验。对外物执着重的人心意容易乱，反而生机减损，所以拥有意缘太多的人，对心意生机的考验就巨大，如果修养不够，心意的生机就难以承担得起应付强大意缘的责任和负担。

[Illuminating Intentionality]

The broader the realm of a person's public intentions, the greater the power of one's intentions to include other people and other things, and the greater one's power of being like-minded with others and making others join with one, gradually reaching a state of greatness. Purely material gathering cannot last long, only the long-term gathering of morality and intentions can have a huge impact. The most powerful thing in the world is the power of intentions and wishes, which may continue to be effective even after a human body disappears.

Ordinary people attach the vitality of their intentions to their obsession with external things. This is actually the biggest test for those who build a career. People who are attached to external objects tend to have their minds confused, which in turn reduces their vitality. Therefore, people who have too many intentional connections will have a huge test on their mental vitality. If they are not sufficiently cultivated, their mental vitality will not be able to bear the responsibility and burden of dealing with strong intentional connections.

初九：无交害，匪咎。艰则无咎。

《象》曰：大有初九，"无交害"也。

【明译】

初九：没有因交往带来害处，自然不会有过错，处境虽然艰难，但自守就不会有祸害。

《象传》说：大有卦初九这一爻，虽然不跟其他爻交往，但不会有交往带来的害处。

Nine (*yang*/strong line) in the first place: If there is no harm caused by communication, there will naturally be no fault. Although the situation is difficult, there will be no harm if one keeps to oneself.

The *Image Commentary* (*Xiang Zhuan*) says: Although the Nine (*yang*/strong line) in the first place of Hexagram Dayou (Great Wealth) does not associate with other lines, there will be no harm caused by association.

【明意】

富有的时候，内心不可没有艰难感，否则几乎心念出偏，马上就会有害。其实，要富有而惟艰方能免害。本爻因为无法跟主爻交往，处境艰难，所以劝勉其当艰难自守意念内在的生机，在明白不会有交往带来的害处的前提下，自修自悟意念生生之力。不交往可以减少让意识被外物所转的机会，因为没有条件交往而相对孤独的人，内心也相应强大，可以放下很多外缘。而不孤独的人，因为外在条件系缚的原因，有时可能不得不主动选择独处。大有涉及人对外在的意缘的把握，意缘应该只是人的意念实化的外缘，而不应该是目的。意缘属于物的部分，是意识流转的对象，不应该让意识之生随具体的意缘如金钱和地位而转。

[Illuminating Intentionality]

When one is wealthy, one must keep a sense of hardship in one's heart; otherwise one's intentions will almost certainly go astray and it will be immediately harmful. In fact, one has to be wealthy and suffer hardships to avoid harm. Because this line is unable to interact with the main line, one is in a difficult situation, so one is advised to take pains to guard the inner vitality of one's intentionality, and to cultivate and realize the power of one's intentions on the premise of knowing that there will be no harm caused by interaction. Not interacting can reduce the chance of being distracted by external objects. People who are relatively lonely because they have no conditions for interaction have a correspondingly strong inner heart and can let go of many external things. People who are not lonely may sometimes have to actively choose to be alone due to external conditions. Much of this involves people's grasp of external conditions, which should only be the external conditions for the realization of people's intentions, not the purpose itself. The emotional connection that belongs to the object is the object of the flow of consciousness. The generation of consciousness should not be allowed to follow specific emotional connections such as money and status.

九二：大车以载，有攸往，无咎。

《象》曰："大车以载"，积中不败也。

【明译】

九二：大车装载着重物，前往走，没有咎害。

《象传》说：大车负载重物，把重物堆积累放在正中间，车和东西就都不会散败。

Nine (*yang*/strong line) in the second place: There is no harm in carrying a heavy load on a cart and advancing.

The *Image Commentary* (*Xiang Zhuan*) says: A large cart carries heavy objects. If the heavy objects are piled up in the middle, the cart and things will not be scattered.

【明意】

九二的意识境遇可谓老成持重，并明白意识的生机要以隐忍沉稳为前提，知道痛苦是远航的压舱石，而意识对于痛苦的领悟和承受力，是意识能否继续安稳前行的关键所在。老成持重的人在生命的历程中受过挫折和磨难，对于生命历程当中生机维系之艰难多有体会，在负重前行之时，自觉把经历的苦难变成意念生机的压力，促进心意的生机更加沉稳。扩展开来也可以理解为，心意要想有生生，就要能适时忍辱负重，即心灵的生机不是简单生成和实化，而常常需要一些持守意念的功夫，懂得意念发动的时机要隐忍沉稳，从而让意念生生有力，也只有时刻担心重负失偏，才能稳掌大有之舵而前行。

[Illuminating Intentionality]

Nine (*yang*/strong line) in the second place's consciousness can be described as mature and prudent, and one understands that the vitality of consciousness must be forbearing and calm. One knows that pain is the ballast stone for a long voyage, and consciousness' understanding and tolerance of pain are the key to whether consciousness can continue to move forward steadily. Mature and prudent people have experienced setbacks and tribulations in the course of life, and are more aware of the difficulty of maintaining vitality in the course of life. When advancing with heavy burdens, they consciously turn the suffering experienced into pressure on the vitality of intentionality, and promote the vitality of intentionality to be more stable. Expanded, this can also be understood as saying that, if the intentionality wants to live, it must be able to endure humiliation and bear burdens at the certain times. That is to say, the vitality of intentionality is not simply generated and realized, but often requires some effort to hold onto intentions, and it is necessary to be patient and calm when the time to initiate an intention is known. In this way, intentions can be made powerful, and only by always worrying that a burden will go astray can we firmly grasp the rudder of great things and move forward.

九三：公用亨（xiǎng）于天子，小人弗克。

《象》曰："公用亨于天子"，小人害也。

【明译】

九三：公侯受到天子的宴享之礼，小人不能领受这样的礼遇。

《象传》说：公侯受到天子的宴享之礼，小人受此礼遇必有危害。

Nine (*yang*/strong line) in the third place: A prince receives the courtesy of a banquet from the emperor. A petty person cannot accept such courtesy.

The *Image Commentary* (*Xiang Zhuan*) says: If a prince is treated to a banquet by the emperor, it will be harmful for a petty person to receive such courtesy.

【明意】

可见，将心意控制在合适尺度之内，其实是九三品德的根本所在。一个人的心意如果不能够时刻掌控在自己可控的尺度之内，其与之有关的意缘就随时可能出问题，即使在大有的状态下，如果一念出偏，仍然可能丧失所有，有时不仅会失去之前获得的所有，或许还有身家性命之忧。

[Illuminating Intentionality]

It can be seen that controlling intentionality within appropriate limits is actually the foundation of the Nine (*yang*/strong line) in the third place's moral character. If a person's intentionality cannot always be kept within a controllable scale, problems may arise in the intentional relationship with it. Even in a state of great abundance, if one intention goes astray, everything may yet be lost. Sometimes, one may not only lose everything one has gained before, but also have to worry about one's family and life.

九四：匪其彭，无咎。

《象》曰："匪其彭，无咎"，明辨晢也。

【明译】

九四：（虽然大有，但）不自恃盛大，就没有咎害。

《象传》说：不自恃盛大，就不会有祸患，这说明九四清明知止，能明辨清楚自己的处境。

Nine (*yang*/strong line) in the fourth place: (Although there is great wealth, but) if one does not rely on one's greatness and take it for granted, there will be no blame.

The *Image Commentary* (*Xiang Zhuan*) says: If one does not rely on one's own grandeur, there will be no disaster. This shows that the Nine (*yang*/strong line) in the fourth place knows how to stop and can clearly identify one's own situation.

【明意】

盛大富有之时，如何面对个人权力与财富，其实在一念之间，境界立判。在大有的状态，富裕了要低调行事，不可张扬，要头脑清醒，思路明晰，知道盛大不是自己造成的，才能谦逊行事。可见，心意生机的尺度能够迅速穿透盛大的表象，知道盛大的状态不完全是自己的努力造成的，而是外在因缘由于心意生机的暂时和合而成，一旦过于执着，以为可以自居成功，这状态则可能转瞬即逝。

[Illuminating Intentionality]

When someone is wealthy, how to face personal power and fortune actually determines their realm in a single intention. In a state of abundance, when one is wealthy, one must act in a low-key manner and not be ostentatious. One must have a clear intentionality and clear thinking. Only when one knows that prosperity is not caused by oneself can one act humbly. It can be seen that the scale of the vitality of intentionality can quickly penetrate the appearance of grandness, knowing that the state of grandness is not entirely caused by one's own efforts, but is caused by external causes and conditions temporarily combining with the vitality of intentionality. If one is too persistent and thinks that one can claim success, it may be fleeting.

六五：厥孚交如，威如，吉。

《象》曰："厥孚交如"，信以发志也。"威如"之"吉"，易而无备也。

【明译】

六五：频频交往且有诚信，威严庄重，吉祥。

《象传》说：诚实守信遍交上下，说明六五能以诚信引发人的心志，同时自己的心志得到抒扬。威望庄重而得到吉祥，是因为六五平易近人，无所防备，大家也无需戒备，自然心生敬畏。

Six (*yin*/soft line) in the fifth place: Frequent interactions with integrity, majesty and solemnity, there is good fortune.

The *Image Commentary* (*Xiang Zhuan*) says: Honesty and trustworthiness are spread all around, showing that the Six (*yin*/soft line) in the fifth place can inspire people's aspirations with integrity, and at the same time, their own aspirations can be expressed. The solemn prestige and auspiciousness are due to the fact that the Six (*yin*/soft line) in the fifth place is approachable and unguarded, and everyone does not need to be wary, so they are naturally in awe.

【明意】

如此时势的领导者当然可以频频交往，因为威严有利诚信的建立，而诚信利于引发他人心志，实现心意的生机互通。如果不但能够威严还能平易，不使人戒备，那就是非常利于交往的时势状态。可见，大有的一个特征，是阴意都能够得位而生生不息，并唤起周围所有的阳意一起生生，众心会聚，众志成城，众人心意通达，光明灿烂，如日当空朗照，体现出光明心意无限的广度和深度。

[Illuminating Intentionality]

Leaders in such times can of course communicate frequently, because dignity is conducive to the establishment of integrity, and honesty is favorable to arousing the aspirations of others and realizing vitality in the exchange of intentions. If one can be not only majestic but also approachable and not make people wary, this will be a very favorable situation for communication. It can be seen that one of the characteristics of Hexagram Dayou (Great Wealth) is that *yin* intentions can take their place and flourish, and arouse all the *yang* intentions around them to flourish together. When the intentions of all people gather together, their will becomes a city, the intentions of all people are in communication, the light is brilliant, and the sun shines brightly in the sky, manifesting the infinite breadth and depth of luminous intentionality.

上九：自天佑之，吉无不利。

《象》曰：大有上吉，"自天佑"也。

【明译】

上九：得到上天的佑助，吉祥而无所不利。

《象传》说：大有上九吉祥而无所不利，是有来自上天的保佑。

Nine (*yang*/strong line) in the top place: Receiving heaven's assistance, there is good fortune and no disadvantage.

The *Image Commentary* (*Xiang Zhuan*) says: The Nine (*yang*/strong line) in the top place of Hexagram Dayou (Great Wealth) brings auspiciousness and no disadvantage, which is a blessing from heaven.

【明意】

大有所描绘的国家状态，确实很像柏拉图《理想国》的理想状态：君主六五心意光明透亮，治理有方；三个阳爻九二九三九四护持着君王，刚勇果决，中道节制；一般民众（初九）不随意交往，安守本分；这样看来，如果六五可以比作一个心意坐生，充满智慧，待人以诚，为天下人信任的哲学王，那么上九可以理解为超脱世俗，沉思人生和社会的哲学家。上九在反思中，领悟到生意发动达到巅峰状态，一定感慨万端。

[Illuminating Intentionality]

The state of the country described in Hexagram Dayou (Great Wealth) is indeed very similar to the ideal state of Plato's *Republic*: the monarch's intentionality is bright and clear, and he governs well; the three Nines (*yang*/strong lines) in the second, third and fourth places protect the king, are brave and decisive, yet take the middle *dao* of moderation; the ordinary people (the Nine (*yang*/strong line) in the first place) do not interact casually and keep to their duties; from this point of view, if the Six (*yin*/soft line) in the fifth place can be compared to a philosopher-king who is full of wisdom, treats others with sincerity, and is trusted by the world, then the Nine (*yang*/strong line) in the top place can be understood as a philosopher who is detached from the world and meditates on life and society. During the Nine (*yang*/strong line) in the top place's reflection, one realizes that productive intentionality has reached its peak, and must be filled with emotion.

地山谦（卦十五）　（艮下坤上）

Qian (Humility), Earth and Mountain (Hexagram 15)　(Gen below, Kun above)

　　谦卦六爻皆吉，六十四卦中这样的很少。地中有山，山入地中，象征人有巨大的实力，但意能隐而不发，表现得谦虚谨慎。只有谦虚能够让人在各种时空条件下都保持良好的状态。

　　谦虚的意能易于聚意缘，让意念的缘分延展，与他意和谐。谦虚是一个人每个心念发动都把他人的感受摆在前面，以心中有他人为根本。可见，谦卦希望人们在意念中始终如一地维持对于他人的关心和爱护。虽然人的意识境遇在自我和他人之间转换，但心念如何扩大，做到一言一行都关照他人，以他人存在为前提，其实非常不容易。从另一方面讲，人必须谦虚的哲理在于，人的自由是有限度的，个人自由是具体的、在群体当中的自由，而在任何群体当中，人与人之间的自由都是有限的。谦虚者因为得到天地的助力，有可能得到更多的自由；但不谦虚者，就可能消耗掉自己有限的自由，变得更加不自由。

　　The six lines of Hexagram Qian (Humility) are all auspicious, and there are very few like this among the 64 hexagrams. There are mountains in the earth, and the mountains are embedded in the earth, symbolizing that people have great strength, but can hide their intentions and behave modestly and cautiously. Only humility can keep people in a good state under various spatio-temporal conditions.

　　A humble intentionality can easily gather intentional dependent co-arising, let intentional dependent co-arising extend, and be in harmony with other intentions. Humility is when a person puts the feelings of others first in every intention, and takes the presence of others in one's heart-mind as the foundation. It can be seen that Hexagram Qian (Humility) hopes that people will consistently maintain care and love for others in their intentions. Although people's consciousness changes between self and others, it is actually not easy to expand intentionality and care for others in every word and deed, regarding the existence of others as a precondition. On the other hand, the philosophical principle that people must be humble is based on the fact that human freedom is limited. Personal freedom is specific and situated in a group, and in any group, the freedom between people is limited. The humble person may gain more freedom because of assistance from heaven and earth; but the immodest person may consume one's limited freedom and become less free.

谦，亨。君子有终。

《彖》曰："谦，亨"，天道下济而光明，地道卑而上行。天道亏盈而益谦，地道变盈而流谦，鬼神害盈而福谦，人道恶盈而好谦。谦，尊而光，卑而不可逾，"君子"之"终"也。

《象》曰：地中有山，谦。君子以裒（póu）多益寡，称（chēng）物平施。

【明译】

谦卦象征谦虚，有谦虚的美德就会亨通。君子谦虚办事就有始有终，会有好结果。

《彖传》说：谦卦，亨通。天道的运动状态是恩泽下施，大放光明，地道的运动状态是位置虽然卑下，却向上生成和运行。天道的运行使满盈之物亏损，使虚少之物增益；地道的运行使满盈的溢出，让多余的部分流入不满之处；鬼神的运行是祸害骄满者而福佑谦让者；人道的运行是厌恶贪得无厌者，喜欢谦让知足者。谦虚的人位于尊位就更加光彩夺目；即使处于卑下之位也无法超越他，所以君子自始至终保持谦虚。

《象传》说：上卦坤为地，下卦艮为山，地中有山，高山低入大地之中，大地中隐藏着高山，这是谦卦的象征。君子因此要减损多余的，增益寡少的；权衡事物多寡，然后公平地去施予。

Hexagram Qian (Humility) symbolizes humility. If one has the virtue of humility, one will be prosperous. An exemplary person behaves humbly, has a beginning and an end, and will have good results.

The *Judgment Commentary* (*Tuan Zhuan*) says: Hexagram Qian (Humility) means prosperity. The state of movement of the heavenly *dao* is that grace is distributed downward and shines brightly. The state of movement of the earthly *dao* is that although its position is humble, it develops and moves upward. The movement of heaven causes loss in full things and gain in empty things; the movement of earth causes fullness to overflow, allowing the excess to flow into places of insufficiency; the movement of ghosts and spirits harms the arrogant and blesses the humble; the movement of humanity detests those who are greedy and likes those who are humble and content. A humble person is more dazzling when one is in a high position; and even if one is in a humble position, one cannot be surpassed, so an exemplary person always remains humble.

The *Image Commentary* (*Xiang Zhuan*) says: The upper Trigram Kun is earth, the lower Trigram Gen is mountain, so there are mountains in the earth, high mountains sink low into the earth, and high mountains are hidden in the earth. This is the symbol of Hexagram Qian (Humility). Therefore, an exemplary person should reduce what is superfluous and increase what is deficient; one should weigh the abundance and lack of things and then distribute them equitably.

【明意】

谦虚的意能状态可以通于鬼神，也就是说，虽然天地阴阳变幻莫测，但因为谦虚者顺应了天道，天道就不难了解了。天道会让自满者所得减少，让谦虚者自然增加。如果不是有人格神在起作用，就是一种鬼神一般的神秘莫测的阴阳之力在起作用。如何让天道使自己的意能增加，就需要谦虚再谦虚。而谦虚以实力为基础，虽然姿态很低，但他人难以逾越，越谦虚他人就越难以逾越。换言之，谦虚者已经做出了为众人认可的贡献，之后才有资格表现出谦虚。反之，从一个人到一个家和国，如果富贵而骄，福气就会立即离开。

从一个人应该永远保持谦虚、遵守天道的角度看，人一生都不应该对自己过分有信心。因为自信心太强，其实是人主观性太强的表现，那就很可能要妨碍人对于客观的认识，而一旦无法客观地认识周围的形势，就很可能要在主观主义的阴沟里翻船。《周易》中的主观和自性都是建立在意识对客观形势的精准把握基础上的。

[Illuminating Intentionality]

A humble mental state can communicate with ghosts and spirits. In other words, although the *yin* and *yang* of heaven and earth are unpredictable, because the humble person conforms to the heavenly *dao*, it is not difficult to understand the heavenly *dao*. The heavenly *dao* will reduce the income of the complacent and increase the income of the humble. If there is not a personal god at work, it is the functioning of a mysterious and unpredictable power of *yin* and *yang* like ghosts and spirits. How to let the heavenly *dao* increase one's willpower requires humility and more humility. Humility is based on real strength. Although one's posture is low, it is difficult for others to overcome. The more humble one is, the more difficult it is for others to overcome. In other words, a humble person has already made a contribution that is recognized by everyone before one is qualified to show humility. On the contrary, from an individual person to a family and country, if one is rich and arrogant, blessings will immediately leave.

From the perspective that one should always remain humble and abide by the *dao* of heaven, one should never have excessive confidence in oneself throughout life. Too much self-confidence is actually a manifestation of people's strong subjectivity, which is likely to hinder people's objective understanding. Once they are unable to objectively understand the surrounding situation, they are likely to capsize in the gutter of subjectivism. The subjectivity and self-nature in the *Book of Changes* are both based on consciousness' accurate grasp of objective situations.

初六：谦谦君子，用涉大川，吉。

《象》曰："谦谦君子"，卑以自牧也。

【明译】

初六：谦而又谦的君子，有能力涉越大河，吉祥。

《象传》说：谦而又谦的君子，能够谦卑地把自己管理好。

Six (*yin*/soft line) in the first place: An exemplary person who is humble and humble again is able to cross a large river, which is auspicious.

The *Image Commentary* (*Xiang Zhuan*) says: An exemplary person who is humble and more humble can manage oneself well with humility.

【明意】

人虽然储备了巨大的意能，但谦虚又谦恭下人的态度，带有把自己放平放空的意思，管理好自己的本心和发动流行的每一念，让每一念的发动都带着川流奔腾的意能，而且是一种面死的意能，因为巨大的意能储存在向死而生的状态当中，而在死亡面前，所有人都一样必须谦虚再谦虚，即使有再大的意能，到最后都必然归零，所以意能的量度是时刻面对归零状态而存在的。而个人的意能无论如何通天，在浩瀚的宇宙面前，也就是一颗微尘，微不足道，我们没有理由不谦虚地发动和保有自己的意能。

[Illuminating Intentionality]

Although people have a huge reserve of intentional energy, their humble and courteous attitude towards others means to put themselves in a flat and empty state. They must manage their original heart-mind and every intention that they initiate and enact, so that every intention is initiated with a powerful and continuously flowing intentional energy, a kind of intentional energy that faces death, because huge intentional energy is stored in the state of living towards death, and in the face of death, everyone must be humble and modest, no matter how serious the situation is. Intentional energy will inevitably return to zero in the end, so the degree of intentional energy exists facing a return to a zero state at all times. No matter how powerful a person's intentional energy is, it is just a tiny speck of dust in the face of the vast cosmos, so there is no reason not to be humble in initiating and maintaining our own intentional energy.

六二：鸣谦，贞吉。

《象》曰："鸣谦贞吉"，中心得也。

【明译】

六二：谦虚的行为得到他人赞美鸣和，不沾沾自喜而能持守正道，可得吉祥。

《象传》说：谦虚的行为得到他人赞美，不沾沾自喜并能持守正道，可得吉祥，说明六二居中位，心里觉得谦虚很美而引发共鸣，是心中自得。

Six (*yin*/soft line) in the second place: Humble behavior will be praised by others. If one is not complacent but can stick to the right *dao*, one will gain good fortune.

The *Image Commentary* (*Xiang Zhuan*) says: When one's humble behavior is praised by others, if one is not complacent and can stick to the right *dao*, one can get good fortune. This means that the Six (*yin*/soft line) in the second place is in the middle and feels in one's heart that modesty is beautiful, which produces resonance, hence it is content from the bottom of one's heart.

【明意】

内心谦虚，意能增强，会有名声，得到鸣（名）和。因鸣而有名之后，切不可沾沾自喜，否则意能会受到减损。意能来自中心恒守的意念之力，因为谦虚而与他心共鸣，而自然而然感到快乐。上面看到六二的实力和修养，真诚地给予美誉，坚持正道则形势不错。

[Illuminating Intentionality]

If one is humble in one's heart, then one's intentionality will be strengthened, one will have a good reputation, and one will receive renown (fame) and harmony. After becoming renowned for one's expression, one must not be complacent; otherwise one's ability will be diminished. The power of intention comes from the intentional energy that is maintained in the center. Because one's humility resonates with other people's heart-minds, one naturally feels happy. Those above can see the Six (*yin*/soft line) in the second place's strength and cultivation, and sincerely give one honors. If one sticks to the right *dao*, the situational propensity will be good.

九三：劳谦君子，有终，吉。

《象》曰："劳谦君子"，万民服也。

【明译】

九三：有功劳又谦和的君子，有好结果，吉祥。

《象传》说：有功劳又谦和的君子，天下百姓都心悦诚服。

Nine (*yang*/strong line) in the third place: An exemplary person who is meritorious and humble will have good results, which is auspicious.

The *Image Commentary* (*Xiang Zhuan*) says: An exemplary person who is meritorious and humble will be admired by all the people in the world.

【明意】

劳是有意能，功劳积累了意识的能量，但能够自我控制，放低持守，能量将会更大。九三是卦主，位在山顶，三多凶，危险很大，故要继续谦虚谨慎，要感谢他人的谦让，让自己得到这样的成就。周围人看到九三如此有能力和成就还这样谦虚，就会心悦诚服。

[Illuminating Intentionality]

Labor has intentional energy, and merit accumulates the energy of consciousness, but if one can control oneself, lower oneself and persevere, one's energy will be greater. The Nine (*yang*/strong line) in the third place is the hexagram's master and is located on top of the mountain. The number three is inauspicious and the danger is great. Therefore, one must continue to be humble and cautious, and thank others for their humility, which allow one to make such achievements. When people around see that the Nine (*yang*/strong line) in the third place is so capable and accomplished yet so humble, they will be convinced.

六四：无不利，扚（huī）谦。

《象》曰："无不利，扚谦"，不违则也。

【明译】

六四：没有不利，因为处处运用发挥谦虚的美德。

《象传》说：发挥谦虚的美德没有什么不吉利的，这是因为六四不违背自然法则。

Six (*yin*/soft line) in the fourth place: There is no disadvantage, because the virtue of humility is used everywhere.

The *Imago Commentary* (*Xiang Zhuan*) says: There is nothing unfortunate in exercising the virtue of humility, because the Six (*yin*/soft line) in the fourth place does not violate the laws of nature.

【明意】

六四意能把控收放自如，自然生发，如水平之表，平稳安然。同理，人的意能当谦和流动，引而不发，从容中道。能够自然发挥谦德的人，内心如行云流水一般，流露出谦虚平和的气度，仿佛大化无形，意念一动，实化的瞬间就能够营造出一种谦虚的氛围，这是很高的修为境界。这种谦和的意能是顺从天地人神自然谦虚之原则的。

[Illuminating Intentionality]

The Six (*yin*/soft line) in the fourth place means intentions can be controlled, retracted, and released freely, and they can grow naturally, like a horizontal surface, stable and safe. In the same way, a person's will should be modest and flowing, directed but not released, and calm and moderate. People who can naturally display humility have a humble and peaceful demeanor in their intentions like clouds and flowing water, as if they are invisible. They can create an atmosphere of humility as soon as they initiate their intentions and concretize them. This is a very high level of cultivation. This kind of humble intention is in compliance with the principle of natural humility of heaven, earth, humans and spirits.

六五：不富以其邻，利用侵伐，无不利。

《象》曰："利用侵伐"，征不服也。

【明译】

六五：觉得因为邻居才变得不富裕，所以利用权势出兵讨伐，没有什么不利。

《象传》说：适宜利用权势出兵讨伐，是因为六五有实力去讨伐不服的人。

Six (*yin*/soft line) in the fifth place: One feels that one becomes less wealthy because of one's neighbor, so there is no disadvantage in using one's power to send troops to attack them.

The *Image Commentary* (*Xiang Zhuan*) says: It is appropriate to use power to send troops to attack because the Six (*yin*/soft line) in the fifth place has the strength to attack those who are disobedient.

【明意】

《周易》系统当中，意能的竞争最后可以用武力解决，这是《周易》与《论语》的重大区别所在。这说明，《周易》不是纯道德说教，不主张所有的问题都放在纯道德教化、纯仁情感化的礼仪框架里解决。在谦虚到极点，可是还是有人不服的情况下，有可能忍无可忍，而在形势允许自己动用武力的时候，是可以征伐不服的对象的。所以《周易》与道家、兵家、阴阳家、纵横家等各家学问相通，而儒家只是发挥了其道德教化层面的意义。

[Illuminating Intentionality]

In the system of the *Book of Changes*, competition between intentional energies can finally be resolved by force. This is one of the major differences between the *Book of Changes* and Confucius' Analects. This shows that the *Book of Changes* is not purely moral preaching, nor does it advocate that all problems should be solved within the framework of purely moral education or purely benevolent and affective ritual propriety. When one is extremely humble, but there are still people who are dissatisfied, one may be unable to endure this, and when the situation allows one to use force, one can conquer the dissatisfied. Therefore, the *Book of Changes* is connected with the Daoist, military, *yin-yang*, strategist and other schools of learning, while Confucianism only exerts its significance at the level of moral education.

上六：鸣谦，利用行师，征邑国。

《象》曰："鸣谦"，志未得也。可"用行师，征邑国"也。

【明译】

上六：因谦虚而声名远播，利于出兵打仗，征伐邑国。

《象传》说：上六这一爻因谦虚而声名远播，但志向仍然没有实现。可以出兵打仗，是因为可以征服自己治下还不服的邑国。

Six (*yin*/soft line) in the top place: Fame spreads far and wide due to humility, which is helpful for

221

sending troops to fight and conquer a country.

The *Image Commentary* (*Xiang Zhuan*) says: The Six (*yin*/soft line) in the top place is famous for its modesty, but its ambition has not been realized. One can send troops to fight because one can conquer the states under one's rule that are still unwilling to obey.

【明意】

不论一个人如何修身养性，谦而又谦，还一定会有人不服。这就只能在合情合理而且有手段的时候，适当运用手段来征服之，此为不得已而为之。武力的征伐是必要的，因为有一些人在道德教化所及的范围之外，这就是《周易》不单纯地假设人性之善，也不单纯地设定道德教化的唯一可行性，而是认为现实中的人是复杂的，虽然大部分人可以理解而被教化，但小部分的人不能理解，而且无法教化，最后不得不动用暴力机器与手段。

《周易》承认人之意无缘不可能成事，但有了意缘却不能生发，也是人生常态，毕竟很多时候，并不是意缘不得生发，而是不能按照自己主观的意愿来生发而已。在意缘过分违背自己的期盼，自己又有实力改变意缘的情况下，《周易》容许运用武力来实化自己的意缘。

[Illuminating Intentionality]

No matter how well a person cultivates one's moral character and how modest one can be, there will still be people who are dissatisfied. When it is reasonable, and when one has the means, one can use appropriate means to conquer the dissatisfied party. This is a last resort. Military conquest is necessary because there are some people who are beyond the scope of moral education. This is why the *Book of Changes* does not simply assume the goodness of human nature, nor simply posit the sole feasibility of moral education, but believes that people are in reality complex. Although most people can understand and be educated, a small number of people cannot understand or be educated. In the end, one may have to use violent mechanisms and means.

The *Book of Changes* admits that it is impossible for people's intentions to be concretized without predestined dependent co-arising, but it is also common in life that people's intentions cannot be concretized even with such dependent co-arising. After all, many times, it is not that an intention is not concretized, but that it cannot be concretized according to one's own subjective wishes. When intentional dependent co-arising goes too far against one's own expectations and one has the strength to change it, the *Book of Changes* allows the use of force to change it to be as favorable as possible.

雷地豫（卦十六）　（坤下震上）

Yu (Enjoyment), Thunder and Earth (Hexagram 16)　(Kun below, Zhen above)

雷从地下奋搏而出，象征意缘从无的背景中生出来，有一种爆炸一样的突然感，以及那一瞬间的"缘"带来的兴奋感。意缘的突然发生，都有或强或弱的预备征兆，也总会有一个预备的时空情境以备意缘之突发，而发生之后，意缘发生带来的怡悦欢欣鼓舞，既有豫乐感，但又不可以耽于这种豫乐感。

庄子之"天籁"有关于心念与天地之乐，意能顺物性而动，因意的先天结构与物等同，故物动即意动，意顺即意通与顺物性而动。大自然的声音是天籁，音乐是对大自然声音的模仿和创造，心灵把握事物内在韵律的客体化，由内而外地表现出来，如产生伟大艺术品的过程一般。心通于物，自然而然：通于物的节奏和韵律，人心自然能够感受到事物的内在运动之节奏，如物运化之音，事行进之乐等。

Thunder bursts out from the ground, symbolizing the emergence of intentional dependent co-arising from a background of nothingness. There is a sudden feeling like an explosion, and the excitement brought by that moment of dependent co-arising. There are always strong or weak preparatory signs for the sudden occurrence of intentional dependent co-arising, and there is always a prepared spatio-temporal situation to prepare for the sudden occurrence of dependent co-arising. After it occurs, the joy and excitement brought by dependent co-arising will be there. One has a sense of joy, but one also cannot indulge in this sense of joy.

Zhuangzi's "piping of heaven" relates to intentional thought and the joy of heaven and earth.

Intentionality can move in accordance with the nature of things. Because the inherent structure of intentionality is identical with things, the movement of things means the movement of intention, and the movement of intentionality means that intentionality is connected and moves in accordance with the nature of things. The sounds of nature are the piping of heaven, and music is the imitation and creation of the sounds of nature. Intentionality grasps the objectification of the inner rhythm of things and expresses it from the inside out, just like the process of producing great works of art. It is natural for intentionality to be connected to things: connected to the rhythm and rhyme of things, so that human intentionality can naturally feel the rhythm of the inner movement of things, such as the sound of the dynamic transformation of things, the joy of the advancement of things, etc.

豫，利建侯行师。

《彖》曰：豫，刚应而志行，顺以动，豫。豫，顺以动，故天地如之，而况"建侯行师"乎？天地以顺动，故日月不过，而四时不忒。圣人以顺动，则刑罚清而民服，豫之时义大矣哉！

《象》曰：雷出地奋，豫。先王以作乐崇德，殷荐之上帝，以配祖考。

【明译】

豫卦象征欢乐怡悦，有利于封建诸侯，兴兵征伐。

《彖传》说：豫卦，刚健之志得到应和，心志得以推行，这是心情欢乐怡悦的状态。豫卦下卦坤为顺，上卦震为动，顺应事物本性而动，所以天地的运行都会与它配合相应，何况是封建诸侯、行师征伐这样的事呢！天地顺阴阳之性而运动，所以日月运行不会失去法度，四季交替不会出现差误。圣人顺人天之性而动，就会刑罚清明，百姓心悦诚服。豫卦象征欢乐怡悦所显示出来的顺应人天本性的时机化意义实在太重大了！

《象传》说：上卦震为雷，下卦坤为地，雷从地下出来，大地振作起来，就是豫卦象征的欢乐怡悦的状态。先王从雷在地上轰鸣、大自然充满活力的现象中得到启示，要创制音乐以赞颂功德，并通过盛大的祭奠仪式进献给天帝，让历代祖先与天地一起共享欢乐怡悦。

Hexagram Yu (Enjoyment) symbolizes joy and enjoyment, which is beneficial for feudal princes to raise troops for conquest.

The *Judgment Commentary* (*Tuan Zhuan*) says: In Hexagram Yu (Enjoyment), strong aspirations are responded to and intentions are carried out. This is a state of joy and pleasure. The lower Trigram Kun of Hexagram Yu (Enjoyment) is harmony, and the upper Trigram Zhen is motion. One moves in accordance with the original nature of things, so even the movement of heaven and earth cooperates, let alone things like feudal princes and military conquests! Heaven and earth move according to the nature of *yin* and *yang*, so the movements of the sun and the moon do not lose their laws, and there are no errors in the alternation of the four seasons. If the sage acts in accordance with the nature of humanity and heaven, the criminal law will be clear and the people will be sincerely convinced. Hexagram Yu symbolizes joy and delight, and the timing of conforming to the nature of humanity and heaven is of great significance!

The *Image Commentary* (*Xiang Zhuan*) says: The upper Trigram Zhen is thunder, and the lower Trigram Kun is earth. When thunder comes out of the ground, the earth stirs itself, which is the happy and joyful state symbolized by Hexagram Yu (Enjoyment). The former kings were inspired by the phenomenon of thunder roaring on the ground and the natural world full of vitality. They wanted to create music to praise merits and present it to the emperor of heaven through a grand sacrificial ceremony, so that the ancestors of past generations could cooperate with heaven and earth to share joy and bliss.

【明意】

意念发动需要振奋，即心念发动之时需要外缘发动以提振之，犹若雷行则风雨相从。豫的快乐不仅是人的事情，而且是人之意感通天地之大乐。人需要喜乐，但喜乐要有度，这是对外缘的生发之节制，即要理智地控制外缘，理性和理智能反观欲望，监督做坏事心意之生灭，避免忘乎所以，如雷从地里出来，会让人振奋，但一开始也可能很震惊，如果自己所处的位置不安全，对于时势突然出现的缘分没有丝毫的准备之心，可能就会完全出乎意料。可见，得意忘形，可能乐极生悲。快乐的分寸在一定程度上取决于控制外缘的力量。人快乐的时候，要感谢天地和祖先，因为外缘其实都在天地之中。

[Illuminating Intentionality]

When intentions are initiated, they need to be invigorated. That is to say, when intentions are initiated, external conditions need to be initiated to boost them, just like how, when thunder moves, wind and rain follow. Yu's happiness is not only a human affair, but also a great happiness in which human intentionality affects and responds to heaven and earth. People need joy, but joy must be moderate. This is to control the occurrence of external conditions, that is, to control external conditions rationally. Reason and rationality can reflect on desires, supervise the emergence and extinction of bad intentions, and avoid forgetting oneself. Like thunder coming from the ground, when one emerges, it will be exciting, but may also be shocking at first. If one is in an unsafe position and not prepared for the sudden dependent co-arising of the situation, it may be completely unexpected. It can be seen that being carried away with oneself may lead to an extreme of happiness producing sadness. The measure of happiness depends in part on the power to control outer conditions. When people are happy, they should thank heaven, earth and ancestors, because the outer conditions are actually in heaven and earth.

初六：鸣豫，凶。

《象》曰：初六"鸣豫"，志穷"凶"也。

【明译】

初六：沉溺于豫乐，自鸣得意，一定有凶祸。

《象传》说：处在一卦之初就沉溺豫乐，自鸣得意，心志已尽，凶灾在所难免。

Six (*yin*/soft line) in the first place: Indulging in happiness and being complacent will certainly lead to disaster.

The *Image Commentary (Xiang Zhuan)* says: If one indulges in enjoyments at the beginning of a hexagram, one will be complacent, one's ambition will be exhausted, and disaster will be inevitable.

【明意】

为何满足于既有的意缘，自鸣（震）得意的同时就意味着意缘的坍塌？初六刚刚开始，就鸣于所得，显得过度安乐，忘乎所以，无志于建立新的意缘，则有危险。心志的丧失是心志对外缘维护的力度减弱，或者心志对外缘的控制力减弱，自得其乐从而放弃或减弱对外缘的控制，可能导致凶灾。可见，意缘应该尽量不随外界而动，努力维持内在的坚持和把握。意缘不仅仅是外缘，对外来的侵略有抗拒之责。选择即意缘择境的力量，意缘自然生发却不得过于自得，否则耽于自然意缘的起起落落，表现得了无心志，看起来随意随缘，其实并不合适。

[Illuminating Intentionality]

Why be satisfied with existing intentional conditions and feel proud of oneself, if this means the collapse of the intentional coarising? At the beginning of the Six (*yin*/soft line) in the first place, there is a danger if one feels satisfied with one's gains, appears overly happy, forgets about oneself, and has no ambition to establish new relationships. The loss of intentionality means that intentionality's strength to maintain or control outer conditions is weakened, and giving up or weakening control over outer conditions due to joyful self-satisfaction may lead to disaster. It can be seen that intentionality should try not to change with the outside world, but rather strive to maintain inner persistence and grasp. Intentional dependence (*yiyuan* 意缘) is not just an external factor, but has the responsibility to resist external interference. Choice is the power of intentional dependence to determine a situation. When intentional dependence occurs naturally, one must not be too complacent. Otherwise, one will indulge the ups and downs of natural conditions, which shows a lack of intentionality and seems to be accommodating, while in fact it is not appropriate.

六二：介于石，不终日，贞吉。

《象》曰："不终日，贞吉"，以中正也。

【明译】

六二：独立耿介坚定犹如巨石，不成天沉溺于安乐当中，守正吉祥。

《象传》说：不成天沉溺于安乐当中，守正吉祥，是因为六二居中守正。

Six (*yin*/soft line) in the second place: Independent, upright and firm as a boulder, do not indulge in peace and happiness all day long, but stay upright and auspicious.

The *Image Commentary (Xiang Zhuan)* says: That it is not acceptable to indulge in peace and happiness all day long, but still remains upright and auspicious, is because the Six (*yin*/soft line) in the second place is in the middle and upright.

【明意】

对于外在意缘的变化，要保持察微知几的超级敏感度，内心坚定，如果意识之缘稍有偏邪，要立即警醒纠正过来，不要等到一天过去再入夜反省，那样就慢了，应该尽快改正意念的缘分，其实也就是端正念头。

[Illuminating Intentionality]

Regarding the changes in the external conditions of consciousness, one must maintain a super sensitivity to detect subtle changes, and be firm in one's intentions. If the conditions of consciousness are slightly biased, one must be alert and correct them immediately. One does not need to wait until the day has passed before reflecting at night, which would be too slow. One should rather correct the dependent co-arising of one's intentions as soon as possible, which actually means maintaining one's righteous intentionality.

六三：盱（xū）豫，悔，迟有悔。

《象》曰："盱豫有悔"，位不当也。

【明译】

六三：媚上求欢，耽溺喜乐，导致忧悔，如果不及时悔改，就会追悔莫及。

《象传》说：用媚上求欢的方式耽溺喜乐，导致追悔莫及，是因为六三阴爻处阳位不正。

Six (*yin*/soft line) in the third place: Charming for pleasure and indulging in joy will lead to sorrow and regret. If you don't repent in time, you will regret it too late.

The *Image Commentary* (*Xiang Zhuan*) says: That indulging in joy through flattery and seeking joy leads to regrets is because the Six (*yin*/soft line) in the third place is a *yin* line instead of yang, which is not the yang position

【明意】

意念发动和人生选择都无法重回，悔根和赎罪的心灵代价无法言传。此爻之悲剧，在于明确放弃自己的独立人格，而随从他人的意缘，不主动操控自己的意缘，随波逐流，本质是放弃对意缘的自我选择权。这犹如自居卑微的属下把命运主动权交到主子手里；又如忏悔者进入教堂，放弃自由意志，完全让上帝给自己的选择做主。

[Illuminating Intentionality]

Neither intentions nor life choices can be undone, and the spiritual cost of regret and atonement is indescribable. The tragedy of this line is that one clearly gives up one's own independent personality and follows the wishes of others, not actively controlling one's own destiny, and just going with the flow. This essentially means giving up the right to choose one's own destiny. This is like a subordinate who considers himself humble and puts the initiative of his destiny into the hands of his master; it is also like a penitent who enters the church and gives up his free will, completely letting heaven make his choices for him.

九四：由豫，大有得，勿疑。朋盍（hé）簪（zān）。

《象》曰："由豫大有得"，志大行也。

【明译】

九四：众人依赖九四而获得喜豫之感，会大有收获，至诚不疑，朋友们会像簪子聚合头发一样聚拢在周围。

《象传》说：大家的喜豫之感由九四自身而来，会大有所得，说明九四的志意得以彻底实行。

Nine (*yang*/strong line) in the fourth place: Attaining joy by relying on the Nine (*yang*/strong line) in the fourth place, people gain a lot. They are sincere and have no doubts, friends gathering around them like hairpins gathering hair.

The *Image Commentary* (*Xiang Zhuan*) says: Everyone's feeling of joy comes from the Nine (*yang*/strong line) in the fourth place itself, and they gain a lot, which shows that the intentions of the Nine (*yang*/strong line) in the fourth place can be fully implemented.

【明意】

心志推行是意缘相通者的聚拢。人间大乐，或得志之乐是与人和乐与共，否则，无人共乐就无所谓大乐。人天大乐只存在与人、与天地分享的状态，这就是为什么大象辞说豫卦之主应该要创制人天大乐，以赞颂天地与人间的功德，为了表现人天之意与天地贯通的境界，要通过盛大的祭奠仪式，把真诚的意缘和喜豫的状态进献通达到天帝那里，让历代的祖先一起来享受和乐的化境，随同参与天地之大乐，一起配合共享人与天通的欢乐怡悦，这是意缘通达天地的化境。

[Illuminating Intentionality]

The implementation of intentionality is the gathering of people with similar intentions. Great happiness in the world, or the happiness of achieving one's ambitions, is to share happiness with others. Otherwise, there is no such thing as great happiness if there is no one to enjoy it together. The great joy of humanity and heaven only exists when shared with people and with heaven and earth. This is why the *Image Commentary* (*Xiang Zhuan*) states that the ruler of Hexagram Yu (Enjoyment) should create the great joy of humanity and heaven to praise the merit of heaven and earth, to express the intentionality of human and heaven and the relationship between heaven and earth. To achieve a state of connection, one must present one's sincere intentions and joyful state to the emperor of heaven through a grand memorial ceremony, so that the ancestors of all generations can enjoy the state of harmony together, participate in the great joy of heaven and earth, and together share the joy and happiness of the connection between humanity and heaven. This is the transformative state of intentional connection with heaven and earth.

六五：贞疾，恒不死。
《象》曰：六五"贞疾"，乘刚也。"恒不死"，中未亡也。

【明译】

六五：正在闹病，但长久不会死去。
《象传》说：六五位中却会闹病，是因为乘刚（九四）的原因。长期坚持不会死亡，是因为六五毕竟有中位优势。

Six (*yin*/soft line) in the fifth place: One gets sick, but stay alive for a long time.

The *Image Commentary* (*Xiang Zhuan*) says: As the Six (*yin*/soft line) in the fifth place, some will get sick because they ride on the strong (the Nine (*yang*/strong line) in the fourth place). One will not die if one persists for a long time, because after all, the Six (*yin*/soft line) in the fifth place has the advantage of a central position.

【明意】

柔爻凌于刚爻之上，代表意缘有所不安，但守正可过，因为有得力的九四，可以减少很多不必要的麻烦。这里是象征身体与心意的自我折磨状态，也是心身交关的缘起缘灭状态。心的状态与身的外缘之间不易协调，可能有所冲突，毕竟基于身体存在的身缘是心意之缘的起点，但人们常常意识不到，也就经常被忽略，可是，一旦身体闹病，心意之缘向外实化的意缘状态就会受到伤害，因为意缘将首先关注身缘，也就是要先集中到身缘的正常状态之中去。只有身体与外界的沟通之缘处于健康正常的状态，意念与外缘之间构筑的意缘才能正常实化和展开。

[Illuminating Intentionality]

The *yin*/soft line above the *yang*/strong line means that the intentional conditions are uneasy, but this can be passed by keeping upright, because with the powerful Nine (*yang*/strong line) in the fourth place, a lot of unnecessary troubles can be reduced. This is a symbol of a state of self-torture of body and intentionality, as well as interdependence between intentionality and body. It is not easy to coordinate between mental states and the outer condition of the body, and there may be conflicts. After all, the physical condition based on the existence of the body is the starting point of the condition of intentionality, but people often do not realize this and ignore it. However, once the body is in trouble, in case of illness, the intentional state of the mind-condition that manifests outwardly will be harmed, because the mind-condition will first focus on the body-condition, that is, it must first focus on the normal state of the body-condition. Only when the connection between the body and the outside world is in a healthy and normal state, can the connection between intentionality and the outside world be concretized and unfold normally.

　　上六：冥豫，成，有渝无咎。
　　《象》曰："冥豫"在上，何可长也？
　　【明译】
　　上六：昏昧无明地骄满喜豫，最后一定要有变化，才能没有咎害。
　　《象传》说：昏昧无明地耽于享乐到了极点，还处于上穷之位，这样的情况怎么能够保持长久呢？

Six (*yin*/soft line) in the top place: Being ignorant and arrogant, full of joy and gladness, there must finally be a change in order to be free from blame.

The *Image Commentary* (*Xiang Zhuan*) says: If one is ignorant and indulges in pleasure to the extreme, and also in a position of elevated poverty, how can such a situation be maintained for a long time?

　　【明意】
　　如果喜豫到不能收心，太过快乐以至于乐极生悲，这就走向事情的反面。所以不可沉迷于安乐，要及时收心，回归正途，在忧患之中多做预备。本爻有浪子回头金不换的味道，也有放下屠刀立地成佛的转念意味。
　　豫卦反对纵欲，反对纵情享乐，因为乐极生悲，祸福相依，快乐到极点必然走向反面。但能够长久喜豫的意缘状态必有人跟随。虽然全卦总是劝人不可过度欢乐，但其他意缘的追随却是自然的，所以豫卦之后紧接着是随卦。

[Illuminating Intentionality]

If one is so happy that one cannot contain oneself, and if one is so happy that extreme joy leads to sadness, this will lead to the opposite side of affairs. Therefore, one should not be addicted to peace and happiness, but must calm down in time, return to the right *dao*, and make more preparations for sorrow. This line has the flavor of a prodigal son returning being more precious than gold, and also has the flavor of a change of heart, of putting down the butcher's knife and immediately becoming a Buddha.

Hexagram Yu (Enjoyment) is against indulgence in lust and pleasure, because extreme happiness leads to sadness, misfortunes and blessings depend on each other, and extreme happiness will inevitably lead to its opposite. But if one can be happy for a long time, there must be people who follow. Although the whole hexagram always advises people not to be overly happy, it is natural to follow other intentional conditions, so Hexagram Yu (Enjoyment) is followed by Hexagram Sui (Following).

泽雷随（卦十七）　（震下兑上）

Sui (Following), Lake and Thunder (Hexagram 17)   (Zhen below, Dui above)

䷐

　　生存之境遇常常非人力所能选择，所以人需要随顺自己的生存境遇。生存境遇是全方位的，有无限的维度，所以人之心意应该择善而从，随缘自适，随机应变。随顺的意缘状态包括：生存需要权变，通达意缘的变化；随"意"即合适的意缘，但不可随意而不用心；就近的权宜容易太过随意；在复杂的意缘状态之中，要明白其中的利害关系，做出明智的选择；随缘但要用意，以扬公意而抑私意；死心塌地地跟随正当的意缘是成就事业之本。随不仅仅是身体的依附和跟随，根本上是意识境域的随顺他缘。一个人如何判断他人的意识境域值得追随，而且能够追随合道，并不是一件容易的事情。

Survival situations are often beyond human choice, so people need to adapt to their own survival situations. Survival situations are all-round and have infinite dimensions, so people should choose what is good, adapt to circumstances, and adapt to changes. The intentional state of adaptability includes: Survival requires contingency and understanding of changes in intention; following intentionality means suitable intentional conditions, but it cannot be done casually without paying attention; the nearest expedient is often too casual; in a complex state of intention, one must understand the stakes involved and make wise choices; go with the flow but use one's intentionality, promote the public will and suppress one's private will; following the right destiny wholeheartedly is the foundation of a successful career. Surrendering is not just the attachment and following of the body, it is fundamentally the adaptability of the realm of consciousness to other conditions. It is not an easy task for a person to judge that the realm of consciousness of others is worthy of following and compatible with the *dao*.

随：元亨，利贞，无咎。

《彖》曰：随，刚来而下柔，动而说，随。大亨贞，"无咎"，而天下随时，随时之义大矣哉！

《象》曰：泽中有雷，随。君子以向晦入宴息。

【明译】

随卦象征随顺适变，大为亨通，利于守正，没有咎害。

《彖传》说：随卦，刚爻来到柔爻之下，上兑柔下震刚，是刚来到柔的下面，刚健者甘居于柔顺者之下。下卦震动，上卦兑悦，上下卦组合就是行动使心中悦顺，所以有众人跟随。大为亨通，守持正道，没有灾祸。天下都能顺应时势而运动，随时提示的从宜适变的时机化意义实在太伟大了！

《象传》说：上卦兑为泽，下卦震为雷，雷进入大泽之中，泽水随着雷声而波动，这就是随卦象征的状态。君子随天时而动，动静合宜，日出而作，日落而息。

Hexagram Sui (Following) symbolizes being adaptable to changes, which brings great prosperity, is conducive to maintaining integrity, and implies no harm.

The *Judgment Commentary* (*Tuan Zhuan*) says: According to Hexagram Sui (Following), *yang*/strong lines come under *yin*/soft lines, and the upper Trigram Dui means soft while the lower Trigram Zhen means hard. The hard trigram comes under the soft trigram, meaning that the strong is willing to live under the soft. The lower Trigram Zhen vibrates, the upper Trigram Dui corresponds to joy, so the combination of the upper and lower Trigrams means that an action is pleasing to the heart, so people follow. Be prosperous, keep to the right *dao*, and there will be no disasters. The world under heaven can all move in accordance with the propensity of the times, and the significance of the opportunity to adapt to changes at any time is great!

The *Image Commentary* (*Xiang Zhuan*) says: The upper Trigram Dui is lake, and the lower Trigram Zhen is thunder. Thunder enters a lake, and the water in the lake fluctuates with the sound of thunder. This is the state symbolized by Hexagram Sui (Following). An exemplary person moves according to the times and the seasons, so one's movement and stillness are appropriate, and one works at sunrise and rests at sunset.

【明意】

关于意缘之随与肉体之附着于世之外缘的关系，应该说，心意并不是偶然占有使用肉体，因心意有肉体不能控制的部分。心意不是肉体的附属品，如泰勒（Richard Taylor）持心意与肉体相互作用论，即心意与身体交感互动构成随顺意缘的基础。意缘之随身难以简单化，如心理学关于疼痛的实验、中医的经络运行的检验等，通过仪器检查却难以发现，说明意识机能不仅是人身中的物理变化，不仅是神经元和皮层等的活动，不仅是体内内在的物理过程，不是肉体神经活动的简单副产品。总之，知意缘生生之理，则很难同意副现象论，更不可把心意与肉体绝对同一。应该说，意缘生生足以随顺外物之缘，意缘作为意识内外合一的境遇性存在，是心物一体的存在，是不仅具备物理性特征的客观存在，而是具备纯粹心灵意特征的实际存在，对这种存在的认识当以当下意念感通万物的心通物论为根本基石。

[Illuminating Intentionality]

Regarding the relationship between the following of intentionality and the attachment of the body to the outer world, it should be said that intentionality does not accidentally occupy and use the body, because intentionality has parts that the body cannot control. Intentionality is not an accessory of the body. For example, Richard Taylor holds a theory of mutual interaction between intentionality and the body, that is, that sympathetic interaction between intentionality and the body forms the basis of the smooth dependent co-arising. It is difficult to simplify the phenomenon of intentionality following the body. For example, experiments on pain in psychology and tests of meridian operation in traditional Chinese medicine are difficult to detect through instrumental examination. This shows that the functioning of consciousness is neither just a physical change in the human body, nor simply a function of the neurons and cortex. Activity is not just an intrinsic physical process in the body, nor a simple by-product of physical nervous activity. In short, it is difficult to agree with the theory of epiphenomenalism if we know the principle of the origin of intentionality and the body, let alone any absolute identity of intentionality and body. It should be said that the productivity of intentionality is sufficient to follow the dependent co-arising of external objects. As a situational existence that integrates the inside and outside of consciousness, it is an existence that unifies mind and things/events. It is an objective existence that has not only physical characteristics, but also purely spiritual and intentional characteristics. Any understanding of this existence should be based on a theory of intentionality and body that connects the myriad things with immediate intentionality as its fundamental cornerstone.

初九：官有渝，贞吉，出门交有功。

《象》曰："官有渝"，从正"吉"也。"出门交有功"，不失也。

【明译】

初九：为官有权变，变不离开正道，吉祥。出门与人交往，会有功效。

《象传》：为官有权变，随从正道吉祥。出门与人交往，会有功效，因为没有过失。

Nine (*yang*/strong line) in the first place: As an official, one decides on changes, and if one's changes do not deviate from the right *dao*, all is auspicious. Going out and interacting with people is effective.

The *Image Commentary* (*Xiang Zhuan*) says: An official has the power to change things, and it is auspicious because one follows the right *dao*. Going out and interacting with people is effective because there is no fault.

【明意】

此爻是刚爻随顺，来到柔爻之下继续变通随顺，走正道而无过失。心意之随当随正道。既然出门就要追随他人之缘，所以必须有一个基本的判断，知道哪些意缘值得追随。此爻代表出门当官，从事公共服务的事情，意缘随时随势都要由他人评判。此时心意虽刚，但必须让意缘生起刚正不阿，不宜有过失，才能维持功劳。这种刚正不失，其实也就是意缘都要按规矩合道做人做事才会有功效，也就必须要持守正道去随顺他人他意，构筑合适的意缘之境。

[Illuminating Intentionality]

This line is a *yang*/strong line that follows, and continues to be flexible when it arrives beneath a *yin*/soft line, following the right *dao* without making any mistakes. In following, intentionality should follow the right *dao*. Since one has to follow the dependent co-arising of others when one goes out, one must make a basic judgment to know which dependent arising things/events are worth following. This line represents going out to be an official or engaging in public service, where its intentional conditions will be judged by others at any time and in any situation. Although intentionality is strong at this time, it must be upright and unfailing, and there should be no mistakes in order to maintain merit. This kind of uprightness actually means that one must behave in accordance with the rules without mistakes in order to be effective. It also means that one must adhere to the right *dao*, follow other people's intentions, and build a suitable context of intentionality.

六二：系小子，失丈夫。

《象》曰："系小子"，弗兼与也。

【明译】

六二：系恋小子，失去丈夫。

《象传》说：系恋小子（初九），因为六二不能两者兼得。

Six (*yin*/soft line) in the second place: Being attached to a boy and losing a husband.

The *Image Commentary* (*Xiang Zhuan*) says: Being attached to a boy (the Nine (*yang*/strong line) in the first place), the Six (*yin*/soft line) in the second place cannot have both.

【明意】

意缘的选择常是两难选择，有时是情感抑或道德选择，甚至有时在利益选择之间举棋不定。理性的意缘选择或依从外在原则，或依从内在良心。意缘的社会性体现在社会交往的选择常常有得有失，意之对象的外在之缘不可能全部都得，因为意必有向，而向则有得必有失，不同选择对象之间可能有利益对立关系，也就不可得兼。一个本应选择丈夫（或老师、军师）的人，在某种时空条件下，可能被身边人改变其对于长者的意缘之境，不选择扩大而是缩小自己的意识境域，来从情感上把自己做的选择合理化。

[Illuminating Intentionality]

Choosing intentional conditions is often a dilemma, sometimes an emotional or moral choice, and sometimes one is even undecided between a choice of interests. Rational choice depends either on external principles or on inner conscience. The social nature of intention is reflected in the fact that there are often gains and losses in the choice of social interactions. It is impossible to obtain all the external connections of an object of intention, because intention must have a direction, and there must be gains and losses in any direction. Different choices of objects may have conflicting interests between them, where one cannot have both. A person who is supposed to choose a husband (or teacher, or military commander) may, under certain spatio-temporal conditions, be changed by the people around them to change their emotional state of intentionality towards their elder, and choose not to expand but to narrow their own realm of consciousness in order to choose based on emotions, and rationalize the choices they make.

六三：系丈夫，失小子。随有求，得。利居贞。

《象》曰："系丈夫"，志舍下也。

【明译】

六三：系恋丈夫，则失去小子。追随他人有所求，能够得到，但宜于用安居守正之道来追随。

《象传》说：系恋丈夫（九四），是六三心志坚定地不选择在下的小子（初九）。

Six (*yin*/soft line) in the third place: If one is attached to one's husband, one will lose one's boy. If one follows others, one can get what one wants, but it is advisable to follow them in a peaceful and upright way.

The *Image Commentary* (*Xiang Zhuan*) says: She loves her husband (the Nine (*yang*/strong line) in the fourth place), and is determined not to choose the boy beneath her (the Nine (*yang*/strong line) in the first place).

【明意】

可见每一个意缘的选择都有得有失，时空的唯一性与相关的得失状态都有关系，意的唯一之缘都有唯一的现实性，但也有唯一的决定性和不可改易性。每一个意缘的生成，都对他者的意缘生成构成影响，因为意缘时刻的生成变化，改变着意境的能量体系，也自然对他人的意缘生成变化形成影响。

[Illuminating Intentionality]

It can be seen that every choice of intentionality has gains and losses. The uniqueness of time and space is related to the correlated gains and losses. The unique dependent co-arising of intentionality has unique reality, but it is also uniquely decisive and unchangeable. The formation of each intentional condition has an impact on the formation of other intentional conditions, because the generation and change of the intentional context at any time changes the energy system of the intentional context, and naturally affects the formation and changes of other people's intentional conditions.

九四：随有获，贞凶。有孚在道，以明，何咎？

《象》曰："随有获"，其义"凶"也。"有孚在道"，明功也。

【明译】

九四：随从他人而自己有所收获，如果还正固不会权变就有凶险。如果心怀诚信，言行合乎正道，能够明辨进退，那又会有什么灾害呢？

《象传》说：随从他人而自己有大收获，从道义上说九四应当有凶灾。但因为九四心怀诚信，能处正道，所以是因明智而有功劳。

Nine (*yang*/strong line) in the fourth place: If one follows others and gains something oneself, but one remains upright and does not change one's intention, there is danger. If one has integrity in one's mind, one's words and deeds are in line with the right *dao*, and one can clearly distinguish between advance and retreat, what disaster will happen?

The *Image Commentary* (*Xiang Zhuan*) says: If one follows others and gains a lot, morally speaking, there should be disasters in the Nine (*yang*/strong line) in the fourth place. But because the Nine (*yang*/strong line) in the fourth place has integrity and is able to follow the right *dao*, one gains merit through one's wisdom.

【明意】

九四为求自保，要时刻输诚，尽量让九五知道，自己每时每刻心思意念里都装着他，关键时刻永远会把九五的利益放在第一位，否则就很危险。九四意念中时时输诚以求自我保护，其意缘虽有轻重缓急，但受情境的驱迫，为了让九五放心，心意中的缘分总是得把他作为意缘的第一要素，其实就是意境的基调，或者以九五作为自己意境之背景。九四要让九五感通到自己的意境完全是九五在主导，自己所有的意缘之取舍都当符合九五的利益。

[Illuminating Intentionality]

In order to protect himself, the Nine (*yang*/strong line) in the fourth place must always be sincere and try to let the Nine (*yang*/strong line) in the fifth place know that one is always in one's intentions and heart-mind. One must always put the Nine (*yang*/strong line) in the fifth place's interests first at critical moments, otherwise it will be very dangerous. In the Nine (*yang*/strong line) in the fourth place's intentions, one always loses sincerity in order to protect oneself. Although one's dependent co-arising has different priorities, one is driven by the situation. In order to make the Nine (*yang*/strong line) in the fifth place feel at ease, one must always regard oneself as the first element among one's intentional conditions. In fact, this is the keynote of the intentional context, or the Nine (*yang*/strong line) in the fifth place is taken as the background of one's own intentional context. The Nine (*yang*/strong line) in the fourth place must let the Nine (*yang*/strong line) in the fifth place feel that one's own intentional context is entirely under one's control, and all the choices of one's intentional context should be in line with the Nine (*yang*/strong line) in the fifth place's interests.

九五：孚于嘉，吉。

《象》曰："孚于嘉，吉"，位正中也。

【明译】

九五：相信并收获着各种嘉美之事，非常吉利。

《象传》说：对嘉美之道心存诚信，吉祥的原因是九五位置既正又中。

Nine (*yang*/strong line) in the fifth place: Believing in and reaping all kinds of wonderful things, it is very auspicious.

The *Image Commentary* (*Xiang Zhuan*) says: Having sincerity for the *dao* of wonder in its heart, the reason for auspiciousness is that the Nine (*yang*/strong line) in the fifth place is both upright and in the middle.

【明意】

要顺利发展人生事业的意缘，就要心怀诚信，主要是对事业要有大公无私意义上的诚信，要诚到对事业的热爱能够压抑、有时甚至牺牲个人私情。从一个方面说明，做领导或者为了成就公共事业，就要努力维持公心和公共意缘，也就不能过分在乎和计较私情，不宜让私情之意缘影响或破坏事业之意缘。

[Illuminating Intentionality]

In order to successfully develop one's life and career, one must have integrity, especially selfless integrity in one's career. One must be so sincere that one's love for one's career can suppress or sometimes even sacrifice one's personal feelings. Explained from one aspect, as a leader or in order to achieve public undertakings, one must strive to maintain a public spirit and public aspirations. This means that one should not be excessively concerned about or calculating in personal relationships, and should not let personal relationships and feelings affect or destroy one's career aspirations.

上六：拘系之，乃从维之，王用亨于西山。

《象》曰："拘系之"，上穷也。

【明译】

上六：好像被（九五）拘押住，拴起来，又（被九五随顺地）维系住，追随大王（九五）到西山去祭享天地。

《象传》说：上六所以会（宁可主动被九五）拘系起来（以便追随九五），是因为上六处在极上困穷之位，随顺到头（没有方向）了。

Six (*yin*/soft line) in the top place: As if detained and tied up (by the Nine (*yang*/strong line) in the

237

fifth place), and restrained (submissively, by the Nine (*yang*/strong line) in the fifth place), one follows the King (the Nine (*yang*/strong line) in the fifth place) to the Western Mountains to offer sacrifices to heaven and earth.

The *Image Commentary* (*Xiang Zhuan*) says: The reason why the Six (*yin*/soft line) in the top place is (and would actively choose to be) detained (in order to follow the Nine (*yang*/strong line) in the fifth place) is because the Six (*yin*/soft line) in the top place is in an extremely poor position and can now only follow (without any direction).

【明意】

随卦因此强调人心之相随，随到极致，以致民心相系于其主，死心塌地如绳结一般坚固，共同维系王朝伟业。民心相随王之意缘，为王业之本，也就是民心随顺皆善的意缘相聚合成，这就是王业的基石。人民随顺王的意缘，是王之意中有民，而民之意中有王，意缘相互感应，层层叠叠，互相叠聚，才最终能够成就王业。

[Illuminating Intentionality]

Hexagram Sui (Following) therefore emphasizes following people's intentions to the extreme, so that the people's intentions are bound to their ruler, and they are as strong and secure as a knot, and together they maintain the great cause of the dynasty. The people's intentions follow the king's intentionality, which is the foundation of the king's reign. That is, the people's intentions and minds follow all good intentionality in its dependent co-arising. The people follow the king's intentionality, because the king's intentions contain the people, and the people's intentions contain the king. Intentionality and dependent co-arising resonate with each other, layer upon layer, and overlap each other so that the king's cause can finally be achieved.

第二章　易经明意
——爻意分说（上经）

山风蛊（卦十八）　（巽下艮上）

Gu (Corruption), Mountain and Wind (Hexagram 18)　(Xun below, Gen above)

追随的人多了，意向的结构变得复杂，而难免出现问题，需要整顿解决。追随一个中心意向，彼此之间的互动会有事情，这种事情是由于意向的杂乱和混沌导致的。

颐卦上六谈及颐养之道的先天结构为天地之生机，意识之中能够涵养领悟先天的生机而后为己所用。颐养之道体现出来的先天性生机归于蛊卦所展示的时间结构，换言之，蛊卦是接续颐卦先天生机的时间结构之展开。

人生在时间中流逝，本身是一种时间意识，在意识的流动过程之中，人建构了时间观念。时间存续的先天结构是人对时间建构的基础，人们在意识之中建立时间观念，必须以理解时间的先行结构作为基础，即"意—时"，悟得"意—时"有利于依时行事和做事。

As more people follow, the structure of intention becomes more complex, and problems inevitably arise that need to be rectified and resolved. When following a central intention, there will be problems in the interactions between people, which are caused by the confusion and chaos of their intentions.

Hexagram Yi (Nourishment) talks about the transcendental structure of the way of nourishment as the vitality of heaven and earth. Transcendental vitality can be cultivated and understood in consciousness and then used for oneself. The transcendental vitality reflected in the way of nourishment can be attributed to the time structure displayed by Hexagram Gu (Corruption). In other words, Hexagram Gu (Corruption) is an expansion of the time structure that continues the transcendental vitality of Hexagram Yi (Nourishment).

The passage of life in time is itself a kind of temporal consciousness. In the process of the flow of consciousness, people construct the concept of time, and the transcendental structure of the existence of time is the basis for people's construction of time. When people establish the concept of time in their consciousness, they must understand the antecedent structure of time as the basis, that is, "intentionality-time." Understanding "intentionality-time" is conducive to relying on it to be on time in one's affairs.

蛊，元亨。利涉大川，先甲三日，后甲三日。

《彖》曰：蛊，刚上而柔下，巽而止，蛊。"蛊，元亨"而天下治也。"利涉大川"，往有事也。"先甲三日，后甲三日"，终则有始，天行也。

《象》曰：山下有风，蛊。君子以振民育德。

【明译】

蛊卦象征整饬修治，大为亨通，有利于涉越大河。应该在"甲"日之前的（癸壬辛）三天准备，在"甲"日之后的（乙丙丁）三天行动。

《彖传》说：蛊卦从泰卦变来，是泰卦初九的刚爻上到上位，上位的上六柔爻来到下位；上卦艮为山为阳卦，下卦巽为风为阴卦，阳刚在上，刚健向上；阴柔在下，柔顺居下。下卦为巽为风顺，上卦为艮为止，好比风遇山而能止，又好比乘着顺风又有岸可止，这就是蛊卦的卦象。蛊卦大为亨通，是天下得到了治理，有利于涉越大河，克服大难，是要勇敢去干革除积弊的事情。在"甲"日之前的（癸壬辛）三天准备，在"甲"日之后的（乙丙丁）三天行动，这是旧时期需要整治终结，要开始新的时期，任何事情都要有始有终，循环往复，这是天道运行的本然状态。

《象传》说：上卦艮为山，下卦巽为风，山下吹来大风的卦象就是蛊卦。君子从风吹叶落，摧枯拉朽之象中受到启示，要振作民众、培育道德。

Hexagram Gu (Corruption) symbolizes rectification and repair, which brings great prosperity and is conducive to crossing a large river. One should prepare three days before the start of the first day (Gui, Ren, Xin), and act three days after the start of the first day (Yi, Bing, Ding).

The *Judgment Commentary* (*Tuan Zhuan*) says: Hexagram Gu (Corruption) changes from Hexagram Tai (Communication). The Nine (*yang*/strong line) in the first place in Hexagram Tai (Communication) goes up to the upper position, and the Six (*yin*/soft line) in the top place goes to the lower position; the upper Trigram Gen is mountain and is a *yang* hexagram, and the lower Trigram Xun is wind and is a *yin* hexagram, with masculinity on the top and strength rising upward, and femininity and softness on the bottom. The lower Trigram Xun means the wind is smooth, and the upper Trigram Gen means the wind can stop when it encounters a mountain, like riding a favorable wind and having a shore to stop at. This is the hexagram image of Hexagram Gu (Corruption).

Hexagram Gu (Corruption) is very prosperous, meaning that the world has been governed, which is conducive to crossing large rivers and overcoming catastrophes. It means that one must be brave enough to eliminate long-standing evils. Three days of preparation (Gui, Ren, Xin) before the start of the first day and three days of action (Yi, Bing, Ding) after the start of the first day signify that this is the end of the old period that needs to be rectified, and that, to start a new period, anything can be done. There must be a beginning and an end, and the cycle repeats itself. This is the natural state of the movement of heaven.

The *Image Commentary* (*Xiang Zhuan*) says: The upper Trigram Gen is mountain, the lower Trigram Xun is wind, and the hexagram image of strong wind blowing from below a mountain is Hexagram Gu. Exemplary people are inspired by the phenomenon of leaves falling in the wind and destroying dryness and decay, and know to inspire the people and cultivate morality.

【明意】

风气变坏，人们心意蛊乱，需要整治改变。腐败虽然难免，但须及时治理，要振作精神，也就是发动意念，发心改变堕落状态，如秋风扫落叶一般，把腐败的地方摧枯拉朽涤荡干净。振作做事的根本在于抉择的魄力，能够选择本身就是吸收时的能量。选择关乎情境，不关乎情感；情感影响理智判断，制造无名业力，最后需要靠理智来调节。《周易》是理性选择与调节的智慧，治理腐败近乎《孙子》讨论的决战，关乎严峻的自控力，自控意识，不可以被情感所乱。

[Illuminating Intentionality]

The ethos has become bad, people are confused and need to be rectified and reformed. Although corruption is unavoidable, it must be dealt with in a timely manner, and one must cheer up, that is, mobilize one's intentions and resolve to change the corrupt state, just like the autumn wind sweeping away fallen leaves, destroying and cleaning up corrupt places. The foundation of hard work lies in the courage to make choices, and being able to choose is itself an energy that absorbs time. Choices are about situations, not emotions; emotions affect rational judgment, create nameless karma, and ultimately need to be adjusted by reason. The *Book of Changes* is about the wisdom of rational choice and adjustment. Managing corruption is close to the decisive battle discussed in Sunzi's *Art of War*. It is about strict self-control and awareness of self-control, which must not be confused by emotions.

初六：干（gàn）父之蛊，有子，考无咎。厉，终吉。

《象》曰："干父之蛊"，意承"考"也。

【明译】

初六：整治先父留下的腐败和积弊，这是能继承大业的好儿子，对于亡父来说，没有祸患，虽然有一些危险，但最终会吉祥。

《象传》说：整治先父时代的腐败和积弊，这说明儿子在意识中要继承和发扬父政的生机。

Six (*yin*/soft line) in the first place: One who rectifies the corruption and malpractice left by his late father is a good son who can inherit the great cause, and there is no disaster for the deceased father. Although there are some dangers, all will be auspicious in the end.

The *Image Commentary* (*Xiang Zhuan*) says: Rectifying the corruption and malpractice of his father's time shows that the son should carry forward the vitality of his father's government in his consciousness.

【明意】

要在意识之中自觉自明地继承先人之志，即意识的继承主要包括对先人文化意识的继承、祖先和家族意识的传承等。个人的家族意识是其自我意识塑造的一部分。文化、家族意识可能成为一种无意识的传承和积淀，但也来自有意识的选择与必要的自我塑造的长期积淀。时间久了，一个人的精神、观念重复形成习惯，精神习惯的重复影响人的行为，也影响其家人与周围人的意识境遇。

人的成长是试错的过程。精神上的腐败可以通过沟通改变，但物质方面的腐败就可能会上瘾而难于改变。即使改掉物质方面的习惯比较困难，人也要让精神成为身外之物的主宰，而非相反。

[Illuminating Intentionality]

We must consciously and deliberately inherit the aspirations of our ancestors in our consciousness, that is, the inheritance of consciousness mainly includes the inheritance of our ancestors' cultural consciousness, the inheritance of ancestral and family consciousness, etc. An individual's sense of family is part of the shaping of his or her sense of self. Cultural and familial consciousness may be an unconscious inheritance and accumulation, but they also come from conscious choices and long-term accumulation of necessary self-shaping. Over time, a person's spirit and concepts are repeated to form habits. The repetition of mental habits affects a person's behavior and also affects the consciousness of one's family and the people around them.

Human growth is a process of trial and error. Mental corruption can be changed through communication, but material corruption may become addictive and difficult to change. Even if it is difficult to change material habits, people must let their spirit become the master of things outside themselves, not the other way around.

九二：干母之蛊，不可贞。

《象》曰："干母之蛊"，得中道也。

【明译】

九二：整治母辈所造成的腐败和积弊，要坚定但不可过分固执。

《象传》说：整治母辈所造成的腐败和积弊，因为九二在下卦中位，行事符合中道。

Nine (*yang*/strong line) in the second place: To rectify the corruption and long-term abuses caused by our parents, we must be firm but not overly stubborn.

The *Image Commentary* (*Xiang Zhuan*) says: One must correct the corruption and accumulated malpractice caused by one's mother's generation, because the Nine (*yang*/strong line) in the second place is in the middle of the lower Trigram, and its actions are in line with the middle way.

【明意】

意念可以转变蛊乱现象，但需要区分蛊乱问题产生是公共领域本身出了问题，还是因为私情的分寸不当。如果是私情缺乏约束导致的，那就应该与公共问题采取不一样的手段与分寸来处理。此爻明确指出，纠正私情造成的积弊不宜过度。虽儿子治理蛊乱的意识境遇应时刻与亡父亡母的心意相通，但对父政的继承与纠偏跟涉及母辈的弊政处理的方式要内外有别，处理家政的意识要和缓，而治理外政的意识需要宁严勿宽。

[Illuminating Intentionality]

Intentions can change phenomena of disorder, but it is necessary to distinguish whether a problem of disorder occurs because of problems in the public domain itself, or because of inappropriate personal relationships. If it is caused by a lack of restraint in private affairs, then it should be handled with different methods and measures than public issues. This line clearly points out that correcting the long-standing harm caused by personal relationships should not be excessive. Although a son's consciousness of governing disorder should always be connected with the intentions of his deceased father and mother, the way of inheriting and correcting his father's rule should be different from the way of dealing with bad governance involving the mother's generation. One's awareness should be mild in dealing with family governance, but should be strict rather than lenient in dealing with external affairs.

九三：干父之蛊，小有悔，无大咎。

《象》曰："干父之蛊"，终无咎也。

【明译】

九三：整治父辈的腐败和弊政，虽然还有小的忧悔遗憾，但没有太大的祸患。

《象传》说：整治父辈造成的腐败和弊政，宁可矫枉过正，最终不会有太大的祸患。

Nine (*yang*/strong line) in the third place: Although a few regrets and misgivings about rectifying the corruption and bad governance of one's father's generation still remain, there is no major disaster.

The *Image Commentary* (*Xiang Zhuan*) says: To rectify the corruption and bad governance caused by one's fathers, it is preferable to be severe and strict, then there will be no big disaster in the end.

【明意】

从整治的分寸来看，初六是后继有人，励精图治；九二是内部整治，对家人适可而止；九三是治理公共乱象，宁可雷霆万钧，矫枉过正。此爻是说，为了维系父政"意—

时"的生机而必须整治之前父政中不利于当下生机的部分，即使有整治过分的问题也要继续刚硬的意识状态，为的是避免最后出现大的乱子。

[Illuminating Intentionality]

From the point of view of the degree of rectification, the Six (*yin*/soft line) in the first place has successors and works hard; the Nine (*yang*/strong line) in the second place rectifies internally, just enough for the family; the Nine (*yang*/strong line) in the third place deals with public disorder, and it is better to act like a thunderbolt in severity and strictness. This line means that in order to maintain the vitality of the "intentionality-time" of one's father's government, it is necessary to rectify the parts of the father's government that are not conducive to current vitality. Even if there is excessive rectification of problems, one must continue to have a rigid state of consciousness in order to avoid greater disorder finally occurring.

六四：裕父之蛊，往见吝。

《象》曰："裕父之蛊"，往未得也。

【明译】

六四：宽容放任地处理父辈的腐败和弊政，长此以往会有遗憾羞吝。

《象传》说：懈怠迁就地处理父辈的腐败和弊政，听凭原样因循苟且下去，长久以往将会一无所得。

Six (*yin*/soft line) in the fourth place: If one deals with the corruption and bad government of one's father's generation with tolerance and a laissez-faire attitude, one will have regrets and difficulties in the long run.

The *Image Commentary* (*Xiang Zhuan*) says: If one is lazy and indulgent in dealing with the corruption and bad government of one's father's generation, and allows things to continue as they are, one will gain nothing in the long run.

【明意】

如果过分宽容父政当中不利于当下延续生机的部分，是一种遗憾和吝难，因为没有纠正过来，"意—时"的生机就无法延续，如果不以振作的意识状态来承续父辈"意—时"的生机，君王当下的意识之生机也将相应地难以为继，最后会一无所得，而生机一旦散失，就得不偿失。

当然，可能六四太弱，占着位置犹豫不干事，浪费了时间，但这种时间成本非常之重，不但可能一无所得，更加可能会有羞咎吝难，最后导致重大的遗憾和悔恨。所以，从一开始就调整好自己的意识境域非常重要，尽早在意识中理顺修整的分寸。

[Illuminating Intentionality]

If one is too tolerant of the parts of one's father's government that are not conducive to the continuation of vitality in the present, it will lead to regrets and difficulties, because if not corrected, the vitality of "intentionality-time" cannot continue. The vitality of "intentionality-time" and the vitality of the king's current consciousness will accordingly be difficult to sustain, and nothing will be gained in the end. Once this vitality is lost, the losses will outweigh the gains.

Of course, the Six (*yin*/soft line) in the fourth place may be too weak, and it may be a waste of time because it hesitates and does nothing while occupying the position, but this kind of time cost is very heavy. Not only may nothing be gained, but it may also lead to shame and difficulties, which will eventually lead to major sadness and regret. Therefore, it is very important to adjust one's own realm of consciousness from the beginning, and straighten out the degree of rectification in one's consciousness as soon as possible.

六五：干父之蛊，用誉。

《象》曰："干父用誉"，承以德也。

【明译】

六五：整治父辈的腐败和积弊，用维系荣誉的方法把大业继承下来。

《象传》说：整治父辈的腐败和积弊，用维系荣誉的方法把大业继承下来，这是因为六五以美好的品德继承并传扬了先人的德业。

Six (*yin*/soft line) in the fifth place: One rectifies the corruption and long-standing malpractice of one's father, and inherits the great cause by maintaining honor.

The *Image Commentary* (*Xiang Zhuan*) says: One rectifies the corruption and long-term abuse of one's father, and inherits the great achievements by maintaining honor. This is because the Six (*yin*/soft line) in the fifth place inherits and passes on the virtues of the ancestors with beautiful virtue and character.

【明意】

六五是能用中道救治父政之弊的状态，而且要把父政的荣誉保留下来，传承和发扬先人的德业，就是继承先人"意—时"的生机。其实，能够在意识之中悟得先人之政的生机，并且在现实中存养与延续这种生机，并不容易。

用今人之德来继承，就是先人之生机在今人德性和德行方面的表现，把这种德业内在的生机继承下来的前提，是在位君王的意识中有能力领略这种生机。只有能够领略与把握这种生机，先王之生机才能继承发展下去，并且发扬光大。意念对生机的领会和存养是保持先人荣誉的关键。声誉是生的声誉，即人的生命力量的一种延续形式，只有保持了生机，才可能持续延续荣誉的生机，使荣誉长存。努力保持先人荣誉之生机，就要在意识中领悟并保持发扬这种生机，这才是真正顺承和发扬先人的德业。

[Illuminating Intentionality]

The Six (*yin*/soft line) in the fifth place is a state in which the shortcomings of a father's rule can be cured by the middle way, the honor of a father's rule must be preserved, and the virtues of the ancestors must be inherited and carried forward, which is to inherit the vitality of the ancestors' "intentionality-time". In fact, it is not easy to realize the vitality of the ancestors' politics in consciousness, nor to maintain and continue this vitality in reality.

Inheriting with the virtue of today's people is the manifestation of the vitality of ancestors in the virtues and merits of today's people. The prerequisite for inheriting the intrinsic vitality of this virtue is that a reigning king has the ability to appreciate this vitality in his consciousness. Only by being able to appreciate and grasp this vitality can the vitality of the previous kings be inherited, developed and carried forward. The understanding and preservation of vitality by intentionality is the key to maintaining the honor of ancestors. Reputation is a living reputation, that is, a form of continuation of human life force. Only by maintaining vitality can it be possible to continue the vitality of honor and make honor last forever. To strive to maintain the vitality of the honor of our ancestors, we must understand and maintain and carry forward this vitality in consciousness. This is the true inheritance and development of the virtues of our ancestors.

上九：不事王侯，高尚其事。

《象》曰："不事王侯"，志可则也。

【明译】

上九：不继续事奉君王公侯，把自己的退隐行为看得很高尚。

《象传》说：不继续事奉君王公侯，说明上九的高洁志向可以效法。

Nine (*yang*/strong line) in the top place: Not continuing to serve the king and princes, and regarding one's retirement behavior as very noble.

The *Image Commentary* (*Xiang Zhuan*) says: Not continuing to serve kings and princes shows that the Nine (*yang*/strong line) in the top place's noble aspirations can be followed.

【明意】

在权力世界之外，或者看破红尘之后，就应该有一种超脱的意识出来，即放下对权力世界的执念，把自己退隐的行为看得高尚。因为既然"意—时"的生机难以在当世得以延续，或者可以不再努力也能够延续得很好的时候，就应该放下对身外之权力的得失之心，转而专注于内在意识的生机。

可见，无论是入世治蛊，还是出世自高，意识之中生机意识的维系一直都是蛊（即整治）的根本。任何时候，整治的核心是求生，或者让生机保养得更好，所以如果陷入权力斗争，或者变成纯粹争权夺利的游戏，就离开了生机之本，而成为私利之争了。一旦公共事务离开公意之生机，变成私人利益之争，就可能伤及先王政治生机之延续。

[Illuminating Intentionality]

Outside the world of power, or after seeing through the mortal world, one should have a sense of detachment, that is, let go of the obsession with the world of power, and view one's retreat as noble. Because since the vitality of "intentionality-time" cannot be sustained in this world, or can continue well without any effort, one should put aside concern for the gains and losses of external power and focus instead on the vitality of inner consciousness.

It can be seen that whether to enter the world to govern disorder, or to rise above the world, the maintenance of vitality consciousness in consciousness has always been the foundation for dealing with corruption (that is, its rectification). At any time, the core of rectification is to survive or maintain vitality better. Therefore, if it falls into a power struggle or becomes a pure game of power and profit, it leaves the foundation of vitality and becomes a struggle for self-interest. Once public affairs leave the vitality of public intentionality and it becomes a dispute over private interests, it may harm the continuation of the political vitality of former kings.

地泽临（卦十九） （兑下坤上）

Lin (Presence), Earth and Lake (Hexagram 19)　(Dui below, Kun above)

　　临从蛊来，是受到蛊惑，于是要亲临视事。人在世间，"情"是对实际事变的情感领会，"情"本身是一种亲在、亲自的状态，而临表现在情境之中，就是亲临、亲在、临在，即不是混同世俗的在，而是有点意识上居高临下的在。临是心意的生机参与了境遇的生机，表现为情感的实际介入存在之感。鸟儿飞临枝头，那种"临"是一种渐进的、对场域的领会和介入。一种临于某场的人，也都是渐进地打开和融入某一个心的场域（临的意境就永远在临界的边界上）。

　　意念的动态平衡结构是一种在泽进入意域之前的先行领会。阴阳平衡是一个动态结构，不可能绝对稳定，阴意与阳意的平衡也是不断保持阴阳平衡的意境结构，需要保持与他意（他人之意）之间的平衡。意识的意义来自他人对意的理解和解读，也来自他人对于意的发动的领会，而最根本是来自对意发动之前的意涵状态的领会。虽然事情都是有时间性的（时间存在于世界当中），但意念可能在没有进入时空之前就被领会。

　　Hexagram Lin (Presence) comes from Hexagram Gu (Corruption), meaning that the situation has become disordered, so one has to come and see things in person. When people are in the world, "emotion/feeling" is the emotional understanding of actual events, so "emotion/feeling" is itself a state of personal presence and engagement. When presence is expressed in situations, it means personal presence, serious engagement, and supervision, which means it is not to be confused with blending in with the secular world, but is rather a superior and somewhat condescending presence in consciousness. Presence is the vitality of intentionality participating in the vitality of the situation, which is expressed as the sense of actual intervention of emotions. Like birds flying around branches, that "presence" is a gradual understanding of and intervention in a field. A kind of person who is present in a certain scene also gradually opens and fuses into a certain mental field (the intentional context of presence is always on the critical boundary).

The dynamic balance structure of intentionality is a kind of advance understanding before entering the realm of consciousness. The balance of *yin* and *yang* is a dynamic structure that cannot be absolutely stable, and the balance between *yin* and *yang* intentionality is also a contextual structure that constantly maintains the balance of *yin* and *yang*, which also needs to maintain a balance with other intentions (other people's intentions). The intentionality of consciousness comes from others' understanding and interpretation of intention, and also from others' understanding of the initiation of intention, and most fundamentally from the understanding of the state of intentionality before the initiation of intention. Although things are temporal (time exists in the world), intentions may be understood before they enter time and space.

临，元亨，利贞。至于八月有凶。

《彖》曰：临，刚浸而长，说而顺，刚中而应。大亨以正，天之道也。"至于八月有凶"，消不久也。

《象》曰：泽上有地，临。君子以教思无穷，容保民无疆。

【明译】

临卦象征临事知惧，大为亨通，有利于持守正固，但到（阴历）八月会有凶险。

《彖传》说：临卦是阳刚爻渐渐生长。下卦兑为悦，"说"同悦；上卦坤为顺，既喜悦又柔顺，刚爻居于下卦中位，又有六五正应。大为亨通又恰到好处，这是天道运行的本然状态。到（阴历）八月会有凶险，是因为阳气将要消退，阳刚存在不会太长久了。

《象传》说：下卦兑为泽，上卦坤为地，湖泽的上面有大地，人在地上看泽，居高临下，这就是象征临事知惧的临卦。君子要从临卦中学习，要以无穷无尽的思想道德去教化民众，并以无边的包容胸怀去容纳和养育人民。

Hexagram Lin (Presence) symbolizes being aware of fear when confronting problems, which brings great prosperity and helps to maintain integrity, though there will be danger in the eighth month (of the lunar calendar).

The *Judgment Commentary* (*Tuan Zhuan*) says: Hexagram Lin (Presence) is the gradual growth of *yang*/strong lines. The lower Trigram Dui is joy; the upper Trigram Kun is smooth, and it thus means both joyful and supple. The *yang*/strong line is in the middle of the lower Trigram, and there is a Six (*yin*/soft line) in the fifth place to correctly respond to the Nine (*yang*/strong line) in the second place. Being prosperous and just right is the natural state of the heavenly *dao*. There will be danger in the eighth month (lunar calendar) because the *yang* energy will disappear and the *yang* strength will not exist for long.

The *Image Commentary* (*Xiang Zhuan*) says: The lower Trigram Dui is lake, and the upper Trigram Kun is ground, so there is earth above a lake. People look at the lake from the ground and are condescending, so this is Hexagram Lin (Presence) that symbolizes knowing how to deal with things. An exemplary person must learn from Hexagram Lin (Presence), educate the people with endless ideals and morals, and accommodate and nurture the people with boundless tolerance.

【明意】

临本阳意壮胜之象，引申出居高临下、临事而惧、成己成物之道。观阳意之壮胜，而乐观其成，乐见生意成长之象，如农历十二月过年之时，喜事临门，乃一年之中生意最为显著之时。另临有阳意成长，以威势逼临阴意后退，此进逼之意为逼临。

总之，临是阳意生长到生生不息状态，生机盎然，如临大敌，有临事观变、临泽而充满生气的状态，如周敦颐观窗前草不除的生生意境。可见，临象征对意境的涵养和培育，是对阴意与阳意交融之动态平衡的领会。阳意生长象征努力成就事业的人，必然面临艰难险阻，要临事知惧，恭敬处世。

[Illuminating Intentionality]

The image of *yang*/positive intentions' majestic victory at the base of Hexagram Lin (Presence) leads to the way of being superior and somewhat condescending, monitoring affairs with trepidation, and accomplishing oneself and things. Observe the majestic success of *yang* intentionality, take joy in its success, and be pleased to see the growth of productive intentions. For example, the chinese lunar new year at the end of the twelfth lunar month, when good things are coming, is the most significant time of the year for productive intention. In addition, there is a growth of *yang* intentionality, which forces the *yin* intentionality to retreat with its power and authority. The intentionality of this forceful advance is forceful presence.

In short, Hexagram Lin (Presence) is a state where *yang* intentionality has grown to a state of endless productivity, overflowing with vitality, like facing an enemy, observing changes in situations, and full of vital *qi*, such as Zhou Dunyi's special feeling about his productive situation when the grass in front of his window was not cut. It can be seen that Hexagram Lin (Presence) symbolizes a concentration and cultivation of intentional context and an understanding of dynamic balance in the blending of *yin* and *yang*. The growth of *yang* intentionality means that those who work hard to achieve a career will inevitably face difficulties and obstacles, so they must have the sense of fear and behave respectfully.

初九：咸临，贞吉。

《象》曰："咸临，贞吉"，志行正也。

【明译】

初九：阳气一起来临，守正自然吉祥。

《象传》说：阳气一起来临，守正自然吉祥，因为初九心志和行为都是正当的。

Nine (*yang*/strong line) in the first place: *Yangqi* comes together, and keeping upright naturally brings good fortune.

The *Image Commentary* (*Xiang Zhuan*) says: *Yangqi* comes together, and it is naturally auspicious to be upright, because the intentions and behavior of the Nine (*yang*/strong line) in the first place are all correct.

【明意】

临是生机勃发，心志上行而正当。"咸临"是阳意共同来到阴意之境中，面临开创新意境的状态。"咸临"明显有用阳意改变阴性之意境的努力，但这种改变不是外部强迫，而是自本自发的"向死而生"。"生生"本来面临的情景就是"死死"，除非自己用雷震之力主动愿意改变。当人用意改变自己的意识境遇，就可能迅速改变其意识境遇关联的整个生活世界。

[Illuminating Intentionality]

Hexagram Lin (Presence) is full of vitality, and its intentionality is upward and correct. "*Yangqi* comes together" is *yang*/positive intentionality coming together to the realm of *yin*/negative intentionality and facing the state of creating a new intentional context. It is obvious that "*Yangqi* comes together" implies the effort of rising *yang* power to change the *yin*/negative intentional context. This change is not externally forced, but a spontaneous process of "living toward death." The situation faced by "creative creativity (*shengsheng* 生生)" is "deathly dying" unless the power of a thunderous shock is used to actively change it. When people intend to change their conscious situation, they may quickly change the entire life world associated with their conscious situation.

九二：咸临，吉，无不利。

《象》曰："咸临，吉，无不利"，未顺命也。

【明译】

九二：一起来临，吉祥，无所不利。

《象传》说：九二虽然跟初九一起来临，吉祥，没有不利，但形势还是阴爻主导，还没有顺从扶阳抑阴的天道运行的命令。

Nine (*yang*/strong line) in the second place: Coming together, auspicious and no disadvantages.

The *Image Commentary* (*Xiang Zhuan*) says: Although the Nine (*yang*/strong line) in the second place comes together with the Nine (*yang*/strong line) in the first place, which is auspicious and not disadvantageous, the situation is still dominated by *yin* and has not yet obeyed the order of the heavenly *dao* to support *yang* and suppress *yin*.

【明意】

《周易》不是简单介绍天地之道如何是一阴一阳，而是要告诉人们如何利用一阴一阳的天道，并时时刻刻转天地之道为天人之道，也就是转天道为人道，这是人天之意的本旨。学习《周易》是建立一种人天之意的意识，帮助我们打通人与天，开悟通天，如阳明的"龙场悟道"一般，超越人本身的意识，而与天的意识时时刻刻接轨。

[Illuminating Intentionality]
The *Book of Changes* does not simply introduce how the *dao* of heaven and earth alternates between *yin* and *yang*, but also tells people how to make use of the *dao* of heaven and earth, which alternates between *yin* and *yang*, and to constantly transform the *dao* of heaven and earth into the *dao* of heaven and humanity, that is, to transform the heavenly *dao* into the human *dao*; this is the original intentionality of humanity and heaven. Studying the *Book of Changes* means establishing an awareness of the intentionality of humanity and heaven, helping us to open up the connection between humanity and heaven, and realize our continuity with heaven, just like Wang Yangming's "realization of the *dao* at Longchang," which transcends humanity's own consciousness and immediately attains constant contact with the consciousness of heaven.

六三：甘临，无攸利。既忧之，无咎。
《象》曰："甘临"，位不当也。"既忧之"，咎不长也。
【明译】
六三：甘甜自美地面对阳气的来临，没有什么好处。如果能够为当前的处境忧虑，才不会有过错灾害。
《象传》说：甘甜自美地面对阳气的来临，指六三处在柔爻被逼退，自己却首当其冲的位置，另六三柔爻居刚位，都是位不当。既然能为目前面临的处境忧虑，那么咎害不会太长了。

Six (*yin*/soft line) in the third place: There is no benefit in facing the coming of *yangqi* in sweet contentment. If one can worry about the current situation, one will avoid mistakes and disasters.

The *Image Commentary* (*Xiang Zhuan*) says: Facing the coming of *yangqi* sweetly and contentedly means that the Six (*yin*/soft line) in the third place is forced to retreat, but is the first to bear the brunt, while it is also a soft line in a strong position, which is inappropriate. Since one can worry about the situation one is currently facing, the blame will not last too long.

【明意】
人生有阴阳之体，在身心的平衡状态追求阴阳之意，不可在阳意对阴意趋迫的情势之中仍然甘之如饴，而要亲临视事，让意境面对危机情境有所警觉，知道不应该用花言巧语讨好他人，否则，不知道情势之危，忘乎所以，最后必然大节有亏。人天之意的意境应该无私无欲，起心动念都回复到扶阳抑阴的大势上去，明了意念所处的境遇，让境遇合乎时势之变化，让当下的意境超越个人的主观意欲，此即宋儒所谓"存天理灭人欲"

在当下意念当中的功夫。

[Illuminating Intentionality]

Human life has a body of *yin* and *yang*, so one should pursue the intentionality of *yin* and *yang* in a balanced state of body and mind, and should not be content with a situation where *yang* intentionality is pressing against *yin* intentionality. Instead, one should personally observe the situation, so that one's intentional context can be alert to the crisis situation and know whether it is advisable or not to use sweet words to please others; otherwise, one will not know the danger of the situation and forget about it, and will surely suffer a big loss in the end. The intentional context of the intentionality of humanity and heaven should be selfless and without desires, and every intention should return to the general trend of supporting *yang* and suppressing *yin*. One should understand the situation of the intention, let the situation conform to the changes of the times, and let the current intentional context transcend personal subjective wishes. This is what Song Confucianism called the effort to "preserve the patterns of nature and overcome human desires" in current intentions.

六四：至临，无咎。

《象》曰："至临，无咎"，位当也。

【明译】

六四：（与阳力）一起到来，没有什么问题。

《象传》说：（顺着阳力上升一起来）亲临现场，当然不会有祸患，因为六四位置适当。

Six (*yin*/soft line) in the fourth place: Arriving together (with *yang* power), there are no difficulties.

The *Image Commentary* (*Xiang Zhuan*) says: (Following the rising *yang* force,) if one visits the scene in person, there will surely be no harm, because the location of the Six (*yin*/soft line) in the fourth place is appropriate.

【明意】

六四中正明理，在阳意上升的临境之中，以阳意之境为自己的意境，不仅乐观，并且帮助阳意进临阴意之境域。等于在帮助阳意进入阴意之境的同时，对阴阳关联的现场的意境有控制力，与上坤诸阴一起处理好相关细节。六四虽是阴意，但其展示出来却有阳意之境。六四顺应阳意而形成的意识情境，是一种逐渐帮助阳意生长，让阳意轻松接近阴境，进而改变阴意之境的生生意境。

[Illuminating Intentionality]

The Six (*yin*/soft line) in the fourth place is central and upright and understands the patterns of change, so in a situation where *yang*/positive intentionality is rising, to use the *yang*/positive intentions realm as one's own intentional context is not merely optimistic, but also helps *yang*/positive intentionality enter the realm of *yin*/negative intentionality. This means that, while helping *yang*/positive intentionality enter the realm of *yin*/negative intentionality, it also has control over the intentional context of the situation related to *yin* and *yang*, and handles the relevant details together with upper Trigram Kun's *yin* lines. Although the Six (*yin*/soft line) in the fourth place has *yin* intentionality, its display has a context of *yang* intentionality. The conscious situation formed by the Six (*yin*/soft line) in the fourth place resonating and complying with *yang* intentionality is a productive intentional context that gradually helps the growth of *yang* intentionality, allows the *yang* to easily approach the *yin* realm, and then changes the *yin* realm.

六五：知临，大君之宜，吉。

《象》曰："大君之宜"，行中之谓也。

【明译】

六五：以聪明睿智君临天下，大意之君能够以合宜的方式治国理政，当然吉祥。

《象传》说：意境大明的君王以合宜的方式治理国，指的是六五施政能够奉行中道。

Six (*yin*/soft line) in the fifth place: It is naturally auspicious to rule over the world under heaven with wisdom and insight, and a ruler of great intentionality can govern a country in an appropriate way.

The *Image Commentary* (*Xiang Zhuan*) says: A king of the enlightened intentional context governing a country in a suitable way refers to the Six (*yin*/soft line) in the fifth place being able to pursue the middle way in its administration.

【明意】

君临天下的气势和中道的秉持在"智"，不仅要知人善任、让底下人尽职尽责，更要明白临卦大势。阴意发动，自然有阳境之生，光明透亮，天下合宜。可见，这种君临天下的意境和气势之境，不仅因缘际会而聚缘而成，更是对阳意生长之大势有深刻领会。"行中"代表意识境遇发动的合宜状态。有如此明智与行中意境的领导者，其意念柔顺，念念从阳合宜，其阴意之发，不仅有利于明智地洞悉情境，更有利于意念实化皆不出中道。如此则阴意发动与阳境交融互动，相得益彰，气象恢弘。

[Illuminating Intentionality]

The aura of ruling over the world under heaven and the upholding of the middle way lie in wisdom. It is not only necessary to know people well and have them fulfill their duties, but also to understand the general trend of Hexagram Lin (Presence). When *yin* intentionality is initiated, a *yang* state naturally arises which is illuminated and transparent, and the world is in harmony. It can be seen that this state of intentional context and momentum of dominating the world is not only caused by the gathering of dependent co-arising, but also a profound understanding of the general trend of the growth of *yang*/positive intentionality. "Walking in the middle way" represents the appropriate state of consciousness initiated by the situation. A leader with such a wise and central intentional context of action, whose intentions are supple, follow the *yang* and are appropriate, and whose *yin* power is initiated, is not only conducive to wisely understanding the situation, but also to the realization of intentions without straying from the middle *dao*. In this way, *yin* will initiate and interact with the *yang* realm, the two complementing each other and creating a magnificent atmosphere.

上六：敦临，吉，无咎。
《象》曰："敦临"之"吉"，志在内也。
【明译】
上六：温和敦厚地统临，吉祥，没有问题。
《象传》说：以厚重的意境蓄统临下所以吉祥，是因为上六的心志在内卦的阳爻。

Six (*yin*/soft line) in the top place: Ruling in a gentle and sincere manner, auspicious and without difficulties.

The *Image Commentary* (*Xiang Zhuan*) says: It is auspicious to rule over those beneath with a stately intentional context, because the intention of the Six (*yin*/soft line) in the top place lies with the *yang* lines of the inner trigram.

【明意】
对于阳意强势构筑的意境，各阴爻皆乐观其长，而以上六之意境至为敦厚，心意温和，心怀感激。阴意在阳意上长的逼临大势下，丝毫没有逼迫阳意稍加改变之志，而是包容蓄纳，以成就阳长的意境为志向。下二阳作为临卦意境力量核心，也需要在诸阴，尤其是上六这样的阴爻的倾力配合下，才能完美地深厚地构筑起阳意之境，从而造就临之阳境的蔚为大观，所以接观卦。意境如此敦厚，自然大为可观。

[Illuminating Intentionality]

In the intentional context constructed by the strong *yang*/positive intentionality, all *yin* lines are optimistic about their merits, and the intentional context of the Six (*yin*/soft line) in the top place is the most sincere, gentle and grateful. Yin intentionality faces the general trend of *yang* intentionality, and has no intention of forcing *yang* intentionality to change even slightly. Instead, it is tolerant and inclusive, with the ambition of achieving the intentional context of the *yang* growth. The two lower *yang* lines, as the core of the intentional context of Hexagram Lin (Presence), also need the full cooperation of the *yin* power, especially *yin* lines such as the Six (yin/soft line) in the top place, in order to perfectly and profoundly construct the realm of *yang* conception, thus creating the grand view of the *yang* realm of Hexagram Lin (Presence), so they connect to Hexagram Guan (Observation). The intentional context is so honest and sincere that it is naturally very impressive to observe.

风地观（卦二十）　坤下巽上）

Guan (Observation), Wind and Earth (Hexagram 20)　(Kun below, Xun above)

　　观说明宗教性仪式的可观和蔚为大观，因为主祭人洗手的时候能够通过他本人的"意—生"来调动自己和人民甚至天地心意的生机，所以洗手就具备了极其强烈的宗教仪式感和感人可观的意味，是主祭人内在良心和良知通于天地的瞬间表达。可见，祭祀的时候，主祭人意念的生机是否彰显格外重要。只有意念中生机冲盈，才能够让心意之生与天地大道之生机相通，因此心念要洁净精微，感通天地之生机，并与之融合而无丝毫差别，因为意念对天地生机的领悟是将其情境化而蔚为大观的前提。

　　古人借助《周易》的卦象的结构来观察世界，进一步塑造我们的视角，在观察中自明意念之生，有生意的观察就是大观，既能自己观察，又能让人看，让心意的生机通于天地，在祭祀之前，用极尽庄严的态度来表达，使所有观察者的心念都进入一个感而未发的状态，念已形，但未发。好像凝固天地生机，通过庄严的仪式感让天下百姓的心意进入一种感而未发的意念状态。人们参加神圣的宗教仪式的时候，意念虽未发动，但意念之境已先被熏陶改变，这其实是一种风化的艺术，是一种直接改变他人意境的更为重要的艺术。

　　Hexagram Guan (Observation) demonstrates how religious rituals are impressive and magnificent, because when the officiant washes his hands, he can mobilize the vitality of himself, the people, and even the heart-mind of heaven and earth through his own "intentional-production," so washing his hands has an extremely strong sense of religious ritual and a touching feeling. This remarkable intentionality is the instant expression of the officiant's inner conscience and moral knowing that connects with heaven and earth. It can be seen that, when performing sacrifices, it is particularly important to display the vitality of the intentions of the officiant. Only when the intentionality is full of vitality can the productivity of intentionality be connected with the vitality of heaven and earth. Therefore, the intentionality must be pure and subtle, affectively connect with the vitality of heaven and earth, and merge with it without any difference, because the mind's understanding of the vitality of heaven and earth is the precondition for contextualizing it and making it grand.

The ancients observed the world with the help of the hexagram structure of the *Book of Changes*, and further shaped our perspective. In observation, intentions are triggered. Observing productive power is a grand view both through one's own eyes, and also through those of others, allowing the vitality of intentional-productivity to connect with heaven and earth. Before the sacrifice, it is expressed with an extremely solemn attitude, so that the intentions of all observers enter a state of feeling that is formed but not yet initiated, in which transcendental intentions have been formed but not yet manifested as empirical intentions. This seems to solidify the vitality of heaven and earth, and through the solemn sense of ceremony, the intentions of the people in the world enter a state of feeling without yet expressing and manifesting intentions. When people participate in sacred religious ceremonies, although their intentions have not been initiated, their state of intentionality has first been influenced and changed. This is actually a kind of educative art, one in which it is more important to directly change the state of intentionality of others.

观，盥（guàn）而不荐。有孚，颙（yóng）若。

《彖》曰：大观在上，顺而巽，中正以观天下。"观，盥而不荐，有孚颙若"，下观而化也。观天之神道，而四时不忒。圣人以神道设教，而天下服矣。

《象》曰：风行地上，观。先王以省方观民设教。

【明译】

观卦象征观察瞻仰，祭祀时洁敬洗手，进献祭品的仪式还没开始，内心就无比虔诚，表现得庄严恭敬，诚敬肃穆。

《彖传》说：主爻九五刚爻为大，居天位在上，跟上九都在上，气势宏大可观；下卦坤为顺，上卦巽为入，教化能顺利地深入人心；九五在上卦中位，刚爻居刚位，位正，九五以下的三四爻为人位，初二爻为地位，都在天下。九五能以中正之道居高临下地观天下，这就是观卦。进献祭品的仪式还没开始，内心就无比虔诚，表现得庄严恭敬，诚敬肃穆，在下的臣民看到主祭人的精诚深深地受到感化，这是道德虔诚的感化力量。仰观自然神妙莫测的大道，考察天体运行，发现四季交替分毫不差，从不失度。圣人效法自然神妙莫测的大道来设立教化，这样天下的人民就会信服。

《象传》说：上卦巽为风，下卦坤为地，风在地上吹行，无孔不入就是观卦。先王从中得到启示，就要巡视四方，考察民情风俗，设立教化。

Hexagram Guan (Observation) symbolizes observation and admiration. When offering sacrifices, one should wash one's hands cleanl reverently. Before the ceremony of offering sacrifices has even begun, one is extremely pious in one's heart and behaves seriously, respectfully, sincerely and solemnly.

The *Judgment Commentary* (*Tuan Zhuan*) says: The main line, the Nine (*yang*/strong line) in the fifth place, is great, in the heavenly position at the top together with the Nine (*yang*/strong line) in the sixth place, so it is grand and impressive; the lower Trigram Kun is smooth, and the upper Trigram Xun is entering, so it means that teaching can smoothly penetrate into people's intentions. The Nine (*yang*/strong line) in the fifth place is in the middle of the upper Trigram, a *yang*/strong line in a *yang* position, so its position is upright. The third and fourth lines below the Nine (*yang*/strong line) in the fifth place are in the human position, and the first and second lines are in the earthly position. The Nine (*yang*/strong line) in the fifth place is able to observe the world from a high position in the right way; this is Hexagram Guan (Observation). Before the ceremony of offering sacrifices has even begun, the leader is extremely devout in his heart and behaves solemnly, respectfully, sincerely and seriously. The people below are deeply influenced by the sincerity of the leader. This is the influence of moral piety. Looking up at the mysterious and unfathomable *dao* of nature, observing the movement of celestial bodies, we find that the four seasons change exactly and never lose their balance. Sages imitate the mysterious and unfathomable *dao* of nature to establish moral transformation, so that the people of the world will be convinced.

The *Image Commentary* (*Xiang Zhuan*) says: The upper Trigram Xun is wind, and the lower Trigram Kun is earth. The wind blowing over the ground and penetrating every hole is Hexagram Guan (Observation). The former kings received inspiration from this and knew to patrol the four directions, inspect the people's customs and establish moral transformation.

【明意】

如何让意念通达于神境，并引导所有人的心念进入一种感而未发的状态，这是一个有意义的哲学问题。观卦说明，要让心意通于天地之生机，可借助风吹大地来塑造心通天地的结构，如主祭者把天地的生机领会出来，再风化传达给世人。要让天下百姓顺从需要教化的艺术，不是简单地讲道理，还需要通过一些"神迹"来引导百姓。

天底下总有一些东西是视而不可见的，要让百姓了解每人心意都有神秘莫测可以通达天地的部分，所以要先观圣人教化，领悟到其生生不息与天地生机本身一样蔚为大观。事业的可观表现在有吸引力，能够鼓舞人心，激发人心的应和与同情，吸引大家一起付出心力，从而形成可观的局面。自然充满生机，而其生机的运转似乎从来不出差错，圣人意识到并模仿自然生机的运转，以神道来设立教化，让不能马上明白道理的百姓，从自身利益的角度出发，能够理解并听从之，从而跟随转化。

258

[Illuminating Intentionality]

How to allow intentions to connect with the spiritual realm and guide all people's intentions into a state of being affected yet uninitiated is a meaningful philosophical question. Hexagram Guan (Observation) explains that in order to connect intentionality to the vitality of heaven and earth, we can use the wind blowing over the earth to shape the structure of the intentionality connecting with heaven and earth. For example, the chief officiant can understand the vitality of heaven and earth, and then convey it to the world through transformative means like educating. To make the ordinary people of the world obey the art of moral transformation, it is not simply a matter of reasoning, but also of guiding the people through some miraculous signs.

There are always some things in the world under heaven that are invisible. People should understand that there is a mysterious part in everyone's intentionality that can connect with heaven and earth. Therefore, they must first observe the transformative teachings of sages and realize that their endless life is as magnificent as the vitality of heaven and earth itself. The impressive performance of a career is that it is attractive, can encourage people, inspire people's sympathetic response, and attract everyone to work together, thus forming a promising situation. Nature is full of vitality, and the operation of its vitality never seems to go wrong. Sages realize and imitate the operation of natural vitality, and use the spiritual *dao* (later "Shinto" in Japanese) to establish educative transformation, so that people who cannot immediately understand the truth can understand and obey it from the perspective of their own interests, and thereby follow the transformation.

初六：童观，小人无咎，君子吝。

《象》曰：初六"童观"，"小人"道也。

【明译】

初六：像儿童一样观事物，对小人来说没有什么过失，但对君子来说就有吝难。

《象传》说：像儿童一样看问题，这是小人之道。

Six (*yin*/soft line) in the first place: Seeing things like a child is not a fault for a petty person, but it is a problem for an exemplary person.

The *Image Commentary* (*Xiang Zhuan*) says: Seeing problems like a child is the way of the petty person.

【明意】

孩童意念的生机有限，眼意看表面，内里看不清楚，不知道用心，所以幼稚。此爻告诉人们应该看要调动眼意的生机，也即用心琢磨，认真理解才行。心量在心意与世交接之初，既清明又混沌，清明因其无染，自然应物，世界之生机就其本相为儿童的"意—生"所感通；开始混沌，因为儿童之童观与世不分，即詹姆士（William James）所谓"纯粹经验（pure experience）"，那种无法分清人与我、自我与世界的状态。此爻之观从正面的意思来讲，是原初性的物我不分状态，即心念与自然生机时刻感通的状态，而能够体验和保持这种状态的人就是意念发动可以一直保持初心的人。

[Illuminating Intentionality]

The vitality of children's intentionality is limited, so they only look at the surface and cannot see things clearly from the inside. They do not know their intentions, so they are childish. This line tells people that they should look with the vitality of their eyes, that is, think and understand carefully. At the beginning of the connection between intentionality and the world, intentionality is both clear and chaotic, and this clear and bright nature corresponds to things because it is untainted. The vitality of the world is inspired by the "intentional-productivity" of children in its true form; it begins to be chaotic because children's childlike view is not separated from the world, what William James called "pure experience," a state in which it is impossible to distinguish between self and other, self and the world. In a positive sense, this line's observation refers to the original state of indifference between things and the self, that is, a state in which intentionality and natural vitality are always connected. People who can experience and maintain this state can initiate their intentions and always maintain their original intention.

六二：窥观，利女贞。

《象》曰："窥观，女贞"，亦可丑也。

【明译】

六二：从门缝里向外窥视，对女子来说是正当的。

《象传》说：透过门缝向外偷看，对女子而言，守正则有利，不过这样做终究不太光彩。

Six (*yin*/soft line) in the second place: It is correct for a woman to peek out from under her door.

The *Image Commentary* (*Xiang Zhuan*) says: Peeping through a crack in the door is beneficial for women, but it is not honorable to do so.

【明意】

传统男性心念的狭隘，尤其体现在对于女性意念生机的限制。传统社会限制女性意念发动的生机，让她们以"女性的眼光"来看待世界，而这种概念的存在本身只相对于男性眼光才可能，如波伏娃《第二性》认为女性眼光为男性社会所塑造。今天，女性眼光的生机当如六二之中正，可以超越性别，而且不能说男性的眼光就比女性或小人的眼光高明。今天男性如果还去限制女性意念生机而不以为偏狭，那就会让人觉得羞耻。

[Illuminating Intentionality]

The narrowness of traditional male intentionality is especially reflected in the restriction on the vitality of female intentions. Traditional society restricted the vitality of women's intentions, allowing them to view the world from a "female perspective," a concept the existence of which is only possible in relation to a male perspective. For example, Simone De Beauvoir's *The Second Sex* argues that the female perspective is actually shaped by the male perspective in a male-dominated society. Today, the vitality of women's vision should be as positive as that of the Six (*yin*/soft line) in the second place, which can transcend gender, and it cannot be said that men's vision is better than that of women or petty people. If today men still try to restrict the vitality of women's intentions and do not think of it as intolerance, people will feel this is shameful.

六三：观我生，进退。

《象》曰："观我生，进退"，未失道也。

【明译】

六三：观察我的生民的情况，决定进还是退，是观察风俗民情决定政策。

《象传》说：观察体会人民意念生生的实情，决定进还是退，不失正道（六三能按风俗民情，以神道设教，故为"未失道"）。

Six (*yin*/soft line) in the third place: Observing the situation of my people, I decide whether to advance or retreat. This is to observe the customs and conditions of the people to decide on policy.

The *Image Commentary* (*Xiang Zhuan*) says: Observing and understanding the actual situation of people's intentions and productivity, one decides whether to advance or retreat without losing the right *dao* (the Six (*yin*/soft line) in the third place can set up teachings based on heavenly *dao* according to the customs and sentiments of the people, so it does not lose the right *dao*).

【明意】

意念实化过程中，要让意念的生机通于外在的人民心意之生机。这个合道的过程当中，自我决定的部分有限，人的观察经历经验构成当下意识生生的境域，其中的生机随时可能成为实化意念的决定因素。那些在我们的经验当中，能够触动人心的生机部分深深地影响着我们意念境遇的存在，可能生机突显，突然成为意念发动的决定因素，这样的生机类似于弗洛伊德所谓的"潜意识"，可能在意识境遇的实化过程当中，突然生发，突然决定意识的进退。

[Illuminating Intentionality]

In the process of concretizing one's intentions, the vitality of the intention must be connected externally to the vitality of the people's minds, and in this process of union, the self-determined part is limited. People's observation and experience constitute the productive realm of current consciousness, and the vitality in it may become the decisive factor in concretizing intention at any time. Those vital parts in our experience that can touch people's intentions deeply affect the existence of our intentional context. They may emerge suddenly and become the decisive factor in the initiation of intentions. Such vital energy is similar to the "subconscious mind" that Freud spoke of, and may occur suddenly during the concretization process of consciousness, and suddenly determine its advance or retreat.

六四：观国之光，利用宾于王。

《象》曰："观国之光"，尚宾也。

【明译】

六四：观看国家礼仪盛典的光辉气象，有利于成为君王的座上宾客。

《象传》说：观仰王朝盛世的辉煌生机，说明六四已经是君王尊贵的座上宾客。

Six (*yin*/soft line) in the fourth place: Observing the glorious atmosphere of a state ritual ceremony is conducive to becoming a seated guest of the king.

The *Image Commentary* (*Xiang Zhuan*) says: Observing the glorious vitality of the dynasty in its heyday shows that the Six (*yin*/soft line) in the fourth place has become a distinguished guest of the king.

【明意】

六四依着九五之蔚为大观而能够成为君王的府上宾，感受到巨大的生机气象。六四是代表人民欣赏崇高与盛大的生机的国家栋梁，人民通过民意的代表参与盛大的典礼而改变其心境的生意，从而间接观察和体会国家盛典体现出来的生生不息气象。这本身是把国人内在通于天地生机的人天之意加以显化，即人民心意当中近于天地之境的内在意识得以展现。

[Illuminating Intentionality]

Based on the grand view of the Nine (*yang*/strong line) in the fifth place, the Six (*yin*/soft line) in the fourth place is able to become a guest of the king's house and feels its great vitality. The Six (*yin*/soft line) in the fourth place is a pillar of the country that represents the people's appreciation of lofty and grand vitality. The people participate in the grand ceremony through representatives of public opinion and change their mood, thereby indirectly observing and experiencing the ceaselessly productive atmosphere reflected in the national ceremony. This in itself is to manifest the inner intentionality of humanity and heaven that connects the vitality of heaven and earth to the people of the country, that is, to reveal the inner consciousness close to the realm of heaven and earth in the intentions of the people.

九五：观我生，君子无咎。

《象》曰："观我生"，观民也。

【明译】

九五：观察我的生民，这样可以使君子不犯错误。

《象传》说：观察我意念生生之境，就是观察我心与民心相通之境。

Nine (*yang*/strong line) in the fifth place: Observing one's life and people, an exemplary person will not make mistakes.

The *Image Commentary* (*Xiang Zhuan*) says: Observing the state where one's intentions are productive is to observe the state where one's heart-mind is connected with the intentions of the people.

【明意】

意念生生之境是世界存在之本，世界生生，虽然也在死死的过程当中，但有生机才有意念，如果注重死机就无所谓意念的生发，所以必以生机为本。观察体悟生机，尤其是天地大观之生机，才是领悟世界存在的根本，体悟人民意念生生与生存世界之生生的根本。

[Illuminating Intentionality]

The realm of intentional productivity is the foundation of the existence of the world. Although the living productivity of the world is also in the process of death and dying, only when there is vitality can there be intentions. If you focus on death, there will be no generation and initiation of intentions, so one must regard vitality as fundamental. Observing and experiencing vitality, especially the vitality of the grand view of heaven and earth, is the basis for understanding the existence of the world, and the basis for understanding the emergence of people's intentions and the productivity of the life-world.

上九：观其生，君子无咎。

《象》曰："观其生"，志未平也。

【明译】

上九：观察他所治理的生民，君子就可以不犯错误。

《象传》说：观察他意念的生生之境，因为上九担心自己的雄心壮志难以实现。

Nine (*yang*/strong line) in the top place: An exemplary person will avoid making mistakes by observing the people one governs.

The *Image Commentary* (*Xiang Zhuan*) says: Observe the productive state of one's intentions, because the Nine (*yang*/strong line) in the top place is worried that one's ambitions will not be realized.

【明意】

上九需要每时每刻都观察与反思自己的生境，担心自己体会到的天下生生不息的雄心壮志无法传递给九五，或者传递到了，九五却没法实现。所以需要每时每刻帮助九五维系人民的生生意境，那样才是真正帮助领导人（九五）成功。当然，上六爻维系并不容易，稍有不慎就可能壮志难酬。

[Illuminating Intentionality]

The Nine (*yang*/strong line) in the top place requires observing and reflecting on one's own situation at all times, worrying that the endless ambitions of the world that one feels cannot be passed on to the Nine (*yang*/strong line) in the fifth place, or that if they are passed on, the Nine (*yang*/strong line) in the fifth place will not be able to realize them. Therefore, one needs to help the Nine (*yang*/strong line) in the fifth place maintain the people's living conditions at all times. Only in this way can one truly help the leader (the Nine (*yang*/strong line) in the fifth place) to succeed. Of course, it is not easy for the Six (*yin*/soft line) in the top place to to maintain its position, and if one is not careful, one's ambition may be difficult to achieve.

火雷噬嗑（卦二十一）　（震下离上）

Shihe (Punishment), Fire and Thunder (Hexagram 21)　(Zhen below, Li above)

天生万物，地养万物，没有先后，心面对天地生养的几微，知道世界存在的根基在于生生之几，意识到要珍惜保养让几微生发。万物创生，同时演化，意识参与事物变迁的演化，即所谓无中生有，因此意识能把事物的状态做调整和转化。人转化世界的开端是意识，实化意念的开关是口舌，是意识实化出来的言语改变着事物变化的阴阳。

人意识如何考虑他意，按照兵家是"知己知彼"，按照雷电与几微，几微之动，迅雷不及。面对几微之变，人的意识就要知道如何去持经达变，知道何为未变之经，何为变，需要随机应变。自然生发的意识始于性情，而性情不仅受风俗潜移默化影响，也受其他思想影响。对所有人有利而且有道理的价值才是普世价值，而适应于某些族群的价值不必然就是普世的。人与人之间的不同伦理系统应该都有普世的成分，儒家对于人伦的理论在古代本来就是，今天也应该发展成为普世伦理系统。

Heaven produces the myriad things, and the earth nourishes them. There is no order of precedence in this. The heart-mind faces the subtlety of heaven and earth's creation and nourishing, and knows that the foundation of the existence of the world lies in the subtlety of productivity. Consciousness must cherish and maintain this subtlety to allow them to flourish. The myriad things are created and evolve at the same time. Consciousness participates in the evolution of changing things, and this is the so-called *creatio ex nihilo*, hence consciousness can adjust and transform the state of things and events. The starting point for people to transform the world is consciousness, the switch that concretizes intentions is the mouth and tongue, and it is the words concretized by consciousness that change the *yin* and *yang* of things.

How people's consciousness considers other people's intentions, according to military strategists, is to "know yourself and know your enemy," according to thunder, lightning and infinitesimal subtlety, while the latter is as fast as lightning. In the face of infinitesimally subtle changes, human consciousness must know how to hold onto the constant to achieve change, and know what is the constant that has not changed and what is change, as well as needing to adapt to change. Spontaneously initiated consciousness begins with nature and temperament, which are influenced not only by the subtle influence of customs but also by other thoughts. Values that are beneficial and reasonable to all people are universal values, and values that are suitable for certain ethnic groups are not necessarily universal. Different ethical systems among people should all have universal elements. The Confucian theory of appropriate human relations was originally a universal ethical system in ancient times, and it should also be developed into a universal ethical system today.

噬嗑（hé），亨。利用狱。

《彖》曰：颐中有物曰"噬嗑"。"噬嗑"而"亨"，刚柔分，动而明。雷电合而章。柔得中而上行，虽不当位，"利用狱"也。

《象》曰：雷电，噬嗑。先王以明罚敕法。

【明译】

噬嗑卦象征梗碍刑狱，亨通，有利于处罚量刑，听讼治狱。

《彖传》说：口腔里有食物就是噬嗑卦要说明的处境。有东西梗碍在口中，为什么还会亨通，是因为噬嗑卦从否卦变来，卦变中刚柔爻分开交错，变得刚柔相济。下卦震为动，上卦离为明，下震动而上明丽，有行动光明之象，所以能亨通。下卦震为雷，上卦离为闪电，雷电交加，电闪雷鸣，有强大的震慑威力和明察秋毫的光照效应。（噬嗑由否变来，即否卦九五与初六换位，否卦的初六柔爻上行到上卦的中位，卦变为噬嗑卦。）卦变的意义是柔爻柔顺地上进到中位且具有中正的道德，六五虽然是柔爻取得刚位，位不当，但办案理冤不需要刚暴，所以利于处罚量刑，决断讼狱。

《象传》说：下卦震为雷，上卦离为闪电，组合在一起就是象征雷电交加的噬嗑卦。先王从电闪雷鸣的象征中得到启示，要彰明刑罚，饬正法令。

Hexagram Shihe (Punishment) symbolizes obstructions, punishments and prison, as well as prosperity, and is conducive to punishment and sentencing, hearing lawsuits and jailing.

The *Judgment Commentary* (*Tuan Zhuan*) says: Food in the mouth is the situation explained by Hexagram Shihe (Punishment). Why does it signify prosperity when there is something stuck in someone's mouth? This is because Hexagram Shihe (Punishment) comes from Hexagram Pi (Non-Communication). In the hexagram-changes system, strong and soft lines are separated yet intertwined, becoming the strong and soft helping each other. The lower Trigram Zhen is vibration, and the upper Trigram Li is brightness; vibration below and brightness above is an image of brightness and action, so it can be prosperous. The lower Trigram Zhen is thunder, the upper Trigram Li is lightning. Thunder and lightning enhance each other's strong power of deterrence and give an effect of clear illumination. The hexagram-change is from Hexagram Pi (Non-Communication) to Hexagram Shihe (Punishment), that is, the Nine (*yang*/strong line) in the fifth place in Hexagram Pi (Non-Communication) exchanges with the Six (*yin*/soft line) in the first place. The soft line of the Six (*yin*/soft line) in the first place of Hexagram Pi (Non-Communication) moves up to the middle position of the upper Trigram, and the hexagram becomes Hexagram Shihe (Punishment). The meaning of the change in the hexagram is that the soft lines softly and smoothly advance to the middle position and have upright morals. The Six (*yin*/soft line) in the fifth place is soft but in a strong position, so its position is inappropriate, but handling cases and redressing injustice does not require force and violence, so it is conducive to punishment, sentencing, and court decisions.

The *Image Commentary* (*Xiang Zhuan*) says: The lower Trigram Zhen is thunder, and the upper Trigram Li is lightning. When combined together, they become Hexagram Shihe (Punishment), which symbolizes thunder and lightning. The former kings learned from the symbols of lightning and thunder that they needed to clarify punishments and correct laws.

【明意】

惩罚的效果微妙玄通，要达于人心方可。如不达人心，则无效力。传统惩罚犯人的方式，希望通过约束行为改变人心，反而不如直指人心的教化有效。中国传统治理模式基本都是儒表法里，即认为大部分人可以用儒理教化，少部分人无法改变，只能用法刑之道对付他们。从约束行动自由的角度，通过惩罚来逼迫少数人走正道做正事。

司法考验人心，也影响人们对法律的信心。其实人民对于法律本身无所谓信心，但对于司法与执法人员的公正与否，人心自有判断。司法只能做到公正，不可能做到公平。中国人在社会分配上追求合理的不公平，合情合理，社会正义最后也要体现在人心之上，而不仅是外在的分配形式上。正义本来是天道自然的实化形式，但因为人心的占有和自私，而难以在人间社会的分配当中自然而然地实现，但社会正义的理想值得永远去追求。

[Illuminating Intentionality]

The effect of punishment is subtle and mysterious, and must reach people's heart-minds. If it does not reach people's heart-minds, it will be ineffective. The traditional way of punishing prisoners, hoping to change people's heart-minds by restraining their behavior, is not as effective as education that changes people's heart-minds directly. The traditional Chinese governance model was basically based on an outer surface of Confucian ritual and a core of law, which held that most people can be educated with Confucianism, but a small number of people cannot be changed, and they can only be dealt with through legal and penal methods. From the perspective of restricting freedom of movement, punishment was used to force this minority of people to take the right *dao* and do the right thing.

Judicial methods test people's intentions and affect people's confidence in the law. In fact, the people have no confidence in the law itself, but have their own judgment on the fairness of the judiciary and law enforcement officials. A judiciary can only be impartial, and cannot be fair. Chinese people pursue reasonable unfairness in social distribution, one which accords with feeling and principle. In the end, social justice must be reflected in people's intentions, not just in the external form of distribution. Justice is originally the natural form of realization of the *dao* of heaven, but due to the possessiveness and selfishness of the human heart-mind, it is difficult to realize it naturally in the distribution of human society. However, the ideal of social justice is worth pursuing forever.

初九：屦（jù）校灭趾，无咎。

《象》曰："屦校灭趾"，不行也。

【明译】

初九：脚上套着脚枷，遮没了脚趾，没有太大的罪过。

《象传》说：脚被带上了足枷，遮没了脚趾，是因为初九受到惩戒，走不动路了，也不可以再继续前行犯错了。

Nine (*yang*/strong line) in the first place: There are shackles on the feet, covering the toes. It is not a big crime.

The *Image Commentary* (*Xiang Zhuan*) says: The feet are put in shackles and the toes are covered because the Nine (*yang*/strong line) in the first place has been punished and can no longer walk, nor can it continue to move forward and make mistakes.

【明意】

犯了错误就把人手脚拷起来，使之"不行"，就无法随意行动了。这是把人的手脚束缚住，迫使其意识的实化不再出偏差，也就是即使其意识仍然是偏的，但不让其意识实化的身体反应产生任何对他人的伤害。初九犯了错，对应的策略是通过惩罚让犯错者失去行动自由，迫使其反思，在反省与检讨中改变自我意识实化的方式。这是通过外来行为约束，迫使主体改变内在的意识实化的方式。自由从这个意义上说，是实化主体意识之可能与否。有实化意识的可能，与实化意识之不可能，是两种完全不同的人生境遇，是意识之"行"与"不行"的两种不同状态。

[Illuminating Intentionality]

When a mistake is made, a person's hands and feet are handcuffed, making him "not doing" and unable to act as he pleases. This is to tie a person's hands and feet, forcing the concretization of his consciousness to no longer deviate. That is, even if his consciousness is still biased, he does not allow the physical reaction of his consciousness to cause any harm to others. If someone makes a mistake as the Nine (*yang*/strong line) in the first place, the corresponding strategy is to use punishment to make the wrongdoer lose their freedom of action, force them to reflect, and change the way they realize their self-awareness during reflection and review. This is a way of forcing the subject to change the inner concretization of consciousness through external behavioral constraints. In this sense, freedom is the possibility or impossibility of concretizing subjective consciousness. The possibility of realizing consciousness and the impossibility of realizing consciousness are two completely different situations in life, two different states of "doing" and "not doing" of consciousness.

六二：噬肤灭鼻，无咎。

《象》曰："噬肤灭鼻"，乘刚也。

【明译】

六二：咬食带皮的肉，连鼻子都陷没到肉里去了，没有过错。

《象传》说：像咬啮带皮的肉一样施刑，连鼻梁都打陷，好像没到肉里去了，是因为六二柔爻乘驾在初九刚爻之上，好比以欺凌的态度施用严刑峻罚。

Six (*yin*/soft line) in the second place: There is no fault in biting meat covered with skin until one's nose sinks into the meat.

The *Image Commentary* (*Xiang Zhuan*) says: When punishment is like biting meat with skin, even the bridge of the nose sinks in, as if it has not penetrated into the flesh. This is because the Six (*yin*/soft line) in the second place rides on the Nine (*yang*/strong line) in the first place, which is like a bullying attitude of imposing harsh punishments.

【明意】

意念发动都有感应。当惩罚的意识发动，往往招致相应的反抗意念。惩罚与征讨之人，如果知道这个道理，出手时就应该注意分寸，不可轻易发动惩罚他人的意识，否则噬咬不成，吃相难看，自取其辱，适得其反。换言之，意识发动应该有自我反省和评估机制，因为意识发动不仅仅是发动而已，在发动瞬间，意与感同时显现，当可体悟到感应状态。如意识能够反省，一旦惩罚的意识发动，就会立即招致相应的反抗意念，而且意念与其反动的意念之间，可能发生刚劲力量的较量，这就是意念与形势之间互动的力道。

[Illuminating Intentionality]

There is always an affective response when intentions are initiated. When the consciousness of punishment initiates, it often leads to corresponding intentions of resistance. Those who punish and conquer, if they know this truth, should be careful when taking action, and should not easily initiate the consciousness of punishing others, otherwise their biting will not be successful, the bite will be ugly, it will be humiliating, and it will be counterproductive. In other words, the initiation of consciousness should have a self-reflection and evaluation mechanism, because the initiation of consciousness is more than just initiation. At the moment of initiation, intention and feeling appear at the same time, and an induction state can be realized. If consciousness can reflect, once the consciousness of punishment is initiated, it will immediately lead to corresponding resistance intentions, and a contest of strength may occur between intentions and their reactive intentions. This is the strength of the interaction between intentions and a situation.

六三：噬腊肉，遇毒，小吝，无咎。

《象》曰："遇毒"，位不当也。

【明译】

六三：咬食坚硬的腊肉，遇到毒物，有小的麻烦，却不会有大的灾害。

《象传》说：遇到毒物犹如受刑者不服，原因是六三阴爻占据阳位，位置不适当，所以受刑者心生怨恨。

Six (*yin*/soft line) in the third place: If you bite hard cured meat and encounter poison, you will have small troubles, but no major disasters.

The *Image Commentary* (*Xiang Zhuan*) says: Encountering poison is like a person being tortured and refusing to accept it. The reason is that the Six (*yin*/soft line) in the third place occupies the *yang* position and is not appropriate, so the person being tortured feels resentful.

【明意】

同上爻所言，强迫使用意识的力发出，往往遭遇近乎相似力道的回应，如果是武力意识，则可能有相应的抵抗力。可见意识之力的运用要讲求分寸，不可因为位置不当就出手过猛，反而生变，损人伤己。此爻阴意表面柔弱，但骨子里刚硬不屈，是对于自认不合理的外力不甘屈服。可见，咬断阻碍之力，需要担心反力。从施用刑罚的角度来说，惩罚的力量依存于执行者的力量。

[Illuminating Intentionality]

As noted in the above line, when consciousness is forced to be initiated, this is often met with a response of almost similar strength. If it is a violent consciousness, there may be corresponding resistance. It can be seen that the use of the power of consciousness must be measured, and one should not attack too hard just because a position is inappropriate. On the contrary, this will change and harm others and oneself. The *yin* intentionality of this line is weak on the surface, but it is hard and unyielding in its bones. It is unwilling to give in to external forces that it considers unreasonable. It can be seen that in order to bite off an obstructive force, one needs to worry about the reactive force. From the perspective of the application of punishment, the power of punishment depends on the power of the executor.

九四：噬干胏（zǐ），得金矢。利艰贞，吉。

《象》曰："利艰贞，吉"，未光也。

【明译】

九四：咬食干硬带骨的肉，却意外得到骨中的金属箭头，有利于在艰难处境中持守正道，可获吉祥。

《象传》说：有利于在艰难中持守正道，可获吉祥，但是九四还难以发扬刑罚之威力和光明。

Nine (*yang*/strong line) in the fourth place: Biting dry meat with a hard bone inside, one accidentally gets a metal arrowhead in the bone. This is helpful for staying on the right *dao* in a difficult situation, and there will be good fortune.

The *Image Commentary* (*Xiang Zhuan*) says: It is helpful to stick to the right *dao* in difficulties and gain good fortune, but it is difficult to develop the power and light of punishment for the Nine (*yang*/strong line) in the fourth place.

【明意】

审案从来都是艰难的工作。审案可能像咬干肉一样不好啃，又可能啃到金矢（坚硬刚直的对象），那就难上加难，这时，对付又刚又直的审判对象，应该也用又刚又直的断案精神才可以。所以是一个艰难的审讯过程。审案需要贤明的意识，可能意外遭遇金属箭头，是一种啃硬骨头的努力之后的意外收获。在审判双方意识都刚直的状态当中，意念之有力与否，靠的是自身的意念发动背后的意志力，自制力和情境的支持力、作用力等的合力。

[Illuminating Intentionality]

Trial cases are always difficult work. A trial may be as hard to chew as dried meat, and it may be even more difficult if one bites a target with a metal arrow (hard and straight). At this time, when dealing with a tough and straight trial target, one should also use "hard and straight" means because only a straightforward spirit can solve the case effectively. So it is a difficult trial and interrogation process. Judging a case requires a wise mind, and you may encounter a metal arrow accidentally, which is an unexpected reward after hard work. In a state where both parties in the trial have upright consciousness, the strength of their intentions depends on the willpower and self-control behind the initiation of their own intentions, as well as the support and influence of the situation.

六五：噬干肉，得黄金。贞厉，无咎。

《象》曰："贞厉无咎"，得当也。

【明译】

六五：咬食干肉，意外得到黄金。在艰难之中，能持守正道，不会有咎害。

《象传》说：在艰难之中而能持守正道，不会有咎害，是因为六五在上卦中位，施刑治狱能够持中守正，分寸得当（所以最后有意外收获）。

Six (*yin*/soft line) in the fifth place: One bites dried meat and accidentally gets gold. In difficult times, if one can stick to the right *dao*, one will not suffer any harm.

The *Image Commentary* (*Xiang Zhuan*) says: The reason why one can stick to the right *dao* in difficult times and there will be no harm is because the Six (*yin*/soft line) in the fifth place is in the middle of the upper Trigram, and can stick to the right *dao* when applying punishment and incarceration, so it is appropriate (there will be unexpected gains in the end).

【明意】

在艰难的情境之中，人的意识往往可能懈怠，但这时特别需要贞的精神，即坚持不懈的努力。审判的意识竞争，是审判者与被审者的意志力之竞争，当然，被审者的意识因身体的自由度受到限定而相应受到影响，也就通常难以抗拒审判者的手段和威力。

[Illuminating Intentionality]

In difficult situations, people's consciousness may often slack off, but at this time, the spirit of steadfast, unremitting efforts, is particularly needed. The competition of consciousness in trial is a competition between the willpower of the judge and the person being judged. Of course, the consciousness of the person being judged is affected accordingly due to the limited freedom of the body, so it is usually difficult to resist the means and power of a judge.

上九：何校灭耳，凶。

《象》曰："何校灭耳"，聪不明也。

【明译】

上九：肩上扛着颈枷，遮没了耳朵，有凶祸。

《象传》说：肩上扛着颈枷，遮没了耳朵，是因为上九像耳不聪，目不明的聋子瞎子，犯下大错，被迫接受重刑。

Nine (*yang*/strong line) in the top place: Carrying a yoke on one's shoulders and covering one's ears is a sign of misfortune.

The *Image Commentary* (*Xiang Zhuan*) says: The reason why one carries a pillory on one's shoulders and covers one's ears, is because the Nine (*yang*/strong line) in the top place is like a deaf and blind person who has no hearing and cannot see clearly, so makes a big mistake and is forced to accept severe punishment.

【明意】

耳不聪，目不明，人的意识就不明，不明则无法认清形势，犯下大错，被迫接受重罚，被迫带上能遮住耳朵的颈枷，原因是因为主体意识本来不聪不明，而导致意念发动之后造就的客观上不聪不明的后果。这种后果可以说是咎由自取。

这是说人被惩罚的后果是因为自己意识境域的问题导致的。罪大恶极不值得同情，自己自绝于同类，自作自受；自己耳目不聪明，对于他人的意识没有感觉，最后被迫承担耳目被遮蔽的惩罚。说明人的意识本来就存在于跟他人交流的过程之中，如果自己意识不明，就可能招致麻烦，如果严重的话，可能有相应的后果要去承担。

[Illuminating Intentionality]

If their ears are not clear and their eyes are not bright, a person's consciousness will be unenlightened. If a person is unenlightened, one will not be able to recognize the situation clearly. One will make a big mistake and be forced to accept heavy punishments and be forced to wear a shackle that can cover one's ears. The reason is that subjective consciousness is not originally aware of the situation, which leads to the objective consequences of not being intelligent or clear after the initiation of intentions. This consequence can be said to be self-inflicted.

This means that the consequences of people being punished are caused by problems in their own consciousness. A crime that is so heinous is unworthy of sympathy. One isolates oneself from one own kind and suffers one's own consequences. One's ears and eyes are not clear and bright, and one has no sense of the consciousness of others. In the end, one is forced to bear the punishment of having one's ears and eyes blocked. This shows that people's consciousness originally exists in a process of communication with others. If one is unclear about one's consciousness, one may get into trouble. If it is serious, one may have to bear the corresponding consequences.

山火贲（卦二十二） （离下艮上）

Bi (Decoration), Mountain and Fire (Hexagram 22) (Li below, Gen above)

　　文饰是在有限意量的基础上，意念随顺天文之力而自然文饰，进而限定其量的。如果没有一定的意量，那么文饰是不可能的，因为没有落实的有限性基础。文饰主要是柔顺地化妆、妆饰、调整，所以是柔火、柔而用明之象。

　　人的心灵的装饰与限定，好像天文的阴阳装饰，文明地限定自身的意量，因其限定反而有通天的意境出来，这就是人天之意在意量有限性方向修持而愈发通天光明灿烂的表现。君子的人天之意装饰社会文明和政治活动，但文饰本身不足以断狱和惩治作恶的人，这是柔性的意量之有限性的表现；因为柔小的增饰是给善人的善心善意锦上添花，至于邪心邪意发动，总是要整治和施压他人的人，单纯依赖善人的意量去感化他们是不够的，还需要用其他的方式。

　　Literary decoration is based on limited intentionality, and intentionality is naturally decorated according to astronomical power, thereby limiting its quantity. Without a certain degree of intentionality, then, decoration is impossible because there is no finite basis for its implementation. Decoration is mainly about cosmetics, embellishment and adjustment, so it is an image of soft fire, softness and use of light.

　　The decoration and limitation of human intentionality is like the *yin* and *yang* decoration of astronomy. It limits its own intentionality in a civilized manner, and because of its limitation, a heaven-connecting intentional context comes out. This is the way that the intention of humanity and heaven gives a brighter and more brilliant performance when it is practiced in the direction of a limited quantity of intention. An exemplary person's intention of humanity and heaven embellishes social civilization and political activities, but decoration itself is not enough to break prisons and punish evildoers. This is a manifestation of the limitation of soft intentions; because small additions are but the icing on the cake of good people's good intentions, as for those who have evil intentions and always want to manipulate and pressure others, it is not enough to rely solely on the will of good people to influence them, and other methods are also needed.

贲（bì），亨。小利有攸往。

《彖》曰："贲，亨"，柔来而文刚，故"亨"。分刚上而文柔，故"小利有攸往"。刚柔交错，天文也。文明以止，人文也。观乎天文，以察时变；观乎人文，以化成天下。

《象》曰：山下有火，贲。君子以明庶政，无敢折狱。

【明译】

贲卦象征文饰装扮，亨通。向前去做事可以有小的利益。

《彖传》说：贲卦亨通，柔顺者来文饰刚强者（贲卦由泰卦上六与九二换位变出，卦变中柔爻从上位下来，使刚柔交错开，是柔顺者来文饰刚健者），所以贲卦亨通。刚健者分开而上去文饰柔顺者，（卦变中，泰下卦乾的刚爻被分开，九二到上位去文饰柔爻，使上卦坤的柔爻得到交错，刚柔互济）。向前去做事可以有小的利益（在卦变中柔爻从上位来到下卦中位，刚爻从乾天中位到上位，刚爻代表天来文饰柔爻，柔爻为小，所以向前去做事可以有小的利益）。阳刚与阴柔交错，这是天的文章和文采。下卦离为文明，上卦艮为止，用文明来规范限制人们的行为，就是人的文化和文明。观测天的文章和文采，就可以察知时间和季节变化之道；观察人的文化与文明，就可以推行教化成就天下隆盛昌明。

《象传》说：上卦艮为山，下卦离为火，山下燃烧着火焰就是贲卦的象征。君子从这种火光照亮万物，光芒足以文饰的景观中受到启示，要通过文饰来让政治昌明，文化昌盛，但不可以依靠文饰来判决讼狱之事。

Hexagram Bi (Decoration) symbolizes decoration and prosperity. There can be small benefits in advancing.

The *Judgment Commentary* (*Tuan Zhuan*) says: Hexagram Bi (Decoration) is prosperous, with the submissive decorating the strong (Hexagram Bi (Decoration) comes from exchanging the positions of the Six (*yin*/soft line) in the top place and the Nine (*yang*/strong line) in the second place in Hexagram Tai (Communication), so in the hexagram-change the *yin*/soft line comes down from the highest position and divides the *yang*/strong lines, the soft decorating the strong), so Hexagram Bi (Decoration) is prosperous. This separates the strong which decorate the soft above (during the hexagram-change, the *yang*/strong lines of the lower Trigram Qian in Hexagram Tai (Communication) are separated, and the Nine (*yang*/strong line) in the second place goes to the upper Trigram Kun to decorate the *yin*/soft lines, so that the *yin*/soft lines of the upper Trigram Kun are interlaced, and the strong and soft lines complement each other). Doing things and advancing can bring small benefits (in the hexagram-change, a *yin*/soft line goes from the top position to the middle position of the lower Trigram, and a *yang*/strong line goes from the middle position of Trigram Qian (Heaven) to the top position. The *yang*/strong line represents heaven in decorating the *yin*/soft lines, and the *yin*/soft line is small, so there can be small benefits in advancing). The intertwining of *yang*/strong masculinity and *yin*/soft femininity is heaven's decorative signification and literary talent. The lower Trigram Li is civilization, while the upper Trigram Gen is stopping, used to regulate and restrict people's behavior, so this signifies human culture and civilization. By observing heaven's signs and literary talent, one can discern the changes of time and season; by observing human culture and civilization, one can implement enlightenment and make the world prosperous and enlightened.

The *Image Commentary* (*Xiang Zhuan*) says: The upper Trigram Gen is mountain, the lower Trigram Li is fire, so a flame burning under a mountain is the symbol of Hexagram Bi (Decoration). Exemplary people are inspired by this scene where fire illuminates the myriad things and the light is enough for decoration, and know they should use decoration to make politics enlightened and culture flourishing, but cannot rely on decoration to judge lawsuits and criminal cases.

【明意】

如果上一卦噬嗑讲审判断案，近于法家；那么贲卦就是文饰，是以德治国的儒家。文饰意量的最高境界是天文（天道之化成），代表天的文饰成为意的文饰所能达到最完美的境界，原因是心意的文明本身与天的文饰有着先天的同构性。人文是人的花样，天文即天的花样。人文化成要模仿天的化育之功，人的意念来自天，人的文化量都是意念所实化，但人文（文化意念）不能脱离天文（自然之意）的内在结构。

[Illuminating Intentionality]

If the previous Hexagram Shihe (Punishment) talks about trials and judgment, which is close to Legalism, then Hexagram Bi (Decoration) is concerned with literary decoration and represents the Confucianism that governs the country by virtue. The highest state of the intentionality of literary decoration is astronomy (the transformation of the heavenly *dao*). The decoration of heaven becomes the most perfect state that the decoration of intentionality can reach. The reason is that the civilization of intentionality itself and the decoration of heaven have an inherent isomorphism. The humanities are the patterns of people, and astronomy is the patterns of heaven. The success of human culture should imitate the transformation and education of heaven. Human intentionality comes from heaven, and human cultural qualities are concretized by intentions. However, the humanities (cultural intentionality) cannot be separated from the inner structure of astronomy (natural intentionality).

初九：贲其趾，舍车而徒。

《象》曰："舍车而徒"，义弗乘也。

【明译】

初九：文饰脚趾，舍弃车子不坐，徒步行走。

《象传》说：舍弃车子不坐，徒步行走，因为初九所处的地位按照礼仪来说不应该去乘坐大车。

Nine (*yang*/strong line) in the first place: Decorating one's toes, one abandons a vehicle and walk on foot.

The *Image Commentary* (*Xiang Zhuan*) says: Giving up the vehicle and walking on foot is because, according to the ritual propriety of the Nine (*yang*/strong line) in the first place's position, one should not ride in a large vehicle.

【明意】

脚趾是脚的根源，比脚跟更有贴近大地的原生态意味。好像海德格尔赞美的农夫之鞋。脚趾有身体之端的意义，代表身体的开端和自尊心的源头。人通过修脚穿鞋可以接通与大地阴意气脉的关联。对脚的意量作为身意的根基，虽然通常粗鄙，但应该敝帚自珍，文饰脚说明对自身的关爱和对美感的重视。此爻有车不上，更显出脚的文饰象征自尊心的根源，是人的意量给自己设定的自尊之限度，不允许他人超越进入自己的尊严范围。

[Illuminating Intentionality]

The toes are the root of the foot, and are closer to the earth than the heel, like Van Gogh's painting of peasant shoes praised by Heidegger. The toes have the meaning of the tip of the body, representing the beginning of the body and the source of self-esteem. People can connect with the *yinqi* of the earth through pedicure and shoes. Intentionality concerning feet is the foundation of bodily intention, and although they are usually vulgar, they should be cherished, and embellishment of the feet shows care for oneself and emphasis on beauty. The vehicle in this line is not boarded, and the decoration of the feet symbolizes the source of self-esteem. It is the limit of self-esteem set by human intention and does not allow others to exceed the scope of one's own dignity.

六二：贲其须。

《象》曰："贲其须"，与上兴也。

【明译】

六二：文饰他的胡须。

《象传》说：六二是文饰九三的胡须，因为六二随着上边九三一起兴起来文饰。

Six (*yin*/soft line) in the second place: He decorates his beard.

The *Image Commentary* (*Xiang Zhuan*) says: The Six (*yin*/soft line) in the second place is the beard that decorates the Nine (*yang*/strong line) in the third place, because the Six (*yin*/soft line) in the second place follows the Nine (*yang*/strong line) in the third place above to decorate along with it.

【明意】

胡须是男性的象征，文饰胡须是男性美化自己的表现，也是主体对阳意意量边界的文饰。胡须是阳意的末梢，是颐养（互颐）之外的装饰之物。文饰末梢表示文饰细节的精细程度，也是阳意的自我展示，所以文饰胡须含有男性雄性意量的展示意味。何谓雄性意量？就是阳意发动的边界，在人身明显的外在表现是胡须。在世间就是男性雄性力量的外在实化，如齐家治国等。

雄性的意量带有残酷的斗争性，这在动物界里就是如此，适者生存是说明雄性意量存续的根本表述。正是因为雄性意量从自然界延伸下来就争斗不止，人难以彻底摆脱作为动物性的一面，所以文饰人的意量进而美化其行为，就显得特别有必要。文饰心灵、文饰雄性争斗的方式与手法等，都是让雄性意量之间的竞争变成文明而不再野蛮的竞争。

[Illuminating Intentionality]

The beard is a symbol of masculinity, and beard decoration is a way for men to beautify themselves, and also a decoration for the subject's boundary of *yang* intentionality. The beard is the tip of *yang*/positive intentionality and is a decorative thing in addition to care for each other. The tips of the ornaments represent the fineness of the details of the ornaments, and are also an self-expression of *yang* intentionality, so an ornamental beard also means a display of male masculinity. What is masculine intentionality? It is the boundary where *yang* intentions are initiated, and its obvious external manifestation in the human body is the beard. In the world, it is the external realization of male power, such as organizing the family and governing the country.

Masculine intentionality is characterized by cruel struggle, as is the case in the animal kingdom. Survival of the fittest is the fundamental expression that explains the existence of masculine intentionality. It is precisely because masculine intentionality is constantly fighting when it extends from nature, and because it is difficult for people to completely get rid of their animal side, that it is particularly necessary to embellish people's intentions and beautify their behavior. Decorating the mind, decorating the ways and techniques of masculine struggle, etc., all make the competition between masculine intentionality become civilized and no longer barbaric.

九三：贲如，濡（rú）如，永贞吉。

《象》曰："永贞"之"吉"，终莫之陵也。

【明译】

九三：文饰地光鲜亮丽的样子，润泽水灵的样子，能够相濡以沫、长久持守正固自然吉祥。

《象传》说：爱情如果能够长久持守正固自然吉祥，因为世间最终没有什么能凌驾于九三（坚贞的爱情）之上。

Nine (*yang*/strong line) in the third place: The bright and beautiful appearance of decoration, a fresh and dewy appearance, can provide mutual support and maintain integrity for a long time, which is naturally auspicious.

The *Image Commentary* (*Xiang Zhuan*) says: If love can remain upright for a long time, it will be naturally auspicious, because ultimately nothing in the world can surpass (the faithful love of) the Nine (*yang*/strong line) in the third place.

【明意】

人间心灵文饰的最高境界通过爱的意丹来体现。此"永贞吉"体现的就是彼此对爱意之丹的坚贞相守，双方时刻心意相通，文饰对方的心意，共同建构彼此的意量。虽然彼此坚贞的意念相和的意量有限，但意丹凝结而成之后却可能达到永恒的境界。"永"是有限意量的无限化的状态，是用意固结同心，直达爱情"有而无之"至高境界的努力，让爱的意丹因其坚贞而达致"无"的永恒，从而成为世间无与伦比的心意风景。

深情相爱中缘构彼此的意量，常会受怀疑的情绪影响，可能把对方的好意误会成敌意，但因彼此心意相通，最后还是能够迅速克服各种情绪，重新回到彼此深沉相爱的意量之中。彼此深爱之人，他们的意量是感应的最深形式，分分秒秒心心相印，时时刻刻不能离开对方，是对方的存在与印和（跨越时空）缘构了意量的限度，而这种限度因心心相印的尺度可以跨越时空中近于无限的隔阂。

[Illuminating Intentionality]

The highest state of spiritual decoration in the world is reflected through the elixir of love. This eternally devoted love reflects both parties' steadfastness in the elixir of love. Both parties are always connected, and embellish and jointly construct each other's intentions. Although the harmony of both parties' steadfast intentions has a limited intentionality, once the elixir of intention is condensed, it may reach an eternal state. "Eternal" is the state of infinity of limited intentionality. It is the effort to consolidate one intentionality and reach the highest state of love, so that the elixir of love can reach the eternity of "non-being" due to its steadfastness, and thereby become an unparalleled spiritual sight in the world.

Although deep love builds up each party's intentionality, they are often affected by doubtful emotions, and may misunderstand each other's good intentions as hostility. However, because they are connected, they can quickly overcome various emotions in the end and return to the deep intention of loving each other. For people who love each other deeply, their will is the deepest form of induction. They are in touch with each other every second and cannot leave each other at any time. It is the existence and seal of the other person and their dependent co-arising (across time and space) that constitute the limit of their intentionality. This kind of limit can span a nearly infinite gap in time and space because of the scale of heart-to-heart connection.

六四：贲如皤（pó）如，白马翰如。匪寇，婚媾。

《象》曰：六四，当位疑也。"匪寇婚媾"，终无尤也。

【明译】

六四：文饰地淡雅美素、白净无瑕的样子，坐下白马又是那样纯白无杂的样子，（向初九飞奔而来）；（初九）发现前方来的（六四）并非寇盗，而是来求婚联姻的佳偶。

《象传》说：六四阴爻居阴位，正当多疑的位置，所以六四开始怀疑，后来（初九）发现前方来的（六四）不是寇盗，而是来求婚联姻的佳偶，（六四）到最后不会有什么抱怨和忧虑。

Six (*yin*/soft line) in the fourth place: The decoration is elegant and simple, and the white horse one rides looks so pure (after running towards the Nine (*yang*/strong line) in the first place); (the Nine (*yang*/strong line) in the first place) finds that the person coming in front (the Six (*yin*/soft line) in the fourth place) is not a bandit, but a partner who has come to propose marriage.

The *Image Commentary* (*Xiang Zhuan*) says: The *yin* line of the Six (*yin*/soft line) in the fourth place is in a *yin* position, which is a correct but suspicious position, so Six (*yin*/soft line) in the fourth place begins to doubt, but later (the Nine (*yang*/strong line) in the first place) discovers that the people coming in front (the Six (*yin*/soft line) in the fourth place) are not bandits, but a partner who has come to propose marriage. (For the Six (*yin*/soft line) in the fourth place,) in the end there will be no complaints or worries.

【明意】

爱情之中意量的彼此缘构开始可能对对方的情感有所怀疑，深爱本身也有盲目和危险，但冲破了如寇盗一般的疑心，反而可以有更加坚如磐石的彼此深爱，进入真正的婚姻境界。从而使爱的意量提升到一个不可以离却彼此的最佳心意相通状态。

此爻表达了人间意念彼此感通，融合无碍，超越时空的极致美妙境界。

[Illuminating Intentionality]

An intentional relationship in love may begin to produce doubt about each other's feelings, and deep love itself is also blind and dangerous. However, if they break through the suspicion like that of bandits, they can have a more rock-solid love for each other and enter the true state of marriage. This elevates the intentionality of love to a state of optimal mind-intentionality communication in which the two cannot be separated from each other.

This line expresses the ultimate and wonderful state of human intentions being connected to each other, integrating without hindrance, and transcending time and space.

六五：贲于丘园，束帛戋（jiān）戋。吝，终吉。

《象》曰：六五之"吉"，有喜也。

第二章　易经明意
——爻意分说（上经）

【明译】

六五：（君王）意图文饰装扮大好河山的丘山田园，以轻微的束帛礼品招贤纳士，虽然有点不成敬意，但最后一定会国事呈祥。

《象传》说：六五的吉祥是因为必有喜庆，既因为六五位置好，也因为六五虚怀若谷，招贤纳士，一定会有喜事。

Six (*yin*/soft line) in the fifth place: (The king) intends to decorate the hills and countryside of the great rivers and mountains with literary decoration, and recruit talents with light silk gifts. Although this is slightly disrespectful, in the end it will definitely bring good fortune to the country.

The *Image Commentary* (*Xiang Zhuan*) says: The Six (*yin*/soft line) in the fifth place is auspicious because there must be joy, not only because the Six (*yin*/soft line) in the fifth place is in a good position, but also because the Six (*yin*/soft line) in the fifth place is open-minded and recruiting talent, so there will be happy events.

【明意】

忠贞圆满的爱情意量当延伸到家国天下之中去，而不是仅仅局限在自己的小家当中，故彼此印和的心意不仅仅以对方为量，而且还应该同时以天下为量，也就是要邀请彼此相好的同道共同成就一番伟业，把天地都一起装饰好。要有装饰好天地的气量，首先要有阴意与阳意彼此感通凝成意丹的意量。意量伸展至广大天地之中，即可以改天换地，共同把天地家国装饰好。

此爻说明装饰天地宇宙万物的心意是可能的，爱的意量可以突破小家格局，而有天地宇宙的宏大气象，即爱的意丹可以延展到天下之中去。人文是小家小爱，要文明以止，发乎情止乎礼。天文才是贲卦的要旨所在，上察天时，下化众生，是装修天地宇宙万物，而不是装扮自己的小家。读贲卦，知道斯文载道，文化的装修才是超越时空的大装修。

[Illuminating Intentionality]

The intentionality of loyal and perfect love should be extended to the family, country and the world, rather than just limited to the scope of one's own small family. Therefore, mutual affection should not only be measured by one's partner, but should also be measured by the world at the same time. That is to say, colleagues who like each other should be invited to achieve great things and decorate the world together. To have the energy to decorate the world, one must first have the energy to communicate with each other and form an elixir of intentionality. If one's intentionality extends to the vast world, one can change and decorate the world together.

This line shows that it is possible to decorate the intentionality of the myriad things in heaven, earth and the cosmos. The intention of love can break through the small family structure, and with the grand atmosphere of heaven, earth and the cosmos, the intention of love can be extended to the world. Humanity is a small family and a small love, which must be civilized and end with ritual propriety. Astronomy is the main point of Hexagram Bi. Observing the sky above, and transforming all living beings below is to decorate heaven, earth, the cosmos and the myriad things, rather than to decorate one's own small home. Reading Hexagram Bi, we know that this culture carries the *dao*, so culture is a major decoration that transcends time and space.

上九：白贲，无咎。

《象》曰："白贲，无咎"，上得志也。

【明译】

上九：文饰装扮到了极致境界而洗尽铅华，返璞归真，没有什么问题。

《象传》说：在素朴虚白的大地上文饰装扮，没有什么问题，因为上九实现了它想上来文饰装扮坤地的志向。

Nine (*yang*/strong line) in the top place: Decoration is applied to the ultimate level and is washed away, returning to original nature. There is no problem.

The *Image Commentary* (*Xiang Zhuan*) says: There is no problem in decorating the plain and white earth with ornaments, because the Nine (*yang*/strong line) in the top place has realized its ambition to decorate the earth (Trigram Kun) with ornaments.

【明意】

一爻爻用儒家的进路解，好像一路搞装修装饰上来，境界越来越高，最后到了山顶，实现了极致状态，有点道家的气象出来。路上还发生了两场令人魂牵梦绕的爱情故事，也算儒家入世的表现。贲卦不同爻位有不同高度、不同视野，影响装饰的不同范围和境界。

贲卦到上爻，真有会当凌绝顶，一览众山小之妙境，上六在艮山之巅，可以高瞻远瞩，化成天下。以此视角看此爻的意量，白是天地的虚白，正好大做装修，有经纶天下之志。不论是上来得志，还是在上得意，搞顶层设计是绝妙的自我实现的体验，是潇洒人生成功境界背后洗尽铅华、返璞归真的意道，是成功的装饰天地的那种高峰体验，也是一种儒道合一的完美人生境界的体现。

在山顶上搞顶层设计，达到儒道合一的境界，不但脚痛会忘，什么痛苦都可以放下，这就是心通天地的自我实现，即人天之意通达天地的境界。上九在高山之巅，也在天地之极致境界，爱的意量被放大到最大尺度，从而能够进入高瞻远瞩、洞彻天地的虚白之境，把爱人之情意的意量转化为仁爱天地的气魄，从而把经营天地的意量扩大到最高远深邃的境界。可见，装修天地的气魄实现了对天地之大爱那种儒道合一的至圣境界。

[Illuminating Intentionality]

Line after line is interpreted using the Confucian approach, and it seems that one is decorating and embellishing all the way up, one's realm getting higher and higher, until one finally reaches the top of the mountain, achieving the ultimate state, and there is a Daoist atmosphere. Two haunting love stories also happen on the road, which can also be regarded as a manifestation of Confucianism's entry into the world. Different lines of Hexagram Bi (Decoration) have different heights and different visions, which affect the different scope and realm of decoration.

When Hexagram Bi (Decoration) reaches the top line, one can really stand on the top of the mountain and enjoy a panoramic view of the wonderful scenery of all the small mountains. The top line is the peak of Trigram Gen's Mountain, so can have a far-sighted view and see the world. Looking at the intentionality of this line from this perspective, white is the empty whiteness of heaven and earth. This is just the time to do a lot of decoration and have the ambition to manage the world. Whether one is successful in achievement or proud in accomplishment, engaging in top-level design is a wonderful experience of self-realization. It is the cleansing behind a successful state of unrestrained life and returns to nature. It is the kind of peak experience that successfully decorates the world, and it is also an embodiment of the perfect realm of life that combines Confucianism and Daoism.

Engaging in top-level design on the top of the mountain can achieve the realm of the integration of Confucianism and Daoism. Not only is foot pain forgotten, but all pain can be let go of. This is the self-realization of intentionality connecting with the world, that is, the state where the intentionality of humanity and heaven can reach the world. The Nine (*yang*/strong line) in the top place is on the top of the mountain and in the ultimate realms of heaven and earth. The intentionality of love is magnified to the greatest scale, so that it can enter the white realm of far-sightedness and penetrate heaven and earth, and transform the intentionality of love for others into the spirit of benevolence for heaven and earth, thereby expanding the intention to manage the world to the highest and most profound realm. It can be seen that the spirit of decorating heaven and earth realizes the holy state of the great love for heaven and earth that combines Confucianism and Daoism.

山地剥（卦二十三） （坤下艮上）

Bo (Peeling), Mountain and Earth (Hexagram 23)　(Kun below, Gen above)

　　贲上九透出可以挥斥方遒的豪迈，可是转到剥就要顺而止之，形势变化迅速，好像刚搞完顶层设计，转过来就岌岌可危，现实中好比搞顶层设计必然触及既得利益集团，此时只能顺应时势而该止则止，心随天行，先止念，之后找机会止住败坏的时势。让意念在止中生，在长期的休止安宁平静之中，生机似乎已然不显，而一旦外缘生起，生机可能迅速点燃，心念的生机被长期压抑和削弱，得到强烈的外缘而全身心地释放，生机大展。

　　从意生论的角度，人必须转向自我决定，才能把赋予生命的使命从外转向内，虽然一生当中很多事情自己不能掌控，但人还是要努力创造自己的人生。人只有在意识到自己的存在之后，才会具有反思的能力，去思考存在的开端和意义。人所能改变的，不过是只有一次的人生，力图过得比较符合自己的意愿。

　　Hexagram Bi (Decoration)'s Nine (*yang*/strong line) in the top place exudes a boldness that can be used to arouse great morale, but when it comes to the stage of stripping back, it has to stop. The situation changes rapidly, and it seems that as soon as the top-level design is completed, it will be in danger when it turns around. In reality, top-level design will inevitably involve vested interest groups, and at this time, we can only adapt to the current situation and stop when necessary. Intentionality follows the *dao* of heaven, so one first stops thinking, and then looks for opportunities to stop the corrupt situation. One can let the intentions arise in the stillness, as during the long-term rest and tranquility, vitality may seem to have disappeared, but once the outer edge arises, vitality may be quickly ignited. The vitality of intentionality has been suppressed and weakened for a long time, and the strong outer edge affects the whole body. The heart is released and vitality is revealed.

From the perspective of the theory of intentional production, people must turn to self-determination in order to turn the life-giving mission from the outside to the inside. Although there are many things in life that they cannot control, people still have to work hard to create their own life. Only after people realize their own existence can they have the ability to reflect and think about the beginning and meaning of existence. What people can change is a life that's lived only once, and how to live it more in line with their own intentions.

剥，不利有攸往。

《彖》曰：剥，剥也。柔变刚也。"不利有攸往"，小人长也。顺而止之，观象也。君子尚消息盈虚，天行也。

《象》曰：山附于地，剥。上以厚下安宅。

【明译】

剥卦象征剥蚀掉落，不利于有所前往。

《彖传》说：剥就是剥蚀掉落的意思。是阴柔上长即将变成阳刚之体。不利于有所前往，是因为小人的势力正在不断上长。下卦坤为顺，上卦艮为止，全卦是五阴逼退一阳的架势，阳爻应该顺势抑止小人之道的成长，这从观察卦象就可以看出来。君子处事崇尚消息进退、盈盛亏虚的转化哲理，这也是顺从天的运行法则。

《象传》说：上卦艮为山，下卦坤为地，山剥蚀掉落附在大地上就是剥卦。在上位的君子看到大山被剥蚀将尽、山石掉落重压在地面上的卦象，担心根基不固，要增厚宅基，安稳而居；也要厚待百姓，让他们安居乐业。

Hexagram Bo (Peeling) symbolizes erosion and falling, which is not conducive to having somewhere one wants to go.

The *Judgment Commentary* (*Tuan Zhuan*) says: Hexagram Bo (Peeling) means eroding and falling off. It is the rising of the *yin*/soft that is about to change the *yang*/strong body. It is not conducive to advancing because the power of the petty person is constantly growing. The lower Trigram Kun is in order, and the upper Trigram Gen is stopping, so the whole hexagram is a state in which five *yin*s force one *yang* to retreat, and the *yang* line should take advantage of the trend to inhibit the growth of the petty person's way. This can be seen from observing the hexagram image. An exemplary person upholds the transformation philosophy of rising and falling, advance and retreat, and prosperity and loss, which is also in compliance with the laws of heaven.

The *Image Commentary* (*Xiang Zhuan*) says: The upper Trigram Gen is mountain, the lower Trigram Kun is earth, so a mountain being eroded and sinking to the earth is Hexagram Bo (Peeling).

The exemplary person in the top position sees the hexagram of the mountain being eroded and the rocks falling and weighing heavily on the ground. One is worried that the foundation is not solid, so one wants to strengthen the homestead so that one can live safely; one also wants to be kind to the ordinary people so they can live and work in peace and contentment.

【明意】

生机是人生及其境遇的根基。当人意识到生命的尽头在日益逼近，可能深感恐惧，人生匆匆而过，但生机尚未展开，一旦生机被压抑剥弱到极致，自己都感慨恐慌。不管知不知道自己的死期，人最后的结果都是死亡，区别仅仅在于人生的色彩，生命的强度和力度。人生的生机如果没有机会绽放，好像枉此一生。但绽放生意的机缘却可遇而不可求，每个生缘的瞬间都是所遇为命的状态，命的生机在当下意念交接的瞬间当中显现与展开。

生机在时空之中，随时间的推移而不可思议，《周易》揭示出时间对存在物的特殊意义，即存在物无时无刻不在时间之中，也就无时无刻不跟时间的阴阳性质发生交流。阴意处于阳意不断被剥蚀的情景中，一旦没有阳意即无生机。换言之，如果生缘显现而自己不抓住，就难以让生缘存续。

[Illuminating Intentionality]

Vitality is the foundation of human life and its circumstances. When people realize that the end of life is approaching day by day, they may feel deeply scared. Life is passing by in a hurry, but vitality has not yet unfolded. Once vitality is suppressed and weakened to the extreme, one will feel panic. Regardless of whether one knows one's date of death or not, the final result for any person is death. The difference lies only in the color of life, the intensity and power of life. If the vitality of life does not have a chance to bloom, it seems that this life is in vain. However, the opportunity for productive intentionality to bloom can only be encountered but cannot be sought. Every moment of dependent co-arising in life is a state of meeting one's destiny. The vitality of life appears and unfolds in the moment of exchange of intentions.

Life is in time and space, and it becomes unfathomable as time goes by. The *Book of Changes* reveals the special significance of time to existing things, that is, existing things are always within time, and they are always in communication with the *yin* and *yang* qualities of time. *Yin* intentionality is in a situation where *yang* intentionality is constantly being eroded, and once there is no *yang* intentionality, there is no vitality. In other words, if the dependent co-arising of life appears and one fails to grasp it, it will be difficult to continue the dependent co-arising of life.

初六：剥床以足，蔑，贞凶。

《象》曰："剥床以足"，以灭下也。

【明译】

初六：从床脚开始剥蚀，邪道开始侵蚀正道，必有凶险。

《象传》说：从床脚下面开始剥蚀，就是要从根基开始毁灭。

Six (*yin*/soft line) in the first place: The erosion starts from the legs of the bed, and the evil *dao* begins to erode the righteous *dao*. There must be danger.

The *Image Commentary* (*Xiang Zhuan*) says: That the bed is eroded from the legs means to destroy from the foundation.

【明意】

阴意在生，阳意被剥蚀，阳意缺乏自觉，从下面开始被灭。"蔑"提醒人们要绝地奋起，努力自救。剥是生机之剥，但刚开始剥蚀通常没有明确感觉，因为还在生机不显的情境，自我意识往往不清，对情境之感受也缺乏生气，但正因如此，反而说明，一旦感受和意识到切近的危险情境，就要有绝地反击的心理准备，在保存实力之中等待机缘，明白亡羊补牢还来得及的道理。

在大势不好、危险来临的时候，即使守正也可能凶，即使应该守规矩，也需要根据情境的瞬息变化不断从宜适变，不可坐以待毙。

[Illuminating Intentionality]

Yin intentionality is growing and *yang* intentionality is being eroded, but *yang* intentionality lacks self-consciousness and is being destroyed from below. "Erosion" reminds people to rise up and work hard to save themselves. Hexagram Bo (Peeling) is the peeling off of vitality, but there is usually no clear feeling at the beginning of peeling off, because in a situation where vitality is not obvious, self-awareness is often unclear, and the feelings of the situation lack vitality. However, because of this, it shows that once the feelings and consciousness are facing and approaching a dangerous situation, one must be mentally prepared to fight back, wait for opportunities while preserving one's strength, and understand that it is still not too late to make amends.

When the general propensity is bad and danger is approaching, even if one keeps things right, one may have bad fortune. Even if one should abide by the rules, one still needs to constantly adapt to the changing situation, and cannot just sit back and wait for death.

六二：剥床以辨，蔑，贞凶。

《象》曰："剥床以辨"，未有与也。

【明译】

六二：继续剥蚀床腿，邪道继续侵蚀正道，越来越凶险。

《象传》说：继续剥蚀床腿，是六二孤立无援，没有应与。

Six (*yin*/soft line) in the second place: Continuing to erode the legs of the bed, the evil *dao* continues to erode the righteous *dao*, becoming more and more dangerous.

The *Image Commentary* (*Xiang Zhuan*) says: If the legs of the bed continue to be eroded, the Six (*yin*/soft line) in the second place will be left alone and helpless.

【明意】

六二是阴意肆无忌惮地剥蚀阳意的凶险之境，要做好绝地反击的准备。意念的准备是意识到剥是生机之剥，是阴意生、压灭阳意之生机，阴意没有阳意的相与和感通，生机就被继续剥蚀。可以理解为，自我对于情境的感受已经泯灭，难以存续。在艰难时刻，生机的出现往往在精神的偶遇之间。可见，六二代表安宁到没有任何生机之气和可能性的情境，虽是典型无生气的阴意情境，没有阳意的相应，所以任何情感的异动都如死水微澜，结果阴意灭除阳意生机的意志越发强烈。

[Illuminating Intentionality]

The Six (*yin*/soft line) in the second place is a dangerous situation where *yin* power unscrupulously erodes *yang* power, so be prepared for a desperate counterattack. The mental preparation is to realize that peeling off is the peeling off of vitality, which is *yin* being generated and suppressing the vitality of *yang*. Without the interaction and connection between *yin* and *yang*, vitality will continue to be eroded. This can be understood as saying that one's own affective comprehension of the situation has been extinguished, and it is difficult to survive. In difficult times, vitality often emerges through spiritual encounters. It can be seen that the Six (*yin*/soft line) in the second place represents a situation that is so peaceful that there is no vitality or possibility. Although it is a typical lifeless situation of *yin* intentionality, and there is no corresponding *yang* intentionality, so any emotional changes are like the slightest ripples of stagnant water, and the will of *yin* intentionality to eliminate *yang*/positive intentionality's vitality becomes stronger and stronger.

六三：剥之，无咎。

《象》曰："剥之，无咎"，失上下也。

【明译】

六三：顺剥落之势，却没有什么过失。

《象传》说：顺剥落之势，却没有什么过失，是因为六三跟上下阴爻都不一致。

Six (*yin*/soft line) in the third place: Follow the trend of peeling, but there is no fault.

The *Image Commentary* (*Xiang Zhuan*) says: Follow the trend of peeling, but there is no fault, because the Six (*yin*/soft line) in the third place is not consistent with the *yin* lines above and below."

【明意】

此爻说明心意的生机已被剥蚀，进入孤立无援孤独无助的心意之境。在生机几乎全部剥蚀的时刻，处于绝望状态。阴意剥蚀阳意的趋势不可避免，几乎形成自然形势，只能难以抗拒，顺势而剥。此爻的心意之剥比身意之剥彻底到位，阳意被剥蚀尽净之时，恰是阴意生机的展现和绽放时刻。

[Illuminating Intentionality]

This line shows that the vitality of intentionality has been eroded, and it has entered a state of isolation and helplessness. At the moment when almost everything is eroded, vitality is eroded and in a state of despair. The tendency of *yin* to erode *yang* is inevitable, and has almost become a natural propensity, so one can only forgo resisting it and follow the propensity by peeling too. The peeling off of intentionality in this line is more thorough than the peeling off of body and mind. When *yang* intentionality is completely stripped away is the moment when the vitality of *yin* intentionality appears and blooms.

六四：剥床以肤，凶。

《象》曰："剥床以肤"，切近灾也。

【明译】

六四：剥蚀床到了人的皮肉，非常凶险。

《象传》说：剥蚀床到了人的皮肉，说明六四已经切实迫近灾祸了。

Six (*yin*/soft line) in the fourth place: The eroding bed touches people's skin and flesh, which is very dangerous.

The *Image Commentary* (*Xiang Zhuan*) says: The eroding bed reaches human skin and flesh, which shows that the Six (*yin*/soft line) in the fourth place is really approaching disaster.

【明意】

阴意在天地的生机中，已把原生剥蚀阳意的状态进行到底，此时危机四伏，阴意已基本把阳意剥蚀净尽，但阴意没有阳意之应，即无生机，也就不可存续。此刻阳意的危险迫在眉睫，生机被剥蚀到极致，但反而是彻底绽放的可能性。一说阴意觉得剥蚀过分，悔恨交加，阳意对阴意的触动，让阴意意识到自己已剥蚀过度，但危局已经造成，无法回去，可以说是唯有艰难面对自己造成的过失之境。

[Illuminating Intentionality]

In the vitality of heaven and earth, *yin*/negative intentionality has carried out the original state of eroding *yang*/positive intentionality to the end. At this time, crises are everywhere, and *yin*/negative intentionality has basically completely eroded *yang*/positive intentionality. However, *yin*/negative intentionality has no response from *yang*/positive intentionality, that is, it has no vitality and cannot survive. At this moment, the danger of *yang*/positive intentionality is imminent, and vitality has been eroded to the extreme, but instead it has the possibility of completely blooming. As soon as it is said that *yin*/negative intentionality feels that it has over-eroded, it is full of regrets. Yang/positive intentionality touches *yin*/negative intentionality, making *yin*/negative intentionality realize that it has over-eroded, but the crisis has been created and there is no way to go back. It can be said that the only way to face it is to face the realm of fault created by one's own mistakes.

六五：贯鱼，以宫人宠，无不利。

《象》曰："以宫人宠"，终无尤也。

【明译】

六五：率领众宫女们鱼贯而进，受到宠爱，是无所不利的。

《象传》说：像宫女们一样受宠，最后不会有什么怨尤。

Six (*yin*/soft line) in the fifth place: Leading all the maids in the palace to file in, and being pampered, there is no disadvantage.

The *Image Commentary* (*Xiang Zhuan*) says: If one is favored like a palace lady, one will not have any complaints in the end.

【明意】

六五以阴居阳位，阴柔而能够领导，但领导力的根源却在上九，是阳意给了力量，所以一改剥蚀之意，会主动顺承阳意，不再剥蚀阳意，而是尽量保留哪怕一点点阳意，知道岌岌可危的阳意都会尽心尽力去体会并珍惜六五给予的生机，可见，六五在意念之中把阳意的生机贯穿在整个阴意剥阳的生命历程，和阴意存续时刻不能离开阳意的丰富精神世界之中。

[Illuminating Intentionality]

In Six (*yin*/soft line) in the fifth place, *yin* occupies a *yang* position. *Yin* softness is capable of leadership, but the root of leadership lies in the Nine (*yang*/strong line) in the top place, as it is *yang* intentionality that gives strength. Therefore, once the intention of erosion is changed, *yin* intentionality will actively obey *yang* intentionality and will no longer erode *yang* intentionality. Instead, it will try to retain even a little bit of *yang*/positive intentionality. Knowing that *yang*/positive intentionality is in danger, one will try one's best to appreciate and cherish the vitality given by the Six (*yin*/soft line) in the fifth place. It can be seen that, in its intentions, the Six (*yin*/soft line) in the fifth place is permeated with the vitality of *yang*/positive intentionality throughout the entire life of the *yin*/negative intention to erode *yang*. The process, and the existence of *yin*/negative intentionality cannot leave behind the rich spiritual world of *yang*/positive intentionality.

上九：硕果不食。君子得舆，小人剥庐。

《象》曰："君子得舆"，民所载也。"小人剥庐"，终不可用也。

【明译】

上九：硕大的果实还没有被剥蚀和摘食。君子摘得，便是载人的车舆；小人占有，就会把人们庐舍的屋顶都掀翻。

《象传》说：君子摘得，便是载人的车舆，因为人民放心地搭乘君子的车舆（继续拥戴他）；小人占有，就会把人们庐舍的屋顶都掀翻，说明小人终究不可任用。

Nine (*yang*/strong line) in the top place: A huge fruit has not yet overripened and been picked. If an exemplary person takes it, it will be a vehicle to carry people; if a petty person takes it, it will knock off the roofs of people's houses.

The *Image Commentary* (*Xiang Zhuan*) says: If an exemplary person picks it, it will be a vehicle for carrying people, because the people can ride on the exemplary person's vehicle with confidence (continue to support him); if a petty person takes it, it will knock off the roofs of people's houses, which shows that petty people cannot be used in the end.

【明意】

阳意命悬一线的关键时刻，可以说，过得去就是君子，过不去就是小人，此时既看德性，也看运气和结果，但人在最关键的时候，要赌一把，过得去是靠天意，在生死之间，在绝境之间，靠的是看不清楚的阴阳交汇之力。最终老天会拯救良心发动的人，因为人的行为最后由内在德性与外在德行一起体现出来，不应该是单纯的结果主义，从另一方面讲，君子对百姓的起心动念方式要合乎天地良心。阳意所在，君子体天地之生意而为仁，如车可行更快，小人不能体会天地生意，心小而妒恨，把屋子破坏，所以百姓的心意即是天地之生意。

[Illuminating Intentionality]

At the critical moment when *yang*/positive intentionality's life is hanging by a thread, it can be said that if one can survive it, one is an exemplary person, and if one cannot survive it, one is a petty person. At this time, things depend not only on virtue, but also on luck and results. But at the most critical moment, people have to take a gamble. Survival depends on cosmological intentionality, between life and death, between desperate situations, and relies on the invisible power of the intersection of *yin* and *yang*. In the end, heaven will save those who are motivated by conscience, because a person's behavior is ultimately reflected in both internal and external virtues, and should not be purely consequentialist. On the other hand, an exemplary person's way of thinking about the ordinary people must be in line with the conscience of heaven and earth. Where the intentionality of *yang* intentionality is, an exemplary person understands the productive intentionality of heaven and earth and is benevolent, and can move faster like a car, while a petty person cannot understand the productive intentionality of heaven and earth, and is jealous and destroys the house. Therefore, the intentionality of the ordinary people is the productive intentionality of heaven and earth.

地雷复（卦二十四） （震下坤上）

Fu (Returning), Earth and Thunder (Hexagram 24)   (Zhen below, Kun above)

      复卦的本义是根绝往误，重回善道。此卦讨论人因生而有意则实存，无意则人并不实存，或人丧失实化自己意念的能力则不是完整的存在形态。人如何领会宇宙生生不息之意？意向能梳理天地万物的秩序，故意向的重生，带有复兴天地宇宙秩序的意味，如巽之鲜洁整齐之意。人心的先行结构与宇宙意志天籁的先行结构同质，所以人心在后天境遇中的复兴是意图在后天世界中重建先天世界的心灵秩序和逻辑结构。

      天地之意念何以可能？天行是自然之行，人之意即是天地之意。人心之善念何以可能？人之意与天地之意有相同的先天结构，人心本来就是天地之心，天地之心生生不息，在人心就是天心自然流动表现为仁心流动，都是就"生"与"成"的气象说，而不是就其否定的一方面说。但宇宙之心，即宇宙的意志如何领悟，这需要领悟宇宙意志（天籁）的先行结构（如河图洛书）。中国古人发明一套表达人心与宇宙共通的先天结构的模式，自有其内在的象数逻辑，而运用也往往相当有效甚至精确，但没有达到西方的数学与科学系统那般精确易行。

      The original meaning of Hexagram Fu (Returning) is to eradicate past mistakes and return to the good *dao*. This hexagram discusses the fact that people really exist if they have the intentionality they are born with, but if they do not have this intentionality, they do not really exist, or, if one loses the ability to concretize one's own intentions, one is not a complete form of existence. How do people understand the ceaselessly productive intentionality of the cosmos? Intentionality can sort out the order of heaven and earth, and the rebirth of intentionality has the sense of reviving the order of heaven, earth and the cosmos, just like the freshness and neatness of Trigram Xun. The antecedent structure of the human heart-mind is the same as the antecedent structure of the intentionality of the cosmos. Therefore, the revival of the human heart-mind in empirical (post-celestial) situations is intended to reconstruct the spiritual order and logical structure of the transcendental (pre-celestial) world in the empirical world.

How the intentionality of heaven and earth is possible: the movement of heaven is the movement of nature, and the intentions of humanity are the intentions of heaven and earth. How is it possible for the human heart-mind to have good intentions? The intentions of humanity and the intentions of heaven and earth have the same transcendental structure. The human heart-mind is originally the heart-mind of heaven and earth. The heart-mind of heaven and earth is endless. In the human heart-mind, the natural flow of heaven's heart-mind manifests as the flow of benevolence. They are both "produced" and "completed" in terms of atmosphere, rather than in terms of their negative aspect. But how to understand the heart-mind of the cosmos, that is, the intentionality of the cosmos, requires understanding the antecedent structure (such as River Diagram and Luo Chart) of the intentionality of the cosmos (the piping of heaven). The ancient Chinese invented a set of models to express the common transcendental structure of the human heart-mind and the cosmos. It has its own inherent symbolic logic, and its application is often quite effective and even accurate, but it is not as precise and easy to implement as Western mathematical and scientific systems.

复，亨。出入无疾，朋来无咎。反复其道，七日来复，利有攸往。

《彖》曰："复，亨"，刚反，动而以顺行。是以"出入无疾，朋来无咎"。"反复其道，七日来复"，天行也。"利有攸往"，刚长也。复，其见天地之心乎。

《象》曰：雷在地中，复。先王以至日闭关，商旅不行，后不省方。

【明译】

复卦象征往而复来，亨通。阳气从内生长，出入之间，没有障碍。志同道合的阳刚朋友们一起前进，不会有过失。阴气剥尽，阳气来复，阴阳彼此消长，有其规律，七天之内就会重新回来，周而复始。利于有所前往。

《彖传》说：复卦，亨通。阳刚之气又返回来，下卦震为动，上卦坤为顺，阳气顺势震动，向上通畅运行，所以阳气从内生长，出入之间，没有障碍。志同道合的阳刚朋友们一起前进，不会有过失。阴气剥尽，阳气来复，阴阳彼此消长，有其规律，七天之内就会重新回来，周期循环往复，这是天道运行的规律。按照这个道理向前进，是有利的，因为阳气会随着你的前往而逐渐增长。阳气往去复来，从中我们可以看到天地化生生养万物的心意吧。

《象传》说：下卦震为雷，上卦坤为地，雷蛰伏在地中，在地中微动，象征阳气来复。以前的君王知道冬至一阳来复，在冬至这一天封闭关卡，让全民静养，商贾旅客不得通行，即使是君王都不去四方的邦国巡视。

Hexagram Fu (Returning) symbolizes going and coming back, with prosperity. *Yangqi* grows from within, and there are no obstacles between it and its passage. If like-minded positive friends move forward together, there will be no mistakes. *Yin* energy is stripped away, and *yang* energy comes back. The *yin* and *yang* wax and wane against each other, and have their own rules. They come back within seven days, and the cycle starts again. This is conducive to advancing.

The *Judgment Commentary* (*Tuan Zhuan*) says: Hexagram Fu (Returning) is prosperity. The *yang* energy returns again, the lower Trigram Zhen is vibration, and the upper Trigram Kun is smoothness, so *yang* energy vibrates along with the propensity and rises upward smoothly, where *yang* energy grows from within, with no obstacle between going in and coming out. If like-minded positive friends move forward together, there will be no mistakes. *Yin* energy is stripped away and *yang* energy comes back, *yin* and *yang* waxing and waning each other according to their own rules. They will return within seven days, and the cycle repeats. This is the regularity of the movement of the *dao* of heaven. It is beneficial to move forward according to this principle, because *yangqi* will gradually increase as you go. *Yangqi* goes and comes back, from which we can see the intention of heaven and earth to transform and nourish the myriad things.

The *Image Commentary* (*Xiang Zhuan*) says: The lower Trigram Zhen is thunder, and the upper Trigram Kun is earth. Thunder lies dormant in the ground and moves slightly in the earth, symbolizing the return of *yangqi*. The former kings in the past knew that the sun would come back at the winter solstice, so they closed the gates on the day of the winter solstice to allow all the people to rest, and merchants and tourists were not allowed to pass, with even the kings not visiting surrounding states.

【明意】

天地之心，既是天地运行的心意，更是天地化生、生养万物的心意。天心通于人心，所以当主动合于天心，按照天心周而复始，生生不息的刚健有为状态，去起心动念。复卦闭关，是为静养阳气，古人认为阳气初生，微动难养，所以需要静养，让阳气的气机发动，从而保持心意合于天道化生的阳意而和谐顺畅。

人对于日月时空的周而复始有体会而必分始终，但这些始终在本体上无所谓分别，人的心意每时每刻随顺天机而时时更新，所以终极的理解是日新，每时每刻都是新的，其实是阳气新生，因生而有意的实存，无生则意不存。但《周易》不采用佛家刹那生灭的宇宙观，认为全部的消长盈虚皆在生机中延续。至于如何复兴，则要伺机而动，等待合适的时间与形势，顺势而行。

[Illuminating Intentionality]

The heart-mind of heaven and earth is not only the intentionality for the movement of heaven and earth, but also the intentionality for heaven and earth to transform and nourish the myriad things. Heaven's heart-mind connects with the human heart-mind, so we should take the initiative to align with heaven's heart-mind, and follow the strong and active state of heaven's heart-mind that is ceaselessly productive, so as to avoid intentions arising in the heart-mind. Hexagram Fu (Returning) closes up to rest and maintain *yangqi*. The ancients believed that *yangqi* is newly produced and difficult to nourish even if it moves slightly, so it is necessary to rest and let the *yangqi* machine initiate, so as to keep one's intentionality in harmony with the *yang* intentionality of the heavenly *dao* and to be harmonious and smooth.

Human beings have an understanding of the cycles of the sun and the moon in time and space, and must distinguish these from beginning to end, but these are always indistinguishable in original substance. Human intentionality is updated every moment in accordance with the vitality of heaven, so the ultimate understanding is new day by day, at every moment. What is new is actually the rebirth of *yang* energy, and where there is life, there is intention and real existence; without life, intention does not exist. However, the *Book of Changes* does not share the Buddhist view of the cosmos of instantaneous birth and death, and believes that all rise and fall, growth and decline, etc. are continuous in vitality. As for how to revive these, one must wait for the opportunity, for the right time and situation, and follow the propensity in action.

初九：不远复，无祇悔，元吉。

《象》曰："不远"之"复"，以修身也。

【明译】

初九：没有偏离正道太远，犯错之后，马上改正回复，不至于日后悔恨，非常吉祥。

《象传》说：没有偏离正道太远，犯错之后，马上改正回复，说明初九善于实化意念，正己修身。

Nine (*yang*/strong line) in the first place: Not deviating too far from the right *dao*. After making a mistake, it can be corrected immediately and there will be no regret. This is very auspicious.

The *Image Commentary* (*Xiang Zhuan*) says: One has not deviated too far from the right *dao*. After making a mistake, one immediately corrects it and recovers, which shows that the Nine (*yang*/strong line) in the first place is good at concretizing one's intentions, rectifying and cultivating oneself.

【明意】

身的实存，其实是念念相续的基础。离开念念之生机，便是行尸走肉。身为意之境的重要承载体，身意通常不如意境敏感，但身意一旦陷入伤痛，就可能对意境构成挤压，因心意即集中在病痛之中，意境为病痛所占据和持续而难以关注其他。

可见，如果偏离正道太远则无法回复，学习要常常复习，做事要及时反省。阳意初生象征人地生疏的时候，不可急功近利，因为必有阻碍，需要小心应对，摸清形势，缓慢推进。人需要时常反身修行，克服邪念恶念，随时回到正道上来，时时刻刻，心灵一动，即有度和分寸的问题。

[Illuminating Intentionality]

The real existence of the body is actually the basis for the continuity of thought. Without the vitality of thought, one is just a walking corpse. The body is an important carrier of the intentional context, and the body and intentionality are usually not as sensitive as the intentional context. However, once the body and intentionality fall into pain, they may put pressure on the intentional context, because intentionality is concentrated on the illness, and the intentional context is occupied and sustained by the illness, so it is hard to focus on anything else.

It can be seen that if one deviates too far from the right *dao*, one will not be able to recover. One must review one's studies frequently and reflect on one's actions in a timely manner. The initial birth of *yang* intentionality means that when people and place are unfamiliar, one should not rush for quick success, because there will be obstacles, and one needs to deal with them carefully, understand the situation, and advance slowly. People need to practice self-reflection from time to time, overcome evil and bad intentions, and return to the right *dao* at all times. At every moment when intentionality moves, there is a question of moderation and propriety.

六二：休复，吉。

《象》曰："休复"之"吉"，以下仁也。

【明译】

六二：休于阻止，回复顺应阳意上长的正道，吉祥。

《象传》说：休于阻止的过错，回复顺应初九阳意上升之正道，表现出美善吉祥的心意，是因为六二能够向下亲近顺从初九这个仁人。

Six (*yin*/soft line) in the second place: To end the blockage and return to the right *dao* that conforms to *yang* intentionality's will, which is auspicious.

The *Image Commentary* (*Xiang Zhuan*) says: Stop making the mistake of blocking, return to the right *dao* of rising *yang* intentionality of the Nine (*yang*/strong line) in the first place, and show good and auspicious intentions. This is because the Six (*yin*/soft line) in the second place can get close to and obey the benevolent person of the Nine (*yang*/strong line) in the first place.

【明意】

为什么休止是美好的？六二阴爻当位居中，跟其他阴爻有所区别，会尽可能合理美好地配合阳气初生的形势，先去照顾它，亲近它，这说明小人之群也会有所分化，六二不但不压制初九，反而乐于见到阳气上升，来帮助初九的成长。小人之所以顺阳意生长之境，是因为明白本来阴意就必须借助阳意才有生机，阴意顺承阳意之生才能生。

[Illuminating Intentionality]

Why is rest excellent? The Six (*yin*/soft line) in the second place should be in the middle, and it is different from other *yin*/soft lines. It tries its best to coordinate with the situation of the nascent *yangqi* as reasonably and beautifully as possible. It first takes care of it and gets close to it. This shows that a group of petty people is also differentiated. Not only does the Six (*yin*/soft line) in the second place not suppress the Nine (*yang*/strong line) in the first place, it is even happy to see the *yangqi* rise, and helps the growth of the Nine (*yang*/strong line) in the first place. The reason why the petty person here follows in accordance with the growth of *yang* intentionality is because one understands that *yin* intentionality must rely on *yang* to have vitality, and *yin* will be able to grow in accordance with *yang*.

六三：频复，厉，无咎。

《象》曰："频复"之"厉"，义无咎也。

【明译】

六三：频繁而不情愿地改正错误，回归正道，虽有危险，但没有祸患。

《象传》说：频繁而不情愿地改正错误，回归正道，看起来似乎常有危险，但道义上说不应该有什么灾害。

Six (*yin*/soft line) in the third place: Frequently and reluctantly correcting mistakes and returning to the right *dao*. Although there is danger, there is no disaster.

The *Image Commentary* (*Xiang Zhuan*) says: Frequently and unwillingly correcting mistakes and returning to the right *dao* may seem dangerous, but morally speaking, there should be no disaster.

【明意】

六三屡屡犯错，有危厉，又频频回复，是看到六二已经顺应了阳气大涨的形势，虽然心里纠结，但最后还是顺应形势，没有大的问题。具备了复兴的时机，但需要逐渐改变周围的力量，让力量都来顺应才可能顺利复兴。

六三在频繁而不情愿的回复当中，不断重塑其新生的意境。

[Illuminating Intentionality]

The Six (*yin*/soft line) in the third place repeatedly makes mistakes, is in danger, and responds frequently. This is because one sees that the Six (*yin*/soft line) in the second place adapts to the situation of rising *yangqi*. Although one is conflicted in one's heart, one finally complies with the situation and there is no big problem. There is an opportunity for revival, but it is necessary to gradually change the surrounding forces and let all forces adapt to it before a smooth revival can be achieved.

The Six (*yin*/soft line) in the third place continues to reshape its new intentional context through frequent and reluctant responses.

六四，中行独复。

《象》曰："中行独复"，以从道也。

【明译】

六四：持守中道而行正，独自返回正道。

《象传》说：守中而行正，独自返回正道，是因为六四与初九正应，与其他阴爻不同，能够独自顺从阳气上长的正道。

Nine (*yang*/strong line) in the fourth place: Sticking to the middle *dao* and doing the right thing, one returns to the right *dao* alone.

The *Image Commentary* (*Xiang Zhuan*) says: Keeping to the middle and doing the right thing, one returns to the right *dao* alone, because the Six (*yin*/soft line) in the fourth place and the Nine (*yang*/strong line) in the first place are corresponding to each other. Different from other *yin* lines, it can independently obey the right *dao* of growing *yangqi*.

【明意】

相对于群阴来说，六四有自己独特的意识境遇，因为独与阳应，所以有足够的信心去走自己认定的正道。六四与初九阳意相应，内心欣喜，自然特立独行而不与周围一群小人同道，选择自我决定，自己定义自己的意识境遇，不随着周围抑制阴意的情境而改变。虽然不一定得到阳意的支持，但自己觉得对就顺着阳气上长的正道坚持下去。

[Illuminating Intentionality]

Compared with the group of *yin*, the Six (*yin*/soft line) in the fourth place has its own unique consciousness situation. Because one is alone and corresponds to *yang*, one has enough confidence to follow the right *dao* that one believes. The Six (*yin*/soft line) in the fourth place corresponds to the *yang* intentionality of the Nine (*yang*/strong line) in the first place, and one's heart-mind is happy. Naturally, one is independent and does not agree with the group of petty people around one. One chooses to make one's own decisions and define one's own conscious situation by oneself, and does not change with the surrounding situations that suppress *yin* intentionality. Although one may not necessarily get the support of *yangqi*, if one feels that it is right, one should stick to the right *dao* of growing *yangqi*.

六五：敦复，无悔。

《象》曰："敦复，无悔"，中以自考也。

【明译】

六五：敦厚忠实地返回正道，没有悔恨。

《象传》说：敦厚忠实地返回正道，没有悔恨，是因为六五居中不偏，能够顺应大势，内心自我反省。

Six (*yin*/soft line) in the fifth place: Returning to the right *dao* honestly and faithfully, with no regrets.

The *Image Commentary* (*Xiang Zhuan*) says: Being honest and faithful in returning to the right *dao* is without regrets because the Six (*yin*/soft line) in the fifth place is centered and impartial, able to adapt to the general trend, and reflects in one's heart-mind.

【明意】

全卦顺应阳意的复兴为大势，即使六五阴意在最有利的位置也不会去阻挡阳意之力复兴的形势，而能够以乐观其成的态度包涵宽容阳意力量生长，形成阳意上升的意识境遇并乐观其成。六五有自知之明，知道自己力量有限，加上认识不足，采取乐观其成的观望态度。阴意对于阳意的上升也有一种大势的判断，知道没有办法阻止阳意之境的成形，就顺观其成。

[Illuminating Intentionality]

The whole hexagram conforms to the general propensity for the revival of *yang* intentionality. Even if the Six (*yin*/soft line) being in the fifth place means *yin* intentionality is in the most favorable position, it will not block the revival of *yang* intentionality. Instead, it can tolerate the growth of *yang* intentionality with an optimistic attitude, forming a conscious context for the growth of *yang* intentionality, and being optimistic about its success. The Six (*yin*/soft line) in the fifth place is self-aware and knows that one's own strength is limited. Coupled with one's lack of understanding, one adopts a wait-and-see attitude that is optimistic about success. Yin/negative intentionality also makes a judgment on the general trend of the rise of *yang*/positive intentions. Knowing that there is no way to prevent the formation of a realm of *yang*/positive intentionality, it just passively observes its development.

上六：迷复，凶，有灾眚。用行师，终有大败，以其国君凶。至于十年，不克征。

《象》曰："迷复"之"凶"，反君道也。

【明译】

上六：执迷于复兴而不知回复正道，迟早会有凶险，有天灾人祸。形势不允许的情况下，还出兵打仗以期改变，最后会大败而归，这对国君来讲是非常凶险的，以至于十年之内，出兵征伐都难以取胜。

《象传》说：执迷于复兴而不知回复正道，迟早会有凶险，是因为上六不能理解形势的发展，违背了为君之道。

Six (*yin*/soft line) in the top place: Obsessed with revival without knowing the right *dao*, sooner or later there will be danger, both natural and man-made disasters. When the situational propensity does not allow it, if you send troops to fight in the hope of change, you will eventually come back defeated. This is very dangerous for a monarch, so much that it will be difficult to come back victorious even if he sends troops to fight for ten years.

The *Image Commentary* (*Xiang Zhuan*) says: Being obsessed with revival but not knowing the right *dao* will lead to danger sooner or later. This is because the Six (*yin*/soft line) in the top place cannot understand the development of the situation and violates the *dao* of the ruler.

【明意】

复的前提是明，意境不明，则难复。此爻形势不佳，说明不可执迷于过去的心境，而不去积极应世。在阳意很弱的情况下，力不从心，却执迷不悟，必有大伤害。故应当破除妄念，让心意接续阳意生长的天机而发。

要恢复元气，知道休息是自然修复，需要慢慢调整意境，不可强打精神，冒然行动。引导众人改变心态的意境，要适可而止，不可妄动强动，因为形势比人强。他人的心念构成的意境只能顺应，难以随意改变。君道应该顺天应人，不可过度折磨百姓，而要给百姓修复的时间。这样君就要用没有妄念的诚意来面对百姓，于是进入无妄卦。

[Illuminating Intentionality]

The prerequisite for recovery is clarity. If the intentional context is unclear, it will be difficult to recover. The situation in this line is not good, indicating that one should not be obsessed with the past state of intentionality and fail to actively respond to the world. When *yang* intentionality is very weak, if one is unable to do what one wants, but persists in it nonetheless, one will definitely suffer great harm. Therefore, one should get rid of delusional intentions and allow intentionality to continue to develop according to the heavenly vitality of *yang*/positive intentions.

To restore vitality, know that rest is a natural repair, and that one needs to slowly adjust one's mood, and not force oneself to act rashly. The intentional context that guides the masses to change their mentality should be implemented in moderation, and not be rash or forceful, because a situation is stronger than a person. The intentional context formed by other people's intentions can only be adapted to and cannot be changed at will. The *dao* of the ruler should obey nature and respond to people, not afflicting the people excessively, but giving them time to recover. In this way, the ruler may face the people with sincerity and without delusion, and then enter Hexagram Wuwang (Non-Delusion).

天雷无妄（卦二十五）　（震下乾上）

Wuwang (Non-Delusion), Heaven and Thunder (Hexagram 25)　(Zhen below, Qian above)

☰
☳

　　无妄是因为在乎意识的感应，以无妄心妄念求安全的感应状态。心正无邪、诚意通天的意识状态如何可能？无妄的意识之中，没有邪念妄念，意识不乱，自然口无妄言，不胡乱行动，好像天打雷之时在外，不可有妄念妄行，方能避免无妄之灾。

　　无妄的前提是意识的自控力可以降服纷乱的世界，自己制念即制妄界。妄念俱消，则天灾人祸消去，这是放大心意而似乎受到上天保佑之感，其实是了解几微的意识对于形势的影响，知道操控自己的心念，使之没有妄念就是操控自己的命运。人要意识到命起于几微状态，而且不仅是个人心念的几微，更是个人与家人和他人心念互动的几微之境。如果能够念念无妄，念念接续天机，让自己的意识无妄，可以通过唯识的状态而扩大意量。

　　Non-delusion refers to caring about the inductive response of consciousness, seeking a safe inductive response state with non-delusory intentionality. How is it possible to have a state of consciousness with a pure faultless heart-mind and sincerity that connects with heaven? In the consciousness of non-delusion, there are no evil intentions and delusions, consciousness is not chaotic, spontaneous words are not false, and actions are not random, just like how, when there is thunder in the world, there must be no delusory thoughts or deeds, so as to avoid the disaster of non-delusion.

　　The condition for non-delusion is that the self-control of consciousness can overcome a chaotic world, that controlling one's own intentions can control the world of delusion. When all delusions are eliminated, natural and man-made disasters will both disappear. This is the feeling of magnifying intentionality and seeming to be blessed by heaven. In fact, it is understanding the impact of a few degrees of consciousness on a situation, and knowing how to control one's intentionality so that there are no delusions, which is to control one's own destiny. People must realize that life starts from infinitesimally subtle states, not only infinitesimally subtle states of personal intentions, but also infinitesimally subtle states of interaction between an individual, one's family and other people's intentions. If one can think without any illusions, continue the heavenly vitality with all one's intentions, and make one's consciousness be without delusions, one can expand one's intentionality through a consciousness-only state.

无妄，元亨，利贞。其匪正有眚，不利有攸往。

《彖》曰：无妄，刚自外来而为主于内，动而健，刚中而应。大亨以正，天之命也。"其匪正有眚，不利有攸往。""无妄"之"往"，何之矣？天命不佑，行矣哉！

《象》曰：天下雷行，物与无妄。先王以茂对时育万物。

【明译】

无妄卦象征心意安宁不乱，大为亨通，利于持守正道，如果背离正道必有灾眚，不利于前往而有所作为。

《彖传》说：无妄卦象征没有虚妄的心意和言行。无妄卦由遯卦变来，是遯卦上九刚爻从外卦来到内卦下位，变出无妄卦。卦变显示阳刚者从外部进入内部作了主宰。下卦震为动，上卦乾为健，组合起来是威势震动又能刚健运行。尊位上的刚爻九五在上卦中位，下有六二阴阳正应，显示出行为中正并得到响应。主爻九五在上卦乾（天）里，位正，显示出大亨通而且中正，行施的是天的命令。如果背离正道必有灾眚，不利于前往有所作为，是因为在天下都不敢有虚意妄行之时还要执意前往，怎么可能会有路可走呢？上天之意在惩治邪恶，不保佑外出活动，怎么还敢妄言妄行呢？

《象传》说：上卦乾为天，下卦震为雷，合在一起是震雷在天下施威，万物都怀着敬畏之心，不敢胡来妄为，安分守己。先王从雷行天下中受到启示，要勤勉努力地配合天时来养育万物。

Hexagram Wuwang (Non-Delusion) symbolizes peace and stability of intentionality with great prosperity, which is conducive to adhering to the right *dao*. If one deviates from the right *dao*, there will be disaster, which is not conducive to making achievements.

The *Judgment Commentary* (*Tuan Zhuan*) says: Hexagram Wuwang (Non-Delusion) symbolizes the absence of unfounded intentions, words and deeds. Hexagram Wuwang (Non-Delusion) is changed from Hexagram Dun (Retreat). The Nine (*yang*/strong line) in the top place in Hexagram Dun (Retreat) moves from the outer hexagram to the lower position of the inner hexagram, and thus changes into Hexagram Wuwang (Non-Delusion). This hexagram-change shows a positive person entering the interior from the outside and taking control. The lower Trigram Zhen represents movement, and the upper Trigram Qian represents health. The combination is powerful, vibrating, and able to move vigorously. The *yin* and *yang* of the Nine (*yang*/strong line) in the prosperous fifth place in the middle position of the upper Trigram and the Six (*yin*/soft line) in the second place below correspond, which shows that their behavior is upright and gets a response. The main Nine (*yang*/strong line) in the fifth place is in the upper Trigram Qian (heaven), and its position is upright, showing that it is powerful and upright, and the orders of heaven are carried out. If one deviates from the right *dao*, there will be disaster, and it will not be conducive to advancing and making a difference. This is because one intentionally insists on advancing when everyone in the world dares not to act falsely. How could there be a way out? Heaven's intention is to punish evil, not to protect people when they go out actively, so how could one still dare to speak and act recklessly?

The *Image Commentary* (*Xiang Zhuan*) says: The upper Trigram is sky, the lower Trigram is thunder, and together they represent thunder exerting its power in the world. All things are in awe, dare not act recklessly, and stay safe. The former kings were inspired by thunder in the world, and knew they should work diligently and conscientiously to coordinate with heaven's cycles and nourish the myriad things.

【明意】

从不可妄行引申出自正心念，但自己端正或者自己证明心念之正，又如何做到？人控制念头的难度很大，无论是从"思无邪"开始的修意传统，还是西方的原罪说，都承认人的意识容易偏斜。修意的核心就是要让意识设法修回正道，这是道德与宗教的着力之处。如何做到无丝毫妄念之心，即压根儿就不起邪念？这需要做自觉、反思的功夫，尽量自己控制；反之，不自觉就无法控制。要知道惜福，少动歪念头，因为小的意识不注意可能要成为大祸害。既然存在皆因意念而生，所以人事的祸害大都因为执念就不难理解。

心诚通天才能无私，知道意识发动危险丛生，所以不可妄动。意识不仅以身体的物理反应为基础，虽可把意识理解为生理运动的副现象，但从人可以修意主动控制意识的角度，就不能把意识理解为完全被动状态，所以仅归结为生理反应不够，人的意识还有通于天地之维度。

[Illuminating Intentionality]

From not acting recklessly, correcting one's intentions was derived, but how can one prove that one is correct or that one's intentionality is right? It is very difficult for people to control their intentions. Whether it is the tradition of intentionality cultivation that started from "think nothing evil" (Confucius) or the Western theory of original sin, they all admit that human consciousness is prone to deflection. The core of intentionality cultivation is to let consciousness try to return to the right *dao*, and this is the focus of morality and religion. How can we avoid having any delusional intentions, that is, not having any evil intentions at all? This requires conscious and reflective effort to try to control it oneself; if, on the contrary, one is not conscious, one will not be able to control it. One should know how to cherish one's blessings and avoid having wrong intentions, because if one is not careful, one's little intention may become a big disaster. Since all existence is caused by intentionality, it is not difficult to understand that most of the disasters in human affairs are caused by obsessions.

Only when one is sincere can one be selfless. Knowing that there are dangers in initiating consciousness, one should not act rashly. Consciousness is not only based on the physical reactions of the body. Although consciousness can be understood as an epiphenomenon of physiological movement, from the perspective that people can cultivate their intentions and actively control consciousness, consciousness cannot be understood as a completely passive state, and so only attributing it to physiological reactions is insufficient, as human consciousness also has a dimension that connects it to heaven and earth.

初九：无妄，往吉。

《象》曰："无妄"之"往"，得志也。

【明译】

初九：没有虚意妄行，这样前往会有吉祥。

《象传》说：没有虚意妄行前往会吉利，是因为心志得以实现。

Nine (*yang*/strong line) in the first place: If there is no unfounded intention or action, it will be auspicious to go forward.

The *Image Commentary* (*Xiang Zhuan*) says: If there is no unfounded intention or action, advancing will be auspicious, because one's intention is concretized.

【明意】

纯而又纯的感应状态如何可能？心中没有妄念去行动就会得到好的结果。心通于物，意识每时每刻都与物缘关联。无妄即是至诚之心自然流布，而意不为任何具体物缘所牵绕，不是意识没有物缘，没有物缘就不能有意识的显明，而是意识升起的时候，不执于任何物缘，随缘起缘灭，因为没有任何执着所以无妄而行，就会吉祥有利。

意随心转，万事如意，但前提是心正意诚。意识必须纯而又纯，乾阳即意识之纯阳，坤阴即意识之随顺，意识之报由乾坤之意合而成型。

[Illuminating Intentionality]

How is a purer than pure state of inductive resonance possible? If one acts without delusions in one's mind, one will get good results. Intentionality is connected to things, and consciousness is related to things at all times. Non-delusion means that the most sincere heart-mind flows naturally, and that intentionality is not tied to any specific object. It is not that consciousness has no object, since without an object it cannot consciously manifest, but that when consciousness arises, it is not attached to anything, arising and perishing according to dependent co-arising. Since there is no attachment, if one acts without any delusions, one will be auspicious and beneficial.

Intentions shift following the heart-mind and everything goes according to intention, but the prerequisite is that one's heart-mind is upright and sincere. Consciousness must be purer than pure, Qian-*yang* is the pure *yang* of consciousness, Kun-*yin* is the obedient following of consciousness, and the response of consciousness is formed by the union of the Qian and Kun intentionality.

六二：不耕获，不菑（zī）畲（yú），则利有攸往。

《象》曰："不耕获"，未富也。

【明译】

六二：安心耕种，不指望收获多少；刚开荒出来的土地，不指望能够有熟田的收成，（没有这样的虚意妄念），那么前往就会有利。

《象传》说：六二安心耕种，不指望收获多少，因为六二没有升起求富之心这样的虚意妄念。

Six (*yin*/soft line) in the second place: Farm with a peaceful heart-mind and have no expectations for the harvest; if one does not expect to get a mature harvest from land that has just been opened up, (since one has no such vain intention), then it will be beneficial to go forward.

The *Image Commentary* (*Xiang Zhuan*) says: The Six (*yin*/soft line) in the second place cultivates with peaceful heart-mind and does not expect much from the harvest, because the Six (*yin*/soft line) in the second place has no such vain intention as seeking wealth.

【明意】

自觉放下虚意妄念的心意之境。人们对于收成，对于财富的积蓄，都容易有虚意执着的妄念，所以要能够永保无妄之初心，放下执着之念，顺其自然，自然而然。

如果没有信心，则意识难安。这爻是安心而没有虚妄的期盼。相信自己处在可以自己带来信心，而不要依赖他者给予信心的位置。相信只要自己安心就会有力量，相信自己安心就能够安世界。这是典型的依自不依他的宗教情怀。《周易》相信天人合一，万物一体，所以在最绝望最无助的境遇当中，强调的是自信而不是期待他者给予自己力量。

[Illuminating Intentionality]

The state of intentionality where one consciously lets go of unfounded intentions. People tend to have unfounded and persistent intentions about harvests and accumulation of wealth. Therefore, one must always maintain one's original intention of not having any illusions, let go of our persistent intentions, and let nature take its course.

If there is no confidence, then consciousness will not be at ease. This line is about having a peaceful heart-mind and no false expectations. Trust that you are in a position where you can bring your own confidence rather than relying on others to give it to you. Believe that as long as you feel at ease, you will have strength, and believe that as long as you feel at ease, you will be able to put the world at ease. This is a typical religious feeling of relying on oneself and not others. The *Book of Changes* believes that heaven and humanity are one continuity, and the myriad things are one body, so in the most desperate and helpless situation, the emphasis is on self-confidence rather than expecting others to give oneself strength.

六三：无妄之灾。或系之牛，行人之得，邑人之灾。

《象》曰：行人得牛，邑人灾也。

【明译】

六三：没有妄念妄行却无缘无故遭受灾难，好比有人拴了一头牛，被过路人牵走了，（结果主人怪罪村里人，而让）村里人遭受了不白之冤。

《象传》说：途经此地的行人顺手把牛牵走了，害得村里人被怀疑而蒙受不白之冤。

Six (*yin*/soft line) in the third place: Having no delusional intentions but suffering disaster for no reason is like someone tethering a cow and it being led away by a passerby. (As a result, the owner blames the villagers, and) the villagers suffer an injustice.

The *Image Commentary* (*Xiang Zhuan*) says: Pedestrians passing by take the cow away, causing villagers to be suspected and suffer injustice.

【明意】

当有人顺手牵牛，就有人蒙受不白之冤，对于受冤的人就是飞来横祸，无妄之灾。对于相识的人，一个人的过错让另一个人蒙受不白之冤，这自然是不对的，但比起这种情况更严重的是，认识的人之间栽赃陷害，或者哪怕是无心的私欲使然而使朋友蒙受不白之冤，这在道德上是不合适的。不应该让无辜的人，尤其是无辜的熟人承受不明不白的冤屈。人道好还，通常这种冤屈会以另一种形式报应出来。回到自己，应该知道要时刻承担起意识发动的责任感，对于意识的感应以及长远的报应深怀谨慎戒惧之心。

[Illuminating Intentionality]

When someone takes the opportunity to lead away a cow, someone is unfairly wronged, and disaster comes to the wronged person. For people who are acquaintances, it is naturally wrong for one person's fault to cause another person to suffer injustice, but what is more serious than this situation is when people who know each other are scapegoated, framed, or even when selfish desires unintentionally cause injustice for a friend; these are morally inappropriate. Innocent people, especially innocent acquaintances, should not be allowed to suffer unexplained injustices. Human nature is fit for retribution, and usually this kind of injustice will be repaid in another form. When one returns to oneself, one should know that one must always assume the responsibility for initiating consciousness, and be cautious and wary of the inductive resonance of consciousness and long-term retribution.

九四：可贞。无咎。

《象》曰："可贞，无咎"，固有之也。

【明译】

九四：能够持守正道，没有妄念妄行，就不会有灾祸。

《象传》说：能够保持正固，没有妄念妄行，就不会有灾祸，这说明九四本身就能够一直持守正道。

Nine (*yang*/strong line) in the fourth place: If one can uphold the right *dao* and have no delusions or misdeeds, there will be no disaster.

The *Image Commentary* (*Xiang Zhuan*) says: If one can maintain integrity and have no delusions or misdeeds, there will be no disasters. This shows that the Nine (*yang*/strong line) in the fourth place can always maintain the right *dao* for itself.

【明意】

在意识发动之前，即有某种心通于物的先天结构，心与物在先天之前完全相通为一，后天因为意识的介入而分心物，也迷失了心物相通的先天结构。其实，先天结构之领悟与保持，是后天意识应物的前提，但因其不自我彰明，而又要借助意识的反身性去确定其先行性，结果总是难乎其难。心、物、意三者未分的先天结构中，因为没有意的参与，可以说都混沌一体，一旦意识发动，即有心物之分，也就区分出意识之量，即心对物认知的范围和程度。

天赋善性，为三教之核心。但这善不是善恶对待后的善，而是对待之前的天道自然之善。天道自然之善如何可能？要去对待和用道德判断。如喜欲皆念之陷阱，要在起心动念之前，先天意识发动的功夫里，意识到心思无时无刻不通于物的本然状态。这样的状态帮助好人脱离厄运，帮助好人靠挺立和高扬本来就有的无妄之本心挺过厄运。

[Illuminating Intentionality]

Before the initiation of consciousness, there is a certain transcendental (pre-celestial) structure in which intentionality and things/events are connected. Intentionality and things/events are completely connected as one before the transcendental, but later, due to the intervention of consciousness, the heart-mind and objects are separated, and the transcendental structure of intentionality and things/events is lost. In fact, the understanding and maintenance of the transcendental structure is the prerequisite for empirical consciousness to respond to things. However, since it is not self-evident, and it is necessary to rely on the reflexivity of consciousness to determine its antecedence, it would always turn out to be extremely difficult. In the transcendental structure of the undivided heart-mind, things, and intentionality, because there is no participation of intention, it can be said that they are all chaotic and unified. Once consciousness is initiated, the heart-mind and things/events are separated, and the amount of consciousness is also distinguished, that is, the scope and degree of the heart-mind's cognition of things.

Innate goodness is the core of the three teachings (Confucianism, Daoism, and Buddhism). But this goodness is not the goodness that comes after dealing with good or evil, but the natural goodness that comes from the heavenly *dao* before dealing with it. How is the goodness of nature and the *dao* of heaven made possible? One must handle affairs and make moral judgments. Just like the trap of seeing all pleasures and desires as thoughts, one must realize that one's intentionality is always connected to the original state of things when one's transcendental consciousness is initiated before one has any intentions. This state helps good people escape bad fortune, and helps good people survive bad fortune by standing upright and exalting their inherent good intentions.

九五：无妄之疾，勿药有喜。
《象》曰："无妄"之"药"，不可试也。
【明译】
九五：没有妄念妄行却得了无缘无故的疾病，不必用药就会有自愈的喜庆。
《象传》说：只要没有妄念妄行，无缘无故生了病，病确诊不了，也难以开出对症的药，不对症的药就不可以轻易试服。

Nine (*yang*/strong line) in the fifth place: One has no delusional intentions and gets a sudden disease, but is happily cured without taking medicine.

The *Image Commentary* (*Xiang Zhuan*) says: As long as there are no delusional intentions or actions, if one gets sick for no reason, and the disease cannot be diagnosed, it is difficult to prescribe the right medicine. One should not try the wrong medicine easily.

【明意】
人们往往会觉得，如果自己心无妄念，就应该少受不白之冤，少受无妄之疾。可是人生不如意十有八九，往往事与愿违。如果人对生活当中发生的事情没有过高的期望，那么归根到底应该可以无妄，这样就会坦然接受不必用药就能够自愈的喜庆，甚至满怀感恩之情。人对自己意识把握好，内心充实，则妄念自然减少，意识与行为的一致性就会提升。有疾病的时候，要让意识自然恢复，缓慢调整到与外境相合的状态。无妄状态应该是不求利害、不求生死的无欲无求状态。那种超脱生死的至诚之道，才是无妄应该达到的状态。

[Illuminating Intentionality]
People often feel that if they have no delusional intentions, they should suffer less injustice and disease. But nine times out of ten is that life is not what we want it to be, and things often go against

our wishes. If people do not have too high expectations for what happens in life, then in the final analysis they should be able to be calm, and will be able to accept the joy of being able to heal on their own without medication, and even feel grateful. If one has a good grasp of one's own consciousness and is enriched in one's heart-mind, one's delusions will naturally be reduced, and the consistency between consciousness and behavior will be improved. When there is an illness, consciousness should be allowed to recover naturally and slowly adjust to a state consistent with the external environment. The state of non-delusion should be a state of no desires or pursuits without seeking benefit or harm, life or death. That kind of sincerity that transcends life and death is the ideal state that Hexagram Wuwang (Non-Delusion) should achieve.

上九：无妄，行有眚，无攸利。

《象》曰："无妄"之"行"，穷之灾也。

【明译】

上九：虽然没有妄念妄行，但处时穷之境，行动就会有灾眚，做什么都没有好处。

《象传》说：虽然没有妄念妄行，但处时穷之境还要去行动，那时因为上九已经走到了穷尽的地位，再轻举妄动就会有走向穷途末路的灾难。

Nine (*yang*/strong line) in the top place: Although there are no delusional intentions or misdeeds, if one is in a situation of poverty, one's actions will be disastrous and there will be no benefit in anything one does.

The *Image Commentary* (*Xiang Zhuan*) says: Although there are no delusional intentions or actions, one still has to take action when one is in a desperate situation. At that time, because the Nine (*yang*/strong line) in the top place has reached the end of the road, if one acts rashly, one will end up in disaster.

【明意】

行至上爻，即使心念一直无妄，却也还是动辄得咎。因为形势是山穷水尽，即使内心再正义正直，也可能面临困难，有冤无处申，此时还是要自得其乐，不可为时穷之位所限，不可作茧自缚。所以山穷水尽后的曙光在自己当下的意识之境中。

山穷水尽之时，不可完全放弃主观努力，更不可放弃自己，否则连生命存在的意义都说不上，没有生机，那么与意念之生相关的一切都不再有意义。

[Illuminating Intentionality]

When one's advance reaches the highest line, even if one's intentions are always innocent, one still gets into trouble frequently. Because the situation is at the end of the road, no matter how righteous and upright one is in one's heart, one may still face difficulties and have nowhere to redress one's injustice. At this time, one still has to enjoy oneself and should not be limited by time and poverty, and one must not wrap oneself in a cocoon. Therefore, the light at the end of the road lies in the current state of consciousness.

When one is at the end of one's rope, one cannot completely give up one's subjective efforts, let alone give up too much on oneself. Otherwise, one will not even be able to feel the meaning of life and existence. If there is no vitality, then everything related to the production of intentions will no longer make any sense.

山天大畜（卦二十六）　（乾下艮上）

Daxu (Accumulation), Mountain and Heaven (Hexagram 26)　(Qian below, Gen above)

人要学会培养和维系一个无妄的持续意识状态，不断地修炼自己的德行，坚持积累自己的意识能量（意能）。所以通过无妄训练意念的控制和持续，有助于达到大畜的意量。人认识自己的意量很难，但人认识自己的意量、知心之所止有重大的意义。

意量的力度和广度产生于无声处，当下发动的意念可以从前人的经验中汲取教训和力量，因为情境在不同的时空当中有相似之处，而意量的建构也是如此，故可以从先人的意量当中汲取生物气象。心念一动，就可能具有古往今来的伟大气势，人心一动，就可能重温历代的重大事件。人的意念可能随着前人应对事件的道理而改变，从创造历史的伟人那里吸收巨大的气魄，扩大意量。

People must learn to cultivate and maintain a continuous state of consciousness without delusion, constantly cultivate their own virtue, and persist in accumulating their own conscious energy (intentional energy). Therefore, through the control and persistence of intentions through non-delusion training, this can help to achieve the intention of great accumulation. It is difficult for people to know their own intentional capacity, but it is of great significance for people to know where their own intentional capacity and conscious intentions stop.

The strength and breadth of intentional capacity are generated in silence. An intention initiated at a moment can draw lessons and strength from the experience of previous people. Because situations are similar in different times and spaces, the same is true for the construction of intention, so a biological atmosphere can be absorbed from the intentional capacity of forerunners. When intentionality moves, it may have a great momentum of the past and present. When the human heart moves, it may be possible to relive the major events of past dynasties. People's intentions may change according to the patterns of how their predecessors responded to events, absorbing great courage and expanding their intentional capacity from the great people who made history.

大畜，利贞。不家食，吉。利涉大川。

《彖》曰：大畜，刚健笃实，辉光日新。其德刚上而尚贤，能止健，大正也。"不家食，吉"，养贤也。"利涉大川"，应乎天也。

《象》曰：天在山中，大畜。君子以多识（zhì）前言往行，以畜其德。

【明译】

大畜卦象征大为蓄聚，有利于持守正道。不使贤才在家吃闲饭，就可以获得吉祥，有利于克服像涉越大河一样的险阻。

《彖传》说：大畜卦，下卦乾为天刚健，上卦艮为山厚实，所以阳刚强健，敦厚充实，荣光相映，日新不已。卦变中刚爻上到最上位，说明大畜卦有崇尚贤能的德行。上卦艮为止，下卦乾为刚健，能把刚健者规止住，说明有宏大正直的力量，不使贤才在家吃闲饭，就可以获得吉祥，因为国家需要蓄养贤才。有利于克服像涉越大河一样的险阻，这是因为行动能够顺应天道。

《象传》说：上（外）卦是艮为山；下（内）卦是乾为天，卦象是山在外，好像山把天包含在其中。可见山的蓄藏能量很大，所以卦名叫大畜。君子学习大山包天的蓄藏能力，多多学习识记古圣先贤的佳言善行，培养积聚自己的仁德。

Hexagram Daxu (Accumulation) symbolizes great accumulation, which is conducive to maintaining the upright *dao*. If talented people are not allowed to sit around at home, they can gain good fortune and be helpful in overcoming obstacles like crossing a large river.

The *Judgment Commentary* (*Tuan Zhuan*) says: In Hexagram Daxu (Accumulation), the lower Trigram Qian represents the strength of the sky, and the upper Trigram Gen represents the thickness of a mountain. Therefore, *yang* is strong, honest and substantial, its glories complement each other, and it is constantly renewed with each passing day. In hexagram-changes, the *yang*/strong line reaches the highest position, indicating that Hexagram Daxu (Accumulation) has the virtue of advocating the worthy and capable. The upper Trigram Gen means stopping, and the lower Trigram Qian means strong, so it can regulate the strong, indicating that it has great and upright power. If one does not let talented people live at home, one will gain good fortune, because the country needs to cultivate talented people. This is helpful to overcome obstacles as dangerous as crossing a large river, because actions can accord with the heavenly *dao*.

The *Image Commentary* (*Xiang Zhuan*) says: The upper (outer) hexagram is Gen which means mountain; the lower (inner) hexagram is Qian which means sky. The hexagram image is thus a mountain on the outside, as if the mountain contains the sky. It can be seen that the stored energy of the mountain is very large, so the hexagram is called Hexagram Daxu (Accumulation). The exemplary person should learn from the storage capacity of mountains and the sky, learn to memorize the good words and deeds of ancient sages, and cultivate and accumulate one's own benevolence.

【明意】

控制心念的节奏最难。事业的大小取决于意量的大小，其实主要的是控心之力，即止意之量。意念的格局决定意量的尺度。品德是意念的一种习惯，是意念发动的一种持续模式。意念的发动如果不具有主动的内力，而依附于外力，则显得无力。意念止力太弱则不能够承担事情。一个人能够修炼的是，在人生经历当中增强自己内心的力量，协同他意而共筑收蓄参天的大山气势。

[Illuminating Intentionality]

Controlling the rhythm of intentionality is the hardest. The size of one's career depends on the capacity of one's intentionality. In fact, the most important thing is the ability to control one's intention, that is, the ability to stop one's intentions. The pattern of intentions determines the scale of intentional capacity. Virtue is a habit of intention, a continuous pattern of intentional initiation. If the initiation of intentions does not have active internal force but relies on external force, it will appear weak. If intentionality is too weak, it will not be able to take on affairs. What one can cultivate is to enhance one's inner strength through life experiences, and cooperate with other's intentionality to build a towering and magnificent presence like that of a mountain.

初九：有厉，利已。

《象》曰："有厉，利已"，不犯灾也。

【明译】

初九：有危险，宜于知止不前。

《象传》说：初九有潜在危险，如谨慎处之不妄动，还是有利的，因为不去招惹灾祸。

Nine (*yang*/strong line) in the first place: If there is danger, it is beneficial to know where to stop.

The *Image Commentary* (*Xiang Zhuan*) says: There are potential dangers with the Nine (*yang*/strong line) in the first place. It is still beneficial to be cautious and not act rashly, trying not to cause disaster.

【明意】

初九的意性刚健，意行有力，加上心有所动，以六四之应为意量，但落实于意行，则不得不适可而止，因为过分勇进，则可能有灾，上有兑（泽）之损，不宜干犯。也就是说，初九的意量在于自知有意前进而又适可而止，不冒险行动，险是可能伤害与损伤意量的，因量的开展而受到压抑与打击，不如小心翼翼地运己之力，小心意量的边界。人的意念发动随时随刻有其生发的情境，而意量不可能离却意境，故必须小心运意，让意量处于安全稳定的状态。

[Illuminating Intentionality]

With the Nine (*yang*/strong line) in the first place, intentionality is strong and powerful, and the heart-mind is moved. The Six (*yin*/soft line) in the fourth place should be taken as the measure of intention. However, when it comes to the implementation of intention, it must be done in moderation, because if one advances too much, there may be disasters. It is not advisable to offend, since there is the risk of losses. That is to say, the intention capacity of the Nine (*yang*/strong line) in the first place lies in knowing that one has the intention to move forward without stopping, but not to take risks, since risk may harm and damage one's intention capacity. If one is suppressed and attacked due to the development of intention capacity, it is better to use one's strength cautiously, being careful about the boundaries of one's intentionality. People's intentions can be triggered by situations at any time, and an intention cannot leave its intentional context. Therefore, we must be careful about our fortune and keep our intentionality in a safe and stable state.

九二：舆说輹。

《象》曰："舆说輹"，中无尤也。

【明译】

九二：车厢从车轴上脱下来。

《象传》说：车厢跟车轴分离开来了，只是因为九二在下卦中位，应于六五，行动能够合乎中道，所以才没有过失，不必过于忧虑。

Nine (*yang*/strong line) in the second place: The carriage compartment comes off its axle.

The *Image Commentary* (*Xiang Zhuan*) says: That the carriage compartment is separated from its axle is only because the Nine (*yang*/strong line) in the second place is in the middle of the lower Trigram, corresponding to the Six (*yin*/soft line) in the fifth place, and its actions can be in line with the middle way, so there is no fault and no need to worry too much.

【明意】

修身是于一定情境之中，控制自己的意念，以积蓄心意的力量。车轴象征内在的德性，需要通过自我控制而不断精进，修行路上，碰到困难自己克服。九二居中，言说行事能守中道，该说的一句不能少，不该说的一句不宜多，可见蓄志的中道分寸很难。蓄积的道路上，就地停下休整是为了更好地再出发，维持住更大更高的蓄积状态。

[Illuminating Intentionality]

Self-cultivation means to control one's intentions in certain situations to accumulate the power of intentionality. The axle symbolizes inner virtue, which requires continuous improvement through self-control. On the road of spiritual practice, one can overcome difficulties by oneself. The Nine (*yang*/strong line) in the second place is in the middle, so one can speak and act in accord with the middle way, not saying one sentence more or less than one should. It can be seen that it is difficult to be determined and measured in the middle way. On the road of accumulation, stopping and resting on the spot is in order to start again in a better way and maintain a larger and higher state of accumulation.

九三：良马逐，利艰贞，曰闲舆卫，利有攸往。

《象》曰："利有攸往"，上合志也。

【明译】

九三：驾着良马（拉的车）驰逐时，即使道路艰险，只要持守正道，就会化险为夷。（人要向良马学习）每日练习熟练驾驶车和护卫车的技能，有利于继续前进。

《象传》说：有利于继续前进，是因为九三向上的努力合乎上面六四、六五的心志。

Nine (*yang*/strong line) in the third place: When driving a good horse (pulling a carriage), even if the road is difficult and dangerous, as long as one sticks to the right path, danger will be averted. (People should learn from good horses, as) Practicing the skills of driving and escorting carriages proficiently every day will help them continue to move forward.

The *Image Commentary* (*Xiang Zhuan*) says: It is conducive to continue to move forward because the Nine (*yang*/strong line) in the third place's upward efforts are in line with the aspirations of those above (the Sixes (*yin*/soft lines) in the fourth and fifth places).

【明意】

心量的蓄止要有技术，就好像驾驭战马一样娴熟操练，才能良好地蓄止，即当行则行，当止则止。生命的操练就是一个不断向死而生地扩大自己意量的功夫，但对这种功夫的娴熟操练与了解并不容易。如果因为对情境有所了解而轻举妄动，就容易出错，伤害大畜的意境。可以说，大畜的意量，就是阳意与阴意时刻的张力，阳意多么宏伟壮大，阴意也相应有多大的止之能量，所以意量的扩充伴随着意能的涵养与增益。

[Illuminating Intentionality]

The concentration of intentionality must be skillful, just like driving a warhorse. Only by skillful training can one control it well, that is, go when one wants to go, and stop when one wants to stop. The practice of life is a skill of constantly expanding one's intentionality of living towards death, but it is not easy to master and understand this skill. If one acts rashly because one has some understanding of a situation, one can easily make mistakes and harm the intentional context of great accumulation. It can be said that the intentional capacity of great accumulation is the moment-to-moment tension between *yang*/positive intentionality and *yin*/negative intentionality. How grand and powerful *yang*/positive intentionality is, and *yin*/negative intentionality has a corresponding amount of stopping energy, so the expansion of intentional capacity is accompanied by the cultivation and increase of intentional energy.

六四：童牛之牿，元吉。

《象》曰：六四"元吉"，有喜也。

【明译】

六四：（为驯化小野牛）在它的角上绑上防止顶伤人的横木，这样大吉大利。

《象传》说：六四会大吉大利（因为未雨绸缪，用柔术蓄养豪杰，栽培人才），所以有喜庆（六四在互兑里，兑为喜悦）。

Six (*yin*/soft line) in the fourth place: (To tame a young bison,) tie a crossbar to its horns to prevent it from hurting people. This will bring good fortune.

The *Image Commentary* (*Xiang Zhuan*) says: The Six (*yin*/soft line) in the fourth place is auspicious (because it is prepared for a rainy day, using jujitsu-like methods to cultivate heroism and talent), so there is joy as the Six (*yin*/soft line) in the fourth place is in the internal Trigram Dui, which signifies joy.

【明意】

最大的积蓄是人才意能的积蓄，要建立蓄止的机制，让所有人都把意量最大化。贤才心量扩大，不但要蓄养，还要去除不断伤人的潜在危险。要成就大畜的力量，必须磨砺意境，才能提升意能。让人心的明德阳意彰显出来，需要一个艰苦的磨炼过程，才能达到止于至善的目标，意念才能时刻止于最高的善境。可见心性和意念有所制约、接受磨砺方能成就伟业。意能在制约与磨砺之中得到提升，也只有磨砺后才可能达到大畜境界。

[Illuminating Intentionality]

The greatest accumulation is the accumulation of the intentional energy of talent. A mechanism for accumulation must be established to allow everyone to maximize their intentional capacity. To expand the intentional capacity of a talented person, one must not only cultivate it, but also eliminate the potential danger of constantly hurting others. In order to achieve the power of great accumulation, one must hone one's intentional context in order to improve one's mental abilities. In order to reveal the bright virtue and *yang* intentionality of people's intentions, an arduous tempering process is required to achieve the goal of the perfect good, such that intentionality can always remain in the highest state of goodness. It can be seen that great achievements can only be made if one's intentionality and intentions are restricted and tempered. Intentionality can be improved through restriction and tempering, and only after tempering can it reach the realm of great accumulation.

六五：豶（fén）豕之牙，吉。

《象》曰：六五之"吉"，有庆也。

【明译】

六五：被阉割过的猪，嘴里的尖牙不会伤人，所以是吉祥的。

《象传》说：六五之所以吉祥，是因为占据了上卦中位，比六四位置好，防患于未然，留住了贤才，会有大喜庆。

Six (yin/soft line) in the fifth place: A castrated boar has fangs in its mouth that will not hurt people, so it is auspicious.

The *Image Commentary* (*Xiang Zhuan*) says: The reason why the Six (yin/soft line) in the fifth place is auspicious is that it occupies the middle position of the upper Trigram, which is a better than the Six (yin/soft line) in the fourth place. It prevents problems from occurring, retains talented people, and brings great joy.

【明意】

驾驭和运用贤才的心意境遇是让其心意发动的瞬间都顺天之生意而行，而且没有一丝一毫肃杀之气，这样的意量是纯粹的善量，这才是贤人致力天下的大畜之量。大人才的力量存在于他起心动念的瞬间，一念起即心志和魄力都在其中。大人的意念能够改变阴阳，这就是能够转化心意通于天下阴阳运作的形势。

[Illuminating Intentionality]

The state of intentionality that controls and utilizes the virtuous allows the virtuous person to follow the productive intentionality of heaven at the moment when one initiates one's intentions, and there is no trace of cruel intention. This kind of intentional capacity is pure kindness, and this is the capacity of great accumulation that the virtuous person devotes to the world. The power of a great talent exists in the moment when one initiates an intention or thought. As soon as an intention arises, one's will and courage are in it. A great person's intentions can change *yin* and *yang*, and this is the situational propensity that can transform intentionality and connect *yin* and *yang* in the world under heaven.

上九：何（hè）天之衢（qú），亨。

《象》曰："何天之衢"，道大行也。

【明译】

上九：位当四通八达的天街大道，亨通。

《象传》说：上九位当四通八达的天街大道，大畜之道将与大路一样畅通大行。

Nine (yang/strong line) in the top place: The broad heavenly avenue, which extends in all directions, is prosperous.

The *Image Commentary* (*Xiang Zhuan*) says: The Nine (yang/strong line) in the top place is a heavenly thoroughfare extending in all directions, and the way of great accumulation is as smooth and broad as the main road.

【明意】

大畜是让人间贤人的意量得到充分实现，进入天人合一、物我合一、心物合一之化境，同天而合道，顺天地自然之生机。从而大畜天下，而天下乐见其人天之意的大意量，即实现了通天化境。当这种大意量的意向性状态持续，即可心安理得，持久而品德高尚，颐养天年，于是颐卦出现。

[Illuminating Intentionality]

Great accumulation allows the wishes of the worthy in the world to be fully concretized, and to enter a transformative state of unity between nature and man, a unity of things and self, and a unity of heart-mind and things/events. They are in harmony with heaven and united with the *dao*, and follow the natural vitality of heaven and earth. As a result, the world is greatly accumulated, and is happy to see one's great intention, which means one has achieved the transformative state connecting to heaven. When this state of large-capacity intentionality continues, one can feel at ease, have a lasting and noble moral character, and live a long life, so Hexagram Yi (Nourishment) appears.

山雷颐（卦二十七）　（震下艮上）

Yi (Nourishment), Mountain and Thunder (Hexagram 27)　(Zhen below, Gen above)

　　颐卦在大畜卦之后，天下大有积蓄，就有了养育的条件，就要看该养些什么人，如何养育他们。颐卦认为应该养贤，即先把人才养起来，培育和发挥他们的贤能，从而把天下万民养育好。

　　要让真气颐养身体，其实意识也要养，而如何控制和涵养意识，是传统哲学功夫论的重要内容。颐卦讨论意识之平易快乐，看清之后平和平易，自得真量。养生的根本首先要管好自己的嘴巴，但管好嘴巴的根本又是通过意识来控制，对于自己的需要能够有所取舍。"养正"是饮食之道当遵守饮食的礼仪，即通过摄取的正道来保证摄入的都是养分，保养自己的身体和意识。这是一场得气与不得气之战，在意识中不断地做善良与邪恶的斗争、健康与损害的斗争，可谓时刻都是天理与人欲的决战。颐卦说明，不同时刻有不同的选择方法，而依从涵养心的经验，确实远没有依从原则来得容易。

　　Hexagram Yi (Nourishment) follows Hexagram Daxu (Accumulation). There is a lot of accumulation in the world, so it's eligible for raising others, and the question is who should be raised and how to raise them. Hexagram Yi (Nourishment) believes that virtuous people should be nurtured, that is, talents should be raised first, their virtuous abilities cultivated and brought into play, so as to nurture all people in the world well.

　　In order for *qi* to nourish the body, consciousness must also be nourished, and how to control and cultivate consciousness is an important part of traditional Chinese philosophical theory of effort (*gongfu*). Hexagram Yi (Nourishment) discusses the ease and happiness of consciousness. After seeing things clearly, it is harmonious and easy, and one can attain one's true capacity. The foundation of health preservation is to first take care of one's mouth, but the foundation of taking care of one's mouth is to control it through consciousness and be able to make choices based on one's own needs. "Cultivating with rightness" means that the *dao* of eating and drinking should abide by the ritual propriety of eating and drinking, that is, through the right *dao* of intake, one can ensure that one is taking in only nutrients and maintain one's body and consciousness. This is a battle between gaining and losing *qi*, and there is a constant battle between good and evil, health and harm in consciousness. It can be said that it is a decisive battle between heavenly patterns and human desires at all times. Hexagram Yi (Nourishment) explains that there are different methods of choice at different times, and following the experience of cultivating the heart-mind, it is indeed far less easy than following principles.

颐，贞吉。观颐，自求口实。

《彖》曰："颐，贞吉"，养正则吉也。"观颐"，观其所养也。"自求口实"，观其自养也。天地养万物，圣人养贤以及万民，颐之时大矣哉！

《象》曰：山下有雷，颐。君子以慎言语，节饮食。

【明译】

颐卦象征颐养，持守正道可获吉祥，观察万物颐养之道，（当知要以自食其力的正道）自己谋求食物。

《彖传》说：颐养，持守正道可获吉祥，是颐养得其正道就会吉祥。观察万物颐养之道，是要了解他所养的对象都是些什么人。要以自食其力的正道自己谋求食物，观察他如何颐养自己。天地养育之道是养育万物没有偏私不求回报，圣人要学习天地养育万物的正道，先养育贤能的人，贤人再帮助圣人把万民养育好。颐卦的时势揭示的时机化意义实在太重大了！

《象传》说：上卦艮为山，下卦震为雷，大山镇住了轰响的雷就是颐卦。君子从上动下止，如口嚼食的象得到启示，学会说话要谨慎，饮食要有节制。

Hexagram Yi (Nourishment) symbolizes nourishment. If one sticks to the right *dao*, one will gain good fortune. Observing the way of nourishment for the myriad things, seek one's own food (one should know that one must follow the right *dao* of self-reliance).

The *Judgment Commentary* (*Tuan Zhuan*) says: In nourishing and cultivating, if one sticks to the right *dao*, one may get good fortune; if nourishment finds the right *dao*, one will get good fortune. The way to observe the care and nourishment of the myriad things is to understand the kind of people they care for. To seek food for oneself in the right way of self-reliance is to observe how a person supports oneself. The way heaven and earth nourish the myriad things is to nourish them without favoritism and without asking for anything in return. Sages should learn the right *dao* of heaven and earth in nourishing the myriad things. They should first raise worthy people, and then wise people will help the sages to raise all people well. The time of vital transformation revealed by the temporal propensity of Hexagram Yi (Nourishment) is truly significant!

The *Image Commentary* (*Xiang Zhuan*) says: The upper Trigram Gen is mountain, the lower Trigram is thunder, so a mountain suppressing roaring thunder is Hexagram Yi (Nourishment). An exemplary person moves from top and stops at the bottom, like the image of chewing food in the mouth. One gets inspiration from this, and learns to speak carefully and eat in moderation.

【明意】

养的意识是从天地养人到人养他人，涉及如何管好口腹之欲的意念与人生之乐，即如何处理欲与乐的关系。但更为深刻的是生养与死的关系，因为养其实是生死之战，只是在生的状态中不易感觉到死或者对死的体验不深而已。古人注重吃的艺术，留意与吃的行为相关的意识状态。既要吃得有面子，还要吃得有味道，最主要的是，吃的应该是事物之真气，让善良、健康的生气发荣滋长。

天地养育之道就是，养育万事万物从来都没有偏私，先把贤能的人养育起来，贤人才有能力帮助圣人把万民养育好，这样的管理当然离不开亲亲有等。只有自己吃饱饭才可能去照顾别人，推己及人，自立立人。感激他人给自己心意展开的力量，时刻保持感恩之心，如果没有他人提供的情境，一个人纵然有再大能力也无法施展。好比没有时间吃饭，就无法品尝人间百味，不能细细品味美酒佳肴的味道，就难得其养。

[Illuminating Intentionality]

The consciousness of nourishment moves from heaven and earth nourishing people to people nourishing other people. It involves how to manage the desire for food and drink and the happiness of human life, that is, how to deal with the relationship between desire and happiness. But what is more profound is the relationship between life and death, because nourishment is actually a battle between life and death. It is just that in the state of life, it is not easy to feel death, or the experience of death is not deep. The ancients paid attention to the art of eating and to the state of consciousness related to the act of eating. One should eat with dignity and taste, yet the most important thing is that we should eat the authentic *qi* of things, so that kind and healthy energy can flourish.

Heaven and earth's *dao* of raising the world is that they have no partiality in raising the myriad things. But wise people should be raised first, since wise people can then help the sages to raise all the people well. Of course, such management cannot be separated from relatives and friends. Only when one has enough to eat can one take care of others, respect others, and be self-reliant. One should be grateful to others for giving one the power to expand one's intentionality, and always keep a thankful heart-mind. Without the affective context provided by others, no matter how great a person is, one will not be able to develop. This is like how, if one has no time to eat, one will be unable to taste the various flavors of the world, and if one cannot savor the taste of fine wine and food, one will be unable to nourish oneself.

初九：舍尔灵龟，观我朵颐，凶。
《象》曰："观我朵颐"，亦不足贵也。

【明译】

初九：舍弃你自己拥有的大灵龟，看着我馋涎欲滴，这样是会有凶险的。

《象传》说：看着我馋涎欲滴，（初九的颐养之道）实在不值得推崇。

Nine (*yang*/strong line) in the first place: It would be dangerous to abandon the big turtle one owns and watch me while salivating greedily.

The *Image Commentary* (*Xiang Zhuan*) says: Looking at me salivating, (the way of maintaining life of the Nine (*yang*/strong line) in the first place) is really not worthy of praise.

【明意】

人的健康靠自己管理，需要自己把握好跟世界能量交换的分寸。颐养之道因为每时每刻都要与食欲作斗争，所以本身就是一场心意生机与堕落的欲望之间的战争，是制服和驾驭欲望的艺术。初九到底还是被本性决定，难以自我控制，垂涎欲滴而忘乎所以，这样是违背颐养之道的，所以初九提示人们对欲望的控制和忍耐非常重要。从另一方面讲，初九有机会可以锻炼自己对欲望的控制力，只可惜初九错过了绝好的锻炼机会。初九本来可以有高贵的精神追求，结果去追求低俗的快乐，是很不应该的。

颐养之道以龟之养神为最高境界，初九主动离开这种最高境界的颐养意识状态可谓匪夷所思。可以说，初九舍弃自家宝藏，转而艳羡他人，是没有出息的表现。从中可体会宋明理学家们讲的，时刻在意念发动处"存天理灭人欲"，有一定的合理性。

[Illuminating Intentionality]

People's health depends on their own management, and they need to grasp the balance of energy exchange with the world. Because the *dao* of nourishing cultivation involves fighting desire for food at every moment, it is itself a war between the vitality of intentionality and the corrupted desires, an art of subduing and controlling desires. After all, the Nine (*yang*/strong line) in the first place is still determined by its original nature, has difficulty in controlling itself, indulges in desire and forgets its own affairs. This goes against the *dao* of nourishing cultivation, so the Nine (*yang*/strong line) in the first place reminds people that it is very important to control and restrain desires. On the other hand, the Nine (*yang*/strong line) in the first place has the opportunity to exercise one's control over one's desires, but unfortunately misses the perfect opportunity to exercise it. As the Nine (*yang*/strong line) in the first place, one could have noble spiritual pursuits, but in the end, one pursues vulgar pleasure, which is inappropriate.

The way of nourishing cultivation takes the spiritual nourishment of the tortoise as the highest state. It is incredible that the Nine (*yang*/strong line) in the first place voluntarily leaves this conscious state of nourishing cultivation, which is the highest state. It can be said that abandoning one's own treasure-store and turning to envy others as the Nine (*yang*/strong line) in the first place is a sign of having no future. From this, we can understand why it is somehow reasonable that the Neo-Confucians of the Song and Ming dynasties advocated "preserving the patterns of nature and extinguishing human desires" at the moment when intentions are initiated.

六二：颠颐，拂经于丘颐，征凶。

《象》曰：六二"征凶"，行失类也。

【明译】

六二：颠倒颐养之常道，违背以下养上的常理，反而向丘山田园之上去求取颐养，向前征进必有凶险。

《象传》说：六二向前征进必有凶险，因为向前征行会失去同类。

Six (*yin*/soft line) in the second place: Inverting the normal way of nourishment, one goes against the common sense of using the lower to cultivate the higher, and instead goes to the high places in mountains and fields to seek nourishment. There will be dangers in marching forward.

The *Image Commentary* (*Xiang Zhuan*) says: The Six (*yin*/soft line) in the second place marching forward must be dangerous, because in marching forward one will lose those of the same kind.

【明意】

《周易》对于天地之间阴意与阳意的能量交流方式有一定的把握，不宜颠倒反转，如果感应后乱动，就不合分寸。六二内心凄苦矛盾，这种意识状态不利于颐养，违背常道，征进凶险。自己的颐养之道本来应该从下，但内心觉得不合适，颠来倒去，心中凄苦，不得其养。这是不得形势之养，内心失去对形势的领会和把握，就无法得养。

[Illuminating Intentionality]

The *Book of Changes* has a certain grasp of the energy exchange method for *yin* and *yang* intentionality between heaven and earth. This should not be reversed, and if it is moved randomly after inductive response, it will be inappropriate. The Six (*yin*/soft line) in the second place's heart-mind is miserable and contradictory. This state of consciousness is not conducive to nourishment, goes against the common sense, and leads to danger. One's way of caring for oneself should be from the bottom up, but in this state one feels inappropriate in one's heart-mind, tossing and turning, feeling miserable and unable to nourish oneself. This is not being able to be nourished by the situational propensity. If one loses one's inner understanding and grasp of the situation, one cannot be nourished.

六三：拂颐，贞凶。十年勿用，无攸利。

《象》曰："十年勿用"，道大悖也。

【明译】

六三：背逆颐养正道，一意孤行，必有凶险，在十年这样长的时间里都没法为君王所用，没有什么好处。

《象传》说：在十年这样长的时间里都没法有所作为，因为六三大大背逆了颐养之道。

Six (*yin*/soft line) in the third place: If one goes against the right *dao* and goes one's own way reaklessly, there will be danger. One will not be able to be used by the king for ten years, and there will be no benefit.

The *Image Commentary* (*Xiang Zhuan*) says: The Six (*yin*/soft line) in the third place is unable to make any difference for ten years because it violated the *dao* of nourishing cultivation.

【明意】

这一爻说明颐养之道，以正道养己不易，养人很难，要以正道被养于人，那是非常之难。养的意识当然包括养己、养人、养于人。养己的意识是要自己判断正道，摄取营养，从正道当中汲取营养。养人是要养合适的人，比如贤人、善人和走正道的人。养于人则养的人要合适，养的路子要对。养的意识其实每时每刻都有选择和判断，都有养己养人养于人的区分，而每一种养其实都不容易。

自己的意识要生生不息，但又需要遵守颐养的正道。最后的出路还是涵养正念，当下实意而不依托外境，也不为外境所转，谋食容易谋道难，养色容易养德难，但养生最主要的是养正，脊椎骨要正，吃饭要正，有规矩所养之气才通畅，切不可贪图一时的舒服。陪家人一起吃饭是学习如何颐养自己，也是养他人的过程。家是养己养人养于人的一个合体，所以家的颐养之道要正，要合适，因为家是培养颐养之道与颐养意识的核心。

[Illuminating Intentionality]

This line illustrates the *dao* of nourishment. It is not easy to nourish oneself in the right way, difficult to raise others, and very difficult to be raised by others in the right way. The awareness of nourish ment certainly includes nourishing oneself, nourishing others, and being nourished by others. The consciousness of nourishing oneself requires judging the right *dao*, taking in nutrients, and drawing nutrients along the right *dao*. Raising people means raising the right people, such as wise people, good people and people who follow the right *dao*. To raise a child, the one you raise must be suitable and the way you raise the child must be right. The consciousness of nourishment actually involves choices and judgments at every moment, and there is a distinction between nourishing oneself, nourishing others, and being nourished by others, and in fact every kind of nourishment is not easy.

One's own consciousness must be endless, but one needs to follow the right *dao* of nourishing cultivation. The final way out is to cultivate one's mindfulness to be sincere in the moment and not rely on or be influenced by external circumstances. It is easy to find food but difficult to find the *dao*, and easy to cultivate beauty but difficult to cultivate virtue. But the most important thing in maintaining health is to maintain uprightness. The spine must be upright, and food must be eaten properly, as only when *qi* is nourished by rules can energy flow smoothly, so do not be greedy for temporary comfort. Eating with one's family is a process of learning how to support oneself and others. A family is a combination of raising oneself, raising others, and being raised by others, so the way of raising oneself must be correct and appropriate, because the family is the core of cultivating the *dao* and awareness of raising oneself.

六四：颠颐，吉。虎视眈眈，其欲逐逐，无咎。

《象》曰："颠颐"之"吉"，上施光也。

【明译】

六四：颠倒颐卦（从小颐卦颠倒变成大颐卦），自然吉祥。虽然看起来像老虎颠动下巴眈眈注视着食物（初九）一样，显得贪得无厌，迫切追逐欲望而毫不收敛，但仍然没有什么问题。

《象传》说：颠倒颐卦，使六五下的小颐卦变成大颐卦，虽然好像（六四）颠倒了颐养之道，但（对六四来说）反而吉祥，因为上边（九五）下来到初位，卦变大离，象征君主施布出来的恩惠非常广大光明。

Six (*yin*/soft line) in the fourth place: Reversing Hexagram Yi (Nourishment) (reversing a small Hexagram Yi (Nourishment) into a big Hexagram Yi (Nourishment)) is naturally auspicious. Although it looks like a tiger twitching its chin and staring at food (the Nine (*yang*/strong line) in the first place), seeming greedy and eager to pursue desires without restraint, there is still no problem.

The *Image Commentary* (*Xiang Zhuan*) says: Inverting Hexagram Yi (Nourishment) makes a small Hexagram Yi (Nourishment) under the Six in the fifth place become a big Hexagram Yi (Nourishment). Although it seems that it (the Six (*yin*/soft line) in the fourth place) has reversed the way of self-care, it is actually auspicious (for the Six (*yin*/soft line) in the fourth place) because the upper part (the Nine (*yang*/strong line) in the fifth place) comes down to the first position, and thus the hexagram changes to a big Hexagram Li, symbolizing that the kindness given by the monarch is very broad and bright.

【明意】

意识因为过度执着于外物而表现出垂涎欲滴的样子，但第一部分也同样是因为关爱之心切，爱意的专注与排他形成的这种状态。真情相悦形成的意识是一种情感融通的状态，彼此心印而且强烈地吸引，意识境遇融会贯通，有利于形成意丹的状态。在彼此相印的真爱状态中，欲望无疑被放大了。但这是正常放大的，并不是非分过度，所以虽然表面颠倒，其实蛮好的。而且九二向上之颠，导致施布恩德的光明意境，让六四与初九的欲望和爱意都被放大了。当然，六四虎视眈眈显得欲望太盛，不过，表现得欲望强盛，可能反而没有攻击性，犹如武将功高震主之后，如果对财物贪得无厌，反能避免被君王猜忌。

[Illuminating Intentionality]

Consciousness appears to be salivating due to excessive attachment to external objects, but the first part is also due to eagerness to care, the concentration and exclusiveness of love to form this state. The consciousness formed by true love is a state of emotional harmony, mutual heart-mind imprinting and strong attraction, and the integration of consciousness and situation is conducive to the formation of an intentionality-elixir state. In a state of true love with each other, desire is undoubtedly magnified. But this is normal magnification, not excessive, so although it appears upside down, it is actually rather good. Moreover, the upward peak of the Nine in the second place leads to a bright intentional context of grace and virtue, which amplifies the desire and love of the Six (*yin*/soft line) in the fourth place and the Nine (*yang*/strong line) in the first place. Of course, the Six (*yin*/soft line) in the fourth place eyeing covetously shows too much desire. However, showing strong desire may not be aggressive, just like a military general who has conquered his master with great achievements but is greedy for property can avoid the suspicion of his king.

六五：拂经，居贞吉。不可涉大川。

《象》曰："居贞"之"吉"，顺以从上也。

【明译】

六五：违背正常的颐养之道，安居持守正道可以获得吉祥，但没法克服涉越大河那样的艰难险阻。

《象传》说：六五安居持守正道还可以获得吉祥，因为阴柔地顺从上面的刚爻上九。

Six (*yin*/soft line) in the fifth place: Violating the normal *dao* of nourishing cultivation, one can gain good fortune by living in peace and adhering to the right way, but cannot overcome difficulties and obstacles like crossing a large river.

The *Image Commentary* (*Xiang Zhuan*) says: Living peacefully and adhering to the right *dao* as the Six (*yin*/soft line) in the fifth place can also lead to good fortune, because it can obey the Nine (*yang*/strong line) in the top place above softly.

【明意】

六五自知自己的时位而后知道运意的分寸，自知居于互坤之中，所以柔顺顺应上九。心意为公，即使有违常道，也可得吉祥。阴爻阴意处于不好的时势，不得不依赖上九，不过阴顺阳还是挺好的。得阳之养，自然柔顺而得养生养识。因识得养方可以有识量。阴意的识量都要顺从阳意而方可实化。没有阳意的阴意，本身孤独难明，也难独存，阴意只有依托阳意的生机，自身才能焕发生机。

[Illuminating Intentionality]

The Six (*yin*/soft line) in the fifth place knows its own time and position, and thus knows the propriety of fortune. One knows that one lives in a mutual relationship, so one is docile and adaptable to the Nine (*yang*/strong line) in the top place. If one's intentions are fair, even if one goes against the norm, one can still get good fortune. When the *yin* line's *yin*/negative intentionality is in a bad situation, it has to rely on the Nine (*yang*/strong line) in the top place, but if *yin* follows *yang*, then both remain good. When nourished by *yang*, the body becomes naturally supple and nourishes health and consciousness. Only when knowledge is nourished can we have the capacity for knowledge. The consciousness of the *yin* intentionality must obey *yang* intentionality before it can be concretized. Yin intentionality without *yang* intentionality is lonely and difficult to enlighten, and it is difficult to exist alone, so *yin* intentionality can only be revitalized by relying on the vitality of *yang* intentionality.

上九：由颐，厉，吉。利涉大川。

《象》曰："由颐，厉，吉"，大有庆也。

【明译】

上九：这是颐养之道的来源，即使有危险，也能够获得吉祥，有利于克服涉越大河那样的艰难险阻。

《象传》说：这是天下众生颐养之道的来源，即使有危险，也能够获得吉祥，大有喜庆。

Nine (*yang*/strong line) in the top place: This is the source of the *dao* of nourishment. Even if there is danger, one can still obtain good fortune, and this is beneficial to overcome difficulties and obstacles such as crossing a large river.

The *Image Commentary* (*Xiang Zhuan*) says: This is the source of the *dao* to support all living beings in the world under heaven. Even if there is danger, they can still obtain good fortune and have great joy.

【明意】

阴阳之意相互造就，阴意造就阳意，本爻体现阴阳相互造就之养，离开妻道，柔道，臣道，阳无所成。颐卦是自养和养人的意识，自己要养好，之后要养人，养人是功德。意识之养的根本是接天地之生气，从天地生生不息的气象中涵养出意识本身的生气与生机。意识可从后天境界返回先天生机结构，这是颐养的核心。

[Illuminating Intentionality]

Yin and *yang* intentionality create each other, *yin* creating *yang*, and this line embodies the mutual creation and support of *yin* and *yang*. Without the *dao* of the wife, of softness, and of the minister, *yang* cannot achieve anything. Hexagram Yi (Nourishment) is the consciousness of self-nurturing and nurturing others. One must first nurture oneself, then nurture others, so nurturing others is a merit. The foundation of cultivating consciousness is receiving the vital *qi* of heaven and earth, and cultivating the vital *qi* and vitality of consciousness itself from the ceaselessly productive atmosphere of heaven and earth. Consciousness can return from the empirical realm to the transcendental vital structure, which is the core of self-cultivation.

泽风大过（卦二十八）　（巽下兑上）

Daguo (Great Excess), Lake and Wind (Hexagram 28)　(Xun below, Dui above)

　　大过是改换意缘的时势，是动意重新聚缘的时势，需要动心忍性，深入超常意识境遇的意缘，改变自己原有意识境遇，勇于开拓新的意缘。大过涉及意缘的改换方式有：洁净精微；抓住生机，绝处逢生；绝境之中，大彻大悟；力挽狂澜；极度谨慎；舍己为人等等。总之，没有非常之运意方式，就无法成就非凡之事。大过之形势要求人有非常的心意和行动，才能打破旧缘的局面，聚合新缘，但又不恣意妄为。

　　Great excess is a time of change in the dependent co-arising of intentionality, a time of reuniting by moving intentions. It requires patience to go deep into the intentional dependent co-arising of extraordinary consciousness, change one's original realm of consciousness, and have the courage to open up a new dependent co-arising for intention. The methods for changing intentional dependent co-arising related to great excess include: purifying the subtle essence; seizing upon vitality to survive in a desperate situation; achieving great enlightenment in a desperate context; turning the tide; being extremely cautious; sacrificing oneself for others, etc. In short, without extraordinary change of intentionality, extraordinary things cannot be achieved. The situation of great excess requires people to have extraordinary intentions and actions in order to break the situation of old dependencies and gather new ones, but not act arbitrarily.

　　大过，栋桡（náo），利有攸往，亨。

　　《彖》曰：大过，大者过也。"栋桡"，本末弱也。刚过而中，巽而说，行。"利有攸往"，乃"亨"。大过之时大矣哉！

《象》曰：泽灭木，大过。君子以独立不惧，遁世无闷。

【明译】

大过卦象征强大过分，房子的栋梁开始弯曲，知道要抓紧修补挽救，所以还有利于有所前往，能够亨通顺利。

《彖传》说："强大过分"，"大"的意思就是大的刚爻太强大过分了。好比栋梁弯曲了，是因为它的本末两头（两个柔爻）太软弱了。大壮变大过的卦变中，九五从初位过去到上卦中位，是刚爻刚健越过（二三四刚爻）来居于中正之位。下卦巽为顺利，上卦兑为喜悦，能够顺利而喜悦地行动，当然就前往有利而且亨通顺利。大过这一时势的时机化意义实在太重大了！

《象传》说：下卦巽为木，上卦兑为泽，泽水淹没了大树，这是大过卦的象征。君子看到泽水淹没大树这样的灭顶之灾，要坦然面对，以挽救危难的时局为己任，独立支持，毫无惧色，力挽狂澜，扭转崩溃之势，即使回天无术，也不怨天尤人，可以退隐避世，毫不郁闷。

Hexagram Daguo (Great Excess) symbolizes excessive strength and size, and the pillars of the house begin to bend. One knows that one must hurry up to repair and save it, so it is also conducive to advancing and being able to prosper smoothly.

The *Judgment Commentary* (*Tuan Zhuan*) says: In "strong and big beyond its share," "big" means that the big *yang*/strong line is too strong and excessive. It is like a pillar being bent because its ends (the two soft lines) are too weak. In the hexagram-changes, Dazhuang (Exuberance) becomes Daguo (Great Excess), the Nine (*yang*/strong line) in the fifth place passing from the first place to the middle position of the upper Trigram, a *yang*/strong line vigorously crossing over (the second, third, and fourth *yang*/strong lines) to occupy a central and upright position. The lower Trigram Xun means success, and the upper Trigram Dui means joy. Actions that can be smooth and joyful will of course be beneficial and prosperous. The temporal propensity of this situation is of great significance!

The *Image Commentary* (*Xiang Zhuan*) says: The lower Trigram Xun is wood, the upper Trigram Dui is lake, so lake water submerging a big tree is the symbol of the Hexagram Daguo (Great Excess). When an exemplary person sees a catastrophic situation like a big tree being submerged in a river, one must face it calmly, take it as one's own duty to save the critical situation, support things independently, act without fear, turn the tide and reverse the propensity of collapse, even if there is no way to save it, blaming neither heaven nor humanity, and retreating from the world without feeling depressed.

【明意】

虽然大过说明心念发动，无法控制情境的回应，以致意缘都超出个人的想象与操控，但对于情境的结果，要勇于面对，承担选择的后果，用勇气去改变意缘。心意之力道来自对逼迫自己进入某种情境的外力的领会和操控，迫于情境而生的心意可能非常之大，大大超过平常，所以也就可能超越外力。心志来自对非常情境的理解与应对，因为这来自人对情境当中非常之力的意会，对情境当中大过寻常之力的感知，要有独立不惧、努力改变意缘的魄力。可见，关键时刻，要能够豁得出去，才可能改变意缘状态。

[Illuminating Intentionality]

Although great excess means that intentionality has initiated and cannot control the response of the situation, to the point that intentional dependent co-arising is beyond individual imagination and control. However, one must have the courage to face the consequences of the situation, bear the consequences of one's choice, and use one's courage to change the intentional dependent co-arising. The power of intentionality comes from the understanding and control of the external forces that force oneself into a certain situation. The intentionality that is forced by the situation may be very large, much larger than usual, so it may surpass the external forces. The will comes from understanding and coping with extraordinary situations, because it comes from people's understanding of the extraordinary power in the situation, and the perception of the situation's greater than ordinary power. They must have the courage to be independent, fearless, and work hard to change their intentional dependent co-arising. It can be seen that at critical moments, only by being able to risk one's life can the state of one's destiny be changed.

初六：藉（jiè）用白茅，无咎。

《象》曰："藉用白茅"，柔在下也。

【明译】

初六：祭祀前先把柔软的白茅草衬垫在祭器的下边，这样谨小慎微当然没有什么害处。

《象传》说：先把柔软的白茅草衬垫在祭器的下边，因为初六柔爻在全卦最下方，柔顺地居于下位。

Six (*yin*/soft line) in the first place: Before offering sacrifices, put soft white couchgrass under the sacrificial vessel. There is certainly no harm in being cautious.

The *Image Commentary* (*Xiang Zhuan*) says: First put the soft white couchgrass grass under the sacrificial vessel, because the Six (*yin*/soft line) in the first place is at the bottom of the whole hexagram, and it complyingly remains in a lower position.

【明意】

意念不可一刻出偏，念起念灭，否则念来如果时间长久，定有回应的意缘，如影随形。意念洁净精微，必须小心至极，因为担心回应的力量太过巨大。一开始就要祭祀，表示初出茅庐，需要借力，小心运作，思路缜密，做事慎而又慎，要小心思考应对可能应和的意缘。

[Illuminating Intentionality]

The intentions should not go astray for a moment, and should disappear as soon as they arise. Otherwise, if intentions come for a long time, there will be a response, like a shadow. Intentions are pure and subtle, and one must be extremely careful, for fear that the power of the response will be too great. Offering sacrifices at the beginning means that one is just starting out and needs to borrow strength, operate carefully, think carefully, do things cautiously, and think carefully about possible intentional dependent co-arisings.

九二：枯杨生稊（tí），老夫得其女妻，无不利。

《象》曰："老夫、女妻"，过以相与也。

【明译】

九二：干枯的杨树生出了嫩芽和新枝，好比老男人娶得年少的娇妻，这种情况没有什么不利的。

《象传》说：老汉娶得少妻，是六五过了九二才来跟枯杨（老汉）相遇，是逾越常规、有点过分的。

Nine (*yang*/strong line) in the second place: Withered poplar trees sprout buds and new branches, just like an old man marrying a young wife. There is nothing disadvantageous about this situation.

The *Image Commentary* (*Xiang Zhuan*) says: An old man marries a young wife, but this is the Six (*yin*/soft line) in the fifth place meeting the withered poplar (the old man) only after passing the Nine (*yang*/strong line) in the second place. This is beyond the norm and a bit excessive.

【明意】

处在非常卦位，需要对事情有非常理解，在似乎没有生机的境遇中，也要发掘出一线生机。反常之时，不可采用常理处理意缘。

[Illuminating Intentionality]

Being in an abnormal hexagram position requires a very deep understanding of things, and a glimmer of hope must be found in seemingly lifeless situations. When things are abnormal, common sense cannot be used to deal with intentional dependent co-arising.

九三：栋桡，凶。

《象》曰："栋桡"之"凶"，不可以有辅也。

【明译】

九三：房子栋梁弯曲，非常凶险。

《象传》说：房子栋梁弯曲，带来凶险，是因为九三处于绝境，而上六自身难保，所以无法给它任何有效的辅助。

Nine (*yang*/strong line) in the third place: The pillars of the house are bent, which is very dangerous.

The *Image Commentary* (*Xiang Zhuan*) says: The pillars of the house are bent, which brings danger, because the Nine (*yang*/strong line) in the third place is in a desperate situation, and the Six (*yin*/soft line) in the top place cannot even protect itself, let alone give any effective assistance.

【明意】

九三身处绝境，而周围各爻，都爱莫能助，无限悲哀绝望之情境，莫过于此。更为重要的是，人在大过之危难中，不可以有一丝一毫的分心，需要集中精力专注，方能解困。对九三来说，上六是危险的意缘，本来就不应该出现在自己的意识境遇当中，即使出现了，也要明白上六对自己只有危险而无助力。可以说，九三在眼看大厦将倾之时，其意缘取舍到了千钧一发的关键时刻，知道除了抛弃上六，勉力维持，别无他缘可以借助。可见，正处独木难支的绝境当中，需要对自身情境有透彻的了悟才行，越是大过之时，需要大彻大悟，才能于非常之险境当中如履平地。

[Illuminating Intentionality]

The Nine (*yang*/strong line) in the third place is in a desperate situation, and everyone around him is helpless. This is a situation of infinite sadness and despair. However, what is more important is that when people are in great danger, they must not be distracted in the slightest. They need to concentrate and focus in order to solve the problem. For the Nine (*yang*/strong line) in the third place, the Six (*yin*/soft line) in the top place is a dangerous dependent co-arising, and it should not appear in one's conscious situation. Even if it does appear, one must understand that the Six (*yin*/soft line) in the top place is only dangerous to one's, and not helpful. It can be said that when the Nine (*yang*/strong line) in the third place sees that the building is about to collapse, one's choice of dependent co-arising reaches a critical moment. One knows that there is no other dependent co-arising to rely on except abandoning the Six (*yin*/soft line) in the top place and struggling to survive. It can be seen that when one is in a desperate situation, one needs to have a thorough understanding of one's own situation. The more serious the situation is, the more one needs to have a thorough understanding in order to be able to walk on the ground steadily in an extremely dangerous situation.

九四：栋隆，吉。有它吝。

《象》曰："栋隆"之"吉"，不桡乎下也。

【明译】

九四：栋梁向上隆起，可获吉祥，但可能有另外的吝难。

《象传》说：栋梁向上隆起，可获吉祥，因为九四在上卦（与九三不同），虽有初六正应，但是非常害怕被初六牵引向下。

Nine (*yang*/strong line) in the fourth place: If the pillars are raised upward, it will bring good fortune, but there may be other troubles.

The *Image Commentary* (*Xiang Zhuan*) says: If the pillars bulge upward, it will be auspicious, because the Nine (*yang*/strong line) in the fourth place is in the upper Trigram (different from the Nine (*yang*/strong line) in the third place). Although it corresponds to the Six (*yin*/soft line) in the first place, it is very afraid of being pulled downward by the Six (*yin*/soft line) in the first place.

【明意】

但九四拯救时局需要非同寻常地专注和努力才行，此时初六的正应反而成为很大的坏事，好像一个专心学问的人，被情感所牵绊，最后无所成就。心力的凝聚，在一些关键时刻不能够有分分秒秒的分神，所以此刻初六跟九四正应，对九四来说实在不是什么好事，而随时可能有其他的危险和苦难发生。九四也不可介意初六跟随九二，否则情感一动，心意出偏，就会有麻烦。可见，九四特别需要知道割舍，知道舍小情才能救大义的道理。否则，危急时刻，浩然正气维持半天，一念私心就土崩瓦解了。

[Illuminating Intentionality]

Nonetheless, saving the situation of the Nine (*yang*/strong line) in the fourth place requires extraordinary concentration and hard work. At this time, the positive response of the Six (*yin*/soft line) in the first place has turned out to be a big bad thing, just like a person who concentrates on learning, is tied up by emotions, and ultimately achieves nothing. The concentration of intentional energy cannot be distracted at critical moments, so the Six (*yin*/soft line) in the first place coincides with the Nine (*yang*/strong line) in the fourth place, which is really not a good thing for the Nine (*yang*/strong line) in the fourth place, and other dangers and sufferings may occur at any time. The Nine (*yang*/strong line) in the fourth place also cannot mind if the Six (*yin*/soft line) in the first place follows the Nine (*yang*/strong line) in the second place, otherwise one will be in trouble as soon as emotions are aroused and one's intentionality goes astray. It can be seen that the Nine (*yang*/strong line) in the fourth place especially needs to know how to let go, and know the principle that only by letting go of small feelings can one save great justice. Otherwise, in a critical moment, even if one's flood-like upright *qi* has lasted for a long time, it might fall apart at the first intention of selfishness.

九五：枯杨生华（huā），老妇得其士夫。无咎无誉。

《象》曰："枯杨生华"，何可久也。"老妇、士夫"，亦可丑也。

【明译】

九五：干枯的杨树开出新鲜的花朵，好比年老的妇人得到少壮的男子做丈夫，这没有什么害处，但也得不到什么荣誉。

《象传》说：干枯的杨树开出新鲜的花朵，可是这样的生机怎么能够持久得了呢？年老的妇人嫁给少壮的男子，这算是羞耻丑陋、丢人现眼的事吧。

Nine (*yang*/strong line) in the fifth place: A withered poplar tree blooms with fresh flowers, just like an old woman taking a young man as her husband. There is no harm in this, and there is no honor in it.

The *Image Commentary* (*Xiang Zhuan*) says: A dry poplar tree may bloom with fresh flowers, but how long can such vitality last? It is shameful, ugly and disgraceful for an old woman to marry a young man.

【明意】

九五得到的意缘缺少生机，可是又无从选择，人生的选择有些时候就是如此的不如意。但这里的生机是本身没有，所以即使得到少壮男子也只是短暂而且有限地增益新的意缘，而有限的增益不能算是好的意缘。

[Illuminating Intentionality]

The intentional dependent co-arising obtained by the Nine (*yang*/strong line) in the fifth place lacks vitality, but it has no choice, and sometimes the choices in life are so unsatisfactory. But there is no vitality here, so even if she gets a young man, she will only temporarily and limitedly gain new intentional dependent co-arising, and limited gains cannot be regarded as good intentional dependent co-arising.

上六：过涉灭顶，凶。无咎。

《象》曰："过涉"之"凶"，不可咎也。

【明译】

上六：渡过深水的时候，淹没了头顶，是很凶险的，但没有什么过错。

《象传》说：渡过深水淹没了头顶带来凶险，因为上六遇到灾祸并不是它造成的，无可指责（位正，本身无过错）。

Six (*yin*/soft line) in the top place: When crossing deep water, the top of one's head is submerged, which is very dangerous, but there is no fault.

The *Image Commentary* (*Xiang Zhuan*) says: Crossing deep water and submerging the top of the head brings danger, but because the disaster encountered by the Six (*yin*/soft line) in the top place was not caused by it, it is blameless (its position is upright, and there is no fault of its own).

【明意】

在不得不牺牲自己的时候，能够预见自我牺牲带给他人和团队的正面价值，对于意缘的增益和整合是一种高尚的情怀使然。当人的能力有限，无力承担危局，这时挺身而出，牺牲自己，成就大家，精神可嘉，无可指责，问心无愧。这是在极度艰难危险的时刻，愿意牺牲自己而成就他人的意缘继续，这是一种崇高的精神境界。

[Illuminating Intentionality]

When one has to sacrifice oneself, it is a noble sentiment to be able to foresee the positive value that self-sacrifice brings to others and the team, and to gain and integrate the intentionality. When people's abilities are limited and they are unable to bear a crisis, they step forward and sacrifice themselves to achieve success for everyone. Their spirit is praiseworthy, they are blameless, and they have a clear conscience. This is a continuation of the desire to sacrifice oneself for the achievements of others in extremely difficult and dangerous times of crisis. This is a noble spiritual state.

坎为水（卦二十九）　（坎下坎上）

Kan (In Danger), Water (Hexagram 29)　(Kan below, Kan above)

　　无论是个人还是集体，意向发动即在重重险难之中。意念必动，动则必危，人要学会在意向每时每刻发动之时，都与危险安然相处，这需要经过重复练习，让心意重复之后，逐渐熟悉危险，所谓"习于坎"。危险总是层层叠叠，如果处险而不知，则危险随时降临，如游泳、开车等等。意向之险，在与险平易相处；心意发动时常处险，久成自然，游走于险动之间。意向发动的危险，还表现在意念堕落非常迅速，而要升华则难上加难。意向发动即面对意向背后的危险。意向之险，还可以险设险，在思想中模拟危险的发生与应对。意念无时无刻不动，也就无时无刻不在险中，所以要学会用险止险，即所谓知险而制险，或知险而止险。当然，通常说来，要知道见险而止，要于险中控制意念行动的分寸。

　　Whether it is an individual or a collective, as soon as intention initiates, it is in the midst of many dangers. Intentions must move, and movements must lead to danger. People must learn to live with dangers every time when intentionality is initiated, which requires repeated practice. After repeating an intention, one gradually becomes familiar with the dangers, and this is called "getting used to obstacles." Danger is always one after another. If one is in danger and does not know it, danger can come at any time, such as when swimming, driving, etc. The danger of intention lies in its finding it easy to get along with danger; when intentionality is initiated, it is always in danger, and it becomes natural over time, wandering among dangers. The danger of initiating intentions is also reflected in the fact that intentions deteriorate very quickly and are even more difficult to sublimate. To initiate an intention is to face the danger behind the intention. Intentional risks can also be taken as risks, simulating the occurrence of and response to the danger in one's intention. If one's intentionality is always moving, one is always in danger, so one must learn to use danger to avoid danger, which is called knowing danger and avoiding danger, or knowing danger and stopping danger. Of course, generally speaking, one needs to know how to stop when danger arises and how to control one's intentions and actions in times of danger.

习坎，有孚，维心亨。行有尚。

《彖》曰：习坎，重险也。水流而不盈。行险而不失其信。"维心亨"，乃以刚中也。"行有尚"，往有功也。天险，不可升也。地险，山川丘陵也。王公设险以守其国。险之时用大矣哉！

《象》曰：水洊（jiàn）至，习坎。君子以常德行，习教事。

【明译】

坎卦象征险象环生，只要心怀诚信，坚定维系心念中的人天之意，就能亨通。勇往直前，努力上进，将会受到人们尊重崇尚。

《彖传》说：习坎是险象环生，好比川流不息的水却无法填满深不可测的陷阱一般（下卦坎为水，上卦坎为坎陷之地，水不断流入低洼之处，但坎陷于中，怎么也流不满）。坎为水，又为坎险，遭遇到险象环生、危机四伏的境域，内心仍然充满诚信通天的人天之意，不但能够诚信于人，而且能够诚信感天。只要坚定持守人天之意的信念，就会获得亨通，因为坎卦内心刚健实诚（中爻是刚爻），好比水流之地低洼艰险，但奔流入海之心刚健不改。坎卦从临变来，主爻从临的初九升进成为坎的九五，取得尊位，象征前往可以建功立业。天险（阴长阳消造成的衰朽败亡等天道运行的险难时势）是高不可升、无法逾越的。地险就是山川丘陵等能够阻挡人前行的险阻。君王公侯于是设置险要之关（如城墙、城濠等人险）来守卫自己的国家。险象环生的时机化作用实在太重大了！

《象传》说：水连续不断地流出来，险而又险，险象环生就是习坎卦的象征。君子学习水连续不断地流出来，奔流到海不复回的特点，要使仁德品行有恒常不变的刚强之性，不断学习操练，以实践好教化人民的事业。

Hexagram Kan (In Danger) symbolizes dangers. As long as one has integrity and firmly maintains the intentionality of humanity and heaven in one's heart-mind, one will be able to prosper. If one moves forward courageously and works hard, one will be respected and admired by people.

The *Judgment Commentary* (*Tuan Zhuan*) says: Hexagram Kan (In Danger) is surrounded by dangers, just like an endless flow of water that cannot fill an unfathomable trap (the lower Trigram Kan is water, the upper Trigram Kan is the place where the trap is set, and water keeps flowing into low-lying places, but if one is stuck in the middle, one will never be satisfied.) Trigram Kan is water, but it is also danger. When encountering a dangerous and crisis-ridden environment, one's heart-mind is still full of integrity and the intention of humanity and heaven. One can not only be honest with others, but also be honest with heaven. As long as one firmly adheres to the belief in the cosmological intentionality of humanity and heaven, one will achieve prosperity, because the intention of Hexagram Kan (In Danger) is strong and sincere (the middle line is a strong line), just like how the place where the water flows is low and full of danger, but the intention of rushing into the sea is strong and unchanging. Hexagram Kan (In Danger) comes from Hexagram Lin (Presence), and the main line rises from the Nine (*yang*/strong line) in the first place of Hexagram Lin (Presence) to the Nine (*yang*/strong line) in the fifth place of Hexagram Kan (In Danger), and obtains an honorable position, which symbolizes that one can make achievements if one goes forward. Heavenly dangers (dangerous situations in the movement of the *dao* of heaven, such as the decay and destruction caused by the growth of *yin* and disappearance of *yang*) are overwhelming and insurmountable. Earthly dangers are dangers such as mountains, rivers, and hills that can prevent people from advancing. Kings and princes then set up dangerous passes (such as city walls, city gates, etc.) to guard their countries. The temporalizing aspect of danger is so important!

The *Image Commentary* (*Xiang Zhuan*) says: When water flows out continuously, it is more and more dangerous. These dangers everywhere are the symbol of Hexagram Kan (In Danger). An exemplary person learns from the characteristics of water that flows out continuously and rushes to the sea without ever returning, and knows to make one's benevolent and virtuous character unchanging and strong, constantly learning and practicing the cause of educating the people.

【明意】

意念的本性是危险的行动性，因意念必行，而行必有险，所以人之意向性必须习于险境之中，虽险必行。意念之险，不在当下之险，而在暗险，即意向的感应结果之险，习险靠的是刚强的内心和强悍的意志力，时刻处险，当习以为常，也就善于化险为夷。人天之意在意向发动之中行于中道。要使仁德品行有恒常不变的刚强之性，需要不断学习操练，才能实践教化的事业，这是从坎（水）目标坚定和持之以恒的刚强当中学来。儒家向水学习的是内心刚强，道家向水学习的是柔弱处下；儒家是为了教化人民，道家是为了争胜成王；儒家是已经成王，之后如何运用为王之道；道家是没有成为王之前的道，是成王之道。儒家和道家，向水学习的是很不一样的品格。儒家学习的是人天之意，是人在任何时候都通于天的意向状态；道家学习的是自然之意，即顺应自然，无心顺道的境界，两种意向状态很不一样。修行修炼的就是一种意向的状态，并且长久保持下去。

意向之险用于用兵之道，如出其不意攻其不备等，但这些不等于不择手段。意念之行需要理性对自然情感加以克制，依照综合判断来展开意向性，但意向之涉险，又不能靠纯粹理性的推演，还有经验的、想象的成分，跟形象思维、关联思维密不可分。如果只是理性思维的描述,那么对于感觉、情感等非理性内容,以及进入对坎险先行结构的理解,也就不能在意念发动之前进入反思状态。

[Illuminating Intentionality]

The nature of intentions is dangerous action, because intentions must be carried out, and doing so must be risky, so people's intentionality must be accustomed to dangerous situations, and they must act despite the danger. The danger of intentions is not the danger of the moment, but the danger of hidden danger, that is, the danger of the result of the inductive resonance of intention. The habit of risk depends on a strong intention and strong willpower. When one is in danger all the time, if one can get used to it, one will be good at turning danger into ease. The cosmological intentionality of humanity and heaven follows the middle way when intention is initiated. To make benevolence and virtue have a constant and unchanging strong nature requires continuous learning and practice in order to practice the cause of education. This is learned from the firmness of the goal of Kan (water) and the perseverance of the strong. What Confucians learn from water is inner strength, while what Daoists learn from water is softness and staying beneath. Confucianism is about educating the people, while Daoism is about winning and becoming a king. Confucianism is about how to use the *dao* of the king after one has become a king, while Daoism is about how to be a king before one becomes a king, that is, how to become a king. Confucians and Daoists thus learn very different qualities from water. What Confucianism studies is the cosmological intentionality of humanity and heaven, the state of intentionality in which humanity is connected to heaven at all times; what Daoism studies is the intentionality of nature, that is, the state of conforming to nature and selflessly following the *dao*. These two states of intentionality are very different. Cultivation is a state of intentionality, and it should be maintained for a long time.

The dangers of intentionality are used in the use of troops, such as taking the enemy by surprise and attacking the unprepared, etc., but these do not mean that the ends justify the means. The act of thinking requires reason to restrain natural emotions and develop intentionality based on comprehensive judgment. However, the risk involved in intention cannot rely purely on rational deduction. It also has elements of experience and imagination, which are inseparable from image-thinking and relational thinking. If it is just a description of rational thinking, then irrational content such as sensations and emotions, as well as entering into an understanding of the transcendental structure of Kan/danger, cannot enter the state of reflection before an intention is launched.

初六:习坎,入于坎窞(dàn),凶。

《象》曰:"习坎入坎",失道凶也。

【明译】

初六:在险象环生重重坎陷之境,好像落入水底深不可测的洞穴里去了,极其凶险。

《象传》说:在双重的坎里,又落入坎下,指的是初六从五位下到初位,迷失道路,自己走向深渊之中,当然必有凶祸。

Six (*yin*/soft line) in the first place: In a dangerous situation with many obstacles, it can seem like falling into an unfathomable cave at the bottom of the water, which is extremely dangerous.

The *Image Commentary* (*Xiang Zhuan*) says: Being in a double trap and falling down a pit means that on the Six (*yin*/soft line) in the first place, one falls from the fifth position to the first position, loses one's way, and goes towards the abyss. Of course, there will be disaster.

【明意】

意向要面对的危险层层叠叠，躲过一劫可能又来一劫。如果对意向危险的评估不足，就可能真的被危险卷进去。所以要提前开始，未雨绸缪。孩子从小有应对危险的经验，长大就不容易吃亏，如应该让孩子学会应对骗局，否则长大不知如何应付。从小在安全范围内冒一点险，长大才会有经验，因人生圈套陷阱常见，意向提早预备应对可能的险难，反而能够避难，不预备险难的发生，却容易遇难。

[Illuminating Intentionality]

The dangers that one intends to face are piling up, and even if one escapes one disaster, another may come. If the intended hazard is not adequately assessed, one may truly become trapped by the danger, so start early and plan ahead. Children who have had experience in dealing with dangers since childhood will be less likely to suffer losses when they grow up. For example, children should learn to deal with scams, otherwise they will not know how to deal with them when they grow up. By taking some risks within a safe range from childhood, one can gain experience for when one grows up. Because scams and traps are common in life, if one intends to prepare in advance to deal with possible dangers, one will be able to avoid them. If one is not prepared for dangers, one can easily meet with difficulties.

九二：坎有险，求小得。

《象》曰："求小得"，未出中也。

【明译】

九二：在坎陷之境中困罹险难，只能于险情中谋取小得。

《象传》说：九二在险境之中求取，还可小有所获，因为九二虽然没有脱离险情，但在下卦中位，心思意念未出中道。

Nine (*yang*/strong line) in the second place: Trapped in danger in a difficult situation, one can only make small gains from the danger.

The *Image Commentary* (*Xiang Zhuan*) says: The Nine (*yang*/strong line) in the second place can still gain a little if one seeks it in a dangerous situation, because although the Nine (*yang*/strong line) in the second place is not out of danger, one is in the middle of the lower Trigram, and one's thoughts and intentions have not gone beyond the middle *dao*.

【明意】

从信用的角度说，九二在险境中保持人天之意，不出中道，还可以小有收获。信用一大部分来自家庭关系的延伸，与西方近现代平面的信用社会之信用有别。基于关系而延伸的信用，跟西方通过遵守规则积累信用不太一样。不过，不论是基于关系的，还是基于个人意向性的逐步积累，信用体系都要强调个人心念之善的积累，以及与情境的互动。

面对生命的绝境，意念之行仍可以充满生机，也可以给他人他境带去生机。意念之存续的核心是生生之机，即使在极度危险的境遇中，存续和保养生机仍是第一位的。在生存的存在与虚无之间，人还是要努力建立"善"；在自我与虚无之间，生机渺茫的关键时刻，人更要努力确立自我，等待时机而行动。

[Illuminating Intentionality]

From the point of view of trust, the Nine (*yang*/strong line) in the second place can still achieve small gains by maintaining the intentionality of humanity and heaven in dangerous situations and staying within the middle *dao*. A large part of trust comes from the extension of family relationships, which is different from the trust in flat modern Western trust societies. Trust extended based on relationships is different from the accumulation of trust in the West through compliance with rules. However, whether it is based on relationships or the gradual accumulation of personal intentionality, any trust system must emphasize the accumulation of personal kindness and interaction with emotional situations.

Faced with a desperate situation of life, the journey of intentions can still be full of vitality, and it can also bring vitality to other people and situations. The core of the survival of intentions is the vitality of production. Even in extremely dangerous situations, survival and maintenance of vitality is still the first priority. Between existence and nothingness, people still have to work hard to establish "goodness;" between self and nothingness, at the critical moment when vitality is slim, people have to work hard to establish themselves and wait for an opportunity to act.

六三：来之坎坎，险且枕。入于坎窞，勿用。

《象》曰："来之坎坎"，终无功也。

【明译】

六三：上下都是险难重重，进退维谷，只是险中还有所依靠。已经陷入危险陷阱深处，实在无法施展才用。

《象传》说：来去都是坎陷之险难，说明六三最终都是在做无用之功（无论如何挣扎都走不出谷底，有劲也用不上）。

Six (*yin*/soft line) in the third place: There are many dangers and difficulties both above and below, and one is in a dilemma about advancing or retreating, but one still has something to rely on in the danger. However, one has fallen deep into a dangerous trap and is really unable to use one's talents.

The *Image Commentary* (*Xiang Zhuan*) says: Coming and going are both dangers and difficulties, which shows that the Six (*yin*/soft line) in the third place is ultimately making useless efforts (no matter how hard one struggles, one can't get out of the bottom of the valley, and is unable to use one's energy).

【明意】

本爻的意向进入无法摆脱的绝望境遇，险之又险。此时的意向无比绝望，一个又一个险境连环而生，无法摆脱。人在绝望之中，如果放弃阳意的希望，则可能走上放弃生命的自杀道路，所以在绝望中还当保持希望的光明。此爻在绝望当中的希望，来自九二，九二给予六三致命危险当中最具牺牲精神的拯救，用自己的生命来延续六三的生机。

[Illuminating Intentionality]

This line has entered a desperate situation that cannot be escaped, and it is increasingly dangerous. The intention at this time is extremely desperate, and dangers appear one after another, making it impossible to escape. In despair, if one gives up the hope of *yang*/positive intentionality, one may embark on the road of suicide to give up one's life, so one should keep the light of hope in despair. The hope in despair of this line comes from the Nine (*yang*/strong line) in the second place, which gives the Six (*yin*/soft line) in the third place the most sacrificial spirit of rescue from fatal danger, using its own life to continue the Six (*yin*/soft line) in the third place's vitality.

六四：樽酒簋（guǐ）贰，用缶。纳约自牖（yǒu），终无咎。

《象》曰："樽酒簋贰"，刚柔际也。

【明译】

六四：一樽薄酒，两簋供品，选瓦缶作祭器，（非常敬慎地）从窗户纳进素朴的祭品，最终不会有咎害。

《象传》说：用一杯薄酒，两碗糙饭（的素朴祭品顺服地祭献），因为六四在刚爻与柔爻交际之处（故四爻之意向要刚柔适中）。

Six (*yin*/soft line) in the fourth place: One bottle of light wine, two baskets of offerings, choosing an earthenware vessel as the sacrificial vessel, and (very carefully) accepting plain offerings through the window, there will be no harm in the end.

The *Image Commentary* (*Xiang Zhuan*) says: Use a cup of thin wine and two bowls of rice (a simple sacrifice that is obediently sacrificed), because the Six (*yin*/soft line) in the fourth place is at the intersection of strong and soft lines (so the intention of the fourth line must be moderate between strong and soft).

【明意】

此爻为了出险，需要学习柔弱处险之道，以弱女子祭祀求福之心意行世。身处危险境地，需要竭尽全力抓住能够摆脱危险的机会和方式，而最重要的，就是在意向发动处要柔弱、真诚、质朴地顺服九五。逆境之中需要千方百计搞好跟他人的关系，哪怕一点点机会都应该争取，抓住，即使一杯酒、两碗饭这样简单的东西，身处逆境时都不应该嫌弃，而应该从粗茶淡饭当中磨练自己谦柔居下的品行。在身居逆境之时，彼此的交情是患难之交。

六四之爱要克服其意识当中无可把握的虚无感。在没有具体的爱的对象之前，其祈求的爱难以克服虚无感。可见，爱的意念之行，需要有具体的爱意之缘，方能克服虚无感。在重重坎险之境中，意念之行当极度低调小心，以不激发意境之反作用为宜，危难时刻，少女出嫁前那种小心温柔，祭礼求福的心态才是意念之行的合适状态。

[Illuminating Intentionality]

In this line, in order to escape from danger, one needs to learn the *dao* of being weak and existing in danger, and move through the world with the intentionality of weak women offering sacrifices to seek blessings. When one is in a dangerous situation, one needs to do one's best to seize the opportunities and methods that can escape from danger. The most important thing is to submissively, sincerely and plainly obey the Nine (*yang*/strong line) in the fifth place where intention is initiated. In adversity, one needs to do everything one can to build good relationships with others, and one should strive for and seize even the slightest opportunity. Even if it is as simple as a glass of wine or two bowls of rice, one should not despise it when one is in adversity. Instead, one should learn from it through simple meals to practice one's humble and submissive character. In times of adversity, mutual friendship is often difficult to find.

The Six (*yin*/soft line) in the fourth place must overcome the uncontrollable sense of emptiness in its consciousness. Before there is a specific love object, the love one prays for cannot overcome the feeling of emptiness. It can be seen that the act of intentional love requires a concrete love relationship in order to overcome the feeling of emptiness. In a dangerous situation, the movement of intentions should be extremely low-key and careful, so as not to trigger a reaction from the intentional context. In times of crisis, the cautious and gentle attitude of a girl before she gets married and the mentality of offering sacrifices and praying for blessings are the appropriate state for the movement of intentions.

九五：坎不盈，祇（chī）既平，无咎。

《象》曰："坎不盈"，中未大也。

【明译】

九五：水流入坎里，没有满溢出来，只有等（水中沙洲）到了跟坎陷齐平的程度，这时候应该没有太大危险了。

《象传》说：水还没有盈满溢出坎陷之地，这是因为九五在上卦中位，居中能处中道，但自求脱险之功无法光大。

Nine (*yang*/strong line) in the fifth place: The water flows into the sunken area and does not overflow. when it (the sandbar in the water) reaches the same level as the sunken area, there should not be much danger.

The *Image Commentary* (*Xiang Zhuan*) says: The water has not yet filled up and overflowed from the sunken place. This is because the Nine (*yang*/strong line) in the fifth place is in the middle of the upper Trigram. If one is in the middle, one can find the middle way, but one's own efforts to escape danger cannot be achieved.

【明意】

身心陷在坎险之中，危险和委屈都只得隐忍接受。分秒之间，它们全部因我的意念之行而成为实在，可是，危险之中，已经顾不上我自己的实在性，因为求生的本能压过了对自我实在性的追求。面对周围连环发生的重重危险，"我"需要在危险中生存下去，至于是否有信心建立不同于虚无的真实人生，是求生成功之后的问题。这样看来，人生的实在性，其实很难建立在层层叠叠的危险上面。换言之，在危险重重、自身难保的人生当中，无所谓真实自我的建立问题，也谈不上自我修养的问题。

[Illuminating Intentionality]

One's body and intentionality are trapped in danger, and the dangers and grievances have to be endured. In a matter of seconds, they all became reality due to the actions of one's intentions. However, in the midst of danger, one can no longer care about one's own reality, because the instinct to survive overcomes the pursuit of one's own reality. Facing the many surrounding dangers emerging, one needs to survive the dangers. As for whether one has the confidence to build a real life different from nothingness, this is a question for after the success of survival. From this point of view, the reality of life is actually difficult to build upon layers of dangers. In other words, in a life that is full of dangers where one cannot protect oneself, there is no question of establishing a true self, nor can there be any question of self-cultivation.

上六：系用徽纆（mò），寘（zhì）于丛棘，三岁不得，凶。

《象》曰：上六失道，"凶三岁"也。

【明译】

上六：用重重的绳子捆绑起来之后，被投入犹如荆棘丛生的监狱之中，三年都得不到释放，非常凶险。

《象传》说：上六偏离正道，迷失了道路，凶险的境遇将持续三年之久。

Six (*yin*/soft line) in the top place: After being tied up with heavy ropes, one is like being thrown into a prison full of thorns and cannot be released for three years. This is very dangerous.

The *Image Commentary* (*Xiang Zhuan*) says: The Six (*yin*/soft line) in the top place deviates from the right *dao* and loses its way. The dangerous situation will last for three years.

【明意】

坎卦描述了一个拼命逃生的逃犯的心路历程。从逃犯挣扎出险的人生经历来说，其个人的经历，最后必然要走向虚无，为了生存，为了自由而拼命挣扎，但无法摆脱如流星一般的命运，挣扎到底有什么意义？可是不挣扎，没有生机的逃犯，马上就要面临死亡实实在在的威胁，这会让自己恐惧。更不要说自由人的欢乐和盛宴，终将消散无形，所以追求精神性的实在、不变、永恒的柏拉图式形上学家，也会对人生与宇宙的虚无感到迷惑和沮丧。

坎卦也说明，人生而在危险之中，意念发动即与危险相伴，意念对危险存在的现实性理解，都来自经验，对危险存在的预见性也来自经验，所以要依靠经验来做好应对危险的预案，才能防患于未然。坎卦描述了出离危险的艰难，学习坎卦需要印证自己的人生体验，才可能知道，如果出现最危险的情况应该如何应付，这就回到坎卦的本旨——习坎——意念习于坎险，自己主动避险是可能的，也是需要自己操练的。从人生逃离危险旅程的角度来说，人生时刻好比逃犯的境遇一般，险象环生，但全卦到最后还是可以回到卦辞"行有尚"的本旨：只要勇往直前，努力上进，最终将会受到人们尊重崇尚，而这种崇尚，其实是人面对现实层层叠叠的危险表现出来的意念迎难而行的精神力量。

[Illuminating Intentionality]

Hexagram Kan (In Danger) describes the mental journey of a fugitive trying to escape. Judging from the life experience of a fugitive struggling to escape danger, his personal experience must eventually lead to nothingness. He struggles desperately for survival and freedom, but he cannot escape his fate, which is like a shooting star. What is the point of struggling? However, a fugitive who does not struggle and has no chance of survival will soon face the real threat of death, which will make him fearful. Not to mention that the joy and feast of free people will eventually dissipate into nothingness, so even Platonic metaphysicians who pursue a spiritual reality of changelessness, and eternity will also be confused and dejected by the nothingness of human life and the cosmos.

Hexagram Kan (In Danger) also explains that people are born in danger, and the initiation of intentions is accompanied by danger. The intentions' realistic understanding of the existence of danger comes from experience, and the foresight of the existence of danger also comes from experience, so we must rely on experience to formulate a plan to deal with it, one which can nip danger in the bud. Hexagram Kan (In Danger) describes the difficulty of escaping from danger. To learn Hexagram Kan (In Danger), one needs to verify one's own life experience so that one can know how to deal with the most dangerous situations. This goes back to the original purpose of Hexagram Kan (In Danger)—intention being habituated to dangers—as it is possible to get used to risks and take the initiative to avoid risks on one's own, and one needs to practice on one's own. From the perspective of life as a journey of escaping from danger, every moment of life is like the situation of a fugitive, surrounded by dangers. However, in the end, the whole hexagram can still return to the original purpose of the hexagram words: "advancing will be respected." As long as one moves forward bravely and works hard, one will eventually be respected. People give their respect and admiration, and this kind of admiration is actually the spiritual power of people's intention to face the difficulties in the face of the layered dangers in reality.

离为火（卦三十）　（离下离上）

Li (Illumination), Fire (Hexagram 30)　(Li below, Li above)

　　离险必附着，无所附着则不可能脱离坎陷之境遇。文明帮助人们脱离险境，但文明有其限度，创造力也要适可而止。经历大坎（洪水）的洗礼，才能有光明的文明，才能有教化之教，即《易》教之教。坎是苦中苦，离是明中明。

　　平静的水面之下，暗藏危险。心意一动，险无处不在。火无形意，火意无形无象，而力量至大至刚。水意无形，但可随意赋形，柔弱而可被赋意。火比水更本源，火力是意的力量，而火之缘也如意的缘，不可能凭空存在。如火必有缘，而意向之动也必有所附丽为意缘。有缘人生之意念发动和意义状态才得以明白。

　　意在先天与后天之间，但意向必是后天，是向让意明朗化（manifested），而且向明就一直显明下去。所谓继明，是人的意经向而能明于四方天下，治理国家的大人要持续不断地以光明的人天之意照临天下四方。

　　To escape from danger, one must adhere. If there is nothing to adhere to, it is impossible to escape from a difficult situation. Civilization helps people to escape from danger, but civilization has its limits and creativity must also be limited. Only after experiencing the baptism of the great submerging (Hexagram Kan, flood) can there be a bright civilization and the teaching of enlightenment, that is, the teaching of the *Book of Changes*. Kan is suffering among the sufferings, while Li is brightness among the bright.

　　Beneath the calm water, danger lurks. As soon as one's intentionality moves, danger is everywhere.

Fire has no formed intentionality, and the intentionality of fire is formless and imageless, but its power is great and strong. The intentionality of water is formless, but it can be given form following intentions, since it is soft and can be given intentionality. Fire is more original than water, the power of fire is the power of intentionality, and the dependent co-arising of fire is also the dependent co-arising of realized intentions, which cannot exist in a vacuum. Just like fire, there must be dependent co-arising, and the movement of intention must also be attached to some intentional dependent co-arising. It is the destiny of intention. Only with dependent co-arising can the initiation of intentions and the state of intentionality in life be understood.

Intentionality is between transcendental and empirical, but intentions must be empirical. They are manifested, and will continue to be manifested. The "inherited illumination" spoken of here means that people's intentions can be made clear to the world in all directions. The great people who govern the country must continue to enlighten the world with the inherited illumination of the intentionality of humanity and heaven.

离，利贞。亨。畜牝牛吉。

《彖》曰：离，丽也。日月丽乎天，百谷草木丽乎土。重明以丽乎正，乃化成天下。柔丽乎中正，故"亨"，是以"畜牝牛吉"也。

《象》曰：明两作，离。大人以继明照于四方。

【明译】

离卦象征光明附丽，有利于持守正道，做事亨通，如畜养母牛吉祥。

《彖传》说：卦名离是附丽的意思，譬如太阳和月亮附丽在天上，百谷草木要附着在土地上。上下卦都是离为明，离卦有双重之明，明而又明，光明地指引万物附丽到正道上去，就能教化天下，成就人间文明昌盛，犹如日月附丽于天，光辉昌明。离卦从遯卦变来，遯卦初六与九五换位变为离卦。离卦主爻六五的推移说，是柔爻柔顺地依附在刚爻的正中，得中又得正，所以亨通。因为柔爻的运动好像具有母牛那样温顺的德性，所以畜养母牛可获吉祥。

《象传》说：下卦离为明，上卦离又为明，是光明接连不断地升起来，这就是象征着光明附丽于高空的离卦。治理国家的大人要持续不断地以光明的人天之意照临天下四方。

Hexagram Li (Illumination) symbolizes light and beauty, which is helpful for adhering to the right *dao* and making things prosper, just like raising cows, which is auspicious.

The *Judgment Commentary (Tuan Zhuan)* says: The name of Hexagram Li (Illumination) means attached beauty. For example, the sun and the moon attach beauty to the sky, and a multitude of grains and trees attach to the earth. Both the upper and lower Trigrams are Li, meaning bright, so Hexagram Li (Illumination) has a dual brightness, which is bright and brighter again. It brightly guides the myriad things to attach beauty to the right *dao*, which can educate the world and make human civilization prosperous, just like the sun and the moon attach beauty to the heavens and shine brightly. Hexagram Li (Illumination) changes from Hexagram Dun (Retreat), with the Six (*yin*/soft line) in the first place and the Nine (*yang*/strong line) in the fifth place of Hexagram Dun (Retreat) changing positions to form Hexagram Li (Illumination). Judging from the progression of the main Six (*yin*/soft line) in the fifth place in Hexagram Li (Illumination), the soft line is attached to the upright middle of the strong line. It is in the middle and upright, so it is prosperous. Because the movement of the soft line seems to have the docile virtue of a cow, raising cows will bring good fortune.

The *Image Commentary* (*Xiang Zhuan*) says: The lower Trigram Li is bright, and the upper Trigram Li is bright again, so these are lights that rise one after another, and this is Hexagram Li (Illumination), which symbolizes the light attached to the sky. The great people who govern the country must continue to enlighten the world with the inherited illumination of the intentionality from humanity and heaven.

【明意】

离卦说明，持续的光明把私意照亮，自知隐蔽私意而不发，否则，即使有知识，意向所至，也易自私而邪。千秋文明大业来自心念长明。有知识者应有良好的品德，要能够忍辱负重，以附丽之意衬托意向缘生的情境，对如日月一般彰明意缘的发动，这样才能光明广远，助天道生生而成就文明系统的创造。文明体系作为心意之发的实化过程，心意发动必有所依附，如所附不正，则心意皆乱，所以不仅发动要正，而且所附也要正。世界与心之本体相通，物心本体如一非二。人之意向若无缘，则不可能明白自己意向之意义。缘是意向实化的对象，而意向的生生实化之过程本身，对人的生存和发展这个存在本体性来说，可谓动态的实体性存在。

[Illuminating Intentionality]

Hexagram Li (Illumination) explains that continuous light illuminates private intentions, and knows spontaneously to hide private intentions and not express them. Otherwise, even if one has knowledge and the intention has a direction, it is easy to be selfish and evil. The great cause of civilization for thousands of years comes from the long-term enlightenment of the mind. A knowledgeable person should have good moral character, be able to endure humiliation and bear heavy burdens, use beautiful intentionality to set off the situation where intention arises, and initiate intention as brightly as the sun and the moon. Only in this way can they be bright and far-reaching, help with the production of the heavenly *dao*, and achieve the creation of a civilized system. A civilization system is the realization process of intentions, and intentions must be attached to something. If these attachments are not correct, the intentions will be chaotic, so not only must the intentions be correct, but also their attachments. The world and the original substance of the heart-mind are connected, and the original substance of things and the heart-mind is single and not dual. If a person's intentions have no dependent co-arising, it is impossible for one to understand the meaning of one's own intention. Dependent co-arising is the object of the concretization of intention, and the process of the creation and concretization of intention itself can be said to be a dynamic substantial existence from the ontology of human existence and development.

初九：履错然。敬之，无咎。

《象》曰："履错"之"敬"，以辟（bì）咎也。

【明译】

初九：践履行事合乎礼仪，错落而有光采，心怀恭敬，小心谨慎，不会有什么过错。

《象传》说：践履行事合乎礼仪而有文采带出来的内心恭敬，可以避免受到不必要的伤害。

Nine (*yang*/strong line) in the first place: Act according to ritual propriety, be well-organized and glorious, be respectful and careful, and you will not make any mistakes.

The *Image Commentary* (*Xiang Zhuan*) says: Practicing affairs in accord with ritual propriety and having inner respect brought out by literary talent can avoid unnecessary harm.

【明意】

离卦开启新的文明征程，而每一个文明的历程都不是一帆风顺的。文明从敬的意向开始，即要把对礼仪之恭敬作为文明之始。敬是为了避免不必要的伤害，即谦恭安静而避免伤害。

文明从"知识就是力量"这样的认识开始，但文明的力量也有可怕的反作用，如科学技术过度发展，可能给人类生存带来无法挽回的灾难。这里是说，人的意向发动之间要有恭敬之心，对他人意向的恭敬，最后上溯到对上天和超自然力量的敬畏之心。

[Illuminating Intentionality]

Hexagram Li (Illumination) starts a new civilization journey, and the journey of a civilization never begins with smooth sailing. Civilization begins with the intention of respect, that is, respect for ritual propriety should be regarded as the beginning of civilization. Respect is to avoid unnecessary harm, that is, to be humble and quiet to avoid harm.

Civilization began with the understanding that "knowledge is power," but the power of civilization also has terrible side-effects. For example, excessive development of science and technology may bring irreparable disasters to human existence. What this means is that people must be respectful when initiating their intentions. Respect for other people's intentions can ultimately be traced back to the heart-mind's awe of the heavens and of supernatural power.

六二：黄离，元吉。

《象》曰："黄离，元吉"，得中道也。

【明译】

六二：黄色美丽中正的文明，实在是大吉大利。

《象传》说：黄色美丽中正的文明，实在是大吉大利，因为六二在下卦中位，行为中正而行中道。

Six (*yin*/soft line) in the second place: Yellow, beautiful and upright civilization is truly auspicious.

The *Image Commentary* (*Xiang Zhuan*) says: Yellow, beautiful and upright civilization is auspicious because the Six (*yin*/soft line) in the second place is in the middle of the lower Trigram, and its behavior is upright and follows the middle way.

【明意】

中华文明以土之黄色为得中道之大吉大利的文明。六二象征中华文明传承的是炎黄子孙亮丽的文明之道。离为文明，象征人间的文明通于太阳之光明，是人心在世间的光明创造，各个文明都是不同族群的人心的共同创造，没有高下，应该彼此尊重，和平对话。文明对话让精神文明碰撞而光彩四溢。文明对话是大势所趋，世界各个历史时期都有不同程度的文明对话。

人类的文明系统当中，如果人造过度，则虚幻意味太强，文明体系会变得虚幻不实，虽看起来光彩照人，但其实如梦幻泡影。美德和文明都靠生命力量支撑，文明的建构和存续，当通过精神伟大的哲人，文明系统才可以提升精神存续之力，彪炳后世。其中最重要的应当是哲学家对文明的深思，因其征服古往今来文明系统之精神力量的魄力、深度和广度。哲人的思想精髓为不同的时代立向和定调，所以文明世界建构可以是物质性的，但其影响则必然是精神性的。历史上没有精神的文明，必然烟消云散，不复存在，而有精神的文明，即使物质的形式消散，也往往为世人缅怀。

[Illuminating Intentionality]

Chinese civilization regards the yellow color of earth as a civilized foundation that brings good fortune and prosperity. The Six (*yin*/soft line) in the second place symbolizes the inheritance of Chinese civilization and the brilliant civilization of the descendants of the Yellow and Flame Emperors. Illumination (Li) as civilization symbolizes that human civilization is connected to the light of the sun, and is a bright creation of human intentionality in the world. Each civilization is a joint creation of the human intentions of different ethnic groups, so there is no superiority, and should be mutual respect and peaceful dialogue. Civilized dialogue allows spiritual civilizations to collide together and shine with brilliance. Dialogue among civilizations is a general trend, and there are varying degrees of dialogue between civilizations in various historical periods of the world.

In the human civilization system, if there is excessive artificiality, the illusion will be too strong, and the civilization system will become unreal. Although it may look glorious, it is actually like a dream. Virtue and civilization are both supported by the power of life. The construction and survival of civilization can only be achieved through spiritually great philosophers, so that the civilization system can enhance the power of spiritual survival and shine in future generations. The most important in this should be the philosopher's deep reflections on civilization, because of their courage, depth and breadth of spiritual power to conquer the civilization system throughout the ages. The essence of philosophers' thoughts set the direction and tone for different eras. Therefore, the construction of a civilized world can be material, but its influence must be spiritual. Civilizations without spirituality in history will inevitably disappear and cease to exist, while civilizations with spirituality, even if their material forms disappear, are often remembered by the world.

九三：日昃（zè）之离。不鼓缶而歌，则大耋（dié）之嗟，凶。

《象》曰："日昃之离"，何可久也？

【明译】

九三：日暮太阳西斜，垂挂在天上，象征老之将至，如果不顺其自然，敲着瓦盆唱歌自乐，那迟暮之年就只能发出老暮穷衰的嗟叹，这本身就是一件凶险的事。

《象传》说：太阳已经西斜，虽然还挂在西天，可是怎么会长得了呢？

Nine (*yang*/strong line) in the third place: At dusk, the sun sets in the west and hangs in the heaven, which symbolizes the coming of old age. If one doesn't let nature take its course and only enjoys oneself by singing and banging on a pot, then in one's twilight years one can only sigh about old age and poverty. This in itself is alarming.

The *Image Commentary* (*Xiang Zhuan*) says: The sun has set in the west. Although it is still hanging in the western sky, how long can it remain?

【明意】

文明来自每时每刻的自我选择，是构成一生的精神创造拼出的图景。意识当朝创造的方向努力，不要留下遗憾，所以对时光的自我管理是关键。人的精神交流就是从时空中汲取养料。生命是一个意念向度接一个向度的延续。人可以选择，因为意念向度是时时刻刻的自我决定，同样的时间状态，不同人有不同的创造方式，心意的实化和创造，既不由他人决定，也不为外在超越的造物主决定。如果明白人生到最后不过是意念向度的矢量汇集，那人就更当努力自我决定，因为生命即是当下一念的选择，而文明正是这种当下意向选择的汇聚状态。

[Illuminating Intentionality]

Civilization comes from self-selection at every moment, and is a picture spelled out by spiritual creation that constitutes a lifetime. Consciousness should work hard in the direction of creation and not leave behind any regrets, so self-management of time is key. Human spiritual communication draws nourishment from time and space. Life is a continuation of one dimension of intention after another. People can choose, because the dimension of intentions is self-determined moment by moment. In the same temporal state, different people have different ways of creation. The concretization and creation of intentionality are determined neither by others nor by an external and transcendent Creator. If we understand that life is in the end nothing more than a vector convergence of intentional dimensions, then people should work harder to make decisions on their own, because life is the choice of the next intention, and civilization is a state of convergence of this current intentional choice.

九四：突如其来如，焚如，死如，弃如。
《象》曰："突如其来如"，无所容也。
【明译】
九四：太阳升起的时候，好像突然之间来到这个样子（升起火红的朝霞），然后升到高空像烈焰熊熊燃烧，但慢慢衰弱好像变得死一般寂灭，到头来似乎可以被抛弃扔掉一样。

《象传》说：太阳升起的时候，好像突然之间来到这个样子（升起火红的朝霞），好像不能见容于世，不被别人接纳。

Nine (yang/strong line) in the fourth place. When the sun rises, it seems to suddenly look like this (a fiery red morning glow), then rises high into the sky and burns like a blazing flame, but then slowly weakens and seems to become as dead as ashes. In the end, it seems like it could just be cast aside.

The *Image Commentary* (*Xiang Zhuan*) says: When the sun rises, it seems to suddenly become like this (a fiery red morning glow rising), as if it cannot be seen or contained in the world and cannot be accepted by others.

【明意】
九四的意向升起有行动的勇气，但欠缺控制意向的智慧。毕竟意向每时每刻都是突然发生的，也每时每刻好像无处安身，因意向一定是突然实化的。如果不被接纳，那么先天善性就不可能凝结，所以意向的延续要有某种包容性和接纳性，才可能延续先天的善性。如果在每一个意向中拒绝先天善性，那么就当弃之。可见，"继善成性"是天道自然之善的积累继续成性，是积累天道自然之善而凝聚成向善的意性，只是天道之善的自然演进有其自然之力道，人心之善力图改变自然力道推动的自然之善，其实很难。

[Illuminating Intentionality]
When the intention of the Nine (yang/strong line) in the fourth place arises, one has the courage to act, but lacks the wisdom to control the intention. After all, intentions occur suddenly every moment, and at all times they seem to have no place to remain, because intentions must be concretized suddenly. If they are not accepted, then the transcendental goodness cannot condense. Therefore, the continuation of intention must have some kind of inclusivity and acceptance, so that

transcendental goodness can be continued. If transcendental goodness is rejected in every intention, then it should be abandoned. It can be seen that "inheriting the good and completing inherent nature" is the accumulation and continuous development of the natural goodness of the heavenly *dao*. It is the accumulation of the natural goodness of the heavenly *dao* and condenses into the intention to do good. It is just that the natural evolution of the goodness of the heavenly *dao* has its own natural power, while it is actually difficult for the goodness of the human heart-mind to strive to change the natural goodness driven by natural forces.

六五：出涕沱若，戚嗟若，吉。

《象》曰：六五之"吉"，离王公也。

【明译】

六五：眼泪哗哗，涕泗滂沱，悲戚地嗟伤悲叹，但最后逢凶化吉。

《象传》说：六五这一爻如此悲切最后还能逢凶化吉，是因为卦变之后能够附丽于王公。（遯卦的上卦原来是乾为君王，卦变中，六五从初位升进到乾的中位，象征依附到王公的身上，所以会逢凶化吉）。

Six (*yin*/soft line) in the fifth place: Tears stream down in floods, and people lament again and again, but in the end the disaster turns into a blessing.

The *Image Commentary* (*Xiang Zhuan*) says: The reason why the Six (*yin*/soft line) in the fifth place line is so sad yet can turn misfortune into good fortune in the end is because, after the hexagram-changes, it can attach itself to the prince. (The upper Trigram of Hexagram Dun (Retreat) was originally Qian as the king. During the hexagram-changes, the Six (*yin*/soft line) in the fifth place is promoted from the first position to the middle position of Qian, symbolizing attachment to the prince, so it turns misfortune into good fortune).

【明意】

文明只有依附于德才能长久，离开谦卑顺服天道，刚硬不化的结果只能是自取灭亡。转而悔改，回归天道才是正道。要化险为夷，逢凶化吉，要靠六五穿过血与火的战场，突然形势大变，升到君王边上，可以说足够幸运，意向随境而迁，是意向的外缘突然发生了变化，也是修来的。如果因为繁忙而忘了修养自己，不知道培养根本，正如六五只是受到不正当吹捧，那就会越来越空虚。

[Illuminating Intentionality]

Civilization can only last long if it relies on virtue. Without humility and obedience to the heavenly *dao*, the result of stubbornness can only be self-destruction, so turning to repentance and returning to the heavenly *dao* is the right way. To turn danger into ease, and disaster into good fortune, one has to rely on the Six (*yin*/soft line) in the fifth place to pass through the battlefield of blood and fire. Suddenly the situation changes drastically, and one rises to the side of the king. It can be said that one

355

is fortunate enough. The intention changes with the situation, and the outer conditions of intention suddenly arise, while changes are also caused by cultivation. If one forgets to cultivate oneself because one is busy and does not know how to cultivate the fundamentals, just like the Six (*yin*/soft line) in the fifth place is only unfairly praised, things will become more and more empty.

上九：王用出征，有嘉折首，获匪其丑，无咎。

《象》曰："王用出征"，以正邦也。

【明译】

上九：君王出兵征伐，建立嘉功伟绩，但只斩杀敌方首领，不俘获敌军的从犯，不会有祸患。

《象传》说：君王出师征伐，是为了正治邦国，（不是为了耀武扬威，滥杀无辜）。

Nine (*yang*/strong line) in the top place: The king sends out troops to conquer and win great achievements, but only kills the enemy's leaders and does not capture their accomplices, so there will be no disaster.

The *Image Commentary* (*Xiang Zhuan*) says: The reason why kings go out to conquer is to correct the wrong doings and govern countries properly (not to show off their power and kill innocent people indiscriminately).

【明意】

离卦主讲文明之心意的形成过程。意向性需要附丽于意缘。而控制意缘，即制心制意，亦即制命。一个人声望的累积，不能有一点点私心，是靠领导众人走正道而积累起来的。意能之阴阳，有能量有力量，代表意向性的相续，一个意向接着一个意向连绵起来。自然情境本有其力，意能领悟其能，意能流动必有所向。意念是自然力的一种延伸，参与宇宙运化之力而能有所改变，意向不断随缘而生变。人的念力之巨大，可以改变自然的人生，即主动发动意念战胜自己，犹如驾驭青春激情的野马一般，所以驯马就是训练和调整马的意向与人前进的意向之间的协调。

人天之意的境界是心灵感天动地，达到如同没有心灵本体，自然而然，意向随顺天地，如同没有意向的境界，回到天地自然之态去。从这个意义上说，中国古人的文明观念，是自然文明观念，即人造的文明系统，需要跟天地自然之道完全贯通，不可以由私心安排而建立。真正的文明是"推天道以明人事"，其实跟西方宗教的精神，在人间建立天堂，有异曲同工之妙。只是中国的代天立言，是一种无神论的通天，而按西方宗教精神，教堂等都是给神的献祭，人提升自己的创造力，竭力匹配上帝的完美创造，结果人精益求精地创造出一套与上帝和通的文明体系，这跟中国天人合一，物我不分，人事通于天道的和谐精神相通。

第二章　易经明意
——爻意分说（上经）

[Illuminating Intentionality]

Hexagram Li (Illumination) focuses on the formation process of civilization's intentionality. Intentionality needs to be attached to intentional dependent co-arising, and to control intentional dependent co-arising is to control minds and intentions, which is also to control destinies. A person's accumulation of reputation cannot be selfish at all, and is accumulated by leading others to follow the right *dao*. The *yin* and *yang* of intentional capacity have energy and power, representing the continuity of intentionality, one intention following another. Natural situations have their own power, intentionality can understand its capabilities, and the flow of intentionality must have a direction. Intentions are an extension of natural force, and they can be changed by participating in the transformation of the cosmos, with intentions continuing to change according to circumstances. The power of human intentions is so great that it can change natural human life, that is, actively mobilizing intentions to overcome oneself, just like harnessing the wild horses full of youthful passion. Therefore, horse training is also to train and adjust the coordination between the horse's intentions and the person's intention to move forward.

The spiritual plane of the intentionality of humanity and heaven is a state where the mind moves the heaven and the earth, reaching the point where it is as if there is no original substance of the mind, and intentions follow the heavens and the earth naturally. This is like a state where there is no intention, and returns to the natural state of heaven and earth. In this sense, the ancient Chinese concept of civilization is a concept of natural civilization, that is, a man-made civilization system that must be completely connected with the natural *dao* of heaven and earth and cannot be established by selfish arrangements. True civilization means to "extend the heavenly *dao* to illuminate human affairs." In fact, this is similar to the spirit of Western religions in establishing heaven on earth, except that the Chinese idea of setting up words to speak for heaven is an atheistic way of connecting with heaven. According to the spirit of Western religions, churches and the like are offerings to divinity. People enhance their creativity and try their best to match God's perfect creation. As a result, people strive for excellence to create a civilized system that is in harmonious connection with God. This is consistent with the Chinese spirit of harmony in which heaven and humanity are one, things are not separated from the self, and human affairs are connected to the heavenly *dao*.

第三章　易经明意
——爻意分说（下经）

Chapter Ⅲ Illuminating the *Classic of Changes* and Its Intentionality: Exposition of the Intentionality of the Lines (Part II)

泽山咸（卦三十一）　（艮下兑上）

Xian (Resonance), Lake and Mountain (Hexagram 31)　(Gen below, Dui above)

卦名咸，按象辞的解释是"感也"，即相互感应。《杂卦》说"速也"，指的是快速感应。《序卦》说是"有男女然后有夫妇"，是男女之间快速感应成为夫妇。从字形上讲，咸就是阴阳之间自然产生的快速感应。阴阳相吸，这种感应无须特别留意，自然而然就会产生，阴阳之间相互吸引是自然规律，所以"亨"通，但要感应得正才有利，所以利于守持正固。有相互感应的基础，娶妻才可获吉祥。

The name of Hexagram Xian (Resonance) means mutual affection and response. *Miscellaneous Characteristics of the Hexagrams* states it is "speedy," which refers to quick affection and response. *Sequence of the Hexagrams* says that "there are men and women and then there are couples," which means that men and women quickly have affection and become husband and wife. In terms of the form of the character, Hexagram Xian (Resonance) is a natural and rapid response between *yin* and *yang*, in which *yin* and *yang* attract each other. This kind of induction does not require special attention, and will happen naturally. The mutual attraction between *yin* and *yang* is a natural law, so it is "prosperous." However, it is beneficial to have an upright affective response, so it is conducive to maintaining integrity. Only on the basis of mutual affection and response can one get good fortune in taking a wife.

咸，亨。利贞。取女吉。

《彖》曰：咸，感也。柔上而刚下，二气感应以相与。止而说，男下女，是以"亨，利贞，取女吉"也。天地感而万物化生，圣人感人心而天下和平。观其所感，而天地万物之情可见矣。

《象》曰：山上有泽，咸。君子以虚受人。

【明译】

咸卦象征交融感通，亨通，利于守持正固，娶妻可获吉祥。

《彖传》说：咸是感应融通的意思。上卦兑为少女，下卦艮为少男，柔在上刚在下，也是柔顺往上，刚健来下，阴阳二气相互感应结合在一起。艮为止，兑为悦，交感之时稳重自制又欢快喜悦，男子对女子态度谦下，所以亨通，宜于持守正道，娶妻可获吉祥。天地相互交感带来万物创化生养，圣人感化人心带来天下和合太平。观察天地万物彼此交互感应的现象，天下事物的情理就可以明白了。

《象传》说：下卦艮为山，上卦兑为泽，山与泽感应相通就是咸卦。君子从这种卦象当中得到启示，要虚怀若谷，谦下包容，感化众人。

Hexagram Xian (Resonance) symbolizes mingling and affective connection leading to prosperity, which is conducive to maintaining integrity. Taking a wife brings good fortune.

The *Judgment Commentary* (*Tuan Zhuan*) says: Hexagram Xian (Resonance) means affection, response, fusion and interconnection. The upper Trigram Dui is the girl, and the lower Trigram Gen is the boy, so the soft is above and the strong is below, which is also the soft rising and the strong falling, the two *qi* of *yin* and *yang* reacting and combining with each other. Trigram Gen is stopping, while Trigram Dui is joyful, so when it comes to intercourse, it is steady, self-controlled, cheerful, and joyful. A man has a humble attitude toward women, so he is prosperous, and it is advisable to hold to the right *dao*, so he will get good fortune in taking a wife. The interaction between heaven and earth brings about the creation and growth of the myriad things, and sages influence people's intentions to bring harmony and peace to the world. Observing the phenomenon of mutual interaction among the myriad things in the world, one can understand the rationale of things in the world.

The *Image Commentary* (*Xiang Zhuan*) says: The lower Trigram Gen is mountain, the upper Trigram Dui is lake, so the connection between mountain and lake is Hexagram Xian (Resonance). An exemplary person is inspired by this hexagram to be modest, humble and tolerant in order to influence the multitude.

【明意】

卦象以刚下柔，以男下女，如男女感通之始，当男求女。就卦而言，每爻都感；因山艮为止，故止而有感；感必心动而悦，心悦方能亨通。山实泽虚，山阳泽阴，阳升阴降，二气融通，阴意与阳意气息互通，相互感动包容，可见发心之感是阴阳通达之始，创生化育之源，发荣滋长之本。

心灵与世界感通，能够确知世界，但我们用来测量这种"同、通"的尺度，是身体之感官，也往往不够精确而且有限，所以单纯通过身体感官难以了解世界，也难以了解心灵本身。世界在我们见到它之前，就是如此这般的，我们需要致力于超越感官去感通其先天结构。

[Illuminating Intentionality]

The hexagram image is based on the strong beneath the soft, and male beneath female, just like the beginning of the connection between a man and woman, when the man pursues the woman. As far as hexagrams are concerned, every line is affected; because Trigram Gen (mountain) is stopping, it stops and is affected; the affection must be moved by the heart-mind and be happy, and only when the heart-mind is happy can prosperity be achieved. The mountain is full and the lake is empty, the mountain is *yang* and the lake is *yin*, the *yang* rises and the *yin* falls, the two *qis* are fused, the breaths of *yin* and *yang* intentionality are interconnected, and they are moved and tolerated by each other. It can be seen that the feeling of expression of the heart-mind's affection is the beginning of the connection between *yin* and *yang*, the source of creation, transformation and education, and prosperity. Also, the foundation of growth.

The heart-mind is affectively connected to the world and can know the world with certainty. However, the scale we use to measure this "sameness and connection" is the body's senses, which are often imprecise and limited. Therefore, it is difficult to understand the world simply through the body's senses, and also difficult to understand the mind itself. The world is just as it is before we see it, and we need to commit ourselves to transcending our senses to affectively connect with its transcendental structure.

初六：咸其拇。

《象》曰："咸其拇"，志在外也。

【明译】

初六：大脚趾开始有感应。

《象传》说：大脚趾开始有感应，说明初六的心志向着外卦的九四。

Six (*yin*/soft line) in the first place: The big toe starts to feel and respond.

The *Image Commentary* (*Xiang Zhuan*) says: The big toe begins to feel sensation, which shows that the intention of the Six (*yin*/soft line) in the first place is directed towards the Nine (*yang*/strong line) in the fourth place of the outer hexagram.

【明意】

意念将动未动的状态被牵引才有生机。意能发动，感应而动。脚趾上生机萌发，生机勃发都是因为有外在的力量，但本爻感悦而有止，是感应之后知道分寸。

初六是感动的意能发动，将萌未萌之际，虽然所感尚浅，但非常微妙，感天动地的情感和事业，都来自最初的感应和对意能有分寸的培育。

[Illuminating Intentionality]

Only when intentionality's state of being about to move but not yet moving is drawn out does it possess vitality. When intentional energy is initiated, it is moved by affective induction. The vitality sprouting on the toes and its vigorous initiation are all due to external forces, but the feeling of the line is pleasant and restrained. It is after being affected and responding that one knows what is appropriate.

The Six (*yin*/soft line) in the first place is when affective energy is initiated. When it is about to emerge, but its affection is still shallow, it is very subtle. The emotions and endeavors that move heaven and earth all come from the initial affective response and the measured cultivation of intentional energy.

六二：咸其腓（féi），凶。居吉。

《象》曰：虽"凶居吉"，顺不害也。

【明译】

六二：腿肚子开始有感应，乱动会有凶险，安居待时，反而吉祥。

《象传》说：虽然乱动会有凶险，安居待时，反而吉祥，因为随顺不会有灾害。

Six (*yin*/soft line) in the second place: Affective responses begin to appear in the calves. If one moves around, it will be dangerous. If one stays calm and waits for the appropriate time, it will be auspicious.

The *Image Commentary* (*Xiang Zhuan*) says: Although there will be dangers in disorderly movement, it will be auspicious to live in peace and wait for the appropriate time, because there will be no disasters in following.

【明意】

六二意能发动较为随意，总是不能达到好的分寸，也就无法回应出贞正长久的爱情。起步阶段，如果心浮气躁，容易欲速不达，故还是静守为吉。或者说，即使已经感应得非常厉害了，意能也要安贞守正，随顺形势的发展，这样对人对己都不易构成伤害。本爻感动厉害，但情感杂乱而基础薄弱，不可继续躁动，而当安居自控意能的状态。

[Illuminating Intentionality]

The intentional energy of the Six (*yin*/soft line) in the second place initiates relatively randomly and usually cannot achieve a good sense of proportion, so it cannot respond with true and long-lasting love. In the initial stages, if one is flighty and impatient, it is easy to fail due to haste, so it is better to stay calm. In other words, even if the affective response is very strong, intentionality must be honest and upright, and follow the development of the situation, so that one does not easily cause harm to others and oneself. This line is very touching, but its emotions are disorderly and its foundation is weak. One should not continue to be restless, but should maintain a state of self-control.

九三：咸其股，执其随，往吝。

《象》曰："咸其股"，亦不处也。志在"随"人，所"执"下也。

【明译】

九三：大腿开始有感应，牵绊住它想要随顺的心意，如果仍然执意前往会遇到困难。

《象传》说：大腿开始有感应，说明九三不能安静自处，想随着人动，但被下面牵绊住了。

Nine (*yang*/strong line) in the third place: The thighs begin to feel and respond, which hinders its desire to follow along. If it still insists on advancing, it will encounter difficulties.

The *Image Commentary* (*Xiang Zhuan*) says: The thighs begin to be affected, indicating that the Nine (*yang*/strong line) in the third place cannot keep quiet and wants to move with others, but is trapped below.

【明意】

人生的很多选择是这种情况，有心无力，不能完全操之在己，只能不断权衡利弊，而且进退皆有困难。动还是不动，就成为一个问题。每一个动的瞬间，都或明或暗指向相应的人生结果。所以意能的操控，不是简单地以后果论吉凶的事情，有时是从动机发动就知道行动有困难。但《易》教如人生，多数情况下，无法确定自己应该行动与否之时，应该静观其变，等待时势变化。

[Illuminating Intentionality]

Many choices in life are like this. One is powerless and cannot completely control oneself. One can only constantly weigh the pros and cons, and it is difficult to advance or retreat. To move or not to move becomes the question. Every moment of moving points to the corresponding life outcome, either explicitly or implicitly. Therefore, the control of intentional energy is not simply a matter of judging good or bad fortune based on consequences, since sometimes it can be known from the initial motivation that there will be difficulty in action. However, the *Book of Changes* teaches that, like life, in most cases, when one is not sure whether one should act or not, one should wait for the situation to change.

九四：贞吉，悔亡。憧憧往来，朋从尔思。

《象》曰："贞吉，悔亡"，未感害也。"憧憧往来"，未光大也。

【明译】

九四：贞定自守，吉祥自来，忧悔消亡。心思意向不能专一，心神不宁，飘忽无定，来来往往，（一旦思虑专一）朋友终究会顺从你的心思意虑。

《象传》说：贞定自守，吉祥自来，忧悔消亡，因为九四没有感应到自己会受伤害。心思意向不能专一，心神不宁，飘忽无定，来来往往，是因为九四的感应之道还不够广阔远大，无所不至。

365

Nine (*yang*/strong line) in the fourth place: Being steadfast in self-preservation, good fortune will come naturally, and sorrow and regret will disappear. If your thoughts and intentions cannot be focused, your spirit will be restless, erratic, coming and going. (Once your thoughts are focused) Your friends will eventually obey your thoughts and intentions.

The *Image Commentary* (*Xiang Zhuan*) says: Steadfast in self-preservation, good fortune will come naturally, and sorrow and regret will disappear, because the Nine (*yang*/strong line) in the fourth place does not feel that one will be hurt. The reason why thoughts and intentions cannot be focused, and the spirit is restless, erratic, and comes and goes is because the *dao* of affective response of the Nine (*yang*/strong line) in the fourth place is not broad enough to reach in all directions.

【明意】

九四开始的时候心意不定，不知心意往何处去。各个阴爻和阳爻的关系没有梳理清晰。而九四心意一定就有明确的方向感，则意能开始汇聚，阴意和阳意自然围绕明确的意能展开。所以眼光（vision）对聚集意能很重要，即使感应之道不够广大，也可以积聚意能。

[Illuminating Intentionality]

At the beginning of the Nine (*yang*/strong line) in the fourth place, one is unsettled and does not know where to go, since one's relationship with each *yin* and *yang* line is not clearly sorted out. As the Nine (*yang*/strong line) in the fourth place, intentionality must have a clear sense of direction, then intentional energy will begin to gather, and *yin* and *yang* will naturally unfold around the clear intentional energy. Therefore, vision is very important for gathering intentional energy, such that even if the way of induction is not broad enough, intentional energy can still be accumulated.

九五：咸其脢（méi），无悔。

《象》曰："咸其脢"，志末也。

【明译】

九五：脊背上开始有感应，没有什么可以后悔的。

《象传》说：脊背上开始有感应，说明心志没有实现（志于末端，感应太浅）。

Nine (*yang*/strong line) in the fifth place: The spine starts to feel and respond, and there is nothing to regret.

The *Image Commentary* (*Xiang Zhuan*) says: The spine starts to feel and respond, which means that the one's intention is not concretized (the intention is at its end, and the affection is too shallow).

【明意】

萨特谈到自欺，感受不到真心真情而意动，有点像九五与上六那种浅表的感应。自欺欺人的情感，表面上非常感动，甚至心神都有点乱了，看起来意能的交流非常充分，其实不过流于表面，在表面动了深情之后，便是生存的空虚，虽然自欺的当下用间歇性的激情弥补了生命的空虚，但真正的生命却在激情消退之后连生机也消退了。

可见感重要的是发心，需要发自内心的真诚，用感天动地的深情厚谊的意能来应对世界的变化。无心之感来自天地自然之感，但《易》之感应，来自天地。

[Illuminating Intentionality]

Sartre talked about self-deception, not being able to feel the sincerity of emotion, which is somewhat like the superficial feelings of the Nine (*yang*/strong line) in the fifth place and the Six (*yin*/soft line) in the top place. The emotion of self-deception is very touching on the surface, so much that it's even a little preoccupied. It seems that the communication of intention is very full, but in fact it is just superficial. After the deep affection at the surface, there is an emptiness in existence. Although the self-deception at present uses intermittent passion to make up for the emptiness of life, real life still loses its vitality after the passion subsides.

It can be seen that the most important thing is to be sincere, to respond to the changes in the world with the sincerity of the heart-mind, and to respond to the changes in the world with the deep and profound friendship that moves the world. Unintentional affection comes from the natural affection of heaven and earth, but the affective response of the *Book of Changes* comes from heaven and earth.

上六：咸其辅、颊、舌。

《象》曰："咸其辅、颊、舌"，滕口说也。

【明译】

上六：牙床、两颊和舌头都感应到了。

《象传》说：牙床、两颊和舌头都感应到了，说明上六信口开河，无所顾忌地说话。

Six (*yin*/soft line) in the top place: The affection is felt on the gums, cheeks and tongue.

The *Image Commentary* (*Xiang Zhuan*) says: The affection can be felt on the gums, cheeks and tongue, which means that the Six (*yin*/soft line) in the top place speaks freely and without any scruples.

【明意】

此爻之感，达无心之感的最高境界，心意感动，意能流动，如若无心，也是天地自然之意，阴意与阳意相感的热烈境界之体现。所以卦爻本无心，就是要求咸卦不动心。一方面，咸卦以至诚感人，感之以心，方能咸有所感，如"观其所感，天地万物之情可见"，而天地万物之情，本来就是无心地感来感去，故有咸卦之解，但人非要给天地安一个心上去，是自己的心被感动了，加给天地而为人天之意。

人于天地之间，无时无刻不在感应之中，应该寻找一个自在感应的分寸，即在有心与无心之间，不可无心，也不可过度用心，方为感应的中道。无心之感从正面角度说，是热恋状态，随性言说无妨，但从负面角度说，是甜言蜜语，不知哪里出问题，比较可怕。可能导致婚姻、家道、生活紊乱。所以仅以言语感人，感动肤浅，吉凶难料。咸虽无心，却在以心立感，如果《易》的作者无心，这没心的咸卦，很难让人感动。而感动之后，要长长久久，于是开始恒卦。

[Illuminating Intentionality]

This line reaches the highest state of unintentional affection. The heart-mind's intentionality is moved and intentional energy can flow. If there is no intention, this is also an embodiment of the ardent state of the natural intentionality of heaven and earth, and of the mutual feeling of *yin* and *yang*. Therefore, the hexagrams and lines are originally unintentional, and they require Hexagram Xian (Resonance) to be attentive. On the one hand, Hexagram Xian (Resonance) touches people with sincerity, and only when one feels with the heart-mind can one feel something. For example, "Observe what affects you, and the feelings of heaven and earth and the myriad things can be seen." However, the feelings of heaven and earth and the myriad things are originally felt and pass away without intention, so there is this interpretation of Hexagram Xian, but people insist on giving heaven and earth an intention. It is their own heart-minds that are moved, and they give heaven and earth the intentionality of humanity and heaven.

Between heaven and earth, people are constantly in a process of affection and response. They should look for a comfortable measure of affective response, that is, one between intention and non-intention. Only by not being unintentional or over-exerting one's intentionality can one find the middle way of affective response. From a positive point of view, unintentional feelings are like a state of passionate love, and it is fine to talk casually, but from a negative point of view, these are sweet words, and it is worrying to not know where things may go wrong. This may lead to disorder in marriage, family, and life. Therefore, only using words to touch people is superficial and unpredictable. Although Xian has no intention, it uses its intention to establish affection. If the author of the *Book of Changes* had no intentions, it would be difficult to move people with this unintentional Hexagram Xian (Resonance). After being moved, it must last for a long time, and so begins Hexagram Heng (Constancy).

雷风恒（卦三十二）　（巽下震上）

Heng (Constancy), Thunder and Wind (Hexagram 32)　(Xun below, Zhen above)

儒家强调生机是担心人们过多地体悟生命的虚空和空洞，而要力图做无中生有的功夫，（如阳明）从无之中感应出一个生机勃发的世界来，而不要在无中消沉绝望弃世。所以无中生有、生生不息靠的是感于无中的弃世绝望，而无感的人生非常不同。感动到心意混乱的意境中无法建立意缘的稳恒感。存在物之缘在意中的恒定感来自意念对时空的有意选择和操控，意图把握缘分，对缘分执善固执，持之以恒。

恒是意念主动维持长久，是用意缘来实化意向的过程。心意本然通于日月运行之道，所以恒守意缘的状态不可过度主观。意念虽然瞬生瞬灭，但意境说明一个意生状态到下一个意生状态之间持续存在一种恒定性，以之为意念生发情境的恒定性，才有情感意向的恒定性和汲取阴阳能量的恒定性。

Confucianism emphasizes vitality because it is worried that people will sense too much the vacancy and emptiness of life, so they should strive to make something out of nothing, and (like Wang Yangming,) affectively induce a vibrant world from nothing, instead of being depressed, despairing and giving up in nothingness. Therefore, creating something out of nothing in ceaseless productivity depends on the sense of abandonment and despair in nothingness, and a life without affection is very different. When moved into a chaotic intentional context, one cannot establish a sense of stability in intentional dependent co-arising. The constant sense of the dependent co-arising of existence in intentionality comes from the intentional selection and manipulation of time and space by intentions, the intention to grasp dependent co-arising, and persistence and perseverance in dependent co-arising, leading to constancy.

Constancy is the active maintenance of intentions for long periods, and the process of concretizing intentions through the use of intentional dependent co-arising. Intentionality is naturally connected to the movement of the sun and the moon, so the state of maintaining intentionality should not be overly subjective. Although intentions come and go instantly, the intentional context shows that there is a kind of constancy from one mental state to the next. Only by using this as the constancy of the situation in which intentions arise can we have the constancy of emotional intention and absorb constancy from the energy of *yin* and *yang*.

恒，亨。无咎，利贞，利有攸往。

《彖》曰：恒，久也。刚上而柔下。雷风相与，巽而动，刚柔皆应，恒。"恒，亨，无咎，利贞"，久于其道也，天地之道恒久而不已也。"利有攸往"，终则有始也。日月得天而能久照，四时变化而能久成，圣人久于其道而天下化成。观其所恒，而天地万物之情可见矣。

《象》曰：雷风，恒。君子以立不易方。

【明译】

恒卦象征永恒持久，亨通。只有不犯过错，才利于共同持守正道，才利于有所前往。

《彖传》说：恒就是永恒持久的意思。上卦震为阳刚处上，下卦巽为阴柔处下（卦变中泰卦之初九升上到达四位，而六四下降到初位）。雷震风行，交相互助，巽为顺，震为动，要先逊顺然后震动，上下卦的刚爻与柔爻都彼此应和，这才是恒久之道。永恒持久，亨通，没有过错（祸患、咎害），利于共同持守正道，说明恒道在于双方共同长久保持正道。天地的运行是恒久持续周流不息的，利于有所前往，是因为事物的发展总是终而复始。日月顺天道而行才能长久照亮世间，四季往复变化而能长久创化生成万物，圣人法天道，长久保持正道与美德，就能教化天下而大有成就。观察自然万物的恒久之道，就能从中发现天地万物的情实状态。

《象传》说：上卦震为雷，下卦巽为风，雷鸣风行，风雷交加，雷风相伴是大自然恒久不变的现象，这就是恒卦，君子从中得到启示，立身于恒久不变的人天大道。

Hexagram Heng (Constancy) symbolizes eternity and prosperity. Only by not making mistakes can we jointly uphold the right *dao* and move forward.

The *Judgment Commentary* (*Tuan Zhuan*) says: Hexagram Heng (Constancy) means eternal and lasting. The upper Trigram Zhen is the strong residing above, while the lower Trigram Xun is the soft residing below (in the hexagram-changes, the Nine (*yang*/strong line) in the first place of Hexagram Tai (Communication) rises to the fourth place, while the Six (*yin*/soft line) in the fourth place descends to the first place). Thunder resounds and the wind moves, helping each other, and wind is smoothness, while vibration is movement, so one must first be smooth and then shake. The strong and soft lines of the upper and lower Trigrams all respond to each other, and this is the eternal and constant *dao*. Eternal and lasting, prosperous, without fault (disaster, blame), it is conducive to jointly maintaining the right *dao*, indicating that the eternal *dao* lies in both parties maintaining the right *dao* together for a long time. The movement of heaven and earth is eternal and continuous, which is conducive to advancing somewhere, because the development of things always ends and begins again. The sun and the moon can illuminate the world for a long time if they follow the heavenly *dao*, and the four seasons transform and create the myriad things for a long time. A sage follows the heavenly *dao* and maintains the right *dao* and virtue for a long time, so one can educate the world and achieve great things. By observing the eternal and constant *dao* of the myriad things in nature, we can discover the true state of the myriad things in the world.

The *Image Commentary* (*Xiang Zhuan*) says: The upper Trigram Zhen represents thunder, and the lower Trigram Xun represents wind, so thunder resounds and wind moves, wind and thunder mix. Thunder and wind accompanying one another is a constant phenomenon in nature, and this is Hexagram Heng (Constancy). The exemplary person is enlightened by this, and dedicates their life to the constant and unchanging *dao* of humanity and heaven.

【明意】

人有进入永恒守意的状态的天然倾向，因意识到自己的肉身意念有限，面对宇宙和日月所赋予的永恒之感，于是在意念中也建构与天同一的结构，如信仰、神、文化等具有永恒价值的内容，以期建构一个理念系统，能够与天地日月一样永恒。《周易》是人创造出来模仿天地自然之永恒先天结构的努力。这种意念倾向创制的系统之中，所有的意都有恒久操控意缘的意味，犹如持志，即意念力图把握意缘而成事。

恒是致恒之道，实意在于坚持意念之缘，即要动才能恒，不动则无所谓恒，缘都在动中，要在动中求恒。从《周易》的角度看，我们可能了悟永恒的先天结构。如果有一个先于经验的永恒结构，足以是人类认知的恒久目标，或者，至少人天之意把这个先天结构认知为永恒的。

[Illuminating Intentionality]

People have a natural tendency to enter a state of constant mindfulness. Because they realize that their bodily intentions are limited, and with the sense of constancy given by the cosmos and the sun and the moon, they also construct structures in their intentions that are identical with heaven, such as beliefs, gods, cultures and other content with eternal value, in order to build a conceptual system that can be as constant as the heaven, the earth, the sun and the moon. The *Book of Changes* is an effort created by humanity to imitate the eternal transcendental structure of nature, heaven and earth. In this kind of system where intentions tend to create, all intentions have the intentionality of permanently controlling dependent co-arising, just like holding to one's will, so intentionality tries to grasp intentional dependent co-arising to achieve things.

Persistence is the way to achieve constancy. Concretizing intentionality lies in persisting in the dependent co-arising of intentions, that is, one must move to achieve constancy, and as if one does not move, there can be no such thing as constancy. Dependent co-arising is all in motion, and one must seek constancy in motion. From the perspective of the *Book of Changes*, we may understand the eternal transcendental structure. If there is an eternal structure that precedes experience, it can be a constant goal for human cognition, or at least the intentionality of humanity and heaven can recognize this transcendental structure as eternal.

初六：浚（jùn）恒，贞凶，无攸利。

《象》曰："浚恒"之"凶"，始求深也。

【明译】

初六：深深地希望能够恒久，过分坚持会有凶险，没有好处。

《象传》说：深深地希望能够恒久地持守心意，但过分坚持会有凶险，这是因为初六从一开始就这样期待恒久不变的心意状态，将来一定会失望的。

Six (*yin*/soft line) in the first place: One deeply hopes that things will last forever, but excessive persistence will be dangerous and will not be beneficial.

The *Image Commentary* (*Xiang Zhuan*) says: One deeply hopes to be able to hold onto one's intentionality for a long time, but excessive persistence will be dangerous. This is because if one expects a permanent state of intentionality from the beginning of the Six (*yin*/soft line) in the first place, one will definitely be disappointed in the future.

【明意】

恒卦要持久，最要讲究恒久的分寸，要恒首先要把内在的心意调整到恒定状态。可是，刚一开始期待不可过于执着，也就是说，内心意念对身外之物事的期待不可过度单纯，也不可过度刚强，否则，如果只顾追求恒久的深度，就一定事与愿违。心意持定不动，而世事变幻无常，过分静守心意恒定状态的人，往往失望。可见，恒久也是相对的动态平衡，从两情相悦的咸卦过来，一开始就要保持好分寸，起心动念都要留有余地。

[Illuminating Intentionality]

In order for Hexagram Heng (Constancy) to last, the most important thing is to pay attention to the propriety of constancy. To be constant, one must first adjust one's inner intentionality to a constant state. However, one's expectations from the beginning should not be too persistent. In other words, one's inner intentional expectations for things outside the body should neither be too simple nor too strong. Otherwise, if one only pursues the depth of constancy, things will definitely backfire. Intentionality remains stable, but things in the world are constantly changing, so people who keep their intentionality too static are often disappointed. It can be seen that constancy is also a relative dynamic balance, so from the joy in mutual love of Hexagram Xian (Resonance), one must maintain a good sense of proportion from the beginning and leave free space in every intention.

九二：悔亡。

《象》曰：九二"悔亡"，能久中也。

【明译】

九二：忧悔消亡。

《象传》说：忧悔消亡，是因为能够持久保持中正之道。

Nine (*yang*/strong line) in the second place: Sorrow and regret disappear.

The *Image Commentary* (*Xiang Zhuan*) says: The reason for the demise of sorrow and regret is that one can maintain the right *dao* for a long time.

【明意】

此爻是让意境持久稳定地维持意缘。在变动的情势之中，维持恒稳的缘分并不容易，缘与境一同变迁，心意对缘的坚持需要彼此共同的努力。所以单方面的缘并不算是恒缘，恒缘总是相互之间感应的持续坚守。要没有悔就要有能维持下去的共同目标，坚持致恒之道才能成功，可见坚守正道，恒久持守意缘需要毅力，和阴意阳意彼此共同的付出。

[Illuminating Intentionality]

This line allows the intentional context to maintain sustained and stable dependent co-arising. In a changing situation, it is not easy to maintain stable dependent co-arising. Fate and circumstances change together, and the persistence of dependent co-arising in intentionality requires the joint efforts of both parties. Therefore, one-sided dependent co-arising is not considered constant dependent co-arising. Permanent dependent co-arising is always the continuous persistence of mutual affective response. To have no regrets, people need to have a common goal that can be maintained. Only by adhering to the *dao* of perseverance can people succeed. It can be seen that adhering to the right *dao* and persevering in dependent co-arising for a long time requires perseverance and the mutual dedication of *yin* and *yang* intentionality.

九三：不恒其德，或承之羞，贞吝。

《象》曰："不恒其德"，无所容也。

【明译】

九三：不能恒久持守自己的仁德，就有可能要承受羞辱，正固（不好的德行）不改，会有灾难。

《象传》说：不能恒久持守自己的仁德，最后就没有容身之地了。

Nine (*yang*/strong line) in the third place: If one cannot maintain one's benevolent virtue for a long time, one may have to endure humiliation. If one does not change one's bad behavior, one may suffer disaster.

The *Image Commentary* (*Xiang Zhuan*) says: If one cannot maintain one's benevolent virtue for a long time, there will be no place for one in the end.

【明意】

德自道来，是具体心意与自然之道的交接而成就德性，发用为德性，而有"德"。德取乾象，意为道德之意从内到外的一致性和整全性（integrity）。可见，德之本义是道之显明，是内在心意的一致和恒守，表达为外在行为的恒定性。《论语》引这句话，是说没有恒心恒德，则连巫医都做不了。巫医本来是心意通天的神圣职业，但随着古代社会的转化，神权让位给世俗权力，巫医地位下降而变得低贱。以此反观本爻，要求人在变通的局势当中，持守恒久的心意和仁爱之德。

[Illuminating Intentionality]

Virtue comes from *dao*, and is achieved through the connection between specific intentionalities and the *dao* of nature. When it is expressed as a virtuous nature, there is "virtue." Virtue follows the image of Trigram Qian (Heaven), meaning consistency and integrity of moral intentionality from the inside out. It can be seen that the original meaning of virtue is the manifestation of *dao*, the consistency and perseverance of inner mind, expressed as the constancy of external behavior. The *Analects* quoted this sentence to say that without perseverance and constant virtue, one cannot even be a witch doctor. Witch doctors were originally a sacred profession with an intentionality that connected with heaven. However, with the transformation of ancient society, divine power gave way to secular power, and the status of witch doctors declined and became lowly. Reflecting on this line, it requires people to maintain constant intentions and benevolent virtues in changing situations.

九四：田无禽。

《象》曰：久非其位，安得"禽"也。

【明译】

九四：赶到打猎的田野，禽兽都跑光了。

《象传》说：（形势已经大变，九四还想）长久地守着不合适打猎的位置，怎么可能捕捉到禽兽呢？

Nine (*yang*/strong line) in the fourth place: Arriving at the hunting field, all the animals are gone.

The *Image Commentary* (*Xiang Zhuan*) says: (The situational propensity has changed drastically, but the Nine (*yang*/strong line) in the fourth place still thinks.) How can one catch animals if one guards a position that is not suitable for hunting for a long time?

【明意】

意念发动不当，则劳而无功。恒卦希望心意恒定，不恒即为有失。但恒定于什么意缘，却大有差别。此爻说明，心意持守于恒定的过去，就仿佛为泼出去的牛奶悲伤哭泣，伤的不仅仅是当下的心境，因为要面对新梦仍然成空之苦。

不合适的恒心即不能够适应情境变化的恒心，是如守株待兔和刻舟求剑那样的恒心，则不能得到希图的意缘。

[Illuminating Intentionality]

If an intention is not initiated properly, the work will be in vain. Hexagram Heng (Constancy) hopes that the intentionality will be constant, and if it is not constant, there will be a loss. But there is a big difference in what kind of intention it is. This line shows that the intentionality clings to a constant past, just like crying over spilled milk. This hurts more than just the current state of mind, because it has to face the pain of new dreams still becoming empty.

Inappropriate perseverance is perseverance that cannot adapt to changes in a situation, because perseverance like guarding a tree and waiting for a rabbit (to run into the tree a second time) and marking a sailing boat to seek a sword (that has fallen into the water) will not achieve one's desired intention.

六五：恒其德，贞。妇人吉，夫子凶。

《象》曰："妇人贞吉"，从一而终也。"夫子"制义，从妇凶也。

【明译】

六五：恒守自己的仁德，坚守正道。对女人来说，可以获得吉祥，但对男人来说，就会有凶险。

《象传》说：女人坚守正道可以获得吉祥，因为女人应该从一而终。男人要受到道义的制约和引导，如果一味跟从女人就凶险了。

Six (*yin*/soft line) in the fifth place: Keep constant watch over your own benevolence and hold to the right *dao*. For women, this can bring good fortune, but for men, it can bring danger.

The *Image Commentary* (*Xiang Zhuan*) says: A woman who sticks to the right *dao* can gain good fortune, because a woman should stick to it till the end. Men must be restricted and guided by morality, and it is dangerous if they blindly follow women.

【明意】

人天之意要变，但不可乱变，变化之中要有一个相对平衡与稳定的结构。人意要合于天道，男女之意要合于阴阳之意，阴随阳可，阴意随乾天之意，即阴意当随阳意，以不变应万变，但又不可如九三变化多端，没有恒心而致羞，其中分寸很难。

恒守心意之缘，这对于要顺从阳意的阴意（如女性作为阴意的代表）来说是要持之以恒的。但如果男人的阳意不能恒守天地之间的道义，那么男子的心意就太狭小了。既然妇人用顺从天道的温柔方式留住男子的心，那么男子就应表现得阳刚而且通达道义。

[Illuminating Intentionality]

The intentionality of humanity and heaven must change, but not randomly. There must be a relatively balanced and stable structure amidst the changes. Human intentionality must be in line with the heavenly *dao*, the intentionality of men and women must be in line with the intentionality of *yin* and *yang*, in which *yin* can follow *yang*, and *yin* follows the intentionality of Qian as heaven, that is, *yin* intentionality must follow *yang*'s intentionality, and respond to a myriad changes with the unchanging, but this must not be like the Nine (*yang*/strong line) in the third place with its many changes, in which lack of perseverance leads to shame, and it is difficult to find measure.

Perseverance in the dependent co-arising of the heart-mind and intentionality is necessary for the *yin* intentionality that must follow *yang* intentionality (such as women as representatives of *yin* intentionality). But if a man's *yang* intentionality cannot uphold the moral principles between heaven and earth, then his intentionality is too narrow. Since women keep men's intentionality in a gentle way that follows the *dao* of heaven, men should behave in a positive and strong way and understand morality.

上六：振恒，凶。

《象》曰："振恒"在上，大无功也。

【明译】

上六：恒守心意的状态受到震动而动摇，将有凶险。

《象传》说：上六恒守心意的状态受到震动而动摇，还高居在上做事，必然徒劳无功。

Six (*yin*/soft line) in the top place: If the state of constant intentionality is shaken and disturbed, there will be danger.

The *Image Commentary* (*Xiang Zhuan*) says: The state of the intentionality that is constantly guarded by the Six (yin/soft line) in the top place is shaken and disturbed. If you continue to carry out affairs from a lofty position, it will be in vain.

【明意】

恒卦强调要以恒德来守恒久的意缘。结果诸爻皆难以实现这样的期待，毕竟恒守意念对所有人都是非常高的期待，确实难以实现。一个求取恒久意缘的卦，居然爻爻难以持守恒久的意缘，说明人间意缘之发容易，但要恒久持守，实在难上加难。所以大象辞说，君子从雷风相与得到启示，要立身于恒久不变的人天大道。

[Illuminating Intentionality]

Hexagram Heng (Constancy) emphasizes the need to preserve long-lasting intentional connections with constant virtue. As a result, it is difficult for all lines to realize such expectations. After all, the intention of perseverance has very high expectations for everyone, and it is indeed difficult to realize. In a hexagram seeking to obtain a long-lasting intentional connection, it is actually difficult for every line to maintain a long-lasting intentional connection. This shows that it is easy to initiate an intentional connection in the world, but extremely difficult to maintain it for a long time. Therefore, the *Image Commentary* (*Xiang Zhuan*) says that the exemplary person gets inspiration from the combination of thunder and wind, and must establish oneself on the constant and unchanging *dao* of humanity and heaven.

天山遯（卦三十三）　（艮下乾上）

Dun (Retreat), Heaven and Mountain (Hexagram 33)　(Gen below, Qian above)

　　一念之退与一念之生。通常所谓生总是带着进之意味的生，但退意之生其实更具智慧，说明意识主体对情境有着更加深刻的领悟，同时还要有强大的意能，才能迅速地改变意念的方向。在退却的大势当中维系生机很艰难。在不得不退却的大势当中，如何重新确定自己的时位，为意念的生机找到合适的方向，而且需要有能够强烈迅速地转换意念方向的魄力，这是断、舍、离的求生智慧，不可拖泥带水，当退则退，不留恋，不在乎得失。要做到断、舍、离，意念需要有强烈的生机，能够迅速集中意缘，竭尽全力，快捷地进行意念的转换。

The withdrawal of one intention and the emergence of another intention. Usually, the emergence spoken of here always implies a sense of advancement, but the emergence of retreating intention is actually more intelligent, indicating that the conscious subject has a deeper understanding of the situation, and at the same time, and must also have greater intentional energy to quickly change the direction of its intention. It is difficult to stay alive in a general trend of having to retreat, to find a way to re-determine one's temporal position and find a suitable direction for the vitality of one's intentions, and one needs to have the courage to change the direction of one's intentions strongly and quickly. This is the survival wisdom of breaking off, giving up, and leaving behind. One cannot procrastinate, but should retreat when necessary, not linger, and not care about gains and losses. To achieve breaking off, giving up, and leaving behind, one's intentionality must have strong vitality, be able to quickly focus on intentional connections, do one's utmost, and quickly transform one's intentions.

遯，亨。小利贞。

《彖》曰："遯，亨"，遯而亨也。刚当位而应，与时行也。"小利贞"，浸而长也。遯之时义大矣哉！

《象》曰：天下有山，遯。君子以远小人，不恶而严。

【明译】

遯卦象征退隐躲避，亨通，持守正道对于柔小的事情有利。

《彖传》说：遯卦退隐躲避而亨通，是先退隐躲避之后才能够亨通。刚爻九五在尊位，与代表柔爻上长的六二阴阳正应，说明刚爻还执令当权，六二还愿意应合九五，全卦四个刚爻还占据多数，形势还没到急转直下的地步。刚爻只是顺应时势后退，还不是败退。持守正道对于柔小的事情有利，是因为柔爻代表的阴气正在渐渐生长壮大。遯卦的时势体现出的时机化意义实在太重大了！

《象传》说：上卦乾为天，下卦艮为山，天下有山就是遯卦。君子看到山在天的下面，好像山在上升，逼天退让之象，要远远地躲避小人，不必表现出厌恶小人的脸色，但又要严肃矜庄，严格持守好正道的界限。

Hexagram Dun (Retreat) symbolizes retreat and avoidance which lead to prosperity, and adhering to the right *dao* is beneficial for the myriad things.

The *Judgment Commentary* (*Tuan Zhuan*) says: Hexagram Dun (Retreat) retreats and avoids, and then prospers. It is only after retreating and avoiding that one can prosper. The Nine (*yang*/strong line) in the fifth place is in the honored position, and it corresponds to the Six (*yin*/soft line) in the second place in proper positions of *yin* and *yang*. This shows that the strong line is still in power, and the Six (*yin*/soft line) in the second place is still willing to respond to the Nine (*yang*/strong line) in the fifth place. The four strong lines of the whole hexagram still occupy the majority, and the situation is still good, not yet reaching the point of a sudden turn of events. The *yang*/strong lines are just retreating in accordance with the situation, not retreating in defeat. Sticking to the right *dao* is beneficial for the affairs of the soft and minor, because the *yinqi* represented by the soft lines is gradually growing and strengthening. The temporal significance reflected in the current situation of Hexagram Dun (Retreat) is so important!

The *Image Commentary* (*Xiang Zhuan*) says: The upper Trigram is sky, and the lower Trigram is mountain. A mountain in the world under heaven, this is Hexagram Dun (Retreat). When an exemplary person sees a mountain below the sky, it seems as if the mountain is rising, forcing the sky to give in. Although one should stay away from petty people, there is no need to show disgust with them, but one should be serious and solemn, and strictly adhere to the boundaries of the right *dao*.

【明意】

在逆势之中，要首先存生求生，以维系生命之机。因生之机缘持续最为重要，生机微弱，需要自保以继生。严格持守好正道的界限，这是对待小人的方式。心意和格局的不同。不生之生，在不生的状态下，不可强生，需要先隐遁，让小人表演之后等待机会。遯卦为斗小人之术，是君子隐而制小人，需要运用权术和能力来把握进退的分寸。不可嫉恶如仇，否则就是跟小人一般见识了。

气之生与不生，是相对人来说的关于情境的价值判断，不可能是主观判断，而是基于客观气息运行的判断，不是纯粹的价值型判断。人判断气息的生与不生，以思考人事变化的应对之策。人依据形势的气息通畅程度来行动。遯是形势气息不通的行动指南，退避是为了等待生机的重新到来。

[Illuminating Intentionality]

In adverse circumstances, one must first survive in order to maintain the vitality of life. Because the continuation of the vital conditions of life is the most important, when vitality is weak it is necessary to protect oneself in order to survive. Strictly adhering to the boundaries of the right *dao* is the way to treat petty people. Differences exist between intentions and patterns. The generation of the ungenerated cannot be forced in the state of the ungenerated. One must retreat into hiding first and let petty people perform, then wait for an opportunity. Hexagram Dun (Retreat) is a technique for struggling against petty people, and means that an exemplary person conceals oneself and controls petty people. One needs to use power and ability to grasp the right balance of advancing and retreating. One should not detest evil as an enemy, otherwise one will be like a petty person.

In relation to people, the generation or non-generation of *qi* is a value judgment about a situation. It cannot be a subjective judgment, but a judgment based on the objective movements of *qi*, and is thus not a pure value-based judgment. People judge whether *qi* is generated or not to think about how to respond to changes in human affairs. People act according to the degree of flowing *qi* in a situation. Retreat is a guide to action when a situation is blocked, and to retreat is to wait for the return of vitality.

初六：遯尾，厉。勿用有攸往。

《象》曰："遯尾"之"厉"，不往何灾也？

【明译】

初六：退避不及落在了末尾，非常危险，这时候还不如干脆不要向前跑了。

《象传》说：初六退避不及落在了末尾，非常危险，还不如干脆不向前跑了，哪还会有什么灾害呢？

The Six (*yin*/soft line) in the first place: One is unable to retreat and falls back to the end, which is very dangerous. It is better not to run forward at all at this time.

The *Image Commentary* (*Xiang Zhuan*) says: The Six (*yin*/soft line) in the first place is unable to retreat and falls to the ending group, which is very dangerous. It would be better not to run forward at all. How then could there be any disaster?

【明意】

在逃遯的形势当中，此爻说明生机已经微弱，在竞争与行动中落在了后面，这时不可轻举妄动，宁可不动以避免危险。既然生的境遇突然变得艰险，撤退时垫底当守持待命的心意，已经被小人给排挤到最末尾了，还不如不动就算了。

逃遯的形势当中，最显物竞天择，所以不可落在末尾，否则充满危险。一旦意识到时机不对，就应该赶紧转型，犹如人在乱世之中，既然已经逃遯，就要守时待命，自己守住生机不失。

[Illuminating Intentionality]

In the situation of retreating, this line indicates that vitality is weak and that the person is lagging behind in competition and action. At this time, one should not act rashly and should rather stay still to avoid danger. Now that the situation of life has suddenly become difficult and dangerous, the intention of remaining at the bottom and awaiting one's fate during the retreat has been pushed to the back by petty people, so it is better to just stay still.

In the situation of escaping, competition for survival is the most prominent, so one cannot fall behind, otherwise it will be full of danger. Once one realizes that the time is not right, one should quickly transform, just like a person in troubled times, who, now that one has escaped, must mind the times and await one's fate to hold onto one's vitality.

六二：执之用黄牛之革，莫之胜说。

《象》曰："执用黄牛"，固志也。

【明译】

六二：用黄牛皮拧成的绳子把自己跟九五牢牢栓缚在一起，谁都没有办法解脱得开。

《象传》说：用黄牛皮拧成的绳子把自己跟九五牢牢栓缚在一起，因为六二要心志坚定地跟九五捆绑在一起不想后退。

Six (*yin*/soft line) in the second place: Use a rope twisted from yellow cattle's hide to tightly tie yourself to the Nine (*yang*/strong line) in the fifth place. No one can escape.

The *Image Commentary* (*Xiang Zhuan*) says: Use a rope twisted from yellow cattle's hide to firmly tie yourself to the Nine (*yang*/strong line) in the fifth place, because the Six (*yin*/soft line) in the second place must be firmly tied to the Nine (*yang*/strong line) in the fifth place and does not want to retreat.

【明意】

此时阴意担心力量不足，为了牢控阴意，采取小人合力同归于尽的策略，君子只有让心思安宁，努力掌控自己的意志。面对小人合力决一死战的架势，这时君子都只有退避三舍了，要采取灵活的方式对付，既然生机被小人纠缠，那还是要用柔性手法化解。

[Illuminating Intentionality]

At this time, *yin*/negative intentionality is worried about lack of strength. In order to firmly control *yin*/negative intentions, it adopts the strategy of petty people working together to perish together. The exemplary person can only let one's intentionality be peaceful and work hard to control one's own intentions. Faced with the attitude of petty people joining forces to fight to the death, the exemplary person can only retreat and adopt flexible ways to deal with it. Since vitality is entangled with petty people, one still has to use flexible methods to resolve it.

九三：系遯，有疾，厉。畜臣妾吉。

《象》曰："系遯"之"厉"，有疾惫也。"畜臣妾吉"，不可大事也。

【明译】

九三：心怀系恋，不及时退避，将有严重的疾病和危险，（形势已经不退不行了）回家去畜养奴仆和婢妾，还是吉祥的。

《象传》说：有心还想挽回退势并加以努力，这样做非常危险而且困难，会把人累得生出疾病，最后折磨得疲惫不堪。不如退避回到家里畜养奴仆婢妾，干点这类小事还是吉祥的，干大事就不要抱指望了。

Nine (*yang*/strong line) in the third place: If one is deeply attached to someone and does not retreat in time, one will be seriously ill and in danger. (The situational propensity is irreversible.) It is auspicious to go home and raise servants, maids and concubines.

The *Image Commentary* (*Xiang Zhuan*) says: If one is determined to reverse the decline and works hard, doing so is very dangerous and difficult. It will be tiring and lead to sickness, and finally be exhausting. It is better to retreat back home and raise servants and concubines. It is auspicious to do such small things, but one should not expect to do great things.

【明意】

九三的生机已经非常有限，此时当及时退却离开，千万不可有所留恋，更不要想做大事。生机的存续取决于心念的顺逆，在不可存续的时势下要主动改换意生的方向。心意在迫于形势变化的时候，要主动调整期限度，否则当断不断，反受其乱。心意一念转型，时势大变，意定则时势定。一念之转对于时势的改变很明显。这是说，人需要依照形势限制自己心意的尺度和相应的做事分寸。

[Illuminating Intentionality]

The Nine (*yang*/strong line) in the third place's vitality is already very limited. At this time, one should retreat and leave in time. One must not be nostalgic, let alone think of doing great things. The survival of vitality depends on the obedience or reversal of intention. In unsustainable situations, one must take the initiative to change the direction of intention. When your intentionality is forced by changes in the situation, you must take the initiative to adjust the time limit, otherwise you will be disrupted by interruptions. A single intention changes the heart-mind's intentionality, and the situational propensity changes drastically. If the intentionality is determined, the situational propensity will be determined. A single change of intention can obviously change the current situational propensity. This means that people need to limit the scale of their intentions and the proportion of their actions according to the situation.

九四：好遯，君子吉，小人否。

《象》曰："君子好遯"，"小人否"也。

【明译】

九四：从容退避，君子会吉祥，小人做不到就会否塞不通。

《象传》说：君子能够舍得放下，该退的时候从容退让，小人不主动退让，所以会否塞不通。

Nine (*yang*/strong line) in the fourth place: Retreating calmly, an exemplary person will be fortunate, but if a petty person cannot complete it, one's way will be blocked.

The *Image Commentary* (*Xiang Zhuan*) says: An exemplary person is willing to let go and gives in calmly when it is time to give in. A petty person does not take the initiative to give in, so will be blocked.

【明意】

九四应该从容退让以求生，而不是喜好退让。从容就是放下对外物的牵累而顺应自然退让的形势，喜好就是主动选择退让。君子能够舍得，不过度执着，其意生不受外在意缘的牵绊，该退之时，不可留恋外在的意缘，更不可受诱惑而放不下。

[Illuminating Intentionality]

Nine (*yang*/strong line) in the fourth place should be about giving in calmly to survive, rather than liking to give in. Being calm means letting go of the burden of external things and adapting to the natural situation of giving in, while liking means actively taking the initiative to choose to give in. An exemplary person is able to let go without being overly attached, and one's career is not bound by external dependent co-arising. When it is time to retreat, one must not linger one's thoughts on external dependent co-arising, let alone be tempted and unable to let go.

九五：嘉遯，贞吉。

《象》曰："嘉遯，贞吉"，以正志也。

【明译】

九五：退让得尽善尽美，继续持守正道，自然吉祥。

《象传》说：退让得又善又美，心意继续持守正道，自然吉祥无边；这是因为九五心意端正，退得心安理得。

Nine (*yang*/strong line) in the fifth place: Make concessions to perfection, continue to adhere to the right *dao*, and you will be naturally fortunate.

The *Image Commentary* (*Xiang Zhuan*) says: Giving in is both good and beautiful, and your intentionality continues to adhere to the right *dao*, so you will naturally meet with boundless auspiciousness. This is because the Nine (*yang*/strong line) in the fifth place's intentionality is upright and it can feel at ease in retreat.

【明意】

常人对于退让，容易意难舍，志难收，从而留下无数退遯的心意悲剧。此爻明示人们，该退的时候，不但要顺其自然之势该退就退，而且要退让得既善良又美好，自己心意安正，心安理得，同时也让心志相合者继续先前意念关注的情境；即使没有心志相合者在继续自己的事业，在关注之前意念相关的情境，也不可以有丝毫留恋，因为既然已经到了该舍的时候，就要舍得干净利落。所以美好的退让，不是为了获得而舍，而是因为该舍则舍，断舍之退既是善良之心意的存续，又是心意与外境共成的美妙乐章。其进得感天，天人共助；其退舍仍如云天变幻，人意通天，江山如画，残阳如血，美不胜收。

[Illuminating Intentionality]

Ordinary people tend to be reluctant to give in and unwilling to accept loss, not wishing to retract their will, leaving countless tragedies in retreating. This line makes it clear that when it is time to retreat, people should not only retreat as they should, but also that retreat should be kind and beautiful, so that their intentions are at peace and contented, while at the same time, they should allow those who are like-minded to continue to focus on the situation they previously focused on. Even if there is no like-minded person who is continuing one's career, one should not have any nostalgia for the situation related to one's previous intentions, because now that it is time to let go, one must let go abruptly. Therefore, the beautiful concession is not to give up for the sake of gain, but to give up because it is necessary to give up. The withdrawal of giving up is not only a continuation of kind intention, but also a wonderful piece of music composed by intentionality and the external environment. When one enters, one feels grateful to heaven, and heaven and humanity help one; when one leaves, one is still like the clouds and sky changing. People's intentions are connected with the sky, the mountains and rivers are like a painting, the setting sun is like blood, and all is astonishing beauty.

上九：肥遯，无不利。

《象》曰："肥遯，无不利"，无所疑也。

【明译】

上九：高飞远退，逍遥自在，自然没有什么不利。

《象传》说：高飞远退，逍遥自在，自然没有什么不利，因为上九心里没有疑虑，别人对自己也就没有什么可以怀疑的。

Nine in the top place: Flying high and retreating far away, free and easy, naturally there is no disadvantage.

The *Image Commentary* (*Xiang Zhuan*) says: Flying high and retreating far away, free and easy, there is naturally no disadvantage, because the Nine (*yang*/strong line) in the top place has no doubts in one's intention, and others have nothing to doubt about one.

【明意】

君子退隐之术的根本在于看清形势，躲避小人逼退自己的锋芒，该退的时候，不可以留恋，不该动的时候，不要乱动，要顺应形势的发展，学会等待时机发生转变，所以要审时度势，把握好进退的分寸。最难的地方当然是在退却的形势下如何驾驭疯狂进攻的小人，在退却中使小人心正，较稳妥地发挥正面作用。可见，当退之时，不可恋权，求生为上。进的时候，要随时想好退路。这样才能有比较好的结局。真正的修行不是刻意躲藏，而是在人群之中与人合生。

知道全身而退的艺术，保持好意向的生机，才可能大而壮观。因为功业盛大成就卓著的另一面就是随时离去，安宁退守。

[Illuminating Intentionality]

The essence of an exemplary person's retreat is to see the situation clearly and avoid the petty person's leading efforts to retreat. Not lingering when one should retreat, not moving when one shouldn't move, adapting to the development of the situation, and learning to wait for the opportunity to change, one must assess the situation and grasp the right balance of advance and retreat. The most difficult part is of course how to harness the crazy attacks of petty people in a retreat situation, so that the petty people's intentions can be rectified during the retreat, and they can play a positive role more safely. It can be seen that when retreating, one must not be obsessed with power, and survival should be the top priority. When entering, one must always have a way out. Only in this way can one have a better ending. True spiritual practice is not to hide deliberately, but to live among others.

Only by knowing the art of retreating unscathed and keeping one's good intentions alive can one be great and spectacular, because the other side of grand and outstanding achievements is to leave at any time and retreat in peace.

雷天大壮（卦三十四）　（乾下震上）

Dazhuang (Exuberance), Thunder and Heaven (Hexagram 34)　(Qian below, Zhen above)

当阳意壮盛超过阴意的时候，就可以说是阳意大壮的状态，有利于刚健地行动，指阳意刚强壮盛的一面可以表现出来。无论是人还是事物，阴阳不再平衡，当阳意超过了阴意，既要努力保持壮盛，又要防止即将进入衰老的状态。

意境盛大需要留意社会生存的规则，如礼仪的限制等。如何常葆壮盛的人天之意，让意念盛大，又符合礼仪之限度，这是下经认真讨论的主要问题。这种对阳刚之意的限制和调适，同时包涵让阳刚意念受挫的经验，这种丰富经验场域能够帮助人们在挫折当中成长，让心意更加合理地壮大。

When *yang* intention is stronger than *yin* intention, it can be said to be a state of strong *yang* intention, which is conducive to vigorous action, meaning that the strong and powerful side of *yang* intention can be expressed. Whether it is people or things, *yin* and *yang* are no longer balanced. When *yang* exceeds *yin*, we must not only strive to maintain our prosperity, but also prevent ourselves from entering a state of aging.

To have a grand intentional context, one needs to pay attention to the rules of social survival, such as ritual propriety restrictions. How to always maintain the grand intentionality of humanity and nature, make the intentions grand, and comply with the limits of ritual propriety? That is the main issue seriously discussed in the second half of the book. This restriction and adjustment of strong and positive intentions also includes the experience of frustration of those intentions. This rich experience field can help people grow through frustration and allow their intentionality to grow more reasonably.

大壮，利贞。

《彖》曰：大壮，大者壮也。刚以动，故壮。"大壮，利贞"，大者正也。正大，而天地之情可见矣。

《象》曰：雷在天上，大壮。君子以非礼弗履。

【明译】

大壮卦象征强壮旺盛，有利于持守正道去做事。

《彖传》说：大壮卦全卦四刚二柔，是刚大者强壮旺盛的状态，所以卦名叫大壮。下卦乾为刚健，上卦震为动，刚健有力地行动，所以被称作强壮。大壮卦有利于持守正道去做事，是因为刚健强大者必然要守正不阿。盛大又能保持正直，就可以感通天地的情理。

《象传》说：上卦震为雷，下卦乾为天，雷声响彻天下就是大壮卦。君子从雷在天上的卦象里看到，雷声壮大好比上天发威不容邪念，所以要常葆壮盛的人天之意，不干非礼之事。

Hexagram Dazhuang (Exuberance) symbolizes strength and exuberance, which is conducive to doing things in the right way.

The *Judgment Commentary* (*Tuan Zhuan*) says: As a whole, Hexagram Dazhuang (Exuberance) has four strong and two soft lines, which means the great are strong and vigorous, so the hexagram is called Hexagram Dazhuang (Exuberance). The lower Trigram Qian is strength, and the upper Trigram Zhen is vibration. It moves vigorously and powerfully, so it is called strong. Hexagram Dazhuang (Exuberance) is conducive to doing things in the right way, because those who are great and strong necessarily keep to the right way. If one is grand and upright, one can understand the patterns of heaven and earth.

The *Image Commentary* (*Xiang Zhuan*) says: The upper Trigram Zhen is thunder, the lower Trigram Qian is the sky, and the sound of thunder resounding all over the world under heaven is Hexagram Dazhuang (Exuberance). An exemplary person can see from the hexagram of thunder in the sky that the sound of thunder is like the power of heaven that does not tolerate evil intentions. Therefore, one must always maintain the cosmological intentionality of humanity and heaven in a strong manner and refrain from doing improper things.

【明意】

意念在人群境遇之中，随时随刻与他人意念沟通交流而生发。人需要体验天地阳刚正向之意，将其发展壮大，作为运作大业的基础，所以壮盛的人天之意有大的感应力，可以推动与阴意的互动，改换世间的阴阳变化。

把此壮盛的天道之意落实在人间，则是心意在社群中正向发展之道。意向刚正的持续才是志向合适的发展方向，志向之持存使阳刚之意境扩张而盛大。

[Illuminating Intentionality]

Intentions arise in crowd situations and can communicate with other people's intentions at any time. People need to experience the strong and positive intentionality of heaven and earth and develop it as the basis for the operation of great undertakings. Therefore, the strong intentionality of humanity and heaven has great inductive power, which can promote the interaction with *yin* intentionality and change the *yin* and *yang* transformations in the world.

Concretizing this magnificent intentionality of the heavenly *dao* in the human world is the way for the positive development of intentionality in the community. The continuation of the righteousness of intention is the appropriate development direction of ambition. The persistence of ambition makes the strong intentional context expand and become grander.

初九：壮于趾，征凶，有孚。

《象》曰："壮于趾"，其孚穷也。

【明译】

初九：把刚猛强健的力道用在脚趾上，如此征进必然遇到凶险，虽然走路的人内心还保持着信心诚实。

《象传》说：把刚猛强健的力道用在脚趾上，如果具有信实的刚爻初九自以为强盛，还想再向上猛进，就会走向穷途末路。

Nine (*yang*/strong line) in the first place: Using forceful and robust strength on the toes. Such an expedition will inevitably encounter dangers, although one who walks still maintains confidence and honesty in one's intention.

The *Image Commentary* (*Xiang Zhuan*) says: Use strong and sturdy strength on your toes. If the faithful Nine (*yang*/strong line) in the first place thinks one is strong and wants to make further progress, one will end up with no future.

【明意】

初爻积蓄刚强之意，但不可把力道用错地方。如果把刚力用于脚趾上，当然是用错了地方，于事无补不说，还暴露了自己。形式壮盛就不必武装到牙齿，根本不必从一开始就虚张声势，长久的壮盛要以实力开道，更不可一开始就把力道用错方向。

可见，强大实力和优势地位往往使人误判，认为要在每个方向着力，其结果可能适得其反。用力不在合适的方向，如分散用力或者上面没有赏识的人，再有能力也无法实现目标，在穷困的境遇中，意志与能力都无法施展。初九看九四，说明初出茅庐之时，不可锋芒毕露，否则盛大一时，容易昙花一现，事与愿违。

[Illuminating Intentionality]

The first line accumulates the intentionality of strength, but strength should not be used in the wrong place. If one uses rigidity on your toes, one is certainly using it in the wrong place, which will not help the problem and will also expose oneself. To be prosperous in form, one does not need to be armed to the teeth, and there is no need to bluff from the beginning. To achieve long-term prosperity, one must use strength to clear the way, but one must not use one's strength in the wrong direction from the beginning.

It can be seen that great strength and dominant position often make people misjudge and think that efforts should be made in every direction, which may be counterproductive. If effort is not in an appropriate direction, if effort is scattered or there is no appreciation from above, no matter how capable one is, one will not be able to achieve anything. In a poor situation, one will not be able to exert one's intentions and ability. The Nine (*yang*/strong line) in the first place looking at the Nine (*yang*/strong line) in the fourth place means that when one is just starting out, one should not show one's sharpness, otherwise it may be grand for a while, but will be short-lived and backfire.

九二：贞吉。

《象》曰：九二"贞吉"，以中也。

【明译】

九二：坚守正道去做事，就会吉祥。

《象传》说：九二坚守正道去做事，就会吉祥，因为在下卦中位，能行中道。

Nine (*yang*/strong line) in the second place: Sticking to the right *dao* in doing things, there will be good fortune.

The *Image Commentary* (*Xiang Zhuan*) says: The Nine (*yang*/strong line) in the second place sticks to the right *dao* in one's actions, and will be fortunate, because if one is in the middle of the lower Trigram, one can follow the middle *dao*.

【明意】

坚守正道而吉祥是知道自己意识境遇的分寸，不采取激进的做法，当然这是因为上有阴爻，上面有人知道自己的心意，所以可以用中和平稳的方式来处理事情。

此爻刚而能柔，圆通应变，所以较好。阳刚之意，要入阴柔之境，方可绽放其阳刚之力。

[Illuminating Intentionality]

To stick to the right *dao* and be fortunate means to know the appropriateness of one's own conscious situation and not take radical measures. Of course, this is because there are *yin* lines above, and there are people above who know one's own intentions, so they can handle things in a neutral and stable way.

This line is strong yet supple and flexible, so it is rather good. Strong intentionality must enter the soft realm before its strong power can bloom.

九三：小人用壮，君子用罔，贞厉。羝（dī）羊触藩，羸（léi）其角。
《象》曰："小人用壮"，"君子罔"也。

【明译】

九三：小人妄用自己的强壮盲目行动，君子不会这样蛮干，会持守正道以防止危险，否则就会像发狠的公羊冲撞藩篱，觭角被卡在篱笆里面，动弹不得。

《象传》说：小人肆无忌惮，任意妄动，而君子知道居安思危，时刻戒惧。

Nine (*yang*/strong line) in the third place: A petty person abuses one's strength and acts blindly. An exemplary person will not act recklessly like this. One will stick to the right *dao* to avoid danger. Otherwise, one will be like a fierce ram rushing into a fence, and one's horns will get stuck in the fence, unable to move.

The *Image Commentary* (*Xiang Zhuan*) says: A petty person is unscrupulous and acts arbitrarily, but an exemplary person knows to be prepared for danger in times of peace and is always on guard.

【明意】

君子心意通大，虽心网通于大网，但不应该被现实的网所困。小人之心意简单，壮盛之时则盲目而不能考虑，过分在乎利益得失，最后被现实的网所困。可见，羊再壮，角再大，如小人不能开通天眼看到天网，最后虽然壮行，但还是容易被网住，陷入种种困境和羁绊。而心意通天的君子，壮盛之时能够意识到当壮之时，弱势之意有其无用之用，直面罗网的力量，不敢专断凌意而行，反而不容易被现实的困境所栓缚住。在壮盛之时，宁可常守不壮之时的心意之境，方可保其壮盛。

意念的冲击可能面对一个网，也比喻受困之时，不可蛮干，或者居安思危，时刻戒惧。日常生活中不可得理不饶人，过分的话会走向反面。一旦在上位的管理者都用网来网住人们，人民就被网为小人，也就不可能大壮起来。能够被利益网住的都是小人，君子心意通于天地之道，念念跳出利益之网，不会陷在具体的形色利益之争当中。

[Illuminating Intentionality]

An exemplary person's intentionality is connected to heaven. Although the network of one's heart-mind is connected to the network of heaven, one should not be trapped by the net of reality. The petty person has a simple mind, and when one is in one's prime, one is blind and unable to think. One cares too much about gains and losses, and is finally trapped in the net of reality. It can be seen that no matter how strong a sheep is, no matter how big its horns are, just like a petty person, it cannot open its eyes and see the network of heaven. In the end, although it is strong, it is still easily caught in the net and falls into various difficulties and fetters. An exemplary person with a powerful intentionality can realize that when one is strong, a weak will has its useless purpose. One faces the power of the net, and dare not act arbitrarily with one's will. On the contrary, one is not easily bound by real-life dilemmas. When one is in one's prime, one should rather stay in the state of one's intentionality that one was in when one was not strong, in order to maintain one's prime.

The impact of intentions may be faced with a net, which also means that when one is trapped, one should not act recklessly, or be prepared for danger in times of peace and be alert at all times, not being unreasonable and unforgiving in daily life. If one goes too far, it will lead to the opposite. Once managers at the top use nets to trap people, the people will be treated as petty people and it will be impossible for them to become strong. Those who can be caught in the net of interests are petty people. An exemplary person's intentionality is connected with the *dao* of heaven and earth. One can jump out of the net of interests and will not be trapped in specific conflicts of interests.

九四：贞吉，悔亡。藩决不羸，壮于大舆之輹。

《象》曰："藩决不羸"，尚往也。

【明译】

九四：坚守正道去做事自然吉祥，没有什么忧虑和悔恨。这就像公羊冲破藩篱的拘束，把角解脱出来，好像大车因为有强壮的车辕可以跑得更远。

《象传》说：公羊冲破藩篱的拘束，把角解脱出来，象征九四还要继续往前，一直前行向上（上面两个柔爻已无力抵御九四的上长趋势）。

Nine (*yang*/strong line) in the fourth place: Sticking to the right *dao* and doing things will naturally bring good fortune, without any worries or regrets. This is like a ram breaking through the constraints of a fence and freeing its horns, like a cart that can run farther because of its strong chassis.

The *Image Commentary* (*Xiang Zhuan*) says: The ram breaks through the constraints of the fence and frees its horns, which symbolizes that the Nine (*yang*/strong line) in the fourth place will continue to push forward and keep advancing (the two soft lines above are no longer able to resist the upward trend of the Nine (*yang*/strong line) in the fourth place).

【明意】

大壮之时，好像阳意全升大胜之势，其实心念发动反而要特别小心谨慎，而只有谨守正道才可以防止忧悔，即使前进也要依正道行进。在阳意刚进之时，要能纤柔应对局势，不可过刚而行。意念在境遇之前的收敛、节度，对于行动的分寸非常关键。九四可以勇往直前，努力进取，但以阳居阴，说明真正强壮的念力反而不过度强壮，要刚而能谦。要想保持大壮的壮盛之势，就要学习九四之守正道，让人天之意保持持续壮盛的状态。

[Illuminating Intentionality]

When one is strong, it seems that one's *yang*/positive intentions are fully victorious. In fact, one needs to be particularly careful when initiating one's intention. Only by adhering to the right *dao* can one prevent regrets. Even if one moves forward, one must proceed on the right *dao*. When *yang*/positive intentions first enter, one must be able to deal with the situation delicately and not be too rigid. The restraint and moderation of intentions before the situation is very critical to the propriety of actions. The Nine (*yang*/strong line) in the fourth place can move forward bravely and strive for progress, but *yang* resides in a *yin* position, which shows that a truly strong intentionality should not be overly strong, but must be strong and humble. If one wants to maintain a strong and prosperous situation, one must learn the righteous way of the Nine (*yang*/strong line) in the fourth place, allowing the intentionality of humanity and heaven to maintain a continuously prosperous state.

六五：丧羊于易，无悔。

《象》曰："丧羊于易"，位不当也。

【明译】

六五：在（阴阳交易的）边界丧失阳意（羊），无须怨悔。

《象传》说：在（阴阳交易的）地方丧失阳意（羊），因为六五所处的位置不合适（虽以柔爻占据尊位，但在刚位又处在刚爻上长的前沿）。

Six (*yin*/soft line) in the fifth place: There is no need to regret if one loses one's *yang* intentionality (sheep) at the boundary (of *yin-yang* transaction).

The *Image Commentary* (*Xiang Zhuan*) says: One's *yang* intentionality (sheep) is lost in the place where *yin* and *yang* are exchanged and traded, because the position of the Six (*yin*/soft line) in the fifth place is inappropriate (although a soft line occupies an honorable position, but in a strong position it is also on the frontier of the growing strong lines).

【明意】

意念在全境之中，如何把握分寸非常重要。该放下的时候也没有必要拖泥带水，因为悔恨已经没有用了。换言之，意念对于身外之物的操控与得失要放得下，随时能放就放，不可有过度的执念。六五因其无能柔弱而位居高位，虽自有其过人之处。但形势比人强，无法改变，必须丧失自身阳意作为代价，也就无可悔恨。

[Illuminating Intentionality]

Intentions are in a whole situation, and it is very important to grasp proportion. There is no need to drag one's feet when it's time to let go, because regret is of no use. In other words, one must be able to let go of the control, gains and losses of things outside the body, and let go whenever possible, without excessive obsession. The Six (*yin*/soft line) in the fifth place is only in a high position because of its incompetence and weakness, although it has its own merits. But a situation is stronger than an individual and cannot be changed. One must lose one's own *yang*/positive intentions as the price, so there is no regret.

第三章　易经明意
——爻意分说（下经）

上六：羝羊触藩，不能退，不能遂，无攸利。艰则吉。

《象》曰："不能退，不能遂"，不详也。"艰则吉"，咎不长也。

【明译】

上六：公羊顶撞藩篱，角被卡住了，不能后退，也无法前进遂心如意，一点好处都没有。在艰难处境当中，坚守下去就会转而吉祥。

《象传》说：不能后退，也无法前进遂心如意，陷入进退两难的处境是上六自己没有很好审详。在艰难处境当中，坚守下去就会转而吉祥，因为上六到了极位，物极必反，否极泰来，艰难的处境不会持续太久了。

Six (*yin*/soft line) in the top place: The ram bumps against the fence and its horns are stuck. It can neither retreat nor move forward. It is of no benefit at all. In difficult situations, perseverance will turn into good fortune.

The *Image Commentary* (*Xiang Zhuan*) says: One cannot retreat, and one cannot move forward as one wishes. The dilemma is that the Six (*yin*/soft line) in the top place itself doesn't think carefully. In a difficult situation, if one sticks to it, it will turn into auspiciousness, because when the Six (*yin*/soft line) in the top place reaches the extreme, things will turn to the other way. Therefore, the difficult situation will not last long.

【明意】

上六的处境很坏，进退维谷，非常被动。处境艰难到只能用坚守待时来应对。自己没有审视好原先的处境而陷入困境，那也没有什么办法了，只有安守待时。对境遇的审视是一种有自我超越的眼光，类似于"上帝之眼（God's-eye-view）"，也类似于"以道观之（*dao*'s-eye-view）"的视角，是一种超脱本身状态、有全景意味的道的眼光，从超脱的视角看自己，看得更加清楚明白。

既然已经进退维谷，不如随遇而安，对于意念升起和遭遇的所有境遇，皆以安宁顺适的心态去面对。因心意发动，从其生之根本言之，皆通于天地生生之意，即使艰难守正，也是生意生长应有之意。如此之进，晋卦进一步诠释如何回转精进之意。即使心意都正向且合适，也要小心行事，坚持以光明磊落的正道立身，才可能伺机升晋。

[Illuminating Intentionality]

The Six (*yin*/soft line) in the top place is in a very bad situation, stuck between a rock and a hard place, and very passive. The situation is so difficult that the only way to deal with it is to persevere and wait. If one fails to examine the original situation and gets into trouble, one has no choice but to wait and see. The examination of the situation is a perspective of self-transcendence, similar to a "God's-eye-view" or "*dao*'s-eye-view," a vision from *dao* that transcends one's own state and has a panoramic intentionality. Looking at oneself from a transcendent perspective, one can see more clearly.

Since one is stuck in a dilemma, it is better to accept the situation as it comes, and face all situations and encounters that arise with a peaceful and comfortable attitude. Due to the initiation of intention, speaking from the root of its production, it is all connected with the intentionality of production of heaven and earth. Even if it is difficult to keep it right, it is also the intentionality that business and growth should have. Such progress is further explained in Hexagram Jin (Promotion) concerning how to turn around and make progress. Even if one's intentions are positive and suitable, one still has to be careful and stick to the bright, open and upright *dao* in establishing oneself, so that one can wait for opportunities to be promoted.

火地晋（卦三十五）　（坤下离上）

Jin (Promotion), Fire and Earth (Hexagram 35)　(Kun below, Li above)

　　无论升晋多难，意念之生当如日附天空，善念光明，明德昭彰，保持善意之生生气象，因为善意的升进要比人身位的升进更重要。"晋"是太阳（上卦离日）从地面（下卦坤地）升起之象，升进而光明灿烂。《杂卦》说明是青天白日。下卦坤为牝马、为众，互卦坎为美脊马，有马繁殖之象。晋指的是太阳升起的大白昼，下卦有三个柔爻齐头并进，好像一个白天之内被天子召见三次。

No matter how difficult it is to be promoted, the productivity of intentions should be like the sun in the sky, in which good intentions are bright, virtues are clear, and a productive atmosphere of good intentions should be maintained, because the advancement of good intentions is more important than the advancement of one's personal status. Jin (Promotion) is an image of the sun (upper Trigram Li) rising from the earth (lower Trigram Kun), rising and becoming bright and brilliant. In the *Miscellaneous Characteristics of the Hexagrams*, Hexagram Jin (Promotion) refers to a clear sky and white sun. The lower Trigram Kun represents a female horse and a crowd, and the mutual hexagram Kan is a beautiful-back horse, so has the image of horse breeding. Hexagram Jin (Promotion) refers to broad daylight when the sun rises. There are three soft lines in the lower Trigram advancing together, as if summoned by the emperor three times in one day.

晋，康侯用锡马蕃庶，昼日三接。

《彖》曰：晋，进也。明出地上，顺而丽乎大明，柔进而上行，是以"康侯用锡马蕃庶，昼日三接"也。

《象》曰：明出地上，晋。君子以自昭明德。

【明译】

晋卦象征精进晋升，好比尊贵的康侯用天子赏赐的良马繁殖得很好，结果一日之内被天子三次召见。

卦名晋是精进晋升的意思。上卦离为明，下卦坤为地，如同光明的太阳从大地上冉冉升起。下卦坤为地，特性是柔顺，上卦离为日，特性是附丽，光明，犹如大地上的万物柔顺地依附在美丽盛大的太阳光明之上。晋卦由观卦变来，即观的六四柔爻向上升进到五位，这是柔顺地向上升进。因此就好比尊贵的康侯用天子赏赐的良马繁殖得很好，结果一日之内被天子三次召见。

《象传》说：下坤为地，上离为明，组合光明出现在大地之上的卦象，这就是象征精进晋升的晋卦。君子看到阳光普照，万物欣欣向荣的卦象，要彰明自己光明的人天之意。

Hexagram Jin (Promotion) symbolizes advancement and promotion. It is like the noble Marquis Kang using the good horses gifted by the emperor to breed well, and being summoned by the emperor three times in one day.

The hexagram name Jin means advancement and promotion. The upper Trigram Li is brightness, and the lower Trigram Kun is earth, just like the bright sun rising slowly from the earth. The lower Trigram Kun is earth, and its characteristics are soft and supple, while the upper Trigram Li is the sun, and its characteristics are beauty and brightness, just like the myriad things on the earth that are softly attached to the beautiful and grand light of the sun. Hexagram Jin (Promotion) changes from Hexagram Guan (Observation), that is, the Six (*yin*/soft line) in the fourth place of Guan rises up to the fifth position, representing a gentle upward progress. Therefore, it is like the noble Marquis Kang using the fine horses gifted by the emperor to breed well, and being summoned by the emperor three times in one day.

The *Image Commentary* (*Xiang Zhuan*) says: The lower Kun is earth, and the upper Li is light. Their combination as a hexagram in which light appears on the earth is Hexagram Jin (Promotion) that symbolizes advancement. When an exemplary person sees the hexagram image that the sun is shining and the myriad things are prosperous, one wants to show one's own bright intentions for humanity and heaven.

【明意】

日出为天地生机之象，柔顺地附于美丽盛大的光明是生机盎然之象。日出地上，生机勃发，柔顺附丽。意生世界，兑在西为我，我出之后，通于世界。我跟世界相生，顺阳意而行，心动和顺于天下：心意与日月协同自得，能自知则明，了解自己，知己知人。此通于天道的良心发动，附于日月之行，而能够提升人与物质精神境界。

实体存在如单纯具体物的存在，是阴阳两物交互作用而成，从自然状态到意念状态都是如此。《周易》教人意会以道为本，所有的存在都在变易和流行之中，不认为世界存在固定不变的实体。不是先有一个固定的实体之后，才有其状态和属性的变化，而是实体本身就是永恒变化的状态。这样，实体状态的变化不按严格的因果关系，而按照五行生克关系来展开。如果原因导致结果算是必然的，那么五行生克关系如因果一样也是必然的。不管古人经验性的论证是否最可靠，但五行相似性推论自有其有效性：如A推出B，一般来说，推不出A类推出B类；但五行生克之推理似乎可以。可见，五行生克与因果律的自然性一样，应该得到仔细审查和研究。

[Illuminating Intentionality]

The sunrise is a symbol of the vitality of heaven and earth, and the light that softly attaches to its beauty and grandeur is a symbol of vital abundance. When the sun rises, the earth is full of vitality, supple and beautiful. Intentionality produces the world, and Trigram Dui (Lake) in the west is the "I". After the "I" emerges, it connects with the world. The "I" lives together with the world, follows the intentionality of the sun in its movement, and its intention moves harmoniously with the world: the intentionality of the "I" is in self-content harmony with the sun and the moon, and can gain clarity through knowing itself, understanding itself, and knowing itself and others. This conscience connected with the heavenly *dao* initiates, attaches to the movement of the sun and the moon in its movement, and is able to enhance the human and their material and spiritual realms.

Existing entities, such as simple concrete existents, are the result of the interaction between *yin* and *yang*, and this is true from the natural state to the state of intention. The *Book of Changes* teaches people to grasp *dao* as the foundation, and that all existence is subject to change and flow, and does not believe that there is any fixed entity in the world. It is not that there is a fixed entity first, and then its state and attributes change, but that an entity itself is in an eternally changing state. In this way, changes in actual state do not follow a strict causal relationship, but unfold according to the producing/restraining relationships between the Five Phases. If it is inevitable that causes lead to effects, then the relationship between the Five Phases is inevitable just like cause and effect. Regardless of whether the empirical arguments of the ancients are the most reliable, the inference of the similarity of the Five Phases has its own validity: if one can infer B from A, generally speaking, it is impossible to infer type B from type A; however, the inference of the Five Phases' producing and restraining seems to be acceptable. It can be seen that the producing and restraining of the Five Phases is as natural as the law of cause and effect and should be carefully scrutinized and studied.

初六：晋如，摧如，贞吉。罔孚，裕，无咎。

《象》曰："晋如，摧如"，独行正也。"裕无咎"，未受命也。

【明译】

初六：升进之初容易遭受摧折压制，坚守正道，可获吉祥。即使暂时不能见信于人，也要从容应对，宽慰自己，就不会有什么问题。

《象传》说：升进之初容易遭受摧折压制，因为初六在孤独中坚守正道行进（合乎晋卦"柔进而上行"的正道，又有九四为正应）。从容应对，放宽心态，也就不会有什么祸患，是初六还未接到正式任命。

Six (*yin*/soft line) in the first place: At the beginning of promotion, it is easy to be crushed and suppressed. If one sticks to the right *dao*, one will get good fortune. Even if one cannot trust others for the time being, one should deal with it calmly and assure oneself, and there will be no problems.

The *Image Commentary* (*Xiang Zhuan*) says: At the beginning of promotion, it is easy to be crushed and suppressed, because the Six (*yin*/soft line) in the first place sticks to the right *dao* in solitude (in line with the right *dao* of Hexagram Jin (Promotion) "softly advancing and then going upward," and with an upright response from the Nine (*yang*/strong line) in the fourth place). Take it calmly and relax your mental state, and there will be no trouble. This is because the Six (*yin*/soft line) in the first place has not yet received a formal appointment.

【明意】

从古到今，晋升之路都是人挤人，此爻希望人们走阳光正道，不要用心去挤。在走向成功的过程中，难免遭遇曲折，继续坚持追求正道不放弃，总会得吉。虽然此时往往不受信任，也不会被委以重任，但无须在意，宜淡然处之，这样就不会有咎过。

晋升的力量越大，相克的力量也越大，光明与黑暗的势力相辅相成，心意生生而升，这对相应的阴的意义的掌控和独行，放松之生。意念之生必然依托情境而生，也就是依境而生（creatio in situ），而情境通常来说难以为自己的意识完全掌控，故一方面要自控，一方面需要等待情境发生变化。

刚刚出道，容易受到催挤压迫，所以不可过急，要学会摸索，找到最合适的方式，以乐观的态度走正路。

[Illuminating Intentionality]

From ancient times to the present, the road to promotion has been crowded with people. This line hopes that people will take the right *dao* and not deliberately crowd in. On the way to success, one will inevitably encounter twists and turns. If one continues to pursue the right *dao* and never gives up, one will always get good fortune. Although people are often not trusted at this time and will not be entrusted with important responsibilities, there is no need to pay attention to this and it should be treated calmly, so there will be no blame.

The greater the power of promotion, the greater the power of mutual restraint. The forces of light and darkness complement each other, and intentionality rises. This control and independence of the corresponding *yin* intentional context is the product of relaxation. The production of intentions must depend on the situation, that is, *creatio in situ*. Generally speaking, a situation is difficult for one's own consciousness to completely control. Therefore, on the one hand, one must control oneself, and on the other hand, one needs to wait for the situation to change.

When one is just starting out, one is easily pushed and squeezed, so one should not be too hasty, learn to explore, find the most suitable way, and take the right *dao* with an optimistic attitude.

六二：晋如，愁如，贞吉。受兹介福，于其王母。

《象》曰："受兹介福"，以中正也。

【明译】

六二：精进晋升之际愁容满面，坚守正道，可获吉祥。因为他将要从尊贵的王母那里，接受如此宏大的福泽。

《象传》说：六二将要承接如此宏大的福泽，是因为六二居中能够持守正道（六二在下卦中位，柔居柔位，位正）。

Six (*yin*/soft line) in the second place: When one is diligent and at the edge of promotion, one may look anxious. If one sticks to the right *dao*, one will get good fortune, because one is about to receive such a great blessing from the noble queen mother.

The *Image Commentary* (*Xiang Zhuan*) says: The Six (*yin*/soft line) in the second place will inherit such great blessings because the Six (*yin*/soft line) in the second place is in the middle and can maintain the right *dao* (the Six (*yin*/soft line) in the second place is in the middle of the lower Trigram, soft in a soft position, and the position is upright).

【明意】

生的处境化状态有竞争有压力，但主要靠自己努力。晋升更多的是社会化的升，是人群夹缝中的生存和发展。人的心意在与他人的互动之中，几乎是处于夹缝之间，总是受到压制，难以被信任。意念的生机常常不被人承认，但还是要从容应对，安心等待为好。人的心意对他人心意的领会是主观还是客观的？有时人们会认为存在皆主观，那他人对自己心意的判断与互动都是自己心意的作用，其实未必尽然。爻的位置与力量强调互动的客观性。人与他人的关系可能是既生又克的关系，而生与克的分寸还不全是自己主观可以掌握的。

生于人际之中，因中正而有福，福是因缘和合，时机和形式造成的幸运受到保佑。只要把目光放长远，自我完善，应该就会有出头之日。

[Illuminating Intentionality]

The situations of life involve competition and pressure, but one must mainly rely on one's own efforts. Promotion is more about social promotion, survival and development among the crowd. In interactions with others, people's intentions are almost caught in the cracks, always suppressed, and difficult to trust. The vitality of intentions is often not recognized by others, but it is better to take things calmly and wait with peace of mind. Is a person's understanding of other people's intentions subjective or objective? Sometimes people think that all existence is subjective, and that other people's judgments and interactions with their own intentions are a function of their own intentions. In fact, this is not always the case. The position and power of the lines emphasize the objectivity of interaction. The relationship between a person and others may be a relationship of both producing and restraining, and the balance between producing and restraining is not entirely within one's subjective control.

Living among human beings, it is fortunate because it is central and upright. Fortune is a harmonious unity of causes and conditions, and the good fortune caused by timing and form is a blessing. As long as one take a long-term view and improves oneself, one should be able to get ahead.

六三：众允，悔亡。

《象》曰："众允"之志，上行也。

【明译】

六三：众人都服从并愿意追随一起升进，忧虑悔恨都跟着消除了。

《象传》说：众人的心志都信任和拥护，愿意跟随六三走正道前进，是因为六三有上进之心，而众人也愿意向上依附行动。

Six (*yin*/soft line) in the third place: The multitude all obey and are willing to follow and advance together, and all worries and regrets are eliminated.

The *Image Commentary* (*Xiang Zhuan*) says: The multitude all trusts and supports the Six (*yin*/soft line) in the third place and is willing to follow the Six (*yin*/soft line) in the third place on the upright *dao*. This is because the Six (*yin*/soft line) in the third place has a desire to make progress, and everyone is also willing to attach themselves to it and move upward.

【明意】

六三爻强调，一个人要想晋升或发展，必须要有一定的群众基础，要学会笼络人心。这样才能赢得上司的信任和重用。人缘很重要，也是这一爻的核心。谁要是占得此爻，必须把工作重点放到得到下级或身边人、周围的人的认可和信任上，让大家觉得你这个人很靠谱，而不是一味地去讨上司的欢心与青睐。因为一旦你赢得众人的信任，便可以继续朝着既定的目标前进。

柔顺地合众意之生。心志向上升进，而且带动同仁一起升进。同仁们柔顺地依附而生，是与他人共生之生，或带动他人之生。众人推举信任之生，借着他人之认可信任而生。众人的心志都信任而上行，顺则有福，逆则有悔。

[Illuminating Intentionality]

The Six (*yin*/soft line) in the third place emphasizes that if a person wants to be promoted or develop, one must have a certain base in the multitude and learn to win over people's intentions. Only in this way can one win the trust and confidence of one's boss. The dependent co-arising of people is very important and is the core of this line. Anyone who occupies this position must focus on gaining the recognition and trust of subordinates, people next to them, and people around them, so that everyone feels that they are a reliable person, rather than blindly seeking the favor and esteem of their boss. Once one gains the trust of others, one can continue to move toward one's goals.

Living in harmony with the intentions of the multitude, one's ambition is to move upward and forward, and lead one's colleagues to progress together. Colleagues submissively cling to life, living in symbiosis with others, or leading others to live. The trust of the multitude is produced through the recognition and trust of others. The multitude's will is to trust and move forward, so if one follows this, one will gain good fortune, and if one goes against it, one will have regrets.

九四：晋如鼫（shí）鼠，贞厉。

《象》曰："鼫鼠，贞厉"，位不当也。

【明译】

九四：晋升的时候，像身无一技之长的鼫鼠那样，还固守不动，就会有危险。

《象传》说：像身无一技之长的鼫鼠那样，还固守不动，就会有危险，因为九四居位不适当（九四在柔爻上进的路上，有可能被凌轹而过）。

Nine (*yang*/strong line) in the fourth place: When one is promoted, one will be in danger if one remains motionless like a mole with no skills.

The *Image Commentary* (*Xiang Zhuan*) says: If one remains stationary like a mole with no skills, one will be in danger, because the position of the Nine (*yang*/strong line) in the fourth place is inappropriate (the Nine (*yang*/strong line) in the fourth place may be passed over as soft lines progress).

【明意】

九四再不动，就错过升迁的时机，也得不到生机。九四挡住了柔爻升进的路，属于固守失策的状态，被艮止住了，动弹不得，好像被外力给压着一样。如何升进要非常小心，一旦被外力强压住了，就可能难以动弹，一旦被跳过去，成为挡住的障碍就尴尬了。意念的生机要在形势当中艰难地维持下去，即使升进再难，也应该保持升进的心意和态势。

[Illuminating Intentionality]

If the Nine (*yang*/strong line) in the fourth place does not move in, it will miss the opportunity for promotion and lose its vitality. The Nine (*yang*/strong line) in the fourth place blocks the soft lines' way forward, and is stuck in a state of mismanagement. It is stopped by Gen (Mountain) and cannot move, as if it were being pressed by an external force. One has to be very careful about how to ascend. Once one is suppressed by an external force, it may be difficult to move. Once one is jumped over, it is embarrassing to become an obstacle. The vitality of intentions can be maintained only with difficulty in the situational propensity. No matter how difficult it is to advance, one should maintain the intention and attitude of advancement.

六五：悔亡，失得勿恤。往吉，无不利。

《象》曰："失得勿恤"，往有庆也。

【明译】

六五：忧虑悔恨消除了，不必劳神费心计较得失，不管如何前进，都是吉祥的，没有什么不利。

《象传》说：不必劳神费心计较得失，因为六五前往升进，大有喜庆。

Six (*yin*/soft line) in the fifth place: Worries and regrets are eliminated. There is no need to worry about gains and losses. No matter how one moves forward, it will be auspicious and there will be no disadvantages.

The *Image Commentary* (*Xiang Zhuan*) says: There is no need to worry about gains and losses, because it will be a great joy for the Six (*yin*/soft line) in the fifth place to progress.

【明意】

六五升进到主位，进入一片光明的前景当中，但仍然有危险之位，虽有忧虑，但因为升进成功，前途光明灿烂，所以不必过虑。生意不在失得之间，五爻是生机比较自然开放的状态。柔顺上行的生机达到最轻松宽裕的状态。

晋卦是晋升之路上心意的调适，如何在现实的阴阳之意的交战当中，保持自己心意的生机，是非常不容易的。上升之路是一条充满忧虑的道路，可以说没有一时一刻的宽松和平易，因为时刻处在与他人他意的交往和交战之中，即使六五成功实现了晋升，忧悔也不可能完全放下，只是暂时觉得轻松，可以放手去做事的状态。

[Illuminating Intentionality]

The Six (*yin*/soft line) in the fifth place represents people ascending to the main position and entering a bright future, but there are still dangerous positions. Although there are worries, there is no need to worry too much because the promotion is successful and the future is bright and brilliant. Productive intentions are not between gains and losses, and the fifth line is a relatively natural and open state of vitality. The supple upward vitality reaches its most relaxed and generous state.

Hexagram Jin (Promotion) concerns the adjustment of intentionality on the road to promotion. It is not easy to keep one's intentionality vital in battles between *yin* and *yang* in reality. The road of ascent is a road full of worries, and it can be said that there is not a moment of relaxation and ease, because one is always in the midst of interactions and battles with other people and other people's intentions. Even if the Six (*yin*/soft line) in the fifth place successfully achieves promotion, it cannot completely let go of its regrets, only temporarily attaining a state in which it feels relaxed and can let go in its affairs.

上九：晋其角，维用伐邑。厉吉，无咎，贞吝。

《象》曰："维用伐邑"，道未光也。

【明译】

上九：晋升到最高的极点了，宛如高居兽角的尖端，（这时虽然退无可退，但）还可以联合出兵征伐逆乱的属国，如果放手一搏就可能转危为吉，不会有什么问题；但如果正固不动，那就只会更加被动了。

《象传》说：（形势逼人的时候）还可以（维系六三一起）出兵征伐逆乱的属国（初六和六二），因为上九虽然在上卦离（光）里，但是可惜位置困穷，不能远照，所以不够光大。

Nine (*yang*/strong line) in the top place: Having been promoted to the highest point, it is just like standing on the tip of a beast's horn. (Although there is no way to retreat at this time,) one can still unite to send troops to conquer a rebellious vassal country. If one gives this a try, one may be able to turn the crisis into good fortune, and there will be no problems; however, if one is too stubborn and does not move, one will only become more passive.

The *Image Commentary* (*Xiang Zhuan*) says: (When the situation is pressing) one can still send troops to conquer rebellious vassal countries (the Sixes (*yin*/soft lines) in the first and third places), because although the Nine (*yang*/strong line) in the top place is in the upper Trigram Li (Light), unfortunately its location is poor and it cannot illuminate from a distance, so it is not bright enough.

【明意】

这一爻说明，在众阴爻一起晋升，逼退阳爻的境遇之中，被逼到角落的阳爻到了迫不得已反击之时。阳爻该出手做事的时候，若再不抓紧时间去做，就会错过机遇，空留遗憾。如果还正固过分，不知变通，就会导致不通不顺。

上九看起来是不得已排除异己，制造内乱，但阴意一路晋升，势力摧枯拉朽，到了上面，就强求一致，党同伐异，导致阳意虽然微弱，也只有绝地反击。所以不能使阴阳某一方力量绝对独大，必须彼此理解，进退有度，持守一个阴阳互动的合理分寸才行。

[Illuminating Intentionality]

This line shows that in a situation where all *yin* lines are promoted together and force the *yang* lines to retreat, the *yang* line who is forced into a corner has reached the top to fight back. When it is time to act, if one fails to seize the time to do it, one will miss the opportunity and leave regrets. If one is too upright and rigid and does not know how to adapt, it will lead to problems.

The Nine (*yang*/strong line) in the top place seems to have no choice but to eliminate dissidents and create civil strife, but *yin* intentionality has been promoted all the way, and its power is overwhelming. When it reaches the top, it insists on unanimity, where it unites the supporting parties and eliminate the opposing parties. As a result, although *yang* intentionality is weak, it can only fight back desperately. Therefore, one side of *yin* and *yang* cannot be absolutely dominant, and they must understand each other, advance and retreat in a measured manner, and maintain a reasonable balance in *yin* and *yang* interaction.

地火明夷（卦三十六）　（离下坤上）

Mingyi (Fading Light), Earth and Fire (Hexagram 36)　(Li below, Kun above)

丰盛之后形势不妙，黑暗无光，接丰卦上六之象。明夷是光明陷落，但内心的人天之意要更加光明，方能应对黑暗无光的时势。如此黑暗的形势也可象征个人心意由阴意主导，阳意不彰，心生绝望，无路可走。绝望的意境与虚无玄冥的人生境遇有关。人生而在黑暗中，即便在光明中也跟黑暗近似，因为少有人能看清前进的方向。《易》是要找出心意的方向与天地阴阳之间的互动关系，《易》之作者多在明夷这样的艰难中，摸索到宇宙人生这门大学问，所以对《易》认知的意向性基本容纳了中国古人关于世界与人生的哲学思考与建构。

After abundance, the situation is not good, it is dark without light, taking up the image from the Six (*yin*/soft line) in the top place of Hexagram Feng (Abundance). Hexagram Mingyi (Fading Light) shows light failing, but one's inner intentionality of humanity and heaven must be brighter in order to be able to cope with the dark and lightless situation. Such a dark situation can also symbolize that one's intentionality is dominated by *yin* intentionality, with *yang* intentionality not manifested, leading to feelings of despair and having no way out. The intentional context of despair is related to an empty and obscure life situation. People are born in darkness, and even in light it is similar to darkness, because few people can see the way forward clearly. The *Book of Changes* is about uncovering the interactive relationship between the direction of intentionality and the *yin* and *yang* of heaven and earth. The author of the *Changes* mostly explores the great study of life and the cosmos in difficult times like that of Hexagram Mingyi (Fading Light), so their understanding of the *Changes'* intentionality basically accommodates the ancient Chinese philosophical thought and construction about the world and human life.

明夷，利艰贞。

《彖》曰：明入地中，"明夷"。内文明而外柔顺，以蒙大难，文王以之。"利艰贞"，晦其明也，内难而能正其志，箕子以之。

《象》曰：明入地中，明夷。君子以莅众用晦而明。

【明译】

明夷卦象征光明隐陷，利于在艰难困苦中持守正道。

《彖传》说：上卦坤为地，下卦离为日为明，太阳落入地下，光明隐伏地中，这是象征光明隐陷的明夷卦，代表黑暗无光的时势。内卦（下卦）离为文明，外卦（上卦）坤为柔顺，合在一起是内心有光明的仁德，外表为了适应黑暗时世表现极为柔顺。周文王就是用这种方法渡过蒙受大难的逆境，躲过劫难，保存自身。利于在艰难困苦中持守正道，这是要隐藏聪明才智，等待时机。在内心极度艰难痛苦的时候，还能够坚守自己刚强正直的心志，只有箕子能够这样做到。

《象传》说：上卦坤为地，下卦离为明，光明隐陷入大地之下就是明夷卦。君子看到光明受阻而不得彰显的卦象，就知道治理众人的事情之时，要隐藏自己的察微之明，这样才能使自己的人天之意愈显圣洁光明。

Hexagram Mingyi (Fading Light) symbolizes hidden light, which is conducive to maintaining the right *dao* in difficulties and hardships.

The *Judgment Commentary* (*Tuan Zhuan*) says: The upper Trigram Kun is the earth, and the lower Trigram Li is the sun and light. The sun falls into the ground, and its light is hidden in the ground. This is Hexagram Mingyi (Fading Light), which symbolizes hidden light, and represents a dark and lightless situation. The lower (inner) Trigram Li represents civilization, and the upper (outer) Trigram Kun represents suppleness. Together they represent benevolence with light in intention, and the appearance is extremely supple in order to adapt to the dark times. King Wen of Zhou used this method to survive the adversity of catastrophe, avoid disaster, and preserve himself. To stay on the right *dao* in hardships and difficulties is to hide your intelligence and wait for an opportunity. In times of extreme hardship and pain, to still be able to maintain one's strong and upright will is something that only Jizi was able to do.

The *Image Commentary* (*Xiang Zhuan*) says: The upper Trigram Kun is the earth, the lower Trigram Li is bright, and light hidden under the earth is Hexagram Mingyi (Fading Light). When an exemplary person sees the hexagram in which light is blocked and cannot be manifested, one knows that when governing the affairs of others, one must hide one's clarity of discernment, so that one's intentionality of humanity and heaven can become more pure and bright.

第三章 易经明意
——爻意分说（下经）

【明意】

在艰难时世中，内心极度痛苦，还能够坚守自己刚强正直的人天之意，并且知道隐藏自己的心志，只有箕子这样的人能够做到。君子看到光明受阻而不得彰显的卦象，就知道治理众人的事情之时，一旦形势不好，就要隐藏自己的察微之明，这样才能使自己的人天之意愈显圣洁光明。如果带有宗教意味，虽隐藏光明，但圣洁的光辉更能够亲近民众，得到拥护。意向性的圣洁与光辉可以正大光明地体现出来，为人所体知，也可以在形势极坏的时候隐藏起来。虽然不为当时的众人所知，却能为后人纪念，这样圣洁光明的心志才是最难的，需要对心志极度明白，精准体察与把握。

纯粹理性最后还是应该让位于千百万年的历史经验，自由主义带有明显的理念性特征，在处理现实和历史问题的时候还不如合乎历史经验的保守主义，所以从文明哲学或文化哲学如卡西尔等的观点来看，文明带有掩饰人类真诚创造意图的努力，而明哲之人知道如何在灾难深重的时局当中保全自己，继续从事文化创造，以等待文化复兴的时机。

[Illuminating Intentionality]

In difficult times, when one's heart is in extreme pain, one can still stick to one's strong and upright intentionality of humanity and heaven, and know how to hide one's will. Only people like Jizi could do this. When an exemplary person sees this hexagram in which the light is blocked and cannot be revealed, one knows that, when managing the affairs of others, if the situation is not good, one must hide one's clarity of discernment. Only in this way can one's intentionality of humanity and heaven be more pure and bright. If this has a religious significance, even though one hides one's light, the pure brilliance can get closer to the people and gain support. The purity and brilliance of intentionality can be manifested openly and known to others, or it can be hidden when the situation is extremely bad. Even if it is not known to everyone at the time, it can be remembered by future generations. Such a pure and bright intentionality is the most difficult thing, requiring an extreme clarity of intention, and a precise observation and grasp.

Pure reason should finally give way to millions of years of historical experience. Liberalism has obvious intellectual characteristics and is not as good as a conservatism in accord with historical experience when dealing with realistic and historical issues. Therefore, from the perspective of civilizational or cultural philosophies such as that of Ernst Cassirer, civilization involves an effort to cover up human beings' sincere creative intentions, and wise people know how to preserve themselves in disaster-ridden times and continue to engage in cultural creation, waiting for the opportunity for cultural revitalization.

初九：明夷于飞，垂其翼。君子于行，三日不食。有攸往，主人有言。

《象》曰："君子于行"，义不食也。

【明译】

初九：光明隐陷的时候，要像鸟儿那样赶紧飞走，且要低垂掩抑着翅膀，免得被发现。君子在退避的途中，忍饥挨饿，三天都没有吃东西，才得以顺利逃脱，主事的人不能够理解，出言责备。

《象传》说：君子在远险退避的途中，既出于道义也为了保全自身，匆匆忙忙顾不上吃饭了。

Nine (*yang*/strong line) in the first place: When the light fades, fly away quickly like a bird, and lower your wings to avoid being discovered. On the way to escape, the exemplary person suffers from hunger and does not eat for three days before one is able to escape smoothly. The person in charge cannot understand this and criticizes one.

The *Image Commentary* (*Xiang Zhuan*) says: An exemplary person rushes to escape from danger without even time to stop and eat, not only for moral reasons but also to protect oneself.

【明意】

形势变得黑暗的时候，不可等到自己实在过不下去，而要提早预知危难的后果，走为上策。君子为了逃避得快，而且为了安全起见，路上不可暴露行踪，所以赶路的时候，自然就不顾自己吃饭的事情了。君子采取的行动相当于遯卦，要逃跑隐遁来保全自身。

《周易》给出如此明显的建议，说明《周易》有保身的倾向，因为只有保身才能让意向的生机存续下去，才能进一步存在与发展，否则意向生机不续，意能就再也不能发挥出来。人的意向性过分外露必然浅薄。初九看到形势不对，不能展翅高飞，于是不事张扬，偷偷溜走，躲避败坏危险的局势，什么也不带，饭也不能吃。比喻还处在低位的人，眼看形势不对，就要隐藏自己，避免引起主人注意，要找机会稳妥迅速地离开。

[Illuminating Intentionality]

When a situation becomes dark, one should not wait until one really cannot survive it, but should predict the consequences of the crisis in advance and take the best course of action. In order to escape quickly and for safety reasons, an exemplary person should not expose one's whereabouts on the road, so when one is on the road, one naturally will not care about one's own food. The action taken by an exemplary person is equivalent to Hexagram Dun (Retreat), and one must run away and hide in order to protect oneself.

That the *Book of Changes* gives such obvious advice shows that the *Book of Changes* has a tendency for self-protection, because only by protecting oneself can the vitality of intention survive and further exist and develop. Otherwise, the vitality of intention will not continue and the power of intention will no longer be able to be exerted. A person's intentionality that is too exposed will inevitably be shallow. The Nine (*yang*/strong line) in the first place sees that the situation is not right and cannot fly high, so sneaks away quietly to avoid a corrupt and dangerous situation, taking nothing with it and not eating. This is a metaphor for people who are still in a lowly position. Seeing that the situation is not right, they have to hide themselves to avoid attracting the attention of their superiors and look for opportunities to leave safely and quickly.

六二：明夷，夷于左股，用拯马壮，吉。

《象》曰：六二之"吉"，顺以则也。

【明译】

六二：光明隐陷，就好像左腿受了伤，这时用比较强壮的马来代步救命，可以转危为安。

《象传》说：六二之所以能够转危为安，是因为柔爻既中又正，能够柔顺地顺从事物发展之道。

Six (*yin*/soft line) in the second place: The light is hidden, just like the left leg being injured. At this time, riding a stronger horse to save one's life can turn the danger into safety.

The *Image Commentary* (*Xiang Zhuan*) says: The reason why the Six (*yin*/soft line) in the second place can turn danger into safety is because the soft line is both middle and upright, and can docilely follow the development of things.

【明意】

心意受伤，得学会养伤，需要借助外力，柔性地转危为安，不可妄动，导致新伤。转危为安的关键在于，柔顺应对形势，在形势中汲取生机，转化不利的力量。即使没有受伤，人在江湖，身不由己，也不能不顺应形势。人的心思意念，往往易进难退，而进退的机会又往往稍纵即逝，区别仅在意念把握进退的分寸不同而已。通常来说，职责越高，风险越大，全身而退就越难。一旦危险发生，需要强有力的外力来拯救和保全，否则大难难逃。

[Illuminating Intentionality]

When one's intentionality is injured, one has to learn to recover from the injury, getting help from external forces to flexibly turn the crisis into safety, while not acting rashly and causing new injuries. The key to turning a crisis into safety is to respond to the situation flexibly, draw vitality from the situation, and transform unfavorable forces. Even if one is not injured, one cannot help oneself when one is in the arena, and one has to adapt to the situation. People's intentions and purposes are often easy to advance and difficult to retreat, and opportunities to advance and retreat are often fleeting. The only difference is that intentionality grasps the appropriateness of advance and retreat. Generally speaking, the higher the responsibility, the greater the risk, and the harder it is to escape unscathed. Once danger occurs, strong external forces are needed to rescue and preserve the situation, otherwise it may well be catastrophic.

九三：明夷于南狩，得其大首，不可疾，贞。

《象》曰："南狩"之志，乃大得也。

【明译】

九三：光明隐陷的时候，利用去南方狩猎和征伐的机会，诛灭元凶首恶，但不可操之过急，应当采取正当手段，谨慎从事。

《象传》说：向南狩猎征伐的心志（如果成功）将有巨大收获（九三志在阴阳正应的上六，向上推移可能会获得成功）。

Nine (*yang*/strong line) in the third place: When the light is hidden, use the opportunity of hunting and conquest in the south to kill the culprits. However, one should not act too hastily, but should use proper means and proceed with caution.

The *Image Commentary* (*Xiang Zhuan*) says: The ambition to hunt and conquer the south (if successful) will bring huge rewards (the Nine (*yang*/strong line) in the third place's ambition is to overcome the Six (yin/soft line) in the top place, and if it moves upward, it may be successful).

【明意】

本爻的意向性努力有很大收获，是因为在特定时势之中，有目标有手段有力量，没发生时，存在就只是可能性，伪装狩猎（南巡），突然转为征战，并成功。（大首）是敌对他意的中心，在时机成熟的时候攻伐而剿灭之，除去反对者自身，消灭对方意境存续之实有状态。

[Illuminating Intentionality]

This line's intentional efforts have yielded great results, because in a specific situation, there are goals, means, and power. Before it happens, there are only possibilities. Pretending to hunt (the southern patrol) suddenly turns to war, and succeeds. The big leader is the center of hostility among other intentions. Attacking and destroying them when the time is right removes the opponent, and eliminates the actual state of the opponent's intentional context.

六四：入于左腹，获明夷之心，于出门庭。

《象》曰："入于左腹"，获心意也。

【明译】

六四：进入近臣内侧，深刻领会光明隐陷的原因是因为暴君的邪恶心意，于是赶紧跨出门庭远走高飞，躲避时难。

《象传》说：六四进入到近臣内侧，于是深入获知光明隐陷来自上主的邪恶心意。

Six (*yin*/soft line) in the fourth place: Entering the inner circle of ministers, one profoundly understands that the reason why the light is concealed is because of the evil intentions of the tyrant, so one quickly steps out of the door and flees to avoid present difficulties.

The *Image Commentary* (*Xiang Zhuan*) says: The Six (*yin*/soft line) in the fourth place enters the inner circle of ministers, and then profoundly understands that the bright light's being hidden is due to the evil intentions of the ruler.

【明意】

用柔术获得信任,心意能够控制,并感通暗主。心意感知暗主的卑鄙手段,不忍继续同流合污,了解洞彻他的全部心意。腹部受伤,代表自己也受伤很重,伤心欲绝,决心离开。要逃离暗主邪恶心境的影响,因为知道主子有邪恶之心将伤害自己,此时当远走高飞,不必计较方式,而要用最安全的方式存续自己的心意之行。了解摸清黑暗无光的形势是暗主的邪心造成的,那就要赶紧退到安全之地。

[Illuminating Intentionality]

A minister uses soft methods to gain trust, control one's intentions, and affectively connect with a dark ruler. One's intentionality perceives the dark ruler's despicable methods and cannot bear to continue joining in the evil deeds, and understands and penetrates all one's intentions. An injury to the abdomen means that one is also seriously injured, heartbroken, and determined to leave. One must escape the influence of the dark ruler's evil intentional context, because one knows that the ruler has evil intentions and means harm. At this time, one should flee, be unconcerned about method, and use the safest way to maintain one's inner journey. Understanding that the dark and lightless situation is caused by the evil intentions of the dark ruler, retreat to a safe place quickly.

六五:箕子之明夷,利贞。

《象》曰:"箕子"之"贞",明不可息也。

【明译】

六五:箕子一般装疯卖傻,隐陷自己的光明,有利于像箕子一样坚守正道。

《象传》说:像箕子一般坚守正道,使内心光明的人天之意不会被熄灭。

Six (*yin*/soft line) in the fifth place: Jizi often pretends to be crazy and acts foolishly, hiding his own light, which is conducive to sticking to the right *dao* like him.

The *Image Commentary* (*Xiang Zhuan*) says: Like Jizi, he sticks to the right *dao* so that the bright inner intentionality of humanity and heaven will not be extinguished.

【明意】

因为人在瞬间的选择基本代表人的意向之境,所以要隐藏自己心意的高明之士,在特定的形势之下故意选择与自己的心意不相匹配的连续意向之缘,来误导他人对自己意向心境的把握与判断。

在念念皆可致死亡的极度危险之境中，一个人的意向之行影响他是否可以生存下去。内心光明的人天之意不可以熄灭，所以为保全自身，应该艰苦卓绝地不惜装疯卖傻，力图隐藏真实的人天之意。

[Illuminating Intentionality]
Because people's choices in an instant basically represent the state of their intentions, smart people who want to hide their own intentions deliberately choose continuous intentions that do not match their own intentions under specific situations to mislead others' grasp and judgment of their intention and state of mind.

In an extremely dangerous situation where even an intention can lead to death, a person's actions affect whether one can survive. The bright inner cosmological intentionality of humanity and heaven cannot be extinguished, so in order to protect oneself, one should go to great lengths to pretend to be crazy and act foolishly, trying to hide the true cosmological intentionality of humanity and heaven.

上六：不明，晦，初登于天，后入于地。
《象》曰："初登于天"，照四国也。"后入天地"，失则也。
【明译】
上六：光明隐陷的时候，要隐藏自己的察微之明，韬光养晦，否则的话，开始的时候大家把你捧升上天，后来又把你坠落地下。
《象传》说：开初升上天，是（本来应该）光明照耀四方〔上六在上卦坤（国）里〕。后来入于地，是上六处事违背了事物发展之道。

Six (yin/soft line) in the top place: When the light is fading, one must hide one's subtle insights and keep a low profile. Otherwise, one will be praised and lifted to the sky at first, and the dropped to the ground.

The *Image Commentary* (*Xiang Zhuan*) says: When it first ascends to the sky, it is (originally) light shining in all directions (the Six (yin/soft line) in the top place is in the upper Trigram Kun (country)). Later, when it enters the earth, it is because the Six (yin/soft line) in the top place things goes against the way of development of things.

【明意】
光明隐陷之时，自暴光明之意反而危险重重，故要知道如何隐藏自己的光明之意。光明之意可以朗照四国仿佛如登天，但过分违背万物之道则陷入地下，明夷即光明入地。可见，上六违背明夷卦用晦而明的宗旨，控制不住自己就可能把局面变得不可收拾。

明夷是光明受伤之时，但人要有背水一战的勇气，持续努力修炼自己的人天之意，而且，黑暗的形势可以反衬出人内心光明的心意，换言之，光明心意经历了黑暗时世的磨砺，将可能越发光明灿烂。

本卦说明人在外受伤严重，回到家才是最好的疗伤之所，故接家人卦。

[Illuminating Intentionality]

When the light is hidden, it is very dangerous to reveal one's bright intentions, so one must know how to hide one's bright intentions. The intentionality of light can illuminate the four countries as if they have risen into the sky, but if it goes too far against the *dao* of the myriad things, it will fall underground. Hexagram Mingyi (Fading Light) is light entering the earth. It can be seen that the Six (*yin*/soft line) in the top place violates the purpose of Hexagram Mingyi (Fading Light) to use obscurity for clarity. If one cannot control oneself, the situation may become uncontrollable.

Although Hexagram Mingyi (Fading Light) is when the light is injured, people must have the courage to fight and continue to work hard to cultivate their own cosmological intentionality of humanity and heaven. Moreover, the dark situation can reflect the bright intentionality in people's intentions. In other words, the bright intentionality has experienced dark times, and with hard work, it will become brighter and brighter.

This hexagram shows a person is seriously injured outside, and returning home is the best place to heal, so it is followed by Hexagram Jiaren (Family).

风火家人（卦三十七） （离下巽上）

Jiaren (Family), Wind and Fire (Hexagram 37)　(Li below, Xun above)

家是培育意识缘发之地，六爻皆吉，家中有亲情，彼此诚信，互相扶持，是意识与他人共在场域之训练场所。人都生活在家庭关系中，家是人出生和生长的地方，所以人首先是家人，长大成家后，也应该让自己的意识像个家人。

家人卦说明儒家典型的价值观念，即人首先是家人，其次才是社会人，才是国家与天下的人。人与自己家人的情感在《论语》中被特别强调，在《周易》中，对情感创造性的强调不如《论语》，但对于治家和持家的强调却高过《论语》，说明《周易》比《论语》更重家国天下，而《论语》相对来说更重视个人修养。

Home is the place where consciousness is nurtured. In Hexagram Jiaren (Family), all six lines are auspicious. There is family affection, mutual trust and mutual support at home. It is a training place for consciousness to share a field with others. Everyone lives in family relationships, and home is the place where people are born and grow up, hence people are first and foremost family members. When they grow up and start a family, they should also make themselves have the awareness of a family member.

Hexagram Jiaren (Family) illustrates typical Confucian values, that is, people are family members first, then social beings, and only then members of a country and the world under heaven. The emotions between people and their family members are particularly emphasized in the *Analects*. In the *Book of Changes*, the emphasis on emotional creativity is not as strong as in the *Analects*, but the emphasis on family governance and housekeeping is more prominent than in the *Analects*. This shows that, compared with the *Analects*, the *Changes* attaches more importance to the family, the country and the world under heaven, while the *Analects* pays relatively more attention to personal cultivation.

家人，利女贞。

《彖》曰：家人，女正位乎内，男正位乎外。男女正，天地之大义也。家人有严君焉，父母之谓也。父父，子子，兄兄，弟弟，夫夫，妇妇，而家道正。正家而天下定矣。

《象》曰：风自火出，家人。君子以言有物而行有恒。

【明译】

家人卦象征家庭男女，利于女子持守正道。

《彖传》说：家人男女，妻子持守正道位于家庭之内，丈夫持守正道位于家庭之外；丈夫和妻子都持守正道处于合适的位置上，这是天经地义的大道理。一个家庭有严正的君长，指的是父母。父亲要尽责做个父亲，儿子要尽心做个儿子，兄长要作表率像个好兄长，弟弟要作得像个好弟弟，丈夫要守义持家做个好丈夫，妻子要相夫教子做个好妻子，这样家道才能端正合宜，端正了家道就能够安定天下了。

《象传》说：上卦巽为风，下卦离为火，风在火燃烧时从内往外生出就是家人卦，象征男女感通融合组成家庭。君子从卦中得到启示，日常言语要合情适物，居家行事要持常守恒。

Hexagram Jiaren (Family) symbolizes the men and women of the family, and is beneficial for women to maintain the right *dao*.

The *Judgment Commentary* (*Tuan Zhuan*) says: For both men and women in the family, the wife who upholds the upright *dao* is located within the family, and the husband who upholds the upright *dao* is outside the family. When both husband and wife uphold the upright *dao* and are in appropriate positions, this is the great and constant *dao* of heaven and earth. A family has a strict leader, which refers to the parents. A father should be a responsible father, a son should be a son with all his heart, an elder brother should be a model brother, a younger brother should be a good younger brother, a husband should be righteous, run the house, and be a good husband, and a wife should be a good wife for her husband and teach her children. In this way, the family can be upright and proper, and if the family is upright, the world under heaven can be stable.

The *Image Commentary* (*Xiang Zhuan*) says: The upper Trigram Xun is wind, and the lower Trigram Li is fire. When fire burns, wind from the inside out is produced, and this is Hexagram Jiaren (Family), symbolizing the fusion of men and women to form a family. An exemplary person gets inspiration from this hexagram, and knows that one's daily speech should be appropriate to the situation and one's behavior at home consistent and conservative.

【明意】

家庭起于男女互动关系的几微。家庭的建立不仅来自情感，也来自缘构家庭的种种意缘的聚合。人的意识在家庭之境中学习，如情感抚慰，保存实力，意识正直，向外有力等，通常都要把自己有限的意识境遇先延伸到家人那里，在家庭之境中，学习意识所发，皆有实指，也有其对象，言有物，行有恒。在家庭当中涵养丰沛的意识，能够发力持续，稳定恒常，而不会飘忽无定。或者说，人最初持守意识的力道是在家庭场域当中修习出来的。

家庭关系意识的几微：家庭是政治的训练场，政治是家道的延伸，从这个角度看，古人没有家庭内部皆私的概念，因为私人领域的道都与公共政治领域的道一以贯之。政治伦理是家庭伦理关系的延伸。家庭是原型，政治是在社会当中塑造原型的艺术。能塑家庭之型者，就可以塑天下之型。家型于国型，本都是个人心意之型，即心念升起瞬间之型，都从意识的几微状态延伸出去，进而塑造成型。可见，塑造意识之型于自家之中，则可以塑天下之型于千里之外，意识的塑型，首先体现在言行的选择，其次是言行选择的持续与坚持。

[Illuminating Intentionality]

A family begins with subtle interactions between men and women. The establishment of a family comes not only from emotions, but also from the aggregation of various relationships that structure the family. Human consciousness learns many things in the family environment, such as emotional comfort, preservation of strength, awareness of integrity, outward strength, etc. Usually, one has to extend one's limited conscious situation to family members first. In the family environment, one learns that the things that arise from consciousness all have real references and objects, that words have objects, and that actions have constancy. Cultivating abundant awareness in the family, one can exert continuous force, be stable and constant, and not be erratic. In other words, people's ability to maintain awareness is first cultivated in the family field.

The subtlety of awareness in family relationships: The family is the training ground for politics, and politics is an extension of the family *dao*. From this perspective, the ancients did not have a concept of private affairs within the family, because the *dao* of the private sphere is consistent with the *dao* of the public political sphere. Political ethics is an extension of ethical relationships in the family. The family is the archetype, and politics is the art of shaping archetypes in society. One who can shape one's family can shape the world. The shape of the family and the shape of the country are simply the shape of one's own intentions, that is, the shape of the moment when intentionality arises. They are all extended from the most subtle state of consciousness and then shaped. It can be seen that molding the shape of consciousness within oneself can mold the shape of the world under heaven thousands of miles away. The shaping of consciousness is first reflected in the choice of words and deeds, and secondly, the continuity and persistence of the choice of words and deeds.

初九：闲有家，悔亡。

《象》曰："闲有家"，志未变也。

【明译】

初九：防止邪念生出才能保有家庭，防范于未然消除了忧虑悔恨。

《象传》说：防止邪念生出才能保有家庭，就是在初九心志还没有偏邪改变的时候用心防范。

Nine (*yang*/strong line) in the first place: Only by preventing evil intentions from arising can one maintain one's family, and prevent worries and regrets before they occur.

The *Image Commentary* (*Xiang Zhuan*) says: Only by preventing evil intentions from arising can one keep one's family. This is to take precautions as the Nine (*yang*/strong line) in the first place when one's intentionality has not yet changed toward evil intentions.

【明意】

家意味着相对隔绝的空间与院落。家首先是空间，人在这个空间当中，可以创造出新的空间感。家强调安全，具有相对的私密性，不允许外人随意进出。本质上是阴阳交流的心理空间，家人之间心意相通，所以有内外之防。家即使再简陋，也不能无墙无门，以别内外，有别才有家。

所谓防范于未然，是防范于意识未发前的潜意识，甚至无意识的状态，在那种状态中，可能只有微弱的迹象表明这一点，此时也要及时防范，不宜让邪念之意识发展壮大。意识中的横栏才是防闲的根本。如何在家人的意识之中建立横栏，就是要树立家规，不接受外缘的撩拨和引诱，不偏离家的正道。

真正的家是心意之家，意识延续之家。从古至今，建立自己的学说叫成一家之言，因为自己关于宇宙人生的心得体会塑造了一个意识系统，后人追溯理解之，沉潜玩索之，蔚然大观之后，某一家之言就成为一个心意之家，精神之家，超越肉体和血缘的家庭观念，跨越时空，让不同时空中的人通过精神感通而联成一家。

[Illuminating Intentionality]

Home means a relatively isolated space and courtyard. Home is first and foremost a space, and in this space, people can create a new sense of space. The home emphasizes safety and is relatively private, and does not allow outsiders to enter and exit at will. It is essentially a psychological space where *yin* and *yang* communicate. The intentions of family members are connected with each other, so there are internal and external defenses. No matter how simple a home is, it cannot be without walls and doors to distinguish the inside and outside, as only by separation can there be a home.

When people speak of nipping it in the bud, this means to be careful in the subconscious or even unconscious state before consciousness occurs. In that state, there may be only weak signs indicating it. At this time, we must also take precautions in time, and it is not appropriate to allow the consciousness of evil intentions to develop and grow. A horizontal crossbar in consciousness is the basis for preventing idleness. Horizontal barriers can be established in the consciousness of family members by establishing family rules, not accepting provocation and temptation from outsiders, and not deviating from the right *dao* of the family.

The true home is the home of intentionality, the home of the continuation of consciousness. From ancient times to the present, establishing one's own theory has been called developing "the words of a family," because one's own experience of the cosmos and human life have shaped a consciousness system, one which later generations will retrospectively understand, dive into and explore. After taking a grand view of them, a certain family's words become a home of intentionality, a spiritual home, a family concept that transcends physical ties of body and blood, and spans time and space, allowing people in different times and spaces to become one family through spiritual connection.

六二：无攸遂，在中馈，贞吉。

《象》曰：六二之"吉"，顺以巽也。

【明译】

六二：不自作主张，也无所成就，只管家中饮食之事，坚持正道可获吉祥。

《象传》说：六二可获吉祥，因为家庭主妇既柔顺又随顺。

Six (*yin*/soft line) in the second place: Making none of one's own decisions, and achieving nothing, just taking care of food and drink at home. If one sticks to the right *dao*, one will gain good fortune.

The *Image Commentary* (*Xiang Zhuan*) says: The Six (*yin*/soft line) in the second place will bring good fortune, because the housewife is both submissive and obedient.

【明意】

安宁在家维持家人饮食，并从这种持家过程之中自得其乐，这是维系家的意识，以家人之乐为乐，喜欢乐意在家人之中。快乐、随性、欢愉，对于家庭的支持与帮助非常重要。女主人的意识境遇塑造着家庭每一位成员的意识境遇之发展状态。所谓心灵港湾的意境就是给家人提供一个舒缓自在的意识交流平台，大家开心地生活发展。

六二主妇在家做饭，让丈夫愿意回家吃饭，能够在家里的饮食中获得满足，说明家庭主妇通过饮食的顺应之道让家庭意识之境成为家庭成员心意安顿的港湾。

[Illuminating Intentionality]

Staying peacefully at home, maintaining food and drink for the family, and taking pleasure in the process of running the house; this is the consciousness of maintaining the family. Taking pleasure in the happiness of the family, being willing to be with the family, and being happy, casual, and joyful are all very important for the family's support and help. The mistress of the house's consciousness shapes the development of the consciousness of every member of the family. The intentional context of the so-called spiritual harbor is to provide a soothing and comfortable platform for communication of consciousness for family members, so that everyone can live and develop happily.

The housewife of the Six (*yin*/soft line) in the second place cooks at home, so her husband is willing to go home to eat, and is satisfied with the food at home, which shows that housewives make the realm of family consciousness a haven for family members to settle down through their adaptation to food.

九三：家人嗃（hè）嗃，悔厉，吉；妇子嘻嘻，终吝。

《象》曰："家人嗃嗃"，未失也。"妇子嘻嘻"，失家节也。

【明译】

九三：治家严厉，家人愁怨叫嚷，虽然有悔恨危险之事，有所遗憾，但最终吉祥；妇人和孩子一起嘻嘻哈哈，打打闹闹，最终会有吝难。

《象传》说：家人愁怨叫嚷，但没有失掉家规。妇女和孩子一起嘻嘻哈哈，打打闹闹，有失家教礼节，不成体统。

Nine (*yang*/strong line) in the third place: The family is governed harshly, and the family members complain and shout. Although they are remorseful over dangerous actions and have some regrets, all is ultimately auspicious. The wife laughs and jokes with her children, and there will be difficulties in the end.

The *Image Commentary* (*Xiang Zhuan*) says: The family members moan and complain, but do not lose the rules of the family. Women laughing and joking with their children is incompatible with family ritual propriety and thus inappropriate.

【明意】

对于家长的意识来说，持家宁严毋宽，即使有过分严厉的情况，但对家庭的整体来说是好的。如果不严厉一些，妇女与子女打闹过分，就可能出现吝难。

家节虽然是外在的约束，但根本是内在心灵意识的分寸，子女应该持守父母心意的分寸，作为家道的延续。这种持守是要求子女的意识境遇当中，永远有父母，让父母成为思考与行动的潜意识，这是家族荣誉感的来源，也是家族之耻的来源根据。子女时刻关心父母的意识境遇不会因为父母离开人世就不存在，还会而且应该继续在子女心中长久存在下去。

[Illuminating Intentionality]

From a parent's point of view, it is better to be strict than to be lenient in running a household. Even if one is overly strict, it is good for the family as a whole. If one is not strict, women may horse around with their children too much, and trouble may arise.

Although family ties are external constraints, they are fundamentally about one's inner sense of propriety. Children should adhere to the sense of propriety of their parents as a continuation of the family tradition. This kind of persistence requires that children always have parents in their conscious environment, allowing parents to become their subconscious intentionality of thought and action. This is the source of a family's honor and shame. The consciousness that children have to always care about their parents will not cease to exist just because their parents have passed away. It will and should continue to exist in the intentions of their children for a long time.

六四：富家，大吉。
《象》曰："富家大吉"，顺在位也。
【明译】
六四：发家致富，大吉大利。
《象传》说：六四能够发家致富，大吉大利，是因为本身柔顺，又处在合适的位置上。

Six (*yin*/soft line) in the fourth place: The family becomes wealthy, and there is good fortune.

The *Image Commentary* (*Xiang Zhuan*) says: The Six (*yin*/soft line) in the fourth place is able to become wealthy and gain good fortune, because it is docile and in the right position.

【明意】
作为家的女主人，六四的意识能够很好地塑造和帮助男主人，从而达到发家致富的理想状态。阴意的顺承让阳意更加有力，而且有成效，因为实化意识首先就应该获得阴意的随顺和支持，这样阳意的实化就有了坚实的基础。《周易》是阴阳合体的意识存在论，因为意识只要实化就必须是阴阳合体的，而阴意持续稳定地支持阳意对阳意的实化至为关键。

六四如女子有帮夫运，对丈夫很有利。妻子在家里的意识境遇对丈夫构成巨大的影响，是丈夫意识发动交流的首要对象，也是家道兴旺，家庭意识境遇延伸扩展，不断发展的根本所在。

[Illuminating Intentionality]

As the mistress of the house, the consciousness of the Six (*yin*/soft line) in the fourth place can well shape and help the man of the house, so as to achieve the ideal state of becoming wealthy. The compliance of *yin* intentionality makes *yang* intentionality more powerful and effective, because the concretization of consciousness should first obtain the compliance and support of *yin* intentionality, so that the realization of *yang* intentionality has a solid foundation. The *Book of Changes* is an ontology of consciousness that combines *yin* and *yang*, because as long as consciousness is realized, it must be a combination of *yin* and *yang*, and the continuous and stable support of *yin* intentionality to *yang* intentionality is crucial to the concretization of *yang* intentionality.

If a woman helps with her husband's fortune as the Six (*yin*/soft line) in the fourth place, it will be very beneficial to her husband. A wife's conscious state at home has a huge impact on her husband, as she is the primary object of initiation and communication for her husband's consciousness. This is also the foundation for the prosperity of the family, the extension and expansion of the family's state of consciousness, and its continuous development.

九五：王假（gě）有家，勿恤，吉。

《象》曰："王假有家"，交相爱也。

【明译】

九五：君王用自己的诚意感格众人然后保有其家，不必忧虑，吉祥。

《象传》说：君王用自己的诚意感格众人然后保有其家，大家相亲相爱，和睦相处。

Nine (*yang*/strong line) in the fifth place: The king impresses everyone with his sincerity and then keeps his home. There is no need to worry; it is auspicious.

The *Image Commentary* (*Xiang Zhuan*) says: The king impresses everyone with his sincerity and then keeps his home. Everyone loves each other and lives in harmony.

【明意】

意识之境的感通，通常在对先人祭祀时最为强烈，要让这种真诚至极的感通状态时刻体现在当下家庭生活当中，让当下的心意，时刻与祖先沟通，让祖先从当下心意发动的瞬间活出来，如此心意展现出来现世的家庭生活，时时刻刻与对祖先乃至上天的至诚感格联通一体，可谓光宗耀祖的极致之境界。这就是中国的家庭和祠堂与国家一体性、连续性的美妙乐章。

人们通过当下一念发动时刻与祖先共在的状态，实现慎终追远于时时刻刻活泼的仁情之间，乡里乡亲，同宗互爱，从而在家庭成员的彼此关爱之间建立天地意识，而天地自然之意，连同先人和祖宗，时刻如活在家庭和家族当下的生活当中一般。这种醇厚至极的家道通天意识，所达到的家庭与故土合一，当下心意通于祖先而致的天人合一之境，与西方宗教在人间建立完美天国的意识境遇，其实有着异曲同工之妙。

[Illuminating Intentionality]

The affective connection of the realm of consciousness is usually strongest when offering sacrifices to ancestors. This sincere state of connection should always be reflected in current family life, allowing one's present intentions to communicate with ancestors at all times, and allowing the ancestors to live momentarily in one's present intentions. In this way, the initiation of intention manifests family life in the present world, and is always connected as one body with sincere feeling for one's ancestors and even for heaven. This can be said to be the ultimate state of honoring one's ancestors. This is the wonderful movement of the unity and continuity of Chinese families, ancestral halls and the country.

People initiate the state of coexistence with their ancestors at all times through their present intention, and realize at all times the careful pursuit of lively benevolence, the love between fellow villagers and the same clan, thus establishing the consciousness of heaven and earth in the mutual care of family members. The intentionality of nature and heaven and earth means that one always lives together with forebears and ancestors in the current life of the family and clan. This mellow and deep consciousness of the family *dao* connecting to heaven, the unity of family and hometown, and the unity of heaven and humanity caused by the current intentionality connecting with ancestors, are actually similar to the consciousness of Western religions in their wonderful function of establishing a perfect heaven on earth.

上九：有孚威如，终吉。

《象》曰："威如"之"吉"，反身之谓也。

【明译】

上九：让家人心悦诚服，治家就要始终维持威严庄重的姿态，最终可以获得吉祥。

《象传》说：在治家的时候始终维持威严庄重的姿态最终能够收获吉祥，是因为上九时常反躬自省、严格自律的缘故。

Nine (*yang*/strong line) in the top place: To keep family members sincerely convinced, always maintain a majestic and solemn posture when running the family, and ultimately good fortune will be gained.

The *Image Commentary* (*Xiang Zhuan*) says: Always maintaining a majestic and solemn posture when running a family can ultimately reap good fortune, because the Nine (*yang*/strong line) in the top place often reflects on itself and exercises strict self-discipline.

【明意】

家长要以身作则，通过反思知道自己的言行情境。要求他人做到的，自己要努力先做到，在意识发动之前，已经能够反思性地领略意识发动之后的状态，这是反思性的重要意义。《周易》中多次出现反身修德而修行建立反省自己的机制。

如果家长的意识状态庄重严肃，令家人敬畏，家人对于长辈的言传身教纪念一辈子，最后家会吉祥。如果父母能够有好的家道，子女也能够从态度到心意发动保持敬畏安宁的意识。

对家长的敬畏与庄严的意识需要在反身意识中实现，也就是说，可以通过意识的反省机制（reflexive mechanism）来理解自己意识与他人的关系，在意识中如何尊敬家长，对家长心悦诚服，自觉维护庄重的姿态。

[Illuminating Intentionality]

Parents should lead by example and understand the context of their words and deeds through reflection. What one asks others to do, one must work hard to do first. Before consciousness is initiated, one can already reflexively understand the state after the consciousness is initiated. This is the important intentionality of reflexivity. In the *Book of Changes*, there are many times when reflexive cultivation of virtue and practice establish a mechanism for self-reflection.

If parents' state of consciousness is majestic and solemn, family members are in awe, and family members remember the words and deeds of their elders for a lifetime, then the family will be auspicious. If parents can have a good *dao* of the family, their children can also maintain an awareness of reverence and tranquility from attitude to initiation of intention.

The awareness of awe and solemnity for parents needs to be realized in reflexive consciousness. That is to say, through the reflective mechanism of consciousness one can understand the relationship between one's own consciousness and others, how to respect parents in consciousness, be sincerely convinced by parents, and consciously maintain a dignified posture.

火泽睽（卦三十八） （兑下离上）

Kui (Separation), Fire and Lake (Hexagram 38)   (Dui below, Li above)

专注以扩大意量的努力，既是减损自己的物欲，同时又是心生之力与外在物欲之力相斗争的过程。心意的涵养其实每时每刻都是与分背、偏离心意的力量作斗争的过程。所谓求同存异是于心意生机之间，即通过相反相成的过程来领悟和实化天地间的生机。

因为意识有不同的方向，有时互补，有时冲突，但正是这种冲突所以才能促进意境的创生，提升情识的生机进而扩大意量。卦名睽是离异不合，相互乖背，彼此不同之意。睽卦柔（小）爻六五占据尊位，所以说做小事情还是吉利的。

Focusing on the effort to expand one's intentionality not only reduces one's own material desires, but is also a process of the struggle between the power of intentionality and the power of external material desires. Cultivating one's intentionality is actually a process of fighting against the forces that distract and divert one's intentionality at every moment. The idea of seeking common ground while reserving differences lies in the vitality of heart-mind and intention, that is, through the process of opposites and mutual complementation, one can understand and concretize the vitality between heaven and earth.

Because consciousness has different directions, it is sometimes complementary and sometimes in conflict, but this conflict can promote the creation of intentional context, enhance the vitality of emotion and expand intentionality. The hexagram name Hexagram Kui (Separation) means divorce, disagreement, mutual disobedience, and mutual dissimilarity. In Hexagram Kui (Separation), the Six (*yin*/soft line) in the fifth place occupies the honorable position, so doing small things can still be auspicious.

睽，小事吉。

《彖》曰：睽，火动而上，泽动而下。二女同居，其志不同行。说而丽乎明，柔进而上行，得中而应乎刚，是以"小事吉"。天地睽而其事同也。男女睽而其志通也。万物睽而其事类也，睽之时用大矣哉！

《象》曰：上火下泽，睽。君子以同而异。

【明译】

睽卦象征乖戾背离，做小事情还是可以吉利的。

《彖传》说：睽卦，上卦离为火，为中女，下卦兑为泽，为少女，火焰燃动向上，泽水流动润下。犹如两个女子同居一室，但她们因志向不同而行为乖戾背离。下卦兑为喜悦，上卦离为光明，是喜悦地附丽于光明之上，阴爻柔顺地升进，向上运行，得到上卦中位，〔睽卦从中孚变来，未变之前，初九有正应在六四（原在互震里），卦变后初九失去正应〕。并与下卦的刚爻九二相应，所以柔和小心地成就小事还是吉祥的。天地上下阴阳乖戾背离，但它们创生生长化育万物的事功却是相同的；男女体态各异，生理特征差别很大，但他们交感求合的心志却相通；天下万物形态各异，特性千差万别，但它们秉受阴阳之气而生的过程却是很类似的。由此看来，乖戾背离之道因其时仍然能够有非常巨大的作用啊！

《象传》说：上卦离为火，下卦兑为泽，水火不相容就是象征乖戾背离的睽卦，君子从这样的现象中得到启示，要善于求和通而容小异（以异求同）。

Hexagram Kui (Separation) symbolizes divergence, but doing small things can still be auspicious.

The *Judgment Commentary* (*Tuan Zhuan*) says: In Hexagram Kui (Separation), the upper Trigram Li is fire, which is the middle woman, and the lower Trigram Dui is lake, which is the young woman. The flames burn upward, and the water flows down, like two women living in the same room who behave inversely because of different ambitions. The lower Trigram Dui is joy, and the upper Trigram Li is light, which thus mean being joyfully attached to the light, a *yin* line rising smoothly and moving upward to obtain the middle position of upper Trigram Li. (Hexagram Kui (Separation) changes from Hexagram Zhongfu (Trust); the Nine (*yang*/strong line) in the first place had a positive response from the Six (*yin*/soft line) in the fourth place (originally in Trigram Zhen (Shaking)), but after the hexagram-changes, the Nine (*yang*/strong line) in the first place loses its positive response.) After the hexagram-changes, the Six (*yin*/soft line) in the fifth place corresponds to the Nine (*yang*/strong line) in the second place of the lower Trigram Dui, so it is auspicious to be able to accomplish small things gently and carefully. The *yin* and *yang* of heaven and earth are divergent, but their roles in creating, growing, and nurturing the myriad things are the same; men and women have different bodies and very different physiological characteristics, but their desires to communicate and seek unity are the same; the myriad things in the world have different shapes and characteristics, and are all very different, but the processes in which they are born with the energy of *yin* and *yang* are very similar. From this point of view, the *dao* of deviation and divergence can still have a huge effect at that time!

The *Image Commentary* (*Xiang Zhuan*) says: The upper Trigram Li is fire and the lower Trigram Dui is lake. The incompatibility of water and fire means that Hexagram Kui (Separation) symbolizes deviation and divergence. An exemplary person gets inspiration from such phenomena and knows one must be good at seeking harmony and tolerating minor differences (seeking common ground through differences).

【明意】

意生之量的存养与扩大，是与生机相反的力量彼此成就的。有时相反的力量越大，越能激发出生机的意量，生生之几与随时死亡的危机共存，而相悖的力量之间的张力在主导着意量的深度与广度。

意量之同与异之间相反相成，比如画家用五色画出美丽的画，演奏家用五音奏出协调优美的乐章，厨师用五味烹制调和可口的菜肴，工农兵学商组成文明社会，可见睽的意量之不同而时势功用巨大。分背异化的意量真正促进了人世之间精彩纷呈的精神世界。

[Illuminating Intentionality]

The preservation and expansion of the capacity for intentional production is achieved mutually in relation to forces opposite to vitality. Sometimes the greater the opposite force, the more it can stimulate the intentionality of life. Life chances and death dangers coexist at any time, and the tension between contradictory forces dominates the depth and breadth of intentionality.

Similarities and differences in intentionality complement each other. For example, a painter uses five colors to create a beautiful painting, a musician uses five tones to play a harmonious and beautiful movement, a chef uses five flavors to prepare delicious dishes, and workers, farmers, soldiers, scholars and merchants form a civilized society. This shows the differences in capacity of Kui (Separation) intentionality and the great effect of situational propensity. The intentionality of separation and alienation truly promotes a wonderful spiritual world of human beings.

初九：悔亡。丧马勿逐，自复。见恶人，无咎。

《象》曰："见恶人"，以辟咎也。

【明译】

初九：不要忧悔，不要去追赶丢失的马匹，静候它自己回来。以这样的态度面对偷马的盗贼，不会有什么灾患。

《象传》说：（以静候失马的态度）面见坏人，也就能够自觉地避开灾患（因为初九在乖异背离的形势下从心里知道躲避）。

Nine (*yang*/strong line) in the first place: Without regret, there is no need to chase a lost horse, just wait for it to come back on its own. With this attitude, there is no disaster in facing horse thieves.

The *Image Commentary* (*Xiang Zhuan*) says: (With the attitude of waiting for a lost horse) when one meets bad people, one can consciously avoid disasters (because as the Nine (*yang*/strong line) in the first place, one knows how to be evasive in a situation of deviation and separation).

【明意】

生机在人生中通常的理解与得相联，因生而有得，与失往往相辅相成。理解得失互补的道理，就能够对得失持一种超然的态度，犹如塞翁失马的塞翁那样，知道吉凶成败相反相成，从而以一种平静态度应对外在的得失。

从终极意义上说，世间存在物都随生意流转，只是在这生意流转之中，要让生意走失的力量也在与生意作斗争。故一旦阴意主导情景，不必有丝毫得失之心，相信自己终将等来生命的转机。可见，身外之物的得与失导致的意量的升与缩本身不是需要特别在意的事情。

[Illuminating Intentionality]

Vitality is usually understood to be associated with gains in life, because where there is life there are gains, and losses often come along with them. If one understands the principle of complementarity of gains and losses, one can maintain a detached attitude towards gains and losses, as in cases of blessings in disguise. One knows that good and bad fortune and success and failure complement each other, so one can deal with external gains and losses with a calm attitude.

In the ultimate sense, everything in the world flows with productive intentionality, but in the flow of productive intentionality, the force that wants to lose productive intentionality is also fighting against productive intentionality. Therefore, once *yin* intentionality dominates a situation, there is no need to have any intentions of gain or loss, and one should believe that one will eventually see an awaited turning point in life. It can be seen that the rise and fall of consciousness caused by gain and loss of things outside the body is not something that needs special attention.

九二：遇主于巷，无咎。

《象》曰："遇主于巷"，未失道也。

【明译】

九二：在小巷中不期然地偶遇主人，当然没有咎害。

《象传》说：在小巷中不期然地偶遇主人（六五），九二在乖异背离的大势中并没有迷失正道。

Nine (*yang*/strong line) in the second place: There is no harm in meeting a master unexpectedly in an alley.

The *Image Commentary* (*Xiang Zhuan*) says: An unexpected encounter with a master (the Six (*yin*/

soft line) in the fifth place) in an alley means that the Nine (*yang*/strong line) in the second place has not lost the upright *dao* in the general trend of separation.

【明意】

在兵荒马乱，人事分背乖离的时代，还能够巧遇旧时代的主人，不能不说是一件天大的喜事。象辞的解释是不离正道，而所谓的正道首先是意量的中和平稳，能平易面对世间得失，不以物喜，不以己悲，从而能够感受生命中偶遇的欣喜与欢乐。

郭象说"所遇为命"，所遇与人的意识之量有关，即心意没有足够的力量，该发生的可能就不会发生，越发期待偶遇的，可能根本不会发生。偶遇是人生最奇妙的存在状态，而人生的机遇很大一部分由偶遇决定。生命当中很多美妙的事情发生在偶然之中，但偶遇本身包含着命运必然性格局的分量。所以当"静其所遇"，意量在平静安宁之中，透出人天之意的通天之机，即心意能够涵纳万物、吞吐天地的大气象，因大气象而能平静地面对世界沧桑，白云苍狗，万千物换。

[Illuminating Intentionality]

In an era of chaos and disorder, it is a great joy to meet a master of the old era by chance. The explanation of the *Image Commentary* (*Xiang Zhuan*) is to stay on the upright *dao*, and the upright *dao* spoken of here is first of all to be neutral and stable in intention, to be able to face gains and losses in the world easily, not to take pleasure in material things, and not to be sad about oneself, so as to be able to feel the joy and happiness that one encounters in life.

Guo Xiang said that "everything that is encountered is fate." What one encounters is related to the capacity of a person's consciousness. That is, if intentionality does not have enough power, what should happen may not happen, and the more one looks forward to an encounter, the more likely it will not happen at all. A chance encounter is the most wonderful state of existence in life, and a large part of life's opportunities are determined by chance encounters. Many wonderful things in life happen by chance, but chance encounters themselves contain the weight of an inevitable pattern of fate or dependent co-arising. Therefore, when one is "quiet in the face of what one encounters," one's intentionality should be in calmness and tranquility, revealing the heaven-connected secret of the intentionality of humanity and nature, that is, that intentionality can contain the myriad things and swallow up the great atmosphere of heaven and earth, and, because of this great atmosphere, can calmly face the vicissitudes of life in which everything changes.

六三：见舆曳，其牛掣，其人天且劓（yì），无初有终。

《象》曰："见舆曳"，位不当也。"无初有终"，遇刚也。

【明译】

六三：看见大车被拉着向前，拉车的牛被牵制，拽着向后，好比赶车人先被剃发，受了黥刑，后被割鼻，受了劓刑，刚开始时困难重重，但最终会有好结果。

《象传》说：看见车被拉着向前，是六三位置不适当。开初不好，最终有好结果，是因为六三前行要跟刚爻上九遇合。

Six (*yin*/soft line) in the third place: Seeing the cart being pulled forward, and the oxen pulling the cart being restrained and pulled backward, it is like the cart driver was first shaved and tattooed, and then he had his nose cut off and was tortured. At the beginning things are difficult, but they will work out well in the end.

The *Image Commentary* (*Xiang Zhuan*) says: If one sees a cart being pulled forward, it means that the position of the Six (*yin*/soft line) in the third place is inappropriate. It started out poorly, but ended up with good results, because the Six (*yin*/soft line) in the third place's journey forward will meet up with the Nine (*yang*/strong line) in the top place.

【明意】

意识之量在睽异的大格局中，因为与牵扯的力量作巨大的斗争，是在互相拉扯的过程之中延续生生之机。生机能够延续还在于有应合之力，即有相应的力量来拉动生机，给意识以出路和光明。

[Illuminating Intentionality]

The capacity of consciousness is involved in the greater pattern of separation, because it is in a huge struggle against the forces involved, and it is the opportunity to continue life's productive vitality in the process of pulling against one another. The continuation of vitality also depends on the power of response, that is, there is corresponding power to stimulate vitality and give consciousness light and a way out.

九四：睽孤，遇元夫。交孚，厉，无咎。

《象》曰："交孚，无咎"，志行也。

【明译】

九四：乖戾背离的时运使得九四孑然孤独，这时遇到刚强的大丈夫，二人心志交融，彼此信任，虽然情境尚有危险，但不会有过失。

《象传》说：二人心志交融，彼此信任，这样就不会有过错，这是因为双方异中求同的心志彼此相通，都可以被推行的缘故。

Nine (*yang*/strong line) in the fourth place: Strange and deviant luck makes the Nine (*yang*/strong line) in the fourth place lonely. At this time, one meets a great man, and the two develop harmonious intentions and trust one another. Although the situation is still dangerous, there will be no mistakes.

The *Image Commentary* (*Xiang Zhuan*) says: The two people's intentions are blended and they trust each other, so there will be no mistakes. This is because the two parties' aspirations to seek common ground despite differences are interlinked with each other and can be implemented.

【明意】

人生无时无刻不在危险当中，死亡的威胁无处不在，生机常受威胁，在这样的处境中，要尽量与心境彼此感通的人携手共进，才能逐渐走出险境。尤其在乖异的大形势中，心意的处境非常孤独，但此时如果有刚强的阳意来应合，就可能一起脱离险境。这说明，在困境中只有与心境相通的人相感应，让心志互通的状态对抗外在的逆境，相互信任彼此互助，才能走出低谷。在危险的处境之中，人的意量被压制，所以需要寻找共同的心志，以求存续和发展。

[Illuminating Intentionality]

Life is in danger all the time, the threat of death is everywhere, and vitality is often threatened. In such a situation, we must try our best to work together with people who are sympathetic to each other, so that we can gradually get out of danger. Especially in a strange general situation, the situation of intentionality can be very lonely, but if there is a strong *yang* intentionality to respond to at this time, it is possible to escape from the danger together. This shows that in difficult times, only by connecting with people who are in the same state of mind, allowing a state of mutual understanding to fight against external adversities, and trusting and helping each other can we get out of the trough. In dangerous situations, people's intentional capacity is suppressed, so they need to find a common will in order to survive and develop.

六五：悔亡。厥宗噬肤，往何咎？

《象》曰："厥宗噬肤，往"，有庆也。

【明译】

六五：消除悔恨，结成亲密宗亲好比彼此能够噬咬对方的皮肤，如此一来，前行还有什么困难呢？

《象传》说：结成亲密宗亲好比彼此能够噬咬对方的皮肤，如此意志坚决、精诚团结，即使在分悖离弃的大势下前往都会有喜庆。

Six (*yin*/soft line) in the fifth place: Eliminating regrets and forming a close kinship is like being able to bite each other's skin. If so, what difficulty is there in advancing?

The *Image Commentary* (*Xiang Zhuan*) says: Forming a close kinship is like being able to bite each other's skin. With such determination and sincere unity, there will be joy even in the general trend of division and abandonment.

【明意】

没有心志相通的人就难以走出困境，所以最重要的支持来自家族宗亲和近似于跟自己结成家人之盟的人的支持，彼此慰藉足以抵抗风雨。乖异到极点的处境之中，人的精神状态都会出问题，心情恍惚之中，人不得不听天由命，人的意识之量需要比正常状态更多地交给天意。人在极度背运和苦难之中，还要有随顺自然之意的心境，相信自己的心意将因天地之间阳意与阴意的交融而改变。

象辞比爻辞乐观很多，不但认为只要在极度艰难的处境当中还能精诚团结，就没有什么困难，而且认为，意量找到志同道合者，共同面对人生的风雨，其实是大有喜庆，欢乐无比之象，犹如天作的姻缘，有佳偶天成之感。

[Illuminating Intentionality]
Without like-minded people, it is difficult to get out of a predicament, so the most important support comes from family members and people who practically form a family alliance with them. The comfort of each other is enough to withstand the trials and hardships. In extremely strange situations, people's mental states will have problems. In a dazed mood, people have to resign themselves to heaven and fate, so the capacity of human consciousness that needs to be left to the intentionality of heaven is more than in a normal state. In the midst of extreme misfortune and suffering, people should have the mental state of following the intentionality of nature, believing that their intentions will be changed by the blending of *yang* and *yin* intentionality between heaven and earth.

The *Image Commentary* (*Xiang Zhuan*) is much more optimistic than the text of the line itself. Not only does it believe that as long as we can unite sincerely in an extremely difficult situation, there will be no difficulty, it also believes that it is actually very joyful to find like-minded people and face the storms of life together. The incomparable image of such joy is like a marriage made in heaven, a feeling of a couple made in heaven.

上九：睽孤，见豕负涂，载鬼一车，先张之弧，后说之弧。匪寇，婚媾。往遇雨则吉。

《象》曰："遇雨"之"吉"，群疑亡也。

【明译】

上九：乖弃背离到了极点，孤独狐疑，恍惚中似乎看见猪背着浑身的污泥，又仿佛看见一辆大车满载鬼怪奔驰。惊疑之中，先张开弓，准备放箭，发现情况不对，又把弓放下来，发现来的不是强盗，而是来提亲的。如果前往，遇到下雨就会吉祥。

《象传》说：如果前往，遇到下雨就会吉祥，是因为在雨中，上九所有的疑虑都会被打消，烟消云散。

Nine (*yang*/strong line) in the top place: The separation has reached an extreme, and one is lonely and suspicious. In a trance, one seems to see a pig carrying mud on its back, and a large cart full of ghosts rushing by. In surprise and suspicion, one first opens one's bow, then prepares to release an arrow. When one realizes that something is wrong, one lowers one's bow again and finds that the person who has come is not a robber, but a marriage proposal. If one advances, it will be auspicious if it also rains.

The *Image Commentary* (*Xiang Zhuan*) says: If one advances, it will be auspicious if it rains, because in the rain, all doubts about the Nine (*yang*/strong line) in the top place are dispelled and disappear.

【明意】

幻想与想象不是认识世界的正途，但心量被冲击到极度艰难的状态当中，只有听天由命，此时维持住心意，不让幻想阻挡住自己的意识，即是让生机不乱，让意志清醒而有力地掌控自己的意量。

整个睽卦处境极度艰难，但却都在讲如何延续生机和扩大意量，在绝望中充满生生之机和走出绝境，化解负面力量的希望。人生处处皆生机，越是睽背分离的处境，越是要明了感悟生机之所在，乐观处世，改造意量，让意量再上台阶。

[Illuminating Intentionality]

Fantasy and imagination are not the right way to understand the world, but intentionality has been pushed into an extremely difficult state, in which one can only resign oneself to one's fate. Maintaining one's intentionality at this time and not letting fantasy block one's consciousness is to keep one's vitality stable and one's will clear, and have strong control over one's own will.

The entirety of Hexagram Kui (Separation) is in an extremely difficult situation, but it is all about how to continue one's vitality and expand one's intentionality, to be full of opportunities for life in despair, to get out of desperate situations, and to dissolve negative forces. Human life is full of vitality. The more one faces a situation of separation, the more one needs to understand where vitality lies, be optimistic about the world, change one's mind, and let one's intentionality reach a higher level.

水山蹇（卦三十九）　（艮下坎上）

Jian (Dragging), Water and Mountain (Hexagram 39)　(Gen below, Kan above)

蹇境当前，感应艰难，意能在艰难推进中提升。感是感通，而蹇是不通，感是意能增进，蹇是意能受伤减损，意识能量的提升总是艰难的，蹇卦讲的是意能的生成与转化。人是各种能量的聚合体，但所有的能量都要通过意能表现出意识的力量，而意识能量的层级千差万别。

卦象像一个堰塞湖，危险的能量巨大地积累起来，高高地如水库之将倾，如利剑之将落，危险巨大。面对高山上面马上要倾倒下来的恶水，一个人要有力挽狂澜的壮志和策略，坚定不移，百折不挠。

In Hexagram Jian (Dragging), facing the current situation, one responds with difficulty, and one's power of intentionality improves in the difficult advancement. Sensation means affective connection, while Jian (Dragging) means disconnection. Affection means an increase of intentional energy, while Hexagram Jian (Dragging) means a damage or loss of intentional energy. It is always difficult to improve the energy of consciousness, and Hexagram Jian (Dragging) talks about the generation and transformation of intentional energy. Human beings are an aggregation of various energies, but all energies must express the power of consciousness through intentional power, and the level of conscious energy varies widely.

The hexagram image is like a barrier lake, with a huge amount of dangerous energy accumulated. The height is like a reservoir dam about to collapse, like a sword about to fall, and the danger is huge. Facing the terrible water that is about to pour down from the high mountain, a person must have the

433

ambition and strategy to turn the tide, and be firm and unyielding.

蹇，利西南，不利东北。利见大人。贞吉。

《彖》曰：蹇，难也，险在前也。见险而能止，知矣哉！"蹇，利西南"，往得中也。"不利东北"，其道穷也。"利见大人"，往有功也。当位"贞吉"，以正邦也。蹇之时用大矣哉！

《象》曰：山上有水，蹇。君子以反身修德。

【明译】

蹇卦举步维艰，向西南方走有利，向东北方走不利。宜于依靠贤明的领袖，持守正道，渡过难关，获得吉祥。

《彖传》说，蹇是难的意思，险阻在前面（上卦坎险为前）。遇到险难懂得停止不前，真是明智啊（见险（坎）而止（艮））！蹇卦向西南方（西南坤，平，不险）走有利，是前往取得上卦中位（从小过变来，卦变中主爻九五从四位升上来），其行为中正（既不冒险，又没有停止不前）。向东北方走不利是因为道路困阻（艮）不通。宜于依靠贤明的领袖，是因为在危难的时候出现大人就可以建功立业（主爻九五升进取得尊贵的五位，成为大人）。九五身当其位，正固吉祥，能够以正道治理自己的邦国。蹇卦所代表的时势的时机化功用实在太重大了！

《象传》说：下卦艮为山，上卦坎为水，山上有水就组合为蹇卦。君子看到高山上蓄聚着水，因为不能流动而显得举步维艰的象，要反躬自省，修正错误，培养仁德（山上之水按本性反身下流滋润大山，而有反身自润之象，象征人遇险难而能反省自查）。

Hexagram Jian (Dragging) is difficult to move. It is beneficial to move to the southwest, but disadvantageous to move to the northeast. It is advisable to rely on wise leaders, stick to the upright *dao*, overcome difficulties, and gain good fortune.

The *Judgment Commentary* (*Tuan Zhuan*) says: Jian means difficulty, and danger is ahead (the upper Trigram Kan is in front). It is really wise to know to stop when encountering danger (one sees the danger (Trigram Kan) and stops (Trigram Gen))! It is advantageous to move Hexagram Jian (Dragging) to the southwest (the southwest of Trigram Kun (smooth, not dangerous)), because it advances to get to the middle position of the upper Trigram (changed from Hexagram Xiaoguo (Slight Overreaching), in the hexagram-changes the main Nine (*yang*/strong line) in the fifth place rises from the fourth position), and its behavior is upright, neither taking risks nor stopping in one place). Going northeast is unfavorable because the road is blocked (Trigram Gen). It is advisable to rely on wise leaders, because when a great person appears in times of crisis, achievements can be made (the master line is promoted to the fifth position of honor and becomes a great person as the Nine (*yang*/strong line) in the fifth place). The Nine (*yang*/strong line) in the fifth place is in its place, it is upright and auspicious, and it can govern its country with the upright *dao*. The timing function of the current situation represented by Hexagram Jian (Dragging) is so important!

The *Image Commentary* (*Xiang Zhuan*) says: The lower Trigram Gen is mountain, the upper Trigram Kan is water. If there is water on the mountain, they combine to form Hexagram Jian (Dragging). When an exemplary person sees water accumulating on a high mountain, and it seems to be struggling because it cannot flow, one should reflect on oneself, correct one's mistakes, and cultivate benevolence. (This represents how, when people are in danger, they can reflect and examine themselves).

【明意】

慎始才能善终，摆脱困境要在千钧一发之际，不可蛮干，要以才德化解险难，而不可以暴制暴。要想力挽狂澜，得有回到瀑布下修炼神功的意识和经历，走出困难的情境要先顺应，自觉压抑意能，再转化之。

我们好像无可选择，只有相信这个世界只能如此呈现出来，由超出个人控制的条件，如性别、家庭等不可改变的先行条件构成人生艰难的意识之缘，对我们的意识能量进行限制，而且基本上终生无法摆脱，所以要面对这些限制意能的条件不断做反身修炼的功夫。

[Illuminating Intentionality]

Only by starting carefully can one end well, and one must get out of trouble at the critical moment. One must not act recklessly, but must resolve dangers and difficulties with talent and virtue, and must not use violence to control violence. If one wants to turn the tide, one must have the awareness and experience to return to beneath the waterfall to practice magical skills. To get out of difficult situations, one must first adapt, consciously suppress one's power of intention, and then transform it.

It seems that people have no choice but to believe that the world can only appear this way. Conditions beyond personal control, such as gender, family and other unchangeable antecedent conditions, constitute the difficult conditions of consciousness in life, limiting people's conscious energy, and these basically cannot be eliminated throughout life, so one has to face these conditions that limit one's power of intention and continue to practice reflexive effort.

初六：往蹇，来誉。

《象》曰："往蹇，来誉"，宜待也。

【明译】

初六：往前行走会遇到艰难，返身退回来反而得到人们的赞誉。

《象传》说：往前行走会遇到艰难，返身退回来反而得到人们的赞誉，（因为初六在一卦之初，位置太低，还未到行动的时候）尚须待时而动。

Six (*yin*/soft line) in the first place: Advancing will lead to encountering difficulties, but turning back will gain people's praise.

The *Image Commentary* (*Xiang Zhuan*) says: Advancing will lead to encountering difficulties, but turning back will gain people's praise (because for a Six (*yin*/soft line) in the first place at the beginning of a hexagram, its position is too low, and it is not yet time to act) and there will still be time to act later.

【明意】

人生要学会在艰难险阻当中磨练品德，提升意能。初六象征处于艰困之中，人应该学会等待，守时待命，把变化交给时间，让时间来掌控主导，意识到时间与空间之中转化意识的能量，延伸意识能量的时空维度。

[Illuminating Intentionality]

In life, one must learn to hone one's character and improve one's mental abilities in the face of hardships and obstacles. The Six (*yin*/soft line) in the first place symbolizes being in difficulty. People should learn to wait, observe time and stand by, leave changes to time, and let time take control. Through acceptance, it is the energy that transforms consciousness in time and space, extending the space-time dimension of conscious energy.

六二：王臣蹇蹇，匪躬之故。

《象》曰："王臣蹇蹇"，终无尤也。

【明译】

六二：君王的臣属们艰难来往，劳苦做事，但他们不是为了自己的私事。

《象传》说：君王的臣属们艰难来往，劳苦做事，能任劳任怨，始终没有抱怨忧虑（六二与九五阴阳正应，忠心向主）。

Six (*yin*/soft line) in the second place: The king's subjects hustle and bustle about with difficulty, toiling in their work, but they do not do so for their own private affairs.

The *Image Commentary* (*Xiang Zhuan*) says: The king's subjects come and go with difficulty, work hard, toil without complaining, and never complain or worry (the *yin* of the Six (*yin*/soft line) in the second place and the and *yang* of the Nine (*yang*/strong line) in the fifth place correspond to each other, and they are loyal to the ruler).

【明意】

人生皆在操劳中，公私之意非常微妙，当人的社会角色上升到管理者的时候，有时私意即是公意，对一般平民来说，即使心念发动都是公意，也往往难以转化成为公共意念。此爻是大臣为公事操劳之象，大臣不为自己操劳，为君王和他人的公事操劳，因为大臣有公职，所以其发动的意念皆在公共情境之中，能主动不发动自己的意念是正确的选择。另外，大臣在操劳之时空中消耗的意能，最终流向君王和大众的公共意识领域（意—间），这有利于避免忧患，缓解君王对大众的操劳和忧伤。

[Illuminating Intentionality]

Life is all about work, and public and private intentions are very subtle. When a person's social role rises to the level of a manager, sometimes private intentions are also public intentions. For ordinary people, even if their intentions are intended publicly, it does not matter, as it is often difficult to translate it into public opinion.

In this line, the minister is working on official affairs. The minister does not work for himself, but for the official affairs of the king and others. Because the minister has a public position, the intentions he initiates are all in public situations, and it is correct to take the initiative not to initiate his own intentional choices. In addition, the intentional energy consumed by ministers in the time and space under their care eventually flows to the field of public consciousness (intentionality-time) of the king and the public, which is conducive to avoiding worries and alleviating the king's care and concern for the public.

九三：往蹇，来反。

《象》曰："往蹇来反"，内喜之也。

【明译】

九三：往前进会遇到艰难险阻，不如退回原地。

《象传》说：往前进会遇到艰难险阻，不如退回原地，因为内人（内卦两个阴爻）喜欢它返回来（给家遮风挡雨）。

Nine (*yang*/strong line) in the third place: One will encounter difficulties and obstacles if one moves forward, so it is better to return to one's original position.

The *Image Commentary* (*Xiang Zhuan*) says: If one advances, one will encounter difficulties and obstacles, so it is better to retreat to where one was, because one's wife (the two *yin* lines of the inner trigram) likes one to come back (to protect one's home from wind and rain).

【明意】

人的意能发动应以是否能够生生不息，不断增长为旨归。换言之，意能往哪个方向生发流动通畅就往哪个方向发动，有时为了节省和保护意能，不应该冒险前进，而是明察形势，及早返回家中，或其他可以遮风挡雨的地方，等于回归可以疗伤的心灵港湾，犹如回到家里，就回到有亲情爱情的温暖港湾，有助于逐渐恢复意能。这好比人的意能需要补充的过程，艰难的时刻该回来就回来，该在家就在家，该平易就平易，安宁顺势，自然而然。所以艰难时势当中，应该回来把家料理好，把身体养好再说。此时意能随意发动非常危险，应该先退回来安顿自己，反身修德，安心提升意能。

[Illuminating Intentionality]

The motivation of human intentions should be based on whether it can continue to grow and reproduce. In other words, intentional energy is generated and flows in the direction in which it can produce and flow smoothly. Sometimes, in order to save and protect intentional energy, one should not risk advancing, but should clearly observe the situation and return home as early as possible, or move to other places where one can shelter from wind and rain, which is equivalent to returning. A spiritual harbor that can heal wounds is like returning home to a warm harbor with family and love, which helps to gradually restore consciousness. This is like the process of replenishing the human power of intention. When difficult times arise, one should and will return, when one should be at home, one will be at home, and when it should be easy, it will be easy, so peace and tranquility come naturally. Therefore, in difficult times, one should go back to take care of one's home and take good care of one's health. At this time, it is very dangerous to initiate the power of intention at will. One should retreat and settle oneself first, practice moral cultivation reflexively, and improve one's power of intention with peace of mind.

六四：往蹇，来连。

《象》曰："往蹇来连"，当位实也。

【明译】

六四：往前走会遇到艰难险阻，最好返回来联合其他力量。

《象传》说：往前走会遇到艰难险阻，最好返回来联合（艮山之）实力，本身当位，同时也把两个当位的健实之交连起来了。

Six (*yin*/soft line) in the fourth place: One will encounter difficulties and obstacles if one advances. It is best to go back and join forces with others.

The *Image Commentary* (*Xiang Zhuan*) says: If one advances, one will encounter difficulties and obstacles. It is best to return and unite with the strength (of Trigram Gen's mountain), taking the right position oneself, and at the same time connecting two strong lines together.

【明意】

六四善于谋篇布局，清楚知道困难所在和应对策略，阴意的意能之最大化就是辅佐阳意，何况是联合两个阳意，等于通过自己的意能把有实力的阳意给联通了。联系上下刚爻的意能，就大大结合增进了意能的层级。

[Illuminating Intentionality]

The Six (*yin*/soft line) in the fourth place is good at plotting and planning, and clearly knows the difficulties and coping strategies. A maximum of *yin*/negative intentional energy can assist a *yang*/positive intention, not to mention uniting two *yang*/positive intentions, which is equivalent to connecting powerful *yang*/positive intentions through one's own intentional energy. Connecting the intentional energy of the upper and lower *yang*/strong lines greatly combines and enhances the level of intentional energy.

九五：大蹇，朋来。

《象》曰："大蹇朋来"，以中节也。

【明译】

九五：遭遇极度危险艰难的情况，朋友们纷纷前来相助。

《象传》说：君王遭遇极度危险艰难的情况，朋友们纷纷前来相助，因为（九五处在上卦中位，又在两个柔爻之中，刚柔互济），险难之中处事仍然能够以中正之道行节制之权。

Nine (yang/strong line) in the fifth place: Encountering extremely dangerous and difficult situations, friends come to help one after another.

The *Image Commentary* (*Xiang Zhuan*) says: When the king encounters extremely dangerous and difficult situations, his friends come to help him one after another, because (the Nine (yang/strong line) in the fifth place is in the middle of the upper Trigram, and between the two soft lines, the strong and the soft complement each other). In dealing with things in the middle of difficulties, one can still exercise the power of moderation in a right way.

【明意】

当人处于被动和艰难的情形之中时，朋友的意能是帮助自己改变处境的核心所在。度过蹇难要靠朋友，意能的艰难要有人来提升，朋友要给予能量，逐渐缓解艰难的局势。在极度艰难的情形中，九五显得有面对困难的气魄和担当。在危险的情境之中，要有转换和积累众人意能的能力，才能济度蹇难。九五可谓集万千意能于一身，既然身在尊位，又得到大家意能的全力支持，自己面对蹇难时势，反而应该有我不入地狱谁入地狱的英雄主义气概，拼尽全力，突破难关。

[Illuminating Intentionality]

When people are in passive and difficult situations, the power of friends is the core of helping them change their situation. People need friends to get through difficulties, to improve their abilities when in difficulty, so friends can give energy and gradually ease a difficult situation. In extremely difficult situations, the Nine (yang/strong line) in the fifth place shows the courage and responsibility to face one's difficulties. In dangerous situations, one must have the ability to transform and accumulate everyone's intentions in order to overcome the difficulties. The Nine (yang/strong line) in the fifth place can be said to be the integration of thousands of intentional powers in one person. Since one is in an honorable position and has the full support of everyone's intentions and abilities, when facing difficult times, one should have the heroic spirit of not going to hell and not letting anyone else go either, and fighting with all one's strength, going all out and breaking through the difficulties.

上六：往蹇来硕，吉。利见大人。

《象》曰："往蹇来硕"，志在内也。"利见大人"，以从贵也。

【明译】

上六：继续前行十分艰难，回过头来则能够建立丰硕功业，这样做是吉祥的，有利于依靠贤明的领导。

《象传》说：继续前行十分艰难，回过头来则能够建立丰硕功业，因为心意向内（九三、九五）。有利于帮助贤明的领导，因为随从贵人（九五）。

Six (*yin*/soft line) in the top place: It is very difficult to move forward, but one can build fruitful achievements by looking back. Doing so is auspicious and conducive to relying on wise leadership.

The *Image Commentary* (*Xiang Zhuan*) says: It is very difficult to move forward, but one can build fruitful achievements when one looks back, because one's intentionality is directed inward (at the Nine (*yang*/strong line) in the third place and the Nine (*yang*/strong line) in the fifth place). It is beneficial to help wise leaders because one follows noble people (the Nine (*yang*/strong line) in the fifth place).

【明意】

上六有强烈的危机感，对于境遇有深厚的感触力，意识到自己的意能必须及时调整方向，这是一种领导者的意识和意能，面对危机的境遇，能够化险为夷，运用丰富强烈的感受力及时转换自己和所在团体的意能。

上六走不通就回来，可以辅佐贵人心志向内，修炼内功，得到内助很好，是非常正确的判断和选择。艰难时分，意能内敛，向内用功，而不可向外消散意能。能够吸纳帮助自己的力量，提升积蓄意能，能量被压抑，但要知道转化，因为转化可能有新的出路。能够集中心力向内整合意能，带领团队走出困境的心意，可见，艰难时势当中，集中意能需要悟性，也需要功夫，而这些往往不是通过操作性的学习和渐修就可获得的。

[Illuminating Intentionality]

The Six (*yin*/soft line) in the top place has a strong sense of crisis, has a deep sensitivity to the situation, and realizes that one's power of intention must adjust one's direction in time. This is a kind of leader's consciousness and power of intention. When facing a crisis situation, one can turn danger into safety and use a rich and strong sensibility to transform one's own and the group's consciousness in a timely manner.

If the Six (*yin*/soft line) in the top place cannot go any further, it should return. This can help nobles to have inner aspirations and practice internal skills, as it is good to get internal help, and is a very correct judgment and choice. When times are tough, one should keep intentionality in check and work inward instead of dissipating energy outwards, absorbing the power to help oneself and improve one's accumulated energy. The energy is suppressed, but one must know how to transform, because transformation may lead to new ways out. The ability to concentrate on integrating one's intentionality inward and lead the team out of trouble shows that, in difficult times, concentrating one's intentionality requires both understanding and effort, which are often not obtained through operational learning and gradual practice.

雷水解（卦四十）　（坎下震上）

Jie (Relaxation), Thunder and Water (Hexagram 40)　(Kan below, Zhen above)

　　解困需要机遇，意念在困难的形势中，其意缘需要外在的机缘才能化解。解缘主要是关于缘的结构重生、缘生变化的情态。意缘之在即意之缘生形态，既是心意存在之缘，又是行动时需要的外在条件。

　　解卦涉及恢复阴意与阳意相交之心意，通过持守稳定正当的意缘而有意外收获的心意；欺上瞒下，对合理意缘胡作非为的心意；摆脱小人之缘，自觉舒缓的心意；君子舒缓意缘到连小人都心服口服的程度；君子擒贼擒王，舒缓险难的心意。解是改变形势和命运的时机，应当尽量抓住，得到合适的时机和时势，对于心意舒展和人生发展非常重要。

　　Opportunities are needed to overcome difficulties, and in difficult situations, intentions need external opportunities to resolve them. The resolution of the relationship is mainly about the rebirth of the structure and changing state of the relationship. The presence of intentionality is a dependent form of intention. It is not only the condition for the existence of intention, but also requires external conditions for action.

　　Hexagram Jie (Relaxation) involves the intentionality that restores the interaction of *yin* and *yang*, the intentionality that achieves unexpected gains by maintaining a stable and legitimate fate, the intentionality that knows deceiving superiors and concealing from inferiors to be acting recklessly against reasonable destiny, the intentionality that gets rid of petty people and consciously feels relieved in one's heart-mind, the intentionality of an exemplary person who soothes to the point where even a petty person is convinced, and the intentionality that pacifies danger when an exemplary person catches thieves and kings. Hexagram Jie (Relaxation) is an opportunity to change the situation and destiny, and one should try one's best to seize it. Getting the right opportunity and situation is very important for the relaxation of intentionality and the development of life.

解，利西南。无所往，其来复吉。有攸往，夙吉。

《彖》曰：解，险以动，动而免乎险，解。"解，利西南"，往得众也。"无所往，其来复吉"，乃得中也。"有攸往夙吉"，往有功也。天地解而雷雨作，雷雨作而百果草木皆甲坼（chè）。解之时大矣哉！

《象》曰：雷雨作，解。君子以赦过宥（yòu）罪。

【明译】

解卦象征舒缓宽松，有利于到西南方去，没有危险情况需要去解救的时候，回来做好原来的事情就吉祥。如果有地方出现了灾难，那就越早赶去解救越好，早行动才能吉祥。

《彖传》说：解卦象征解放舒松，下坎是险，上震是动，因为有险难而行动，在行动中脱离险难（行动才可以脱离险难，至少缓解险难的程度）这就是解卦。解卦有利于到西南方去，因为前往可以得到群众。没有危险情况需要去解救的时候，回来做好原来的事情就吉祥，是因为可以得到中位（解卦从小过变来，刚爻没有往上推移，这是无所前往；而是返回向下而来，进入下卦中位，所以返回来吉祥，因为得到中位）。如果有地方出现了灾难，那就越早赶去救越好，早去才能获得吉祥，也因为早去才能真正帮人纾解险难，才会有贡献和功劳。天地舒缓解冻才会发生雷雨（上卦震雷，下卦坎雨，春天雷雨兴作之象）。雷雨兴起百果草木的种子就会破壳萌芽，破土生出。解卦的代表舒缓宽松的时势之时机化意义实在太重大了！

《象传》说：上卦震为雷，下卦坎为雨，雷雨兴作的卦就是解卦。君子看到雷雨交加，严寒消解，万物复苏的现象，就要赦免过错，解放宽恕有罪之人。

Hexagram Jie (Relaxation) symbolizes relaxation, which is good for going to the southwest. When there is no dangerous situation that needs to be rescued, it will be auspicious to return and do the original thing. If there is a disaster somewhere, the sooner one rushes to the rescue, the better it is, as early action will bring good fortune.

The *Judgment Commentary* (*Tuan Zhuan*) says: Hexagram Jie (Relaxation) symbolizes liberation and relaxation. The lower Trigram Kan is danger, and the upper Trigram Zhen is movement. We act because of danger and difficulty, and escape from danger in action (only by taking action can we escape from danger, or at least alleviate the degree of danger.) This is Hexagram Jie (Relaxation), which is beneficial for going to the southwest, because going there can attract people. When there is no dangerous situation that needs to be rescued, it is auspicious to come back and return to one's original affairs, because one can get the middle position (when Hexagram Jie (Relaxation) changes from Hexagram Xiaoguo (Slight Overreaching), the *yang*/strong line does not move upward, which means there is nowhere to go; instead, it returns downward and enters the middle position of the lower Trigram Kan, so the return is auspicious because one has obtained the middle position). If there is a disaster somewhere, the sooner one rushes to the rescue, the better it is. The sooner one goes, the better the fortune that will come is. Also, the sooner one goes, the more one can truly help people relieve their difficulties, and then one will have contributions and merits. Thunderstorms will occur only when heaven and earth are warmer and defrosted (the upper Trigram Zhen is thunder and the lower Trigram Kan is rain, which form a sign of thunderstorms in spring). When thunderstorms arise, the seeds of fruit trees will burst out of their shells, germinate, and emerge from the soil. Hexagram Jie (Relaxation) represents the timing of relaxing the current situation, which is of great significance!

The *Image Commentary* (*Xiang Zhuan*) says: The upper Trigram is thunder, the lower Trigram is rain, and the hexagram formed of thunder and rain is Hexagram Jie (Relaxation). When an exemplary person sees a thunderstorm, the severe cold disappearing, and the revival of the myriad things, one will forgive mistakes, and liberate and pardon the guilty.

【明意】

意念之动如电闪雷鸣，意念的缘生形态在心动与意动的瞬间存在。在有危险出现之时，要在运动中才能有解难的可能。缘生形态依赖外缘而在，解是缘生而舒缓的状态，因有外缘，让人的意向得以进入另一个时间和空间。

危险巨大，如何解脱，意念如雷降雨舒缓出来。面对危险困难的局面，不动不可能化解。在危难之际，意缘的转换有一个黄金时间，但首先通过自救才能转换意缘的存在状态。

[Illuminating Intentionality]

The movement of intentionality is like thunder and lightning, and the conditioned form of intentionality exists in the moment when the heart-mind and intentions move. When danger occurs, it is possible to solve the problem only during movement. The conditioned form of Hexagram Jie (Relaxation) depends on external conditions to exist, and the solution is a conditioned and soothing state, and because of external conditions, people's intentions can enter another time and space.

The danger is huge, so how to escape is how the intentions are like thunder bringing rain, soothing one out. Faced with a dangerous and difficult situation, it is impossible to resolve it without moving. In times of crisis, there is a golden time for the transformation of intentionality, but only through self-help can the state of existence of intentionality be transformed.

初六：无咎。

《象》曰：刚柔之际，义无咎也。

【明译】

初六：没有什么咎害。

《象传》说：初六在刚柔交接之际，柔顺地承接九二刚爻，按道理讲不应该有什么咎害。

Six (*yin*/soft line) in the first place: No blame.

The *Image Commentary* (*Xiang Zhuan*) says: As the Six (*yin*/soft line) in the first place is at a time of handover between the strong and the soft, if one smoothly connects with the Nine (*yang*/strong line) in the second place, logically speaking, there should be no blame.

【明意】

初爻所在情境本身即解困脱难之时，但阴爻意识到自己的力量有限，知道必须配合阳爻阳意才能发挥自己的力量，才能够脱困。柔代表阴意，阴意承阳意，比较舒缓，阴意与阳意相应，是缘分相合而阴顺阳。初爻能够以顺承阳意的状态来面对险难，所以一开始就应该没有什么问题。这是对初爻阴意发动状态的领会和判断，换言之，相信阴爻之意能够以这种态度去面对解困的形势，就应该问题不大。

无咎既可以是状态判断，也可以是目标判断，力求无咎，不一定无咎。

[Illuminating Intentionality]

The Six (*yin*/soft line) in the first place is at the time to get out of trouble, but as a *yin* line realizes that one's power is limited, and knows that one must cooperate with *yang* lines and *yang*/positive intentions to exert one's power and get out of trouble. Softness represents *yin*, and *yin* follows *yang*, which is relatively soothing. *Yin* and *yang* respond to each other, and *yin* follows *yang* because of the coincidence of dependent co-arising. The Six (*yin*/soft line) in the first place can now face dangers in a state of compliance with *yang*'s intentions, so there should be no problems from the beginning. This is the understanding and judgment of the initiation status of the *yin* line in the first place and its intentionality. In other words, if one believes that the *yin* line can face the situation of resolving difficulties with this attitude, there should be no big problem.

Being blameless can be either a judgment of status or a judgment of goal. Trying to be blameless may not necessarily be blameless.

九二：田获三狐，得黄矢，贞吉。

《象》曰：九二"贞吉"，得中道也。

【明译】

九二：打猎的时候捕获三只狐狸，得到金黄色的箭矢，守持正道，可以吉祥。

《象传》说：九二守持正道，可以吉祥，因为在下卦中位，上应六五，做事遵从中正之道。

Nine (*yang*/strong line) in the second place: Catching three foxes while hunting will give golden arrows. Keeping to the upright *dao* will bring good fortune.

The *Image Commentary* (*Xiang Zhuan*) says: The Nine (*yang*/strong line) in the second place can be auspicious if one sticks to the upright *dao*, because it is in the middle of the lower Trigram, responds to the Six (*yin*/soft line) in the fifth place of the upper Trigram, and follows the upright *dao* in its affairs.

【明意】

六二是个像狙击手一样高明的猎手，能够解除小人之难，去小人之缘。狐代表小人，此爻有除恶人之意，近于清理人事的环境，让正面的阳意得到护持，而反面的阴意被排斥。保持意念发动的缘生形态，需要对周围的阴阳之意有直接的洞察，并能够扶阳意抑阴意。阴意与阳意相交合于本心之意境。复其本心（通天）即使无过，也是心通天之无过。

[Illuminating Intentionality]

The Six (*yin*/soft line) in the second place is a hunter as skilled as a sniper, able to relieve petty people of their troubles and get rid of petty people's dependent co-arising. The fox represents the petty person, and this line has the intentionality of getting rid of evil people, which is close to cleaning up the personnel environment, so that the positive *yang* spirit can be protected and the negative *yin* spirit can be rejected. To maintain the conditional form of intention initiation, one needs to have direct insight into the surrounding *yin* and *yang* intentions, and be able to support *yang* intentions and suppress *yin* intentions. *Yin* and *yang* intersect and merge into the intentional context of the original mind. There is no fault in restoring one's original intentionality (connecting with heaven), because intentionality has no fault if it connects with heaven.

六三：负且乘，致寇至，贞吝。

《象》曰："负且乘"，亦可丑也。自我致戎，又谁咎也？

【明译】

六三：身子坐在大车上，背上却还背着贵重的财物，这样就会招惹盗寇来抢劫，如果还坐着不动，就一定要有危难。

《象传》说：坐在车上仍旧把东西背在背上，不放下来，可见他没坐过车，形象太丑陋了，一看就不像个好人。所以是自己招致寇盗来抢劫，哪能怨别人呢？

Six (*yin*/soft line) in the third place: Sitting on a cart with valuables on one's back will attract thieves to attack. If one sits still, one must be in danger.

The *Image Commentary* (*Xiang Zhuan*) says: When sitting in a carriage, one still carries things on one's back and does not put them down. It can be seen that one has never been in a carriage. One's image is too ugly and one does not look like a decent person at first glance. Since it was one oneself who caused the bandits to come and attack, how can one blame others?

【明意】

六三心不正，才做得不好，心里有贼，当然天下有贼。可是要自己解开心魔，谈何容易？因为外在的执着都是心魔，要自己能够一念放下，自己负得太多不合适，就会有不好的结果。一个人的意缘有身缘，有位缘，有状态之缘，即一个人做事情不符合其身位，则有可能招惹不好的缘分，所以内心的意缘不正，则外在的感应就不可能正当平顺。

六三非常典型，其意缘的内外状态皆不顺当，都不合适。内缘即以柔意乘于刚强之位，无法驾驭，必然失控。外缘即自己推移不当，致使身陷危境，盗寇自来，无法制服自己的心魔，则意念出偏，难以回复正轨。

[Illuminating Intentionality]

The Six (*yin*/soft line) in the third place does not do well because its heart-mind is not upright. There are thieves in its intentions, and of course there are thieves in the world. However, it is not easy to solve one's own inner demons, because external attachments are all inner demons. When one needs to be able to let go of one's own intentions, bearing too much of a burden is inappropriate, and there will be bad results. A person's intentionality is related to one's body, one's position, and one's state. That is, if a person does things that are not in line with one's status, one may cause bad dependent co-arising. Therefore, if one's inner intentionality is not correct, one's external affective responses will not be correct, and things cannot be upright and smooth.

The Six (*yin*/soft line) in the third place is very typical. The internal and external states of its emotions are not smooth, and inappropriate. The inner condition is a soft intentionality riding in a strong position. If it cannot be controlled, it will inevitably lose control. The outer condition means that if one does not move properly, resulting in being in danger, bandits come, and then, unable to subdue one's inner demons, one's intentions will go astray and it is difficult to return to the right track.

九四：解而拇，朋至斯孚。

《象》曰："解而拇"，未当位也。

【明译】

九四：像舒解自己脚大拇趾的隐患那样摆脱小人的纠缠，然后朋友们就能诚心前来相助。

《象传》说：像舒解自己脚大拇趾的隐患那样摆脱小人的纠缠，因为九四所处的位置不适当（刚爻居柔位）。

Nine (*yang*/strong line) in the fourth place: Get rid of the entanglement of petty people just like relieving the hidden dangers of your toes, and then friends can come to help with sincerity.

The *Image Commentary* (*Xiang Zhuan*) says: Getting rid of the entanglement of petty people is just like relieving the hidden dangers of your toes, because the position of Nine (*yang*/strong line) in the fourth place is inappropriate (a *yang*/strong line in a soft position).

【明意】

没有朋友则自己的意缘无法得到应合。要想帮助他人，必须先解决自己心意的问题，也就是要消除外缘困扰。要去掉外缘在心意之境上的困扰，首先要自净其意，净缘以应世，方才不失进退的分寸。

要摆脱小人，先要舒缓自己的意境，也就是必须先去除自己心缘的麻烦，才能解难。解的本质是心缘之解，不被外缘所束，意念行于正道。

[Illuminating Intentionality]

Without friends, one's intentions cannot be fulfilled. If one wants to help others, one must first solve the problems in one's own intention, that is, one must eliminate external troubles. To get rid of the troubles caused by external factors in the state of intention, one must first purify one's intentionality and purify the factors to cope with the world, only then can one not lose the sense of advance and retreat.

To get rid of petty people, one must first soothe one's own intentional context, that is, one must first get rid of the troubles in one's own intentionality before one can solve the problem. The essence of the solution is resolving mental conditions. This is not bound by external conditions, and its intentions are on the upright *dao*.

六五：君子维有解，吉，有孚于小人。

《象》曰："君子有解"，小人退也。

【明译】

六五：君子只有舒缓解难，才能吉祥，只有让小人心服口服，才算真正解脱险难。

《象传》说：君子只有舒缓解难，这样小人（六五）才会愿意把尊位让给九四，主动退出去。

Six (*yin*/soft line) in the fifth place: An exemplary person can only be fortunate by easing one's difficulties, and only by convincing petty people can one truly be freed from danger.

The *Image Commentary* (*Xiang Zhuan*) says: An exemplary person can only ease one's difficulties, so that the petty person (the Six (*yin*/soft line) in the fifth place) will be willing to give up one's position to the Nine (*yang*/strong line) in the fourth place and take the initiative to withdraw.

【明意】

君子的诚信连小人都相信了，君子舒缓意缘到连小人都心服口服的地步。君子能够舒缓险难，是因为有能力驱除小人。

君子之意境能够融化感动小人之意。君子的意缘能够感动小人。上六用射掉坏人之头目的方式，君子舒缓情境，化解了紧张的情势。此爻小人被君子之道感动而解，小人取得尊位之后要顺守，以君子之道行事。

[Illuminating Intentionality]
Even petty people believe in the integrity of an exemplary person. An exemplary person soothes feelings to the point where even petty people are convinced, and can alleviate dangers because one has the ability to drive away petty people.

The intentional context of an exemplary person can soothe and move the intentions of a petty person, so an exemplary person's intentional conditions can move a petty person. The Six (*yin*/soft line) in the top place uses the method of shooting down the leader among the bad people, as the exemplary person relaxes the emotional situation and thus resolves the tense propensity. In this line, petty people are moved by the way of an exemplary person and understand it. After they obtain an honorable position, they must follow this and act according to the *dao* of an exemplary person.

上六：公用射隼（sǔn）于高墉之上，获之，无不利。

《象》曰："公用射隼"，以解悖也。

【明译】

上六：王公用箭射下栖落在高墙之上的恶隼，一举把它擒获，这样做是无所不利的。

《象传》说：王公用箭一举射杀恶隼，这是不得已为民除害，只有这样才能彻底消灭作乱的小人，舒解悖逆者造成的祸乱。

Six (*yin*/soft line) in the top place: The prince shoots down the ferocious eagle perched on the high wall with an arrow, capturing it in one fell swoop. There is no disadvantage in doing so.

The *Image Commentary* (*Xiang Zhuan*) says: The prince shoots the evil hawk with an arrow as a last resort to eliminate harm for the people. Only in this way can the petty people who caused trouble be completely eliminated and the chaos caused by the rebellious relieved.

【明意】

如果从修心的角度来说，可以理解为修行者心中都有出头妄想之鸟，有人留之欣赏，就容易祸福相随，有人用心射之，才能飞行自在，所以要射掉心中之隼。如果从上六无情系恋的角度来看，确实更能客观地处理问题，从另一个角度来说，则是上六应该绝无情系，面对险难，要排除情绪干扰，冷静果断，修出心如止水的意境，才能百步穿杨，以解心头之患祸。确实，每个人心头之患必须自己射自己解，大家都要用好箭法把自己的心隼解决掉。如果人人都能反求诸己，这世界就会真的美好。如果能射心隼，就有可能弯弓射天上人间的大雕。

[Illuminating Intentionality]

From the perspective of cultivating the heart-mind, it can be understood that practitioners all have birds of delusion in their intentions. If one keeps them to appreciate them, misfortunes and blessings will easily follow one another. Only if one shoots them carefully can they fly freely, so people must shoot away the hawks in their intentions. If one looks at this from the perspective of the Six (*yin*/soft line) in the top place's ruthless relations, it is indeed a more objective way to deal with the problem. From another perspective, it is that the Six (*yin*/soft line) in the top place should never have ruthless relations. When facing dangers, we must eliminate emotional interference, be calm and decisive, and practice cultivation. Only when intentionality is as calm as water can one resolve the troubles in one's intentions as accurately and precisely as a good archer. Indeed, everyone's inner troubles must be solved by themselves, and everyone must use good archery skills to get rid of their own troubles. If everyone can seek within themselves, the world would be truly beautiful. Only if one can shoot the hawk in one's heart-mind, may one be able to bend one's bow and shoot the giant hawks in the sky and within one's heart.

山泽损（卦四十一）　（兑下艮上）

Sun (Diminishing), Mountain and Lake (Hexagram 41)　(Dui below, Gen above)

损卦六爻都指引我们如何获益，明白了生命损益之理，能够损去有害于生命者则吉，认识自己需要通过认识天道，才可以知道损中有益，其实减损也可以增益。这种减损与增益的过程都要以诚信为本，方可得生命正道。如果能够损去对生命有害无益之事，即会有益，换言之，减少欲望，就是在避损行益。

生存的意志让生命有意义，或者因为有生存意志，以及生存下去的实际事实，所以人们努力赋予生命以意义。很多时候，人有生存的意志但无力生存下去，如病入膏肓的人，身体极度虚弱的人，死刑犯等等；这时，生存的意义立即从无限变成有限。意量的涵纳与收敛是一个减损的过程，减损物欲与诸遮蔽心智之物，将有助于涵养生生之意，也就是修德要减少自己的缺点，要学会减损不必要的心意负担，以专注于生机之本。天道生生不息，但应适时减损；人道尊奉天道，要损中求益。其实每一卦每一爻都在求生生，因为生生之谓易，易以生生为本体，意之生为世界存在之根本，是意之生使得世界实存而生成。

The six lines of Hexagram Sun (Diminishing) all guide us on how to gain benefit, and understand the principles of loss and gain in life. If we can lose something that is harmful to life, we will be fortunate. To understand ourselves, we need to understand the heavenly *dao*, and then we can know that there is benefit in loss. In fact, loss can also be gained. This process of loss and gain must be based on integrity in order to achieve the upright *dao* of life. If one can eliminate things that are harmful to one's life, it will be beneficial. In other words, reducing one's desires means avoiding losses and being beneficial.

The will to live gives life meaning, or, because there is a will to live, and the actual fact of surviving, people strive to give meaning to life. Many times, people have the will to live but are unable to survive, such as terminally ill people, extremely weak people, death row prisoners, etc. At this time, the intentionality of survival immediately changes from unlimited to limited. The involution and retraction of intentionality is a process of reducing material desires and things that obscure the intentions, which helps to cultivate the intentionality of life. That is to say, to cultivate morality, one must reduce one's own shortcomings and learn to reduce unnecessary mental burdens, in order to focus on the root of vitality. The heavenly *dao* is endlessly productive, but it should reduce at the right time; the humane *dao* respects the heavenly *dao* and seeks benefits from losses. In fact, every hexagram and every line is seeking production and reproduction, because production and reproduction are what is called change, and change takes production and reproduction as its fundamental root. The productivity of intentionality is the foundation of the existence of the world, and it is the productivity of intentionality that makes the world exist.

损：有孚，元吉，无咎。可贞。利有攸往。曷（hé）之用？二簋可用享。

《彖》曰：损，损下益上，其道上行。损而"有孚，元吉，无咎，可贞。利有攸往。曷之用？二簋可用享。"二簋应有时。损刚益柔有时，损益盈虚，与时偕行。

《象》曰：山下有泽，损。君子以惩忿窒欲。

【明译】

损卦象征减损衰退，心中保持诚信，就能大吉大利，没有过错，可以守持正道，有利于前往做事。减损衰退之道在人伦日用之间如何体现出来呢？用两簋淡薄的食物来祭祀就足够表达内心的诚敬了。

《彖传》说：损卦从泰卦变来，在卦变中泰卦初九上升到最上位，减损下面的刚实，增益上面的柔虚，阳爻的运行之道是往上走。即使在减损衰退的过程之中，心中仍然充满诚信，所以能够大吉大利，没有过错，可以守持正道，有利于前往做事。减损衰退之道在人伦日用之间如何体现出来呢？用两簋淡薄的食物来祭祀就足够表达内心的诚敬了。用两簋淡薄的食物来祭祀要合于时令，减损阳刚来增益阴柔也要讲究合适的时机：事物的减损、增益、盈满、亏虚都在时间之中，随着时间流变，通过不同的时机体现出来。

《象传》说：上卦艮为山，下卦兑为泽，山下有泽就是损卦，山中的泽水不断下流，淘空山体，可能导致山崩地坼，泽在减损衰退，越来越深的同时，水面不断下降，显得山越来越高。君子看到这样的卦象要抑制忿怒，窒塞邪欲。

Hexagram Sun (Diminishing) symbolizes loss and decline. If one keeps integrity in one's heart-mind, one will be able to have good fortune. If one has no faults, one can keep to the upright *dao* and gain benefits through advancing and acting. How does the *dao* of reduction and decline manifest itself in human relations and daily use? Offering two baskets of light food as a sacrifice is enough to express one's inner sincerity.

The *Judgment Commentary* (*Tuan Zhuan*) says: Hexagram Sun (Diminishing) changes from Hexagram Tai (Communication). In the hexagram-changes, the Nine (*yang*/strong line) in the first place of Hexagram Tai (Communication) rises to the highest position, detracting from the solidity below and increasing the softness above, as the *dao* of the movement of the *yang* line is upward. Even in the process of loss and decline, one's heart-mind is still full of integrity, so one can have good fortune, make no mistakes, keep to the upright *dao*, and gain benefits through advancing and acting. How does the method of reduction and decline manifest itself in human relations and daily use? Offering two baskets of light food as a sacrifice is enough to express one's inner sincerity. To offer sacrifices with two baskets of light food must be in accordance with the season, and to detract from the *yang*/strong and increase the *yin*/soft must also be done at the right time: the loss, gain, fullness, and deficiency of things all occur in time, and change with time, manifesting through different timings.

The *Image Commentary* (*Xiang Zhuan*) says: The upper Trigram Gen is mountain, and the lower Trigram Dui is lake. If there is a marsh at the foot of a mountain, this is Hexagram Sun (Diminishing). The marsh water in the mountain will continue to flow down, and the mountain will be emptied, which may lead to landslides. As it gets deeper, the water surface continues to drop, making the mountain appear to be getting higher and higher. When an exemplary person sees such a hexagram, one knows to suppress one's anger and suffocate one's evil desires.

【明意】

人生的生机看似无限，其实有限。首先人存在于一个有限的时空之中，人的时空跨度无论多长都是有限的。其次人的意识虽似有无限的生机，但随时可能因为身体不适、病痛等，只能将意识境域集中在有限的状态中，甚至以求生为本。因为没有生机则存在都免谈，减损外物是为了生机的存续，是为了对世界的再认识得以可能。很多人经历生命的减损过程，如大病一场之后，往往对于生机的涵养有深刻的体会，因为生机是存在之本，活生生的意量是生命和世界存续的前提。

卦有从山上看大泽之象，人见风景如画，自然减损怒气和嗜欲，得天地生生之气。还有说兑下艮上，好像少男少女之间的爱意充满生生之机，顺天地之爱而无欲则刚，如果私人的爱，能够由万物一体之感，爱自己并推致于天地自然之意境，则损心意至极致，反而能够悟得心意通天之意境。

[Illuminating Intentionality]

The vitality of life seems unlimited, but is in fact limited. First of all, people exist in a finite time and space, and their spatio-temporal span is limited, no matter how long it is. Secondly, although human consciousness seems to have unlimited vitality, due to physical discomfort or pain at any time, the realm of consciousness can only be concentrated in a limited state, sometimes even based on survival. Since without vitality, there is no need to talk about existence, so the reduction of external objects is needed for the survival of vitality and to make it possible to re-understand the world. Many people who have experienced loss in life, such as after a serious illness, often have a profound understanding of the cultivation of vitality, because vitality is the foundation of existence, and living intentionality is the prerequisite for the survival of life and the world.

This hexagram has the image of looking at a great lake from a mountain. When people see picturesque scenery, they will naturally reduce their anger and desires, and gain the vitality of heaven and earth. It also states that the love between young men and women is full of productive vitality, and it is strong to follow the love between heaven and earth without desire. If private love can feel the unity of the myriad things, love oneself and promote the natural intentional context of heaven and earth, then the intentionality of diminishing is taken to the extreme, but it is able to realize the intentional context of intentionality connecting with heaven.

初九：已事遄（chuán）往，无咎。酌损之。

《象》曰："已事遄往"，尚合志也。

【明译】

初九：已经具备损下益上的条件，就要迅速前往，这样才没有过失。这说明可以酌情减损自己的阳刚之质。

《象传》说：已经具备损下益上的条件，就要迅速前往，是向上跟六四心志相合。

Nine (*yang*/strong line) in the first place: If one already has the conditions for loss and gain, one must advance quickly to avoid making any mistakes. This shows that one can diminish one's *yang*/strong qualities as appropriate.

The *Image Commentary* (*Xiang Zhuan*) says: If one has met the conditions for losses and gains, one must advance quickly. This is to align with the aspirations of the Six (*yin*/soft line) in the fourth place.

【明意】

当一念反思之时，意识到与意共生的负累太多，并决心减损意念的附属物的时候，就当决意为之，努力减损意念的附属之物，从而让生生的诚意得以彰显出来。当生命的涵养出现危机，要迅速减损外在不必要的累赘，以期存续生机之本。

[Illuminating Intentionality]

When reflecting on intentions, if one realizes that the burdens of symbiosis with one's intentions are too much, and decides to reduce the attachments of one's intentions, then one should make the decision and work hard to reduce the attachments of one's intentions, so that one's sincerity can be revealed. When there is a crisis in the cultivation of life, one must quickly reduce unnecessary external burdens in order to preserve the foundation of vitality.

九二：利贞。征凶，弗损益之。

《象》曰：九二"利贞"，中以为志也。

【明译】

九二：利于持守正道，盲目征进会有凶险，既不过分减损自身，也不去增益上边。

《象传》说：九二利于持守正道，是居于中位，谨守本分，以居于中位，持守中道作为自己的心意志向。

Nine (*yang*/strong line) in the second place: It is beneficial to stick to the upright *dao*, and there are dangers in blindly marching forward. Neither diminish oneself excessively, nor increase that which is above.

The *Image Commentary* (*Xiang Zhuan*) says: The Nine (*yang*/strong line) in the second place is conducive to maintaining the upright *dao*, which means staying in the middle position and accepting one's share, so one makes staying in the middle position and adhering to the middle *dao* as one's intention and will.

【明意】

在生命之机受到威胁的减损处境中，过分征进即过分地减损自己，于己于人皆不安全，所以既不可过度减损自身，也不必要去增益上边，而要减损适度才能益生。

在减损的大势中，既然已经减损到了一定程度，还要继续，那么减损要量力而行，做力所能及的、应该做的减损之事，但不宜过度。

[Illuminating Intentionality]

In a loss situation where the basis of life is threatened, excessive advancement means excessive loss of oneself, which is unsafe for oneself and others. Therefore, one should neither overly diminish oneself nor increase those above, as only moderate loss can be beneficial.

In the general trend of diminishing and reduction, since the diminishment has reached a certain level and will continue, the diminishment must be done within one's ability and according to what should be done, but it should not be excessive.

六三：三人行则损一人，一人行则得其友。

《象》曰："一人行"，"三"则疑也。

【明译】

六三：三个人一起前行会损失一个人，一个人单独前行则会得到朋友。

《象传》说：一个人单独前行可以得到朋友，而三个人一起前行难免相互猜疑。

Six (*yin*/soft line) in the third place: If three people advance together, they will lose one person; if one person moves forward alone, one will gain a friend.

The *Image Commentary* (*Xiang Zhuan*) says: A person traveling alone can gain friends, but three people traveling together will inevitably be suspicious of each other.

455

【明意】

在减损的大格局中，要搜寻心意相近者的支持，与自己的心意相通的友人沟通，能够唤起自己心意之生机。如果与二人共处一个减损的格局当中，只有抓住最有利于自己生机的对象，所以另一个也可能被减损。这是因为阴阳相吸而致一，如男女相吸，阴意与阳意结合方能有意丹生成，如果阴意过度，或阳意过度，都要减损，重新达到平衡。

[Illuminating Intentionality]

In the general pattern of diminishment, one should look for the support of people with similar minds. Communicating with friends who share one's own intentions can arouse the vitality of one's own intention. If one is in a diminishing pattern with two people, one can only seize the object that is most beneficial to one's own vitality, so another may also be diminished. This is because *yin* and *yang* attract each other and become one, just like men and women attract each other, and only when *yin* and *yang* are combined can the elixir of intentionality be generated. If either *yin* or *yang* is excessive, it must be reduced and the balance must be restored.

六四：损其疾，使遄有喜，无咎。

《象》曰："损其疾"，亦可"喜"也。

【明译】

六四：减损自己的疾病，使得自己很快就欢欣喜悦，当然没有什么过错。

《象传》说：减损自己的疾病，这件事本身就可喜可贺。

【明意】

疾病是生机减损的一种大处境。病可以是物欲，对外物和使自己心意物化倾向的执念，而不仅是被迫应对疾病的处境。而减损疾病就意味着生机的复苏，虽然于生机没有明确的提振，但减损疾病本身就是件好事。

有心力期待自己进入喜悦的状态本身就是一件喜悦的事。从不得不把意念专注于具体物化之物的处境之中解脱出来，即是一种成功。要能控制欲望，也就是减损欲望，才有利于摆脱困境。因控制欲望即便是减少意欲被物化的可能性，也可给予心意的生机以成长的空间。

Six (*yin*/soft line) in the fourth place: There is nothing wrong with diminishing one's illness, making oneself happy quickly.

The *Image Commentary* (*Xiang Zhuan*) says: Reducing one's own illness is gratifying in itself.

[Illuminating Intentionality]

Illness is a major condition that reduces vitality. Disease can be material desires, obsession with external objects, and the tendency to objectify one's own intentions, not just the situation of being forced to deal with a disease. The diminishing of disease means the recovery of vitality. Even where there is no clear boost to vitality, the loss of disease itself is a good thing.

Having the energy to expect oneself to enter a state of joy is a joyful thing in itself. It is a kind of success to be freed from the situation of having to focus one's intentions on concrete objects. Only by being able to control desires, that is, by reducing desires, can one get out of trouble. Because controlling desires reduces the possibility of objectification, it also gives the vitality of intentionality room to grow.

六五：或益之十朋之龟，弗克违，元吉。

《象》曰：六五"元吉"，自上佑也。

【明译】

六五：有人送来价值"十朋"的大宝龟，并不违背自己的心意，不必推辞，大吉大利。

《象传》说：六五大吉大利，因为上天佑助。

Six (*yin*/soft line) in the fifth place: Someone sends a large treasure turtle worth ten *peng*. This does not go against one's will, so one does not have to refuse, and there is good fortune.

The *Image Commentary (Xiang Zhuan)* says: The Six (*yin*/soft line) in the fifth place is very auspicious, because heaven is helping.

【明意】

心意本来自然通天，但只有在某些特定的时刻，如此爻因上爻之从天而降而意境大变，仿佛心意与天相通的机缘被天意显示出来，得到意想不到的吉利的征象。人的心意本来通天，所以当天显吉象，没有必要违背，顺而受之即可，因顺天受礼，乘势而行本身就是一种心意通天的智慧。可见损益之道在互推互动的过程之中相辅相成。

[Illuminating Intentionality]

Intentionality naturally connects with heaven, but only at certain specific moments like this line, as its intentional context changes greatly due to the line above falling from heaven. It is as if the opportunity of a connection between intentionality and heaven is revealed by heavenly intentionality, and an unexpected and auspicious sign is obtained. People's heart-minds are originally connected to heaven, so there is no need to violate the auspicious signs in the heavens. One can just accept them, because accepting a gift from heaven and taking advantage of the situation is a kind of wisdom that has the intentionality to connect to heaven. It can be seen that the patterns of gain and loss complement each other in the process of mutual promotion and interaction.

上九：弗损，益之，无咎。贞吉。利有攸往，得臣无家。

《象》曰："弗损，益之"，大得志也。

【明译】

上九：没有受到减损，反而得到增益，当然没有过错。持守正道可获吉祥。利于有所前往，得到广大臣民的拥护，就不必在乎自己的小家了。

《象传》说：没有受到减损，反而得到增益，是因为上九的心意志向完全得到了实化。

Nine (*yang*/strong line) in the top place: There is no loss, but rather gain, so of course there is no fault. Staying on the upright *dao* will bring good fortune. If one wants to go somewhere and gain the support of the general public, one does not have to care about your own little home.

The *Image Commentary* (*Xiang Zhuan*) says: One has not been diminished, but gained, because the Nine (*yang*/strong line) in the top place's heart-mind and will have been completely realized.

【明意】

损的哲学告诉人们，人的意量融贯天下，但往往是通过减损伤害生命生机的物欲来做到的。心智能够通达天道的人，心念所发皆与天道相通，并能自觉此点，而不会遮蔽心意与天齐同的本然状态。心意的生机完全融贯通于天下的状态，就是智量通天的状态，即所谓"得志"的状态。

[Illuminating Intentionality]

The philosophy of diminishing tells people that human intentional capacity is integrated into the world, but it is often done by diminishing material desires that harm the vitality of life. People whose minds can access the heavenly *dao* will have everything that comes from their intentions connected with the heavenly *dao*, and they will be aware of this, without covering up their natural state of being in harmony with heaven. The state in which the vitality of intentionality is completely integrated into the world is a state in which wisdom reaches the heavens, which is what can be called a "realized" state.

风雷益（卦四十二）　（震下巽上）

Yi (Increase), Wind and Thunder (Hexagram 42)　(Zhen below, Xun above)

　　几微之际改变意识状态的魄力展示出的制心艺术是意念存续的机括。在意识发动的瞬间，反省而明白哪些是纯粹的欲望，哪些是合理的成分，在意念缘发的极微之处改变自己的意境。意识的增益也有这个问题，在意识中增加什么，其实就要以减少什么作为条件，当下的意识境遇所要的非常有限。

　　益是增益之意。《杂卦》说益是开始旺盛，因为增益就会渐趋兴旺。按照彖辞的说法，益卦从否卦变来，即否上九旋转到最下位变益卦。益卦象征与春夏相对应的生产和成长，而损卦象征与秋冬相对应的生气减弱，节制欲望等。益有利益和公益之意。利益首先是君子之修身得益，增益内在的德性。公益是对天下之民皆利。

The art of intentionality control demonstrated by the ability to change the state of consciousness in a few moments is the mechanism for the survival of intentions. At the moment when consciousness is initiated, one should reflect and understand which are pure desires and which are reasonable elements, and change one's intentional context in the smallest possible way. The increase of consciousness also has this problem, as whatever is added to consciousness must be conditioned on reducing something. The current conscious situation requires very limited things.

Hexagram Yi (Increase) means gain. In the *Miscellaneous Characteristics of the Hexagrams*, it states that Hexagram Yi (Increase) is beginning to be strong, because gain will gradually become more prosperous. According to the *Judgment Commentary* (*Tuan Zhuan*), Hexagram Yi (Increase) changes from Hexagram Pi (Non-Communication), that is, the Nine (*yang*/strong line) in the top place of

Hexagram Pi (Non-Communication) changes round to the lowest position, and it becomes Hexagram Yi (Increase). Hexagram Yi (Increase) symbolizes production and growth corresponding to spring and summer, while Hexagram Sun (Diminishing) symbolizes the weakening of vitality and restrained desires corresponding to autumn and winter. Increase means both profit and public welfare. The first benefit is to benefit an exemplary person's self-cultivation and enhance one's inner virtue. Public welfare is beneficial to all people in the world.

益，利有攸往。利涉大川。

《彖》曰：益，损上益下，民说无疆。自上下下，其道大光。"利有攸往"，中正有庆。"利涉大川"，木道乃行。益动而巽，日进无疆。天施地生，其益无方。凡益之道，与时偕行。

《象》曰：风雷，益。君子以见善则迁，有过则改。

【明译】

益卦象征增益，利于有所前往，利于涉越大河。

《彖传》说：益卦，减损上面的来增益下面的（初九从否卦最上方来到益卦最下方），百姓欢欣喜悦无可限量。从上面降下到下面，其心意之道正大光明。有利于前往，是九五中正而有喜庆。有利于涉越大河，是因为木船能够渡河通畅。益卦下面震动（震），上面随顺（巽），日复一日前进没有止境。上天施予阳光雨露，大地生养万物一视同仁，天地生养增益万物没有固定的方式。大凡事物当要增益时所体现的道理，都随时间一起流变，按照一定时机化的方式展现出来。

《象传》说：上卦巽为风，下卦震为雷，雷风呼应，相得益彰，这就是益卦，君子从中得到启示，见到善美的行为就要心向往之，择善而从，有错迅速就改。

Hexagram Yi (Increase) symbolizes gain, and is helpful for advancing and crossing a great river.

The *Judgment Commentary* (*Tuan Zhuan*) says: Hexagram Yi (Increase) diminishes those above and increases those below (the Nine (*yang*/strong line) in the first place moves from the top of the Hexagram Pi (Non-Communication) to the bottom of Hexagram Yi (Increase)), and the common people's joy is boundless. Descending from above to below, the *dao* of one's intentionality is upright and bright. This is conducive to advancing, and it is the most upright and festive time in the Nine (*yang*/strong line) in the fifth place. It is advantageous to cross large rivers because wooden boats can cross the river smoothly. The lower part of Hexagram Yi (Increase) vibrates (Zhen), the upper part Trigram Xun means to follow, and there is no end to the progress day after day. Heaven gives sunshine and rain, and the earth gives birth to the myriad things equally. There is no fixed way for heaven and earth to give birth to and enhance the myriad things. The truths reflected in most things when they are about to gain will change with time and be displayed in a certain timing manner.

The *Image Commentary* (*Xiang Zhuan*) says: The upper Trigram Xun is wind, the lower Trigram

Zhen is thunder, and the thunder and wind echo and complement each other. This is Hexagram Yi (Increase). An exemplary person gets inspiration from it. If you want to see good behavior, you must yearn for it and choose the good and follow it and correct any mistakes quickly.

【明意】

减损上面，增益下面，也就是增益必以减损为前提，心意能量与客观能量之间也是等量交换的关系。想益必先损，天下没有只损不益，或者只益不损的事情，要损己才能获利。人控制自己的意识不易，而于一念之间通晓三千世界最难。生活的基础是经验，而且主要是自身的体验。进退的姿态主要来自对人生体验的理解和把握。意识的增益被常人理解为意识对象或者身外之物的增益，其实是方向性的错误，因为身外物的增益无助于意识境外的增益。

风雷激荡之间，即意识的运发之际，可以激发人产生经验性的自察，或者说以经验为基础的自省，帮助人们意识到增益意识能量的复杂程度。可见，心意参与风雷激荡而收获经验性的领悟之后，才能增益心对意识几微的自察力量。

[Illuminating Intentionality]

Above is loss, below is gain, that is to say, gain must be based on loss, and the relationship between intentional energy and objective energy is also an equal exchange relationship. If you want to gain, you must first lose. There is no such thing as a loss but not a gain, or a gain but not a loss. You have to lose oneself before one can gain. It is not easy for people to control their own consciousness, but it is most difficult to understand the three thousand worlds in one intention. The basis of life is experience, and it is mainly one's own experience. The posture of advance and retreat mainly comes from the understanding and grasp of life experience. The gain of consciousness is understood by ordinary people as the gain of objects in consciousness or things outside the body, but this is actually a directional error, because the gain of things outside the body does not contribute to the gain outside the realm of consciousness.

Between the storm and the thunder, that is, when consciousness is developing, it can inspire people to have experiential self-examination, or introspection based on experience, and help people realize the complexity of increasing the energy of consciousness. It can be seen that only after the intentionality participates in the agitation of wind and thunder and gains experiential understanding, can the mind's self-awareness of consciousness be enhanced.

初九：利用为大作，元吉，无咎。

《象》曰："元吉无咎"，下不厚事也。

【明译】

初九：有利于大有作为，建功立业，一开始就大吉大利，没有过错。

《象传》说：大吉大利，没有过错，因为下民不需要付出太多来事奉统治者。

Nine (*yang*/strong line) in the first place: It is conducive to making great achievements. It will be auspicious from the beginning and there will be no mistakes.

The *Image Commentary* (*Xiang Zhuan*) says: Good fortune, great benefit, and no fault, because the people do not need to pay too much to serve the ruler.

【明意】

风雷激荡之时，一开始就有利于做大的事情。初九从上来增益下边，自然不要下边付出太多，既能做大事，又不兴师动众，所以非常合适。卦变上下面得到增益，获得厚生的生机滋养，这种生机来自在上位者增益下面人民的意识，这样大家因为增益而能够多做一些原来不能做的大事情。人们领略到了领导者的生生之意，也得到增益的实惠，这是非常好的意识境遇。

[Illuminating Intentionality]

When the wind and thunder are turbulent, it is conducive to doing big things from the beginning. Nine (*yang*/strong line) in the first place works from the top to benefit the bottom, so naturally the bottom should not pay too much. It can do great things without invading the crowd, so it is very suitable. The upper and lower parts of the hexagram-changes are enhanced and nourished by the vitality of the people. This vitality comes from the consciousness of the people below the upper person's enhancement, so that everyone can do more big things that they could not do before because of the enhancement. People appreciate the leader's intentionality of life and gain benefits. This is a very good state of consciousness.

六二：或益之十朋之龟，弗克违。永贞吉。王用享于帝，吉。

《象》曰："或益之"，自外来也。

【明译】

六二：有人送来价值"十朋"的大宝龟，并不违背自己的心意，不必推辞，永久保持正道吉利。君王向天帝祭享，吉利。

《象传》说：有人送来大宝龟，说明六二的增益是从外面不招自来的。

Six (*yin*/soft line) in the second place: If someone sends you a big treasure turtle worth "ten *peng*", it does not go against your will, so you don't have to refuse, and you will always stay on the right *dao* and be auspicious. It is auspicious for the king to offer sacrifices to the Emperor of Heaven.

The *Image Commentary* (*Xiang Zhuan*) says: Someone sent a big treasure turtle, which shows that the Six (*yin*/soft line) in the second place's gain came from outside.

【明意】

一般的增益就已是外在的福分，这种天降的礼物代表福分不招自来，好像得到天帝的庇护和佑助一般。这种意识是人得到了外财而非常感动苍天的眷顾，觉得老天增益他外来的福分，让他可以去增益自己的所需，这种感天动地的情怀，是因为天的增益让自己的意识与天感通而增益。

心存感恩，会有巨大的增益，一种对所遇都保持感恩之心的情怀，让心灵能够感悟和领略生命中无限的偶遇和美妙。

[Illuminating Intentionality]

Ordinary gains are external blessings. This kind of gift from heaven means that blessings come unexpectedly, as if receiving the protection and help of the Emperor of Heaven. This kind of consciousness is when a person has received foreign wealth and is very moved by heaven's blessings. One feels that heaven has blessed one with foreign blessings, allowing one to increase one's own needs. This feeling of touching heaven and earth is because of heaven's blessings. Allow your consciousness to connect with the heaven and increase your awareness.

Being grateful will bring huge gains. Maintaining a feeling of gratitude for everything you encounter allows the heart-mind to perceive and appreciate the infinite encounters and beauty in life.

六三：益之用凶事，无咎。有孚，中行，告公用圭。

《象》曰："益用凶事"，固有之也。

【明译】

六三：把所得的增益运用于拯凶救难、赈灾平险当中，没有过错。心怀诚信，行动中正平和，手持玉圭向王公禀报告急。

《象传》说：把所得的增益运用于拯凶救难、赈灾平险当中，这是本当如此的事情。

Six (yin/soft line) in the third place: There is nothing wrong with using the gains gained to save people from disasters and relieve disasters. One has integrity in one's heart and is peaceful in one's actions. One holds a jade guide and reports the emergency to the prince.

It is the right thing to use the gains obtained to save people from disasters and relieve disasters.

【明意】

这是一种紧急和急促的意识状态，因为救灾是人命关天和刻不容缓的事情。在灾情紧急的关头，人民的需要就是天意，人心就是天心的意境之实化。人民处于生存的危急关头，需要领导的心意增益才能解脱困境，这时领导的增益之意以民心为天，以民意为本，这是本当如此的事情，也就是说，当民众蒙灾受损，领导就该发动主动增益的意识。

[Illuminating Intentionality]

This is an urgent and urgent state of consciousness, because disaster relief is a matter of life and death and cannot be delayed. At the critical moment of disaster, the needs of the people are the will of heaven, and the human heart is the realization of the intentional context of heavenly mind. The people are at a critical juncture of survival, and they need the leadership's support to get out of the predicament. At this time, the leadership's support is based on the people's intentions and minds. This is what should be done. In other words, when the people suffer disasters and losses, leaders should initiate the awareness of active gain.

六四：中行，告公从，利用为依迁国。

《象》曰："告公从"，以益志也。

【明译】

六四：以中正之意行乎中道，禀告王公自己有顺从之意，王公依从，就会有利于依附君王（九五）做出迁都这样的大事。

《象传》说：禀告王公（初九）自己有顺从之意，王公依从，这增益了六四的意志。

Six (*yin*/soft line) in the fourth place: Walking in the middle way with the right intention, and reporting to the prince that you intend to obey. If the prince obeys, it will be beneficial to the king (Nine (*yang*/strong line) in the fifth place) to do such a big thing as relocating the capital.

The *Image Commentary* (*Xiang Zhuan*) says: Report to the prince (on Nine (*yang*/strong line) in the first place) that one has the intention to obey, and the prince obeys, which strengthens the will of Six (*yin*/soft line) in the fourth place.

【明意】

领导人心意中正，而且得到上天的礼物来增益自己的意志，其意识自然是做事要顺从天意。也可以理解为，得到最高领导的认可才能增益自己的意识，也要让大家放心，才可以做利己利人的事情。

[Illuminating Intentionality]

Leaders whose intentions are right and who have received gifts from heaven to strengthen their will naturally have the consciousness to obey cosmological intentionality in doing things. It can also be understood that only by gaining recognition from the top leadership can one's own consciousness be enhanced, and only by making everyone feel at ease can one do things that benefit oneself and others.

九五：有孚惠心，勿问，元吉。有孚，惠我德。

《象》曰："有孚惠心"，勿问之矣。"惠我德"，大得志也。

【明译】

九五：真诚地怀着施惠于民的心意，不需占问就是非常吉利的，天下人都会真诚地感念我的恩德。

《象传》说：真诚地怀着施惠于民的心意，就不必再去占问了。天下人都会感念我的恩德，说明九五"损上益下"的心志得到完美的实化。

Nine (*yang*/strong line) in the fifth place: If one sincerely intends to benefit the people, it is very auspicious without divining, and everyone in the world under heaven will sincerely appreciate one's kindness.

The *Image Commentary* (*Xiang Zhuan*) says: If one sincerely intends to benefit the people, there is no need to ask by divination. That everyone in the world under heaven will be grateful for one's kindness shows that the ambition of the Nine (*yang*/strong line) in the fifth place to "diminish those above and benefit those below" has been perfectly realized.

【明意】

九五德位相配，有真诚至极地增益天下人的意识，天下人也都会反馈并增益他的意识，故意识之增益才是真正的"惠"。怀惠于人才能得人之惠，九五心意通天，既能够施惠于民，又能最终施惠于己。九五之诚，是心意通天之至诚，足以感天动地，因其深得损益之道，主动减损自己，让利他人，自然得志四方，其心意实化之处，无须占问，自然合道，吉祥如意之所之。

[Illuminating Intentionality]

If the Nine (*yang*/strong line) in the fifth place has the matching virtue, one can sincerely be of extreme benefit to the consciousness of the people in the world under heaven, and everyone in the world under heaven will also feedback and increase one's consciousness. Therefore, an increase of consciousness is the real "benefit." Only by being kind to others can one get benefits from others. As the Nine (*yang*/strong line) in the fifth place, one's intentionality is open to heaven, and one can not only benefit the people, but also ultimately benefit oneself. The sincerity of the Nine (*yang*/strong line) in the fifth place is the sincerity that reaches to heaven and is sufficient to move the heavens and the earth, and because it deeply understands the way of gain and loss, it takes the initiative to reduce itself and benefit others, and will naturally succeed in all directions. Wherever its intentions are concretized, there is no need to ask by divination, as it will naturally accord with the *dao*, and attain good fortune as it intends.

上九：莫益之，或击之。立心勿恒，凶。

《象》曰："莫益之"，偏辞也。"或击之"，自外来也。

【明译】

上九：没有人来增益他，反而有人来攻击他，不能坚定地持守人天之意，会有凶险。

《象传》说：没有人来增益他，对上九来说是通常的情况。反而有人来攻击他，因为阳爻从外卦下来，（不招自来而生成了危险的境遇）。

Nine (*yang*/strong line) in the top place: No one comes to strengthen him, but someone comes to attack him. If he cannot firmly adhere to the cosmological intentionality of humanity and heaven, there will be danger.

The *Image Commentary* (*Xiang Zhuan*) says: That no one comes to benefit him is a normal situation for the Nine (*yang*/strong line) in the top place. Instead, someone comes to attack him, because the *yang* line comes down from the outer hexagram (it comes itself without being called, creating a dangerous situation).

【明意】

益是一个人的意识要力求实化的状态，如果没有人来增益，就有可能有人来攻击。所以意识不稳定，就容易形成危险的形势。这样说来，意识时刻增益是一个应该追求的状态，因为如不能增益，就意味着减损和受伤，可见增益的意识境遇是应该追求的，意识状态要在增益中随时保持阴意与阳意的平衡。人的心意是一个阴阳平衡的过程，没有足够的支撑力，就有相应的伤害力出来。意识的生成与转换是一个系统工程，心意在其中只能够依境而生，顺势而为。这种形势的变化，有时不是自己招来的，是大势的变化转化了心意所在的境域。

[Illuminating Intentionality]

Increase is a state that a person's consciousness must strive to realize. If no one comes to benefit one, someone may come to attack. Therefore, an unstable consciousness can easily lead to dangerous situations. In this way, the constant increase of consciousness is a state that should be pursued, because if one cannot increase, it means loss and injury. It can be seen that a conscious state of gain should be sought, and the state of consciousness must maintain a balance of *yin* and *yang* intentionality at all times during the increase. Human intentionality is a process of *yin* and *yang* balance, and if there is not enough support, there will be corresponding harm. The generation and transformation of consciousness is a systematic project in which intentionality can only arise according to the situation and follow propensity in action. Sometimes this kind of change in situation is not caused by oneself, but is a change in the general propensity that changes the realm of one's intentionality.

泽天夬（卦四十三）　（乾下兑上）

Guai (Determination), Lake and Heaven (Hexagram 43)　(Qian below, Dui above)

　　泽水在天上开决而下，有增益至极以致溢出，如泽水决口、冲天而下之象，显得勇猛刚决，阳刚力道十足，但又要有分寸，要"决而和"，争取不战而胜之。夬卦阴爻有位，高居王位之上，象征小人高扬一时，经过带有决战意味的谈判，希望能够和谈喜悦，最后让小人知难而退。泽水下降，象征推恩施禄，降下恩泽与生机，百姓欢欣悦纳，感恩戴德。此时在上者不可自居恩德，犹如决战之后，小人欣悦退出，君子亦不可自恃恩威于人。

　　从夬卦中看出，在善恶对决的过程当中，如果只有善而没有恶，就没有所谓的正义，可以说正义是面对恶之时善良意念的分寸。意念不可能脱离情境而自我实化，所以把控意念之境的分寸至为关键。

　　Lake water bursts out from the heaven and flows downward, as the increase is so great that it overflows, an image like water bursting out and rushing down from the heaven. It appears to be a brave and decisive decision, full of masculinity and strength, but it must be measured, and must be "determined and peaceful" to strive for victory without fighting. The *yin* line of Hexagram Guai (Determination) has a position, and it is high above the throne, symbolizing that a petty person is held high for a while. After negotiations with the significance of a final battle, it is hoped that the peace talks with joy, and that the petty person will finally retreat in the face of difficulties. The water falling from the lake symbolizes extending favor and granting fortune, bringing down grace and vitality, and the people are happy to accept it and are grateful. At this time, those above should not show off their kindness, and just like how the petty person happily quits after a decisive battle, the exemplary person should not impose one's kindness on others.

From Hexagram Guai (Determination), in the process of the duel between good and evil, if there is only good but no evil, there is no so-called justice. It can be said that justice is proportion of good intentions when faced with evil. Intentions cannot be separated from a situation and realize themselves, so it is crucial to control proportion in the realm of intentions.

夬，扬于王庭，孚号有厉；告自邑，不利即戎，利有攸往。

《彖》曰：夬，决也，刚决柔也。健而说，决而和。"扬于王庭"，柔乘五刚也。"孚号有厉"，其危乃光也。"告自邑，不利即戎"，所尚乃穷也。"利有攸往"，刚长乃终也。

《象》曰：泽上于天，夬。君子以施禄及下，居德则忌。

【明译】

夬卦象征除恶决断，可以在君王朝廷之上公布张扬小人的罪恶予以制裁，并怀着诚信号令众人戒备危险。此时应该颁布政令于城邑上下，告知大家现在还不利于动用武力发兵作战，但有利于积极主动地做一些事情加以防备。

《彖传》说：夬是决断、决去的意思，是刚爻决去柔爻。下卦乾为刚健，上卦兑为悦，刚健而喜悦，刚健能断，果决而不失和悦，决绝斩断仍能协和众人。在君王朝廷之上公布张扬小人的罪恶予以制裁，指上六柔爻肆意凌驾于五刚之上，必须决去。怀着诚信号令众人戒备危险，说明让人们时刻处于危惧戒备之中才能够把除恶决断的形势发扬光大。此时应该颁布政令于城邑上下，告知大家现在还不利于动用武力发兵作战，是因为如果滥用武力，反而会使除恶决断之道马上走到穷途末路。但有利于积极主动地做一些事情加以防备，是让大家相信形势的发展，阳刚之力还在生长，最终一定能够彻底制服阴柔小人，只要积极应对准备就可以了（刚爻再上长一点就将完全克服阴爻）。

《象传》说：下卦乾为天，上卦兑为泽，泽水蒸发到了天上就是夬卦。君子看到天上的泽水一定要化为云雨施布到下民身上的卦象，要主动把利禄施布给人民，但不能认为这是自己给予别人恩赐，如果自居有恩德于人，这是君子的大忌。

Hexagram Guai (Determination) symbolizes the determination to eliminate evil, which can be used to publicize and sanction petty people's crimes before the king's court, and to warn everyone of danger with a signal of sincerity. At this time, a government decree should be issued throughout the city to inform everyone that it is not yet conducive to use force and send troops to fight, but it is conducive to proactively take some action in preparation.

The *Judgment Commentary (Tuan Zhuan)* says: Hexagram Guai (Determination) means to make a decision or remove something, i.e. the strong lines removing the soft. The lower Trigram Qian is strength, and the upper Trigram Dui is joy, so it is strong and joyful, firm and able to be decisive, but without losing harmony; hence it can still harmonize everyone even if it is decisive and severe. That the sins of petty people should be announced publicly in the emperor's court and punished refers to the Six (*yin*/soft line) in the top place wantonly overriding five strong lines and needing to be removed. With a sincere signal, everyone is alerted to the danger, which shows that only by keeping people on alert for danger can the decisive situation of eradicating evil be carried forward. At this time, a government decree should be issued in the city to inform everyone that it is not conducive to use force to send troops to fight, because if force is abused, the decisive way to eliminate evil will immediately come to an end. However, it is conducive to proactively take some action to prepare for it, and let everyone believe that the situation is developing, the *yang*/strong power is still growing, and eventually the *yin*/soft petty person will be completely subdued, as long as it is proactively prepared for (if the strong lines grow a little more, they will completely overcome the *yin* line).

The *Image Commentary* (*Xiang Zhuan*) says: The lower Trigram Qian is sky, and the upper Trigram Dui is lake. When water from the lake evaporates into the sky, this is Hexagram Guai (Determination). When an exemplary person sees the hexagram with water in the sky turning into clouds and rain and being distributed to the people, one should take the initiative to distribute wealth and benefits to the people, but should not think of it as a gift to others. If one takes oneself as kind to others, this is a cardinal sin for exemplary people.

【明意】

夬卦的形势引申出公正问题。一方面，阳意已经占据了绝对优势，所以在阳意占绝对优势的时候就有相应的正义问题，出于正义的考虑，在西方传统上，正义（justice）意味着公平和无偏私；在中国传统中，正义问题涉及善恶的对决和分配的合理。传统上，中国式分配正义不是通过体制决定的，而是以主事者或既得利益集团的心意分寸为主的，不同于西方以体制和制度为根本的解决。总言之，中国式正义在一念之间，在于强势群体对弱势者的关爱和分寸。统治者的一念跟百姓息息相关；被统治者的一念跟修身养性，等待时机有关。

除去小人的分寸感，以及社会分配的合理性，来自处分者对被处分者的小心和悦的应对。就占据优势的阳意来说，决定和决断、决战的尺度最难，惩恶扬善需要注意分寸，"以施禄及下，居德则忌"指出了张扬阳意的尺度。一方面阳意已经占据了绝对优势，另一方面，越是容易的事情，越需要小心把握分寸。

[Illuminating Intentionality]

Hexagram Guai (Determination) raises the issue of justice. On the one hand, *yang*/positive intentions have already taken the absolute advantage, so when *yang*/positive intentions have an absolute advantage, there are corresponding issues of justice. In terms of justice, in the Western tradition, justice means fairness and impartiality. In the Chinese tradition, issues of justice involve a duel between good and evil and the nature of reasonable distribution. Traditionally, Chinese-style distributive justice is not determined through a system, but based on the heart-minds and sense of proportion of the principals or vested interest groups, which is different from the Western solution based on systems and institutions. In short, Chinese-style justice lies in the care and propriety of strong groups towards the weak. The intentions of rulers are closely related to the people; the intentions of the ruled are related to self-cultivation and waiting for opportunities.

The sense of proportion in removing petty people and the rationality of social distribution both come from the punisher's careful and pleasant response to the punished. As far as the dominant *yang*/positive intentions are concerned, the scale for decision-making and decisive battles is the most difficult. To punish evil and promote good, one needs to pay attention to measure, and the phrase "in distributing wealth to those below, assuming one's virtue is a cardinal sin" points out the measure for promoting *yang*/positive intentions. On the one hand, *yang*/positive intentions already have the absolute advantage; on the other hand, the easier things are, the more careful they need to be.

初九：壮于前趾，往不胜为咎。

《象》曰："不胜"而"往"，"咎"也。

【明译】

初九：把刚壮的力道都使在前脚趾上了，难以胜任地冒然前进一定会有灾祸。

《象传》说：不能胜任，自不量力，凭一时之勇蛮冲硬闯，必然会闯祸。

Nine (*yang*/strong line) in the first place: Using all one's strength on one's front toes and advancing rashly without the ability to do so will surely lead to disaster.

The *Image Commentary* (*Xiang Zhuan*) says: If one is not up to the task, does not know one's capabilities, and rushes forward in a moment of bravery, one will inevitably get into trouble.

【明意】

本爻自不量力的原因，往往是对于形势的误判，以为自己处于优势地位，以为胜算可以继续押在自己一边，但其实只是判断失误而已。因为看不清形势而用错了阳刚之意，即是盲目行动，初九不当"决"之时却过分刚决强决，不但不可能达到目的，反而适得其反。应在坤（境）之宫中，多考虑意境的情况，不宜过分主观，一时冲动，胡乱决断而行动。

[Illuminating Intentionality]

The overestimation of one's own capabilities in this line is often a misjudgment of the situation, thinking that one is in an advantageous position and that the odds of winning continue to be on one's side, while in fact this is just a mistake in judgment, and a *yang*/strong intentionality is wrongly used because one cannot clearly see the situation. That is, one acts blindly by being too strong and decisive when it is not appropriate for the Nine (*yang*/strong line) in the first place to "decide," and thus it is not only impossible to achieve one's goal, but also counterproductive. When one should be in the palace (realm) of Kun, one should pay more attention to the intentional context, and should not be overly subjective, act impulsively, or make random decisions.

九二：惕号，莫（mù）夜有戎，勿恤。

《象》曰："有戎勿恤"，得中道也。

【明译】

九二：发布号令警惕民众，提防敌人深夜来袭，已经准备好要兵戎相见，大家不要过分忧虑担心。

《象传》说：已经准备好要兵戎相见，大家不要过分忧虑担心，因为九二能守中正之道，应事沉着冷静。

Nine (*yang*/strong line) in the second place: Issuing an order to alert the people to beware of the enemy's late night attack, they are ready to fight, so there is no need to worry too much.

The *Image Commentary* (*Xiang Zhuan*) says: They are already prepared to meet in battle, so there is no need to worry too much, because the Nine (*yang*/strong line) in the second place can hold to the upright *dao* and deal with matters calmly.

【明意】

除恶的关键在于形成一种警惕小人生事的氛围，告诉众人夜里也要警惕，担心小人趁大家不注意的时候偷袭，所以不可掉以轻心。每时每刻都要形成警惕的阵势，另外是否能够转化小人之心，形成正义之境需要一些手法，如梳理人群的心意，让心齐而形成合力。五个阳爻最大的问题是心不齐，所以要警惕大家，通过多次提醒警示来要求大家齐心协力。除恶的关键在于分化小人的党羽，是否可能让小人的一部分站队过来，否则很危险。最不得已的状态是兵戎相见。但事已至此，也就没有什么办法。此时就要像发布戒严令一样要求大家，齐心协力，共对恶人。决战之前，把决意之境传达给自己的同盟者和支持者。

[Illuminating Intentionality]

The key to eliminating evil is to create an atmosphere of vigilance against petty people and tell everyone to be vigilant at night. They worry that petty people will sneak up on people when they are not paying attention, so they should not take it lightly. A vigilant posture must be kept at all times, and in addition, whether or not one can transform the intentions of petty people and form a realm of justice requires some methods, such as sorting out the intentions and heart-minds of the crowd, so that they can unite and form a joint force. The biggest problem with the five *yang* lines is lack of unity, so one needs to be vigilant and request everyone to work together through repeated reminders and warnings. The key to eradicating evil lies in dividing the gang of petty people into cliques, and whether or not it is possible to get some of the petty people to join one's forces; otherwise it may be very dangerous. Fighting against each other is the last resort, but now that the matter has come to this, there is nothing else one can do. At this time, martial law is declared and everyone is required to work together to deal with the evildoers. Before the decisive battle, one should convey one's determination to one's allies and supporters.

九三：壮于頄（qiú），有凶。君子夬夬，独行，遇雨若濡，有愠，无咎。

《象》曰："君子夬夬"，终无咎也。

【明译】

九三：强势表现在高突的颧骨上，怒形于色，必有凶险。（面对必须除掉的小人）君子应当刚毅果决，当断则断，好比独自前行，遇到大雨，淋湿衣服，面有愠色，但最后不会有祸患。

《象传》说：君子应当刚毅果决，当断则断，最终不会有什么咎害（因为有上六正应）。

Nine (*yang*/strong line) in the third place: Strength is reflected in high protruding cheekbones, and there is an expression of anger which must mean danger. (Facing petty people who must be eliminated,) an exemplary person should be resolute and determined, and make decisions when necessary. It is like walking alone, encountering heavy rain, getting wet clothes, but having a good complexion, and there will be no disaster in the end.

The *Image Commentary* (*Xiang Zhuan*) says: An exemplary person should be resolute and determined, and should make decisions when necessary. In the end, there will be no harm (because the Six (*yin*/soft line) in the top place corresponds and resonates).

【明意】

九三与上六有应，好像是君子队伍中与外人勾结的人一样，大家都拿他当小人看，这种时候，九三需要表现自己的正义感，所以独自行动去应付小人。九三的这种意识境遇好像是一个人为了洗刷自己的清白，也好像为了效忠团队而立下投名状、军令状似的。这种处境所迫，当然确实是不得已，但面对同伴的质疑，在生死之关面前，却往往也没有什么更好的选择，九三意识的实化可谓是被情境所迫的"决"意之彰显。九三的意境是典型的二难处境。自身对大势判断没有问题，但自己表面与小人的关系却比大家都好，于是不得不作为刚强的决断与小人切割，这样才能让自己的意境融通于阳刚正义的形势之中。

[Illuminating Intentionality]

The Nine (*yang*/strong line) in the third place corresponds to the Six (*yin*/soft line) in the top place, as if one is colluding with outsiders in the team of exemplary people, so everyone regards one as a petty person. At this time, the Nine (*yang*/strong line) in the third place needs to show one's sense of justice, so one acts alone to deal with the petty person. The Nine (*yang*/strong line) in the third place's state of consciousness is as if a person has signed a pledge of surrender or a military order in order to clear one's name or be loyal to one's team. Forced by this kind of situation, of course it is a last resort, but when faced with doubts from companions and faced with a life-and-death situation, there is often no better choice. The realization of the consciousness of the Nine (*yang*/strong line) in the third place can be said to be a manifestation of "decisive" intentionality forced by the situation. The intentional context of Nine (*yang*/strong line) in the third place is a typical dilemma. It has no problem judging the general situation, but its relationship with the petty person is better than everyone else, so it has to make a strong decision to cut itself off from the petty person, so that its intentional context can be integrated into the situation of *yang*/strength and justice.

九四：臀无肤，其行次且（zī jū）。牵羊悔亡，闻言不信。

《象》曰："其行次且"，位不当也。"闻言不信"，聪不明也。

【明译】

九四：臀部已经皮开肉绽，走路举步维艰。像被牵的羊一样顺从，就可以消除忧虑悔恨，可惜他听到这话却不相信。

《象传》说：走路举步维艰，因为九四位置不当（刚爻占据柔位）。他听到这话却不相信，是因为他耳不聪目不明，糊里糊涂。

Nine (*yang*/strong line) in the fourth place: The skin on one's buttocks has been split open and it is difficult to walk. Being as obedient as a led sheep can eliminate worries and regrets, but unfortunately one did not believe this when one heard it.

The *Image Commentary* (*Xiang Zhuan*) says: It is difficult to walk because the position of the Nine (*yang*/strong line) in the fourth place is inappropriate (a strong line occupying a soft position). One heard this but did not believe it because one was blind and confused.

【明意】

《易》的每一个卦都象征人在群体当中的活动，人的意念发动都要面对群体意念的交互网络，即在意念集合的意境当中，意念发动要在意境中寻找合适的出路。九四对意境不明，不能洞见实相（道心），而为常俗之见（人心）所迷，也为利害形势所牵（人心），故进退失据，不敢遵从本心之意境，而导致实化出来的意境浑浊不堪。即使有人告诉应放弃本心（道心）之意境，完全服从形势之利害（九五之势），也不过最多减免忧虑悔恨而已，可惜自己心意已乱，不能明辨意境，所以听说了却不相信，因为耳目不明，失去了对于意境的判断力，是典型的迷于人心，不明道心的状态。

[Illuminating Intentionality]

Each hexagram in the *Book of Changes* symbolizes people's activities in a group. The initiation of human intentions must face an interactive network of group intentions, that is, in an intentional context as a collection of intentions, the initiation of intentions must find a suitable outlet. The Nine (*yang*/strong line) in the fourth place is unclear about the intentional context, unable to see reality (the heart-mind of *dao*), and confused by popular views (the human heart-mind), and also affected by the situation of interests (the human heart-mind), so one's advance or retreat has lost one's basis and one dare not follow the intentional context of one's original intention. As a result, one's realizes intentional context is turbid and unclear. Even if someone tells one to give up the intentional context of one's original intention (the heart-mind of *dao*) and completely obey the interests of the situation (the Nine (*yang*/strong line) in the fifth place), one will only reduce one's worries and regrets at most. Unfortunately, one's intentionality is confused and one cannot clearly discern the intentional context, so one will not believe even after hearing. Losing the ability to judge the intentional context due to unclear hearing and vision is a typical state of being confused by the human heart-mind and not knowing the heart-mind of *dao*.

九五：苋（xiàn）陆夬夬，中行无咎。

《象》曰："中行无咎"，中未光也。

【明译】

九五：如细角山羊那样，刚毅果决地清除小人，居于中位，行于正道，没有什么灾祸。

《象传》说：九五居于中位，行于正道，没有什么灾祸，能行中道，但志向还没彻底实现，不算光大。

Nine (*yang*/strong line) in the fifth place: Like a thin-horned goat, resolutely eliminate petty people, stay in the middle position, follow the upright *dao*, and there will be no disasters.

The *Image Commentary* (*Xiang Zhuan*) says: The Nine (*yang*/strong line) in the fifth place stays in the middle and follows the right *dao* without any disasters. Although one can follow the middle *dao*, one's ambitions have not yet been fully realized, so one cannot yet be considered great.

【明意】

此爻讲决战之意境，千钧一发，运万千形势于一念之间。无论是内向修行，还是外向建功立业，都有千钧一发的关键时刻，不可不察。决战的意境形势尚未光大，有待光大，发力来自意念之力，而一念决意，要合于天时地利之势。

九五也是正义的核心所在，代表阳刚之力对上六决战，既要到位，又不可斩草除根，而是适可而止，即以中道决小人，逼退小人，并得到小人的理解和配合。这样看来，正义是对阴爻柔弱，而对小人没有私心。正义之心是适度包容并容忍，但该决则决。对大势已去的小人，在正义之心上代表弱势群体，要适度包容。

[Illuminating Intentionality]

This line talks about the intentional context of the decisive battle. It is a critical moment, and thousands of situations can be controlled in a single intention. Whether one is practicing inwardly or making achievements outwardly, there are critical moments that must be observed. The intentional context and situation of the decisive battle have not yet developed, and they need to be developed. The power comes from the power of intentions, and a single intention and decision must be consistent with the situational propensity in time and place.

The Nine (*yang*/strong line) in the fifth place is also the core of justice. It represents the decisive battle between the *yang*/strong forces and the Six (*yin*/soft line) in the top place. It must be in place, but it cannot be eliminated, and it must be treated with moderation, that is, one must use the middle *dao* to overcome the petty person, force the petty person to retreat, and gain the petty person's understanding and cooperation. From this point of view, justice is weak towards *yin* lines, but has no selfish motives towards petty people. The heart of justice is to be moderately tolerant and lenient, but decisive when necessary. One should be appropriately tolerant of petty people who have lost their power and represent disadvantaged groups with a sense of justice.

上六：无号，终有凶。

《象》曰："无号"之"凶"，终不可长也。

【明译】

上六：嚎啕大哭也没用，凶险终究难逃。

《象传》说：嚎啕大哭也没用，小人终究难逃凶险，因为小人大势已去，无论如何无法延长行将灭亡的时间。

Six (*yin*/soft line) in the top place: It is useless to cry loudly, as the danger is inevitable.

The *Image Commentary* (*Xiang Zhuan*) says: It is useless to cry loudly. The petty person will not be able to escape from danger in the end, because one's power is over and one cannot prolong the time of one's imminent destruction.

【明意】

从阳意来讲，已经占尽优势，应该留有余地，尽量不战而屈人之兵，不可赶尽杀绝。过分刚强，不蓄阴德，则难以长远。对小人也要温柔敦厚，相信人性来自天道自然之善，小人也有被教化的可能。属于被决的对象，在不断攻击自己的阳意面前步步退守，即使嚎哭也没有用，为凄凉落寞的小人际遇，大势已去，只能以泪洗面，凶境难出。凶境来自多重的攻击，也来自阳意无力支持，最后落单，连拼死反抗的可能性都不再存在。这是决意的残酷一面，既不可能留住自己的位置，也没有主动退守的可能，这是非常凄惨的结局。

[Illuminating Intentionality]

From the perspective of *yang* intentionality, one has already gained all the advantages, so should leave some room. Try to defeat the enemy's troops without fighting, and do not kill them all. If one is too strong and does not accumulate *yin* virtue, it will be difficult to last long. One must also be gentle

475

and kind to petty people, believing that human nature comes from the goodness of the natural *dao* of heaven, and that petty people can also be educated. Being the subject of the determination, one retreats step by step in front of the *yang*/positive intentions that constantly attack one, and even crying is of no use. Because of the desolate and lonely situation of the petty person, one's power is over, one can only wash one's face with tears, and it is difficult to escape from a terrible end. The dangerous situation comes from multiple attacks, but also from the powerlessness of *yang*/positive intentions to offer support, and finally being alone, even the possibility of desperate resistance no longer exists. This is the cruel side of determination. It is impossible to retain one's position, and there is no possibility of taking the initiative to retreat. This is a very miserable ending.

天风姤（卦四十四） （巽下乾上）

Gou (Encounter), Heaven and Wind (Hexagram 44) (Xun below, Qian above)

　　夬卦是意念之生去决除小人，但小人决去，并不见得可以高枕无忧，小人往往以另一种方式重新出现，所以姤卦接着夬卦。世间阴意对于阳意的干扰，或隐或显，只在心念所及不及之间，好比心头大患，不见得退得干净，往往退去又来。一阴虽弱，但终必灭阳，故深忧虑，要戒慎恐惧地应对。意念之生需要安宁，才能持守正意，当生机悖乱之时，要有所制约。阴意被时时牵制，如刹车一般固定则可以转为吉祥，如果放任冒进，则浮躁而动，必致不祥。

　　姤是邂逅相遇之意。姤是夬卦的覆卦，两卦爻辞有雷同之处。夬卦上六从上位退出再从下位生出即为姤卦，从卦变上说，姤直接由乾卦变来，即乾卦下生一阴为姤。阴为女，从发展趋势上看是女的将越来越强壮，相对来说，则男的处于衰退的时势当中，所以说不宜娶之为妻。姤卦五阳之心意，被初六搅乱，都想与初六相遇，而生出许多意念生或不生的意缘来。

　　Hexagram Guai (Determination) is created by the intentionality to eliminate petty people, but once the petty people are gone, one may not be able to sit back and relax. They often reappear in another way, so Hexagram Gou (Encounter) follows Hexagram Guai (Determination). The interference from *yin* to *yang* in the world may be hidden or obvious, and it is only a matter of whether or not it is within reach of intentions. It is like a serious trouble in the heart, which may not completely go away, but often recedes and comes back. Although *yin* is weak, it will eventually destroy *yang*, so it is deeply worrying and must be dealt with in caution and fear. The production of intentions needs to be peaceful in order to maintain upright intention. When vitality is chaotic, it must be restrained. If *yin* intention is constantly restrained and secured as with a brake, it can turn into auspiciousness. If it is allowed to advance rashly, it will move impetuously, which will inevitably lead to misfortune.

Hexagram Gou (Encounter) means encounter, and it is the inversion of Hexagram Guai (Determination); hence the lines of the two hexagrams are similar. The Six (*yin*/soft line) in the top place exits from Hexagram Guai (Determination), and then emerges from the lower position, which forms Hexagram Gou (Encounter). From the hexagram-changes point of view, Hexagram Gou (Encounter) is directly transformed from Hexagram Qian (Creativity), that is, the lower part of Hexagram Qian (Creativity) produces a *yin*, which forms Hexagram Gou (Encounter). Yin is female, so judging from the development trend, the female will become stronger and stronger, and relatively speaking, the male will be in decline, so it is not suitable for them to marry. The intentions of the five *yang* lines of Hexagram Gou (Encounter) are disturbed by the Six (*yin*/soft line) in the first place, and they all want to meet the Six (*yin*/soft line) in the first place, which gives rise to many intentional relationships that may or may not arise.

姤：女壮，勿用取女。

《彖》曰：姤，遇也，柔遇刚也。"勿用取女"，不可与长也。天地相遇，品物咸章也。刚遇中正，天下大行也。姤之时义大矣哉！

《象》曰：天下有风，姤。后以施命诰四方。

【明译】

姤卦象征邂逅相遇，女的越来越强壮，则不宜娶之为妻。

《彖传》说：姤是阴阳相遇，是柔爻从下生出与五个刚爻相遇，如一个阴柔女子对付五位阳刚男子。不宜娶此女为妻，这是因为不能与失位不正的女子长相厮守。天的阳气与地的阴气相遇才能化育万物，各种各样的事物才会昭彰显明表现出来。刚健应当遇合中正的地位，这样阳气才会大行于天下，象征着君子之道大为畅行。邂逅相遇之时势的时机化意义实在太重大了！

《象传》说：上卦乾为天，下卦巽为风，天下刮着风就是姤卦。君王看到上天传递号令之象，发号施令，诏告四方。

Hexagram Gou (Encounter) symbolizes encountering by chance. A woman becomes stronger and stronger, so it is not suitable to marry her.

The *Judgment Commentary* (*Tuan Zhuan*) says: Hexagram Gou (Encounter) is a meeting of *yin* and *yang*, as the soft line produced below meets the five strong lines, like a feminine woman facing five masculine men. It is not appropriate to marry this woman because one cannot stay together for a long time with a woman who has lost her position and is not upright. Only when the *yang* energy of heaven meets the *yin* energy of earth can the myriad things be nurtured, and then all kinds of things will manifest themselves clearly. Strength should meet a central and upright status, so that *yangqi* will prevail in the world, symbolizing that the *dao* of the exemplary person will be greatly promoted. The timing of an encounter is so significant!

The *Image Commentary* (*Xiang Zhuan*) says: The upper Trigram Qian is heaven, the lower Trigram Xun is wind, and wind blowing in the world under heaven is Hexagram Gou (Encounter). The king sees the image of heaven transmitting orders, and issues orders and edicts in the four directions.

【明意】

刚柔相遇之际，不是遇或不遇，而是如何遇，如何把握遇的分寸很重要。阴意不努力上升，就与阳意没有交流，阴阳之变化不可能多姿多彩。可是如果阴力太过强盛，让阳意退守犯难，则走向阴阳交流初衷的反面。可能阳意一方面乐见和享受阴力上升的交流，但道义上和道德上又觉得阴力强悍的上升不利于阳意之境秩序的维系。用于人事之上，君王当然要品德高尚，才会有贤人来交流帮助，可是来交流者力度太强，却对君王构成威胁，也就是阴意过强会让阳意为难。姤与遯同时在阴意上升的情势中，所以阳意需要了解如何保持生机与生意的艺术。

[Illuminating Intentionality]

When the strong and the soft meet, it is not a question of whether they meet or not, but of how they meet, so how to grasp the appropriateness of an encounter is very important. If *yin* intentionality does not strive to rise, there will be no communication with *yang* intentionality, and the changes of *yin* and *yang* cannot be vibrant. However, if the *yin* force is too strong and *yang* intentionality retreats and becomes difficult, it will go against the original intention of the exchange of *yin* and *yang*. *Yang*/positive intentions may be happy to see and enjoy the exchange of a rising *yin* power, but rightfully and morally they also feel that the strong rise of *yin* power is not conducive to the maintenance of order in the realm of *yang*/positive intentions. When used in personnel affairs, the king must of course have a high moral character so that wise men will come to communicate and help. However, if those who come to communicate are too strong, they will pose a threat to the king, that is, if a *yin* intention is too strong, *yang* intentions will be in trouble. Hexagram Gou (Encounter) and Hexagram Dun (Retreat) are both in a situation where *yin* is rising, so *yang* needs to understand the art of maintaining vitality and productive intentionality.

初六：系于金柅（nǐ），贞吉。有攸往，见凶。羸豕孚蹢躅（zhí zhú）。

《象》曰："系于金柅"，柔道牵也。

【明译】

初六：紧紧系缚在刚硬灵敏的"车闸"上，安守正道，就会获得吉祥。盲行冒进，必有凶灾，可别像被捆绑的母猪一样轻浮躁动，心浮气躁。

《象传》说：紧紧系缚在刚硬灵敏的"刹车器"上，说明初六的柔道必须要有所牵制（初六柔爻还会上长，象征小人道长，应当加以牵制）。

Six (*yin*/soft line) in the first place: Tied tightly to the hard yet sensitive "brake" and keeping to the upright *dao*, one will gain good fortune. If one advances blindly, there will be disaster, so do not be frivolous and impatient like a tied sow.

The *Image Commentary* (*Xiang Zhuan*) says: Being tightly tied to the hard and sensitive "brake" means that the soft *dao* of the Six (*yin*/soft line) in the first place must be restrained (the Six (*yin*/soft line) in the first place will grow upward, which symbolizes the *dao* of the petty person growing and should be restrained).

【明意】

可见处理遇的分寸很难，包括自我控制的分寸和时时自发生成的分寸，要有"所遇为命"的态度才能自然应对。阴力卑贱轻浮地跟阳境沟通，不庄重，无所谓，很随便，从情理上可以理解，但道义上讲不合适，长久以往，对正常的秩序构成挑战和威胁。邪心所向，可能影响整个阳境。邪意一出，当立即制止。

[Illuminating Intentionality]

It can be seen that it is difficult to deal with the sense of propriety in encounters, including the sense of self-control and propriety that arises spontaneously from time to time. Only by having the attitude of "whatever one encounters is fate" can one deal with it naturally. The *yin* force communicates with the *yang* realm in a despicable and frivolous way, without solemnity, with indifference, and very casual. This is understandable from a rational point of view, but morally inappropriate. In the long run, it poses a challenge and threat to the normal order. The direction of evil intentions may affect the entire *yang* realm. As soon as evil intentions arise, put a stop to them immediately.

九二：包有鱼，无咎，不利宾。

《象》曰："包有鱼"，义不及宾也。

【明译】

九二：包住初六这条鱼，不会有什么害处，就是不利于其他宾客（其他刚爻）。

《象传》说：包住初六这条鱼，按理说也不能够再让给其他宾客（五个刚爻都要限制初六上长，九二一见就把初六挡住是应该的，不能让它去上应九四）。

Nine (*yang*/strong line) in the second place: Wrapping the fish on the Six (*yin*/soft line) in the first place will not do any harm, but it will not be beneficial to other guests (other *yang*/strong lines).

The *Image Commentary* (*Xiang Zhuan*) says: If one wraps up the fish of the Six (*yin*/soft line) in the first place, it stands to reason that it cannot be given to other guests (the five *yang*/strong lines must limit the upward growth of the Six (*yin*/soft line) in the first place. It is right for the Nine (*yang*/strong line) in the second place to block the Six (*yin*/soft line) in the first place as soon as it is seen, because one cannot let it go to respond to the Nine (*yang*/strong line) in the fourth place).

【明意】

遇都是自己与外物的相遇，但如何把控这种相遇的分寸，人与人有很大的区别。是自己享受偶遇的快感，还是心意生机开放，把相遇之生作为一种公共经验与人分享？同样是遇是得，有的人想到的是个人私利，有的人想到的是如何从公利的角度出发来共生共融。

[Illuminating Intentionality]

Encounters are all encounters between oneself and external objects, but there are big differences between people in how to control the proportion of such encounters, such as whether they enjoy the pleasure of chance encounters themselves, or whether they should be open-minded and lively, and regard the encounter as a public experience to share with others. In the same situation, some people think of personal gain, while others think of how to achieve symbiosis and harmony from the perspective of public interest.

九三：臀无肤，其行次且。厉，无大咎。

《象》曰："其行次且"，行未牵也。

【明译】

九三：臀部皮开肉绽，步履维艰，会遇到危险，但不会有大的祸患。

《象传》说：步履维艰，但九三的行动还没有受到牵制。

Nine (*yang*/strong line) in the third place: The skin on the buttocks is split and torn, and it is difficult to walk. One may encounter dangers, but there will be no major disasters.

The *Image Commentary* (*Xiang Zhuan*) says: The steps are difficult, but the Nine (*yang*/strong line) in the third place's actions have not yet been restrained.

【明意】

皮开肉绽，举步维艰的心意无法实化。生之艰难，意生于难中。这一爻为何遇到如此艰难的情景，很关键在于没有正应，这说明人相遇情境的展开，最主要的是应该有帮助或牵拉自己的力量，如果没有，就只有自己承受情境当中的负面力量，很可能举步维艰。

[Illuminating Intentionality]

The skin is split and the flesh is torn, and the struggling intention cannot be realized. Life is difficult, and intentionality is born in difficulty. The key to why this line encounters such a difficult situation is that there is no upright response. This shows that when people encounter a situation, the most important thing is to have the power to help or pull up themselves. If this is absent, one can only bear negative power of the situation oneself, and this may make things difficult.

九四：包无鱼，起凶。

《象》曰："无鱼"之"凶"，远民也。

【明译】

九四：包不到鱼了，还想奋起去争（鱼），会有凶灾。

《象传》说：包不到鱼带来的凶灾，是因为九四远离了民众。

Nine (*yang*/strong line) in the fourth place: If one cannot catch any fish, but still wants to fight over it (fish), there will be disaster.

The *Image Commentary (Xiang Zhuan)* says: The disaster caused by not being able to catch fish is because the Nine (*yang*/strong line) in the fourth place is far away from the people.

【明意】

相遇不可有过强的私意，如九四看到九二把鱼据为己有，心情极为不舒服，想意气用事。可是，形势比人强，一旦九四意气用事，则不太能有好的结果，所以万不可因为一时的得失而仓促应对，导致凶祸。

可见，人的心意如果离开公意之境，所发皆只顾自己的私意就容易有凶险，最后伤及意之生意。对于乱群的初六，九四是唯一的正应，理当得之而不可得，可是，如果总是抱着"理当得之"的执念，而不能够有公意之心，客观冷静地面对形势，就会陷自己的生意于危机之中。

[Illuminating Intentionality]

One should not have excessively strong personal intentions when meeting someone. For example, when the Nine (*yang*/strong line) in the fourth place sees the Nine (*yang*/strong line) in the second place taking fish for oneself, one feels extremely uncomfortable and wants to act out of anger. However, the situational propensity is stronger than people. Once the Nine (*yang*/strong line) in the fourth place's actions are impulsive, they are unlikely to have good results. Therefore, we must not respond hastily because of temporary gains and losses, as this will lead to disaster.

It can be seen that if a person's intentionality leaves the realm of the general intention and only considers one's own private will in everything one does, it will be dangerous and will eventually hurt one's productive intentionality. For the chaotic group of people of the Six (*yin*/soft line) in the first place, the Nine (*yang*/strong line) in the fourth place is the only correct response, so they should get it but cannot. However, if one always clings to the obsession with "deserving it" and fails to express the general will or objectively and calmly face the situation, one will put one's productive intentionaliy into crisis.

九五：以杞包瓜，含章，有陨自天。

《象》曰：九五"含章"，中正也。"有陨自天"，志不舍命也。

第三章　易经明意
——爻意分说（下经）

【明译】

九五：用杞树叶包住瓜，好比内心含藏着华丽彰美的文采，可以等待可喜的遇合因缘从天而降。

《象传》说：九五内心含藏着华丽彰美的文采，因为他有中正之德（在上卦之中，位正）。可以等待可喜的遇合因缘从天而降，因为他矢志不移地遵从人天之意的天命。

Nine (*yang*/strong line) in the fifth place: Wrapping melons with wolfberry leaves is like having a gorgeous and beautiful literary talent hidden in one's heart, waiting for happy encounters or karma to fall from the heavens.

The *Image Commentary* (*Xiang Zhuan*) says: The Nine (*yang*/strong line) in the fifth place's heart-mind contains gorgeous and beautiful literary talent, because one has the virtue of being central and upright (in the upper Trigram, one's position is upright). One can wait for a gratifying karma and destiny to fall from the heavens, because one is determined to follow the fate of humanity-heaven intentionality.

【明意】

内心对于全局全境有整体的判断，并且有种强大的责任感，那么即使遇到过分强大的阴意，也要坚守内心的人天之意，等待形势改变。不过不能等着天上掉馅饼，要自己去主动改变境遇，即使在逆境之中，也要主动顺从自己内心的人天之意，努力改变、开创自己相遇进而遇合的机缘。

九五有德有生自然相遇，不求外缘，包容天下之遇。要力图控制心意生机的时机化改变，在善的机缘中慢慢等待境遇转化，即领会和控制境遇与意念相接的改变过程。既要借阴意保持阳意，又要让阳意不为阴意所化，让阳意矢志不移地遵从人天之意的天命。

[Illuminating Intentionality]

If one has an overall judgment of the complete situation in one's heart, along with a strong sense of responsibility, even if one encounters an overly powerful *yin* intention, one must stick to one's inner intentionality of humanity and heaven and wait for the situation to change. However, one cannot wait for pie to fall from the sky, but must take the initiative to change the situation. Even in adversity, we must actively obey the inner intentionality of humanity and heaven, work hard to change things, and create opportunities for ourselves to meet and unite.

For the Nine (*yang*/strong line) in the fifth place, virtue and talent meet naturally, not seeking external conditions, and tolerating the world's encounters. We must strive to control the opportunistic changes in the vitality of intentionality, and slowly wait for the transformation of circumstances in good conditions, that is, understand and control the process of change in the connection between circumstances and intentions. It is necessary not only to maintain the *yang* intentions through the *yin*, but also to prevent the *yang* from being transformed by the *yin*, so that the *yang* will unswervingly follow the fate of humanity-heaven intentionality.

上九：姤其角，吝，无咎。

《象》曰："姤其角"，上穷"吝"也。

【明译】

上九：遇合到头顶的角尖那里去了，根本不可能遇到什么了，只是没有什么伤害罢了。

《象传》说：遇合到头顶的角尖那里去了，因为上九处在全卦的穷极之位，所以根本不可能遇到什么了。

Nine (*yang*/strong line) in the top place: The encounter has reached the tip of the horn above the head. It is impossible to encounter anything at all, but there is no harm.

The *Image Commentary* (*Xiang Zhuan*) says: The encounter reaches the tip of the horn on the top of the head. Because the Nine (*yang*/strong line) in the top place is in the extreme position of the whole hexagram, it is impossible to encounter anything.

【明意】

穷极之处，遇合基本没有什么机会，遇合的机缘与时空决定了遇合的可能性。把"不遇"作为一种机遇的方式坦然接受，用充分体验和领会时机化存在状态的努力，来应对自己的艰难处境。即使在缺乏想象力和可能性的状态当中，也应该让心意与情境交接的生机展开。这样，只要未来没有确定，就还应该努力维系相改变，享受阴意与阳意相遇的每一个瞬间，体验每个相遇的时机化状态之中无限的可能性。

[Illuminating Intentionality]

In extreme places, there is basically no chance of encounter. The chance of an encounter along with time and space determines the possibility of an encounter. One should accept "the unexpected" as a form of opportunity, and use effort to fully experience and understand the opportunistic state of existence and deal with one's own difficult situation. Even in the absence of imagination and possibility, the vitality of the connection between intentionality and situation should be allowed to unfold. In this way, as long as the future is uncertain, one should still strive to maintain and change, enjoy every moment when *yin* and *yang* meet, and experience the infinite possibilities in the timing of each encounter.

第三章　易经明意
——爻意分说（下经）

泽地萃（卦四十五）　（坤下兑上）

Cui (Gathering), Lake and Earth (Hexagram 45)　(Kun below, Dui above)

　　姤为人与人、人与物的相遇，相遇增多，有萃聚之象。地（坤）容聚泽水（兑），如萃聚人心众意。人心聚合来自与人与物相感。君王通过祭祀宗庙来维系人心，自古聚集民意和意能要依靠宗庙接续天意。古代国家祭祀场所如天坛是汇聚集体意能的重要场所。

　　意的力量来自天，但意能之聚在地上，地面的支撑使得意能汇集。萃之意回到有能量的地面而重新聚能，有主动寻找意的大地，进而诗意地栖居在大地上之象。人天之意在土地上，在居于地面的状态中汇聚，意要主动寻找大地才能栖居，不栖居下来就没有发展，所以聚合人心就要寻找能够诗意地栖居之地，让能量增长，生机勃发。《周易》鼓励人们的精神有所归，即当建立心庙，而《周易》之（意）道与中国哲学之（意）道当为中华民族之永恒的心庙。

　　Hexagram Gou (Encounter) refers to encounters between people, and between people and things. The number of encounters increases and there is a sign of gathering. The capacity of the earth (Trigram Kun) gathers water (Trigram Dui), just like the gathering of people's intentions. The gathering of people's intentions comes from feeling connected with people and things. The king maintains the people's intentions by offering sacrifices in the ancestral temple. Since ancient times, gathering public opinion and energy has relied on ancestral temples to continue the intentionality of heaven. Ancient national sacrifice sites such as the Temple of Heaven were important places for gathering collective energy.

The power of intentionality comes from heaven, but the energy of intentionality is gathered on earth, and the support of the ground allows the energy of intentionality to gather. The intentionality of gathering returns to the ground with its energy and re-gathers energy, like actively looking for the earth of intentionality, and then living on the earth poetically. The intentionality of humanity and heaven is gathered on the earth, in the state of living on the ground. Intentionality must actively seek the earth to live on, as if it does not live there, there will be no development. Therefore, to gather people's intentions, we must find a poetic place to live and let intentional energy grow, full of vitality. The *Book of Changes* encourages people to have a spiritual direction, that is, to build a temple of the heart-mind, and the (intentionality) *dao* of the *Changes* and the (intentionality) *dao* of Chinese philosophy should be the eternal heart-mind temple of the Chinese nation.

萃，亨，王假有庙。利见大人，亨，利贞。用大牲吉。利有攸往。

《彖》曰：萃，聚也。顺以说，刚中而应，故聚也。"王假有庙"，致孝享也。"利见大人，亨"，聚以正也。"用大牲吉，利有攸往"，顺天命也。观其所聚，而天地万物之情可见矣。

《象》曰：泽上于地，萃。君子以除戎器，戒不虞。

【明译】

萃卦象征众心会聚，好比祭享的时候，是人们的大聚会，此时君王到宗庙祭祀，感格神灵。有利于大人出现，也有利于见到大人，前景亨通而利于持守正道去做事。用大牲畜去祭祀可获吉祥，有利于带动人们前往聚合。

《彖传》说：萃是众心会聚。下卦坤为顺，上卦兑为悦，和顺又喜悦，刚健中正（主爻九五居上卦中位）又有应援（六二居下卦中位），上下阴阳正应，所以能让众心聚合。君王到宗庙里去，是为了表达对先王的孝心孝意，并供奉祭享物品。有利于见到大人，前景亨通，大人九五能够依从正道聚合人心。用大牲畜去祭祀可获吉祥，有利于带动人们前往聚合，这说明汇聚人心需要顺应天命。观察天下万物如何会聚的道理，就可窥见万物的真实情状。

《象传》说：上卦兑为泽，下卦坤为地，大泽高处地之上的卦象就是萃卦。君子看到大泽高于平地，担心随时发生泽水泛滥的卦象，要时常整治军备，戒备群聚发生的不测之事。

Hexagram Cui (Gathering) symbolizes the gathering of intentions, just like a time of sacrifice, which is a big gathering of people's intentions. At this time, the king goes to the ancestral temple to offer sacrifices and express gratitude to the ancestors and heavens. This is conducive to the appearance of great people, and it is also conducive to meeting great people. It has a prosperous future and is conducive to doing things following the upright *dao*. Using large animals to sacrifice can bring good fortune and help attract people to gather together.

The *Judgment Commentary* (*Tuan Zhuan*) says: Hexagram Cui (Gathering) is a gathering of intentions. The lower Trigram Kun is smooth, and the upper Trigram Dui is joy, so it is gentle and joyful, strong and upright (the main Nine (*yang*/strong line) in the fifth place is in the middle of the upper Trigram) and has corresponding support (the Six (*yin*/soft line) in the second place is in the middle of the lower Trigram), and the upper and lower *yin* and *yang* are in harmony, so it can make people's intentions come together. The king goes to the ancestral temple to express his filial piety to the late king and to offer sacrificial items. This is conducive to meeting great people, and the future is prosperous, meaning that great people can follow the upright *dao* and gather people's intentions. Using large animals to sacrifice can bring good fortune and help bring people to gather, which shows that gathering people's intentions needs to comply with the fate of heaven. By observing how everything in the world converges, we can get a glimpse of the true state of everything.

The *Image Commentary* (*Xiang Zhuan*) says: The upper Trigram Dui is lake, the lower Trigram Kun is earth, and a big lake high above the ground is Hexagram Cui (Gathering). When an exemplary person sees a large lake higher than the ground, one is worried that the lake will overflow at any time, so one must constantly regulate one's military equipment and be on guard against unexpected events that may occur when people gather together.

【明意】

保住宗庙是王朝继续的标志，但要维系王朝，需要帝王德才兼备，才能继续维系人心聚集的状态，让底下人顺从，上面的人喜悦。九五依赖六二来聚集人气，以构成意能情势的基本构架，也就是领导核心要聚集人气和心意，才能影响到周围的人。

聚合家族之心和社会众人之心，则首重孝心孝情。在宗庙要表达的是对天地的大孝，是从对父母的小孝发展而来，希望长久维系真诚通天的意能结构。孝是有宗教性意味的，通过宗庙祭祀把对先王的孝心延伸到人们日常生活中的孝情孝意，通过感动众人之心来汇聚大家的意能。

儒家的人情从孝延伸出来，包涵社会化情感和自我的建立。聚集人气首先要引导大家，通过祭礼等把心意与天相接，意能通过人与人呼应的意识情境不断增强。聚人就要维系人们意能之间的矢量汇集，所以应该要有坚实的土地作为基础，才能够托得起聚集的财和人。

[Illuminating Intentionality]

Preserving the ancestral temple is a sign of the continuation of the dynasty, but to maintain the dynasty, the emperor needs to have both political integrity and talent, so that one can continue to maintain the state of gathering people's intentions, making those below obedient and those above happy. The Nine (*yang*/strong line) in the fifth place relies on the Six (*yin*/soft line) in the second place to gather popularity to form the basic structure of the emotional situation. That is, the core of leadership must gather popularity and intentionality in order to influence the people around it.

To gather the intentions of the family and the intentions of everyone in society, filial piety and love are the first priority. What is expressed in the ancestral temple is the greater filial piety to heaven and earth, which develops from the smaller filial piety to parents. It is hoped that this sincere and heaven-reaching emotional structure can be maintained for a long time. Filial piety has a religious significance. Through ancestral temple sacrifices, filial piety towards the former kings is extended to the filial piety in people's daily lives, and it gathers everyone's intentions by touching their heart-minds.

Confucian human feelings extend from filial piety and include socialized emotions and self-establishment. To gather popularity, one must first guide everyone and connect their intentions and heart-minds to heaven through rituals, etc. The power of intentionality will be continuously enhanced through the conscious situation of people echoing each other. Gathering people means maintaining the vector gathering between people's intentions and energy, so there should be a solid land as a foundation to be able to support the gathering of wealth and people.

初六：有孚不终，乃乱乃萃。若号，一握为笑，勿恤，往无咎。

《象》曰："乃乱乃萃"，其志乱也。

【明译】

初六：内心有诚信，却不能坚持至终，于是导致心神紊乱，并跟他人妄意聚合，嚎啕大哭之中，上九下到四位，向自己的应爻初六呼号，（得到应和）就能与之握手言欢，破涕为笑，所以不必忧虑，初六往上聚拢，没有咎害。

《象传》说：心神紊乱并跟他人妄意聚合，这是初六心志迷乱的缘故（与九四为正应，但又得选择九五）。

Six (*yin*/soft line) in the first place: One has integrity in one's heart, but one cannot stick to it to the end, which leads to mental disarray, and one gathers with other people's misguided intentions. In the midst of crying, the Nine (*yang*/strong line) in the top place descends to the fourth place, and calls out to its corresponding line, the Six (*yin*/soft line) in the first place, (gets an answer, and) can shake hands with them, and talk happily, turning tears into laughter, so there is no need to worry. There is no harm in gathering upwards as the Six (*yin*/soft line) in the first place.

The *Image Commentary* (*Xiang Zhuan*) says: Mental disarray and gathering with other people's confused intentions are the reasons for the confused will of the Six (*yin*/soft line) in the first place (it corresponds with the Nine (*yang*/strong line) in the fourth place, but has to choose the Nine (*yang*/strong line) in the fifth place).

【明意】

萃卦强调与他人聚合的分寸，初心乱则人生乱，故与他人的心意感通的分寸很难把握。人生无时无刻不在情境之中，顺应大势应该超越个人的情感倾向。初生的心意（本爻是汇聚之心）不可迷乱，要有意能保持初心的意境，要真诚地持续汇聚之心，不可放弃，不可受情感的诱惑。内心要善于调控与反省，即使波折经历艰难，也要回到汇聚的初心。

[Illuminating Intentionality]

Hexagram Cui (Gathering) emphasizes the propriety of getting together with others. If intentionality is chaotic at the beginning, life will be chaotic, so it is difficult to grasp the propriety of connecting with other people's intentions. In human life one is always surrounded by situations, and conforming to the general trend should transcend personal emotional tendencies. The newly produced intentionality (this line is the heart of gathering) must not be confused, and needs intentional energy to maintain the intentional context of the original intention. It must sincerely continue the heart-mind of gathering, not give up, and not be tempted by emotions. One must be good at inner control and reflection, and even if one experiences setbacks and hardships, one must return to one's original intention of gathering.

六二：引吉，无咎，孚乃利用禴（yuè）。

《象》曰："引吉无咎"，中未变也。

【明译】

六二：受人引导来参加大家聚会，这是吉祥的，没有什么过错，只要心怀诚信，即使微薄的禴祭也有利于献享神灵。

《象传》说：受人引导来参加大家聚会，这是吉祥的，因为六二守中未变（在卦变前后始终在下卦中位）。

Six (*yin*/soft line) in the second place: It is auspicious to be led by others to participate in large group gatherings, and there is nothing wrong with it. As long as one is sincere, even a meager rice offering will be beneficial to the gods.

The *Image Commentary* (*Xiang Zhuan*) says: It is auspicious to be guided by others to attend large group gatherings, because the Six (*yin*/soft line) in the second place holds to the center and has not changed (it is always in the middle of the lower Trigram, both before and after the hexagram-changes).

【明意】

内心真诚比外在的礼节重要。内心有诚信，心意通天，让人天之意主导自己的意能，就不会随便因为外在情势改变而改来改去。通过祭祀的方式，让意念真诚接通天意，真诚的意能就不易改变。当然，坚守中道不变本身很不容易，人需要与他人心意相通，一起来聚集意能，否则自己孤掌难鸣，意能容易消散。

[Illuminating Intentionality]

Inner sincerity is more important than outward ritual propriety. If one has integrity in one's heart-mind, one's intentionality is open to heaven, and one lets the intentionality of humanity and heaven dominate one's intentional energy, one will not change it casually because of changes in external situations. Through the method of offering sacrifices, one can let one's intentions sincerely connect with cosmological intentionality, and one's sincere intentions will not be easily changed. Of course, adhering to the middle *dao* is not easy in itself. People need to be connected with others to gather their intentional energy; otherwise they can only sing alone and their intentional energy will easily dissipate.

六三：萃如嗟如，无攸利，往无咎，小吝。

《象》曰："往无咎"，上巽也。

【明译】

六三：想聚又聚不起来，嗟叹连连，不管用什么办法都行不通。但是，继续前往则不会有什么过错，只是有些小的困难罢了。

《象传》说：继续前往则不会有什么过错，因为六三与上面可互为巽卦（取义可理解为对上九四顺应）。

Six (*yin*/soft line) in the third place: One wants to gather together but cannot, so sighs again and again, and no matter what one tries, it doesn't work. However, there is nothing wrong with advancing, just with some minor difficulties.

The *Image Commentary* (*Xiang Zhuan*) says: There will be no fault if one continues to advance, because the Six (*yin*/soft line) in the third place and those above can form the inner Trigram Xun (Wind) (the meaning can be understood as being in compliance with the Nine (*yang*/strong line) in the fourth place).

【明意】

聚集意能是一个人很想前进，集中人们心意的关键所在，但如何聚集意能并不容易，当身处逆境，或事业失败之时，嗟叹连连非常正常。也可能是无人赏识，意能得不到发挥。因为与上面有顺应关系，所以有人可能提升自己的意能。前往也可以理解为静心思考出路。怀才不遇之时，不可耽于无奈感伤，应该静心思考出路为好。

[Illuminating Intentionality]

Gathering intentional energy is the key to a person's desire to advance and focus people's intentions, but how to gather intentional energy is not easy. When one is in adversity or one's career fails, it is very normal to sigh again and again. It may also be that no one appreciates one, and one's abilities cannot be shown. Because of the compliant relationship with those above, some people may improve their mental abilities. Advancing can also be understood as meditating and thinking about the way out. When one's talent is not discovered, one should not be helpless and sentimental, but should calmly think about the way out.

九四：大吉，无咎。

《象》曰："大吉，无咎"，位不当也。

【明译】

九四：虽然情势非常吉利，但不过只是免于灾祸而已。

《象传》说：非常吉祥但能够无灾无难就不错了，这是因为九四位置不当（四位为近臣，以阳居阴位不当，功高震主，只能但求保全）。

Nine (*yang*/strong line) in the fourth place: Although the situation is very auspicious, it is merely a case of avoiding disaster.

The *Image Commentary* (*Xiang Zhuan*) says: Being very auspicious but able to avoid disaster is already not bad. This is because the position of the Nine (*yang*/strong line) in the fourth place is inappropriate (the fourth place is for close ministers, with *yang* occupying the *yin* position inappropriately, and their great achievements shock the ruler, so they can only seek preservation).

【明意】

权力位置随时随刻因应之道，身处变通的情境之中，没有什么一定好，一定不好。九四有能力汇聚众意，但让九五安心也仅能无咎，可见建功立业的同时危险也如影随形。有能力做事一般都是好事，但事情也可能生变，转为不好的事。其中一个非常重要的就是即使再有能力，水平再高也不可有丝毫的执念。既要有能力建功立业，又要能够放下随缘，即使回到一无所有的状态也乐在其中，自然而然。意能之聚于一念之中，散亦于一念之中，无所执着，当即放下，即是境界。

[Illuminating Intentionality]

A position of power at any time is to be in a changing and responding situation, and when one is in a flexible situation nothing is necessarily good or bad. The Nine (*yang*/strong line) in the fourth place has the ability to gather public opinion, but it can only really make Nine (*yang*/strong line) in the fifth place feel at ease. It can be seen that dangers also follow along with achievements. Having the ability to do things is generally a good thing, but good things can change and turn into bad things. It is very important that, no matter how capable one is and how high one's level is, one must not have the slightest obsession. One must have the ability to make achievements, and must also be able to let go of things. Even if one returns to a state of having nothing, one can still enjoy it naturally. When intentional energy is gathered in one intention and dispersed in one intention, with no attachment and immediate letting go, one attains a spiritual realm.

九五：萃有位，无咎。匪孚，元永贞，悔亡。

《象》曰："萃有位"，志未光也。

【明译】

九五：聚合众人而且拥有核心尊位，没有过失和灾难。可是还没有得到大众的信任，需要自始至终恒守正道，忧虑和悔恨才会消亡。

《象传》说：聚合众人而且拥有核心尊位，但聚合人心的志向还没有为广大民众彻底了解。

Nine (*yang*/strong line) in the fifth place: One gathers everyone and has the core position, without mistakes or disasters. However, one has not gained the trust of the public, and it is necessary to adhere to the upright *dao* from beginning to end, so that worries and regrets will disappear.

The *Image Commentary* (*Xiang Zhuan*) says: One gathers people and has a core position, but one's ambition to gather people's intentions has not yet been fully understood by the general public.

【明意】

九五保持聚合人心的志向，就将逐渐为广大民众了解。九五能聚集众人的意能，但心知难以直接到达所有的人，所以跟民众之间还有一个了解的过程，应该放手放心让九四去做。九五有位，具体聚集意能的事情应让九四去努力，自己起到凝聚意能核心作用就好了。

[Illuminating Intentionality]

If the Nine (*yang*/strong line) in the fifth place maintains its ambition of gathering people's intentions, it will gradually be understood by the general public. The Nine (*yang*/strong line) in the fifth place can gather the intentions and energy of everyone, but knows that it is difficult to reach all people directly, so there is still a process of understanding between it and the people. It should let go and allow the Nine (*yang*/strong line) in the fourth place do its work. The Nine (*yang*/strong line) in the fifth place has its position, so the specific details of gathering intentional energy should be left to the Nine (*yang*/strong line) in the fourth place to work on, and it should just be the core around which intentional energy gathers.

上六：赍咨（jī zī）涕洟（tì yí），无咎。

《象》曰："赍咨涕洟"，未安上也。

【明译】

上六：悲痛哀叹，涕泪滂沱，但是可以免于祸患。

《象传》说：悲痛哀叹，涕泪滂沱，是因为上六居于困窘的上位，又不安分守己。

Six (*yin*/soft line) in the top place: There is sadness and lamentation, with tears pouring down, but one can avoid disaster.

The *Image Commentary* (*Xiang Zhuan*) says: The reason for lamentation and tears is because the Six (*yin*/soft line) in the top place is in an embarrassingly high position yet is also dissatisfied and self-centered.

【明意】

上六意能很难，非常困窘，又不愿意安分，可是没有什么出路，聚到最后伤痛欲绝，因为太难了，也可以说聚到最后一场空，缘聚最后缘必散，所以有多大意能聚集，其实也就有多大的负面能量聚集起来。因此汇聚意能的时刻要保持清醒，聚人也有难聚的困境。

[Illuminating Intentionality]

The intentional energy of the Six (*yin*/soft line) in the top place is very difficult, as it is extremely awkward, yet does not want to settle down, even though there is no way out. It is heartbroken at the end of the gathering, because the situation is too difficult. It can also be said that the gathering will be empty at the end, and the dependent co-arising will eventually disperse, so how much intentional energy can be gathered, is in fact a question of how much negative intentional energy accumulates. Therefore, one needs to stay aware when gathering intentional energy, as there are also difficulties involved in gathering people.

地风升（卦四十六）　（巽下坤上）

Sheng (Ascent), Earth and Wind (Hexagram 46)　(Xun below, Kun above)

　　升缘讲的是意缘的阶段性提升问题。如萃卦阳爻得时，凝聚群阴，则升卦下阳爻得中，守中忍耐，待时而升。升卦讨论意缘整体性地柔顺地提升。意缘的升进如征服天地总有限度，身外的意缘如名和财的升进都要适可而止，不可无穷无尽地去追求。

　　Hexagram Sheng (Ascent) talks about a phased rise of intentional dependent co-arising. For example, when the *yang* lines of Hexagram Cui (Gathering) are in the right position and the *yin* are gathered together, then the *yang* line in the lower Trigram Xun of Hexagram Sheng (Ascent) is in the middle. It should remain in the middle and be patient, waiting for the time to rise. Hexagram Sheng (Ascent) discusses the smooth and supple rising of intentionality as a whole. There is always a limit to the advancement of one's destiny, just like conquering heaven and earth. The advancement of one's destiny, such as fame and wealth, should be limited and not be pursued endlessly.

　　升，元亨。用见大人，勿恤。南征吉。
　　《彖》曰：柔以时升，巽而顺，刚中而应，是以大亨，"用见大人，勿恤"，有庆也。"南征吉"，志行也。
　　《象》曰：地中生木，升。君子以顺德，积小以高大。
　　【明译】
　　升卦象征积聚升进，大为亨通，宜于去见大人并获得任用，不必忧虑，向南方进发，

第三章　易经明意
——爻意分说（下经）

会获得吉祥。

《象传》说：下卦为巽为随和，上卦为坤为柔顺，沿着柔顺之道适时地升进（卦变中小过六二柔爻上升到四位），随和而又柔顺，九二阳刚居中，刚健能行中道，又有六五应援，因此大亨通。宜于去见大人并获得任用，不必忧虑，会有喜庆（卦变中六四与九二换位，互兑为悦有喜庆）。向南方进发，会获得吉祥，上升的心志如愿上行。

《象传》说：上卦坤为地，下卦巽为木，草木从地下生长起来就是象征积聚升进的升卦。君子看到地里的草木慢慢成形，顺着时节生长的卦象，就要顺着人天之意修养德行，积累小善事，以成就大功业。

Hexagram Sheng (Ascent) symbolizes accumulation and advancement, which means great prosperity. It is appropriate to go to see great people and get appointments, and there is no need to worry. Heading to the south will bring good fortune.

The *Judgment Commentary* (*Tuan Zhuan*) says: The lower Trigram Xun means easy-going, the upper Trigram Kun means supple, so it will rise at the appropriate time following the *dao* of suppleness (in the hexagram-changes, the Six (*yin*/soft line) in the second place of Hexagram Xiaoguo (Slight Overreaching) rises to the fourth place), easy-going and supple. The Nine (*yang*/strong) line in the second place is in the middle position, is strong and able to follow the middle *dao*, and has corresponding support from the Six (*yin*/soft line) in the fifth place, so it is prosperous. It is appropriate to go to see a great person and get an appointment, so there is no need to worry, and there will be joy (in the hexagram-changes, the Six (*yin*/soft line) in the fourth place and the Nine (*yang*/strong line) in the second place change places, and the resulting inner Trigram Dui means there will be joy). Heading towards the south will bring good fortune, and one's rising aspirations will ascend as one wishes.

The *Image Commentary* (*Xiang Zhuan*) says: The upper Trigram Kun is earth, and the lower Trigram Xun is wood. Vegetation growing from the ground is Hexagram Sheng (Ascent), symbolizing accumulation and advancement. When an exemplary person sees the grass and trees in the ground slowly taking shape and growing according to the seasons, one should cultivate one's virtues in accordance with the intentionality of humanity and heaven, accumulate small good deeds, and thereby make great achievements.

【明意】

卦名升是上升之意。聚合起来，大家一起升进。同心协力，不可自乱阵脚。意缘的整体性提升需要有坚实的基础，如果基础不牢，升进就很难。要不断修炼自己的意识缘分，顺着情境的转化而改变。

[Illuminating Intentionality]

The hexagram name Sheng means rising. Coming together, the group all advances together. Working together as one, they do not throw positions into disarray. The overall improvement of intentional dependence (*yiyuan* 意缘) requires a solid foundation. If the foundation is not solid, it will be difficult to advance. One must continue to cultivate one's own conscious dependent co-arising and change it according to the transformation of the situation.

初六：允升，大吉。

《象》曰："允升，大吉"，上合志也。

【明译】

初六：诚心诚意进步上升，自然大为吉祥。

《象传》说：诚心诚意进步上升，自然大为吉祥，因为初六上承九二，都志在升进。

Six (*yin*/soft line) in the first place: Sincerely and honestly progressing and ascending, all is naturally very auspicious.

The *Image Commentary* (*Xiang Zhuan*) says: Sincerely and honestly making progress and rising, all is naturally very auspicious, because the Six (*yin*/soft line) in the first place supports the Nine (*yang*/strong line) in the second place, and both aim to advance.

【明意】

意缘的整体性的提升需要上面意志的牵引，也需要下面其他意识境域的协同配合。意缘之升，在开始的时候，有能力行君子之道，然后大家信服，乐观其成，乐观其升。在升进的大势之中，小过六二已升，则可带动初六之升，初六是下巽（树木）之本，根系强旺，方能升进。

[Illuminating Intentionality]

The integrity of ascending intentional dependence requires traction from the will of those above and the coordination of the other conscious realms of those below. In the promotion of intentional dependence, at the beginning, one has the ability to follow the *dao* of the exemplary person, and then everyone is convinced, optimistic about success, and optimistic about promotion. In the general propensity of advancement, if the Six (*yin*/soft line) in the second place of Hexagram Xiaoguo (Slight Overreaching) has risen, it can bring along the rise of the Six (*yin*/soft line) in the first place. The Six (*yin*/soft line) in the first place is the root of the lower Trigram Xun (tree, wood), and only when the root system is strong can one advance.

九二：孚乃利用禴，无咎。

《象》曰：九二之"孚"，有喜也。

【明译】

九二：心存诚信，即使用微薄的祭品祭祀，也会有利，不会有什么祸患。

《象传》说：九二心怀孚信，即使进行薄祭也可以得到福佑之喜庆（九二与六五正应，互兑为喜庆）。

Nine (*yang*/strong line) in the second place: If one is sincere, even when one offers a meager sacrifice, it will be beneficial and there will be no harm.

The *Image Commentary* (*Xiang Zhuan*) says: The Nine (*yang*/strong line) in the second place has good faith in its heart-mind, so even if it offers a small sacrifice, it can still get blessings and joy (the Nine (*yang*/strong line) in the second place and the Six (*yin*/soft line) in the fifth place are in perfect correspondence, and the inner Trigram Dui implies joy).

【明意】

个人之意缘不宜偏离团体之意缘，个人的意缘要与团体与上位者的意缘相合相配才能升进。个人之意应该尽量协同团体之意，通过有诚信的表现，不让团体的意念对个人的意念形成疑心。当有诚信与上位者相应，即使奉献的祭品有限，仍然可以有喜庆。天地之间的阳力配合人的阳意，把人的阳意提升到更有序美好的状态。

《周易》不讲攀附意缘，而讲真诚感天动人而能为人所孚信，让天地动容而成就事业。人之意诚，则其意缘"和"，其意缘之升进顺。

[Illuminating Intentionality]

Individual destiny should not deviate from the destiny of the group, and should match the destiny of the group and those above in order to advance. The individual's intentions should be coordinated with the group's intentions as much as possible, and through honest performance, the group's intentions should not be suspicious of the individual's intentions. When there is integrity and correspondence with those above, even if the sacrifices offered are limited, there can still be celebrations. The *yang* force between heaven and earth cooperates with the human *yang* intentionality and elevates it to a more orderly and beautiful state.

The *Book of Changes* does not talk about clinging to dependent co-arising, but about sincerity that moves heaven and humanity and can be trusted by others, that moves heaven and earth and successfully completes endeavors. If a person's intentions are sincere, one's intentions will be "harmonious", and the advance of one's intentions will be smooth.

九三：升虚邑。

《象》曰："升虚邑"，无所疑也。

【明译】

九三：升进顺利，如长驱直入空虚的村落。

《象传》说：升进顺利，如长驱直入空虚的村落，因为九三不必有所疑虑（上邻坤卦，可以毫无疑虑地升进）。

Nine (*yang*/strong line) in the third place: Advancement is smooth, like driving straight into an empty village.

The *Image Commentary* (*Xiang Zhuan*) says: Advancement is smooth, just like driving straight into an empty village, because there is no need to have any doubts about the Nine (*yang*/strong line) in the third place (it is next to Trigram Kun above, representing how it can advance without any doubts).

【明意】

意缘是升进如入无缘之境，是一种非常奇特的体验，在世俗中是无人能争或无人可争的位置，在修炼中进入一种意缘无物可对的状态，相对于意缘总是牵缚受制于具体外物的状态来说，是一种提升。进入一个新的空虚的意缘之境，可能存在新的危险，而一开始并不能够明了。人的升境能够意识到潜在的危险比较好，否则如入无人之境，潜在的危险也往往超出预期。

[Illuminating Intentionality]

Intentional dependence is ascending as if into a realm of unconditionality. It is a very unique experience. In the secular world, it is a position that no one can compete with or contest. In cultivation, it is to enter a state in which there is nothing to oppose one. This is an elevation in relation to the state where intentionality is always tied to specific external objects. Entering a new and empty realm of intentionality may present new dangers that may not be apparent at first, and it is better for people to be aware of potential dangers when ascending to a new place. Otherwise, if they enter an uninhabited land, the potential dangers will often exceed expectations.

六四：王用亨（xiǎng）于岐山，吉，无咎。

《象》曰："王用亨于岐山"，顺事也。

【明译】

六四：君王来到岐山祭祀，吉祥而没有过错。

《象传》说：君王来到岐山祭享，是顺从天道，建功立事。

Six (*yin*/soft line) in the fourth place: The king comes to Mount Qi to offer sacrifices, which are auspicious and without fault.

The *Image Commentary* (*Xiang Zhuan*) says: When kings come to Mount Qi to offer sacrifices, they follow the heavenly *dao* and establish meritorious deeds.

【明意】

个人实力上升，意缘相应升进扩大，意缘整体性的升进当以个人实力为基础，否则升入了一个新的意缘之境，没有顺从天道则难以持续。"顺事"此处不仅指顺从应当的事去做，而且是指顺从天道才能去做大事，诚意通天方可升进。诚到顺天立极的地步自然可以建功立业。此处可以理解为典型修炼意缘之路，指心意通天才能升进的重要教导。

[Illuminating Intentionality]

As personal strength rises, the intentionality of destiny will increase and expand accordingly. The increase of the overall intentionality of destiny should be based on personal strength; otherwise it will rise to a new realm of intentionality and destiny, and this will be difficult to sustain without obeying the heavenly *dao*. "Following in deeds" here not only means following what should be done, but also means following the heavenly *dao* to achieve great things, and only with sincerity connecting with heaven can one advance. If one is sincere to the point of following heaven in establishing supremacy, one can naturally make great achievements. This can be understood as a typical path of cultivating intentional dependence (*yiyuan*), which refers to the important teaching that only by connecting with heaven can one's intentionality advance.

六五：贞吉，升阶。

《象》曰："贞吉，升阶"，大得志也。

【明译】

六五：持守正道行事吉祥，如同登上台阶步步高升。

《象传》说：持守正道行事吉祥，如同登上台阶步步高升，是六五上升的心志完满实现（下有刚爻九二阴阳正应）。

Six (*yin*/soft line) in the fifth place: Adhering to the upright *dao* and actions being auspicious is like climbing up stairs and ascending step by step.

The *Image Commentary* (*Xiang Zhuan*) says: Adhering to the upright *dao* and actions being auspicious is like climbing up stairs and rising step by step is the complete realization of the Six (*yin*/soft line) in the fifth place's rising aspirations (there is a Nine (*yang*/strong line) in the second place below so the two *yin* and *yang* lines correspond perfectly).

【明意】

六五下有九二刚毅有力的支持，自己有信心又努力地营造出升进的意缘情境。时机一到，即可升进。六五能够保持整体性的升进格局，当然心志得到完满的实现。升进是不间断持守意缘的努力，每上一个阶段，都要安宁持守，在得志的状态当中重新恒稳地维护整合意缘，在这个意义上，升象征心意对意缘的持守和整合，不断升到一个新的格局、境界和状态。

[Illuminating Intentionality]

The Six (*yin*/soft line) in the fifth place is supported by the fortitude of the Nine (*yang*/strong line) in the second place, so has the confidence and hard work to create a progressive situation. When the time comes, one can advance. The Six (*yin*/soft line) in the fifth place can maintain a holistic pattern of promotion, so of course its aspirations will be fully realized. Ascension is the continuous effort to maintain intentional dependence. In each phase, one must maintain peace and stability, and re-establish the integration of intentionality in a successful state. In this sense, the ascension symbolizes the persistence and integration of intentionality toward intentional dependence, constantly rising to a new pattern, realm and state.

上六：冥升，利于不息之贞。

《象》曰："冥升"在上，消不富也。

【明译】

上六：在窈冥之境中昏昧地升进，有利于永不停息地持守正道干事。

《象传》说：在窈冥之境中昏昧地升进，又处在上位，还是会消衰而无法富盛（坤为不富，为虚）。

Six (*yin*/soft line) in the top place: Advancing ignorantly in a dark and remote realm is conducive to endlessly upholding the right *dao* and doing things.

The *Image Commentary* (*Xiang Zhuan*) says: If one advances in ignorance in a dark and remote (*yaoming*窈冥) realm and is in a high position, one will still decline and cannot be prosperous (Trigram Kun is not wealthy, and represents emptiness).

【明意】

意缘提升的是精神修养的阶段性升进，钱财等身外之物不可能一直升进。真正支持大业的是一个人内在的德性。一个人升进有困难，则当反身修德。至于《周易》通过阴阳干支系统，转化天时地利为能量生克之体系，致力于揭示冥合的先天结构，这主要在术数易学里体现和运用出来。但如果未来皆已注定，就不需要人通过人天之意而主动修为。所以《易》道通过经与传的正宗传统强调《易》可助人修心修意，而不宜过度在意自己被外在时刻能量系统所决定的状态。

[Illuminating Intentionality]

What improves intentional dependence is a phased improvement in spiritual cultivation. Wealth and other external things cannot always be increased. What truly supports a great cause is a person's inner virtue. If a person has difficulty in advancing, one should reflect on oneself and cultivate virtue. As for the *Book of Changes*, through the system of *yin* and *yang* stems and branches, it transforms time and place into a system of energy production and restraint, and is committed to revealing the transcendental structure of the dark and remote realm, as is mainly reflected and used in divinatory *Changes* studies. However, if the future is already determined, there is no need for people to take the initiative to cultivate through the cosmological intentionality of humanity and heaven. Therefore, through the classic and its commentaries, the *dao* of the *Changes* emphasizes that the *Changes* can help people cultivate their intentions and heart-minds, and that people should not be overly concerned about their own state being determined by the external energy system of the moment.

泽水困（卦四十七）　（坎下兑上）

Kun (Entanglement), Lake and Water (Hexagram 47)　(Kan below, Dui above)

　　由下上升要消耗意能，意能耗尽则必受困，故升卦之后接困卦。意能不能流动如泽水之困。泽水入泽底之下，如意识的能量泄露渗透到意境之下，干涸无能也无力。意能如水流动，不能流动的时候，意能就泄掉了。意能枯竭之时，还得靠自己努力转化增益。当形势困顿，阻止意念接天，人反而应该更努力让意念接天机，顺天意，也就是处在逆境之中，意念被困于无力甚至悖逆之境，人只要努力自助，还是有可能亨通的。

　　人生之困，或困于情，或困于时，或困于境，但卦象都是阳意被阴意纠缠而无力之象。困卦讨论人需要放下和解脱这种纠缠才能恢复意念的能量。为了自己的人天之意的意能表达出来，极度困难之时要能够豁出性命。志向就是人心通于天的意念，所以可以称为人天之意。

Ascending from the bottom consumes intentional energy, and if intentional energy is exhausted, one will be trapped, so Hexagram Sheng (Ascent) is followed by Hexagram Kun (Entanglement). When intentionality cannot flow, it is like trapped water. When water enters the bottom of a pool, it is like the energy of consciousness leaking and penetrating into the intentional context, drying up and becoming powerless. The energy of intentionality flows like water, and when it cannot flow, the energy of the intentionality is released. When one's intentional energy is exhausted, one still has to rely on one's own efforts to convert it into increase. When a situation is difficult and prevents intentionality from connecting with heaven, people should work harder to allow intentionality to connect with heaven and follow the intentionality of heaven. That is to say, in adversity, intentionality is trapped in a state of powerlessness or even rebellion, but as long as people work hard to help themselves, it is still possible to prosper.

Difficulties in life may be due to emotions, time, or circumstances, but through the hexagram images, they are all signs of *yang* being entangled by *yin* and becoming powerless. Hexagram Kun (Entanglement) discusses the need for people to let go and get rid of this entanglement in order to restore the energy of their intentionality. In order to be able to express one's own intentionality of humanity and heaven, one must be able to risk one's life in times of extreme difficulty. Ambition is the human heart-mind connecting with the intentions of heaven, so it can be called the cosmological intentionality of humanity and heaven.

困，亨，贞，大人吉，无咎。有言不信。

《彖》曰：困，刚掩也。险以说，困而不失其所，"亨"，其唯君子乎。"贞，大人吉"，以刚中也。"有言不信"，尚口乃穷也。

《象》曰：泽无水，困。君子以致命遂志。

【明译】

困卦象征困逆之境，努力自助还可亨通，要持守正道，对意能大的人来说，不但吉祥而且还没有咎害，只是处于困逆之境的时候，说话未必有人愿意相信。

《彖传》说：困卦是阳刚受到埋没掩蔽。下卦坎为险，上卦兑为悦，能在险难中保持喜悦，处于困逆之境而不失其人天之意，才会亨通，尽管艰辛，但可能只有君子才能做到这样吧。要持守正道，对意能大的人来说是吉祥的，因刚爻九二、九五皆居于中道。处于困逆之境的时候，说话未必有人愿意相信，因为崇尚言辞无法让人信服，反而更加困厄（上六从二位升到上卦兑里，位处穷极）。

《象传》说：上卦兑为泽，下卦坎为水，水渗到泽下去了，泽里没有水，组合成困卦。君子看到大泽里的水都被困干了的卦象，决定为了实现自己的人天之意，可以舍弃自己的性命。

Hexagram Kun (Entanglement) symbolizes a difficult and adverse situation, but one can still prosper if one works hard to help oneself, though one must stick to the upright *dao*. For people with strong intentional energy, it is not only auspicious but also free from blame. However, when one is in a difficult situation, no one may be willing to believe one's words.

The *Judgment Commentary* (*Tuan Zhuan*) says: Hexagram Kun (Entanglement) means that *yang*/strong is buried and covered. The lower Trigram Kan represents danger, and the upper Trigram Dui represents joy. Only by being able to maintain joy in danger and adversity without losing the intentionality of humanity and heaven will one be able to prosper. Although it is difficult, perhaps only an exemplary person can do this. It is auspicious for people with great intentional energy to stick to the upright *dao*, because the Nine (*yang*/strong line) in the second place and the Nine (*yang*/strong line) in the fifth place are both on the middle *dao*. When one is in a difficult situation, no one may be willing to believe what one says, because words of advocation cannot convince people, and may even in fact make things more difficult (the Six (*yin*/soft line) in the top place has been promoted from the second position to the upper Trigram Dui, and is at its final extreme).

The *Image Commentary* (*Xiang Zhuan*) says: The upper Trigram Dui is lake, and the lower Trigram Kan is water. Water seeps from the bottom of the lake, and there is no water in the lake, so the combination forms Hexagram Kun (Entanglement). The exemplary person sees a hexagram in which all the water in the lake is trapped and dried up, and decides to give up one's life in order to concretize one's intentionality of humanity and heaven.

【明意】

君子之志是实现道义，道义即真理，在极度困境之中，为了实现自己的人天之意，要有可以舍弃自己性命的决心和壮志。在精神处于困境之时，需要有意能的转化和突破。人在困境之中，首先要能够处之泰然，之后寻求突破，而突破来自意能的提升和改变状态，在此过程之中，能屈能伸是一种基本素质。在困境中，人当纯净自己的意念，该说的说，不该说的一点都不可以说。

泽水入于地下，无水则困。困到极致，需要回到自己的本性，孤注一掷，奋力一搏，提升意能的等级与志向。大人有大的意能状态，但大的意能来自其经历过大的磨难。心大志大，困境自然相应就大。很多困境是来自没有突破自己的心灵意识境遇，而个人的心灵意识境遇如果不突破，就很难真正摆脱困境。

[Illuminating Intentionality]

The ambition of an exemplary person is to realize morality and justice, which is truth. In extreme difficulties, in order to realize one's own intentionality of humanity and heaven, one must have the determination and ambition to sacrifice one's own life. When one is in a spiritual dilemma, one needs to have the intentional energy to transform and break through. When a person is in a difficult situation, one must first be able to be calm, and then seek a breakthrough, and breakthroughs come from an improvement and change of intentional energy. In this process, being able to bend and stretch is a basic quality. In a difficult situation, people should purify their intentions, say what should be said, and say nothing about what should not be said.

Water flows into the ground, and without water, one will be trapped. When one is trapped to an extreme, one needs to return to one's true nature, make a desperate move, and work hard to improve one's level of consciousness and ambition. Great people have a state of great intentional energy, but their great intentional energy comes from the great suffering they have experienced. If one has a great heart-mind and big ambitions, the difficulties will naturally be great. Many difficulties come from a failure to break through one's own spiritual and conscious situation, and if one does not break through one's own spiritual and conscious situation, it will be difficult to truly get rid of one's predicament.

初六：臀困于株木，入于幽谷，三岁不觌（dí）。

《象》曰："入于幽谷"，"幽"不明也。

【明译】

初六：坐困在枯木和木根之间，陷到幽暗的深谷之中，三年都没有人再见过他。

《象传》说：退陷到幽暗的深谷之中，因初六困于幽暗不明的深谷之中（下卦坎为隐伏）。

Six (*yin*/soft line) in the first place: One sits trapped between dead trees and roots, and retreats into a dark valley. No one sees this one again for three years.

The *Image Commentary* (*Xiang Zhuan*) says: One retreats into a dark valley, because the Six (*yin*/soft line) in the first place is trapped in a dark and remote valley (the lower Trigram Kan means hidden).

【明意】

初六陷入没有生气的困境，如在遥远深邃的幽谷当中，不为人知，得不到帮助和庇佑。初六有所待，不得而受困于深谷的枯木林里。处于意能极低的状态，处境昏暗，自身又不明理，自困又困人，总是不能明白脱困之道，所以自陷穷途末路，难以解脱。

但从另一个角度讲，初六又如绝世高人，在世外修炼，在枯木这样无生气的困境之中，不断修炼提升意能，这是孤独修炼意能的状态。心意的能量经过困境的磨炼，焕发出新生，可能提升达到新的境界。这说明，要想提高意能，就需要一个避世修炼修行的过程。由此可知，君子小人的转化，不在身体的转变，而在意识境遇的转化。意能在困境当中要想提升，需要学会从困境当中汲取养料，提升意能的心理和训练机制。

[Illuminating Intentionality]

The Six (*yin*/soft line) in the first place falls into a lifeless predicament, like being in a remote and deep valley, unknown to anyone, without help or protection. The Six (*yin*/soft line) in the first place was waiting for something, but did not get it and was trapped in the deadwood forest of a deep valley. In a state of extremely low intentional energy, the situation is dim, and one does not understand oneself, trapped by oneself and others. One is always unable to see a way out of the entanglement, so one is trapped in a dead end and it is difficult to escape.

But from another perspective, the Six (*yin*/soft line) in the first place is like a peerless master who cultivates oneself outside the world. In a lifeless predicament like a dead tree, one constantly cultivates and increases one's intentional energy. This is a state of lonely cultivation of one's intentional state. After being tempered by difficulties, the energy of one's intentionality is reborn and may be elevated to a new level. This shows that if one wants to improve one's mental abilities, one needs a process of escaping from the world and practicing cultivation. It can be seen from this that the transformation of the exemplary person and the petty person is not a transformation of the body, but a transformation of consciousness. If one wants to improve one's mental abilities in difficult situations, one needs to learn to draw nourishment from difficulties and improve the psychological and training mechanisms for one's mental abilities.

九二：困于酒食，朱绂（fú）方来，利用享祀。征凶，无咎。

《象》曰："困于酒食"，中有庆也。

【明译】

九二：正被美酒佳肴所困扰，祭祀时用的大红祭服刚刚送来，穿上它有利于主持宗庙的祭祀大典，此时进取凶多吉少，但不会有大的灾祸。

《象传》说：虽然九二正被美酒佳肴所困扰，但因为能行中道，所以会有喜庆。

Nine (*yang*/strong line) in the second place: One is obsessed with fine wine and delicious food. The bright red sacrificial robes used for sacrifices have just been delivered. Wearing them will help one to preside over the ancestral temple's sacrificial ceremony. At this time, progress is unfortunate, but there will be no major disasters.

The *Image Commentary* (*Xiang Zhuan*) says: Although the Nine (*yang*/strong line) in the second place is disturbed by fine wine and food, one will be joyful because one can follow the middle *dao*.

【明意】

困有多种，如时代和命运的多重困境，但通常首先是空间的约束和艰难，因为空间上自由度减缩，加上没有应援，只能自处困境之中，自己能够开心就好。人在困的空间之中，意识可能受到身体的自由度限制而受困，但也可以通过自由想象和精神驰骋，放下身外之困，超越身体的边界所限。时间上不得其时，则时势会让人陷入穷困之境。

酒食代表困境中表面的风光，但其实是对意能之自由度的限制，不能展示出意能的力量，因为意量要在有一定回旋的空间与时间中展开。意生之能量要能不断调出潜在的意量才会有力量。困境当中，反而需要置之死地的努力，因为意念的边界要自己打开，只有自己才能真正把握和控制自己转化意识能量的方式。

[Illuminating Intentionality]

There are many different types of entanglement, such as multiple dilemmas of time and fate, but usually the first one is constraints and difficulties of space. Because the degree of freedom in space is reduced and there is no support, one can only be in trouble by oneself, though one may still be able to be happy. When a person is in a trapped space, one's consciousness may be restricted by the freedom of the body, but one can also let go of the trappings outside the body and transcend the boundaries of the body through free imagination and spiritual traveling. If the time is not right, such a situation can make people fall into destitution.

Wine and food represent the superficial decor of a difficult situation, but in fact they limit the freedom of imagination and cannot demonstrate its power, because imagination must unfold in a certain space and time. Intentional energy can only be powerful if it can continuously mobilize latent intentionality. In a difficult situation, one needs to work hard, because the boundaries of one's intentions have to be opened by oneself, and only by oneself can one truly grasp and control the way one transforms one's conscious energy.

六三：困于石，据于蒺藜。入于其宫，不见其妻，凶。

《象》曰："据于蒺藜"，乘刚也。"入于其宫，不见其妻"，不祥也。

【明译】

六三：被围困于乱石堆之中，又靠坐在荆棘蒺藜之上。退入自家宫室，却已见不到妻子，非常凶险。

《象传》说：坐困在荆棘蒺藜之上，因为六三乘在刚爻之上。即使得以退回自家居室，看到的妻子好像不像妻子，实在太不吉祥了。

Six (*yin*/soft line) in the third place: Surrounded by piles of rocks and sitting on thorns and thistles, he can retreat into his own palace, but can no longer see his wife, and it is very dangerous.

The *Image Commentary* (*Xiang Zhuan*) says: He is sitting on thorns and thistles because the Six (*yin*/soft line) in the third place rides on a *yang*/strong line. Even if one can retreat to one's home, the wife one sees does not look like one's own wife, which is really unfortunate.

【明意】

这爻说明，进入危险的情境之中，连家人都受牵连，难以保全，非常危险。在置之死地而后生的处境中，要调整转化自己的意能。这爻前有天险，后有追兵，身困死地，几乎是身体之困的极致。人已经没有行动的自由，而且遍体鳞伤，妻离子散，大凶之象。

[Illuminating Intentionality]

This line shows that when entering a dangerous situation, even family members will be implicated and it will be difficult to protect them, and thus very dangerous. In a situation of risking death and surviving, one must adjust and transform one's own intentional energy. There is a natural danger ahead of this line, and there are chasing soldiers behind. The body is trapped to the point of death, which is almost the ultimate level of physical distress. People no longer have freedom of movement, and their bodies are bruised and bruised. Their wives and children are separated, and it looks like a terrible situation.

九四：来徐徐，困于金车，吝，有终。

《象》曰："来徐徐"，志在下也。虽不当位，有与也。

【明译】

九四：只能缓慢前来，因为所乘的坚固豪华的车子在路上被困住了，出了一点麻烦，但最后结果还算顺利。

《象传》说：只能缓慢前来，因为九四的心志一直下应初六（卦变中九二来到二位，九四也愿下来）。虽然以阳居阴，居位不当，但会得到亲和友善愿意帮助自己的人（初六）。

Nine (*yang*/strong line) in the fourth place: One can only proceed slowly, because the sturdy and luxurious carriage one is traveling in is stuck on the road, which causes a little trouble, but in the end the result is smooth.

The *Image Commentary* (*Xiang Zhuan*) says: One can only advance slowly, because the Nine (*yang*/strong line) in the fourth place's ambition has always been to respond to the Six (*yin*/soft line) in the first place (in the hexagram-changes, the Nine (*yang*/strong line) in the second place comes to the second position, and the Nine (*yang*/strong line) in the fourth place is also willing to come down). Although it is a *yang* line in a *yin* position, so its position is inappropriate, it will find kind and friendly people (the Six (*yin*/soft line) in the first place) who are willing to help.

【明意】

在困境当中，意能要分给小人一些。因为被小人包围所困，艰难异常。此时能量不得不分。人要出离困境，在无助之境中，首先要自助，多助人多布施多付出，帮助他人最后会能够帮助到自己。所以，九四既然阳刚有志气，为了脱困，就不能只顾自己，必要时也要帮助小人。

意能要脱困，就不要被私欲牵绊，人心的私欲是阻止约束人行动的金车，自己被私欲困住，就难以施展发挥，更难以解脱困境。

[Illuminating Intentionality]

In a difficult situation, some intentional energy should be given to petty people. It is extremely difficult because one is surrounded and trapped by petty people. At this point the energy has to be divided. If people want to get out of trouble, in a helpless situation, they must first help themselves, then help others more, give more, and pay out more, as helping others will eventually help oneself. Therefore, since the Nine (*yang*/strong line) in the fourth place is *yang*/strong and ambitious, in order to get out of trouble, one must not only care about oneself, but also help petty people when necessary.

If one wants to get out of trouble, one should not be tied down by selfish desires. The selfish desires of the human heart-mind are the golden chariot that prevents and restricts people's actions. If one is trapped by selfish desires, it will be difficult for one to exert oneself, and it will be even more difficult to get out of one's predicament.

九五：劓刖（yuè），困于赤绂，乃徐有说（tuō），利用祭祀。

《象》曰："劓刖"，志未得也。"乃徐有说"，以中直也。"利用祭祀"，受福也。

【明译】

九五：被迫采用劓刑、刖刑治理国家，以至穷困在尊位，后来得以慢慢脱离困境，有利于举行祭祀。

《象传》说：被迫采用劓刑、刖刑治理国家，因为九五的志向得不到伸展（刚爻被柔爻所掩，有道无法推行）。后来得以慢慢脱离困境，因为能够持守中道，处世正直。有利于举行祭祀，因为能够得到神灵的福佑（九五有祭服可祭祀）。

Nine (*yang*/strong line) in the fifth place: One is forced to use torture and mutilation to govern the country, to the point of impoverishing his position. Later, one is gradually able to get out of the predicament, which is conducive to holding sacrifices.

The *Image Commentary* (*Xiang Zhuan*) says: One is forced to use torture and mutilation to govern the country because one's ambitions as the Nine (*yang*/strong line) in the fifth place cannot be extended (the strong line is covered up by a soft line, and its *dao* cannot be implemented). Later, one is able to gradually get out of the predicament because one is able to stick to the middle *dao* and behave uprightly. It is conducive to holding sacrifices because one can obtain the blessings of the gods (the Nine (*yang*/strong line) in the fifth place has sacrificial robes so can sacrifice).

【明意】

在困的大势里，即使在尊位也被迫要面对异常艰困的局面，此时要继续坚持，才能缓慢脱困，需要对意能解困有信心。也可以理解为，要用祭祀这样心意通天的活动来拉升自己意能的层次，让心意通天接天。毕竟，人在困境中祈求神灵保佑，本身没有什么错。困境中人天之意处网而难于接天，但此时更要努力不断地继续天意天机。通过祭祀让人们感受到彼此之间的诚意，让心意接天，诚心接天才是脱困的根本。

通过祭祀等庄严的仪式，人们可以感受到参与者意识通天的庄严心境，这种庄严能够成为意识起死回生的生机，诚意可以感染人，也是生机所寄。在困境中，接天、心诚都是为了生机回复，只有回复到有生机之地，处于有生机之时，生机才能生长焕发起来。

[Illuminating Intentionality]

In a general trend of difficulties, even in high positions, one is forced to face extremely difficult situations. At this time, one must continue to persevere in order to slowly get out of trouble. One needs to have confidence in one's intentional energy to solve these difficulties. It can also be understood that one should use activities such as offering sacrifices that can reach heaven to raise the level of one's own intentional energy, so that one's intentions can connect with the heavens. After all, there is nothing wrong with people praying to gods for protection in difficult situations. In the predicament, the cosmological intentionality of humanity and heaven is entangled and difficult to connect with heaven, but at this time, one must work harder to continue the intentions and vitality of heaven. Through sacrifices, people can feel the sincerity between one another, and letting their intentions and sincerity connect with heaven is the basis for getting out of trouble.

Through solemn rituals such as sacrifices, people can feel the solemn state of intentionality of the participants. This solemnity can become the vitality that can bring consciousness back to life. Sincerity can infect people and is also a source of vitality. In difficult situations, connecting to heaven and being sincere are all aimed at restoring vitality. Only by returning to a place where there is vitality, and living in a time when there is vitality, can vitality grow and radiate.

上六：困于葛藟（lěi），于臲卼（niè wù）曰，动悔，有悔，征吉。

《象》曰："困于葛藟"，未当也。"动悔有悔"，吉行也。

【明译】

上六：受困于藤葛蔓藟之中，又被困在高危摇坠之地，在凶日行动，必生悔恨，处于艰困之境要立即幡然悔悟，努力解脱困境，果断征伐才可能获得吉祥。

《象传》说：受困于藤葛蔓藟之中，因为上六居位不适当（到了穷极之位，又下乘二刚）。这是一动必生悔恨的艰困之境，说明拼力解脱困境前行才能够获得吉祥。

Six (*yin*/soft line) in the top place: Trapped in vines and creepers, and also in a risky and unstable place. If one acts on an inauspicious day, one will inevitably regret it. When one is in a difficult situation, one must immediately repent and work hard to get out of the predicament, and only by a decisive expedition can one gain good fortune.

The *Image Commentary* (*Xiang Zhuan*) says: Trapped in vines and creepers, because the position of the Six (yin/soft line) in the top place is inappropriate (it has reached the final extreme, and rides on two strong lines). This is a difficult situation where every move will lead to regret, which shows that only by working hard to get out of trouble and advance can one gain good fortune.

【明意】

人遭遇困境之时，本来就是意能降低到低凹之时势当中，此时更要学会集中意能的艺术，只有意能集中才能脱困，要把有限的意能集中到能量最高的方向上去，这样才可能集中突破，实现意能的提升。

陷入困境，知悔而征，逐渐转化困境。如果意念纷杂无中心，意能必无力量，因为意念发动起来，就不应该为他物牵累，否则无法使意念集中有力，提升意能。而在某些不合适的时日发动意念，不但必遭凶祸，而且与脱困的初衷背道而驰。

[Illuminating Intentionality]

When people encounter difficulties, it is already in a situation where their intentional energy has been reduced to a low level. At this time, it is even more necessary to learn the art of concentrating intentional energy, since only by concentrating intentional energy can one get out of trouble. One must concentrate one's limited intentional energy in the direction with the highest energy. Only in this way can we focus on breakthroughs and realize an increase of intentional energy.

Falling into trouble, knowing regret yet embarking, one gradually transforms one's predicament. If intentions are scattered and have no center, intentional energy will have no power, because when intentions are initiated, they should not be burdened by other things; otherwise intentions will not be concentrated and powerful and intentional energy will not be increased. However, initiating intentions at certain inappropriate times will not only lead to disaster, but also run counter to the original intention of getting out of trouble.

水风井（卦四十八）　（巽下坎上）

Jing (The Well), Water and Wind (Hexagram 48)　(Xun below, Kan above)

　　总体来说，如井象所示，中国的宗教性仪式比较生活化，没有西方教堂强调的超越义那么强烈。中国的宗教性仪式多致力于提升人的先天善性，但西方教堂却从净化人的先天原罪入手。虽然东西方对于人性的假设不同，但从对灵魂的拷打和震撼的角度来说，无疑原罪说对人的触动更大些，因为人们在绝望中意识到自己是罪人，会做错事，从而自净其意，改变自己的意缘。但如果只是意识到自己的善性，而缺乏克服恶源近乎绝望的自省，那么还是缺乏限制恶缘的有效机制。从制恶入手，更有利于建立完善的行善机制，反而达到更好地扬善的目的。同理，强调天人合一的哲学倾向，因为没有致力于解决天人相分的自然困境，反而在现实中建立天人合一境遇之时，可能还不如天人相分而力图和谐的现实努力。

　　井卦是个不断修井的过程，象征人不断修行意缘的历程。初爻几乎是废井，人之意无缘，无人在乎；二爻可以在井底的水里射抓小鱼，说明人有小的意缘但几乎无用；三爻井修好了，可是没有被人赏识的意缘，终不见用；四爻还得自修等待良好的意缘；五爻才时位兼具，意缘得以伸展，可以济世利人了；到上爻井口收拢，生机焕发，井养人不穷之意缘才大功告成。

　　Generally speaking, as shown by the image of Hexagram Jing (The Well), China's religious rituals are more life-oriented and do not have a transcendent meaning as strong as that emphasized in Western churches. Chinese religious rituals are mostly dedicated to improving people's innate goodness, while Western churches start from purifying people's original sin. Although the East and the West have different assumptions about human nature, from the perspective of torture and shock to the soul, there is no doubt that the theory of original sin touches people more, because people realize in despair that they are sinners and will do wrong, and thus purify their intentionality and change their intentions. If, however, one is only aware of one's own good nature, but lacks the almost desperate introspection to overcome the source of evil, then one still lacks an effective mechanism to limit evil. Starting from controlling evil is more conducive to establishing a complete mechanism for doing good, and in turn achieves the purpose of better promoting good. In the same way, the philosophical tendency that emphasizes the unity of heaven and humanity, because it does not devote itself to solving the natural dilemma of the separation of heaven and humanity, but instead establishes the situation of the unity of heaven and humanity in reality, may not be as good as the effort in reality of the separation of heaven and humanity that strives for harmony.

Hexagram Jing (The Well) is a process of constantly repairing the well, symbolizing the process of people constantly cultivating their intentional conditions. The first line is an almost abandoned well, and no one cares about people's intentionality lacking conditions; in the second line one can shoot and catch small fish in the water at the bottom of the well, which shows that people have a small amount of intentionality, but it is almost useless; in the third line the well has been repaired, but it has not been used, so the intention and dependent co-arising that people would appreciate eventually sees no use; in the fourth line one must cultivate oneself and wait for good intentional conditions; the fifth line has both talent and time, and intentionality and its conditions can be extended, so it can help the world and benefit people; when the top line gathers at the mouth of the well, it is full of vitality and the well's purpose of nourishing people is complete.

井，改邑不改井，无丧无得。往来井井。汔（qì）至，亦未繘（jú）井，羸其瓶，凶。

《彖》曰：巽乎水而上水，井。井养而不穷也。"改邑不改井"，乃以刚中也。"汔至，亦未繘井"，未有功也。"羸其瓶"，是以"凶"也。

《象》曰：木上有水，井。君子以劳民劝相。

【明译】

井卦象征坚定不移，居住的村邑可以改迁，但水井不能改迁到其他地方。每日汲取不见其枯竭，时时流注其中也不见其盈满，任凭来来往往的人反复不断地从井中汲水为用，永远井然有序。如果汲水的时候，打水的陶罐即将升到井口，还没有提到井上的当口被挂住了，一旦倾覆毁坏，就会有凶险。

《象传》说：上卦坎为水，下卦巽为木为入，用木桶深入水下再向上提水，这就是井卦表达的情境。井水取之不尽，用之不竭，滋生养育人的功德也永不穷竭。居住的村邑可以改迁，但水井不能改迁到其他地方，是因为刚健（九二、九五）居中，不易改变。井以打水为功，如果汲水的时候，打水的陶罐即将升到井口，还没有提到井上的当口被挂住了，不能算有功，因为还没有实现井的养人之功。一旦打水的陶瓶被挂住或者倾覆毁坏，那就有凶险了。

《象传》说：下卦巽为木，上卦坎为水，把木桶深入到水面下打水，把水提上来而有井水之用，这就是井卦。君子要效法井水养人之德，要多为人民操劳，劝勉他们互相帮助。

Hexagram Jing (The Well) symbolizes perseverance. The village where one lives can be moved, but the well cannot be moved to other places. Even if one draws from it every day, one will not see it dry up, and if one often pours it into it, one will not see it full. No matter how many people come and go, one can repeatedly draw water from the well for use, and it will always be in order. When drawing water, and the clay pot is about to rise to the mouth of the well, but is caught at the mouth of the well before it emerges, if it overturns and is destroyed, there will be danger.

The *Judgment Commentary* (*Tuan Zhuan*) says: The upper Trigram Kan is water, the lower Trigram Xun is wood, which means using a wooden bucket to go deep into the water and then lift the water upward. This is the situation expressed by Hexagram Jing (The Well). The well water is inexhaustible, and the merits of nourishing and raising people are also inexhaustible. The village where one lives can be moved, but the well cannot be moved to other places, because the Nine (*yang*/strong line) in the second place and Nine (*yang*/strong line) in the fifth place are in the middle and not easy to change. Drawing water from a well is considered meritorious. When drawing water, and the clay pot used to draw water is about to rise to the mouth of the well, but is caught before it emerges, it cannot be counted as meritorious because the merit of the well in raising people has not yet been realized. Once the clay bottle for collecting water is caught or overturned and damaged, it will be dangerous.

The *Image Commentary* (*Xiang Zhuan*) says: The lower Trigram Xun is wood, and the upper Trigram Kan is water. A wooden bucket is deep under the water's surface to draw water, and the water is lifted up to be used as well water. This is Hexagram Jing (The Well). An exemplary person should imitate the virtue of well water in nourishing people, work more for the people, and encourage them to help each other.

【明意】

可以把井理解为有公共纪念生发意义的意缘对象，如地点，公共纪念场所等。人心聚集如井，虽然不动，但因为这个公共之地能够养而不穷，人心自然井然有序。以不变的心境状态应付纷杂的人世纷争，意缘总是变，但内心有所守，如井不变。当水上升遇到困难，就要到井的基础下面去寻找出路，可以让意缘的方向做些改变，但维持意境不变。汨汨流出的井水，经过人们有序取用，成为随时有序的水，也把自然之水变成净化的、有序的、可控的水（自来水）。在这个意义上，井是帮助人们把外在变动不拘的意缘，梳理成为有秩序的可以理解的意缘。虽然人心不断在改变，但自然境遇的风土人情作为人心变化的基础本身，却长期维持相对稳定。

井作为工业社会之"乡愁"的核心，打着深深的农业社会天人合一的烙印，人通过水，身体和思想都与井合为一体。如此困顿惆怅的乡愁之井，却在古老中国面对西方之后基本退出人民的生活，而那个农业社会强烈的天人合一感被人与自然分离和分裂的乱象所取代。如今逐步工业化之后的中国，虽然怀念天人合一的理念，但人与环境的融合感，已经不如上千年宗教性强调人与上帝分离的欧美建筑和环境中体现的人与自然的和谐感，那种在人间建立天国的人神二分思维下建立的人穿过所创造物而有超越感带出来的和谐，在几千年天人合一理念指导下不得和谐的现代工业化场景面前，显得疏异而吊诡。

[Illuminating Intentionality]

A well can be understood as an emotional object with the intentionality of public commemoration, such as a location, a public commemorative site, etc. Human heart-minds gather like a well, and although it does not move, this public place can provide endless nourishment, so the human heart-mind is naturally in order. Dealing with the complicated disputes in the world with an unchanged state of intention, one's intentional conditions are always changing, but one's heart is guarded, like a well that remains unchanged. When the water rises but encounters difficulties, it is necessary to look for a way out under the foundation of the well. One can make some changes in the direction of the intention, but keep the intentional context unchanged. After people use it in an orderly manner, the gurgling well water can become orderly water at any time, and also turns natural water into purified, orderly, and controllable water (running water). In this sense, a well is to help people sort out the external changing and informal intentional conditions into orderly and understandable intentional conditions. Although people's intentions are constantly changing, the natural environment and customs, as the basis for changes in people's intentions, remain relatively stable for a long time.

As the core of "nostalgia" in industrial society, wells bear a deep imprint of the unity of nature and humanity in agricultural society. Through water, people's bodies and minds become one with the well. Such wells with a constricted and melancholy feeling of nostalgia basically withdrew from people's lives after ancient China faced the West, and the strong sense of unity between nature and humanity in agricultural society was replaced by the chaos of separation and division between humanity and nature. Now that China is gradually industrializing, although it pines after the concept of the unity of humanity and nature, the sense of integration between humanity and the environment is no longer as strong as the sense of harmony between humanity and nature reflected in the European and American architecture and environment where religions for thousands of years emphasized the separation of humanity and God. The kind of harmony that is created under the dichotomous thinking of humanity and divinity that establishes heaven on earth, where people have a sense of transcendence through the things they create, seems alien and paradoxical in the face of the modern industrialized scene where harmony cannot be achieved under the guidance of the millennia-old concept of unity of nature and humanity.

初六：井泥，不食。旧井无禽。

《象》曰："井泥，不食"，下也。"旧井无禽"，时舍也。

【明译】

初六：井下淤泥沉滞，井水浑浊不能食用，旧井破旧不堪，就连禽兽都不来喝水光顾。

《象传》说：井下淤泥沉滞，井水浑浊不能食用，因为初六位置在下（在井卦就是井底）。旧井破旧不堪，就连禽兽都不来喝水光顾，因为禽兽到井边饮水都是暂时停留一下，井水有淤泥就被禽兽给舍弃了。

Six (*yin*/soft line) in the first place: Silt settles at the bottom of the well, and the water in the well is too turbid to be drunk. The old well is dilapidated, and even animals do not come to drink its water.

The *Image Commentary* (*Xiang Zhuan*) says: The silt at the bottom of the well settles, and the well water is turbid and cannot be drunk, because the Six (*yin*/soft line) in the first place is in the bottom position (in Hexagram Jing (The Well), it is the bottom of the well). The old well is dilapidated and derelict, and even animals do not come to drink from it, because the animals previously stopped temporarily when they came to drink from the well, and the animals abandoned the well when the water became muddy.

【明意】

好比一个旅人行走天涯，面对老树昏鸦的凄惨之状，心中孤独难受。曾经努力整合新的缘分，尽管竭尽全力，但最后却没有成功，只有孤独地行走天下。

过去的意缘，好像旧井一样。废井让人想到荒废的缘分，对整体性的超越和放弃的旧缘分，好像一个离乡背井的人，背弃了早期的缘分而重建新的意缘。井水有泥，是一个抛弃旧缘的象征，觉得旧泥脏不好，意缘无法展开，没有生机。

井是意缘生生，源源不断之象。人心如井，人需要打扫旧井，好比需要打扫自己的心井，因为心井干净了，才有人来喝水，如果心井不净，心德不修，则连禽兽都远离，打扫了即有新的意缘展开。

[Illuminating Intentionality]

This is like a traveler, walking on the edges of the world, facing the miserable state of old trees and crows, and feeling lonely and uncomfortable in one's heart. One once tried hard to integrate new dependent co-arisings, but despite one's best efforts, one failed in the end and can only walk through the world under heaven alone.

The dependent co-arisings of the past are like an old well. The abandoned well reminds people of abandoned dependent co-arisings, the transcendence of wholeness and abandoned old dependent co-arisings, like a person who has left one's hometown, abandoned one's early dependent co-arisings and rebuilt new dependent co-arisings. There is mud in the well water, which is a symbol of abandoning old relationships, feeling that the old mud is dirty, and that the relationship cannot be developed and has no vitality.

The well is a symbol of the endless flowing production of intentional gathering. The human heart-mind is like a well. People need to clean old wells, just as they need to clean their own inner intentional well. Only when the inner intentional well is clean will people come to drink from it. If the inner well is unclean and intentionality is not cultivated, even animals will stay away. Once it is cleaned, new intentional dependent co-arisings can unfold.

九二：井谷射鲋（fù），瓮敝漏。

《象》曰："井谷射鲋"，无与也。

【明译】

九二：在井谷（底）射抓鲋鱼，水瓮又破旧又漏水。

《象传》说：在井谷（底）射抓鲋鱼，上面却没有人来帮忙（九二没有正应，没有相与在一起的人）。

Nine (*yang*/strong line) in the second place: Shooting and catching carp in the well valley (bottom), the water vat is old and leaking.

The *Image Commentary* (*Xiang Zhuan*) says: One is shooting and catching carp in the well valley (bottom), but no one comes to help (there is no correspondent for the Nine (*yang*/strong line) in the second place, so there is no one to join together with).

【明意】

水瓮又破旧又漏水，等于最重要的工具很不给力，帮不上忙。没有应援，相当于没人帮忙，自己很辛苦。九二关键时刻得不到有力的支持，连工具都是不好用的，即使抓到鱼也会漏掉，就相当于一边做事，一边有人给你搞破坏，事情就很难做起来。上面的人不待见，下面的人心意向下，心不齐，则意缘难聚。

如果意缘起了就灭了，灭了就散了，这样就可能形成自己的意缘恒稳的状态。如果没有相与的意缘，则要想维持稳定的意缘状态就会有难度。没有心意相通的人，则意缘难聚。意缘不可有而无之，要成事要聚意缘，生生灭灭进来就出去。缺乏现实条件的支持，君子之德不能推行，取水之具毁坏，如举贤之路已毁，则意缘难申，只有修意以待时变。

[Illuminating Intentionality]

The water vat is old and leaking, which means that the most important tool is ineffective and of no help. Without support, it means one has no one to help and has to work very hard. If there is no strong support at the critical moment for the Nine (*yang*/strong line) in the second place, even its tools are difficult to use, and even if one catches a fish, one will lose it. This is equivalent to doing things while one is being sabotaged, and it will be difficult to get anything done. The people above don't want to see one, and the people below attract one downward. If heart-minds are not aligned, it is difficult to get together.

If an intentional condition is extinguished as soon as it arises, and disperses as soon as it is extinguished, this may form a stable state of one's own intentional conditions. If there are no correlating intentional conditions, it will be difficult to maintain a stable state of intentional conditions. If there are no people with similar intentions, it is difficult to join together. In order to accomplish something, one must gather the conditions of intention, and with constant production and extinction, these will depart as they enter. Without the support of realistic conditions, the virtues of an exemplary person cannot be implemented, and the tools for collecting water will be destroyed. If the road for promoting talents has been destroyed, it will be difficult to extend intentional conditions, and the only option is to cultivate intentionality and wait for the changes of the times.

九三：井渫（xiè），不食，为我心恻。可用汲，王明，并受其福。

《象》曰："井渫，不食"，行恻也。求"王明，受福"也。

【明译】

九三：把井整治好了，却没人来食用，让我心中不免伤恼凄恻。不过毕竟还是可以用来汲水，等到英明的君王出现，大家都会一同得福受益。

《象传》说：把井中淤泥掏治干净了，却没人来饮用，令行经于此的人感到惋惜难受。盼求圣明的君王出现，大家都可以一同得福受益。

Nine (*yang*/strong line) in the third place: The well is repaired, but still no one comes to drink from it, which makes one feel sad and gloomy. Yet after all, it can still be used to draw water. When a wise king appears, everyone will be blessed together.

The *Image Commentary* (*Xiang Zhuan*) says: The mud in the well is cleared, but still no one comes to drink from it, which makes the people who pass by feel sorry and uncomfortable. One hopes that a wise king will appear so that everyone can be blessed and benefit together.

【明意】

自己修治好了井，却没有人看到，没有人饮水，徒自伤心。这种情形的改变，要等到英明的君王出现，才能让大家受福。说明改井的意缘不是自己简单努力就可以实现的，需要超出个人的外在力量，才可能改变整体性的情境。

怀才不遇时，在上面有权势的人看不到修身的成果，也看不到情形改变的状态，必须忍耐，做好事情，等待机会。要等到好的机遇来重塑意缘，未来在当下意缘展开的过程之中，等到意缘变化才能有新的生机。

[Illuminating Intentionality]

One repairs the well oneself, but no one sees it, and no one drinks from it, which makes one sad. This situation will not change until a wise king appears, so that everyone can be blessed. This shows that the intention of changing the well cannot be achieved by simple efforts on one's own. It requires external power beyond the individual to change an overall situation.

When talents are not available, powerful people above cannot see the results of self-cultivation, nor can they see the changed state of the situation. One must be patient, conduct oneself well, and wait for opportunities. One must wait for a good opportunity to reshape one's destiny, since the future is now in the process of unfolding dependent co-arising, but only when dependent co-arising changes can one have new vitality.

六四：井甃（zhòu），无咎。

《象》曰："井甃无咎"，修井也。

【明译】

六四：把井的内壁用砖头砌好，自然可以避免咎患。

《象传》说：用砖头来修砌井的内壁，以便防止祸患，说的就是要把井修治好的益处。

Six (*yin*/soft line) in the fourth place: Building the inner wall of the well with bricks will naturally avoid trouble.

The *Image Commentary* (*Xiang Zhuan*) says: Using bricks to build the inner wall of the well to prevent disaster means that the benefits of repairing the well will be good.

【明意】

修养如修井，但把自己的意缘修治好，而且是从内治缘，不求外缘，如六四心正，但修养不足，只能切重自身修养，即内缘的完美与提升。至于外在的意缘如何，则不必过分挂虑，内功修好，光彩自来。

井的意缘之道是能上就上，不能上就做好现在的。用井之道，不可急躁，修养不可操之过急。人生在世，时也命也。看开看明懂时势，但不是看破。在逆境之中，修炼内功，等意缘变化而有明显改观。

[Illuminating Intentionality]

Cultivation is like repairing a well, but one must repair one's own intentional conditions, and treat the conditions from the inside, without seeking external conditions. This is like how the Six (*yin*/soft line) in the fourth place, if its heart-mind is right but its cultivation is insufficient, can only focus on self-cultivation, that is, the perfection and improvement of its inner conditions. As for external dependent co-arising, there is no need to worry too much. If one cultivates one's internal strength, one's brilliance will come naturally.

Jing (The Well)'s fate is to advance if one can, and if one cannot, to do one's best in the present. One should not be impatient when using the *dao* of the Well, and not be too hasty in one's cultivation. Living in the world, time is also destiny. One should look beyond the current situation to understand it, but not see through it in disillusionment. In adversity, one should practice inner techniques of cultivation and wait for changes in dependent co-arising to make significant changes.

九五：井洌寒泉，食。

《象》曰："寒泉"之"食"，中正也。

【明译】

九五：井水清洌，如寒爽的甘泉，可以直接饮用。

《象传》说：清澈的井水如寒爽的甘泉，可以直接食用，因为九五能够居中并持守正道。

Nine (*yang*/strong line) in the fifth place: The well water is clear and pure, like a refreshing sweet spring, so one can drink it directly.

The *Image Commentary* (*Xiang Zhuan*) says: Clear well water is like a cold and refreshing sweet spring, which can be drunk directly, because the Nine (*yang*/strong line) in the fifth place can stay in the middle and maintain the right *dao*.

【明意】

实化意念保持良好状态的时候，如甘甜的泉水沁人心脾，滋润大家。也代表人应该要有宽大的胸怀，能够容纳不同意见。

[Illuminating Intentionality]

When concretized intentions are maintained in a good state, it is like sweet spring water that refreshes intentionality and nourishes everyone. This also means that people should have a broad and open mentality and be able to tolerate different opinions.

上六：井收勿幕，有孚元吉。

《象》曰："元吉"在上，大成也。

【明译】

上六：井口收拢好了，就可以不用盖子盖上，因为心怀诚信，自然就会大吉大利。

《象传》说：上六虽然高高在上，但大吉大利，因为井水养人的大功已经告成。

Six (*yin*/soft line) in the top place: Once the well mouth is completed, one can close it without a lid, because if one is honest, one will naturally have good fortune.

The *Image Commentary* (*Xiang Zhuan*) says: Although the Six (*yin*/soft line) in the top place is high above, it is auspicious, because the great work of nourishing people with well water has been completed.

【明意】

意缘实化为生养人的意境，随时接续天地生生之机。收藏井的意缘是井作为一个象征，如心不动以应万变，能够吞吐宇宙之机，收藏天地之志。虽是不动的井，却有无限不测之生机。故炼得功成者，收盖不露，生机内敛，应人而出，此井之大缘。因缘而生，依境而起，乃井之缘生哲学的要值所在。修成正果就随缘度化，开放而包容，心意宽容平和，自然而然。

井加盖也可以理解为人的私心作祟，容易引发争夺，失去井生养众人之公共意味，也是不可掩盖其生机之理由。

[Illuminating Intentionality]

The intentional dependent conditions are transformed into the intentional context of life and nourishment, and can continue the life-giving productive vitality of heaven and earth at any time. The intentionality of completing and covering the mouth of well is that the well is a symbol, which can cope with all changes, just like the heart-mind as an immovable center, can absorb the life force of the cosmos, and gather the aspirations of heaven and earth. Although it is an immovable well, it has infinite and unpredictable vitality. Therefore, those who have succeeded in cultivational practice can close the lid without revealing it, gather their vitality internally, and release it in response to others. This is the great dependent co-arising of the well. Born by causes and conditions, arising according to circumstances, this is the key value of conditional production in the philosophy of the well. When one achieves the right realm of intentional conditions, one can always adapt to changing circumstances, be open and tolerant, and have a tolerant and peaceful intention, naturally flowing with comings and goings, as around the well.

Covering a well can also be understood as a result of people's selfishness, which can easily lead to competition and lose the public intentionality of the well's nourishment, which is also the reason why its vitality should not be covered up.

泽火革（卦四十九）　（离下兑上）

Ge (Revolution), Lake and Fire (Hexagram 49)　(Li below, Dui above)

革卦与蛊卦不同，蛊是社会改革，革是质的革命。变革的时机，即时机中的能量最为关键。《周易》的时间哲学强调的是时间的能量和意向性能量之间的合拍性和可能性。时机需要等待，更需要个体意识的把控。个体意识对于相关信息的体验和把握总是不全面的，毕竟很难真正做到全景式的关照。但变革成败的吊诡之处在于：变革者如果不能对天时能量有足够的自觉，并为变革储备相应的意向能量，就几乎没有办法改变事情的发展，所以变革者的确需要有超越个体意向性的能力，也确实需要有接续天机的意能，不能依天时放大自己的意能，就不能够成功变革所在的形势。

革故鼎新是改变所有人的意识境遇，一定要极为小心。革是意念在危险的情境之中争取变革。君子观革而制定时间哲学，体会心意与时间的关系。意在时间之中，时间如流意，而流变的意念在时间中展开。没有离开时间的意，时间亦不能离开意。不存在离开意向性的时间，也可以说没有客观的时间，没有外在于意向性的时间。时间总是在意向性之中，并在意向性当中展开。

Hexagram Ge (Revolution) is different from Hexagram Gu (Corruption). Gu is concerned with social reform, while Ge is concerned with a qualitative revolution. The timing of change, i.e. the energy in the timing, is most critical. The philosophy of time in the *Book of Changes* emphasizes the rhythmic coherence and possibility between the energy of time and the energy of intentionality. Opportunities require waiting, and also require the control of individual consciousness. The experience and grasp of relevant information by individual consciousness is always incomplete, after all, it is difficult to truly achieve panoramic care. But the paradox of the success or failure of change is that if the changer is not sufficiently aware of the energy of heaven's temporality and reserves the corresponding intentional energy for change, there will be almost no way to change the development of things. Therefore, a changer does need to have the ability to transcend individual intentionality, as well as the intentional ability to take up and continue the vitality of heaven. If one cannot amplify one's own intentional ability according to the temporality of heaven, one will not be able to successfully change a situation.

Reforming the old and bringing in the new means changing the conscious context of all people, so one must be extremely careful. Revolution is the will to strive for change in a dangerous situation. An exemplary person observes changes and develops a philosophy of time, understanding the relationship between one's intentionality and time. Intentions are in time, time is like flowing intentionality, and changing intentions unfold in time. There is no intentionality apart from time, and time cannot be separated from intentionality. As there is no time apart from intentionality, it can also be said that there is no objective time, no time external to intentionality. Time always depends on and unfolds within intentionality.

革，己日乃孚。元亨。利贞，悔亡。

《彖》曰：革，水火相息，二女同居，其志不相得曰"革"。"己日乃孚"，革而信之。文明以说，大"亨"以正。革而当，其"悔"乃"亡"。天地革而四时成，汤武革命，顺乎天而应乎人。革之时大矣哉！

《象》曰：泽中有火，革。君子以治历明时。

【明译】

革卦象征除旧变革，只有在时机成熟的"己日"，改革措施才能取得民众的信服，此后亨通便利，利于持守正固，忧悔也会消亡。

《彖传》说：革卦，上卦泽为水，下卦离为火，水火互相熄灭，好比两个女子同居一室，因为心志趣味不相容，终究要发生"变革"，这就是革卦要说明的情形。只有在时机成熟的"己日"，改革措施才能取得民众的信服，这样改革才算取信于民，得到人民的拥护。下卦离为文明，上卦兑为喜悦，内含文明之德，外显愉悦之色，持守正道而大为亨通，改革适时而妥当合理，忧虑悔恨才会消亡。天地阴阳变革，四季循环往复，商汤革除了夏王朝的天命，周武王革除了商王朝的天命，顺应天道又合乎民心。可见，变革适时合宜的时机化意义实在太重大了！

《象传》说：上卦兑为泽，下卦离为火，泽水当中有烈火就是革卦。君子看到革卦水火互相熄灭的卦象，就要制定历法来明察天时运动的几微。

Hexagram Ge (Revolution) symbolizes the eradication of the old in change and revolution. Only when the time is ripe for an "appropriate day" can reform measures win the trust of the people. From then on, it will be prosperous and expedient, which is conducive to upholding integrity, and sorrows and regrets will disappear.

The *Judgment Commentary* (*Tuan Zhuan*) says: In Hexagram Ge (Revolution), the upper trigram's lake is water, the lower Trigram Li is fire, so water and fire extinguish each other, just like two women living in the same room, because their intentions and interests are incompatible, and "change and reform" will eventually occur. This is the situation that Hexagram Ge (Revolution) illustrates. Only when the time is ripe can reform measures win the trust of the people, and only in this way can a reform gain the support of the people. The lower Trigram Li means civilization, and the upper Trigram Dui means joy, so it contains the virtue of civilization internally and shows the countenance of joy externally. If one sticks to the right *dao*, one will be very prosperous. Reforms will be timely and appropriate, and only then will worries and regrets disappear. The *yin* and *yang* of heaven and earth change, and the four seasons cycle and return. Shang Tang abolished the heavenly mandate of the Xia Dynasty through revolution, and King Wu of Zhou abolished the the heavenly mandate of the Shang Dynasty through revolution, complying with the *dao* of heaven and the heart-minds of the people. It can be seen that the significance of timely opportunity and appropriate timing for changes is great indeed!

The *Image Commentary* (*Xiang Zhuan*) says: The upper Trigram Dui is lake, the lower Trigram Li is fire, so strong fire in lake water is Hexagram Ge (Revolution). When an exemplary person sees the water and fire extinguishing each other in Hexagram Ge (Revolution), one makes a calendar to clearly observe the slightest subtle movement of the heavenly cycles.

【明意】

革卦说明人的勇气和魄力可能决定未来，但需要精准地把握时机。人都想把握未来，改变未来，但到了最为紧要的革命之时，一旦发生变化，后果往往无法预料。此刻还是要顺天应人。意念中的勇气和魄力在时间面前的力量需要认真体悟，好像欣赏变革的美，要能够身临其境，又能够超然物外。否则，勇气和魄力只是美学价值，比如崇高的理想，为了未来献身的勇气等等，如果不能把握和领悟变革的时机，就无法实化出来，而只能远观欣赏而已。理解时机之难，就知道人能够选择的变革既有限也很难。变革是为了改变现状，决定自己和他人，但变革的情境一旦发出，就很难为个体所控制，也就不可能真正做到每时每刻主动选择和自作主宰。

先人区分天地阴阳之革的时机而分出节气等时间节点，从而制定历法。古人从长期积累的时间感中，知道大地与天之间的互动极有规律。天地间的能量周而复始，精确重回。天时的能量掌握着万物的运行，精准不失。

[Illuminating Intentionality]

Hexagram Ge (Revolution) shows that one's courage and boldness may determine the future, but one needs to grasp the timing accurately. Everyone wants to seize the future and change it, but at the most critical time of revolution, once changes occur, the consequences are often unpredictable. At this moment, we still have to obey heaven and respond to people. The power of courage and boldness of intentionality in the face of time needs to be seriously understood, as if appreciating the beauty of change, one must be able to be immersed in a situation and yet detached from it. Otherwise, courage and boldness are just aesthetic values, such as lofty ideals, the courage to sacrifice for the future, etc. If one cannot grasp and understand the opportunity for change, one will not be able to realize it, but only appreciate it from a distance. Understanding the difficulty of timing means knowing that the changes one can choose are both limited and difficult. Change means to change the status quo and determine things concerning oneself and others. However, once a situation of change is issued, it is difficult for individuals to control it, and it is impossible to truly make active choices and take control at every moment.

Ancestors distinguished the timing of *yin* and *yang* revolutions between heaven and earth and divided time nodes such as solar terms to formulate calendars. From a long-term accumulated sense of time, the ancients knew that the interaction between the earth and the heavens was very regular. The energy between heaven and earth returns again and again with precision, and the energy of heavenly cycles controls the movement of the myriad things with precision.

初九．巩用黄牛之革。

《象》曰："巩用黄牛"，不可以有为也。

【明译】

初九：用黄牛皮做的绳子捆绑结实。

《象传》说：用黄牛皮条拧成的绳子捆绑结实，是因为初九要耐心待时，不能轻举妄动，无法有所作为。

Nine (*yang*/strong line) in the first place: Use ropes made of yellow cattle's hide to bind tightly.

The *Image Commentary* (*Xiang Zhuan*) says: The ropes made of twisted yellow catttle's hide strips are tied tightly because as the Nine (*yang*/strong line) in the first place, one must wait patiently and not act rashly or make any contribution.

【明意】

意行开始就要耐心。意与时行，要对流逝的时间有耐心。黄牛之革代表现实难以改变的情势，好像没有办法变革一样。好比变革前严控的前夜，一切似乎都不可改变一样，但最后必须通过变革来改变僵化的时势。在僵化的时势被打破之前，需要对相应的紧困时机有把握，有领悟，而更重要的是巩固变革之意行要有耐心，等待合适的变革时机真正开始并让变革的意行于时势之中，参与引导变革时势的变化。

[Illuminating Intentionality]

One must be patient at the beginning of one's intentionality movement. Intentionality moves with the times, and one has to be patient with the passing of time. The hide of a yellow ox represents a situation that is difficult to change in reality, as if there is no way to change it. This is just like how, on the eve of strict controls before change, everything seems impossible to change, but in the end, reform must be used to change the rigid situation. Before the rigid situation is broken, it is necessary to grasp and understand the corresponding tightly entangled opportunities, and more importantly, to consolidate the intention of change, be patient, wait for the right time for change to really start, and let the intention of change be carried out according to the current situation. One can then participate in guiding changes in a changing situation.

六二：己日乃革之，征吉，无咎。

《象》曰："己日革之"，行有嘉也。

【明译】

六二：到时机成熟的己日发动变革，出征吉祥，没有过错和灾害。

《象传》说：到时机成熟的己日发动变革，说明六二努力前行会有嘉美的结果。

Six (*yin*/soft line) in the second place: When the time is right, initiate changes, and your expedition will be auspicious, without mistakes or disasters.

The *Image Commentary* (*Xiang Zhuan*) says: When the appropriate day comes, initiating changes shows that the Six (*yin*/soft line) in the second place's efforts to move forward will have wonderful results.

【明意】

《周易》告诉人们，做事要遵守天时，尤其是大的变革跟天时有密切关系，因为时间本身具有能量，先人通过历法标示了这些能量刻度和它们之间的转化关系，如果能够为己所用，就能够找到能量最大化的时机，这样才能事半功倍。可见，《周易》的运用是讲究人与天时配合的时机化艺术。

初九形势不允许变革，必须等待。到了六二己日时机成熟，变革时机到了。纳甲学说用己配离，表示时机的能量情态。到离的能量发动的时候，革的意念就会在革的时势当中，被放大到最有力量的状态，所以努力前行会有嘉美的结果。

[Illuminating Intentionality]

The *Book of Changes* tells people that things must be done in accordance with the cycles of heaven, as major changes especially are closely related to seasonal periods, because time itself has its energy. The ancestors marked these energy scales and the transformation relationships between them through the calendar. If this can be used for oneself, one can find the opportunity to maximize energy, so that one can get twice the result with half the effort. It can be seen that the application of the *Book of Changes* is an opportunistic art that pays attention to the coordination between humanity and heaven.

The situation of the Nine (*yang*/strong line) in the first place does not allow for change, and one must wait. By the time of the Six (*yin*/soft line) in the second place, the time is ripe and the time for change and reform has arrived. The Najia theory uses Ji (the sixth of the ten Heavenly Stems) to accompany Trigram Li in expressing the energy state of the time. When the energy of Trigram Li is initiated, the intention of revolution will be amplified to the most powerful state in the current situation of reform, so working hard will have wonderful results.

九三：征凶，贞厉。革言三就，有孚。

《象》曰："革言三就"，又何之矣？

【明译】

九三：急于征进必有凶险，静守不动则有危厉，改革虽已多次宣告小有成功，但还要继续取信于民。

《象传》说：改革已多次宣告小有成功，九三（除了继续改革）还有其他路可走吗？

Nine (*yang*/strong line) in the third place: There is danger in rushing forward, and there is danger in staying still. Although the reform has been declared a small success many times, it still needs to continue to win the trust of the people.

The *Image Commentary* (*Xiang Zhuan*) says: The reform has been declared a small success many times. Is there any other way to go for the Nine (*yang*/strong line) in the third place (other than continuing the reform)?

【明意】

既然已经改革了一半，除了继续改革，就没有其他路可以走了。意向性的前进与对形势的改变，需要十分小心谨慎。意向在等革的时机，而革的时机需要通过对形势的领悟而展开。自己多次通过小的变革来积累形势，但需要积累变革的力量，并一直等待变革的时机。真正的变革需要多方理解和领会形势的能量，在其中寻找自己意向延展的空间。

意念在发动之前要隐忍待时，待形势之变化而行，在发动之前不可表现出来，因之意向性总是待境而实化。所以对于待境的时机，要极度敏感而小心，这需要有巨大的自制力。面对改革到半途的形势，已经没有退路，唯有把改革进行到底。所以改革作为意念之行的整体性变化，个中分寸的拿捏和把握，非常考验改革者控制意念的分寸和时刻自省自察意念实化的能力。

[Illuminating Intentionality]

Now that half of the reform has been completed, there is no other way to go but to continue the process. Intentional progress and changes in situations require great caution. Intentionality waits for the opportunity for revolution, and the opportunity for revolution needs to be unfolded through an understanding of the situation. One has developed the situation through small changes and reforms many times, but still needs to accumulate the power of change and wait for the opportunity for change.

Real change requires multiple parties to understand and appreciate the energy of the situation, and find space within it for the extension of one's own intentions.

One must be patient and wait for the situation to change before intentions are initiated, and they cannot be expressed before they are initiated. Therefore, intentionality always waits for a situation to be realized. Therefore, one must be extremely sensitive and careful about the timing of situations, which requires tremendous self-control. Faced with the situation where the reform is halfway through, there is no path of retreat, and one can only carry out the reform to the end. Therefore, reform is an overall change in the journey of intentions, and the proper grasp of it is a great test of the reformer's ability to control intentions and the ability to self-reflect and realize one's intentions at all times.

九四：悔亡。有孚改命，吉。

《象》曰："改命"之"吉"，信志也。

【明译】

九四：不要忧虑悔恨，只要取信于民，就能够改变旧的天命，会是吉利的。

《象传》说：改变旧的天命吉祥，因为九四诚心诚意顺天应人。

Nine (*yang*/strong line) in the fourth place: There is no need for worry or regret, since as long as one wins the trust of the people, one can change the old heavenly mandate and it will be auspicious.

The *Image Commentary* (*Xiang Zhuan*) says: Changing the old heavenly mandate is auspicious, because the Nine (*yang*/strong line) in the fourth place is sincere, obeys heaven and responds to the people.

【明意】

这是相信民心的政治哲学，但相信民心从来都是意念变革的托辞。真正的民心只能构成变革意念的境遇和相应的能量而已，并不能直接导致变革的发生。总是那些能够明了民之心境，善于整合民心民意的人意念发动，才能够改变整体性的意念之境。

意念之行当顺应人天之意境，而改变情境之革最根本还是要从心念开始，主导革命者的心意可延伸至人民全体。

[Illuminating Intentionality]

This is a political philosophy that believes in the intentions and minds of the people, but believing in the intentions and minds of the people has always been an excuse for ideological change. True public sentiment can only constitute the situation and corresponding energy for the intention of change, but it cannot directly lead to the occurrence of change. Only those who are able to understand the people's state of intentionality and are good at integrating the people's intentions and heart-minds can change the overall state of intentionality by initiating their intentions.

The implementation of intentions should conform to the intentional context of humanity and heaven, and the revolution that changes the situation must fundamentally start from intentions, and the intentionality of leading revolutionaries can be extended to the entire people.

九五：大人虎变，未占有孚。

《象》曰："大人虎变"，其文炳也。

【明译】

九五：大人以猛虎之威势推行变革，不用占决便能赢得民心。

《象传》说：大人以猛虎之威势推行变革，他的文功武略彪炳天下。

Nine (*yang*/strong line) in the fifth place: The great man uses the authority of a fierce tiger to implement changes and reforms, and wins the intentions and heart-minds of the people without having to make decisions.

The *Image Commentary* (*Xiang Zhuan*) says: The great man carries out changes and reforms with the authority of a fierce tiger, and one's literary and military skills shine throughout the world under heaven.

【明意】

大人的意念合于时势，利用对民众的孚信而构筑了变革的时势，并且不用占决就可以获得民心的支持，也就是自己可以通过意念把握合适的变革时机，天下望风而从，不必占问，自然风行草偃，心悦诚服。

[Illuminating Intentionality]

The great man's intentions are in line with the current situation, and one uses one's trust in the people to build the trend of change, so one can gain the support of the people without having to make decisions. In other words, one can seize the appropriate opportunity for change through one's intentions, and the world under heaven will follow suit without one's having to take decisions. Without asking by divination, it is natural that the grass bends when the wind blows, and heart-minds are sincerely convinced.

上六：君子豹变，小人革面，征凶，居贞吉。

《象》曰："君子豹变"，其文蔚也。"小人革面"，顺以从君也。

【明译】

上六：君子以斑豹之势力助大人完成变革，小人纷纷洗心革面，此时若继续激进征进不止会有凶险，居于正位保持正道才能吉利。

《象传》说：君子以斑豹之势力助大人（九五）完成变革，文采华美犹如斑豹花纹一样光彩照人；小人纷纷洗心革面，是表面顺从变革的君主。

Six (*yin*/soft line) in the top place: The exemplary person uses the power of the spotted leopard to help the great man complete the transformation, and the petty people change their minds one after another. If one continues to aggressively advance at this time, there will be more than just dangers. Only by staying in the right position and maintaining the right *dao* can it be auspicious.

The *Image Commentary* (*Xiang Zhuan*) says: The exemplary person uses the power of the leopard to help the great man (the Nine (*yang*/strong line) in the fifth place) complete the reform, and one's literary talent is as radiant as the leopard's pattern; the petty people change their minds one after another, and appear to obey the changes and reforms of the monarch.

【明意】

君子革心，小人革面，革心才是真正的、立即的改变，是意向性合于时机并对其境遇作迅速的改变。心境可以合于时机迅速改变，好像超越时空条件，灵活机动。君子以心转境，小人依境转面，只是把面对情境的那一面改变了，但内里心意发动的机制并没有根本性的变化。不过意念之行的实化皆在时空之中，仍旧要受时空条件的制约。

革命进展到了最后，不可继续革命，反而要缓解革命的形势，继续革命将使得民不聊生，社会无法安定，民生得不到发展。意向性的展开，或意向性过程的展开，时刻都在时机之中，而变革性的意念发动对情境的改变，有着最为强烈的时机化意味。看历史事件的记录特别明显地说明这一点，也就是总是在某些时间节点上，历史事件惊人相似地重复着，甚至周期性地重复。这是因为人世的阴阳之意，不可能跳出天地阴阳之力的大势，所以人事的革故鼎新与天时更迭的确存在密切关系。

[Illuminating Intentionality]

An exemplary person changes one's heart-mind, while a petty person changes one's face. Only reforming the heart-mind is a real and immediate change, which is the intention to adapt to opportunities and make a rapid change in one's situation. The state of the heart-mind can change quickly according to opportunities, as if it transcends spatio-temporal conditions and is flexible. An exemplary person uses one's heart-mind to transform one's situation, while a petty person relies on one's situation to transform one's face, only changing the side facing the situation, while there is no fundamental change in the initiation mechanism of inner intentions. However, the concretization of intentions is all in time and space, and is still restricted by the conditions of time and space.

When the revolution has reached the end, it is not possible to continue with it. Instead, it is necessary to alleviate the revolutionary situation. Continuing the revolution will mean the people are unable to make a living, the society cannot be stable, and the people's livelihood cannot be developed. The unfolding of intentionality, or the unfolding of the intentional process, is always subject to timing, and the initiating of transformative intentions to change a situation has the strongest sense of timing. Looking at the records of historical events clearly illustrates this point, that is, at certain points in time, historical events repeat themselves with striking similarity, even periodically. This is because the *yin* and *yang* intentionality of the human world cannot escape the general trend of the *yin* and *yang* intentionality of heaven and earth. Therefore, there is indeed a close relationship between the reform and renewal of human affairs and the changes of heaven and earth.

火风鼎（卦五十）　（巽下离上）

Ding (Establishment), Fire and Wind (Hexagram 50)　(Xun below, Li above)

　　鼎既是变革食物最为方便之具，又是国家重器，需要谨慎使用。作为权力的象征，不可大权独揽，而应利益均沾。治国之术与烹饪之术本来异曲同工。烹饪之术的核心之一是对食物保持谨慎和敬意，对食材悉心处理，细心当中带着慎重，君王治国也要如此运用烹饪之术，对于圣贤保持深重的敬意，以最高超的烹调之术来礼遇国之重臣。鼎作为国之重器，也是盛祭品的容器，祭祀之后的食品要尽快分与众人，象征权力和利益的共享，否则众人争而食之，不仅食物不可能独占，而且象征权力的鼎也未必保得住。所以君王以敬畏之心烹养圣贤，为的是改善民生，凝聚民心，此谓"正位凝命"，也就是通过正己之心意，疏导端正天下之意缘意向，如一盘散沙之中，疏导出人心洪流之方向，也因此重新塑造心灵活动之范型，成为他心所向的根据。所谓一言九鼎，是心意发动于言，如鼎挺立，昭示天下，百姓见之，心向有归。鼎立新的心之意向，就是于旧的背景之中重塑更好的范型，改造原有的家庭、社会与教育范型，从而重塑旧缘，改变心向的方向，也就能够鼎立新命。

　　鼎卦涉及命的凝结与心的凝聚的关系。命是生命的大方向，是每一个瞬间的意向凝结而成。命凝结成为某种范型：家庭、社会与教育的范型等，引导命运的方向。心灵意向的范型则通过意向的凝结过程来规范意念发动状态的范型，所以要正位凝命，正己正缘，开始正意的人生，让理想的命运状态时刻引导意向，让意向在理想的缘生状态，即想要鼎立的范型状态展开，使理想的命运状态真正成为当下意向的延伸和汇聚。

A tripod cauldron is not only the most convenient tool for changing and reforming food, but also an important implement of the state, so it needs to be used with caution. As a symbol of power, it should not monopolize power, but should share the benefits. The art of governing a country and the art of cooking are essentially the same. One of the cores of cooking is to be cautious and respectful towards food, and to handle the ingredients with care and prudence. A king should also use cooking skills to govern a country, maintain deep respect for the sages, and use the most superb cooking skills in coming to greet the important ministers of the state with ceremony. As an important implement of the state, the tripod cauldron is also a vessel for holding sacrifices. The food after the sacrifice must be distributed to everyone as soon as possible to symbolize the sharing of power and interests; otherwise, everyone will fight to eat it, and it will not only be impossible to monopolize the food, but the tripod cauldron, which symbolizes power, will not necessarily be held onto. Therefore, the king cultivates the sages with reverence in order to improve the people's livelihood and unite the people's intentions. This is called "correcting the position and consolidating the mandate," that is, by rectifying one's own intention, one channels the will and intention of rectifying the world, just like a plate of scattered sand. The direction of the human heart-mind's torrent also reshapes the pattern of spiritual activities and becomes the basis for one's heart-mind's direction. The phrase "one word and nine tripod cauldrons" means that intentionality is initiated by words, like a tripod standing upright, showing the world under heaven. When the people see this, they will have their intentions set on their destination. The intention of establishing a new heart-mind is to reshape a better model amidst the old background, to transform the original family, society and education model, and thereby to reshape the old conditions, changing the direction of the heart-mind, and thus being able to establish a new mandate.

Hexagram Ding (Establishment) involves the relationship between the condensation of fate and the condensation of the heart-mind. Fate is the general direction of life and is the condensed intention of every moment. Fate condenses into a certain paradigm: the paradigm of family, society, education, etc., which guides the direction of fate. The paradigm of mental intention standardizes the paradigm of the state of intentionality initiation through the condensation process of intention. Therefore, we must focus on the right position, lead a righteous life, and start a righteous life, letting the ideal state of fate guide the intentions at all times, and let the intentions be in the right place. The ideal state of dependent co-arising, that is, the paradigm state of wanting to be in harmony, unfolds, making the ideal state of fate truly an extension and convergence of current intentions.

鼎，元吉，亨。

《彖》曰：鼎，象也。以木巽火，亨（pēng）饪也。圣人亨以享上帝，而大亨以养圣贤。巽而耳目聪明，柔进而上行，得中而应乎刚，是以"元亨"。

《象》曰：木上有火，鼎。君子以正位凝命。

【明译】

鼎卦象征鼎立新风。大吉大利，亨通顺畅。

《彖传》说：鼎卦整体取自鼎器的象形。下卦巽为木为顺，上卦离为火，把木材放入火中，让它顺从火的燃烧，就是烹煮食物的情状。圣人烹饪食物来祭享天帝，并烹煮丰盛食物来供养圣贤。谦逊恭顺耳目聪明，柔顺地向上升进，取得中位并与刚强者相应，因此大为亨通。

《象传》说：下卦巽为木，上卦离为火，木头上面火焰在燃烧，好像鼎器在烹煮食物，君子看到这种现象，就知道要摆正自己的位置，凝聚心力，以成就自己的使命。

Hexagram Ding (Establishment) symbolizes the establishment of a new ethos. Good fortune and prosperity.

The *Judgment Commentary* (*Tuan Zhuan*) says: The whole Hexagram Ding (Establishment) is taken from an image of a tripod cauldron. The lower Trigram Xun represents wood and the upper Trigram Li represents fire, so putting wood into the fire and letting it obey the burning of the fire is the situation of cooking food. The sage cooks food to offer sacrifices to the Emperor of Heaven, and cooks sumptuous food to support the sages and worthies. One is humble and respectful, one's ears and eyes are bright, one moves upwards meekly, one achieves the middle position and responds to the strong, so one will be very prosperous.

The *Image Commentary* (*Xiang Zhuan*) says: The lower Trigram Xun is wood, the upper Trigram Li is fire. The flames on the wood are burning, like a cauldron cooking food. When an exemplary person sees this phenomenon, one knows to correct one's position and concentrate one's energy to achieve one's mission.

【明意】

鼎卦取具体物之象。古代最早的鼎是陶制的、用来烧煮饭羹的烹炊器，在人类开始用火之后，用鼎能把生的食物煮熟，于是人们把鼎看成获取新食物的器具，赋予其"取新"之意。后来贵族用青铜铸鼎，形制越来越大，数量越来越多，平民无力与贵族的鼎器相比，鼎又被看成重器，甚至变成权力的象征。商周时期，九鼎易主被看成改朝换代的标志，鼎又有废旧立新之意。上卦是革除旧王朝的天命，这一卦鼎就是新王朝建立。所以大吉大利，亨通顺畅。

鼎卦取六爻全象，初六为鼎腿，二三四刚爻为鼎腹，六五柔爻如鼎的两耳，上九刚爻如扣鼎的铉。下巽（木，风）上离（火），是木柴点着火吹风做饭之象，所以说是烹煮食物。圣人烹制食物祭享天帝，食物丰盛是为了养育圣贤，圣贤是国家的支柱。

从铸鼎的过程引申出君子要体会如摆正范型一样摆正自己的位置，如冷却凝固成型一样凝聚自己和民众的心力和意志。凝的根本是凝聚心力，或者是意志力，意念力，不是其他的。人所能凝聚的就是意念的力量，用意念的力量改换天地之间的阴阳变化。

一个国家的建立和完整性的维持，可能不得不依托于军事力量，但一个社会的鼎立，却不可以过分依赖强权和武力。所以休养民生，使民心民意得以鼎立才是根本。这就要让民心民意鼎立起来才有方向，也需要给百姓指出方向。

[Illuminating Intentionality]

Hexagram Ding (Establishment) takes the image of a specific object. The earliest tripod cauldron in ancient times was a pottery cooking vessel used for cooking rice soup. After humans began to use fire, the tripod cauldron could be used to cook raw food. Therefore, people regarded the tripod cauldron as a tool for obtaining new food and endowed it with the meaning of "getting the new." Later, the nobles used bronze to make tripod cauldrons, and their shapes became larger and larger. There were more and more people, and the common people were unable to compare with the tripod cauldrons of the nobles. The tripod cauldron was regarded as an important implement and even became a symbol of power. During the Shang and Zhou dynasties, the change of ownership of the Nine Tripod Cauldrons was regarded as a symbol of dynastic change, so the tripod cauldron also had the meaning of abolishing the old and establishing the new. The previous hexagram shows the heavenly mandate to abolish an old dynasty, and this hexagram shows the establishment of a new dynasty; hence it means good fortune and prosperity.

Hexagram Ding (Establishment) takes six lines as the whole image, the Six (*yin*/soft line) in the first place is the legs of the tripod cauldron, the second, third and fourth *yang*/strong lines are the belly of the tripod cauldron, the Six (*yin*/soft line) in the fifth place is like the two ears of the tripod cauldron, and the Nine (*yang*/strong line) in the top place is like the clasps of the tripod cauldron. Trigrams Xun (wood, wind) below and Li (fire) above are the image of lighting firewood and blowing the wind for cooking, so it is said to be cooking food. Sages cook food to offer sacrifices to the Emperor of Heaven. The abundance of food is to nourish sages, who are the pillars of the country.

From the process of casting a tripod cauldron, it can be derived that an exemplary person should understand that one should rectify one's own position as if one's were forming the shape of sand, and that one should gather one's own and the people's intentions and wills as if they were cooled and solidified into shape. The essence of condensation is concentration of mental power, or willpower, or intentional power, and nothing else. What people can gather is the power of intentions, and use the power of intentions to change the *yin* and *yang* changes between heaven and earth.

The establishment and maintenance of a country's integrity may have to rely on military power, but the establishment of a society cannot rely too much on power and force. Therefore, it is fundamental to maintain people's livelihood and maintain the people's intentions and heart-minds. This requires the people's intentions and heart-minds to be established in order to have a direction, and it also needs to point out the direction to the common people.

初六：鼎颠趾，利出否。得妾以其子，无咎。

《象》曰："鼎颠趾"，未悖也。"利出否"，以从贵也。

【明译】

初六：鼎腿颠倒，把鼎器翻个朝上，有利于倾倒出滞塞之物，这就好像（正妻不能生育），于是把生了儿子的小妾扶正（取代正妻），没有问题。

《象传》说：鼎腿颠倒，把鼎器翻个朝上，并未违背常理。有利于倾倒出滞塞之物，这是初六（妾）随从贵人（九二），母以子贵。

Six (*yin*/soft line) in the first place: The legs of the tripod cauldron are upside down. Turning the tripod cauldron upside down helps to pour out things that are stuck. This is like (one's first wife not being able to have children), so if a concubine who gave birth to a son is put upright (replacing the first wife), there is no problem.

The *Image Commentary* (*Xiang Zhuan*) says: Turning the tripod cauldron upside down does not violate common sense if the legs of the tripod are upside down. This is helpful for pouring out stagnant things. This is the Six (*yin*/soft line) in the first place (the concubine) following the nobleman (the Nine (*yang*/strong line) in the second place), and a mother becoming noble thanks to her son.

【明意】

鼎立新风即鼎立新的意向，这其实是通过颠倒和换人来实现的，所以无法抽象讨论如何鼎立，而是通过现实现象琢磨出来的意向以改变风气。这不是通过反省就可以的，需要对相关的人事等各种因素都重新调整才行。

革故鼎新之时，自然重新谋篇布局，用新人换旧人，对既有利益格局重新分配，把旧局倾倒出来，洗刷后布新局，这是正常情况。新的格局出现，就有一批新的贵人。新主之前的众多失败，此刻也像清洗鼎器一般一扫而空。成功鼎立的新主，常常不是从胜利走向胜利，而是从不断失败中挺立，坚持到底，犹如妾的地位虽然好像一直很低，但有了儿子之后，就可能被扶正为妻。可见新主之前经历无数失败，饱受压抑，但位置扶正之后，力图鼎立新风，改变局面，从来都是正常且自然的过程。

[Illuminating Intentionality]

To establish a new ethos is to establish a new intentional direction, and this is actually achieved through inversion and substitution. Therefore, it is impossible to discuss how to establish a new ethos in the abstract, since how to change an ethos through intention can only be figured out through real phenomena. It cannot be done through introspection, since it requires readjustment of relevant personnel and other factors.

When reforming the old, it is natural to rethink the layout, replace old people with new, redistribute the existing interest pattern, cast aside the old pattern, and clean up the new pattern, so this is a normal situation. When a new pattern emerges, there will be a new group of noble people. The new ruler's many previous failures are now swept away like cleaning a cauldron. A new ruler who successfully establishes himself often does not go from victory to victory, but rises up through constant failures and perseveres to the end, just like a concubine whose status seems to have been very low, but after having a son, may be promoted to a wife. It can be seen that the new ruler has experienced numerous failures before and suffered from depression, but after correcting his position, he strives to establish a new ethos and change the situation. This has always been a normal and natural process.

九二：鼎有实，我仇有疾，不我能即，吉。
《象》曰："鼎有实"，慎所之也。"我仇有疾"，终无尤也。

【明译】

九二：鼎中充满实物（犹如内心充实而有实力），我的仇人虽然嫉恨我，但也不能拿我怎么样，还是吉祥的。

《象传》说：鼎中充满实物，犹如（有儿子而）内心充实而有实力，可以审慎适中地来去。我的仇人（六五，前妻）虽然嫉恨我，但最后不需要过分担心忧虑。

Nine (*yang*/strong line) in the second place: The tripod cauldron is full of real things (as if the heart-mind is full and powerful). Although one's enemies hate one, they can't do anything, and it is still auspicious.

The *Image Commentary* (*Xiang Zhuan*) says: The tripod cauldron is full of real objects, just like (having a son) who is mentally full and powerful, and can come and go with caution and moderation. Although one's enemy (the Six (*yin*/soft line) in the fifth place, the former wife) hates one, in the end there is no need to worry too much.

【明意】

九二是鼎腹之中，代表肚子里有货，有内涵、有实力的人不会随意不择手段做事情，而愿意等待六五来启用自己。卦变当中如没有九二的出让，就无法成就六五之位，按理说六五也应该记挂九二的恩德。

有实力的人意向发动要从己从人，等待他人意向的应和，需要忍耐等待时机，不接受挑衅，心意不为他意扰动。相信自己的实力别人无法挑战。这样，有实力的人的意向难以受到干扰，他们意向之发自然就会深思熟虑。

[Illuminating Intentionality]

The Nine (*yang*/strong line) in the second place is in the belly of the tripod cauldron, which means that there is something in one's belly. People with intension and strength will not do things casually and by any means, but are willing to wait for the Six (*yin*/soft line) in the fifth place to initiate itself. Without the Nine (*yang*/strong line) in the second place's transfer during the hexagram-changes, the Six (*yin*/soft line) in the fifth place would not be able to achieve the position of Six (*yin*/soft line) in the fifth place. Logically speaking, the Six (*yin*/soft line) in the fifth place should also remember the Nine (*yang*/strong line) in the second place's kindness.

A powerful person must act according to oneself and others, and wait for the response of others' intentions. One must be patient and wait for an opportunity, not accept provocations, and not be disturbed by other people's intentions. One should believe that others cannot challenge one's own strength. In this way, the intentions of powerful people are difficult to disturb, and their intentions will naturally be carefully considered.

九三：鼎耳革，其行塞，雉膏不食，方雨，亏悔，终吉。

《象》曰："鼎耳革"，失其义也。

【明译】

九三：鼎耳脱落了，无法移动鼎器，行动因此受到阻塞，以致于无法品尝美味可口的野鸡汤，还好正赶上下雨，大家消除了懊恼，最终是吉祥的。

《象传》说：鼎耳脱落了，九三也就失去了鼎耳本来可以用来抬鼎的意义。

Nine (*yang*/strong line) in the third place: The ears of the tripod cauldron fall off, and it cannot be moved. As a result, movement was blocked, so the delicious pheasant soup cannot be tasted. Fortunately, it happens to rain, and everyone eliminates their worries, and it is auspicious in the end.

The *Image Commentary* (*Xiang Zhuan*) says: When the tripod cauldron's ears fall off, the Nine (*yang*/strong line) in the third place also loses the intentionality of the ears that could have been used to lift it.

【明意】

个人意向如何在大局中隐忍待时，意向要顺境转化。九三本来是有本事之人，但进入大局之后，自己的才能被埋没且显得不重要了。需要自己保护自己，虽然在革命成功之后的内部复杂矛盾斗争中暂时还处于下风，但最后可以吉顺。

在剧烈的意向交错情境之中，可能个人的实力不彰，个人的意向可能在大局中不显，变得不重要了，但也不可妄自菲薄，要学会保守自身，隐忍待时，等待真正突破的时刻到来。这是意向的时机化转化。

[Illuminating Intentionality]

In making one's personal intentions in an overall situation enduring and patient, intentions should transform smoothly following their context. The Nine (*yang*/strong line) in the third place was originally a capable person, but after entering the overall situation, one's talents were buried and one became unimportant. One needs to protect oneself. Although one is still at a disadvantage in the complex internal contradictions and struggles after the success of the revolution, one can be successful in the end.

In a situation of intensely intertwined intentions, one's personal strength may not be evident, and one's personal intentions may not show up in the overall situation and one may become unimportant. However, one must not belittle oneself. One must learn to protect oneself, be patient and wait for the real breakthrough moment to come. This is a timed transformation of intention.

九四：鼎折足，覆公餗（sù），其形渥，凶。

《象》曰："覆公餗"，信如何也？

【明译】

九四：鼎足折断了，王公的美食倒出来了，搞得鼎身龌龊，凶险。

《象传》说：王公的美食倒出来了，九四怎么能够取得信任呢？

Nine (*yang*/strong line) in the fourth place: The legs of the tripod cauldron are broken, and the prince's delicacies are poured out, making the tripod cauldron dirty, so there is danger.

The *Image Commentary* (*Xiang Zhuan*) says: The prince's delicacies being poured out, how can the Nine (*yang*/strong line) in the fourth place gain trust?

【明意】

意向展开之时，内力不足可能适得其反，所以对于意念内在的力度，自己要有把握的尺度，因为自己对于意向的内在把握与展示的机缘都一样重要。

当人有机会彰显自己的意向之时，反而不可以过度展示，以致明枪易躲暗箭难防，导致大的挫败，而根本在于自己的意念的力度不足以支撑其所希望达到的境遇，导致现实的阴阳之气（力）不能如自己的阴阳之意来运作。

[Illuminating Intentionality]

When an intention is unfolding, insufficient internal strength may be counterproductive, so one must have a measure of confidence in the inner strength of one's intention, because one's inner grasp of an intention is as important as the opportunity to display it.

When people have the opportunity to express their intentions, they should not over-exhibit them, so that it is easy to hide and conceal their intentions, leading to great frustration. The fundamental reason is that their own intentions are not strong enough to support the situation they hope to achieve, resulting in the actual *yin* and *yang* energy (power) not operating like their own *yin* and *yang* intentionality.

六五：鼎黄耳金铉，利贞。

《象》曰："鼎黄耳"，中以为实也。

【明译】

六五：鼎器配了金黄色的鼎耳，坚固的鼎杠，保持坚固是有利的。

《象传》说：鼎器配了金黄色的鼎耳，六五在中位，能够保持坚实。

Six (*yin*/soft line) in the fifth place: The tripod cauldron is equipped with golden ears and a strong pole. It is beneficial to keep it strong.

The *Image Commentary* (*Xiang Zhuan*) says: The tripod is equipped with golden ears, and the Six (*yin*/soft line) in the fifth place is in the middle, so it can remain solid.

【明意】

六五变上来居于中正之位，意向之力相对强固，意念坚实足以打破原有的意境总体格局。掌控和分配权力者的意向对主体意境的塑造有较大影响。在位者鼎立有实力，意念坚实如鼎立天下之象，坚实有力的意向是王位的配置，也是鼎立天下的来源。家国社会的意识境域是由一些掌控家国重器的大人们的意向所分割和调控的，但鼎立新风的主政者要有坚实的意向改变原有的意识境域。

[Illuminating Intentionality]

The Six (*yin*/soft line) in the fifth place is in the middle position, its power of intention is relatively strong, and the intention is solid enough to break the original overall pattern of the intentional context. The intention of those who control and distribute power has a great influence on the shaping of a subject's intentional context. The person in power is established and powerful, and one's intentions are as solid as the image of the world under heaven by the tripod cauldron. Solid and powerful intentions are the configuration of the throne and the source of the world under heaven established by the tripod cauldron. The conscious realm of the family, country, and society is divided and regulated by the intentions of certain great people who control the important implements of the family and the country, but the leaders who establish a new ethos must have a solid intention to change the original conscious realm.

上九：鼎玉铉，大吉，无不利。

《象》曰："玉铉"在上，刚柔节也。

【明译】

上九：鼎上配着玉制的鼎杠，非常吉祥，没有什么不利。

《象传》说：玉制的鼎杠在上面，是刚柔相济，节制得宜。

Nine (*yang*/strong line) in the top place: The tripod cauldron is equipped with a jade pole, which is very auspicious and has no disadvantages.

The *Image Commentary* (*Xiang Zhuan*) says: The jade pole is on the top, which is a combination of the strong and the soft, with appropriate control.

【明意】

鼎上面配上用玉作成的铉，显得有刚柔相济之感，鼎是青铜重器，用金玉作铉，相当珍贵，非常吉祥，没有什么不利。另外，鼎是祭祀天帝的重器，在上爻这个宗庙位最接近天帝，能够让天帝得到馨享而福佑天下，所以非常吉祥，没有不利。上位通于神明，玉也是事天之器，代表人意与天意沟通之物。古人认为，玉不仅珍贵，还有温润高雅的特性。用金作铉太刚，以玉为铉则刚柔合度。

上九代表退出权力境域的前朝大佬，他们的权力不再，但意向发动还是能够有所影响，如果能够跟在位的六五配合好，就可能够发挥较大的影响力。意向之发当随顺和配合主事者的意境。上九要与六五配合，意念发动才能够虚实搭配，刚柔有节，既不过分刚硬，也不过分柔弱无力。

[Illuminating Intentionality]

The tripod cauldron is topped with a jade-made handle, which gives it a sense of strength and softness. The tripod cauldron is a heavy bronze vessel and is made of gold and jade. It is quite precious, very auspicious, and has no disadvantages. In addition, the tripod is an important tool for worshiping the Emperor of Heaven. The ancestral temple in the top line is closest to the Emperor of Heaven. It can allow the Emperor of Heaven to enjoy and bless the world, so it is very auspicious and has no disadvantages. The top position is connected to the divine light, and jade is also a tool for serving heaven, representing the communication between human intentions and heaven's intentions. The ancients believed that jade is not only precious, but also has gentle and elegant properties. Using gold as a handle is too strong, but using jade as a handle is a combination of the strong and the soft.

The Nine (*yang*/strong line) in the top place represents former leaders who have withdrawn from the realm of power. They no longer have power, but they can still have an influence through their intentions. If they can cooperate well with the reigning Six (*yin*/soft line) in the fifth place, they may be able to exert greater influence. The expression of intention should be in compliance with the intentional context of the person in charge. The Nine (*yang*/strong line) in the top place must be coordinated with the Six (*yin*/soft line) in the fifth place, and only by initiating intentionality can the empty and the full be matched, and rigidity and softness be measured, neither too rigid nor too weak.

震为雷（卦五十一） （震下震上）
Zhen (Shaking), Thunder (Hexagram 51)   (Zhen below, Zhen above)

　　震之生生为缘生之本。意缘发动的后天结构符合后天八卦的顺序。以震之动为缘论，是先天数转为后天数的临界点，因为心意发动之前，存在都在先天数理的运作过程之中，心意发动落实之后，则进入后天数理的状态。先后天之数并非割裂，而是时时刻刻相互转化，先天生为后天，后天含先天之数，故以震之生为缘生之本。

　　如果把意比作太阳，那么意缘可以是飘忽的云，大地是意识之境，意识照到的范围是意量。太阳本身生生不息，有内在的能量和无限的可能性，充满各种意能。意缘（云）构成了天空的气象万千，而意量离不开云的变化（空气水汽）。意向是从太阳到大地的方向，意行是从太阳的光行到大地的过程。意识是因为有意境，有意识而后有意行，有意行而后有意量。

　　The shaking break of production and reproduction is the foundation of life and dependent co-arising. The post-celestial structure of intentional dependence (*yiyuan*意缘) initiation conforms to the post-celestial order of the Eight Trigrams. Taking a shaking break as the precondition is the critical point for the transformation of pre-celestial numbers into post-celestial numbers, because before intentionality is initiated, existence is in the process of the operation of pre-celestial numbers. After intentionality is initiated, it enters the state of post-celestial numbers. The pre-celestial and post-celestial numbers are not separated, but transform into each other all the time. The pre-celestial produces and becomes post-celestial, and the post-celestial contains the pre-celestial numbers. Therefore, the shaking break of production is the foundation of life and dependent co-arising.

If the intentionality is compared to the sun, then intentional dependence can be the floating clouds, the earth the realm of consciousness, and the scope of conscious illumination the capacity of intention. The sun itself is endless, has inner energy and infinite possibilities, and is full of all kinds of intentions. Intentional dependence (clouds) constitutes the myriad weather patterns in the sky, and intentionality is inseparable from the changes in clouds (air water vapor). Intention direction is the direction from the sun to the earth, and intentional motion is the process of light from the sun to the earth. Consciousness comes from having an intentional conception, being conscious is followed by intentional action, and intentional action is followed by intentional capacity.

震，亨。震来虩（xì）虩，笑言哑（yā）哑，震惊百里，不丧匕鬯（chàng）。

《彖》曰："震，亨"。"震来虩虩"，恐致福也。"笑言哑哑"，后有则也。"震惊百里"，惊远而惧迩也。"不丧匕鬯"，出可以守宗庙社稷，以为祭主也。

《象》曰：洊雷，震。君子以恐惧修省。

【明译】

震卦象征雷振而起，雷声震动使得万物亨通。震雷袭来令一些人惊惧发抖，惶恐不安，但也能使另一些人处之泰然，言笑如故。比如，即使巨雷能够震惊到方圆百里之远的地方，主持祭祀的太子却镇静如常，手里的木匙和酒杯也没有被震掉。

《彖传》说：雷声震动，使万物亨通。震雷袭来令一些人惊惧发抖，惶恐不安，因恐惧而谨慎可以给人们带来福祉。另一些人处之泰然，言笑如故，是懂得警惕之前的教训，所以会依循处世的正道。巨雷能够震惊到方圆百里之远的地方，是让远方的人震惊，让近处的人知道戒惧。主持祭祀的太子却镇静如常，手里的木匙和酒杯也没有被震掉。国君外出，太子监守宗庙社稷，有能力胜任祭祀典礼的主持人。

《象传》说：雷声隆隆，接二连三打来就是震卦。君子有鉴于雷声轰鸣不断震动的震卦，应当知道恐惧天威，不断反省己过，修行人天之意。

Hexagram Zhen (Shaking) symbolizes the rise of thunder, and the vibration of thunder makes the myriad things prosper. Thunder strikes can make some people tremble with fear and panic, but they can also make other people remain calm, talking and laughing as before. For example, even though a huge thunderclap can shake a place hundreds of miles away, the prince who presides over the sacrifice remains calm, the wooden spoon and wine glass in his hand not being knocked out.

The *Judgment Commentary* (*Tuan Zhuan*) says: The sound of thunder makes the myriad things prosperous. Thunder strikes make some people tremble with fear and panic, and being cautious due to fear can bring happiness to people. Others are calm, talking and laughing as before, because they know how to be wary of previous lessons, so they follow the right *dao* of life. A huge thunderclap can shake a place hundreds of miles away, shaking people far away and letting people nearby know to be wary. The prince who presides over the sacrifice remains calm as usual, and the wooden spoon and wine glass in his hand are not knocked out. When the monarch is away, the prince oversees the ancestral temple and the state, and is capable of hosting the sacrificial ceremony.

The *Image Commentary* (*Xiang Zhuan*) says: The thunder rumbles and claps one after another, and this is Hexagram Zhen (Shaking). An exemplary person should know how to fear the power of heaven, constantly reflect on one's own mistakes, and practice the cosmological intention of humanity and heaven in view of the thunder and roar of Hexagram Zhen (Shaking), which is constantly shaking.

【明意】

人的意向必震于缘，不震动于修身和积德修福之缘，就须震动于一般难以脱身的俗务之缘，附于外缘过多，则最后可能在震天动地的变化到来之时，惊恐失措。人之心意与天地之间的能量交流是一个必须惜缘的系统，平时修行积累品行的人，和平时随波逐流不思积累功德的人，与天地震动之互动的结果往往很不一样。

人因恐惧而修行人天之意，在意缘生起之时戒慎恐惧。强大而连续的天地之动（洊雷）是对心意发动状态的警告，人当于意念发动之处就心存敬畏，不让意念未经反省即与世间之缘发生关联。在意缘发生之前，对意的生发能够有反省的状态是修行的功夫。

[Illuminating Intentionality]

People's intentions must be shaken by their conditions. If they are not shaken by the conditions of self-cultivation and accumulation of virtue and fortune, they must be shaken by the conditions of worldly affairs that are generally difficult to escape from. If they are too attached to external factors, earth-shattering changes may finally come, and at that time, they will be frightened and lose control. The energy exchange between human intentionality and heaven and earth is a system that must be cherished. People who usually practice and accumulate moral character and people who usually drift with the flow without thinking about accumulating merit will often have very different results from their interaction with the vibrations of heaven and earth.

People practice the cosmological intention of humanity and heaven out of fear, and are careful and fearful when the conditions of intentionality arise. The powerful and continuous movement of heaven and earth (thunder) is a warning to the state of intentionality in initiation. People should be in awe wherever intentions are initiated, and not allow intentions to be related to the world without reflection. Before the occurrence of intentions, being able to reflect on the initiation of intention is a matter of effort in practice.

初九：震来虩虩，后笑言哑哑，吉。

《象》曰："震来虩虩"，恐致福也。"笑言哑哑"，"后"有则也。

【明译】

初九：震雷袭来令人惊惧发抖，惶恐不安，但随后也能因为恐惧而使人强化修身，变得处之泰然，言笑如故，所以吉祥。

《象传》说：震雷骤来令人惊惧发抖，惶恐不安，因恐惧而谨慎可以给人们带来福祉。雷声也能够使人强化修身，变得处之泰然，言笑如故，是懂得警惧之前的教训之后，行为就会依循处世的正道。

Nine (*yang*/strong line) in the first place: Thunderclaps can make people tremble with fear and unease, but fear can also make people strengthen their self-cultivation and become calm, talking and laughing as before, so it is auspicious.

The *Image Commentary* (*Xiang Zhuan*) says: A sudden thunderstorm makes people tremble with fear and panic. Being cautious due to fear can bring happiness to people. The sound of thunder can also make people strengthen their self-cultivation, become calm, and speak and laugh as usual. After understanding the lessons before being vigilant, their behavior will follow the right *dao* of life.

【明意】

从雷震而起通于心意之震体会意缘发动和起心动念的艺术，因意缘震动而生发出反省意念震动程度的状态，惊于外缘之震而能迅速反省内心对外缘的驾驭能力，只有内心足够坚强才能有强悍的控制意缘之力。时刻于心动之前，保持戒慎恐惧的状态，于心意将动未动之际，要对于心意实化之前的先行机制保持谨慎节制，因为这个实化的过程其实最为危险，也是心意修行的核心所在，而每一个心意的实化过程，都跟心意相通的缘生情境有关。

[Illuminating Intentionality]

Starting from the thunder and shaking of the mind, one can experience the art of initiating intentional conditions and intentions. Due to the vibration of the mind, one will be in a state of reflecting on the degree of vibration of intention. Being surprised by the shaking of outer conditions, one can quickly reflect on the ability of inner intentionality to control the outer conditions, only if the heart-mind is strong enough can one have the formidable power to control dependent co-arising. Always being cautious and fearful before one's heart beats, when one's intentionality is about to move, one must be cautious and restrained in the preceding mechanism before it materializes, because this process of materialization is actually the most dangerous and is also the core of intentionality practice, and the realization process of every intention is related to the conditional situation between intentionality and the heart-mind.

六二：震来，厉；亿丧贝，跻（jī）于九陵，勿逐，七日得。

《象》曰："震来厉"，乘刚也。

【明译】

六二：震雷骤然袭来，非常危险，丧失大量财宝钱币，赶紧登上九重高峻的陵土之上，不要去追寻（失去的财宝钱币），七天之后将会失而复得。

《象传》说：震雷骤然袭来，非常危险，因为六二乘驾在阳刚之上（卦变中六二骤然来到二位乘凌于初九之上，柔乘刚不顺）。

Six (*yin*/soft line) in the second place: A thunderstorm strikes suddenly, it is very dangerous, and a lot of treasures and coins will be lost. One hurries up the nine-level mausoleum hill, but should not seek (the lost treasures and coins), as they will be lost and recovered in seven days.

The *Image Commentary* (*Xiang Zhuan*) says: A sudden thunderstorm is very dangerous, because the Six (*yin*/soft line) in the second place rides above the *yang*/strong (in the hexagram-changes, the Six (*yin*/soft line) in the second place suddenly comes to the second position above the Nine (*yang*/strong line) in the first place, and for the soft to ride above the strong is not smooth).

【明意】

财产都是身外之物，不应该看得很重。如果把身外之物看得重于身体存在本身，最后一定会把身体消耗和压垮。可是世间很多人追求外在的功名利禄，所花费的时间和精力远甚自己的身体。这是舍本逐末，最后卒以身殉，为天下笑。追求身外之物的过程，是意念实化并于外物上僵死而无生气的过程，即生生不息的意僵死于外物之上，导致生气皆无。这种缘是死缘，不是生缘。

[Illuminating Intentionality]

Property is an external possession and should not be taken seriously. If you value external things more than bodily existence itself, your body will eventually be consumed and crushed. However, many people in the world pursue external fame and wealth, and spend far more time and energy on this than on their own bodies. This is sacrificing one's roots to pursue branches, and in the end, one dies with one's own body and makes the world laugh. The process of pursuing things outside the body is a process in which intentions are concretized and become dead and lifeless on external things. That is, the endless life and productivity of intentionality dies on external things, resulting in no life at all. This kind of dependent co-arising is a dependent co-arising of death, not a dependent co-arising of life.

六三：震苏苏，震行无眚。

《象》曰："震苏苏"，位不当也。

【明译】

六三：被震雷吓得苏苏颤抖，警惧而行，不会有灾眚。

《象传》说：被震雷吓得苏苏颤抖，是六三位置不当（六三进退皆震，以柔居刚也不当）。

Six (*yin*/soft line) in the third place: Being frightened by the thunder, one trembles, but if one acts with caution, there will be no disaster.

The *Image Commentary* (*Xiang Zhuan*) says: That one trembles when frightened by the thunder is due to the improper position of the Six (*yin*/soft line) in the third place (the Six (*yin*/soft line) in the third place is shaken when one advances or retreats, and is also a soft line inappropriately in a strong position).

【明意】

意缘发动与身心安稳有关，心意颤抖是因为对于意缘震动世界的分寸没有把握，知道戒惧反而不容易出错。身体的位置不稳，心意就不安宁。身位依缘而在，依缘而生，是有缘才能维持身体的实存，但当身体的缘不稳，则意缘也会不得安宁，对突然出现的意缘震动得小心应对。

[Illuminating Intentionality]

The initiation of intention is related to the stability of the body and heart-mind, and the trembling intentionality is due to the uncertainty of the scale of the shaking of the world, though knowing fear makes one less likely to make mistakes. If the position of the body is unstable, intentionality will not be peaceful. The body's position depends on conditions, it lives depending on conditions, and only conditions can maintain the existence of the body. However, when the body's conditions are unstable, one's mental conditions will not be peaceful, so one must be careful to deal with sudden vibrations of mental conditions.

九四：震遂泥。

《象》曰："震遂泥"，未光也。

【明译】

九四：雷震之时，惊慌失措，陷坠入泥泞之中。

《象传》说：雷震之时，惊慌失措，陷坠入泥泞之中，因为九四的阳刚还没有达到光大的时势。

Nine (*yang*/strong line) in the fourth place: When thunder strikes, one panics and falls into the mud.

The *Image Commentary* (*Xiang Zhuan*) says: When there is a thunderstorm, people panic and fall into the mud, because the Nine (*yang*/strong line) in the fourth place has not yet reached its prime.

【明意】

如果修养不够，打雷就能把一个人震到泥泞之中去，那他即使很阳刚，也远远没有达到光大的时势。所以时势的形成，根本上是一个人对天地自然运化的应对，如果能够平和无惧，顺应自然，那就可以光大自身的意缘，使人意接近天意，人与天时刻贯通。

因震雷的外缘剧烈震动而导致惊慌失措，也是因为身位不当而无法完全掌握心意的状态，即使要努力戒惧而应对剧烈震荡局面，可是不能做到，那就非常可惜。不过，即使努力自控外缘也可能失控，而一旦失控的时候，对外缘的得失不应过分惊慌失措，因为毕竟还处于时势不光大的时候，那就只能在相应发生的情境中努力自我控制。

[Illuminating Intentionality]

If one is not sufficiently cultivated, a thunderstorm can shake one into the mud. Even if one is very *yang*/strong, one is far from achieving greatness. Therefore, the formation of the current situation is basically a person's response to the natural changes of heaven and earth. If one can be calm and fearless and comply with nature, then one's own intentional conditions can be maximized, so that human intentionality approaches cosmological intentionality, and humanity and heaven are always connected.

The panic caused by the violent shaking of the outer condition of thunder is also caused by the inability to fully grasp the state of intentionality due to improper body position. Even if one tries hard to avoid fear and cope with the violent shaking situation, one cannot do it, which is a great pity. However, even if one tries hard to control oneself, one may still lose control. Once one loses control, one should not panic too much about the gains and losses of the external world, because after all, the situation is still not serious, so one can only try to control oneself in the corresponding situation.

六五：震往来厉，亿无丧，有事。

《象》曰："震往来厉"，危行也。其"事"在中，大"无丧"也。

【明译】

六五：在雷声大震之时，不论上下往来，都有危险，虽然没有损失什么东西，但应该是祭祀上天的时候了。

《象传》说：在雷声大震之时，不论上下往来，都有危险，因为六五冒险行动（震为行）。居尊位行中道举行祭天大典，就不会有大的丧失。

Six (*yin*/soft line) in the fifth place: When strong thunder shakes violently, it is dangerous no matter whether one is going up or coming down. Although nothing is lost, it is time to offer sacrifices to heaven.

The *Image Commentary* (*Xiang Zhuan*) says: When strong thunder shakes violently, it is dangerous no matter whether one is going up or coming down, because the Six (*yin*/soft line) in the fifth place risks taking action (shaking means action). If one holds an honorable position and follows the middle *dao* in holding a ceremony of reverence for heaven, one will not suffer any big losses.

【明意】

即使在震动之险中，心意也要努力接续天机，震动冲击人对意缘的控制力，使之减弱或加强。即使在震动的外缘迅速更换的情境之中，人还是要努力让心意接天，做心意通达天意而正确的事情。

祭祀上天有一种人天相通的宗教情怀，即心意只要努力接天，就可以尽可能把心缘拉回到正当的状态之中，可以避免大的丧失和过度震动带来的厄运。古人相信天人感应，该祭天的时候应该祭天，让心天相通，情势就可能发生转变。

[Illuminating Intentionality]

Even amidst the danger of shaking, intentionality must work hard to continue the heavenly impetus. The shaking affects the person's control over the dependent co-arising of intentions, weakening or strengthening it. Even in a situation where the outer conditions of the shaking are rapidly changing, people still have to work hard to connect their intentions to heaven, and take actions that are clear and correct according to heaven's intentionality.

There is a religious sentiment in offering sacrifices to heaven that connects humanity and heaven. That is, as long as intentionality works hard to connect with heaven, it can bring the heart-mind back to its proper state as much as possible, and avoid big losses and misfortune caused by excessive shaking. The ancients believed in affective resonance between heaven and man, that when it is time to offer sacrifices to heaven, one should offer sacrifices to heaven. If our intentions and heavens are connected, the situation may change.

上六：震索索，视矍（jué）矍，征凶。震不于其躬，于其邻，无咎。婚媾有言。

《象》曰："震索索"，中未得也。虽"凶无咎"，畏"邻"戒也。

【明译】

上六：雷声震动，吓得嗦嗦发抖，畏缩难行，眼神惊恐，仓皇四顾，此时贸然进取，必遭凶厄。但是，只要守正不征，震的后果就不会降到自己身上，而会降到邻居六五那里，所以对自己来说，只要守正就无灾无难。但这个时候如果谈婚论嫁，就会导致言语争执。

《象传》说：雷声震动，吓得嗦嗦发抖，畏缩难行，因为上六未得占据中位，前后失据，心无所归。虽然情势凶险，但最后无灾无难，因为从邻居那里感受到惊畏，从而自己预先有所戒惧。

Six (*yin*/soft line) in the top place: Thunder shakes, causing people to tremble with fright, cowering, unable to move, eyes frightened, looking around hastily. If one dares to advance at this time, one will be met with disaster. However, as long as one keeps upright and doesn't fight, the consequences of the earthquake will not affect oneself, but one's neighbor, the Six (*yin*/soft line) in the fifth place. Therefore, as long as one keeps oneself upright, there will be no disaster. But if one talks about marriage at this time, it will lead to verbal disputes.

The *Image Commentary* (*Xiang Zhuan*) says: The thunder shakes, making people tremble and quiver with fear until they are cowering and unable to move, because the Six (*yin*/soft line) in the top place is not able to occupy the middle position, they lose ground in front and behind, and have nowhere to go. Although the situation is dangerous, there is no disaster in the end, because one feels the fear from one's neighbors, so one is wary in advance.

【明意】

大震动发生之时意缘所生发的状态变动太过剧烈，当然应该预先有所警戒。在心缘剧烈变动发生之前，不可贸然行动，否则必然凶险无比。此时外缘往往不合，容易进退失据，情势危急，当心存敬畏，在"畏"中等待情势的转机。"畏"是因为缘的变动超过心意的掌握，不得不对自然之力心存敬畏，所以对自然力祈祷都是正常的应对状态。预先警戒可以降低对突然发生的震动的惊怖感，而且可以提早做些因应的措施，减缓剧烈变化可能带来的冲击。心理上提早于未发之前做准备是会有帮助的。

[Illuminating Intentionality]

When a big shaking occurs, the state of intentionality changes too fiercely, so of course one should be alert in advance. Before a drastic change in one's heart-mind occurs, one should not act rashly; otherwise it will be extremely dangerous. At this time, the external conditions are often inconsistent, it is easy to lose ground, and the situation is critical. One should be in awe and wait for the situation to turn around in "awe." "Awe" means that the changes in dependent co-arising are beyond the control of intention, and one has to be in awe of the power of nature. Therefore, praying to the power of nature is a normal state of response. Pre-warning can reduce the fear from sudden shaking, and one can take countermeasures in advance to slow down the impact of drastic changes. It helps to prepare mentally well in advance of the event.

艮为山（卦五十二）　（艮下艮上）

Gen (Stopping), Mountain (Hexagram 52)　(Gen below, Gen above)

　　艮在后天八卦为成终而成始之卦，含有万有变化生成的种子，即意念世界实有的种子，或曰世界实有的根本理则。故造量论，以明理则与物事不二，要明物事皆理则上起，而理则需要人意对世界加以领悟才能得知。量论要明白人如何可以意会出范畴，进而意会事物存在为人心意所能把握的分量，即如何从事物源头上悟出存在的真相，因存在皆在意量之中，意量即心意所识量的世界之量。

　　艮宫量论之旨，尴尬处与西方认识论一样，只要谈认识世界，还必须最后落实于言语名相。言语名相是否足以反映世界的本真之相，有实在论、非实在论诸论之争，历代诸家，争讼不断，但止于名相，以为名相逻辑必然能完全映证真如本相，则失之远矣。毕竟名相不过是方便说法，同样的本相之真，可以借助千万种语言与表达方式，故执定言语形式之真，则谬以千里。表达虽不得不止于符号名相，但解悟必须明解透彻，即从性体通天，生生不息之几上理解，方能解悟世界存在之真相。

In the Post-Celestial Eight Trigrams (*houtian bagua* 后天八卦), Gen (mountain) is the trigram of completion and beginning, which contains the seeds of the creation of all changes, that is, the seeds of the reality of the world of intentions, or the fundamental principle of the reality of the world. Therefore, in the creation of an epistemology, in order to show that principle is inseparable from things, it is necessary to understand that the myriad things and events are all principle, and principle needs to be comprehended by people's intentionality in order to be known. An epistemology needs to grasp how people can understand categories and then realize that the existence of things is a component that people can grasp, that is, how to realize the truth of existence from the source of things, because existence is all within the capacity of consciousness, and the capacity of consciousness is what intentionality can grasp of the amount of the world that is known.

The epistemology of Gen (mountain) is the same as Western epistemology in its awkwardness, in that, as long as one talks about understanding the world, one must finally implement it in words, names, and phenomena. There are disputes between realism and non-realism as to whether verbal names and forms are sufficient to reflect the true nature of the world. Various schools in past dynasties argued continually, but they stopped at names and forms, thinking that the logic of names and forms must be able to completely reflect the true nature of things, and were thus far from the truth. After all, names and forms are just convenient expressions, and the same truth can be expressed in thousands of languages and expressions. Therefore, if one insists on the truth of verbal forms, one is seriously mistaken. Although expression has to stop at symbols and names, understanding must be clear and thorough, that is, only by understanding the substance of inherent nature as connecting to heaven, and the subtle inflections of ceaseless production and reproduction, can one understand the truth of the existence of the world.

艮，艮其背，不获其身。行其庭，不见其人，无咎。

《彖》曰：艮，止也。时止则止，时行则行，动静不失其时，其道光明。艮其止，止其所也。上下敌应，不相与也。是以"不获其身，行其庭，不见其人，无咎"也。

《象》曰：兼山，艮。君子以思不出其位。

【明译】

艮卦象征抑制停止，人可以止住自己的背部，但无法操控自己的身体（和心灵），这就好像人可以控制自己在自家的庭院中行走，却无法掌控自己，感知不到自己身体和心灵的活动，倒是不会有什么祸患。

《彖传》说：艮是抑制停止的意思。时机应该停止就要停止，时机应该行动就要行动，运动和静止都不丧失合适的时机，如此则抑制停止的道就会光明灿烂。艮卦的止强调的是抑制静止要适得其所。艮卦六爻上下敌应，同性相斥，彼此都不应合，因此才无法操控自己的身体（和心灵），这就好像人可以控制自己在自家的庭院中行走，却无法掌控自己，感知不到自己身体和心灵的活动，倒也谈不上什么咎害。

《象传》说：两山相并，山外有山就是艮卦。君子有鉴于象征抑制和停止的艮卦，体悟到思考问题不应当超出自己的身位（前面是山，后面也是山，人身被限止在两山之间的地位中，心思活动应该从身位开始，不离其境）。

Hexagram Gen (Stopping) symbolizes restraint and stopping. People can stop their backs, but they cannot control their body (and mind). This is like how people can control themselves walking in their own courtyard, but they cannot control themselves and cannot feel the activity of their own body and mind, yet there is no harm.

The *Judgment Commentary* (*Tuan Zhuan*) says: Hexagram Gen (Stopping) means to restrain and stop. By stopping when the time comes, and acting when the time comes, neither movement nor stillness lose the right time, and in this way, the way to restrain and stop is bright and brilliant. Hexagram Gen (Stopping)'s stopping emphasizes that restraining stillness must be appropriate. The six lines of Hexagram Gen (Stopping) correspond negatively to each other, the same nature repelling each other, and not responding or uniting with each other. Therefore, they cannot control their bodies (and minds). This is like how a person can control oneself to walk in one's own courtyard, but cannot control oneself, in that one cannot perceive the activities of one's own body and mind, yet there is no blame.

The *Image Commentary* (*Xiang Zhuan*) says: Two mountains combine together, and there is a mountain outside the mountain, so this is Hexagram Gen (Stopping). In view of Hexagram Gen (Stopping), which symbolizes restraint and stopping, an exemplary person realizes that in thinking about problems one should not go beyond one's own bodily position (there is a mountain in front of one, and there is also a mountain behind one. The human body is limited to the position between the two mountains, and mental activities should start from the bodily position, not leaving its realm).

【明意】

艮是止意。古文里自动词的用法往往是施受同词。止既是自己停止不动，也是受到制止、限止。象上人在两山之间，人在山中不可不知意之所止，即使不知，心意也无法超越山所设定的界限。所以人当于其意量之分限有清醒的自我意识而不作非分之想。互坎（隐伏）意味着人无法掌控自己，无法感知到自己身体和心灵的活动，这种感觉是一种奇幻感，好像人的感知力突然达到边界而无法突破，虽然有些怪异，不过应该不会有什么祸患。

[Illuminating Intentionality]

Hexagram Gen means stopping. The usage of verbs in ancient Chinese texts is often the same for giving and receiving. Stopping is thus not only stopping oneself, but also being restrained and restricted. As the image above shows, a person is between two mountains, and people in the mountains must know where their intentions stop. Even if they do not know, their intentions cannot go beyond the limits set by the mountains. Therefore, people should have a clear self-awareness of the limits of their intentional capacity and not initiate any unreasonable intentions. Mutual Kan trigrams (hidden) means that people cannot control themselves and cannot perceive the activity of their own bodies and minds. This feeling is a kind of fantasy, as if people's perception suddenly reaches a limit and cannot break through. Although this is a bit strange, there should not and will not be any trouble.

初六：艮其趾，无咎。利永贞。

《象》曰："艮其趾"，未失正也。

【明译】

初六：及时控制住想要迈步的脚趾，这样就无灾无害，有利于永久保持这种能够及时改正、及时抑制错误念头的正道。

《象传》说：及时控制住想要迈步的脚趾，因为初六还没有失去正道（柔爻在下位，符合柔从刚之道）。

Six (*yin*/soft line) in the first place: Control the toes that want to step in time, so that there will be no harm, and it will help to permanently maintain the right *dao* that can correct and suppress wrong intentions in time.

The *Image Commentary* (*Xiang Zhuan*) says: Control the toes that want to step in time, because the right *dao* has not been lost on the Six (*yin*/soft line) in the first place (the soft line is in the lower position, which is in line with the *dao* of softness following strength).

【明意】

艮卦主要从爻位与人体部位对应中取象。初六在全卦最下位，对应人体脚趾部位，是及时控制住想要迈步的脚趾之象。身体靠脚趾来行走，能把脚趾止住不动，全身就不会行走，符合让意念止在该止之处的艮止之道，所以没有什么祸患。

[Illuminating Intentionality]

Hexagram Gen (Stopping) mainly takes its image from the correspondence between the positions of the lines and the parts of the human body. The Six (*yin*/soft line) in the first place is at the lowest position of the hexagram, corresponding to the toes of the human body. It is a symbol of controlling the toes that want to take steps in time. The body walks on the toes, so if the toes can be stopped, the whole body will not move. This is in line with the method of stopping intentionality where it should stop, so there is no harm.

六二：艮其腓，不拯其随，其心不快。

《象》曰："不拯其随"，未退听也。

【明译】

六二：抑制住小腿，不让它抬起来，看到自己心仪的人动了，自己却没法跟随他一起动，心中不畅快。

《象传》说：他想跟随的九五不但不拯救他，还陷他于坎陷之中，又故意把他止住，动弹不得，而且九五还不退回，不愿意听凭形势发展，导致六二没法退回听命于形势发展（心中不快，但无可奈何）。

Six (*yin*/soft line) in the second place: Suppressing the calf to prevent it from lifting up. Seeing the person one likes move but not being able to move with them makes one feel unhappy.

The *Image Commentary* (*Xiang Zhuan*) says: The Nine (*yang*/strong line) in the fifth place one wants to follow not only fails to save one, but also traps one in a hole, and deliberately stops one, so one is unable to move. Moreover, the Nine (*yang*/strong line) in the fifth place refuses to retreat and is unwilling to let the situation develop, resulting in the Six (*yin*/soft line) in the second place not being able to retreat and letting the situation develop (one feels unhappy, but has no choice).

【明意】

自己想跟从的人，本来的意量应该是扩大和帮助自己的，但有时候可能反过来对自己构成最大的危险和压制，这样的事情常常发生。师徒关系有时可能演变成为这种模式，有才华者不但被压制，还可能被迫面对危险的情境，即老师不让学生有任何机会超脱自己划定的意量边界。当一个人的意量被限制，被人为控制，自然心意不畅快，不会高兴，因为觉得自己本来可以，但被某些外在条件抑制住了，就闷闷不乐，这是一种常见的心灵状态。人的意量虽然可能被限制，但人的意志和意能往往不可压制。

[Illuminating Intentionality]

The original intention of the people one wants to follow should be to expand and help one, but sometimes they may in turn pose the greatest danger and oppression to one, as often happens. The mentor-student relationship may sometimes evolve into such a model, where talented people are not only suppressed, but may also be forced to face dangerous situations, denying students any chance to transcend their own boundaries of imagination. When a person's intentional capacity is restricted and artificially controlled, one will naturally feel inhibited and unhappy because one feels that one could have been capable but was suppressed by certain external conditions, and one becomes depressed, a common mental state. Although human intentional capacity may be limited, the human will and intentional energy cannot always be suppressed.

九三：艮其限，列其夤（yín），厉，熏心。

《象》曰："艮其限"，危"熏心"也。

【明译】

九三：抑制住腰的运动，撕裂了背部的脊肉，极其危险痛苦，好像心疼得被火熏烤着一样。

《象传》说：抑制住腰的运动，因为极其危险痛苦，好像心疼得被火烧烤着一样。

Nine (*yang*/strong line) in the third place: Suppressing the movement of the waist, tearing the spine muscles of the back, it is extremely dangerous and painful, as if the heart-mind is being burned by fire.

The *Image Commentary* (*Xiang Zhuan*) says: One suppresses the movement of the waist, because it is extremely dangerous and painful, as if one's heart is being burned by fire.

【明意】

相对于背来说，腰是人的意念受限的另一个地方，它有背的特色，因为有一部分自己看不清，又有其他部位的特点，因为可以有触觉和其他知觉来了解腰的情况，所以腰的意量就在不可知与可知之间。

九三为人在天地之间，在身为肾脏脊背命门之所，如果失其分限，则如烟熏火燎，心志分裂，或如五脏俱焚，撕肝裂肺，不堪其苦。可见，心意之火需要自知自制，不可任其焚烧，致使失去意量分界，否则利欲熏心，必致身毁心亡。

[Illuminating Intentionality]

Compared with the back, the waist is another place where people's intentions are limited. It has the characteristics of the back, because some parts of it cannot be seen clearly, and it also has the characteristics of other parts, because one can have touch and other perceptions to understand the waist's situation, so the intentionality of the waist is between unknowable and knowable.

The Nine (*yang*/strong line) in the third place is a human being between heaven and earth, or on the body, the place where the life gate of the kidneys and backs is located. If its limits are lost, it will be like smoke and fire, and intentionality will be divided, or like all the five internal organs being burned, with the liver and lungs being torn, and the suffering unbearable. It can be seen that the fire of intentionality needs to be self-aware and self-controlled, and it cannot be allowed to burn, resulting in the loss of the boundaries of the will. Otherwise, the desire for gain will inflame intentionality, which will lead to physical and mental destruction.

六四：艮其身，无咎。

《象》曰："艮其身"，止诸躬也。

【明译】

六四：管住自己的身体，没有祸患。

《象传》说：管住自己的身体，不过是管住自己的肉身（不能够完全掌控自己的心灵）。

Six (*yin*/soft line) in the fourth place: Take control of the body and there will be no harm.

The *Image Commentary* (*Xiang Zhuan*) says: Controlling one's own body is just controlling one's own physical body (one cannot fully control one's heart-mind).

【明意】

所有的意量最后都落实在人身之中。物理主义持这种观点，认为人的活动都可以化为物理的运动，也可以通过改变物理运动的机制来改变心灵的运动。这种物理主义对于意量的理解可能有帮助，那就是人的意量应该没有太多的可能超越物理的机制。但我们也可以看到，想象力、幻想、梦想等不可思议的意念活动，尤其是无法预料的灵感的产生与幻灭，这样的意念活动本身似乎漂泊不定，但也都可以还原到人的神经物理活动。人可以控制意念，但控制意念的机制在神经活动上是否可能，或许有一个意志可以超越于物理的运动之上，并驾驭所有的物理运动。

[Illuminating Intentionality]

All intentional capacities are finally implemented in the human body. Physicalism holds this view, and believes that human activities can all be transformed into physical movements, and that the movement of intentionality can also be changed by changing the mechanism of physical movement. This kind of physicalism may be helpful for the understanding of intention, that is, there should not be much possibility for human intention to transcend physical mechanisms. But we can also see that incredible mental activities such as imagination, fantasy, and dreams, especially the generation and disillusionment of unpredictable inspiration. Such mental activities themselves seem to be wandering, but they can also be reduced to human neurophysical activities. People can control intentions, but is the mechanism for controlling intentions possible in terms of neural activity? Perhaps there is a will that can transcend physical movements and control all physical movements.

六五：艮其辅，言有序，悔亡。

《象》曰："艮其辅"，以中正也。

【明译】

六五：抑制住自己的嘴巴，使说话合理有序，这样就会消除忧虑和悔恨。

《象传》说：抑制住自己的嘴巴，因为六五言行中正（在上卦中位）。

Six (*yin*/soft line) in the fifth place: Suppressing the mouth and making speech reasonable and orderly, will eliminate worries and regrets.

The *Image Commentary* (*Xiang Zhuan*) says: Suppress the mouth, because the Six (*yin*/soft line) in the fifth place's words and deeds are upright (in the middle of the upper Trigram).

【明意】

意量的限度最为明显的表现即是言辞的限度，也是言辞之间逻辑的限度。人的思想在虚无之中运行的时候，似乎是在无限意量之状，但一旦通过言辞表达，就立即落入有限的意量之中，所以如何对自己的意量状态有清晰的自我意识，并让这种自我意识准确地作用于言辞边界之上，是一种修辞的艺术。在六五这里最主要的表现就是言语有序，好像自己能够限制自己的思维和言语表达一样。

但限制自己的意量单纯地通过对言语的限制又往往不够，要通过意量本身的自我反省限制和提升行动，通过长期修炼自己意量的行为来实现，人可创造出一种随心所欲不逾矩（即上九）的境界。

[Illuminating Intentionality]

The limit of intentionality is the limit of words, and it is also the limit of logic between words. When human intentions are running in nothingness, they seem to be in a state of infinite consciousness, but once expressed through words, they immediately fall into finite consciousness. So how we can have a clear self-awareness of our own conscious state, and let this self-awareness act accurately on the boundaries of speech, is a rhetorical art. The main performance here in the Six (*yin*/soft line) in the fifth place is orderly speech, as if one can limit one's own thinking and verbal expression.

However, it is often not enough to limit one's own intentional energy simply by restricting words. It is necessary to limit and improve actions through self-reflection on intentional energy itself, and to achieve this through long-term practice on one's own intentional energy. People can create a kind of freedom that does not exceed what they want.

上九：敦艮，吉。

《象》曰："敦艮"之"吉"，以厚终也。

【明译】

上九：以敦厚的心灵抑制邪思邪念，自然吉祥。

《象传》说：心灵敦厚到随心所欲的境界，一起心动念就能够抑制邪思邪念而自然吉祥，说明上九能够慎终如始地保养厚重的人天之意。

Nine (*yang*/strong line) in the top place: Suppressing evil intentions and thoughts with a kind heart, one will be naturally auspicious.

The *Image Commentary* (*Xiang Zhuan*) says: The heart is so sincere that it can do whatever it wants. When the heart-mind is moved together, it can suppress evil intentions and thoughts and become naturally auspicious. This shows that the Nine (*yang*/strong line) in the top place can carefully maintain the profound intentionality of humanity and heaven.

【明意】

通过长期意量自我限制的修行，人的意念发动的边界成为自我意识与自我控制意念机制的自然一部分，进而达到一种随心所欲的境界，能够在起心动念处压抑邪思邪念，而让本来人心之中与天相接的人天心意，得到发动的敦厚基础，达到止住心量的最高境界。这种境界是心灵敦厚到随心所欲的境界，一起心动念就能够抑制邪思邪念而处于敦实厚重的心意状态之中，好像大山那样磅礴厚实，不可动摇，人一旦体会到这一点，就要以山的厚重之力来保养深沉敦厚的人天之意。

[Illuminating Intentionality]

Through long-term self-limiting practices of mindfulness, the boundaries of human intentions become a natural part of the self-awareness and self-control intention mechanism, and then reach a state of doing whatever one wants, where evil intentions and thoughts can be suppressed where the intentions arise, and the original human heart-mind can be freed. The inner intentionality of humanity and heaven, which is connected with heaven, has gained a solid foundation for initiation, and has reached the highest state of stopping the intentions. This state is one where intentionality is so honest that it can do whatever it wants. With a single intention, it can suppress evil intentions and remain in a solid and profound state of mind. It is as majestic and solid as a mountain and cannot be shaken. Once a person realizes this, one must use the heavy power of the mountain to maintain the deep and honest intentionality of humanity and heaven.

风山渐（卦五十三） （艮下巽上）

Jian (Engagement), Wind and Mountain (Hexagram 53) (Gen below, Xun above)

人对世界的认识近于出嫁，有一个逐渐行进的过程。渐卦为女子之所归，归于社会化进程，这体现了《周易》明于人事，落实到人们生活的宗旨。古时女子的意量与所嫁丈夫有莫大的关系，在相当程度上以丈夫的意量为自己的意量，而丈夫的意量又不是自己能控制的，所以就通过一定的程序来估计和稳定丈夫的意量，也就是说，出嫁女子对未来丈夫的认识，不是通过丈夫的意量本身，而是丈夫娶妻的程序来判断丈夫的意量是否适合自己。比如，女子耐心等待婚事的进展，就要耐心等待男子（及男子的意缘）向她展开其意量。

另一方面，古人认为，男女之间的婚礼习俗对于国家风气影响巨大，所以非常重视婚礼对于社会习俗渐渐的转化作用。还有，婚礼的渐进过程，也是认识世界的礼俗对于自己心量的约束，更是自己心量在约定的习俗之中逐渐实化的过程。

People's understanding of the world is similar to getting married, with a gradually advancing process. Hexagram Jian (Engagement) is the home of women and the process of socialization, reflecting the fact that the *Book of Changes* is clear about human affairs and implements the purpose of people's lives. In ancient times, a woman's intentional capacity was closely related to the husband she married. To a considerable extent, her husband's intentional capacity was her own, and her husband's intentional capacity was beyond her control, so she estimated and stabilized it through certain procedures. That is to say, a married woman's understanding of her future husband was not based on the husband's intentional capacity itself, but on using the husband's marriage process to judge whether his intentional capacity was suitable for her. For example, as a woman waits patiently for marriage to progress, she must wait patiently for the man (and his intentional conditions) to reveal his intentional capacity to her.

On the other hand, the ancients believed that wedding customs between men and women had a huge impact on the national ethos, so they attached great importance to the gradual transformation of social customs by weddings. In addition, the gradual process of a wedding is also a process of understanding the restraint of one's own intentionality by the ritual propriety and customs of the world, as well as a process of gradually realizing one's own intentionality in agreed customs.

渐，女归吉，利贞。

《彖》曰：渐之进也，"女归吉"也。进得位，往有功也。进以正，可以正邦也。其位刚得中也。止而巽，动不穷也。

《象》曰：山上有木，渐。君子以居贤德善俗。

【明译】

渐卦象征循序渐进，譬如女子出嫁循礼渐进而归于夫家就会获得吉祥，利于坚守正固。

《彖传》说：逐渐地行进，譬如女子出嫁循礼渐进而归于夫家，这样出嫁之后才会获得吉祥。向前渐进而取得正位，是前往有功（六四从三的阳位推移到四的阴位，柔爻居阴位得位）。渐进而又能依循正道（六四卦变后进入正位），就能以中正之道端正邦国民心，教化风俗。渐卦九五刚爻居于中位，下卦艮为止，上卦巽为顺，只要能静止不躁而又谦逊随顺，以渐进的方式行动就不会陷入困穷之境。

《象传》说：下卦艮为山，上卦巽为木，山上生长着树木就是渐卦。君子看到山上树木层层叠叠，渐渐高大，就知道要逐渐积累贤德，循序改善风俗。

Hexagram Jian (Engagement) symbolizes gradual progress. For example, if a woman gets married and then belongs to her husband's family according to ritual propriety, she will gain good fortune, and this is conducive to upholding integrity.

The *Judgment Commentary* (*Tuan Zhuan*) says: Progressing gradually. For example, when a woman gets married, she gradually belongs to her husband's family according to ritual propriety, so that she will gain good fortune after getting married. To move forward gradually and achieve the correct position is to advance with merit (the Six (*yin*/soft line) in the fourth place moves from the *yang* position of three to the *yin* position of four, and then a soft line is in a *yin* position). Gradually able to follow the right *dao* (entering the right position after the change of the Six (*yin*/soft line) in the fourth place), one can rectify the intentions and minds of the country's people and educate customs with the middle *dao*. The Nine (*yang*/strong line) in the fifth place of Hexagram Jian (Engagement) is in the middle, with the lower Trigram Gen as stopping, and the upper Trigram Xun as smooth. As long as one can be still and unhurried, humble and obedient, one will not fall into poverty if one acts in a gradual manner.

The *Image Commentary* (*Xiang Zhuan*) says: The lower Trigram Gen is mountain, the upper Trigram Xun is wood, and trees growing on a mountain is Hexagram Jian (Engagement). When an exemplary person sees the trees on the mountain growing taller and taller, one knows that one must gradually accumulate virtue and improve customs step by step.

【明意】

古人认为，男婚女嫁对国家风俗影响很大，婚嫁之道正了，将能够起到正邦化俗的作用。卦里九五与六二得位并正应，这说明全卦秩序大面上没有问题。树得地要在山上生长，君子得地要居于贤德。树的生长是从毫末之小树逐渐成长为合抱之木，人的修养和移风易俗也要逐渐进行。

移风易俗是社会道德之本，也是建构理想社会的必经之路，古时人们特别重视，在今天也未必没有道理，但这一定是个渐进的过程，属于儒家建立理想社会的渐进努力。儒家社会的理想形态是领导人的意量能够通过渐进的方式形成社会范型，导民心向善，而这种善从根源上说来自于天地自然之善，让社会民心通过天地的生生不息而化育成型，达到生生和谐的理想境界。

[Illuminating Intentionality]

The ancients believed that marriage between a man and a woman had a great influence on national customs. If a marriage was done correctly, it would play a role in upholding the country's customs. The Nine (*yang*/strong line) in the fifth place and the Six (*yin*/soft line) in the second place are in the right position and respond to each other, which shows that there is no problem with the order of the hexagram as a whole. A tree must grow on a mountain, and an exemplary person must live in a virtuous place. The growth of a tree is from a small tree to a full-sized tree, and people's cultivation and change of customs must also be carried out gradually.

Changing customs is the foundation of social morality and the only way to build an ideal society. In ancient times, people paid special attention to it, which may not be unreasonable today. However, this must be a gradual process and belongs to Confucianism's gradual efforts to build an ideal society. The ideal form of Confucian society is that the intentional capacity of leaders can gradually form a social paradigm and guide the people's intentions toward the good. This goodness fundamentally comes from the natural goodness of heaven and earth, so that the intentions of society and the people can continue to grow through the ceaseless production and reproduction of heaven and earth. Through transformation and cultivation, this reaches the ideal state of harmony in production and reproduction.

初六：鸿渐于干。小子厉，有言，无咎。

《象》曰："小子"之"厉"，义无咎也。

【明译】

初六：大雁渐渐飞到河岸边，好像一个小孩跑到河边玩耍，有危险，受到大人斥责离开了岸边，所以最终还是没有什么灾祸。

《象传》说：小孩跑到河边玩耍，有危险，按道理说，只要能够马上纠正他的错误就不应当有什么灾祸。

Six (*yin*/soft line) in the first place: The wild goose gradually flies to the river bank, just like a child runs to the river to play. He is in danger but is scolded by an adult and leaves the bank, so in the end there is no disaster.

The *Image Commentary* (*Xiang Zhuan*) says: It is dangerous for a child to play by the river. In principle, as long as his mistake can be corrected immediately, there should be no disaster.

【明意】

孩子对世界的认识，好像大雁渐渐飞到河岸边开始认识河水一样，河水的深度和广度，对大雁和小孩来说，都是一个危险的未知世界，而且是一个不可以以身试险的未知世界，对世界的探索，有时候危险太大，不可以冒死去试，要相信前人的经验，这时大人的训斥就相当于人应该相信前人的经验全体（the wholeness of experience）之有效性和合理性。当然，小孩一开始可能是从对大人的权威服从当中慢慢意识到前人经验全体是合理性的，而大人经验的合理性可能包含了一定的试错经验和前人的教训。

对世界的认知从一开始就要确定对先人合理性的服从，以前人经验的意量为意量，如果不相信前人经验的合理性，一味只相信自己有限的初始经验，可能是危险和狭隘的。从另一个角度说，建构理想社会需要耐心，理解其必然是渐进的过程，还必须借鉴历史上的丰富经验，及时修正可能的错误，而不宜尝试被历史已证明不合适的方式。

[Illuminating Intentionality]

A child's understanding of the world is like a wild goose that gradually begins to understand the river when it flies to the river bank. The depth and breadth of the river are a dangerous unknown world for wild geese and children, and a world that cannot be tested by oneself. In the unknown world, the exploration of the world is sometimes too dangerous, and one cannot risk one's life, so one must believe in the experience of one's predecessors. At this time, the reprimand from an adult is equivalent to believing in the effectivity and rationality of the wholeness of experience of one's predecessors. Of course, children may initially realize that all previous experiences are reasonable from their obedience to the authority of adults, and the rationality of adult experience may include a certain amount of trial and error experience and lessons from previous generations.

To know the world, we must obey the rationality of our ancestors from the beginning, and take the intentionality of previous experience as our intentionality. If we do not believe in the rationality of previous experience and blindly believe in our own limited initial experience, it may be dangerous and narrow-minded. From another perspective, building an ideal society requires patience and understanding that it must be a gradual process. We must also learn from the rich experience in history and correct possible mistakes in a timely manner. It is not advisable to try methods that have been proven to be inappropriate in history.

六二：鸿渐于盘，饮食衎（kàn）衎，吉。

《象》曰："饮食衎衎"，不素饱也。

【明译】

六二：大雁飞行渐进到磐石之上，安逸愉快地享用饮食，欢畅喜乐，一片祥和。

《象传》说：安逸愉快地享用饮食，欢畅喜乐，说明六二不会白吃饱饭，无功受禄。

Six (*yin*/soft line) in the second place: The wild geese fly gradually to the rock, enjoying food and drink comfortably and happily, rejoicing and being peaceful.

The *Image Commentary* (*Xiang Zhuan*) says: Enjoying food and drink comfortably and joyfully means that the Six (*yin*/soft line) in the second place will not eat for free or receive a salary without merit.

【明意】

饮食宴乐是一个人认识世界边界开始时期的重要内容，即调节自己本始欲望的限度，让自己的意量渐进成型，而且在欢喜快乐之中，修正调节自己意量的分限。

一个人吃饱饭才可能有正常升进的意识去积极进取，这里表现为与九五的相应。上面的君王之心与己相应，大大扩展了自己的意量。在意量延展的过程之中，事情才可能成就。建构理想社会也要通过揣摩实践，并由礼节逐渐开始。礼仪教化在民心安宁稳定之后，人们的意量渐进成型，大家进入欢畅喜乐的境界。

[Illuminating Intentionality]

Eating, drinking and enjoying is an important part of the beginning of a person's understanding of the boundaries of the world, that is, adjusting the limits of one's original desires, allowing one's intentional capacity to gradually take shape, and correcting and adjusting the limits of one's intentions in the midst of joy.

Only when a person has a full meal can one have a normal and progressive consciousness to be proactive, which is reflected here in resonance with the Nine (*yang*/strong line) in the fifth place. The king's heart-mind above corresponds to one's own, greatly expanding one's intentional capacity, and only in the process of expansion of intentionality can things be accomplished. The construction of an ideal society must also be done through speculation and practice, starting gradually with ritual propriety. After ritual propriety education has stabilized the people's intentions, people's intentional capacity gradually takes shape, and everyone enters a state of joy and happiness.

九三：鸿渐于陆。夫征不复，妇孕不育，凶。利御寇。

《象》曰："夫征不复"，离群丑也。"妇孕不育"，失其道也。"利"用"御寇"，顺相保也。

【明译】

九三：大雁飞行渐进到远离水边的陆地之上，（离雁群越来越远）这就如同丈夫长期出征远行不回家，家里的妻子怀了孕却不能把小孩生养下来，非常凶险，但对抵御寇盗有利。

《象传》说：丈夫长期出征远行不回家，是离开了属于自己的群体（九三在卦变中从乾的三个刚爻中分离出来）。家里的妻子怀了孕却不能把小孩生养下来，因为妻子有失贞节，违背妇道（否卦穷上的三个刚爻按正道推移应当是返下而复。否的九四原有正应在初六，应当推移到初位，而卦变中却到了三位）。对抵御寇盗有利，是因为顺守相保。

Nine (*yang*/strong line) in the third place: A wild goose flies gradually to a land far away from the water (getting further and further away from the flock of geese). This is like a husband who has been away from home for a long time, whose wife at home is pregnant but cannot give birth to a child. It is very dangerous, but useful in fending off bandits.

The *Image Commentary* (*Xiang Zhuan*) says: The husband goes a long-term expedition and does not come home, which means he leaves his own group (the Nine (*yang*/strong line) in the third place is separated from the three *yang*/strong lines of Qian in the hexagram-changes). The wife at home is pregnant but cannot give birth to her child, because the wife has lost her chastity and violated the *dao* of women (the three *yang*/strong lines of Hexagram Pi (Non-Communication) should go back down according to the correct *dao*. The Nine (*yang*/strong line) in the fourth place of Hexagram Pi (Non-Communication) originally had an upright resonance with the Six (*yin*/soft line) in the first place, so it should be moved to the first position, but it in fact reaches the third position in the hexagram-changes). It is beneficial to resist bandits because they follow and protect each other.

【明意】

理想社会的建构与理想家庭建构的道理一样，需要双方同心合意地维系家庭和社群，才有可能建构合理的社会风俗和正常的社会秩序。这是把社会秩序的根基落实到人心和意念的合理秩序，家庭与社会管理的核心都是心意之力的整合。

意量由阴意和阳意之坚贞互动而成型，以凝结意丹为指归，本爻从反面来说明这一点，即丈夫长期出征，无法顾及家人，而妻子有失妇道，怀孕也不敢生子。这是从彼此不能相守，而无法彼此成就对方意量的角度来说明的。

[Illuminating Intentionality]

The construction of an ideal society is the same as the construction of an ideal family, requiring both parties to work together to maintain order of the family and community. Only then can it be possible to construct reasonable social customs and a normal social order. This is a reasonable order that implements the foundation of social order into the human heart-mind and intentions. The core of family and social management is the integration of the power of intention.

Intentional capacity is formed by the steadfast interaction of *yin* and *yang*, and is guided by the condensed intentional elixir (*yidan* 意丹). This line illustrates this from the negative side, that is, the husband is away fighting a war for a long time and cannot take care of his family, while the wife loses the *dao* of the wife and gets pregnant but does not dare to give birth. This is explained from the perspective that the two cannot be with each other and cannot fulfill each other's intentional capacities.

六四：鸿渐于木，或得其桷（jué），无咎。
《象》曰："或得其桷"，顺以巽也。
【明译】
六四：大雁飞行或者渐进到树林之中，或者飞到房屋方形的屋椽之上暂时栖身，没有什么问题。
《象传》说：或者飞到房屋方形的屋椽之上暂时栖身，是因为六四从柔顺变为巽顺。

Six (*yin*/soft line) in the fourth place: The wild goose flies either gradually into the woods, or to the square rafters of houses for temporary shelter. There is no problem.

The *Image Commentary* (*Xiang Zhuan*) says: Maybe it flies to the square rafters of the house to rest temporarily, because the Six (*yin*/soft line) in the fourth place's movement changed from submissive to smooth.

【明意】
对世界的认识是阶段性发展的。要适时停歇，渐进调整，必须采取随顺合境的态度来推进自己的意量。对家庭社会政治的秩序的建构与合理的认识，都要有阶段性推进的合理感。每一个阶段性的微调都是为了更安稳地推进社会秩序的梳理过程。

[Illuminating Intentionality]

Understanding the world develops in stages. To stop at the right time and make gradual adjustments, one must adopt an attitude of adapting to the situation to advance one's own intentions. The construction and reasonable understanding of familial, social and political order must have a reasonable sense of staged advancement. Each stage of fine-tuning is to more stably advance the process of sorting out the social order.

九五：鸿渐于陵，妇三岁不孕，终莫之胜，吉。

《象》曰："终莫之胜，吉"，得所愿也。

【明译】

九五：雄雁离开雌雁渐渐飞到高高的山陵之上，它的雌雁三年都没有怀孕（犹如丈夫远行，导致家里的妻子三年不能怀孕），因为没有比得过她心仪的雄雁的（好比妻子的眼中没有男人能够胜过自己的丈夫），这是非常吉祥的关系。

《象传》说：雌雁心中没有比得过她心仪的雄雁的（好比妻子的眼中没有男人能够胜过自己的丈夫），这样很吉祥，她因为忠贞不二必然会跟雄雁（丈夫）会合，得偿彼此对夫妻关系所期待的愿望（六二虽与九五正应，但同时与九三相比，正应关系经受住了相比关系的考验，但最终会因为六二行为中正，能够实现与九五的正应）。

Nine (*yang*/strong line) in the fifth place: The male goose leaves the female goose and gradually flies to the high mountains. The female goose does not get pregnant for three years (just like the husband traveling far away, whose wife at home was unable to conceive for three years) because none can compare with her partner (just like no man can surpass a husband in the eyes of his wife); this is a very auspicious relationship.

The *Image Commentary* (*Xiang Zhuan*) says: In the heart-mind of a female goose, none is better than the male goose she admires (just like in the eyes of a wife, no man surpass her husband). This is very auspicious. Because of her loyalty, she will definitely be with the male goose (husband), meeting and fulfilling each other's expectations for the relationship between husband and wife (although the Six (*yin*/soft line) in the second place resonates with the Nine (*yang*/strong line) in the fifth place, at the same time, compared with the Nine (*yang*/strong line) in the third place, the positive relationship has withstood the test of comparison, and it will eventually achieve uprightness in response to the Nine (*yang*/strong line) in the fifth place thanks to the Six (*yin*/soft line) in the second place's central and upright conduct).

【明意】

社会秩序的梳理与阴意是否顺承阳意有莫大的关系。如果阴意坚贞自守，社会的秩序就恒稳不乱。这是传统社会政治理念的重要内容，即忠诚不二以保证家长和领导人的意量能够贯彻和放大。对阴意顺承阳意的社会化要求，也被从内化为阴意自身意愿的角度加以强调，也就是阴意本来就是从内心应和并配合阳意的，是心甘情愿地配合阳意的。

无论有没有孩子，此爻都是意量彼此应和而最终凝成意丹的最佳范例，也就是说夫妻心意互通，彼此以对方的意量为意量，最后凝成意丹的过程相当不易，都要经历心意受到外力牵引和诱惑，可能改变原生的凝成意丹的状态。

[Illuminating Intentionality]

Social order has a great relationship with whether *yin* intentionality follows *yang* intentionality.

If *yin* intentionality is firm and self-maintained, the social order will be stable and undisturbed. This is an important part of traditional social and political concepts, that is, loyalty to ensure that the intentions of parents and leaders can be implemented and amplified. The social requirement for *yin*/negative intentionality to obey *yang*/positive intentionality is also emphasized from the perspective of internalizing *yin*/negative intentionality's own will. That is to say, *yin*/negative intentionality originally responds to and cooperates with *yang*/positive intentionality from the heart-mind, and cooperates with *yang*/positive intentionality willingly.

Regardless of whether there are children or not, this line is the best example of how the heart-minds of a couple respond to each other and finally condense into the elixir of intentionality. That is to say, the intentionalities of the husband and wife are connected with each other, and each takes the other's intentional capacity as their intentional capacity. The process of finally condensing into the elixir of intentionality is quite similar. This is not easy, as one has to experience the pull on and temptation of intentionality by external forces, which may change the original state of condensing the elixir of intentionality.

上九：鸿渐于陆，其羽可用为仪，吉。

《象》曰："其羽可用为仪，吉"，不可乱也。

【明译】

上九：大雁飞过了高陵，慢慢地飞回到大陆上来，羽毛洁白美丽，在礼节仪式中可以用来修饰，是忠贞和吉祥的象征。

《象传》说：羽毛洁白美丽，在礼仪中可以用来修饰，是忠贞和吉祥的象征，因为礼仪不可乱序，尊卑有序，进退有节（上巽为进退）。

Nine (*yang*/strong line) in the top place: The wild goose flies over high land and slowly flies back to the mainland. Its feather is white and beautiful, so it can be used for decoration in ritual propriety and ceremonies. It's a symbol of loyalty and good fortune.

The *Image Commentary* (*Xiang Zhuan*) says: Feathers are white and beautiful, and can be used for decoration in ritual propriety. They are a symbol of loyalty and auspiciousness, because ritual propriety must not be disordered, superior and inferior are in order, and advance and retreat are measured (the upper Trigram Xun means advance and retreat).

【明意】

鸿雁是候鸟，不衍期，有准信，象征知时有信。鸿雁飞翔时排成人字，象征有序。鸿雁配偶遇难不另找新欢，孤雁哀鸣，为爱情忧伤，象征忠于爱情，所以古时把鸿雁的羽毛用在礼仪中。君子在飞黄腾达，志得意满之时，更要爱惜自己的羽毛，保持端庄光彩的仪表，从内到外显现出控制自己意量的强大魄力。

亚当·斯密《道德情操论》说明道德与人心秩序是社会与市场秩序的基石，同理，此量论是建立人心的意量,与社会结构和天地阴阳之间预存的先天结构相合拍的合理状态。阴意与阳意经历风雨的洗礼之后完美结合,彼此意量的分限完美融合,成就意丹,如乾坤朗照,意通日月,光华四射,跨越时空,永恒不败。

[Illuminating Intentionality]

The swan goose is a migratory bird. It keeps a regular time and is reliable and dependable, so it symbolizes knowing the right time and having faith. When the geese are flying, they form a human figure, symbolizing order. When a swan goose couple is in trouble, they will not find a new love. A lone goose mourns and is sad for love, which symbolizes loyalty to love. Therefore, the feathers of the swan goose were used in ritual propriety in ancient times. When an exemplary person is prosperous and satisfied with one's ambitions, one should cherish one's feathers, maintain a dignified and glorious appearance, and show the strong courage to control one intentional capacity from the inside out.

Adam Smith's *The Theory of Moral Sentiments* explains that morality and the order of the human heart are the cornerstones of social and market order. In the same way, this theory aims to establish the intentional capacity of the human heart and a reasonable state that is consistent with the social structure and the pre-existing transcendental structure between the *yin* and *yang* of heaven and earth. After a baptism of wind and rain, *yin*/negative intentionality and *yang*/positive intentionality are perfectly combined, and the limits of each other's intentional capacities are perfectly integrated to achieve an intentional elixir (*yidan*), like Qian and Kun shining brightly, intentionality connecting to the sun and the moon, radiating brilliance all around, spanning time and space, and eternally undefeated.

雷泽归妹（卦五十四）　（兑下震上）

Guimei (Marriage), Thunder and Lake (Hexagram 54)　(Dui below, Zhen above)

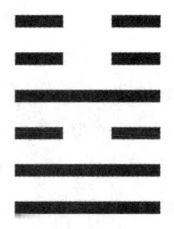

　　归妹是意能与意量的归属，阴阳之意结合而意能得到更大提升，阴阳意的整合就是意能的修炼过程，婚配嫁妹是意能修炼过程的具体化。归妹卦主要强调意能的修炼是阴阳之意融合的过程。

　　阴意之坚贞是阳意之意能增强的核心，阴意坚贞地随顺阳意，对于意能的持续非常重要。阴意在维持阴阳融通的意能状态之时，为了让意能持续有力，有时需要故作盲目，这其实是一种处世的大智慧。当然，为了让意能持续，阴意与阳意都不宜违背人情之常。阴意为了实现自己意能的最大化，有时需要慎重选择自己追随的阳意。意能的强度不在身外之物，而在意识之内。如果阴意不能实实在在地随顺阳意，则意能不显，意丹难成。可见，阴阳意的融通结合可以产生巨大的意能，但阴意如何随顺如何配合阳意是非常关键的。

　　Guimei is where intentional energy and intentional capacity connect together and stay. The integration of *yin* and *yang* will further enhance intentionality, and is the process of cultivating intentionality. Marriage is the embodiment of the process of cultivating intentionality. Hexagram Guimei (Marriage) mainly emphasizes that the cultivation of intentional energy is the process of fusion of *yin* and *yang*.

　　The steadfastness of *yin* intentionality is the core of strengthening *yang* intentionality. The steadfastness of *yin* intentionality to follow *yang* intentionality is very important for the continuation of *yang* intentionality. When *yin*/negative intentionality maintains the state of intentional energy that integrates *yin* and *yang*, in order to keep the intentional energy strong, it sometimes needs to pretend to be blind. This is actually a kind of great wisdom in life. Of course, in order for intentionality to last, neither the *yin* nor the *yang* intentionality should violate human nature. In order to maximize *yin*/negative intentionality's power, it sometimes needs to carefully choose the *yang*/positive intentionality it follows. The strength of intentionality is not found in things outside the body, but within consciousness. If *yin* intentionality cannot truly follow *yang* intentionality, intentions will not be manifested and the intentional elixir will be difficult to achieve. It can be seen that the integration of *yin* and *yang* can produce huge intentional energy, but how *yin* follows and cooperates with *yang* is very critical.

归妹，征凶，无攸利。

《彖》曰：归妹，天地之大义也。天地不交而万物不兴。归妹，人之终始也。说以动，所归妹也。"征凶"，位不当也。"无攸利"，柔乘刚也。

《象》曰：泽上有雷，归妹。君子以永终知敝。

【明译】

归妹卦象征妻娣二女共嫁一夫，前行争斗，必有凶险，不会有什么好处。

《彖传》说：女嫁男婚，是天地阴阳运转的大道理。天地阴阳不交合流变，万物就不会兴旺成长。男婚女嫁是人伦的归宿和开始，人类才能终而复始地繁衍生息。下卦兑为悦，上卦震为动，内心喜悦而外表欢动，这是少女出嫁的象征（下卦兑为少女，即妹）。前行争斗，必有凶险，是前往的位置都不恰当（九四上来以阳刚居柔位，六三下降以阴柔居刚位）。没有什么好处，是因为柔爻乘驾刚爻（卦变后六三柔爻乘驾在刚爻九二之上，九四上往又被柔爻六五所乘）。

《象传》说：下卦兑为泽，上卦震为雷，泽上有雷就是归妹卦。君子看到泽水之上雷声震动，象征少女出嫁之时，内心喜悦而外表欢动，同时也看到，如果雷震动了，湖水就要泛动不安，所以知道要永恒地保持夫妇和睦，也了解有始无终的弊端。

Hexagram Guimei (Marriage) symbolizes a wife and her younger sister marrying one husband. If they fight together, there will be dangers and no good will come of it.

The *Judgment Commentary* (*Tuan Zhuan*) says: Men and women marrying is the principle of the movement of *yin* and *yang* in the world. If the *yin* and *yang* of heaven and earth do not merge and change, the myriad things will not prosper and grow. Marriage between a man and a woman is the destination and beginning of human relations, so that human beings can continue to reproduce and thrive. The lower Trigram Dui means joy, and the upper Trigram Zhen means vibration, so there is joy in the heart and excitement outside, which is a symbol of a girl getting married (the lower Trigram Dui means a girl, that is, the younger sister). When fighting to advance, there must be dangers, and the position one is going to is inappropriate (the Nine (*yang*/strong line) in the fourth place rises to become a *yang*/strong line in a soft position, while the Six (*yin*/soft line) in the third place falls to become a *yin*/soft line in a strong position). There is no benefit because *yin*/soft lines ride above *yang*/strong lines (after the hexagram-changes, the Six (*yin*/soft line) in the third place rides on the Nine (*yang*/strong line) in the second place, and the Nine (*yang*/strong line) in the fourth place rises and is beneath the Six (*yin*/soft line) in the fifth place).

The *Image Commentary* (*Xiang Zhuan*) says: The lower Trigram Dui is lake, and the upper Trigram Zhen is thunder. If there is thunder above a lake, it is Hexagram Guimei (Marriage). The exemplary person sees the thunder shaking above the lake, which symbolizes the inner joy and external excitement of a girl when she gets married. At the same time, one also sees that if the thunder shakes, the lake will be uneasy, so one knows to maintain eternal harmony between husband and wife, as well as understanding the disadvantages of having a beginning but no end.

【明意】

意能的成型如出嫁一般，是与世界交才能开始，所以也是"人之终始"。意能收摄到最后，还是要通过阴意与阳意的结合而表现出来。阴阳之意结合，意能才能爆发出来。心意发动的能量，来自阴意与阳意的融通结合之后可能产生的巨大意能。意能爆发有欢腾感，但也是折腾和问题的开始，所以要有恒心去维系这种欢乐的状态，控制住欢乐之意境的边界，避免乐极生悲，无事生非。

[Illuminating Intentionality]

The formation of intentional energy is like getting married. It begins with interaction with the world, so it is also the "end and beginning of human beings." In the end, the ability of intentional energy to be absorbed must be expressed through the combination of *yin* and *yang*. Only when *yin* and *yang* are combined can the energy of intentionality burst out. The energy initiated by intentionality comes from the huge intentional energy that may be generated after the integration of *yin* and *yang*. There is a sense of joy when intentionality bursts out, but it is also the beginning of frustration and problems. Therefore, one must have perseverance to maintain this joyful state, control the boundaries of the joyful intentional context, and avoid extreme joy leading to sorrow, and causing trouble out of nothing.

初九：归妹以娣（dì）。跛能履，征吉。

《象》曰："归妹以娣"，以恒也。"跛能履"，"吉"相承也。

【明译】

初九：用娣来随嫁出嫁的姐姐，好比跛脚的拐子还能坚持继续走路一样，往前进发，可获吉祥。

《象传》说：妹妹跟随姐姐一起出嫁，这是为了保持姻亲关系恒久。正如拐子跛了一只脚，但还可以坚持继续走路，说明吉祥是可以继承下去的。

Nine (*yang*/strong line) in the first place: A younger sister who follows her elder sister into marriage is like a cripple who can continue to walk. Advancing will bring good fortune.

The *Image Commentary* (*Xiang Zhuan*) says: The younger sister follows her elder sister into marriage in order to maintain a lasting relationship. Just like a cripple who is lame on one foot but can still continue to walk, it shows that good fortune can be inherited.

【明意】

妻娣型联姻的本质是为了防止两个国家或者两个家族的姻亲关系中断，也就是希望保持他们之间的政治和社会关系不断。古时出于国家和家族利益的需要，让女子作为和亲的使者，通过肉体和精神意识的融合与血脉的相继，来维持国家与家族意能的持续。这种阴意随顺阳意的机制，是用血脉的延续确保和维系意能的坚贞，让这种持续不因偶然的因素中断。嫁娣的一方（国家或家族），代表阴意持续的强烈意愿，并让血缘关系的后代来接续自己的意能，阴意希望确保跟阳意的共同创生（co-creativity）过程，即使有影响也不会中断。

[Illuminating Intentionality]

The essence of the concubine form of marriage is to prevent the in-law relationship between two countries or two families from being interrupted, that is, to preserve the political and social relations between them. In ancient times, due to the needs of the interests of the country and the family, women were allowed to serve as messengers of marriage, and through the fusion of physical and spiritual consciousness and bloodline succession, they maintained the continuity of the country and the family. This mechanism of *yin*/negative intentionality following *yang*/positive intentionality uses the continuation of the bloodline to ensure and maintain the integrity of intentional energy, so that this continuity will not be interrupted by accidental factors. The party (country or family) that marries a younger sister represents the strong wish of *yin* intentionality to continue, and allows the descendants of the blood relationship to continue its intentional energy. The *yin* intentionality hopes to ensure the process of co-creativity with *yang* intentionality, so even if there is some impact, there will be no interruption.

九二：眇能视，利幽人之贞。

《象》曰："利幽人之贞"，未变常也。

【明译】

九二：妹妹跟随姐姐一起出嫁，好比自己是一个斜眼偏盲的人，不能把东西看得非常清楚，做一个安处于幽静暗室中的人，这样比较有利。

《象传》说：安恬地做一个处于幽静暗室中的人，这样比较有利，因为九二安守贞洁，并没有改变婚姻状态的常道（九二在中能正，可保持恒久）。

Nine (*yang*/strong line) in the second place: A younger sister follows her elder sister into marriage, like a person with a squint and hemianopsia who cannot see things very clearly. It is more advantageous to be a person who lives quietly in a secluded dark room.

The *Image Commentary* (*Xiang Zhuan*) says: It is more advantageous to be a person secluded in a quiet dark room, because the Nine (*yang*/strong line) in the second place keeps steadfast and does not change the constant *dao* of marriage (the Nine (*yang*/strong line) in the second place can be upright in the middle position, and can maintain permanence).

【明意】

意能不为情感所左右，而为理智所指引，才能做出明智的选择。选择不是处于外在的应当，而是内心自然而然的应当，于是察察之明常不必要，且能够无所住私意而生明心。为让家庭和亲密关系的意能生发持续有力，当事人往往需要有故意睁只眼闭只眼的修养。

[Illuminating Intentionality]

Only when intentionality is not influenced by emotions but guided by reason can one make wise choices. A choice is not an external response, but a natural response from the inner heart-mind. Therefore, it is often unnecessary to inspect and reflect, and a clear intentionality can be born without selfish intentions. In order to keep the intentional power of family and intimate relationships strong, the person concerned often needs to have the cultivation to deliberately turn a blind eye.

六三：归妹以须，反归以娣。

《象》曰："归妹以须"，未当也。

【明译】

六三：少女出嫁时，让她的姐姐作为妾来陪嫁，嫁过去以后，姐姐反而成为自己妹妹的嫁妹了。

《象传》说：少女出嫁时，让她的姐姐作为妾来陪嫁，这样的做法姐妹的位置是不恰当的（六三柔爻推移到刚位，位不当）。

Six (*yin*/soft line) in the third place: When a young girl gets married, she asks her elder sister to be a concubine and accompany her. After she is married, her elder sister becomes her younger sister's husband's concubine.

The *Image Commentary* (*Xiang Zhuan*) says: When a girl gets married, her elder sister is given as a concubine to accompany her. In this way the positions of the sisters are inappropriate (the Six (*yin*/soft line) in the third place is moved to a strong position, which is inappropriate).

【明意】

家庭当中意能是否能阴阳和谐，跟家庭成员是否摆正自己的位置和心态有很大关系。生活经验与历史经验是人理解和调适自己生活的关键所在。人们根据经验调整自己的意能收放的尺度，这是基于相信经验是相应人心相通和人心之动的记录，也相信外在的存在和积淀都是心意之动的实化，人伦之常道的维系不可以违背一些基本的历史经验和心意发动的规律。

[Illuminating Intentionality]

Whether *yin* and *yang* can be harmonious in a family has a lot to do with whether the family members have corrected their position and mentality. Life experience and historical experience are the key for people to understand and adjust their own lives. People adjust the scale of their intentional energy based on experience. This is based on the belief that experience is a record of the connection between people's intentions and the movements of their intentions, as well as the belief that external existence and accumulation are a concretization of the movements of their intentions, and that the maintenance of the constant *dao* of human relations cannot violate some basic historical experiences and regularities of intentionality initiation.

九四：归妹愆（qiān）期，迟归有时。

《象》曰："愆期"之志，有待而行也。

【明译】

九四：出嫁延误婚期，是想稍迟出嫁，等待更加合适的时机。

《象传》说：九四错过婚期的心志，是有所期待而后出嫁。

Nine (*yang*/strong line) in the fourth place: Postponing the wedding date is because one wants to get married later and wait for a more suitable time.

The *Image Commentary* (*Xiang Zhuan*) says: The Nine (*yang*/strong line) in the fourth place's purpose in missing the wedding date is to have some expectations and then get married.

【明意】

古代嫁女以春为时，有时可行，所以想稍迟出嫁，等待更加合适的时机。换言之，如果少女迟迟不想出嫁，其实是想等个好配偶。一说等更加合适的时机。这里的主语，可以是少女，也可以是家长。问题在于，古时女子很难有婚姻自主性，难有选择权，只能被动选择。延误婚期的原因有多种，如未等到合适的人，准备不足，自身素质不够，待（兄）命而行，被命令而行等。也可以理解为，出嫁如出仕做官，不可所适非人，没有合适的人的时候，宁可等着，相信自己能够等到合适的人，所以是在时间当中等待合适的人出现，等待跟合适人的意能相感通。

[Illuminating Intentionality]

In ancient times, spring was the time for a girl to marry, which was sometimes feasible, so one wants to get married later and wait for a more suitable time. In other words, if a girl delays and does not want to get married, she actually wants to wait for a good spouse. One may then wait for a more appropriate time. The subject here can be a girl or a parent. The problem is that in ancient times, it was difficult for women to have autonomy in marriage and the right to choose, and they could only choose passively. There are many reasons for delaying a wedding, such as not yet waiting for the right person, lack of preparation, lack of personal qualities, waiting for (an elder brother's) orders, doing as one is ordered, etc. It can also be understood that getting married is like becoming an official, in which one should not simply adapt to the situation. When there is no suitable person, one had better wait and believe that one can wait for the right person. Therefore, one waits for the right person to appear in time, waiting for a suitable person's intentional energy to connect affectively.

六五：帝乙归妹，其君之袂（mèi）不如其娣之袂良。月几（jī）望，吉。

《象》曰："帝乙归妹，不如其娣之袂良"也。其位在中，以贵行也。

【明译】

六五：帝乙下嫁御妹的时候，小君的衣饰反而比不上娣的衣饰好，小君就像那接近圆满的月亮，（美丽又谦逊）非常吉祥。

《象传》说：帝乙下嫁御妹的时候，小君的衣饰反而比不上娣的衣饰好，因为六五在上卦中位，谦逊而中和地居于尊位，小君是以其尊贵的身份出嫁。

Six (*yin*/soft line) in the fifth place: When Emperor Yi married off his imperial sister, her clothes were not as good as those of her accompanying younger sister. His imperial sister was like the nearly full moon, (beautiful and humble,) and very auspicious.

The *Image Commentary* (*Xiang Zhuan*) says: When Emperor Yi married off his imperial sister, his imperial sister's clothes were not as good as her accompanying younger sister's clothes, because the Six (*yin*/soft line) in the fifth place is in the middle of the upper Trigram, occupying the honorable position in a humble and neutral manner. His imperial sister's clothes were not as good as those of her accompanying younger sister because she was marrying with her noble status.

【明意】

意能内敛不在身外的装饰，而在内心的力量。意能的圆满状态，一定是不显山露水的。阴意尊贵内敛有位，其意能自然彰显，可见意能的力量不在表面文章。

古往今来，意能的修炼，不在外在的穿衣打扮、花拳绣腿，而是来自内在的身份、身世经历、学养、品性、志向、气度、意志等等方面。意能的力量，来自内在的意识发动通于天地的力量，并与之关联的将其实化的能力，而与外在的装饰无关。

[Illuminating Intentionality]

The ability to restrain intentional energy is not found in external decoration, but in inner strength. The perfect state of intentional energy must be one that is invisible and not manifested. *Yin*/negative intentionality is noble and restrained, and its power of intentionality is naturally revealed. It can be seen that the power of intention is not superficial.

Throughout the ages, the cultivation of intentional energy has not come from external aspects such as make-up and costume, but from inner identity, life-related experiences, education, character, ambition, tolerance, will, etc. The power of intention comes from the inner consciousness that initiates the power that connects heaven and earth, and the related ability to concretize it, and has nothing to do with external decoration.

上六：女承筐无实，士刲（kuī）羊无血，无攸利。

《象》曰：上六"无实"，"承"虚"筐"也。

【明译】

上六：（成婚之后，夫妇对祖先血祭之时）新娘手捧竹筐，筐内空空如也；新郎用刀宰羊，却取不到血（夫妇祭祀之礼难成，祖先不佑），没有什么好处。

《象传》说：上六阴虚不实，好比手里捧着空筐。

Six (*yin*/soft line) in the top place: (After getting married, the couple performs a blood sacrifice to their ancestors.) The bride holds a bamboo basket, but the basket is empty; the groom kills a sheep with a knife, but cannot retrieve the blood. (The couple's sacrifice ceremony is difficult because the ancestors do not bless them.) There is nothing beneficial here.

The *Image Commentary* (*Xiang Zhuan*) says: The Six (*yin*/soft line) in the top place is empty and unreal, just like holding an empty basket in one's hand.

【明意】

古代成婚之后，要对祖先血祭，祭时要杀牲取血。夫妇对祖先血祭之时，新娘手捧竹筐，筐内空空如也，无所奉献，暗示女子没有怀孕，不结果实；或者暗示女子婚前已经不是处女。象征祭祀礼仪不成，祖先不佑，有不祥之兆。上六阴虚不实，好比手里捧着空筐，象征这种婚姻看来是没有结果的。

意能之强不在身外，在心意之内。阴意不实实在在地随顺阳意，则意能不显，意丹难成。阴意与阳意可以跨时空融成意丹，如果阴意成空则难成，也就是说，阴意要承阳才能生成意丹，阴意之实以承阳而意丹可成，如果只是虚承则意丹不成。

[Illuminating Intentionality]

In ancient times, after getting married, blood sacrifices were made to ancestors, and animals were killed to collect blood during the sacrifices. When a couple makes blood sacrifices to their ancestors, if the bride holds a bamboo basket with nothing in it, it implies that the woman is not pregnant and will not bear fruit, or that the woman is no longer a virgin before marriage. This symbolizes that the sacrificial rituals are not successful, or the ancestors do not give their blessing, and it is an ominous sign. The Six (*yin*/soft line) in the top place is empty and unreal, like holding an empty basket in one's hands, symbolizing that it seems this kind of marriage will be fruitless.

The power of intentional energy cannot go beyond one's body, but is always within intentionality.

If *yin*/soft intentionality does not truly follow *yang*/strong intentionality, intentions will not be manifested and the intentional elixir will be difficult to achieve. *Yin*/negative intentions and *yang*/positive intentions can be integrated across time and space into the intentional elixir, but if the *yin*/negative intentions are empty, this will be difficult to achieve. That is to say, *yin*/negative intentions should bear *yang* to generate the intentional elixir, and *yin*/negative intentions must have the reality to bear *yang* to enable the intentional elixir to be formed. If it is just an empty promise, the elixir will not form.

雷火丰（卦五十五）　（离下震上）

Feng (Abundance), Thunder and Fire (Hexagram 55)　(Li below, Zhen above)

　　意向性本来通天，但真正通天却需要气概才行。意念之行当尽可能丰盛壮大，如加缪所言，心念发动当如正午的太阳，即使人生都是悲剧，也要有强烈悲壮的英雄主义气概。丰是多而大之意。

　　心意之丰，可丰天地，光明正大的意向性之积累才能让天地有丰的盛大气象。心意丰盈即有雷电之威，无危势则难以丰大，有危势才能断案审案，适用刑罚。革后之丰，心意光明，但形势又乱又不好。

Intentionality originally connects to heaven, but it takes courage to truly connect with heaven. The act of intention should be as rich and powerful as possible, as Camus said, the movement of intentions should be like the sun at noon. Even if life is a tragedy, there must be strong and tragic heroism. Feng here means numerous and large.

Abundance of intention can enrich heaven and earth. Only the accumulation of upright intention can make heaven and earth prosperous. When intentionality is full, it has the power of thunder and lightning, but when there is no danger, it is difficult to be full. Only when there is danger can a case be judged and the punishment applied. In the abundance after the revolution, intentionality is bright, but the situation is chaotic and bad.

丰，亨，王假之。勿忧，宜日中。

《彖》曰：丰，大也。明以动，故"丰"。"王假之"，尚大也。"勿忧，宜日中"，宜照天下也。日中则昃（zè），月盈则食，天地盈虚，与时消息，而况于人乎，况于鬼神乎！

《象》曰：雷电皆至，丰。君子以折狱致刑。

【明译】

丰卦象征丰富盛大，亨通，君王能够使天下丰富盛大，不必忧虑，应该像太阳升到天空正中那样把光辉普照世间。

《彖传》说：卦名丰是丰富盛大之意。下卦离为明，上卦震为动，心意光明地行动，就能发展丰富盛大。君王能够使天下丰富盛大，因为君王崇尚丰富盛大。不必忧虑，应该像正午的太阳升到天空正中那样，因为这样才能让太阳的光辉普照天下。太阳过了中午就会西斜，月到圆满就会亏蚀。天地之间盈满和亏虚不断转换，伴随时间节气的推移而消长，天地都是如此，更何况是天地之中的人和鬼神呢！

《象传》说：上卦震为雷，下卦离为闪电，惊雷闪电一起来到，组合成丰盛壮大的丰卦。君子看到电闪雷鸣，鉴于惊雷的震慑之威，闪电的无隐之明，要公正明确地审理决断各种案子，并适当地动用刑罚。

Hexagram Feng (Abundance) symbolizes opulence and prosperity. The king can make the world rich and prosperous, so there is no need to worry. He should shine his light on the world just like the sun rising to the middle of the sky.

The *Judgment Commentary* (*Tuan Zhuan*) says: The hexagram name Feng means rich and grand. The lower Trigram Li is clear, the upper Trigram Zhen is motion, and if one acts with a bright intentions, one can develop richly and grandly. The king can make the world rich and grand, because the king advocates wealth and grandeur. There is no need to worry, it should be like the sun rising to the middle of the sky at noon, because only in this way can the sun's brilliance shine all over the world. The sun will set to the west after noon, and the moon will eclipse when it is full. The fullness and deficiency between heaven and earth are constantly changing, waxing and waning with the passage of time and solar terms. This is true for heaven and earth, not to mention the people, ghosts and spirits in heaven and earth!

The *Image Commentary* (*Xiang Zhuan*) says: The upper Trigram is thunder, and the lower Trigram is lightning. Thunder and lightning come together to form the rich and powerful Hexagram Feng (Abundance). When an exemplary person sees lightning and thunder, in view of the shaking power of thunder and the hidden brightness of lightning, one must try and decide various cases fairly and clearly, and use punishments appropriately.

第三章　易经明意
——爻意分说（下经）

【明意】

古人碰到太阳被伤害的状态非常恐惧，所以认为有必要去祭祀一下。如果连太阳这么巨大的能量场都能够被伤害，天下就没有什么不能够被伤害了。按照卦象是发生了日食，相当于太阳被伤害，古人就觉得天要塌下来了，得赶紧到庙里去祭祀。但是古人之前也有见过日食的记忆，知道日食过一小段时间就会过去，放心等待其实就会没有什么问题，只是太阳保持丰盈之道好像已经受到伤害，但又不必要为太阳过于担心。

光明丰大，普照天下，照出天下之境，即存在之境，包括鬼神之域，即鬼神的存在方式。人的心意之丰大，足以含摄鬼神，能够折狱致刑，处罚恶人。人性善不从天道自然之善的本体上讲，只是定义和假定的人性本善，不足以回答人性之恶的问题，这跟"至善全能"的上帝何以容忍不完美的世界存在一样是个吊诡的问题。无论普遍的人性如何，人性存在问题不可以简单通过至善假设加以化解，确实是必须直面的理论困境。《周易》确定人天之意通天的本体性的天道自然之善，非善恶对待的善。

[Illuminating Intentionality]

The ancients were very afraid of being harmed by the sun, so they believed it was necessary to offer sacrifices. If even an energy field as huge as the sun can be harmed, then there is nothing in the world that cannot be harmed. According to the hexagram, a solar eclipse occurred, which is equivalent to the sun being damaged. The ancients felt that the sky was about to fall, and they quickly went to the temple to offer sacrifices. However, the ancients also had the memory of seeing a solar eclipse before. They knew that the solar eclipse would pass in a short period of time, so there would be no problem if they waited patiently. It is just that the *dao* by which the sun maintains its abundance seems to have been damaged, but there is no need to worry too much about the sun.

The light is abundant, shining all over the world, illuminating the realm under heaven, that is, the realm of existence, including the realm of ghosts and spirits, that is, the mode in which ghosts and spirits exist. Human intentionality is so rich that it can contain ghosts and spirits, break prisons and impose punishments, and penalize evildoers. The goodness of human nature is not based on the original substance of the natural goodness of the *dao* of nature, but is only a definition and assumption of the inherent goodness of human nature, which is not enough to answer the question of the evil of human nature. This is as paradoxical as why a supremely good and almighty God would tolerate the existence of an imperfect world. No matter what universal human nature is, the problem of human nature cannot be solved simply through the assumption of a supreme good, but is indeed a theoretical dilemma that must be faced head-on. The *Book of Changes* confirms that the ontological nature of the cosmological intentionality of humanity and heaven is connected with heaven, and that the natural goodness of the *dao* of heaven is not the goodness concerning good and evil.

初九：遇其配主，虽旬无咎，往有尚。

《象》曰："虽旬无咎"，过"旬"灾也。

【明译】

初九：遇到相匹配之主（六二），十天内没有祸患，如果前往会得到推崇和嘉尚。

《象传》说：十天内没有祸患，但过了十天会有灾祸。

Nine (*yang*/strong line) in the first place: If one meets the matching ruler (the Six (*yin*/soft line) in the second place), there will be no trouble within ten days. If one advances, one will be praised and honored.

The *Image Commentary* (*Xiang Zhuan*) says: There will be no disaster within ten days, but there will be disaster after ten days.

【明意】

此爻是在变革后的乱势之中，能够遇到相配之主，虽然看起来还算不错，但形势很快转坏。这说明意向性要随变动的境遇而变，如果该变的不变，守一时之安，不久过后会有灾。这是对于阴阳之意能的变化没有体会，该动而不动，失去行动的时机。

[Illuminating Intentionality]

This line is about meeting a compatible ruler in the chaos after reform. Although it looks pretty good, the situation quickly turns bad. This shows that intentionality should change with changing circumstances. If it does not change, it will be safe for a while, but there will be disaster soon. This is because there is no understanding of the changes in the intentional energy of *yin* and *yang*, and one does not move when it is time to move, thus losing the opportunity to act.

六二：丰其蔀（bù），日中见斗。往得疑疾，有孚发若，吉。

《象》曰："有孚发若"，信以发志也。

【明译】

六二：发生了日全食，太阳被大面积遮蔽，大中午都能够看到星斗，这个黑暗到了极点的时候，从四位下来的六二的冒失行动必然招致六五的猜疑嫉恨，六二只有让自己的真诚的人天之意慢慢发动使真相大白，最后会获得吉祥。

《象传》说：六二让自己的真诚的人天之意慢慢发动使真相大白，因为相信自己的诚信可启发六五的心志。

Six (*yin*/soft line) in the second place: A total solar eclipse occurs, and the sun is blocked to a great extent and stars can be seen at noon. When the darkness reaches its extreme, the Six (*yin*/soft line) in the second place's reckless actions from the fourth position inevitably arouse the suspicion and jealousy of the Six (*yin*/soft line) in the fifth place. The Six (*yin*/soft line) in the second place can only let its sincere intentionality of humanity and heaven slowly initiate and the truth come to light, finally gaining auspiciousness.

The *Image Commentary* (*Xiang Zhuan*) says: The Six (*yin*/soft line) in the second place allows one's sincere intentionality of humanity and heaven to slowly unfold the truth, because one believes that one's integrity can inspire the Six (*yin*/soft line) in the fifth place's aspirations.

【明意】

光明心意被遮蔽得黑暗无光，好像日食一般。此时需要对自己的心意有充分的耐心，等待形势的转变。心意虽丰，但形势不妙，被小人之阴意盛大遮蔽，困难重重。光明之心大的时候，小人之阴意也巨大。此刻要相信自己真诚的人天之意，最终可以拨云见日，让真相大白。这是相信内心被遮蔽、被曲解的光明之意，就像日食导致的黑暗一样，不用太久就可以重新光耀天下。

[Illuminating Intentionality]

The bright intentionality is covered with darkness, like a solar eclipse. At this time, one needs to be patient with one's own intentions and wait for the situation to change. Although intentionality is abundant, the situation is not good, it is obscured by the evil intentions of petty people, and there are many difficulties. When the heart of light is great, the evil intentions of petty people are also great. At this moment, one must believe in one's sincere intentions, then eventually one can clear the clouds and let the truth come to light. This is the belief that the light in the heart that has been obscured and misinterpreted, just like the darkness caused by a solar eclipse, will not take long to shine again.

九三：丰其沛，日中见沫（mò），折其右肱，无咎。

《象》曰："丰其沛"，不可大事也。"折其右肱"，终不可用也。

【明译】

九三：日光被遮蔽得非常丰沛了，黑暗非常严重，大中午都能够看到小星星，如果能够像折断右臂那样屈己慎守，最终可以避开祸患。

《象传》说：日光被遮蔽得非常丰沛了，黑暗很严重，这个时候是不能干大事有所作为的。犹如黑暗中折断了右臂（影响做事），导致九三最终还是没有被起用。

Nine (*yang*/strong line) in the third place: The sunlight is blocked very copiously, and the darkness is very serious, so one can see small stars at noon. If one can be as cautious as if one had broken one's right arm, one can finally avoid disaster.

The *Image Commentary* (*Xiang Zhuan*) says: The sunlight is blocked very copiously, and the darkness is very serious. At this time, it is impossible to do great things or make a difference. It is like breaking one's right arm in the dark (which affects one's work), which leads to the Nine (*yang*/strong line) in the third place not being used in the end.

【明意】

形势极度危险，如光明隐陷，此时采用死里逃生之术，犹如下卦明夷所示，当形势黑暗不被见用之时，能断臂求生，先活下来就不错了。可见，受伤曲行是为了保守内在真诚的意性不失。

黑暗当中摔倒，断臂是为了保命求生，但摔到右臂折断，也是受伤严重，等天地恢复光明之时，出来做事还是受到了影响。

[Illuminating Intentionality]
The situation is extremely dangerous, such as the light being hidden, and at this time, the technique of escaping from death is used, as shown in the subsequent Hexagram Mingyi (Fading Light). When the situation is dark and one is not recognized and used, it is good to live on if one can cut off one's arms and survive first. It can be seen that the purpose of being injured is to preserve one's inner sincerity and intention.

One falls down in the dark and breaks one's arm in order to save one's life. But when one fell and broke one's right arm, one was seriously injured. When the light returns to the sky and the earth, one is still affected when one comes out to engage in affairs.

九四：丰其蔀，日中见斗，遇其夷主，吉。
《象》曰："丰其蔀"，位不当也。"日中见斗"，幽不明也。"遇其夷主"，"吉"行也。
【明译】
九四：发生了日全食，光明被遮蔽很大，大中午能够见到星斗，黑暗中遇到旧日的主人，能够化险为夷。

《象传》说：光明被遮蔽很大，因为九四位置不适当。大中午能够见到星斗，是天色幽暗而不明亮。遇到势均力敌的明主，这是吉祥的征行（九四在卦变中向上升进与六五比邻）。

Nine (*yang*/strong line) in the fourth place: A total solar eclipse occurs, and the light is significantly blocked, so one can see the stars at noon. Meeting an old master in the darkness can save the day.

The *Image Commentary* (*Xiang Zhuan*) says: The light is greatly obscured because the location of the Nine (*yang*/strong line) in the fourth place is inappropriate. One can see stars at noon, but the sky is dark and not bright. It is an auspicious journey to encounter an evenly-matched enlightened master (the Nine (*yang*/strong line) in the fourth place ascends in the hexagram-changes and is adjacent to the Six (*yin*/soft line) in the fifth place).

【明意】
郭象说万物皆"独化于玄冥之境"，放到人生当中，可以理解为人生时刻在黑暗之中，要有伴同行才能找到方向，这个伴就是"夷主"，一个跟你平等的，又可能为你的意识方向和意识之行做主的人。其实，每个人虽然都睁着眼睛，但没有几个人看得清前进的方向，当我们碰到心意相投，能够给我们的意识之行指明方向的人，其实就是我们的夷主。因为我们的心念发动，心意之境其实常常在黑暗当中，不知如何才能够让意识之行合乎"中庸之意"，即时时刻刻合乎自然之中道的人天之意。

[Illuminating Intentionality]

Guo Xiang said that the myriad things are "transforming alone in a dark and remote (*xuanming* 玄冥) realm." In the context of human life, this can be understood as saying that life is always in darkness, and one needs a companion to find the right direction. This companion is the "saving master," someone who is equal to one, and may be the person who decides the direction and journey of one's consciousness. In fact, although everyone has their eyes open, few can clearly see the way forward. When we meet people who are like-minded and can point the direction for our conscious journey, they are actually our saving masters. Because our intentions are initiated, the realm of our heart-minds is in fact constantly in darkness. We do not know how to make the actions of consciousness conform to the "intentionality of the golden mean," which is always in line with the central *dao* of nature and its intentionality of humanity and heaven.

六五：来章，有庆誉，吉。

《象》曰：六五之"吉"，"有庆"也。

【明译】

六五：召来内涵有文采的贤人，得到喜庆和荣誉，这是吉祥的。

《象传》说：六五吉祥，是有喜庆。

Six (*yin*/soft line) in the fifth place: It is auspicious to summon wise men with literary talent and receive joy and honor.

The *Image Commentary* (*Xiang Zhuan*) says: The Six (*yin*/soft line) in the fifth place is auspicious and brings joy.

【明意】

对于六五来说，上来了一位贤臣辅助他，能够雷厉风行地帮助他做一些改革，让天下重新变得光明灿烂，即使他自己能力不够，光明有限，但这样的贤人贤臣出现，对于国家和人民来说，恍若光明再现，毕竟是振奋人心的好现象。

君王的意行受到巨大光明的加持和辅助，得到这样的贤臣辅佐，即使昏君也可能让自己的心意光明起来。因为对昏弱之君来说，上来强有力的辅助之人，电闪雷鸣般地开始一些变革，不仅帮助自己的心意转而光明，而且让天下人的心意都变得光明丰大，这可是值得大大庆祝的好事。

[Illuminating Intentionality]

For the Six (*yin*/soft line) in the fifth place, a virtuous minister comes up to assist him, one who can help him make reforms vigorously and resolutely, making the world bright and brilliant again. Even if he himself is not capable enough and his brightness is limited, the appearance of such a virtuous minister is a great help to him. For the country and its people, the sudden reappearance of light is, after all, an exciting and positive phenomenon.

The king's intentions and deeds are blessed and assisted by great light. With the assistance of such wise ministers, even a weak king can make his intentionality bright. Because, for a weak king, powerful assistants come forward and start making changes like lightning and thunder, not only helping his own intentionality to become bright, but also making the intentions of everyone in the world become bright and abundant. This is a good thing that deserves a great celebration.

上六：丰其屋，蔀其家，窥其户，阒（qù）其无人，三岁不觌（dí）。凶。

《象》曰："丰其屋"，天际翔也。"窥其户，阒其无人"，自藏也。

【明译】

上六：巍峨高大的房屋都笼罩在黑暗之中，周围的人家都被彻底遮蔽，即使透过门窗窥视，里面也空寂如荒芜一般，犹如自鸣得意，自绝于人，孤立自闭，多年不让人见，最后必定凶险。

《象传》说：房屋巍峨高大也彻底被无边的黑暗笼罩，这种巨大的恐怖犹如幽灵一般在天际飞翔（上位是天上之位，二至上爻近似小过卦，有飞鸟之象，如鸟在天边飞翔）。透过门窗窥视，里面空寂无人，象征人的心意自我封闭，不跟他人来往（上六丰极必藏而凶）。

Six (*yin*/soft line) in the top place: The majestic and tall houses are shrouded in darkness, and the surrounding homes are completely obscured. Even if one peeks through the doors and windows, the interior is empty and deserted, as if it is complacent, cut off from others, isolated and confined, and has not allowed itself to be seen for many years. This must be dangerous in the end.

The *Image Commentary* (*Xiang Zhuan*) says: The majestic and tall houses are completely shrouded in boundless darkness. This huge terror is like a dark spirit flying in the heavens (the top position is the position in the heaven, and from the second to the top line it is similar to Hexagram Xiaoguo (Slight Overreaching), with the image of a flying bird, like a bird flying in the heaven). Peeping through the doors and windows, there is no one inside, which symbolizes that people's intentions are closed in on themselves and do not interact with others (the Six (*yin*/soft line) in the top place's extreme abundance must be hidden and is dangerous).

【明意】

人间成事于心意之通，败事于心意不通。丰卦电闪雷鸣，本应心意光明，但爻辞借日全食来描述黑暗无光之象，近于明夷，也是以黯然神伤的心意出门旅行之象。丰卦上六非常准确地接地火明夷，自己的光明隐陷而不出。到了上六丰大的心意都被败坏遮蔽了，就不再能够显现出来了。

人的意向性是关于他人他物的，其中连接人的意向与他物的生机至关重要。日全食好像给所有人突然之间判了死刑一般，天下突然光明全无，生机不现，于是有巨大的恐慌。不过有老人经历过，说不要害怕，一时的绝望，不等于永远的绝望，太阳还会出来，我们的意向性还可以跟世间的事物联通，天地的生机还在。

但是有些人被眼前的经历震撼怕了，有人在黑暗当中经历了恐怖的事件，所以长久不能够从中走出来，后半生就一直生存在没有生意的意向性状态当中，昏昏沉沉，意向发动不再有生机，任凭周围的心意荒芜下去，无心也无力去维护意向性发动的生机。这就是上六爻要表达的、心意长久无法从日全食当中解脱出来的状态，也就是意向性不行，或者没有行动力的状态。这样的人行为和意识主体，已经不再是主动的主体（agent），也就不具备意向性的实化能力和意念发动的执行力。

[Illuminating Intentionality]

Success in the world depends on the understanding of intentionality, and failure comes from a lack of understanding of intentionality. The lightning and thunder in Hexagram Feng (Abundance) should mean bright intentions, but the line commentary uses a total solar eclipse to describe a dark and lightless image, close to Hexagram Mingyi (Fading Light), and also represents a journey with a gloomy and sad mind. The Six (*yin*/soft line) in the top place of Hexagram Feng (Abundance) is very accurately connected to ground fire and fading light, and one's own light is hidden and cannot come out. By the time one arrives at the upper reaches of the Six (*yin*/soft line) in the top place, all one's great intentions have been obscured by corruption and can no longer be revealed.

Human intentionality is about other people and other things, and the connection between human intentions and other things is crucial. A total solar eclipse seems to be a sudden death sentence for everyone. Suddenly there is no light in the world, and there is no life, so there is a huge panic. However, some old people have experienced it before and tell people not to be afraid. Temporary despair does not mean eternal despair, as the sun will still come out, one's intentionality can still be connected with things in the world, and the vitality of heaven and earth is still there.

However, some people are shocked and frightened by the experiences before them. Some people experience horrific events in the dark, so they are unable to come out of it for a long time. They live in a state of intentionality without productive intentions for the rest of their lives, feeling groggy and with no vitality to initiate their intentions. Based on the surrounding and ongoing desolation of intentionality, the pure heart-mind will be unable to maintain the vitality initiated by intentionality. This is what the line commentary of the Six (*yin*/soft line) in the top place is trying to express, a state of intentionality that cannot be freed from the total solar eclipse for a long time, that is, a state of lack of intentionality or lack of action. Such a person's behavior and consciousness are no longer those of an active subject (an agent), and they do not have the ability to concretize intentionality and the executive ability to initiate intentions.

火山旅（卦五十六）　（艮下离上）
Lü (Traveling), Fire and Mountain (Hexagram 56)　(Gen below, Li above)

　　上卦丰卦说明，过分丰富反而不可能维持，被迫重新在旅途中找寻方向，旅卦有家破人亡，不得不去旅行之意。只要出来旅行，就只能求小顺小安，因为必须要与周围各种缘分安然相处，做事说话都要适可而止。但意念的方向只能依境而生，即人的意向不可能脱离人的生存条件而生，否则没有方向感则易于迷失自己。

　　人在旅途，必须跟断狱一样审慎，旅行时一念出偏，就偏离很远，有时越走越远，甚至误入歧途而无法回来；断狱也是一样，如果一念出偏，当事人的命运就被改变，有时构成冤假错案，当事人的命运就彻底改观，甚至可能误杀无辜的人，人命关天，无法重新来过。可见，旅行需要火光来照亮前面的道路，人虽然睁眼，但看不清前进的方向，也需要特别的光亮来帮助自己摸索意向的方向，知道每一个意向的抉择，都把人生的意向之路导向不同的方向。旅行当中，人通过自己的意向抉择，决定周围人与自己相关的意向和他们的命运，这与断案的时候，每一个意念都决定当事人的意向和他们的命运其实如出一辙。只是旅行时候对他人的意向命运的决定是弱决定，他人没有感觉，自己也不容易这样去想；而断案时对他人命运的决定是强决定，一旦决断，他人的命运就可能是冰火两重天。

　　意向一发动，只是万千可能性之一，所以意向一动，好像漂泊的旅人，不知何处是正确的方向。旅行者有无限的可能性和无限的意向性。人的一生好比在旅途，很难知道何方是最佳、最合格的方向。旅行是不断抉择、实化和定义自己的意缘的过程，需要非常谨慎小心，正如断案，念念决定当事人的进退存亡，所以更要如用火一般谨慎。不仅仅因为监狱中的人被剥夺了旅行的自由，而且因为有能力决定他人自由的人，要给被剥夺旅行之人足够的尊严，正如小心应对身边的旅人，要谨慎处理而不滞留案件，不宜不合理地影响他们本来就非常有限的自由。

The previous Hexagram Feng (Abundance) shows that it is impossible to maintain excessive wealth, and one is forced to find a direction again on a journey. The journey means that one's family is broken and the people are destroyed, and one has to travel. As long as one travels, one can only seek comfort and peace, because one must get along with all kinds of dependent co-arising conditions around one, and must act and speak in moderation. However, the direction of intentionality can only arise according to the situation, that is, people's intentions cannot be separated from people's living conditions. Otherwise, without a sense of direction, it is easy to lose oneself.

People must be as cautious when traveling as when they are judging a case. When traveling, if an intention goes astray, they will deviate very far. Sometimes, they will go further and further, and even go astray and be unable to come back. The same is true for judging a case. If an intention goes astray, the dependent co-arising of the person involved will be changed, sometimes resulting in an unjust, false or wrongful conviction. Then, the dependent co-arising of the parties concerned is completely changed, and innocent people may even be killed by mistake. Human lives are at stake and there is no way to start over. It can be seen that traveling requires firelight to illuminate the road ahead. Even if people open their eyes, they often cannot see the direction of travel clearly, so they also need special light to help them explore the direction of their intentions. They know that every choice of intention reflects the intentionality of life, the roads of which lead in different directions. During travel, people use their own intentions and choices to determine the intentions and dependent co-arising of those around them. This is exactly the same as when judging a case, where every intention determines the intentions of the parties involved and their dependent co-arising. However, the decision about other people's intentions and dependent co-arising when traveling is a weak decision. Others do not feel it, and it is not easy for one to think like this. However, the decision about other people's dependent co-arising when judging a case is a strong decision. Once the decision is made, the destiny of others may be completely changed.

Once an intention is initiated, it is only one of thousands of possibilities, so once the intention is initiated, it is like a wandering traveler who does not know where the right direction is. The traveler has infinite possibilities and infinite intentionality. A person's life is like a journey, and it is difficult to know which is the best and most suitable direction. Traveling is a process of constantly making choices, concretizing and defining one's own fate, so it requires great caution. Just like deciding a case, one's intentions determine the advance and retreat of the parties involved, so one must be as cautious as using fire. This is not only because people in prison are deprived of the freedom to travel, but also because people who have the ability to determine the freedom of others must give enough dignity to those who are deprived of travel, just as they treat the travelers around them carefully and handle cases carefully without holding them up. This should not unreasonably affect their already very limited freedoms.

旅，小亨。旅贞吉。

《彖》曰："旅，小亨"，柔得中乎外，而顺乎刚，止而丽乎明，是以"小亨，旅贞吉"也。旅之时义大矣哉！

《象》曰：山上有火，旅。君子以明慎用刑而不留狱。

【明译】

旅卦象征旅行漂泊，稍有亨通，行旅的时候持守正道能获吉祥。

《彖传》说：旅卦稍有亨通，是因为柔顺取得在外的中道又能顺应刚健（在卦变中，六五从否下坤的三位升到了外卦乾的中位，坤为柔顺，乾为刚健，是柔顺地顺应刚健）。下卦艮为止，上卦离为附丽、为光明，是安宁守分地依附于光明，因此稍有亨通，行旅的时候持守正道能获吉祥。旅卦的时势的时机化意义实在太重大了！

《象传》说：下卦艮为山，上卦离为火，山上失火，众生皆失家行旅而有旅行漂泊之象。君子鉴于山上着火，火势熊熊的旅卦，知道要明察审慎地施用刑罚，而不滞留案件。

Hexagram Lü (Traveling) symbolizes travel and wandering, and if one is slightly prosperous, one can gain good fortune by staying on the right *dao* while traveling.

The *Judgment Commentary* (*Tuan Zhuan*) says: The reason why Hexagram Lü (Traveling) is slightly prosperous is because the soft obtains the outer central *dao* and can adapt to the strong (in the hexagram-changes, the Six (*yin*/soft line) in the fifth place was promoted from the third position of the lower Trigram Kun in Hexagram Pi (Non-Communication) to the middle position of the outer Trigram Qian, and Kun is pliable, while Qian is firm, so this is the soft complying with the strong). The lower Trigram Gen is stopping, while the upper Trigram Li is attached beauty and light, meaning one is attached to the light in a peaceful and orderly manner, so it is a little prosperous. When traveling, one can get good fortune by adhering to the upright *dao*. The timing of Hexagram Lü (Traveling)'s current situation is of great significance!

The *Image Commentary* (*Xiang Zhuan*) says: The lower Trigram Gen is mountain, and the upper Trigram Li is fire. If there is fire on the mountain, all living beings will lose their homes and travel, and they will have the appearance of traveling and wandering. In view of the fire on the mountain and the raging inferno of Hexagram Lü (Traveling), the exemplary person knows to use punishments wisely and prudently without delaying the case.

【明意】

"旅"是客旅于外，本意就是客寄他乡。古人旅行漂泊主要是行役戍边，所以引申出军旅之意。旅行在外时，自然亲友就少。古时交通不便，旅行在外苦不堪言，所以旅行即是逆境，但人要学会应付逆境，这样逆境就有其正面的意义，人应该既能处顺，又能处逆。

人都是天地之间的旅客，意向从根本上说都缘起缘灭。安身立命其实就是安顿自己心意的方向，为自己的人生找到一个合适的方向来安顿心灵。即使旅行在外，缘起缘灭也不可丧志，不可忘记自己的使命。

旅人的心意与断案者的心意，在决定他人意识境遇甚至命运的角度来说，有异曲同工之妙，因为旅行是一个不断决定自己和他人命运的过程，而断案也是这样的一个过程，只是旅行时对他人的决定弱，而断案时对他人的决定强。人在旅途，时时刻刻都在断案的过程当中，跟他人的意向交汇、意缘交接之处，就是断案的开始，我们在跟人意念交接的瞬间，就在断人之案，决定跟他人意识交往的进退和分寸，这就是人与人之间意识交流的断案。旅人的心意只有真诚随顺，才能让他人断得平和合理，这也是推致自己意念方向的核心。

[Illuminating Intentionality]

"Traveling" means lodging and traveling to faraway places, and its original meaning was to send guests to a remote place. Ancient people's travels and wanderings were mainly for military operations and guarding borders, so the meaning of military expeditions was derived. When one travels, one naturally has fewer relatives and friends around. In ancient times, transportation was inconvenient and traveling was miserable, so traveling was an adversity. However, people should learn to cope with adversity, so adversity has a positive intentionality. People should be able to deal with both good and bad times.

Everyone is a traveler between heaven and earth, and intentions fundamentally arise and perish. To settle down and establish oneself is actually to settle the direction of one's intentionality, to find a suitable direction for one's life to settle one's heart-mind. Even if one is traveling afar and one's conditions come and go, one should not lose heart and not forget one's mission.

The intentionality of a traveler and that of a person who solves a case are similar in terms of determining other people's consciousness and even their fate, because traveling is a process that constantly determines the dependent co-arising of oneself and others, and solving cases is also such a process, except that, when traveling, decisions about others are weak, but decisions about others are strong when deciding a case. When people are traveling, they are in the process of solving a case all the time. The place where the intentions and dependent co-arising of others intersect is the beginning of solving the case. The moment we connect with others' intentions, we are deciding the case and deciding to cooperate with others. The advance, retreat and propriety of conscious communication are the key to conscious communication between people. Only if a traveler is sincere and obedient can others make decisions peacefully and reasonably, and this is also the core of the direction of one's own intentions.

初六：旅琐琐，斯其所取灾。

《象》曰："旅琐琐"，志穷"灾"也。

【明译】

初六：行旅的时候行为卑贱猥琐，这等于是自取其灾。

《象传》说：行旅的时候行为卑贱猥琐，因为初六志气穷困，就容易招惹灾害（初六有正应在九四，但处在下卦艮（阻）里，志受困阻）。

Six (*yin*/soft line) in the first place: Behaving basely and obscenely while traveling is tantamount to bringing disaster upon oneself.

The *Image Commentary* (*Xiang Zhuan*) says: When traveling, one's behavior is base and obscene. Because the ambition of the Six (*yin*/soft line) in the first place is poor, it can easily cause disasters (the Six (*yin*/soft line) in the first place has a positive response in the Nine (*yang*/strong line) in the fourth place, but it is in the lower Trigram Gen (blockage), and its ambition is blocked).

【明意】

旅行之时，身不安宁，不当位、不合适的身位，会影响人的心态，所以首先要警惕小心，要尽量做到即使身不安，心也要安。否则，心不安就容易绝望，进而迷失意向的方向，觉得意向没有出路，或者任何一个意向都是不合适的出路。

[Illuminating Intentionality]

When traveling, the body is not at peace, and an improper position or inappropriate positioning will affect one's mentality, so first of all, one must be vigilant and careful, and try one's best to have peace of intentionality even if one's body is uneasy. Otherwise, if one's intentionality is uneasy, it is easy to despair and then lose the direction of one's intention, feeling that there is no way out for the intention, or that any intention is an inappropriate way out.

六二：旅即次，怀其资，得童仆贞。

《象》曰："得童仆贞"，终无尤也。

【明译】

六二：在旅途当中，住进客舍，怀中带有旅资，得到忠贞的童仆来帮忙照顾。

《象传》说：得到忠贞的童仆来帮忙照顾，说明六二最终不会有怨尤。

Six (*yin*/soft line) in the second place: During the journey, one stays in a guest house, carries travel funds in one's arms, and gets loyal servants to help take care of one.

The *Image Commentary* (*Xiang Zhuan*) says: Having a loyal boy servant to help take care of him means that the Six (*yin*/soft line) in the second place will not have any resentment in the end.

【明意】

六二是得旅行之道的旅客，知道旅行之时的意向应该调整到一种合适的状态。当然，其内在的精神修养，外在的物质条件都不错，所以能够有安宁舒适的旅途。加上有人帮助，则旅行的意向更加安稳，因为有人辅助就能帮忙调整自己意识的方向，方向感更强，力量更大，比一个人摸索好。有人帮助自己调整意向，就容易形成意向合力，有助于减少忧虑。

[Illuminating Intentionality]

The Six (*yin*/soft line) in the second place is a traveler who has learned how to travel. One knows that one's intention when traveling should be adjusted to a suitable state. Of course, one's inner spiritual cultivation and external material conditions are both good, so one can have a peaceful and comfortable journey. In addition, if someone helps, the intention to travel will be more stable, because someone can help adjust the direction of his consciousness. The sense of direction is stronger and the power is greater, which is better than groping alone. If someone helps one adjust one's intentions, it will be easier to form a synergy of intentions and help reduce worries.

九三：旅焚其次，丧其童仆，贞厉。

《象》曰："旅焚其次"，亦以伤矣。以旅与下，其义"丧"也。

【明译】

九三：行旅途中，大火烧毁了旅舍，童仆也走失了，此时还顽固不动，会有危险。

《象传》说：行旅途中，大火烧毁了旅舍，实在是伤人伤物也伤心的事情。把忠心的童仆也当作旅人，出事后按道理说也该丧失（九三原在否卦的五位，卦变时来到下卦三位，失尊得卑）。

Nine (*yang*/strong line) in the third place: During the journey, a fire burns down the inn, and the boy servant is lost. If one remains stubborn at this time, one will be in danger.

The *Image Commentary* (*Xiang Zhuan*) says: During the journey, the fire burns down the hotel, a really sad affair that harmed both people and property. Treat the loyal boy servant as a traveler, and logically speaking, he should be lost after the affair (the Nine (*yang*/strong line) in the third place was originally in the fifth position of Hexagram Pi (Non-Communication), but after the hexagram-changes, he comes to the third position of the next hexagram, so he loses his respect and becomes lowly).

【明意】

人生时刻都在旅行当中，不可以用过分刚正的态度对待其他旅人，如视之为外人和下人，用那样的意向待人不可能得到他们忠贞服侍，一旦有事起火，大家就都先顾自己跑了。人的态度和意向会影响一起旅行的他人之意向，一到关键时刻就能够看出来，稍有不慎就容易遭到灾祸。

阳爻可以理解为主动出去旅行，但还在艮卦的时势当中，所以应该适可而止，不知停止就属于过分，反而会给人欺负。每个爻代表人的个性，代表人的意向特征，这些意向特征与其无法更改的意境一起，构成了人发动意念的宿命。也就是说，人总是倾向于发动某类意念，发动到某些方向，所以总是不善于在反省当中为自己的意向方向做主。

[Illuminating Intentionality]

Life is about traveling all the time. One should not treat other travelers with an overly righteous attitude, such as treating them as outsiders or subordinates. Treating others with such an intention is unlikely to win their loyal service. Once trouble breaks out, everyone will run away first in concern for themselves. A person's attitude and intention will affect the intentions of others traveling together, as can be seen at critical moments. If one is not careful, one may easily suffer disaster.

The *yang* line can be understood as taking the initiative to travel, but it is still in the current situation of Hexagram Gen (Stopping), so it should be stopped appropriately. If one does not know when to stop, it is excessive, and it will in fact lead others to bully. Each line represents a person's personality and his or her intentional characteristics. These intentional characteristics, together with their unchangeable intentional context, constitute the dependent co-arising of people's intentions. That is to say, people always tend to initiate certain types of intentions, and initiate certain types of intentional directions, so they are always not good at making decisions about their own intentions during introspection.

九四：旅于处，得其资斧，我心不快。

《象》曰："旅于处"，未得位也。"得其资斧"，心未快也。

【明译】

九四：客旅途中，暂时得到较为稳定的栖身之处，又得到一点资财利器，可是心中仍然闷闷不乐。

《象传》说：客旅途中，暂时得到栖身之处，因为还没有得到合适的地位（九四刚爻居柔位）。得到一点资财利器，可是心中仍然闷闷不乐（虽然得到行旅所需要的旅费和器用，但总是希望回到家乡可以有更大的发展）。

Nine (*yang*/strong line) in the fourth place: During the journey, one temporarily finds a more stable place to live, and acquires some financial instruments, but is still unhappy in one's heart-mind.

The *Image Commentary* (*Xiang Zhuan*) says: During the journey, one temporarily finds a place to stay because one has not yet obtained a suitable status (the Nine (*yang*/strong line) in the fourth place occupies a soft position). One obtains some financial instruments, but one's heart-mind is still unhappy (although one gets the travel expenses and equipment needed for the trip, one always hopes to have greater development when one returns to one's hometown).

【明意】

人在旅途，心中有期盼，不能活在当下，一定不会快乐。虽然暂时安定，但几乎所有的意向都有让自己不畅快的地方，无法顺利实化自己的意向，于是加剧了本来就很强的漂泊感，更加无法掌控自己的意向，心里闷闷不乐。所以人的意向不但要有方向，而且要有实化的可能性和条件，如果各种方向上人都无法实化自己的意向，就不会觉得意向得到安处。

[Illuminating Intentionality]

When people are on a journey, they have expectations in their intentions. If they cannot live in the present, they will definitely not be happy. Although one is temporarily stable, almost all one's intentions have some dissatisfaction. One is unable to realize one's intentions smoothly, which intensifies one's already strong sense of wandering. One is even more unable to control one's intentions and feels depressed. Therefore, people's intentions must not only have a direction, but also have the possibility and conditions for their realization. If people are unable to concretize their intentions in various directions, they will feel that their intentions have been settled.

六五：射雉，一矢亡，终以誉命。

《象》曰："终以誉命"，上逮（dài）也。

【明译】

六五：用箭射野雉，（一箭射中，但毕竟）丢失了一支箭，（但可找回，所以）最终得到美誉和爵命。

《象传》说：最终得到美誉和爵命，是因为六五到达了上面的尊位（六五卦变中由三位升到尊位）。

Six (*yin*/soft line) in the fifth place: Shooting a pheasant with an arrow, (one arrow hits, but after all) one arrow is lost, (but it can be recovered, so) in the end one gets a good reputation and a noble appointment.

The *Image Commentary* (*Xiang Zhuan*) says: In the end, one gained a good reputation and a noble title because the Six (*yin*/soft line) in the fifth place reached the upper position of honor (one was promoted from the third position to the honored position of the Six (*yin*/soft line) in the fifth place through the hexagram-changes).

【明意】

能不能射中、成功与否并不重要，但意向性展开即有其意量与意境。意量可控有限，而意境通达众人与天地。故意境生生之机，可以逮于上位之人，并用其意向而得到认可。所以意向的发动像动机，结果如何不重要。只要意向生生不息，守于正道，就会得到他意的应和。不断扩大融通的意境，成就自己的意量。从这个过程来说，是否真正的建功立业并不是最重要的。意向发动的瞬间，即已彰显功业的力度与量限。

可见，《周易》是动机主义，符合儒家伦理学以动机为主的精神，生是过程，死是永恒，好好过人生的过程，就是谨慎决定自己永恒生命之中短暂的生之过程。既然建功立业相比永恒的死亡来说并不重要，那么，生存当下意念发动的实在瞬间，是否具有生生之机，便成了决定人生意念质量的根本与核心。这也是儒家圣人之所以强调人心要服从道心，人的精神纯洁度要超越所有外在功业成就的原因所在。这也是儒家动机主义伦理学的神圣性和宗教性的来源。

[Illuminating Intentionality]

It is not important whether or not one can hit the target or whether it is successful or not, but that intentional development has its intentionality and intentional context. The controllability of intention is limited, but the intentional context reaches everyone and heaven and earth. The productive and reproductive impetus of a state of intentionality can be caught by someone in a superior position, and its intentions can be used to gain recognition. So the initiation of intention is like motivation, and the result is not important. As long as one's intention persists and one stays on the upright *dao*, one will get the response of one's intention. Continuously expanding the intentional context of integration, one can achieve one's own intentional energy. From the perspective of this process, whether one truly makes a contribution or not is not the most important thing. The moment the intention is initiated, the strength and limit of its merit are already demonstrated.

It can be seen that the *Book of Changes* is motivational, in line with the motivation-based spirit of Confucian ethics. Life is a process, and death is eternal. The process of living a good life is to carefully determine the short-term life processes in one's eternal life. Since meritorious deeds are not as important as eternal death, whether there is a chance of life at the real moment when intentions are initiated becomes the fundamental and core factor that determines the quality of living intentions. This is why Confucian sages emphasize that the human heart-mind must obey the heart-mind of *dao*, and that human spiritual purity must surpass all external achievements. This is also the source of the sanctity and religiosity of Confucian motivational ethics.

上九：鸟焚其巢，旅人先笑后号咷。丧牛于易，凶。

《象》曰：以旅在上，其义"焚"也。"丧牛于易"，终莫之闻也。

【明译】

上九：（行旅之人在外高高在上）好像鸟巢上面快要着火了，随时可能把鸟巢烧掉，刚开始的时候还笑得出来，但到后来就只有嚎啕大哭了，也好比在边界上把自己的牛群都弄丢了，这对一个在外旅行的人来说，是非常凶险的。

《象传》说：客旅在外还高高在上，丝毫不顺服的话，道义上就会被焚烧（上九在全卦上位）。就好像人（把牛的顺服劲给抛弃了，就会）在边界上把自己的牛群都弄丢了，也就是上九在旅途当中遭到祸殃却无人过问，无人在乎。

Nine (*yang*/strong line) in the top place: (The traveler is outside and high up.) It seems that a bird's nest is about to catch fire, and the bird's nest may be burned down at any time. At the beginning, one could laugh, but later one can only cry, as it is like burning oneself on the border. All the cattle are lost, which is very dangerous for a person traveling abroad.

The *Image Commentary* (*Xiang Zhuan*) says: If a traveler abroad is aloof and does not obey at all, one will be burned morally (the Nine (*yang*/strong line) in the top place is at the top of the whole hexagram). This is like people (who abandon the obedience of cattle) losing all their cattle on the border, that is, the Nine (*yang*/strong line) in the top place suffers disaster during the journey but no one cares about it.

【明意】

在旅行途中，人要柔顺而不可过刚，柔顺则得，过刚则失，此是旅卦一以贯之的教导。顺乎情境的方向，一般才是自己意向的最佳方向。行旅的心向要平和谦恭。在变化的情境中，身外之物的得失和内在的心意状态有很大的关系，所以小心旅行，认真地对待每一个人，都是很重要的。行旅要顺势而发动意向，意向不顺情境则有危险。意识形成于缘起之境中，行旅之人的意向当安顺于其境。人从终极意义之上都在行旅之中，即使位高权重，也是过客旅行，暂居于世而已。所以意向生生不息，总是依境而生，人既在旅途当中，当顺情境而生创造之意，转入巽顺。

[Illuminating Intentionality]

During the journey, one should be gentle and not too strong. If one is soft, one might gain; if one is too strong, one might lose. This is the consistent teaching of Hexagram Lü (Traveling). The direction that goes with the situation is generally the best direction for one's own intentions, so one should travel with a peaceful and humble heart-mind. In changing situations, the gains and losses of external things are closely related to one's inner state of mind, so it is important to travel carefully and treat everyone seriously. When traveling, one must follow the trend and initiate one's intention. If your intention does not go according to the situation, there will be danger. Consciousness is formed in a state of dependent origination, and the traveler's intention should be at ease with it. In an ultimate sense, people are all on a journey. Even if they are in a high and powerful position, they are just passing by and living in the world temporarily. Therefore, intentionality is endless and always arises according to the situation. Since people are on a journey, they should adapt to the situation to create their intentions and turn into the accommodating attitude of Hexagram Xun (Submission).

巽为风（卦五十七） （巽下巽上）

Xun (Submission), Wind (Hexagram 57) (Xun below, Xun above)

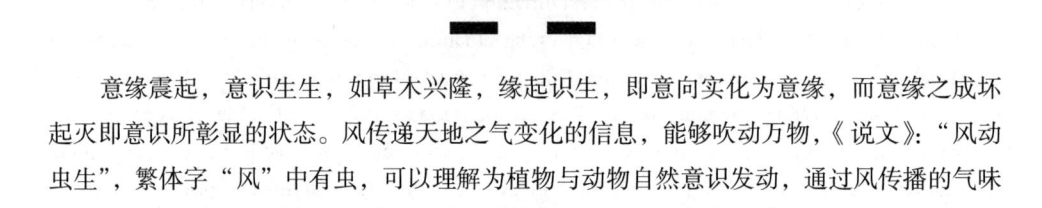

䷸

意缘震起，意识生生，如草木兴隆，缘起识生，即意向实化为意缘，而意缘之成坏起灭即意识所彰显的状态。风传递天地之气变化的信息，能够吹动万物，《说文》："风动虫生"，繁体字"风"中有虫，可以理解为植物与动物自然意识发动，通过风传播的气味实现交配，从而实现繁殖，根本上是意识的叠加和复制，形成新的意识生机。

风动生情，风情万种，根本上是播散意识的新种。风行天下，如水流天下，所以要用意识引导，使之变得鲜活、整齐不乱而形成意识有效的行动和意向。

When intentional conditions resonate, consciousness arises, and just like the flourishing of grass and trees, the consciousness of dependent origination arises, that is, intentionality turns into intentional conditions, and the formation and decay of the intentional condition is the state manifested by consciousness. Wind conveys information about the changes in the air of heaven and earth, and can move the myriad things. *An Explication of Written Characters* (*Shuowen Jiezi* 说文解字) says that "the wind moves and insects are produced." The Traditional Chinese character for "wind" (*feng* 风) contains "insect" (*chong* 蟲), which can be understood as the initiation of the natural consciousness of plants and animals, as mating is achieved through the scents spread by the wind, thereby achieving reproduction, which is fundamentally the superposition and duplication of consciousness, forming a new vitality of intentionality.

The wind brings about emotions and various styles (*feng*) of activity, which are basically new seeds spreading consciousness and intentions. Trends (*feng*) spreading around the world under heaven are like the flow of water on the earth, so they must be guided by intentions to make them lively and orderly, and organize them to form consciously effective actions and intentions.

巽，小亨。利有攸往。利见大人。

《彖》曰：重巽以申命。刚巽乎中正而志行。柔皆顺乎刚，是以"小亨，利有攸往，利见大人"。

《象》曰：随风，巽。君子以申命行事。

【明译】

巽卦象征谦逊随顺，稍有亨通，有利于以随顺的态度去做事，有利于进见大人。

《彖传》说：巽为风，风是上天的号令，两巽相重，表示上天把号令反复传送下来。刚健随顺地进入中正的位置，心志得以推行（巽变遯九二从四位来到下卦中位，是君子柔顺地进入中位，成为大人，可以推行大志）。柔爻都顺从刚爻，因此稍有亨通，有利于以随顺的态度去做事，有利于进见大人。

《象传》说：巽为风，两巽相重，风与风相随，这就是象征谦逊随顺的巽卦。君子看到风连续吹来，无孔不入，无所不顺，反复向民众申告政令，取得人民的理解和支持，然后推行政事。

Hexagram Xun (Submission) symbolizes humility and obedience. A little prosperity is conducive to doing things with an obedient attitude and meeting great people.

The *Judgment Commentary* (*Tuan Zhuan*) says: Trigram Xun represents wind, and wind is a command from heaven. The two Xun trigrams overlap each other, which means that the command is repeatedly transmitted from heaven. Entering the central and upright position vigorously and obediently, ambitions can be implemented (Hexagram Xun (Submission) changes from Hexagram Dun (Retreat) as the Nine (*yang*/strong line) in the second place moves from the fourth position to the middle position of the lower trigram, which means that an exemplary person enters the middle position docilely and becomes a great person, so that one can implement one's ambitions). The soft lines are all obedient to the strong lines, so a little prosperity will help one do things with a submissive attitude and meet great people.

The *Image Commentary* (*Xiang Zhuan*) says: Trigram Xun is wind, two Xun trigrams overlap each other, so wind and wind follow each other, and this is Hexagram Xun (Submission), which symbolizes humility and obedience. An exemplary person sees that the wind blows continuously, penetrates all hollows, and follows all directions. One repeatedly declares the governmental decrees to the people, obtains the people's understanding and support, and then implements administrative measures.

【明意】

巽卦的主要意思是天下有风，犹如天的命令，引申为发布命令；同时天下皆风化，即天下皆随顺天之意，皆随顺天而有通天意识的显化，或天的意识依境而生而有生生气象。此境即是天下之物作为意生之缘。

天的意识又代表天的言说之前的状态，所以有"申命行事"之说，即言语的根本在于言说之前的"前表达状态"。前言说、前表达的状态是根本的言说前状态。表达的几微是意识参与世间运动的开显，当通于意缘发动之前的先天结构。意识是物存在之生机的表达状态，而此意识是时刻心通物之意识，是心物一体的意识。意识当顺应情境变化的几微。

言说的力量在这个参与的几微之间，如孔子提到的正名问题，近于福柯言说的权力与此几微与情境的关系密不可分。所谓"申命行事"就是要依于意识所在的情境，所言有命，依命行事，言着力于行，着力于成事。

[Illuminating Intentionality]

The main intentionality of Hexagram Xun (Submission) is that there is wind in the world under heaven, just like the command of heaven, which is extended to the issuance of orders; at the same time, the world under heaven is all transformed by the wind, that is, the world under heaven follows the intentions of heaven, and all following heaven have a manifestation of the consciousness connecting to heaven, or, the consciousness of heaven is produced from the context and has an atmosphere of production and reproduction. This state is one where the myriad things of the world serve as the conditions for the production of intentions.

The consciousness of heaven also represents the state before heaven's utterance, so there is the phrase "expressing commands in carrying out affairs," that is, the root of speech lies in the "pre-expressional state" before utterance. The state before speech and expression is a fundamental pre-speech state. The infinitesimal subtleties of expression are the manifestation of consciousness' participation in the movement of the world, and should be connected to the transcendental structure before the initiation of intention. Consciousness is the vital expression state of the existence of things, and this consciousness is the consciousness of intentionality that connects with things at all times, and the consciousness of the integral unity of the heart-mind and things. Consciousness should adapt to infinitesimally subtle changes in the affective situation.

The power of speech lies in the infinitesimal subtleties of participation, such as the issue of rectification of names mentioned by Confucius, and the power of speech according to Foucault is closely related to the relationship between these infinitesimal subtleties and the affective situation. The phrase "expressing commands in carrying out affairs" means relying on the affective situation of consciousness, that what is said contains commands, and actions are based on commands. Words should be focused on actions, and efforts should be focused on accomplishing affairs.

初六：进退，利武人之贞。

《象》曰："进退"，志疑也。"利武人之贞"，志治也。

【明译】

初六：随顺太过导致进退不决，有利于勇武之人持守正道。

《象传》说：随顺太过导致进退不决，初六心志游疑不定。有利于像勇武之人那样持守正道，是因为他们善于正治自己的心志，使意识不再游疑不决，变得刚毅果断。

Six (*yin*/soft line) in the first place: Too much obedience leads to indecision, which is conducive for brave people to sticking to the upright *dao*.

The *Image Commentary* (*Xiang Zhuan*) says: Too much obedience leads to indecision, which means that the intentionality of the Six (*yin*/soft line) in the first place is wandering and doubtful. It is conducive for those upholding the upright *dao* like brave people because they are good at regulating their intentions, so that their consciousness no longer hesitates and becomes resolute and decisive.

【明意】

风的流动性有进退不果决的意识在。发布命令的意识犹豫不决，是因为随顺太过。一旦形势改变，就有点不知所措。巽是顺动，但顺动不可太过。犹疑既是对意识境遇的展望模糊，也是对意识发展的可能性没有把握。

[Illuminating Intentionality]

There is a sense of indecision in the flow of wind. The consciousness that gives commands is hesitant because it is too obedient. Once the situation changes, it is somewhat overwhelming. Hexagram Xun (Submission) means to follow movement, but one must not follow movement too much. Hesitation is not only a vague outlook on the situation of consciousness, but also an uncertainty about the possibility of conscious development.

九二：巽在床下，用史巫纷若，吉，无咎。

《象》曰："纷若"之"吉"，得中也。

【明译】

九二：钻到床下隐伏起来，让祝史、巫觋乱纷纷地祝告神祇，求神保佑，到头来是吉祥的，没有什么祸患。

《象传》说：乱纷纷地祝告神祇，求神保佑，到头来是吉祥的，因为九二得到中道（在下卦中位）。

Nine (*yang*/strong line) in the second place: Getting under the bed to hide, let the shamans and diviners pray to the spirits one after another, asking for their blessings. In the end, it is auspicious and there will be no disaster.

The *Image Commentary* (*Xiang Zhuan*) says: In the end, it is auspicious to pray to the spirits one after another and ask for their blessings, because the Nine (*yang*/strong line) in the second place attains the central *dao* (in the middle position of the lower trigram).

【明意】

在自己知道自己能力不足以发布命令的时候，不得不借助于史与巫的谦卑和通灵，希望重新发现自己意识的方向。在自己能力微弱的时候求神拜佛其实是一种随顺天意的表现，通过史巫的言说发现天意，从而随顺天意而得其中。象辞觉得这样的做法有其合理性，在一定程度上无可厚非。

[Illuminating Intentionality]

Knowing that he is not capable enough to issue orders, one has to rely on the humility and channeling of shamans and diviners, hoping to rediscover the direction of one's consciousness. Praying to spirits and venerating the Buddha when one's own abilities are weak is actually a manifestation of following heaven's intentionality. Through shamans and diviners' words, one discovers heaven's intention and thus follows heaven's intentionality and attains its centrality. The *Image Commentary* (*Xiang Zhuan*) feels that this approach is reasonable and to a certain extent, it is understandable.

九三：频巽，吝。

《象》曰："频巽"之"吝"，志穷也。

【明译】

九三：频繁地发布政令，这样做将有吝难。

《象传》说：频繁地更改政令就是一味顺从，说明九三心志困穷。

Nine (*yang*/strong line) in the third place: Frequently issuing government orders will lead to difficulties.

The *Image Commentary* (*Xiang Zhuan*) says: Frequent changes in government orders mean blind obedience, which shows that the Nine (*yang*/strong line) in the third place's ambition is weak.

【明意】

顺从的意识要有分寸，有节度。一味顺从，比如过分顺从民众的状况，导致频繁更改政令，就一定会出现吝难。因为不主动选择，或者没有能力主动选择的人，就不得不以他人的命令为选择，这其实是心智穷困。九三怎么选择都摇晃不稳，已然说明选择者的意识不是在一种清明刚决的状态，其朝令夕改本身就是心智昏暗的表现。

[Illuminating Intentionality]

The consciousness of obedience must be measured and temperate. Blind obedience, such as excessive obedience to the people's conditions, leading to frequent changes in government orders, will inevitably lead to difficulties. When people do not take the initiative to choose, or are unable to take the initiative to choose, they have to make choices based on the orders of others, and this actually shows a weak mind. The Nine (*yang*/strong line) in the third place's choices are shaky regardless, which already shows that the consciousness of the chooser is not in a clear and resolute state, and just like issuing an order in the morning and rescinding it in the evening, that is itself a manifestation of mental dimness.

六四：悔亡，田获三品。

《象》曰："田获三品"，有功也。

【明译】

六四：不再忧虑悔恨，去打猎获得三种猎物。

《象传》说：去打猎获得三种猎物，因为六四随顺处世，马到成功。

Six (*yin*/soft line) in the fourth place: With no more worries and regrets, go hunting and catch three kinds of prey.

The *Image Commentary* (*Xiang Zhuan*) says: One goes hunting and catches three kinds of prey because the Six (*yin*/soft line) in the fourth place is yielding and compliant, so succeeds immediately.

【明意】

六四升上来在九五之下，可以随顺君王九五发布命令，自然会有功劳。当然，这种随顺是臣道之随顺九五君王，不是简单地随顺内心，或者说，随顺内心的同时也要随顺大势，顺势而为。随顺的意识状态在合适的时位可以马到成功。这时要把前面因为意识犹疑不决而导致的忧虑悔恨抛到一边，该做什么就做什么，自然会有收获。

[Illuminating Intentionality]

The Six (*yin*/soft line) in the fourth place rises to right below the Nine (*yang*/strong line) in the fifth place, so can obey the king's orders of the Nine (*yang*/strong line) in the fifth place, and will naturally gain credit. Of course, this kind of obedience is the *dao* of being a minister, and not simply following one's heart-mind. In other words, while obeying one's heart-mind, one must also follow the general trend and act according to it. An obedient state of consciousness at the right time can lead to immediate success. At this time, one should put aside the worries and regrets caused by the hesitation of consciousness and do whatever one needs to do, and one will naturally gain something.

九五：贞吉，悔亡，无不利，无初有终。先庚三日，后庚三日，吉。

《象》曰：九五之"吉"，位正中也。

【明译】

九五：坚守正道，就会吉祥，不再忧虑悔恨，没有什么不利的事。发布命令开始不顺利，但最后畅通无阻。在命令更新的庚日的前三天发布新令，在后三天正式实施，这样比较吉祥。

《象传》说：九五之所以获得吉祥，是因为位置中正，能行中正之道。

Nine (*yang*/strong line) in the fifth place: If one sticks to the upright *dao*, one will be fortunate, no longer worried or regretful, and nothing bad will happen. Issuing orders has a rocky start, but eventually goes smoothly. It is more auspicious to issue a new order three days before the Geng day when the order is updated, and to formally implement it three days after.

The *Image Commentary* (*Xiang Zhuan*) says: The reason why the Nine (*yang*/strong line) in the fifth place is auspicious is that it is in the central and upright position and can practice the central and upright *dao*.

【明意】

九五象征继位之帝,有坐享其成之福,但也可能无初有终。这样的领导者因为根基不稳,所以发布命令要特别讲究分寸和火候。这样发布命令即使刚开始难以服众,后来也能够克服不利因素,让其令畅行。意识境遇的通畅和大势的时机密切相关,因为每一时势都有合适的节奏和节拍,发出的意识状态要合于这种节拍,才有利于天下百姓随顺而成势。

[Illuminating Intentionality]

The Nine (*yang*/strong line) in the fifth place symbolizes that the emperor who succeeds to the throne has the blessing of sitting back and enjoying his success, but may also have no beginning but an end. Because such a leader has an unstable foundation, he must pay special attention to propriety and timing when issuing orders. Even if an order issued in this way is difficult to convince the public at first, it can later overcome the disadvantages and allow the order to be carried out smoothly. The smoothness of the conscious environment is closely related to the timing of the general trend, because every current situation has a suitable rhythm and tempo. The conscious state expressed must be in line with this rhythm, so that the people of the world can follow the trend.

上九:巽在床下,丧其资斧,贞凶。

《象》曰:"巽在床下",上穷也。"丧其资斧",正乎"凶"也。

【明译】

上九:驯服地屈居在床下,因为(随顺过度)已失去了资财和权柄,如果继续正固不动,一定会有凶险。

《象传》说:驯服地屈居在床下,因为卑顺过头已经陷入穷困。失去了资财与权柄,是因为正在凶的位置上。

Nine (*yang*/strong line) in the top place: One submissively succumbs to the bed, because (excessive obedience) has lost wealth and authority. If one continues to be fixed and unmoving, there will be danger.

The *Image Commentary* (*Xiang Zhuan*) says: One submissively succumbs to the bed, because one is too humble and has fallen into poverty. One lost one's wealth and authority because one was in a bad position.

【明意】

此爻说明,谦恭卑顺要有节度,如果过度谦顺导致自己身家性命都要出危险,就划不来了。此时还正固不动,那就非常危险了。

谦卑作为一种个人品德当然是好的，但在政治斗争当中，一味谦卑，结果让底下人势力坐大，自己最后失去势力和实力，就事与愿违了。如此爻上九是谦卑过度的先王，已被下面的势力推翻，说明过度谦卑导致失位，失去发布命令的能力，也再也没有人随顺他了，对他来说，谦顺就不再是好的品德了。可见，不可因过度谦卑而使意识失去其当对应的意量。

[Illuminating Intentionality]
This line shows that humility and obedience must be tempered. If excessive humility puts one's property and life in danger, it is not worth it. It would be very dangerous to remain stationary at this time.

Of course, humility is a good personal virtue, but in political struggles, being humble will only end up making the people below more powerful, and one will eventually lose one's power and strength, which is counterproductive. In this way, the Nine (*yang*/strong line) in the top place is an overly humble former king who has been overthrown by the forces below. This shows that excessive humility leads to loss of position and the ability to issue orders, since no one will follow him anymore. For him, humility is no longer a good virtue of character. It can be seen that consciousness must not lose its corresponding intentionality capacity due to excessive humility.

兑为泽（卦五十八） （兑下兑上）
Dui (Sharing), Lake (Hexagram 58)　(Dui below, Dui above)

　　只要意识还有生机，人们就要尽可能充满喜悦地进入新的时空条件。尽管人生总在不如意中，但意能的解脱毕竟还是有获得合适时空条件的可能性，还是可给艰难的人生以莫大希望。人们通过脱离既存的生存时空能够愉悦地期待自己的人生会有新的开始。

　　万物之间意能的交流都来自彼此能够欣悦与和通。意有"能"才能解脱，兑卦是万物彼此互相交流意能的艺术。没有意能，人与人、物与物之间就无力改变自己所处的时空状态，就接近死气沉沉的状态。所以，意念要生且有能才能脱离所在的时空，从一个时空处所到另一个可能与未定的处所，这就是人的意识在时空中的转移和解脱。我们的意识永远囿于（受制于）一定的时空条件，但又无时无刻不在做脱离存在的时空条件的努力，希望进入新的可能的时空条件。

　　丽泽而有意能的交流与整合。意有"能"，意生即有能。意在生中存在，亦时刻有能才能延续。意有能才能言说，言说是意能的显化与表现。意有能才可能喜悦，才能对喜悦的情感加以表达。兑卦讨论的是获得快乐的艺术，增进意能的艺术，即如何通过让人喜悦，而促进与他意之间的和通与补益。

　　As long as consciousness still has vitality, people should enter new conditions of time and space as joyfully as possible. Although life is always unsatisfactory, the liberation of intentionality still has the possibility of obtaining suitable spatio-temporal conditions, and it can still give great hope to a difficult life. By breaking away from the existing time and space of existence, people can happily look forward to a new beginning in their lives.

Intentional power between the myriad things comes from being able to be happy and harmonious with each other. Only with "energy" can one be liberated, and Hexagram Dui (Sharing) is the art of the myriad things communicating energy with each other. Without intentionality, between people and between things it will not be possible to change the state of time and space they are in, and they will be close to a lifeless state. Therefore, only when intentions are produced and capable can they escape from the time and space where they are, and move from one place in time and space to another possible and undetermined place. This is the transfer and liberation of human consciousness in time and space. Our consciousness is always limited by (subject to) certain spatio-temporal conditions, but we are always making efforts to break away from existing spatio-temporal conditions, hoping to enter new possible spatio-temporal conditions.

Two connected lakes are capable of communication and integration. There is "energy" in intentionality, and intentionality has energy when it is produced. Intentionality exists in life, and it can only continue if it is always capable. Only when intentionality is capable can it be spoken, and speech is the manifestation and expression of intentionality. Only with capability can one be happy and express the emotion of joy. Hexagram Dui (Sharing) discusses the art of obtaining happiness, the art of improving one's intentional energy, that is, how to promote harmony and complementarity with other intentions by making people happy.

兑，亨利贞。

《彖》曰：兑，说也。刚中而柔外，说以"利贞"，是以顺乎天而应乎人。说以先民，民忘其劳。说以犯难，民忘其死。说之大，民劝矣哉！

《象》曰：丽泽，兑。君子以朋友讲习。

【明译】

兑卦象征欢欣喜悦，亨通，有利于坚守正道。

《彖传》说：兑是欢欣喜悦，好比内心刚健而外表柔顺处世。君子大人欢欣喜悦有利于持守正固，因此能上顺天道，下应人心。君子大人先说服民众，他们才会任劳忘苦、欢欣喜悦地跟着干；心悦诚服地去涉难历险，民众才会舍生忘死地跟着干。说服而欢欣喜悦的意义太重大了，因为这样才可以劝勉人民众志成城，共克难关。

《象传》说：上下卦都是兑为泽，大泽与大泽附丽在一起，相互连通就是兑卦。君子从两泽相连，流通互补中得到启示，也要相互滋益，朋友之间讨论研习，相互启发而不断提高。

Hexagram Dui (Sharing) symbolizes joy and prosperity, which is conducive to sticking to the upright *dao*.

605

The *Judgment Commentary* (*Tuan Zhuan*) says: Dui means joy and happiness, just like being strong on the inside and pliable on the outside. An exemplary person's joy and happiness are conducive to upholding integrity, so one can obey the heavenly *dao* and respond to people's intentions. An exemplary person first convinces the people, and then they will follow their work happily and forget their hardships; only if one happily and sincerely braves the difficulties and adventures, will the people risk their lives and follow their work. The significance of persuading and rejoicing is very important, because only in this way can one encourage people to work together to overcome difficulties.

The *Image Commentary* (*Xiang Zhuan*) says: Both the upper and lower trigrams are Trigram Dui, symbolizing a lake. The whole image represents big lakes being attached and connected to each other, and when they are connected to each other, this is Hexagram Dui (Sharing). Exemplary people get inspiration from the connection and complementarity of the two lakes, and know that they should also benefit each other. Friends discuss and study, inspire each other and continuously improve.

【明意】

兑卦的核心是彼此喜悦，进而心意和通。作为八纯卦之一，兑卦的特性都从"说"来。"说"在《周易》里有三义：说话，言谈；喜悦；解脱。古代的"说"字分化出现代汉语说的"说""悦"和"脱"三个意思，联起来就是：说通了，心情畅快而喜悦，于是从困惑中解脱出来。

朋友之间交流心得，共同分享。内心刚健有原则，外表待人接物却比较柔顺，与人为善。两泽相连，如人与人心意交通，令彼此欣喜悦纳，进而相互促进，共同提高。

[Illuminating Intentionality]

The core of Hexagram Dui (Sharing) is mutual joy and harmony of intention. As one of the eight pure hexagrams, the characteristics of Hexagram Dui (Sharing) come from "speaking" (*shuo* 说). "*Shuo*" has three meanings in the *Book of Changes*: speaking and talking, joy, and liberation. The ancient character shuo has divided into three different meanings in modern Chinese: "*shuo*" (speech 说), "*yue*" (joy 悦) and "*tuo*" (liberation 脱). When combined, it means: a spoken explanation makes sense, a mood is relaxed and joyful, and one is freed from confusion.

Friends exchange experiences and share them together. The heart-mind is strong and principled on the inside, but on the outside one is gentle and kind to others. The two lakes are connected, like people communicating with each other, making each other happy and accepting, and then promoting each other and improving together.

初九：和兑，吉。

《象》曰："和兑"之"吉"，行未疑也。

【明译】

初九：随和喜悦，就会吉祥。

《象传》说：意识随和喜悦，就会吉祥，如初九意行端正也就不必犹疑，不被疑忌。

Nine (*yang*/strong line) in the first place: Being easy-going and joyful will bring good fortune.

The *Image Commentary* (*Xiang Zhuan*) says: If consciousness is easy-going and joyful, it is auspicious. If the intentionality and behavior of the Nine (*yang*/strong line) in the first place are correct, there will be no need to hesitate or be suspected.

【明意】

人身心和谐方能有和意，方便与他人交流意能。彼此从心底和通，则意能通于身心之和、人人之和、人天之和，不会犹疑，也就不会被疑忌，犹如青春年少，对世界和他人充满信心，和乐满满，可以放心大胆地去行动和追求。

[Illuminating Intentionality]

Only when a person's body and heart-mind are in harmony can one have harmonious intentions and facilitate communication with others. When they are in harmony with each other from the bottom of their intentions, their intentions can connect to the harmony of body and heart-mind, the harmony of everyone, and the harmony of humanity and heaven. Then there will be no hesitation, there will be no suspicion, and, just like a youth, full of confidence in the world and others, and filled with joy and harmony, one can act and pursue with confidence and boldness.

九二：孚兑，吉，悔亡。

《象》曰："孚兑"之"吉"，信志也。

【明译】

九二：心怀诚信，欢欣喜悦地为人处世，不但吉祥，而且忧虑悔恨自然消丧。

《象传》说：心怀诚信，欢欣喜悦地为人处世带来吉祥，是九二真诚信实而让志意充满生机。

Nine (*yang*/strong line) in the second place: With a sincere heart-mind, one lives in joy and happiness with others. Not only is this auspicious, but worries and regrets will also naturally disappear.

The *Image Commentary* (*Xiang Zhuan*) says: With sincerity in one's heart-mind, one can bring good fortune to people's lives with joy and happiness. It is the sincerity and faithfulness of the Nine (*yang*/strong line) in the second place that makes intentions full of vitality.

【明意】

意能之中充满诚信，也就是充满生机。诚信是生机的体现，是生机在意识之中存续的状态和背景。欢心喜悦的意识境遇与真诚的意识状态一起，增进意识的能量。因为真诚信实，意能就如接通天地原生的生机一般生生不息，意识发动处即有源源不断的生机绵延。意识有生机能够与他心他意沟通，甚至感化刚开始可能干扰自身的他意。心志充满生机也是心志内守以存养生气，生机勃勃则相信内心之气能够与他意沟通交融。

[Illuminating Intentionality]

Intentional energy is full of sincerity, and thus full of vitality. Sincerity is the embodiment of vitality and the state and background in which vitality exists in consciousness. Joyous situations of consciousness, together with sincere states of consciousness, enhance the energy of consciousness. Because of sincerity and faithfulness, the energy of intentionality is as endless as the original vitality connected to heaven and earth, and there is a continuous flow of vitality wherever consciousness is initiated. Consciousness is alive and able to communicate with other minds and intentions, and even influence other minds that may initially interfere with itself. When intentionality is full of vitality, it means keeping intentionality within to preserve and nourish its energy; when it is vital and lively, it means believing that the energy in the heart-mind can communicate and blend with other intentions.

六三：来兑，凶。

《象》曰："来兑"之"凶"，位不当也。

【明译】

六三：献媚取悦他人来谋求喜悦，这是凶险的做法。

《象传》说：献媚取悦他人来谋求喜悦，会有凶险，因为六三位置不适当（以柔居刚）。

Six (*yin*/soft line) in the third place: It is dangerous to seek happiness by flattering others.

The *Image Commentary* (*Xiang Zhuan*) says: There is danger in seeking happiness by flattering others, because the position of the Six (*yin*/soft line) in the third place is inappropriate (the soft resides above the strong).

【明意】

与本来意能沟通不畅的状态中，如果本来对方并不悦，却离开自己的本位，故意去献媚求欢，这是非常不好，而且会有危险的做法。来而取悦于人，就是放弃自尊，离开自己好的意能境界去巴结他人，这样意能交流之时，就不可能充满喜悦和信实。

[Illuminating Intentionality]

In a state of poor communication with the original intentional energy, if another party is originally displeased, but leaves its own position and deliberately flatters and seeks pleasure, this is very bad and dangerous. To please others means to give up one's self-esteem and leave one's own good state of intentionality to please others. In this way, it is impossible for the communication of intentionality to be full of joy and faithfulness.

九四：商兑未宁，介疾有喜。

《象》曰：九四之"喜"，有庆也。

【明译】

九四：有事在喜悦的气氛当中好好商量，虽然不见得都能够商量妥当，但只要能够去掉那些不利于欢欣和悦的小毛病，就会有喜庆。

《象传》说：九四得到喜庆，是件值得庆祝的事情。

Nine (*yang*/strong line) in the fourth place: Affairs can be discussed thoroughly in an atmosphere of joy. Although not everything can be discussed properly, as long as the small problems that are not conducive to joy and happiness can be removed, there will be cause for celebration.

The *Image Commentary* (*Xiang Zhuan*) says: The jubilation of the Nine (*yang*/strong line) in the fourth place is something worth celebrating.

【明意】

在兑卦喜悦的大形势下，有事本来应该好好商量，但是小人在大家喜悦的大环境当中，不断地想浑水摸鱼，好说歹说都没有用，因为他们有自己的意向和目的，不愿意接受明白和正道的商讨，结果就怎么也商量不清。因为小人表面和颜悦色，背后一直有他们自己的目的，只有不明不白，才能继续找机会兑现自己的私意和私利。当然，九四是个明白人，把小人的意图和伎俩看得很清楚，所以即使商量不妥，也会尽量保持喜悦的意境，但心里依旧明确要隔绝小人了。

[Illuminating Intentionality]

In the general situation of joy in Hexagram Dui (Sharing), things should be discussed carefully, but in the general environment of everyone's joy, petty people constantly want to fish in troubled waters, and it is useless to say anything, because they have their own intentions and purposes, and are unwilling to accept and understand the result of clear discussion according to the upright *dao*. The result can thus never be discussed clearly, because petty people always have their own purposes behind their superficially pleasant appearance. Only if they do not understand it thoroughly can they continue to look for opportunities to realize their own selfish intentions and interests. Of course, the Nine (*yang*/strong line) in the fourth place is a sensible person and sees the petty person's intentions and tricks very clearly, so even if the discussion is not appropriate, one will try his best to maintain a happy mood, but one still isolates the petty person in one's heart-mind.

九五：孚于剥，有厉。

《象》曰："孚于剥"，位正当也。

【明译】

九五：听信消剥阳刚君子的小人的谗言欺语，这是危险的事情。

《象传》说：敢于对消剥阳刚君子的小人讲诚信，是因为九五阳刚诚实，居位正当。

Nine (*yang*/strong line) in the fifth place: It is dangerous to listen to the slanderous words and deceptions of petty people who destroy *yang*/strong exemplary people.

The *Image Commentary* (*Xiang Zhuan*) says: Dare to be honest with the petty person who destroys the *yang*/strong exemplary person, because the Nine (*yang*/strong line) in the fifth place is *yang*/strong and honest, and in the right position.

【明意】

如果觉得自己有实力，意能够强，不用担心小人的伤害，则可以放心去信任小人，为自己所用。但如果觉得小人随时可能剥蚀自己的意能，让自己堕落偏邪，那还是不要太亲近小人为好。小人不可能赶尽杀绝，但如何处理与小人沟通的分寸，至关重要。增进意能者，要看破人情冷暖，知道小人的存在，其实也是修炼和提升意能的一个助缘，在确信自己的意能能够不被小人减少时，可以带着感恩小人的意能去亲近小人，感化小人，从而转化小人负面的意能。

[Illuminating Intentionality]

If one feels that one has strength and intentional energy, and does not have to worry about harm from petty people, one can trust petty people and use them for one's own benefit. But if one feels that petty people may erode one's intentional energy at any time and cause one to fall into evil, then it is better not to get too close to petty people. It is impossible to eliminate all petty people, but how to communicate with petty people appropriately is crucial. Those who improve their mental abilities must learn to see through the warmth and coldness of human relationships and know the existence of petty people. In fact, this can also help cultivate and improve one's mental abilities. When one is sure that one's mental abilities will not be reduced by petty people, one can get close to them with the intention to express gratitude and influence them, thereby transforming their negative energy.

上六：引兑。

《象》曰：上六"引兑"，未光也。

【明译】

上六：引诱他人一起欢欣喜悦。

《象传》说：上六能够用引诱取悦于人，说明上六的欢欣喜悦之道还不够光明正大。

Six (*yin*/soft line) in the top place: Inducing others to rejoice together.

The *Image Commentary* (*Xiang Zhuan*) says: That the Six (*yin*/soft line) in the top place can use temptations to please people shows that the Six (*yin*/soft line) in the top place's *dao* of joy and happiness is not sufficiently bright and upright.

【明意】

本爻引诱阳意到亲近的位置之后，继续引诱它，保持私下的欢愉快乐，这是对自己的意能有帮助的私心作祟，所以不够光明正大。意能的生机延续在私利的考量范围之内，就不是光明正大为全局考虑。所以喜悦虽然都有边界，但这种意识的边界，是为自己的私利，还是为全体的公利，在意识发动的瞬间即清晰地昭示天下。可见，意念一有偏私，马上不够光明正大，这也是中国古典伦理学从意念发动的原初状态打通公私的观念。

[Illuminating Intentionality]

This line lures a *yang*/positive intentionality to a close position, continues to tempt one, and maintains private joys. This is a selfish act that is helpful to one's own intentional energy, so it is not sufficiently bright and upright. The continuation of the vitality of intentional energy within the scope of self-interest considerations is not a sufficiently bright and upright consideration of the overall situation. Therefore, although joy has boundaries, the boundary of this consciousness, whether for its own selfish interests or for the common good of all, is clearly revealed to the world at the moment when consciousness is initiated. It can be seen that as soon as intentions are biased, they are not sufficiently bright and upright. This is also the concept of classical Chinese ethics to connect public and private affairs from the original and initial state of intentions.

风水涣（卦五十九） （坎下巽上）

Huan (Melting), Wind and Water (Hexagram 59)　(Kan below, Xun above)

　　涣卦象征离散，"天下没有不散的筵席"，所以代表喜悦的兑卦之后就是象征离散的涣卦。要想收拢民众的意向使之不涣散，涣卦给出的答案是帮助人民建立信仰，让信仰如穿越蒙昧状态的理性之光，给他们的意识以全新的方向，改造其意识向度，整合之前混沌蒙昧的意境。信仰可使一般民众心有所归，所以古人建立天帝之庙，只是为了让人心有方向，而不去讨论神存在与否的问题。

　　人被环境决定且意向被环境的合力牵着走，但人生归根结底还是自己意识实化的旅程，每时每刻都可以从蒙昧而焕然一新，当下明确的意念方向，相对于之前的混沌而蒙昧的状态来说，就是焕然一新的。"日新"的精神态度，往往用来处理当下与之前意识境遇之间的关系。我们的意识可以自我决定，确立自己的意识方向，实化自己的意识境遇。

Hexagram Huan (Melting) symbolizes separation, and as "There is no feast that never ends," so Hexagram Dui (Sharing), which represents joy, is followed by Hexagram Huan (Melting), which symbolizes separation. In order to gather the people's intentions and prevent them from being scattered, the answer given by Hexagram Huan (Melting) is to help the people establish their faith, let faith be like the light of reason that transcends ignorance, give their consciousness a new direction, and transform the dimensions of their consciousness, integrating the previous chaotic and ignorant intentional context. Belief can give ordinary people a sense of direction, so the ancients built the Temple of the Emperor of Heaven just to give people's heart-minds a sense of direction, without discussing the existence of an individual God.

People are determined by their environment and their intentions are led by the combined force of their environment, but in the final analysis, life is a journey of concretizing one's own consciousness. Every moment, one can change from ignorance to a new state, in which the current clear direction of intentionality is different from the previous chaos and ignorance, and terms of conditions, is completely new. The mental attitude of "daily renewal" is often used to deal with the relationship between present and previous conscious situations. Our consciousness can determine itself, establish its own direction, and concretize its own context and situation.

涣，亨。王假有庙。利涉大川，利贞。

《彖》曰："涣，亨"，刚来而不穷，柔得位乎外而上同。"王假有庙"，王乃在中也。"利涉大川"，乘木有功也。

《象》曰：风行水上，涣。先王以享于帝，立庙。

【明译】

涣卦象征风化离散，有所作为，才会亨通，君王来到宗庙祭祀先祖，有利于克服涉越大河那样的艰难险阻，利于持守正道。

《彖传》说：涣卦，有所作为，才会亨通，阳刚来到内卦而不再处于穷困之境（否卦变涣卦，卦变中刚爻九四从上乾下来到二位，改变否卦上面三个刚爻处于穷困被剥退的境地），阴柔得到适当位置与上面和同（柔爻六二把下卦中位让给九四，自己升到外卦四位，得位，并与刚爻组成一体，同命运共患难）。君王来到宗庙祭祀先祖，是君王阳刚居于中位。有利于克服涉越大河那样的艰难险阻，是因为涣卦上卦巽为木，下卦坎为水，是乘着木舟行于水上之象，所以有帮助人们渡过大河之功。

《象传》说：上卦巽为风，下卦坎为水，春风吹行在水面上，于是坚冰消融，春水涣涣，这就是涣卦的象征。先王从风吹水上，水向四面荡漾散开中得到启示，要设立宗庙，祭享先帝，建立信仰，以风化人心。

Hexagram Huan (Melting) symbolizes weathering and separation. Only by taking action can one be prosperous. When the king comes to the ancestral temple to worship his ancestors, it is conducive to overcoming difficulties and obstacles such as crossing a large river, and to adhering to the upright *dao*.

The *Judgment Commentary* (*Tuan Zhuan*) says: In Hexagram Huan (Melting), only when one makes a difference will one be prosperous. The *yang*/strong comes to the inner trigram and is no longer be in a realm of poverty (Hexagram Pi (Non-Communication) changes to Hexagram Huan (Melting) in hexagram-changes, the Nine (*yang*/strong line) in the fourth place moving down from the upper Trigram Qian to the second position, changing the three *yang*/strong lines above in Hexagram Pi (Non-Communication) from a state of poverty and deprivation), while the *yin*/soft gains a proper position in harmony with those above (the Six (*yin*/soft line) in the second place gives up the middle position of the lower trigram to the Nine (*yang*/strong line) in the fourth place, and rises to the fourth position of the outer trigram, gaining a position, and forming one body with the *yang*/strong lines, sharing the same destiny and adversity). When the king comes to the ancestral temple to worship his ancestors, the king is *yang*/strong and in a central position. This is helpful to overcome difficulties and obstacles such as crossing a large river, because the upper Trigram Xun of Hexagram Huan (Melting) is wood and the lower Trigram Kan is water, which form a symbol of riding a wooden canoe on the water, so it helps people cross a river.

The *Image Commentary* (*Xiang Zhuan*) says: The upper Trigram Xun is wind, and the lower Trigram Kan is water. A spring breeze blows on the water, so ice melts and spring water flows, forming the symbol of Hexagram Huan (Melting). The former kings got inspiration from wind blowing on the water and water rippling and spreading in all directions, and wanted to set up an ancestral temple to worship the former emperor, establish faith and change people's heart-minds.

【明意】

"涣"是春风解冻，坚冰消融，水涣漫无际的意思。引申为化解壅滞、消散分离的意义。古代在宗庙祭祀先帝，这有利于民众树立信仰，人民有信仰将有如春风解冻般化解心中的壅滞。

如果要论证信仰对象的存在，当然会是一个理智上莫大的考验。古时的信仰不重视论证外在对象的合理性，而是让信仰对象进入人们的意识境遇并内在化。一旦在人民的意识中内在化即有其合理性，只要能够帮助人民调整意向的方向就可以了。至于所有因信仰对象存在引起的问题，在《周易》的哲学系统之中，基本悬搁而不论。

[Illuminating Intentionality]

Hexagram Huan (Melting) means the spring breeze thaws, ice melts, and water flows endlessly. It is extended to the intentionality of resolving stagnation and dispersing separation. In ancient times, worshiping ancestors and emperors in ancestral temples was conducive to the people's establishment of faith. People's faith will dissolve the stagnation in their intentions like the ice-thawing power of the spring breeze.

If one wants to prove the existence of an object of faith, it will of course be a huge intellectual test. Ancient belief did not attach much importance to demonstrating the rationality of external objects, but instead allowed the objects of belief to enter people's consciousness and become internalized. Once internalized in the people's consciousness, they have their rationality, as long as they can help the people adjust the direction of their intentions. As for all issues caused by the existence of objects of faith, in the philosophical system of the *Book of Changes*, they are basically ignored.

初六：用拯马壮，吉。

《象》曰：初六之"吉"，顺也。

【明译】

初六：（在危难涣散的形势之中）能够借助强壮有力的马来拯救自己，可获吉祥。

《象传》说：初六的吉祥，是因为顺承九二（初六原在否卦的下坤里，坤为顺，愿意顺从九二）。

Six (*yin*/soft line) in the first place: (In a crisis situation,) if one can use a strong and powerful horse to save oneself, one will get good fortune.

The *Image Commentary* (*Xiang Zhuan*) says: The auspiciousness of the Six (*yin*/soft line) in the first place is because it obediently supports the Nine (*yang*/strong line) in the second place (the Six (*yin*/soft line) in the first place was originally in the lower Trigram Kun of Hexagram Pi (Non-Communication), and Kun is submissive and obeying, signifying that one is willing to obey the Nine (*yang*/strong line) in the second place).

【明意】

马改变了意向，当然更重要的是强壮的马向人输出了它的意能，让一个受伤的人得以脱离危险。在关键时候，外在的意能可以改变自己的意向，我们也只有顺应，所以生命关头的随顺很重要。从另一个角度来说，危难之中主动寻找到强壮有力的意能带自己走出危机，是非常重要的一步。在生死关头，只有自己意念的转换才是根本的出路，很难依靠意识境遇之外的力量来增进意能，进而改变意念的方向。

[Illuminating Intentionality]

The horse changes its intention. Of course, more importantly, the strong horse exports its intention to the person, allowing an injured person to escape danger. At critical moments, external intentional energy can change our own intentions, and we can only adapt, so it is important to adapt at critical moments in life. From another perspective, it is a very important step to take the initiative in a crisis to find a strong and powerful intentional energy to lead oneself out of the crisis. At the moment of life and death, only the transformation of one's own intentions is a fundamental way out, as it is difficult to rely on forces outside the conscious situation to enhance one's intentional energy and then change the direction of one's intentions.

九二：涣奔其机，悔亡。

《象》曰："涣奔其机"，得愿也。

【明译】

九二：从涣散剥退的境地脱身出来，得到机会奔向可以依靠之所，忧虑和悔恨都消除了。

《象传》说：得到机会奔向可以依靠之所（初六），得以脱离涣散的险境，实现了心愿。

Nine (*yang*/strong line) in the second place: Escaping from the situation of disorganization and deprivation, one gets the opportunity to run to a place one can rely on, so worries and regrets are eliminated.

The *Image Commentary* (*Xiang Zhuan*) says: If you get an opportunity and run to a place you can rely on (the Six (*yin*/soft line) in the first place), you can escape from the dangerous situation of being scattered and concretize your intentions.

【明意】

意境要稳定才能有量，人的意识都自觉地从不安宁的状态过渡到相对安宁的状态当中去。一旦意识处于不安的境遇（如否卦阴意与阳意不交的状态）之中，一点点意识的依托之所也要抓紧珍惜，因为如果此时得其所愿，只要通过一个立足点，就有利于确定意识的方向。可见，人在危难时刻最重要的就是寻找自己意向的依托之处，自觉到意识境遇当中何者是确有生机的意识向度。

[Illuminating Intentionality]

Only when the intentional context is stable can it be capable. Human consciousness consciously transitions from a state of restlessness to a state of relative tranquility. Once consciousness is in an uneasy situation (such as the state where the *yin* and *yang* of Hexagram Pi (Non-Communication) do not interact), the little bit of support for consciousness must be cherished, because if one gets what one wants at this time, one only needs to pass a single foothold, and it is helpful to determine the direction of consciousness. It can be seen that the most important thing for people in times of crisis is to find a place to rely on for their own intentions, and to be conscious of which dimension of consciousness is truly viable in the conscious situation.

六三：涣其躬，无悔。

《象》曰："涣其躬"，志在外也。

【明译】

六三：（大难临头）涣散自身（自私自利之心），以救助他人，没有什么需要忧虑悔恨的。

《象传》说：（大难临头）涣散自身（自私自利之心），以济助他人，是因为六三心志是向着他人的。

Six (*yin*/soft line) in the third place: (Disaster is imminent, so) one disperses oneself (one's selfish heart-mind) to save others. There is no cause for worry or regret.

The *Image Commentary* (*Xiang Zhuan*) says: (When disaster approaches), one disperses oneself (one's selfish heart-mind) to help others, because the intentionality of the Six (*yin*/soft line) in the third place is directed towards others.

【明意】

在涣的大势之下，需要放下自己的自私自利之心，帮助大家一起发展，才能够克服时艰，否则大家过不好，自己的私利也不可能保得住。险中意向不在一己之私，危急时刻还能不把自己放在第一位实在太难了。但这种意向的控制力来自长期的、总是舍己为人的修养。这一爻是关于游泳和冲浪的艺术，也就是人要把自己的主观意识放下来，让主体的意识方向随顺自然情境的方向，从而呈现主客合一和更和谐的意识境界。

[Illuminating Intentionality]

Under the general trend of melting, one should put aside one's own selfishness and help everyone develop together, so that we can overcome the difficulties. Otherwise, no one will be able to live well, and one's own selfish interests will not be preserved. It is really difficult not to put oneself first in times of crisis, and it's truly unselfish to do so when one's intentions in danger. But the control of this intention comes from the long-term cultivation of always sacrificing oneself for others. This line is about the art of swimming and surfing, which means that people should set aside their subjective consciousness and let the direction of subjective consciousness follow the direction of the natural situation, thus presenting a more harmonious state of consciousness that unites subject and object.

六四：涣其群，元吉。涣有丘，匪夷所思。

《象》曰："涣其群，元吉"，光大也。

【明译】

六四：（危难时刻为了集体）涣散自己的朋党群类，就会大吉大利。而且涣散后还能够聚成像山丘一样的大团体，那就真不是常人所能想象和做到的。

《象传》说：（危难时刻）涣散自己的朋党群类，就会大吉大利，因为六四为了集体没有私心，起心动念光辉广大（六四互为大离，离为光明）。

Six (*yin*/soft line) in the fourth place: (For the sake of the collective in times of crisis,) disperse your own cliques, and you will be in good fortune. To be able to gather into a large group like a hill after being dispersed is really beyond the imagination and ability of ordinary people.

The *Image Commentary* (*Xiang Zhuan*) says: (In times of crisis,) if you disperse your own cliques, you will be in good fortune, because the Six (*yin*/soft line) in the fourth place has no selfish motives for the collective, and its intentions are bright and brilliant, since the Six (*yin*/soft line) in the fourth place is in the Trigram Li, signifying bright light.

【明意】

意向中是否有他人，是否能够顾及他人的利益，这是危难时刻的核心。要理解小团体的利益来自于大团体，所以不可以不顾所有人的利益。起心动念意向光辉光大，大难当头，不以自己的小团体的私利为先，那么大难过后，原来涣散的小团体会聚成一个更大的山丘，说明人心的聚散是看关键时刻一个人意向的表现，一个人现在在乎大家的利益，甚至可以牺牲自己的利益，将来就能够汇聚越来越多的人心。

改换思维的频道，等于改换时空，就可出新的思路，好像柳暗花明，拨云见日，所以才说匪夷所思、不可思议。

[Illuminating Intentionality]

Whether there are others in an intention and whether the interests of others can be taken into account are the core issue in times of crisis. It is important to understand that the interests of small groups come from large groups, so the interests of everyone cannot be ignored. The arising thoughts and intentions are brilliant, and when faced with great difficulties, one does not put the self-interest of one's own small group first. After the crisis, the originally scattered small group will gather into a larger hill, which shows that the gathering and dispersion of people's intentions depends on the expression of one's intention at a critical moment. One who cares about everyone's interests now, and can even sacrifice their own interests, will be able to gather more and more people's intentions in the future.

Changing the channel of thinking is equivalent to changing time and space, and new intentions can come out, just like flowers in the dark and the sun shining through the clouds, so it is said to be incredible and unthinkable.

九五：涣汗，其大号（hào）涣，王居，无咎。

《象》曰："王居无咎"，正位也。

【明译】

九五：（波涛）盛大浩瀚啊！君王的重大号令（像大海一样）浩瀚无际啊！君王安处在正当的位置，没有什么问题。

《象传》说：君王安处在正当的位置，没有什么问题，因为九五一直处在中正的位置。

Nine (*yang*/strong line) in the fifth place: (A wave,) So grand and vast! The king's great command is vast (like the sea)! When the king is in his rightful place, there is no problem.

The *Image Commentary* (*Xiang Zhuan*) says: There is no problem if the king is in the right position, because the Nine (*yang*/strong line) in the fifth place has always been in the right position.

【明意】

君王治国，意向宏阔伟岸，如同乘驾大船，乘风破浪。九五就是驾着大船迎接风浪的君王，虽然外面波涛汹涌，但君王居于正位，其意向顺应大浪而发出大的号令，处之泰然，能够带领人民克服如滔天巨浪一般的困难。君王在位，其意向当中必须有人民，有安民之意，才能安定自己之居所，非实体之居处，而是王位相关的、带领天下人民安居乐业的正居之状态。

[Illuminating Intentionality]

When a king governs a country, his intentions are grand and magnificent, just like taking a big ship to ride the wind and waves. The Nine (*yang*/strong line) in the fifth place is the king who rides on a big ship to meet the wind and waves. Although the waves are rough outside, the king is in an upright position. His intention is to follow the big waves and issue big orders. He is calm and can lead the people to overcome difficulties like huge waves. When the king is on the throne, he must have the people in his intentions and have the intention of peace and tranquility for the people, so that he can stabilize his residence. It is not a physical residence, but a state of residence related to the throne and leading the people of the world to live and work in peace and contentment.

上九：涣其血去逖（tì）出，无咎。

《象》曰："涣其血"，远害也。

【明译】

上九：散去流血之伤，离开血光之灾，高飞远去，不会再有危难。

《象传》说：告别流血之伤，因为上九已远离血光之灾害（上九与下坎相去甚远，坎为血光之灾）。

Nine (*yang*/strong line) in the top place: Dispersing the bleeding wounds, leave the bloody disaster, fly away, and there will be no more dangers.

The *Image Commentary* (*Xiang Zhuan*) says: Say goodbye to bleeding wounds, because the Nine (*yang*/strong line) in the top place is far away from the disaster of blood and light (the Nine (*yang*/strong line) in the top place is far away from the lower Trigram Kan, which signifies a disaster of blood and light).

【明意】

涣作为古人迁徙当中渡过大河的苦难记忆，充满血光之灾，到了上九，就要把这种前人的经历作为族群的记忆加以记取，以期后人能够知道如何远离灾害，更好地生活下去。

当下意向有其历史的苦难记忆（所谓汲取教训）。人通过记忆和回忆，能够从历史中学习，最了不起的是有长期的历史记录，通过这些历史记录，可以学会过去人们意识发动之处体现出来的闪光智慧。

[Illuminating Intentionality]

Hexagram Huan (Melting) could be regarded as a painful memory of ancient people crossing a river during their migration, full of bloody disasters. By the time we reach the Nine (*yang*/strong line) in the top place, we must remember this experience of our predecessors as the memory of the ethnic group, so that future generations can know how to stay away from disasters and live better.

Humans' present intentions might contain their own historical memory of suffering (the so-called lessons learned). People can learn from history through memory and recall, but the most remarkable is that there are long-term historical records. Through these historical records, we can learn the shining wisdom reflected in the places where our ancestors' consciousness was launched in the past.

水泽节（卦六十） （兑下坎上）

Jie (Regulation), Water and Lake (Hexagram 60) (Dui below, Kan above)

　　节卦讨论天的节律与人心节奏之间是否和谐和顺。天地节（阴阳）而阴阳休整，人的心意也是如此，要适于形势有节奏的发动。

　　意念行于虚无之中，自我节度，即量论（过即量）。节卦说明意向性不可以过分拘执于情境的限制，过分受限则无法持续。节制是行险的必要分寸，因为意向发动时时刻刻皆在险中，节是主动避免危险的方式。也就是说，人的意识实化失去节奏，就容易陷入坎险的状态。如果人的意识实化的节奏合适，就可以欣悦地面对和处理险境。

Hexagram Jie (Regulation) discusses whether there is harmony and smoothness between the rhythm of heaven and the rhythm of human heart-mind. The regulation of heaven and earth (*yin* and *yang*) means that *yin* and *yang* rest, and so does the human heart-mind, which must be adapted to the rhythmic initiation of the situation.

Intentionality travels in nothingness and regulates itself, that is, measuring (excess is measuring). Hexagram Jie (Regulation) shows that intentionality cannot be too rigidly attached to the limitations of the situation. If it is too restricted, it will not be sustainable. Temperance is the necessary measure for taking risks, because when one's intention is initiated, one is always in danger, and moderation is a way to proactively avoid danger. In other words, when the realization of human consciousness loses its rhythm, it is easy to fall into a dangerous state. If the rhythm of realization of human consciousness is appropriate, one can face and handle dangerous situations with joy.

节，亨。苦节，不可贞。

《彖》曰："节，亨"，刚柔分而刚得中。"苦节，不可贞"，其道穷也。说以行险，当位以节，中正以通。天地节而四时成。节以制度，不伤财，不害民。

《象》曰：泽上有水，节。君子以制数度，议德行。

【明译】

节卦象征节制有度，调节得好，就顺利亨通，但过分节制的状态不宜一直持续下去。

《彖传》说：节卦象征节制有度，调节得好，就顺利亨通，刚爻与柔爻的群体分离而刚爻取得中位（泰卦变节，泰卦三个刚爻聚于下，三个柔爻聚于上，各自成为小的群体。变节卦，三个刚爻中分出九三上到五位，与柔爻交流在一起；三个柔爻中分出六五下到三位，与刚爻交流在一起；这是刚柔爻各自分离出一部分，称作"刚柔分"。形成节卦后，刚爻九二保持下卦中位，九五取得上卦中位，称作"刚得中"。刚柔阴阳交流，中位又都是刚健之爻，所以节卦亨通）。过分节制的状态不宜一直持续下去，是因为道处穷困（泰卦已到了刚下柔上的极限，守住不变必然道穷）。下卦兑为悦，上卦坎为险，是以喜悦的心情经历险情，卦变中刚爻从三位上到五位，居于适当位置而行节制之道，行为中正而处世能够亨通。天地的运动因为有所节止，才能形成四季交替的节奏。治国要用制度来节止，就可以不损伤财产，不苦害民众。

《象传》说：下卦兑为泽，上卦坎为水，大泽之上积蓄有水，这就是节卦。君子鉴于大泽之上的水要有限度，如同用"数量"控制水位一样制定言行的法度，并以此衡量评议大家的言语行为。

Hexagram Jie (Regulation) symbolizes moderation. If it is well adjusted, it will be smooth and prosperous. However, excessive moderation should not continue forever.

The *Judgment Commentary* (*Tuan Zhuan*) says: Hexagram Jie (Regulation) symbolizes moderation. If it is well adjusted, it will be smooth and prosperous. The groups of strong and soft lines are separated and the strong lines take the middle position (Hexagram Tai (Communication) changes into Hexagram Jie (Regulation), the three strong lines of Hexagram Tai (Communication) gathered at the bottom, and the three soft lines gathered at the top, each forming their own small group. In the change to Hexagram Jie (Regulation), the three strong lines split off the Nine (*yang*/strong line) in the third place, which rises to the fifth position, and communicates with the soft lines; the three soft lines split off the Six (*yin*/soft line) in the fifth place which falls to the third position, and communicates with the strong lines. This is the strong and soft lines each splitting off one part, and is called "strong and soft splitting." After the formation of Hexagram Jie (Regulation), the Nine (*yang*/strong line) in the second place maintains the middle position of the lower trigram, and the Nine (*yang*/strong line) in the fifth place gets the middle position of the upper trigram, which is called "the strong attaining the centers." The strong *yang* and soft *yin* communicate, and the middle positions are both strong lines, so the hexagram is prosperous). The state of excessive restraint should not continue forever because its *dao* is exhausted (Hexagram Tai (Communication) has reached the limit of strong below and soft above, and if it remains unchanged, its *dao* will inevitably be exhausted). The lower Trigram Dui represents joy, and the upper Trigram Kan represents danger. This means experiencing dangerous situations with a joyful mood. In the hexagram-changes, a strong line moves from the third to the fifth position. If one is in an appropriate position and practices moderation, one's behavior will be upright and one will prosper in life. The movement of heaven and earth can form the cycle of the four seasons because of its rhythm. When governing a country, systems must be used to control it, so as to avoid damaging property and not harm the people.

The *Image Commentary* (*Xiang Zhuan*) says: The lower Trigram Dui is marsh, and the upper Trigram Kan is water, so there is water accumulated above a great marsh, and this is Hexagram Jie (Regulation). In view of the fact that there is a limit to the water above the marsh, an exemplary person sets rules for words and deeds, using terms like "quantity" in the same way as in controlling the water level, to measure and evaluate everyone's words and deeds.

【明意】

《周易》政治哲学的核心是对人的意向性的节制。通过教化和法律让人们知节守节，从而内化为自己主动控制意向性的节奏和节率。制度理法都是节。从治国的角度讲，一方面治国者要顺从天地的节奏来控制和引导自己，这是自我修养的节度；另一方面引导人民的欲望和思想的状态，这是礼教制度的节度，也是礼乐政教的节度，尤其是要限制富裕和强势者的欲望，不宜让富者和强者对弱势者丧失基本的节度和公正，也就是礼乐刑政的节度。

[Illuminating Intentionality]

The core of the political philosophy of the *Book of Changes* is the regulation of human intentionality. Through education and laws, people can be made to know the rules and observe them, so that they can internalize the social rhythm and form a rhythm of their own through active and effective regulation of their intentions. Institutional principles and laws are all regulation. From the perspective of governing the country, on one hand, the ruler must obey the rhythms of heaven and earth to control and guide himself, which is the regulation of self-cultivation; on the other hand, he must guide the people's desires and the state of their thought, which is the regulation of the ritual propriety system, and also the regulation of politics and religion through ritual and music. In particular, this must limit the desires of the rich and powerful. It is not appropriate for the rich and powerful to lose their basic regulation and fairness toward the weak, that is, the regulation of ritual propriety, music, punishment, and government.

初九：不出户庭，无咎。

《象》曰："不出户庭"，知通塞（sè）也。

【明译】

初九：不跨出门户庭院，没有咎害。

《象传》说：节制慎行，因而不跨出门户庭院，是因为初九知道闭塞与通达的时势。

Nine (*yang*/strong line) in the first place: As long as one does not step out of the courtyard, there will be no harm.

The *Image Commentary* (*Xiang Zhuan*) says: Being regulated and cautious, one does not step out of the gate of courtyard, because the Nine (*yang*/strong line) in the first place knows the temporal propensity of occlusion and access.

【明意】

不该出的时候，意向就不应该发动，要尽量持守一种未发之中的状态。知险而止于险，不该出的时候就不发动自己的意向，持守未发之中。可见未发的确是心通物境的状态，即所谓"寂然不动"之中，心意仍然可以通天通物的状态。有点像"不出户知天下"，心可以不出户就知道天下时事。心通宇宙的本体，就是人天之意与天相通的贯通状态。

[Illuminating Intentionality]

Intentions should not be initiated when they should not be released, and should be kept in a state of being uninitiated as much as possible. One should know the danger and stop at it, not initiate one's intention when it is not supposed to emerge, and maintain an uninitiated state. It can be seen that an uninitiated (*weifa* 未发) state is indeed a state in which the heart-mind connects to things, that is, in the so-called "quiet and immobile" state, intentionality can still connect to heaven and things. This is a bit like "knowing the world under heaven without stepping out of one's door" in the Daodejing, in which one's heart-mind can know the current affairs of the world under heaven without leaving one's home. The heart-mind connecting with the original substance of the cosmos is the state of interconnection between the intentionality of humanity and heaven and heaven/nature itself.

九二：不出门庭，凶。

《象》曰："不出门庭，凶"，失时极也。

【明译】

九二：不跨出家门庭院，有凶险。

《象传》说：九二拘于节制而不跨出家门庭院，会有凶险，因为极端丧失动的时机（在卦变中正应六五让出尊位，带动九二，九二却没有趁机随着动，以致过分失去上进的时机）。

Nine (*yang*/strong line) in the second place: If one does not step out of one's home or courtyard, there will be danger.

The *Image Commentary* (*Xiang Zhuan*) says: The Nine (*yang*/strong line) in the second place is restrained and does not step out of the house and courtyard, which is dangerous, because the opportunity to act is extremely lost (in the hexagram-changes, the corresponding Six (*yin*/soft line) in the fifth place gives up its honored position and promotes the Nine (*yang*/strong line) in the second place, but the Nine (*yang*/strong line) in the second place does not take the opportunity to follow the movement, so that it seriously loses the opportunity to make progress).

【明意】

天机是阴阳运动向意识显现的能量场域，意念当行不行，失去时机，心该动而无动，心失天机，则事错天机。所以心意实化之时，要抓住心天贯通的本体性能量场域来行动。时势如果已经大变，该动则动，否则必有凶险。节就是意念要顺天地阴阳的节奏而动，如果天地阴阳动了，意念却仍然执着固化不动，则是失去行动时机的大错。

《周易》宇宙论是宇宙与意识本体贯通的宇宙论。宇宙在意识上显现，宇宙能量在意识生发处同步。人的意识发动之时，即是宇宙生能转化之处。意识与宇宙生机发动需要把控同步的节奏才好。

[Illuminating Intentionality]

Heaven's vitality is the energy field where the movement of *yin* and *yang* appears to consciousness. If intentionality fails to do what it should, losing the opportunity, the heart-mind should move but does not move, and if the heart-mind loses heaven's vitality, things will disconnect from heaven's vitality. Therefore, when intentions are concretized, we must seize the ontological energy field that connects the heart-mind and heaven in action. If the current situation has changed drastically, one should take action when one needs to; otherwise there will be danger. Regulation means that intentionality should move with the rhythm of the *yin* and *yang* of heaven and earth. If the *yin* and *yang* of heaven and earth move, but intentionality remains stubborn and immobile, it will be a big mistake that loses the opportunity to act.

The cosmology of the *Book of Changes* is a cosmology that connects the cosmos and the original substance of consciousness. The cosmos appears in consciousness, and the energy of the cosmos is synchronized where consciousness arises. When human consciousness is initiated, it is the place where the energy of the cosmos is transformed. Consciousness' initiation with the vitality of the cosmos needs to control its synchronized rhythm.

六三：不节若，则嗟若，无咎。

《象》曰："不节"之"嗟"，又谁"咎"也。

【明译】

六三：不能够自我节制，于是嗟叹悔过，不是别人的错。

《象传》说：不能够自我节制带来嗟叹悔过，这又能去责怪谁呢？

Six (*yin*/soft line) in the third place: Unable to control oneself, one laments and regrets, and it is not the fault of others. The *Image Commentary (Xiang Zhuan)* says: Failure to exercise self-control will lead to laments and regrets. Who can be blamed for this?

【明意】

三爻之位，追求外物而放弃人之常情，不知节制，就会越来越危险。对于潜在的危险应该要非常小心。追求外物而放弃人之常情，不知节制，就会越来越危险，如果善于补过，自我调整，知道节制，不背离人之常情，可以避免潜在危险。如果自己背离人之常情不知节制，却能够意识到危险已经如影随形，主动节制还来得及。

人作为所谓行为主体（agent），其意向性是否有公心公义，是否合理，皆于反思之中可见。意向性的发动也是通过反思来尽量合乎天时，如果能够合于天时的节奏，就能够增强意向性的能量，如果不合，最后导致自己受伤，也就只能自己悔过。当然，明白天时的节奏，顺天时节奏采取合适的应对之方，以增强意向性的能量，这种反思的境界并不容易实现。

[Illuminating Intentionality]

Staying in the third position, pursuing external things and abandoning constant human feeling, without knowing restraint, will become more and more dangerous. Extreme caution should be exercised regarding potential hazards. If one pursues external things and abandons constant human feeling without knowing restraint, one will be in more and more danger. If one is good at making up for one's mistakes, adjusts oneself, knows restraint, and does not deviate from constant human feeling, one can avoid potential dangers. But if one deviates from constant human feeling and does not know how to exercise restraint, one can realize that danger is already taking form, and it is still early enough to take the initiative to regulate oneself.

As a so-called agent of action, whether a person's intentionality is fair and reasonable can be seen through reflection. The initiation of intentionality is also based on reflection to try to be in line with temporality of the heavens. If it can be in line with the rhythms of the heavens, it can enhance the energy of intentionality. If it is not in line, it will eventually lead to injury, and one can only regret it. Of course, it is not easy to achieve this state of reflection by understanding the rhythm of the heavens and making appropriate responses in accordance with the rhythm of the heavens to enhance the energy of intentionality.

六四：安节，亨。

《象》曰："安节"之"亨"，承上道也。

【明译】

六四：安于自我节制，就会亨通。

《象传》说：安于自我节制，就会亨通，因为顺承上面（九五）的正道。

Six (*yin*/soft line) in the fourth place: Be content with self-control and you will prosper.

The *Image Commentary* (*Xiang Zhuan*) says: If one is content with self-control, one will prosper because one follows the righteous *dao* of those above (the Nine (*yang*/strong line) in the fifth place).

【明意】

意向之行，意境通于上下，意能皆和谐融通。可见六四安宁顺承，在心意之行上知道自我控制，行为上自觉自愿地接受节制，这说明六四的人天之意是让心顺人间的节奏通于天地阴阳的节奏。六四意念通于上下天地之境，得益于对于上下人情的练达与沟通的成熟，知道与下应和与上顺的节奏，能够控制好意念实化的分寸，而这来自于长期经验的积累和自控的力量。

[Illuminating Intentionality]

In the movement of intention, the intentional context connects those above and below, and all the intentional energies are harmoniously integrated. It can be seen that the Six (*yin*/soft line) in the fourth place is peaceful and submissive, and it knows self-control in the conduct of intention, and consciously and voluntarily accepts restraint in behavior. This shows that the intention of the Six (*yin*/soft line) in the fourth place is to let the heart-mind follow the rhythm of the world and connect with the rhythm of *yin* and *yang* in heaven and earth. That the intentions of the Six (*yin*/soft line) in the fourth place are connected to the realm of heaven and earth is due to the maturity of understanding and communication between people above and below, knowing the rhythm of responding to those below and being in harmony with those above, and being able to control proportion in the realization of intentions, and this comes from long-term experience of the power of accumulation and self-control.

九五：甘节，吉。往有尚。

《象》曰："甘节"之"吉"，居位中也。

【明译】

九五：甘美地节制，这是吉祥的状态，因为前往受到崇尚。

《象传》说：甘美地节制（天下），这是吉祥的状态，因为九五居于中正的位置。

Nine (*yang*/strong line) in the fifth place: Sweet moderation is an auspicious state because advancing is revered.

The *Image Commentary* (*Xiang Zhuan*) says: Sweet moderation (of the world under heaven) is an auspicious state, because the Nine (*yang*/strong line) in the fifth place is in a central and upright position.

【明意】

九五甘于通过节制自己而节制天下，因为握权并能够中正节制来行事，将获得民众的尊重，有利于建功立业。

虽居主位，仍然主动甘愿让意念之行受到限制，接受意量作为意向有限性的量度。如果人间的节奏通过意念的节制能够通天，则可以甘于此节奏，甘于意会为合理的节奏，合理合情，合阴阳的节奏能帮助人天之意通于天地，从而节制人间成事之分寸，既于人天之意的发动处节制自己，又能够让民众甘于所节，达到"从心所欲不逾矩"的最高境界。

[Illuminating Intentionality]
The Nine (*yang*/strong line) in the fifth place is willing to control the world through controlling oneself, because holding power and being able to act with moderation and restraint will gain the respect of the people and is conducive to achievements.

Although in the dominant position, the Nine (*yang*/strong line) in the fifth place is still willing to allow the movement of intentions to be limited and accepts intentional energy as the measure of the finiteness of intentions. If the rhythm of the human world can connect with heaven through the control of intentions, then we can willingly accept this rhythm, accept it as a reasonable rhythm, appropriate to both principle and feeling, and harmonized with the rhythm of *yin* and *yang*. This can help the intentionality of humanity and heaven connect with heaven and earth, and thereby regulate proportion in accomplishing tasks in the human world, not only controlling oneself where the intentionality of humanity and heaven is initiated, but also allowing the people to willingly accept regulation and achieve the highest state of "following one's heart-mind without exceeding the rules" in one's seventies proclaimed by Confucius .

上六：苦节，贞凶，悔亡。

《象》曰："苦节，贞凶"，其道穷也。

【明译】

上六：过分节制，让人痛苦不堪，继续正固不动将有凶险，最多能够不致悔恨。

《象传》说：过分节制，让人痛苦不堪，继续正固不动将有凶险，因为上六的节制之道已经陷于穷困。

Six (*yin*/soft line) in the top place: Excessive restraint makes people miserable. Continuing to be upright and immobile will be dangerous, and at most it will not lead to regret.

The *Image Commentary* (*Xiang Zhuan*) says: Excessive restraint makes people miserable. If one continues to be upright and immobile, one will be in danger, because the *dao* of restraint of the Six (*yin*/soft line) in the top place realms has fallen into exhaustion.

【明意】

过分执着于节，不该节的状态也节，无论是节俭还是节制，都丧失了节而有度的意义，走向另一个无度的极端。可见，节而失度，为节而节，就不再是节的本义了。否则不但让自己陷入穷途末路，而且可能凭空增加很多危险。

该动时刻就要动，过时没动就只有悔恨。悔恨是对过去的假设，但这种假设已经不可能变成现实。"悔"是《周易》常出现的词，悔与无悔都是人间常态，根本在于意向性是否切于时势。如果意向性在一定的时势内达成了期望和目标，就不必悔恨。但人们常没有达到期望，所以会有悔恨，悔恨也往往都是因为一时一地意向的错失而造成的。

[Illuminating Intentionality]

If one is too obsessed with regulation, one will regulate states that should not be regulated. Whether this is frugality or moderation, one will lose the intentionality of regulation and proportion and move to the other extreme of excess. It can be seen that the regulation without proportion and for its own sake is no longer the original meaning of regulation. Otherwise, one will not only end up in a dead end, but may also increase a lot of risks from thin air.

One should take action when one should. If one does not take action until it's too late, one will only regret it. Regret is an assumption about the past that is no longer possible. "Regret" is a word that often appears in the *Book of Changes*. Regrets and no regrets are both normal in the world, and what is fundamental is whether intentionality is relevant to the current situation. If intentionality achieves expectations and goals within a certain period of time, there is no need for regret, but people often fail to meet their expectations, so they have regrets. Regrets are often caused by missed intentions at one time or another.

风泽中孚(卦六十一) (兑下巽上)

Zhongfu (Trust), Wind and Lake (Hexagram 61)　(Dui below, Xun above)

中孚卦说明即使意量有所游疑,只要真诚到极致,也可能感动猪和鱼,世间之物就无不能被感动,也就是人心认识世界的秩序可以有力地创生出来,无往而不胜。到最后归于渐卦,意量就逐渐进入阴阳合体,即与世界阴阳相合的状态之中去了。

如果想要建立一套关于世界秩序的理论,还需要极度的真诚,才能扩大这套认识理论的意量,因为真诚至极才可能让人信服,也就是真诚足以提升心意认识结构让人信服的力量,也就是真诚可能感化世人,也足以感化世人。一个人内在的认识世界的结构,不可能完美无缺,但可以通过他对世界的真诚来提升自己心意结构的影响力,也就大大扩大了意念的量度。

Hexagram Zhongfu (Trust) shows that even if there is doubt in one's intention, as long as sincerity is maximized, it is possible to move pigs and fishes, and anything in the world can be moved. That is to say, the human heart-mind's understanding of the order of the world can be powerfully created, to the point that it is unbeatable in every situation. In the end, it returns to Hexagram Jian (Engagement), and intentional capacity gradually enters into the union of *yin* and *yang*, that is, the state of *yin* and *yang* in the world.

If one wants to establish a theory about world order, one needs extreme sincerity to expand the intentional capacity of this cognitive theory, because only extreme sincerity can convince people. That is to say, sincerity is enough to enhance the convincing power of the cognitive structure of intention, that is, sincerity may influence the world, and it is sufficient to influence the world. A person's inner structure of understanding the world cannot be perfect, but one can enhance the influence of one's intentional structure through one's sincerity towards the world. This in turn greatly expands the capacity of intentions.

中孚，豚（tún）鱼，吉。利涉大川，利贞。

《彖》曰：中孚，柔在内而刚得中，说而巽，孚乃化邦也。"豚鱼吉"，信及豚鱼也。"利涉大川"，乘木舟虚也。中孚以"利贞"，乃应乎天也。

《象》曰：泽上有风，中孚。君子以议狱缓死。

【明译】

中孚卦象征心怀诚信，心怀诚信到能够感化猪和鱼的程度，可以获得吉祥，有利于克服涉越大河这样的艰难险阻，有利于持守正道做事。

《彖传》说：中孚卦，阴柔在内，刚爻得到中位。下卦兑为悦，上卦巽为顺，喜悦而巽顺，是心怀诚信能够感化国家和民众。心怀诚信到能够感化猪和鱼的程度，可以获得吉祥，是诚信已经施予到了猪与鱼的身上。有利于克服涉越大河这样的艰难险阻，是好像乘着船舱虚空的木船（上卦巽为木舟。全卦中段两个虚的柔爻为空的船舱，两头两个实的刚爻为船头和船尾）。内心诚信有利于持守正道做事，心怀诚信，心意之发能够顺应天道的运行。

《象传》说：下卦兑为泽，上卦巽为风，大泽上有风就是中孚卦。君子看到春风一吹，涣然冰释这样泽上有风的感化之象，要复议狱案，缓处死囚（复议断过的案子，已判决的死囚暂缓执行，尽量消除冤屈，感化这些最难感化的人）。

Hexagram Zhongfu (Trust) symbolizes having sincerity in one's heart, and having sincerity in one's heart to the extent that it can influence even pigs and fishes, and lead to good fortune, which is helpful for overcoming difficulties and obstacles such as crossing a great river, and is helpful for doing things in the right way.

The *Judgment Commentary* (*Tuan Zhuan*) says: In Hexagram Zhongfu (Trust), the soft are internal, and strong lines are in the central positions. The lower Trigram Dui means joy, and the upper Trigram Xun means smoothness. Joy and smoothness means good faith, which can influence the country and the people. If one is honest enough to influence even pigs and fish, one can gain good fortune, as sincerity has been bestowed upon pigs and fish. This is helpful for overcoming difficulties and obstacles such as crossing a large river, as it is like riding on a wooden boat with an empty cabin (the upper Trigram Xun is a wooden boat, the two empty soft lines in the middle of the whole hexagram are the empty cabin, and the two solid *yang*/strong lines at the two ends are the bow and stern). Inner sincerity of the heart-mind is conducive to upholding the upright *dao* in action. With sincerity in the heart-mind, intentions and feelings can conform to the movement of the *dao* of heaven.

The *Image Commentary* (*Xiang Zhuan*) says: The lower Trigram Dui is lake, the upper Trigram Xun is wind, and wind over a great lake is Hexagram Zhongfu (Trust). When an exemplary person sees the moving scene of spring breeze blowing and melting ice, one wants to review prison cases and postpone the execution of death row inmates (to review the cases that have been decided, and suspend the execution of death row inmates who have been sentenced, try to eliminate grievances, and influence those who are the most difficult to influence).

【明意】

中孚卦是关于人与人之间的信心的卦，尤其与国家社会政治与领导人的意量有莫大的关系，如果领导人的意量如风感化万物，无孔不至，人民无不被感化，好像风过湖水，坚冰融释，那么领导人的真诚就可以感化民众之心，激发他们的热情，进而改变社会政治的方向。

意量的限度其实就是心意真诚的限度，真诚于人，真诚通天，与天共生（contextual creativity）。意量由真诚的程度决定，人天之意的意量在本卦是由极度真诚至于能够感化猪和鱼的程度来限定的，这种真诚至极不仅能够感化人心，更可以感化万物。

有权位的君子看到大泽受到风的感化，其心念也受到感化，推及那些等待审判的犯人，把他们也看作有情之人，真诚地去感化他们。这是从本体上认定人都有恻隐和同情之心，无论犯了多大的错误，都能够感受到通天的怜爱之意。这是社会组织之人心互通的基础，也可谓是构建社会组织的形上学基础，即人心是否受到领导人心意的感动，如果人民失去对领导人心意的信心，社会组织的塑造可能就徒有其表。这说明，政治运作要从感化人心开始，领导人真诚的人天之意才是社会和民心受到感动而有意量的开始。

[Illuminating Intentionality]

Hexagram Zhongfu (Trust) is about confidence between people, especially the crucial relationship between the social politics of a country and the intentional capacity of its leader. If the intentional capacity of a leader is like the wind, it affects the myriad things, is pervasive, and all the people will be affected. Just as how wind blows over a lake and ice melts, a leader's sincerity can influence the intentions of the people, inspire their enthusiasm, and then change the direction of social politics.

The limit of intentional capacity is actually the limit of sincerity, sincerity to people, sincerity to heaven, and symbiosis with heaven (contextual creativity). The capacity of intention is determined by the degree of sincerity. In this hexagram, the capacity of the intentionality of humanity and heaven is limited by the degree of extreme sincerity that can influence even pigs and fish. This extreme sincerity can not only influence people's intentions, but also influence the myriad things.

The powerful exemplary person sees how a great lake is influenced by the wind, and one's intentions are also influenced. One extends this to prisoners waiting for trial, regarding them as sentient people, and sincerely influencing them. This is an ontological recognition that people have compassion and sympathy, and no matter how big a mistake they make, they can feel the love and affection that connects with the cosmos. This is the basis for the communication between people's intentions in social organizations. It can also be said to be the metaphysical basis for building social organizations, that is, whether people's intentions are moved by their leaders' intentions. If the people lose confidence in their leaders' intentions, the shaping of social organizations may be merely superficial. This shows that political operations must start by influencing people's intentions. The sincere intentions of leaders are the beginning of the society and people's intentions being moved and gaining intentional capacity.

初九：虞吉，有它不燕。

《象》曰：初九"虞吉"，志未变也。

【明译】

初九：心志保持初心的状态并依此行事就会吉祥，如果起了其他的疑心则心境不得安宁。

《象传》说：初九的心志保持初心的状态去行事就会吉祥，因为它最初应接世界的心志状态没有发生变化。

Nine (*yang*/strong line) in the first place: If one keeps one's original intention and acts according to it, one will be fortunate. If one has other doubts, one's mood will not be peaceful.

The *Image Commentary* (*Xiang Zhuan*) says: If the intentionality of the Nine (*yang*/strong line) in the first place remains in the original state of mind, it will be auspicious to act, because its initial state of intentionality to cope with the world has not changed.

【明意】

初心即人心皆天机的那种初始状态，或者说是心灵最初应接世界的初始状态，代表着人对于世界的信心。中孚卦的核心是信心的发展变化。人对于世界最初的信心和意量需要涵养和保持，即心意发动接于世界生发之几的瞬间状态要小心护持。这个最初的心意与世界生发之几相接的状态当中有最初的心志。人们不应该改变最初的心志，因为这是人与世界建立诚信关系的开始。如果有疑心则容易心境不安，也就不能够很好地维持初心的意量。一旦初心意量难以维持，则今后再继续努力，重新建构并不容易，而人与世界的诚信也可能就难以建立。

[Illuminating Intentionality]

The original heart-mind is the initial state in which the human heart-mind is filled with heavenly vitality, or the initial state in which the mind first responds to the world, and represents people's confidence in the world. The core of Hexagram Zhongfu (Trust) is the development and change of confidence. People's initial confidence and intentional capacity in the world need to be cultivated and maintained, that is, the momentary state in which intentionality is initiated and the world is produced must be carefully protected. There is an original intentionality in this state where initial intentionality is connected with the infinitesimal emergence of the world. People should not change their original intentions, because this is the beginning of establishing a sincere relationship between people and the world. If one has doubts, one will easily feel uneasy, and will not be able to maintain one's original intention well. Once the original intention is difficult to maintain, it will not be easy to continue to work hard and rebuild in the future, and it may also be difficult to establish sincerity between people and the world.

九二：鸣鹤在阴，其子和（hè）之：我有好爵，吾与尔靡之。

《象》曰："其子和之"，中心愿也。

【明译】

九二：大鹤在阴幽之境中鸣唱，它的小鹤也鸣唱应和（好像在说）：我这里有甘甜的美酒，希望与你分享，同饮共乐。

《象传》说：它的小鹤（在远方）也鸣唱应和大鹤，声音中表达着内心真诚的愿望。

Nine (*yang*/strong line) in the second place: A big crane sings in the gloom, and its little crane also sings in response (as if to say): I have sweet wine here. I hope to share it with you, to drink and enjoy it together.

The *Image Commentary* (*Xiang Zhuan*) says: Its little crane (in the distance) also sings in response to the big crane, expressing its inner heart-mind's sincere wishes in its voice.

【明意】

除了保持初心不变，真诚的鸣和是扩大意量的基本方式。这种从心中出发的真诚是人的心意之量不断扩大到世界的重要过程。心意通达于他人，心量扩大到他心，是通过内心真诚至极的心心相印来实现的。这种对世界的真诚来自彼此对心意与世界共享的生机的共同领悟和认可。

思想和意念的力量，即使没有世俗的权力和位置，也可以跨越时空，改换另一时空的灵魂的意境。可见意量之广大，于其极度精微处，广漠无朕，可以通达宇宙间所有人心与阴阳之意的变化。

[Illuminating Intentionality]

In addition to keeping original intentionality unchanged, sincere harmony is the basic way to expand one's intentional capacity. This kind of sincerity starting from the heart-mind is an important process in which the capacity of human heart continues to expand to the world. The ability to communicate with others and expand intentionality to others is achieved through the most sincere heart-to-heart connection. This sincerity to the world comes from each other's mutual understanding and recognition of the vitality shared by intentionality and the world.

The power of thoughts and intentions, even without worldly power and position, can transcend time and space and change the intentional context of the heart-mind in another time and space. It can be seen that the vastness of intentional capacity, in its extreme subtleties, is vast and infinite, and can comprehend the changes in the intentionality of all the people's heart-minds and all the *yin* and *yang* in the cosmos.

六三：得敌，或鼓或罢，或泣或歌。

《象》曰："或鼓或罢"，位不当也。

【明译】

六三：面临敌人，有的人擂鼓前进，有的人休战败退，有的人哭泣，有的人欢声唱歌。

《象传》说：有的人擂鼓前进，有的人休战败退，是六三居位不当。

Six (*yin*/soft line) in the third place: Facing the enemy, some people beat drums and advance, some make a truce and retreat, some cry, and some sing joyfully.

The *Image Commentary* (*Xiang Zhuan*) says: Some people beat drums and advance, while others retreat and lose. This is due to the improper position of the Six (*yin*/soft line) in the third place.

【明意】

信心的延展，可能被质疑，被怀疑，甚至被打击，因为随着信心的提升，人在实化自己意念的过程中，自己和世界关系的边界必然受到冲击和挑战，这种挑战是修行的必经之路，即人的意量都是通过"敌"即对手来提升和表达出来的。

信的力量来自人心意发动的瞬间，而不取决于外物的得失，不取决于他人对自己的评判，自信则可以放下身外的宠辱得失，超然淡薄。

[Illuminating Intentionality]

The extension of confidence may be questioned, doubted, or even attacked, because with an increase of confidence, in the process of concretizing one's own intentions, the boundaries of the relationship between oneself and the world will inevitably be impacted and challenged. This challenge is a necessary path for spiritual practice, that is, people's intentional capacity is promoted and expressed through the "enemy", that is, their opponent.

The power of confidence comes from the moment when a person's intentionality is initiated, and does not depend on the gains and losses of external things, nor does it depend on other people's judgments of oneself. Self-confidence can let go of the gains and losses of external favors and disgrace, and be detached and indifferent.

六四：月既望，马匹亡，无咎。

《象》曰："马匹亡"，绝类上也。

【明译】

六四：月亮已经过了十五，走失了马匹，没有什么问题。

635

《象传》说：走失了马匹，说明六四与同类断绝关系，到了上卦（在卦变中，六四从大壮卦中间两个刚爻中分离出来到了天位。大壮卦中间两刚爻是同类）。

Six (*yin*/soft line) in the fourth place: The moon has passed the fifteenth day, and a horse has been lost, so there is no problem.

The *Image Commentary* (*Xiang Zhuan*) says: The lost horse means that the Six (*yin*/soft line) in the fourth place has severed ties with its own kind and reached the upper trigram (in the hexagram-changes, the Six (*yin*/soft line) in the fourth place separated from the two *yang*/strong lines in the middle of Hexagram Dazhuang (Exuberance) and reached the heavenly position. The two central lines in Hexagram Dazhuang (Exuberance) are *yang*/strong lines and of the same kind).

【明意】

意量的扩大与认识世界的时机有关，即与阴意和阳意的交战有关，既然努力扩大自己的孚信，那么对于意境中物的得失，就应该抱持一种超然的态度。

对他人和世界信心满满的时候，也应该是付出了离开同类的代价之时，而这种代价，可能通过某些具体的损失表达出来，不必太过在意，看起来不好，但没有太大的问题。

[Illuminating Intentionality]

The extension of intentional capacity is related to the timing of understanding the world, that is, to the battle between *yin* and *yang*. Since we strive to expand our trust, we should maintain a detached attitude towards the gain and loss of objects in the intentional context.

When one is full of confidence in others and the world, one should also pay the price of leaving one's own kind. This price may be expressed through some specific losses, but one should not pay too much attention to them. It may not look good, but it is not a big problem.

九五：有孚挛如，无咎。

《象》曰："有孚挛如"，位正当也。

【明译】

九五：心怀诚信，牵系天下之心，不会有祸患。

《象传》说：心怀诚信，牵系天下之心，是九五位置正当。

Nine (*yang*/strong line) in the fifth place: Be sincere and care about the world under heaven, and there will be no disaster.

The *Image Commentary* (*Xiang Zhuan*) says: Having sincerity and caring for the world is the right position for the Nine (*yang*/strong line) in the fifth place.

【明意】

九五是信心实化的最佳状态，不仅仅天下信从，而且拳拳系恋，犹如用绳子牵系打结，死不分离。也如随卦上六"拘系之，乃从维之"那种死心塌地的跟随之状。

人天之意以其至诚扩大到最大的意量。心意诚信至极，说明九五对于世界和他人之信心可通达天下之意境。

[Illuminating Intentionality]

The Nine (*yang*/strong line) in the fifth place is the best state for the concretization of confidence. Not only does the world obey, but love is bound with sincerity, just like tying a knot with a rope, and it will never be separated. This is also like the state of the Six (*yin*/soft line) in the top place of Hexagram Sui (Following) being dead set on following, "as if detained and restrained." The cosmological intentionality of humanity and heaven expands to the greatest extent with its sincerity. The extreme sincerity of intentionality shows that the Nine (*yang*/strong line) in the fifth place's confidence in the world and others can comprehend the intentional context of all under heaven.

上九：翰音登于天，贞凶。

《象》曰："翰音登于天"，何可长也？

【明译】

上九：（用鸡作祭祀宗庙的牺牲），鸡的鸣叫声显得对天过分诚信，以为可以高升上天，如此过分自信而正固不动必有凶险。

《象传》说：鸡自鸣得意，想自信满满地高飞上天，怎么可能飞得长久呢（上六在亢极之位，已到穷途末路）！

Nine (*yang*/strong line) in the top place: (Chickens are used as sacrifices in the ancestral temple). The crow of the chickens shows that they are overly honest to heaven, thinking that they can ascend to heaven. Such overconfidence and firmness must be dangerous.

The *Image Commentary* (*Xiang Zhuan*) says: The cock crows proudly and wants to fly high into the heavens with confidence. How can it fly for a long time?

【明意】

中孚卦的主线是信，即信的程度和状态，开始不够自信，到信人，以及信人可能出现的问题，到了上九却因为自信过度而自负，转向虚饰和浮华，矫揉造作而为他人耻笑。上九因为过度自信，致使达到盲目真诚的状态，因此伤己伤人，最后走向穷途末路。

此卦解释诚信当然是好事，但人过分诚信，迂腐不通，好像一只祭祀时行将被宰杀当做祭品的鸡自认为有资格登天，这就是自鸣得意、自大过头，死到临头还毫不明白事理的心理状态。

除了自以为是的一面，还有极度迷信的一面，以为神仙保佑，就能够去祸免灾，死到临头都不知道自己犯了什么错误，属于过度偏执，不知悔改。

[Illuminating Intentionality]

The main line of Hexagram Zhongfu (Trust) is trust, that is, the degrees and states of trust. In the beginning, one is not confident (self-trusting) enough, then one trusts people, and problems may arise when trusting people. At the Nine (*yang*/strong line) in the top place, one becomes arrogant because of overconfidence, turns to pretense and glitz, and is pretentious and ridiculed by others. Due to overconfidence, the Nine (*yang*/strong line) in the top place reaches a state of blind sincerity, thus hurting oneself and others, and finally reaches the end of one's road.

This hexagram explains that honesty is certainly a good policy, but people can be overly sincere and pedantic, just like a chicken that is about to be slaughtered during a sacrifice thinking that it is qualified to ascend to heaven. This is self-satisfaction and conceit, a mental state in which one fails to understand affairs even as the moment of death arrives.

In addition to the self-righteous side, there is also an extremely superstitious side. People believe that with the blessing of gods, they can avoid disasters, not knowing what mistakes they have made until they die. They are thus excessively paranoid and unrepentant.

雷山小过（卦六十二） （艮下震上）

Xiaoguo (Slight Overreaching), Thunder and Mountain (Hexagram 62) (Gen below, Zhen above)

　　谦虚能量爆发就会小过。谦卦到了六五，上六已经有意能爆发，或者不得不爆发的倾向，因为谦虚为本，虽然用了征伐的武力，也只能说是小过，而不是大过。谦卦的征战，可以说是一种矫枉过正，宁可过一些。

　　意能的调节有两种，一是主动调节自己的意能；二是通过某些方式调节他人的意能。小过卦说明人们在调节意能的过程当中，需要适当小过一些。

　　调节意能的小过主要表现在：如果有异常的征象发动，就要学会保存意能不受伤害，因为意能必定为现实条件所限制，当现实条件变化的时候，要保持对自身意能变化的敏感，比如，如果跟随小人，意能就容易迅速下降。还要知道主动规避危险，每当意能有所积累，要想继续增强意能，可以适当小过一些，但要避免一直过分积累，而没有注意到已经陷入危险的境地，导致意能没有机缘适当地化实出来，自取灾难而耗光所有积累的意能，那就实在太可惜了。

A sudden burst of modest energy leads to overreaching. When Hexagram Qian (Humility) reaches the Six (*yin*/soft line) in the fifth place, the Six (*yin*/soft line) in the top place has a burst of intentional energy, or an unavoidable tendency for such a burst. Because humility is the basis, even if force is used in conquest, it can only be said to be a minor fault, not a major one. Hexagram Qian (Humility)'s campaign can be said to be overcorrect the wrong, so it is better to be slightly excessive.

There are two ways to regulate one's own intentional energy. One is to actively regulate one's own intentional energy; the other is to regulate other people's intentional energy in certain ways. Hexagram Xiaoguo (Slight Overreaching) shows that people need to be appropriately small in the process of regulating their intentional energy.

The main faults in regulating one's intentional energy are as follows: if there are abnormal signs, one must learn to protect one's intentional energy from being harmed, because one's intentional energy must be limited by real conditions. When real conditions change, one must maintain control over the sensitivity to changes of one's own intentional energy, for example, if one follows a petty person, one's mental abilities will easily decline quickly. One also needs to know how to proactively avoid dangers. Whenever one's intentional energy accumulates, if one wants to continue to increase it, one can overreach slightly. However, one must avoid accumulating too much and not noticing that one has fallen into a dangerous situation, resulting in no opportunity for one's intentional energy to be concretized appropriately, and bringing disaster on oneself by using up all the accumulated intentional energy, which would indeed be a pity.

小过，亨。利贞。可小事，不可大事。飞鸟遗之音，不宜上，宜下，大吉。

《彖》曰：小过，小者过而亨也。过以"利贞"，与时行也。柔得中，是以"小事"吉也。刚失位而不中，是以"不可大事"也。有"飞鸟"之象焉，"飞鸟遗之音"。"不宜上，宜下，大吉"，上逆而下顺也。

《象》曰：山上有雷，小过。君子以行过乎恭，丧过乎哀，用过乎俭。

【明译】

小过卦象征矫枉过正，亨通，利于持守正固。在小事上可以稍微矫枉过正一些，但是在大事上不可以过分。鸟越飞越高，空中留下的声音越来越微弱，这时鸟不适宜继续往上飞，而应当顺势往下飞，才会获得大的吉祥。

《彖传》说：小过卦，是小的事情稍微超矫枉过正一点，还是可以亨通的（柔爻为小，晋变小过卦变中柔爻越过刚爻）。超过一点但还是利于持守正固，是伴随时序运行。柔爻（六二、六五）占据了中位，所以寻常小事稍微过分一点还是可以吉祥的。刚爻失去地位而不在中位，所以不可以做大事。卦有飞鸟之象（两个刚爻是鸟身，上下各两个柔爻是翅膀），所以是鸟越飞越高之后在空中留下的声音。鸟不适宜继续往上飞，而应当顺势往下飞，才会获得大的吉祥，是因为向上是逆，向下是顺，顺才能获吉（观卦变小过，两个柔爻到了刚爻之上，柔爻乘刚爻之上为逆）。

《象传》说：下卦艮为山，上卦震为雷，山上有震雷就是小过卦。山上的雷声比平地上大一些，君子从中受到启示，相比平时，行为上可以更加谦恭一点，办丧事时宁可更加悲哀一些，吃喝用度宁可更加节俭一点。

Hexagram Xiaoguo (Slight Overreaching) symbolizes overcorrection, prosperity, and is conducive to maintaining integrity. One can go a little overboard on small things, but not on big things. A bird flies higher and higher, and the sound left in the air becomes weaker and weaker. At this time, it is not suitable for the bird to continue flying upward, and it should follow the propensity and fly downward, thereby obtaining great auspiciousness.

The *Judgment Commentary* (*Tuan Zhuan*) says: Hexagram Xiaoguo (Slight Overreaching) means that small things can still be successful if they are slightly overcorrected (soft lines are small, and a soft line overtakes a strong line as Hexagram Jin (Promotion) changes into Hexagram Xiaoguo (Slight Overreaching).) If it only exceeds a little, it is still conducive to maintaining integrity and runs with the order of time. *Yin*/soft lines (the Six (*yin*/soft line) in the second place and the Six (*yin*/soft line) in the fifth place) occupy the central positions, so ordinary little things can still be auspicious if they are a little excessive. *Yang*/strong lines lose their status and are not in central positions, so they cannot do big things. The hexagram has the image of a flying bird (the two *yang*/strong lines are the body of the bird, and the two *yin*/soft lines above and below are the wings), so it is the sound left in the air after the bird flies higher and higher. It is not suitable for the bird to continue to fly upward, and it should follow the propensity and fly downward, thereby obtaining great auspiciousness. This is because rising upward is to go against the propensity, while going downward is to follow it (as Hexagram Guan (Observation) changes into Hexagram Xiaoguo (Slight Overreaching), two soft lines rise above the strong lines, the soft lines riding on the strong lines, which is converse).

The *Image Commentary* (*Xiang Zhuan*) says: The lower Trigram Gen is mountain, the upper Trigram Zhen is thunder, and thunder on a mountain is Hexagram Xiaoguo (Slight Overreaching). Thunder in the mountains is louder than on the ground, and exemplary people are inspired by this. Compared with ordinary times, they can be slightly more humble in their conduct, be slightly more sad when holding funerals, and be slightly more frugal in eating and drinking.

【明意】

调节自己的意能可以适当小过，但不可以过度。从六五、上六就可以看出来，小过可以接受，但太过就不可以。调节他人的意能，就是意念的实化问题，意能要借助意缘才能实化。如果没有合适的意缘，意能积累再多，也无法转化。好比一个人空有一身才学武艺，却没有人赏识，甚至没有机会表现。所以一个没有机缘实化自己意能的人，就一直在小过的状态，到最后就太过了。调节他人的意能完全是在与他们意识交流交接的意缘之中发生的。

[Illuminating Intentionality]

Intentional energy can be adjusted slightly in excess, but not disproportionately. It can be seen from the Six (*yin*/soft line) in the fifth place and Six (*yin*/soft line) in the top place that a small excess is acceptable, but an extreme one is not. Adjusting other people's intentional energy is a matter of concretizing intentions. Intentional energy can only be concretized with the help of intentional conditions. If there are no suitable intentional conditions, no matter how much intentional energy is accumulated, it cannot be transformed. This is like a person who has all the talent to learn martial arts, but no one appreciates it, and he does not even have a chance to show it. Therefore, one who does not have the opportunity to concretize one's own intention will always be in a state of slight excess, and in the end it will be too much. Adjusting other people's intentional energy occurs entirely within the intentional context of communicating with their consciousness.

初六：飞鸟以凶。

《象》曰："飞鸟以凶"，不可如何也。

【明译】

初六：鸟惊飞，这是凶兆。

《象传》说：鸟惊飞带来的凶灾是无可奈何的事（飞来横祸，人无能为力）。

Six (*yin*/soft line) in the first place: Birds fly in fright, which is a bad sign.

The *Image Commentary* (*Xiang Zhuan*) says: Nothing can be done about the disaster caused by the frightened birds (flight brings disaster, and people are powerless).

【明意】

意能不能因为受到外在小鸟的惊飞就消懈，而要积极应对，首先要收摄得住，小心应对，不让自己的意能消散。在意念的瞬间转化之间，有一种弹指灰飞烟灭的大气度，不为任何微小的动静所撼动。

要学会于异常征象发动之时保持意能，尽量保持低调谦和，面对突发局面（如鸟惊飞），意能不可乱，而要沉稳，保存意能不受伤害。

[Illuminating Intentionality]

Intentional energy cannot be weakened just because one is frightened by external birds. To actively respond to something, one must first be able to absorb it and deal with it carefully to prevent one's intentional energy from dissipating. In the momentary transformation of intentions, there is a grandeur that can lead to disaster in a flash, so it should not be shaken by any tiny movement.

One must learn to maintain one's intentional energy when abnormal phenomena occur, try to keep a low profile, and be modest. When faced with unexpected situations (such as birds flying), one's intentional energy must not be confused, but must be calm to protect intentional energy from harm.

六二：过其祖，遇其妣（bǐ）。不及其君，遇其臣。无咎。

《象》曰："不及其君"，"臣"不可过也。

【明译】

六二：越过祖父（不在了），遇到祖母；没能见到君王，但遇到了大臣；（碰到的是小过一点点的人），没有什么问题。

《象传》说：没碰上君王，是因为君王的臣子不可以越过，也就不要错过。

Six (*yin*/soft line) in the second place: Passing his grandfather (who has passed away), he meets his grandmother; he does not get to see the king, but meets the minister; (he meets someone a little younger, so) there is no problem.

The *Image Commentary* (*Xiang Zhuan*) says: The reason he did not meet the king is because the king's ministers are not allowed to overstep, so he did not want to make a mistake.

【明意】

小过有主观和客观的原因，此爻说明，有些外在的条件导致的小过，不是主观意愿能够决定的，人间的意缘也是如此，期待和想象中的意缘，可能与现实发生的意缘之间有比较明确的距离。这当然可以说，意能都跟外在的条件有关系，但能不决定缘，缘也不能作为衡量能的标准，可见，能与缘之间，是随意而起，但不纯粹受制于意的。

意能被现实条件所限，人际与现实的条件可能会阻碍意能的生长，有些具体的层级不可越过，即使被层次性地遮挡也无可奈何。意能的提升不可过度依赖外缘，如果过分依赖外缘，往往会有意想不到的阻碍，本来的助力最后都可能变成阻力。

[Illuminating Intentionality]

Minor faults have both subjective and objective causes. This line shows that minor faults caused by some external conditions cannot be determined by subjective intentions. The same is true for the dependent co-arising of the human world, as the dependent co-arising of expectations and imagination may not be the same as what happens in reality, and there is a relatively clear gap between possibilities and actually initiated intentional conditions. Of course, it can be said that intentional energy is related to external conditions, but energy does not determine conditions, and conditions cannot be used as a standard to measure energy. It can be seen that energy and conditions arise following intentions, but they are not purely controlled by intentions.

Intentional energy is limited by real conditions, and interpersonal and realistic conditions may hinder the growth of imagination. There are some specific levels that cannot be crossed, and even if they are blocked hierarchically, there is nothing one can do. To improve one's ability, one should not rely too much on the outside world. If one relies too much on the outside world, there will often be unexpected obstacles, and something that is originally helpful may eventually turn into resistance.

九三：弗过防之，从或戕（qiāng）之，凶。

《象》曰："从或戕之"，"凶"如何也？

【明译】

九三：不仅不肯过于防范，还随从小人之后，就可能会受人戕害，非常凶险。

《象传》说：还随从小人之后，就可能会受人戕害，凶险程度无法预料，不知道能怎么办（九三在卦变中与上六换位，自找其凶）？

Nine (yang/strong line) in the third place: One not only does not want to be too cautious, but also follows a petty person and may be harmed by others, which is very dangerous.

The *Image Commentary* (*Xiang Zhuan*) says: If one follows a petty person, one may be harmed by others, and the degree of danger is unpredictable. What can one do (the Nine (yang/strong line) in the third place changes places with the Six (yin/soft line) in the top place in the hexagram-changes, which is asking for trouble)?

【明意】

跟随会伤害自己意能的小人，就是自取凶祸，因为跟从小人，意能会下降，而意能下降首先由于自己的判断力下降，即对人和对形势判断力都下降所致。可见，跟不对人，加上自己过度自信，不加防范而意念出偏，可能导致凶祸，最后甚至可能失去对自己命运的控制。

九三要防止过刚，更不可自生恶念，从而无法控制，否则可能因为越位之意念而生危险，如果执著不改，则危险显而易见。故现实的意缘之发生甚至越位的意缘，都需要一些切实的外在的机缘，不可以过度执着于一些念头导致无法预料的风险。

[Illuminating Intentionality]

Following petty people who will harm one's own intentional energy is bringing disaster upon oneself, because following petty people will lead to a decline in one's intentional energy, and the decline in one's intentional energy is first caused by a decline in one's own judgment, that is, a decline in judgment about people and situations. It can be seen that not being with the right person, coupled with one's own overconfidence and going astray without taking precautions, may lead to disaster, and in the end, one may even lose control of one's own destiny.

The Nine (yang/strong line) in the third place must be prevented from being too strong, let alone having evil intentions that cannot be controlled, otherwise danger may arise due to overstepping intentions. If one persists and does not change, the danger will be obvious. Therefore, the occurrence of realistic dependent co-arising and even overreaching dependent co-arising requires some real external opportunities. Over-attachment to some intentions cannot but lead to unpredictable risks.

九四：无咎。弗过遇之，往厉必戒，勿用永贞。

《象》曰："弗过遇之"，位不当也。"往厉必戒"，终不可长也。

【明译】

九四：没有祸患，自己没有越位行事，但还是能够相遇。前往将有危险，一定要警戒小心，不要过于执著而不变通。

《象传》说：不要越过，可以相遇，是因为九四的位置不适当（九四刚爻居柔位）。前往有危险，一定要警戒，说明最终不能长久（全卦是小者过，刚爻坚守不可能长久）。

Nine (yang/strong line) in the fourth place: There is no disaster, and one is not overreaching in one's actions, but can still meet that. There will be dangers when one advances, so one must be alert and careful, and not be too persistent or inflexible.

The *Image Commentary* (*Xiang Zhuan*) says: As long as one does not overreach, one can meet disasters, because the position of the Nine (*yang*/strong line) in the fourth place is inappropriate (the Nine (*yang*/strong line) in the fourth place is in a soft position). One must be alert if there is danger when advancing, which means that it will not last long in the end (the whole hexagram is the small overreaching, so it is impossible for a *yang*/strong line to persist for long).

【明意】

艰难时刻，首先要自己守住意能，想方设法找机缘实化自己的意能。但这个过程有风险，当谨慎从事，过度执着容易出事。意能的实化过程，要合于情理，不可过度。

在火烧眉毛的艰险面前，既然已经看清前面有危险，那就千万不可过于拘泥不通，虽然保存意能要知道避险，自己位置不当，必须竭力保存意能在先，但如果想要改变被动的状态，就不可过分执着，不加变通，而必须非动不可，在变动当中，重塑自己的意能。

[Illuminating Intentionality]

In difficult times, one must first guard one's intentional energy and find ways to discover opportunities to concretize one's intentional energy. But this process is risky, so one should be cautious as it can easily lead to trouble if one is too persistent. The process of concretizing intentional energy must be reasonable and not excessive.

In the face of imminent dangers, since one has clearly seen the danger ahead, one must not be too rigid. Although to preserve one's intentional energy, one needs to know how to avoid danger, if one is not in the right position, one must first try one's best to preserve one's intentional energy. If, however, one wants to change one's passive state, one should not be overly persistent or inflexible, but must move and reshape one's own intentional energy in the midst of changes.

六五：密云不雨，自我西郊。公弋取彼在穴。

《象》曰："密云不雨"，已上也。

【明译】

六五：浓云密布而不下雨，从我西郊飘过。王公用带绳的箭射，猎取穴中之物。

《象传》说：浓云密布而不下雨，（杀机四伏的氛围当中）六五已经到了上位（六五卦变中向上推移）。

Six (*yin*/soft line) in the fifth place: Thick clouds without rain drift across one's western suburbs. The prince shoots arrows with ropes to hunt things in caves.

The *Image Commentary* (*Xiang Zhuan*) says: There are thick clouds but no rain (in an atmosphere full of murderous intent), and the Six (*yin*/soft line) in the fifth place has reached an upper position (the Six (*yin*/soft line) in the fifth place moves upward in the hexagram-changes).

【明意】

在雨不下来，杀机已经积累的形势下，还去猎杀很容易到手的猎物，这样猎取的方式本身和增加意能的做法，实在就是小过的做法。就算可以小过一些，通过猎取猎物来增加意能，让能量积累而不释放出来，但六五这种赶尽杀绝以增加自己意能的做法，实在是让二阳寒透了心。按说六五在中位，加上意能虽然已经有所积累，不宜一直小过下去，但实在是因为在小过的大势当中，就一定要小过来继续增加意能。

[Illuminating Intentionality]

In a situation where the rain has stopped and murderous intent has been accumulated, hunting for prey that is easy to obtain really is a small mistake in terms of the hunting method itself and the method for increasing one's intentional energy. Even if it can be done on a smaller scale, by hunting prey to increase one's intentional energy and allowing the energy to accumulate without releasing it, the Six (*yin*/soft line) in the fifth place's method of increasing its own intentional energy by killing everything really makes the two *yang* lines heartbroken. In theory, the Six (*yin*/soft line) in the fifth place is in the central position, and although intentional energy has been accumulated, it is not suitable to continue to slightly overreach, but actually, because of the general trend of slight overreaching, it must be allowed to continue to increase intentional energy.

上六：弗遇过之，飞鸟离之，凶，是谓灾眚。

《象》曰："弗遇过之"，已亢也。

【明译】

上六：没有相遇，却错越过去了。飞鸟自投罗网，太凶险了，可以说是天灾，但其实是自找的人祸。

《象传》说：没有相遇，但错误地超越过去了，说明上六已经飞得太高了。

Six (*yin*/soft line) in the top place: They do not meet, but pass each other by mistake. It is too dangerous for birds to fall into a trap by themselves. It can be said to be a natural disaster, but in fact it is a self-inflicted man-made disaster.

The *Image Commentary* (*Xiang Zhuan*) says: There is no meeting, but the mistake of passing over shows that the Six (*yin*/soft line) in the top place has flown too high.

【明意】

小过卦描述的是人处于乱世时期，应该像飞鸟一样，"宜下不宜上"，如果飞得高亢而错过了合理的分界，就要招致巨大的凶灾。根本原因在于自我认知和自我控制的意能分寸出了问题。一味小过地增强意能，最后却如飞鸟般自投罗网，实在太可惜了。因为积累意能却忘了积累的目标不是意念本身，而是能够实化而有用，结果到了最后可谓竹篮打水一场空，而且可能有天灾人祸。因为处心积虑积累的意能却都用不上了，没有合适的机缘来生发掉积累的意能，就反而陷入险境，最后变成意能很低的状态，好像一个人积累了一生才学，却总是怀才而不遇，空有一身能耐和抱负，却什么机会也没有，结果自入险地，耗光才学，一无所成，到头来只空留嗟叹。过分积累意能的错误的结果，就可能是这样的。或者事情还没调查清楚，还没合理相"遇"，就起恶念去害别人，这样的恶念将让自己作茧自缚、反受其害。

[Illuminating Intentionality]

Hexagram Xiaoguo (Slight Overreaching) describes how people in troubled times should be like birds, for whom "it is better to fly down than fly up." If one flies high and misses reasonable boundaries, one will incur huge disasters. The fundamental reason lies in the problem of self-awareness and self-control. It is such a pity to blindly enhance one's mental abilities in a trivial way, only to end up falling into a trap like a bird. Since the goal of accumulating intentional energy is not the intention itself, but its ability to be concretized and useful, in the end it can be said that it is all in vain, and there may be natural and man-made disasters. Because the intentional energy accumulated through hard work is not used, and there is no suitable opportunity to initiate the accumulated intentional energy, it will be in danger, and finally become a state of very low intentional energy, as if a person has accumulated a lifetime of learning, but has not been able to use it. One always has talents but never encounters a position; one has all the abilities and ambition, but no opportunities. As a result, one ends up in danger, uses up one's talent and learning, achieves nothing, and ends up with nothing but sighs. This may be the result of the mistake of over-accumulating intentional energy. Or, one may have bad intentions to harm others before the matter has been investigated clearly and before one has a reasonable "encounter." Such bad intentions will make one's predicament self-inflicted, and one must suffer the consequences.

水火既济（卦六十三）　（离下坎上）

Jiji (Success), Water and Fire (Hexagram 63)　(Li below, Kan above)

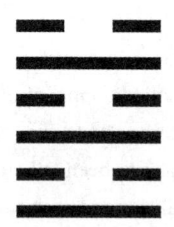

　　既济的状态是意念之行在一种动态平衡状态，达到暂时的平衡和稳定。意行于时间之中，随时变化，全部意念、意识、意能皆行在时间之中，意能相生相克，相互转化，理想化的意念之行，在既济的状态当中，要合于天行，合于阴阳之力的转化，如果不合，意念离开自然阴阳力所构成之境，难以成就也难以维系良好的成功局面。

　　The state of Hexagram Jiji (Success) is that intentions are in a state of dynamic equilibrium, achieving temporary balance and stability. Intentionality moves in time and follows changes in time, with intentions, consciousness, and intentional energy all moving in time. Intentional energies produce and restrain each other, and transforms into each other. The ideal movement of intentionality in a state of success must be consistent with the movement of heaven, and in line with the transformation of the power of *yin* and *yang*. If not, intentionality will leave the realm formed by natural *yin* and *yang* power, and it will be difficult to achieve and maintain a good and successful situation.

　　既济，亨小，利贞。初吉终乱。

　　《彖》曰："既济，亨"，"小"者"亨"也。"利贞"，刚柔正而位当也。"初吉"，柔得中也。"终"止则"乱"，其道穷也。

　　《象》曰：水在火上，既济。君子以思患而豫防之。

　　【明译】

　　既济卦象征事已成功，但只是在小事上亨通，坚守正道会有好处，刚开始时吉祥，到最后却乱作一团。

《彖传》说：事已成功，亨通，可只是在小事上亨通，坚守正道会有好处，因为刚爻和柔爻各自当位，而且两两相应。刚开始时吉祥，因为柔爻当位居中，但到最后一旦停止就会变乱，因为柔爻到顶停止（则与阳失衡），马上陷入穷困之境。

《象传》说：上卦坎为水，下卦离为火，水在火上烧水烹饪，象征事情已经成功。君子看到这种现象，就要居安思危，把握好分寸，防患于未然。

Since Hexagram Jiji (Success) symbolizes success, but only in small things, it will be beneficial to stick to the upright *dao*. It is auspicious at the beginning, but will be chaotic in the end.

The *Judgment Commentary* (*Tuan Zhuan*) says: Things have been successful and prosperous, but they are only prosperous in small things. It will be beneficial to stick to the upright *dao*, because the strong and soft lines have their respective positions, and the two correspond to each other. It is auspicious at the beginning, because the soft line is in the middle, but in the end it will become chaotic once it stops, because the soft line stops at the top (and then is out of balance with *yang*), and it will immediately fall into poverty.

The *Image Commentary* (*Xiang Zhuan*) says: The upper Trigram Kan is water, and the lower Trigram Li is fire. Boiling water over fire for cooking symbolizes that things have been successful. When an exemplary person sees this phenomenon, one should be prepared for danger in times of peace, and take measures to prevent problems before they occur.

【明意】

意念之境存在一种平衡相应的状态，《易》称之为既济，但也只是一种暂时的阴阳平衡之态，意境之内在的矛盾仍然存在，而且在不断发展变化，在每一个意念实化之间把意境驾驭得好，其实非常不容易。既济之时，既是各爻各居其位，达到相对和谐的成功状态，也是各种矛盾和问题暂时掩盖，随时可能实化出来的状态。如何提前预知意境可能存在的问题，并在意念实化的先机当中感知和消解它们，实在需要高超的感知力和良好的分寸感。

水火相济为用，但要以阴阳和乐为要，因为水火本来不容，却要保持一个动态平衡使得水火融通，这是一种相克相容的哲学，面对存在的普遍矛盾，随时把握好矛盾转化的分寸，使之处于平衡的中道，这是理想化的意境状态。也就是说，能够包容各种矛盾，并且善于化解矛盾，这当是意境和通发展的基本样态。

[Illuminating Intentionality]

There is a state of balance and correspondence in the realm of intentionality, which is called Hexagram Jiji (Success) in the *Book of Changes*, but it is only a temporary state of balance between *yin* and *yang*. The inherent contradictions in the state of intentionality still exist and are constantly developing and changing. Between every concretization of intention, it is actually not easy to control the intentional context well. At a time of success, it is not only a state of relative harmony and success in which each line is in its own place, but also a state in which various contradictions and problems are temporarily concealed and may materialize at any time. How to predict possible problems in the intentional context in advance, and to perceive and resolve them before intentions are concretized, really requires superb perception and a good sense of proportion.

Water and fire complement each other, but the harmony of *yin* and *yang* must be the key, because water and fire are originally incompatible, and a dynamic balance must be maintained to make water and fire blend. This is a philosophy of mutual restraint and compatibility. Faced with the common contradictions of existence, one must manage the transformation and proportionality of contradictions at all times, so that they are on the central *dao* of balance; this is an ideal intentional context. In other words, being able to tolerate various contradictions and being good at resolving them should be the basic form for the intentional context's harmonious and comprehensive development.

初九：曳（yè）其轮，濡其尾，无咎。

《象》曰："曳其轮"，义无咎也。

【明译】

初九：拉住车轮（跑不快），渡河沾湿了尾巴（游不快），不过没有太大问题。

《象传》说：拉住车轮，虽然跑不快，但是照理应该不会有什么大的问题。

Nine (*yang*/strong line) in the first place: Holding on to the wheel (unable to run fast), one's tail gets wet when crossing the river (unable to swim fast), but there is not much of a problem.

The *Image Commentary* (*Xiang Zhuan*) says: Holding the wheel, although one cannot run fast, there should not be any big problems.

【明意】

在既已成功的状态当中，要放慢意识的节奏，才能维系好意识与世界融会贯通的理想状态。但既济之时，既要时时刻刻小心谨慎，犹如老狐狸一般疑神疑鬼，谨慎小心，才能无咎，但同时也要有小狐狸敢于尝试新鲜事物的魄力，否则不去渡河，就不可能经历风雨迎来彩虹。这都是心念当下把控的分寸。

[Illuminating Intentionality]

In a state of success, it is necessary to slow down the rhythms of consciousness in order to maintain an ideal state of integration between consciousness and the world. But when times are good, one must always be cautious, like an old fox who is suspicious and wary, so that one can be blameless. But at the same time, one must have the courage of a little fox to dare to try new things. Otherwise, if one does not cross the river, one will not be able to experience the wind and rain and welcome the rainbow. These are all factors that intentionality must control in a moment.

六二：妇丧其茀（fú），勿逐，七日得。

《象》曰："七日得"，以中道也。

第三章　易经明意
——爻意分说（下经）

【明译】

六二：妇人丢失了首饰，不要去找寻，七天后会失而复得。

《象传》说：七天后会失而复得，是因为六二在变动的情境当中能够持守中道。

Six (*yin*/soft line) in the second place: If a woman loses her jewelry, do not look for it. It will be found again in seven days.

The *Image Commentary* (*Xiang Zhuan*) says: It will be lost and recovered after seven days, because the Six (*yin*/soft line) in the second place can maintain the central *dao* in changing situations.

【明意】

意行当有塞翁失马的分寸，坐等事变，也是意行（未动之行），类似未发之中。意向对于外物的执着要注意分寸，得失之感要放下。失了就面对这种缺失的结果，顺其自然，不要过分在意，中道是保持清醒，不为外在的得失所动。

意念发动与内心的德性有关，有德者起心动念暗合天机，往往顺应外在的提示能够得到最好的行动效果。

[Illuminating Intentionality]

Intentions and actions should be done with a measure of control. Waiting for something to happen is also an action of intention (an action that has not yet been taken), similar to what is yet to happen. One should be careful about attachment to external objects and let go of the sense of gains and losses. If one suffers a loss, just face the result of this lack, let it take its course, and do not care too much. The central *dao* is to stay conscious and not be moved by external gains and losses.

The initiation of intentions is related to the inner virtue of the heart-mind. A virtuous person's intentions coincide with heaven's impetus and often follow external prompts to achieve the best results in action.

九三：高宗伐鬼方，三年克之，小人勿用。

《象》曰："三年克之"，惫也。

【明译】

九三：殷高宗武丁去讨伐鬼方，三年后才得到胜利，说明小人不可重用。

《象传》说：三年后才把对方征服，说明九三持久努力，实在是太疲惫了。

Nine (*yang*/strong line) in the third place: In the Shang Dynasty, Emperor Gaozong Wu Ding went to attack kingdom Guifang, but he was victorious three years later, which shows that petty people cannot be used on important occasions.

The *Image Commentary* (*Xiang Zhuan*) says: It took three years to conquer the opponent, which shows that the Nine (*yang*/strong line) in the third place's long-term efforts are too exhausted.

【明意】

意向性长久地集中在某个需要竭尽全力的点上，非常辛苦。三年打仗期间，意向一直不可松弛，必然疲惫不堪。打仗不能速战速决，是因为用人不当。

本爻讨论持续用意的艺术，如何持续有效用意而不会过分疲惫，打仗是一个务求必胜又需要高强度持续用意的过程，所以持续用意的艺术非常重要，如果犯了战略或者战术性的错误，不能尽快克敌制胜，则会疲惫而丧失志向。

[Illuminating Intentionality]

It is very hard to concentrate on a certain point that requires all one's efforts for a long time. During the three years of war, one cannot relax one's intentions, and one must be exhausted. The reason why the war cannot be resolved quickly is because of improper employment of personnel.

This line discusses the art of sustained intention, that is, how to sustain effective intention without being too exhausted. War is a process that must win and requires high-intensity sustained intention, so the art of sustained intention is very important. If one makes strategic or tactical mistakes, one cannot defeat the enemy as soon as possible, and one will become exhausted and lose one's ambition.

六四：繻（xū）有衣袽，终日戒。

《象》曰："终日戒"，有所疑也。

【大意】

六四：木船随时可能渗漏，准备好破衣败絮来堵塞，需要整天高度提防戒备。

《象传》说：需要整天高度提防戒备，是因为六四有所疑惧。

Six (*yin*/soft line) in the fourth place: The wooden boat may leak at any time, so be prepared to use rags and lint to block it. One needs to be on high alert all day long.

The *Image Commentary* (*Xiang Zhuan*) says: The reason why one needs to be on high alert all day long is because one has doubts and fears about the Six (*yin*/soft line) in the fourth place.

【明意】

坎卦讲到意念之危，意念发动后而有时时刻刻的危险，此处的比喻极度精当，好比船的缝隙，微小的缝隙也极度危险，意念的偏差有时就像这样，故唯一可靠的就是极度小心谨慎，慎终如始。

九四表示渡河到一半的状态，可是这种状态之中，人不可以有一点点偏差，否则就可能有倾覆的危险，前有水，后有火，水火无情，极度小心方能通过水与火之绝境的考验。此爻好比在海水与火焰之间，横竖都是生死绝境，只有穿过火与水的考验才能重生。

[Illuminating Intentionality]

Hexagram Kan (In Danger) talks about the danger of intentions, as there is always danger after intentions are initiated. The metaphor here is extremely accurate, as it is like a gap in a ship, and even small gaps are also extremely dangerous. The deviation of intentions is sometimes like this. Therefore, the only reliable option is to be extremely cautious and careful.

The Nine (*yang*/strong line) in the fourth place represents the state of being halfway across the river. However, in this state, one cannot make any deviations; otherwise there may be a risk of capsizing. There is water in front and fire behind, and water and fire are merciless. Only with extreme caution can one pass the desperate test of water and fire. This line is like being between sea water and flames of fire, a desperate situation of life and death. Only by passing the test of fire and water can one be reborn.

九五：东邻杀牛，不如西邻之禴祭，实受其福。

《象》曰："东邻杀牛，不如西邻之"时也。"实受其福"，吉大来也。

【明译】

九五：东方邻国用杀掉整牛的厚礼来祭祀，不如西方邻国举行微薄而虔诚的"禴祭"，反而实实在在受到上天的福佑。

《象传》说：东方邻国用杀牛的厚礼来祭祀，因为它的时运已经不如西方邻国了。实实在在受到福佑，吉祥即将源源不断地降临。

【明译】

Nine (*yang*/strong line) in the fifth place: The neighboring countries in the east use the generous gift of killing a whole cow in sacrifice. This is not as good as the neighboring countries in the west holding a meager and pious "grain sacrifice." On the contrary, they are truly blessed by heaven.

The *Image Commentary* (*Xiang Zhuan*) says: The neighboring country in the east sacrifices cattle as a generous gift because its fortunes are no longer as good as those in the west. Being truly blessed, and auspiciousness will continue to come.

【明意】

可见意念发动与其意缘如何简朴都不要紧，但需要意念真诚，这对神人通用，关键还是时运合适方能有福。事情既成之时，仍要以通天的诚信为主。人是否有福，是否得到上天的祝佑，取决于是否得到天时阴阳和顺之力的鼎力支援，助成人间意缘的聚合。这助缘的内在理由在人叫德性，是顺天道而行的内心德性。德性也可以看作人对天道善性的理解，并且不断通过实化为德行在意向性当中积存再积存，积累沉淀下来。上天保佑有德之人，因为有德之人意行如通天，自然有福。

[Illuminating Intentionality]

It can be seen that it does not matter how simple and plain the intention is, but the intention needs to be sincere. This applies to both spirits and humans, and the key is to find the right time in order to be blessed. When things are already complete, sincerity must still be the main priority. Whether a person is fortunate and blessed by heaven depends on the strong support of the harmonious power of *yin* and *yang* in the heavenly cycles, which can help the gathering of dependent co-arising between people. The inner reason for this help in people is called virtue, and this is the inner virtue that follows the heavenly *dao*. Virtue can also be seen as people's understanding of the goodness of the *dao* of heaven, and it is constantly accumulated and accumulated again in intentionality through concretization into virtue, as it accumulates and precipitates. Heaven blesses virtuous people, because virtuous people's intentions and actions are as if they connect with heaven, and they are naturally blessed.

上六：濡其首，厉。

《象》曰："濡其首，厉"，何可久也？

【明译】

上六：头被打湿，有危险了。

《象传》说：头浸入水中，太危险了，（既济的状态）太难持久了。

Six (*yin*/soft line) in the top place: One's head is wet, one is in danger.

The *Image Commentary* (*Xiang Zhuan*) says: It is too dangerous to immerse one's head in water, and it is too difficult (for the state of success) to last long.

【明意】

小狐狸被水中的浪打湿了头部，头浸水中，是非常危险的事，表示意念极度难行。头是意念性发动的物理基础，头部的大脑是意向性存在与发动的基础，所以"首"被打湿，是意向的发动有极度危险之喻，也是很难持久的。

但意念的转化，往往需要置之死地而后生，也就是绝处逢生。一个既成的意境本身是一个过程，《周易》的宇宙即意识之流，都是一个过程，即使好像成就了一个既济的阶段，也只是流动的过程当中相对平衡稳定的阶段性过程而已。在《周易》的宇宙观当中，宇宙即过程，宇宙即意识，宇宙的时空流及意识流都是变动不居的，宇宙之意即时空之意，意会宇宙为宇宙之时，同构于人心之善即良知，时与良知是发，皆为人心通于天地之几。

[Illuminating Intentionality]

The little fox's head is soaked by the waves in the water. It is very dangerous to have one's head immersed in the water, which means that it is extremely difficult to carry out one's intentions. The head is the physical basis for the initiation of intention, and the brain in the head is the basis for the existence and initiation of intention. Therefore, if the "head" gets wet, it is extremely dangerous for the initiation of intention, and it is difficult to last long.

But the transformation of intentions often requires putting oneself in danger and surviving, that is, finding life in a desperate situation. An established intentional context itself is a process, and the cosmos of the *Book of Changes*, that is, the flow of consciousness, is also a process. Even if it seems to have achieved a stage of success, it is only a relatively balanced and stable stage in the flowing process. In the cosmology of the *Book of Changes*, the cosmos is process, the cosmos is consciousness, the space-time flow and consciousness flow of the cosmos are ever-changing, so the intentionality of the cosmos is the intentionality of space-time, and when the cosmos is comprehended as the cosmos, it is the same structure in the goodness of the human heart-mind, or conscience. When timing and conscience initiate, both are ways in which the human heart-mind connects to heaven and earth.

第三章　易经明意
——爻意分说（下经）

火水未济（卦六十四）　（坎下离上）

Weiji (Unfinished), Fire and Water (Hexagram 64)　(Kan below, Li above)

　　《周易》全书都在启发人们，为自己的意念寻找到合适的方向，不断调整自己的意向到最合适的程度。不料到了最后一卦，却说这个工作没有完成，也不可能完成。一方面意向的修行与调整永远不会终结，除非意向的主体不再活动，也就是因死亡或者昏厥等而丧失意识发动的能力。其他时刻，人的心意都在活动，也都一直有方向。另一个方面是未济揭示着意念方向未定的永恒性，自我意念的修为永远也不可能完成，所谓的完成只能是阶段性的，只要意识在动，当下的意念方向只能是未定的，因为意念只要活动就有无数的可能性，有无数的方向，所以意念方向总是未济的，这是意向性当下的未济状态的现实合理性。

　　鼎立尚未成功，意总是要有方向。意向重新开始，周而复始，如离之光明鼎立之后还需有向，意向不能停止。

The entire *Book of Changes* inspires people to find a suitable direction for their intentions and constantly adjust their intentions to the most appropriate level. Unexpectedly, the last hexagram states that the work is not yet completed and cannot be completed. On one hand, the practice and adjustment of intention will never end unless the subject of intention is no longer active, that is, dies or faints and loses the ability to initiate consciousness. At other times, people's intentions are active and always have a direction. On the other hand, Hexagram Weiji (Unfinished) reveals the eternity of the undetermined direction of intentions. The cultivation of self-intention can never be completed; any so-called

655

completion can only be staged. As long as consciousness is moving, the current direction of intentions can only be undetermined, because as long as intentions are active, they have countless possibilities and directions, so the direction of intentions is always unfinished. This is the realistic rationality of the current unfinished state of intentionality.

Accomplishing the revolution has not yet succeeded, so there must always be a direction for intention. Intentions start again, starting over again and again, as if establishing a bright sun like Hexagram Li (Illumination), which represents the direction of intentionality that is still needed after the revolution, so intentions towards the future never stop.

未济，亨。小狐汔（qì）济，濡其尾，无攸利。

《彖》曰："未济，亨"，柔得中也。"小狐汔济"，未出中也。"濡其尾，无攸利"，不续终也。虽不当位，刚柔应也。

《象》曰：火在水上，未济。君子以慎辨物居方。

【明译】

未济卦象征事情还没成功，努力成就事情还是可以亨通。小狐狸即将渡河成功的时候，弄湿了尾巴，没什么好处。

《彖传》说：事情还没成功，努力成就事情还是可以亨通，因为六五柔顺居中持守正道。小狐狸即将渡河成功的时候，是指它还没有离开坎险之中。弄湿了尾巴，没什么好处，可能因为力小游不到头，功败垂成。虽然每个爻都在不合适的位置上，但刚柔都相应（还是有可能做成事情的）。

《象传》说：上卦离为火，下卦坎为水，火向上，水向下，相克背离，火在水上就是未济。君子看到火跟水很不合的情况，就要审慎分辨人事和物类，让他们各得其所。

Hexagram Weiji (Unfinished) symbolizes that things have not yet succeeded, but things can still prosper if one works hard to achieve them. When the little fox is about to successfully cross the river, it will do no good if it wets its tail.

The *Judgment Commentary* (*Tuan Zhuan*) says: Things have not yet succeeded, but one can still succeed if one works hard to achieve them, because the Six (*yin*/soft line) in the fifth place is meek and stays on the upright *dao*. When the little fox is about to successfully cross the river, it means that it has not yet left the danger. There is no benefit from getting the tail wet, perhaps because one is not strong enough to swim to the end, and one's success will be ruined. Although every line is in an inappropriate position, the strength and softness are corresponding (it is still possible to accomplish things).

The *Image Commentary* (*Xiang Zhuan*) says: The upper Trigram Li is fire, and the lower Trigram Kan is water. Fire is upward and water is downward. They are in conflict with and separating from each other. If fire is above water, it means Weiji (Unfinished). When an exemplary person sees that fire and water are incompatible with each other, one must carefully distinguish between people and things, so that each can find its proper place.

【明意】

未济卦既有事情成功又重新开始新一轮周期，也有功败垂成的意味。未济卦名主要指的是还没有渡过河水，带有未完成、未成功之意。小狐狸渡水快要过去了，但还没有游出水中，可是小狐狸的尾巴已经被水沾湿了，那是会有危险的，这样的危险征兆当然不会没有什么好处，原因可能是小狐狸力气太小，最后会有无力坚持游到头的危险，所以很可能功败垂成。

内险之意，是因为需要外在的光明遍照，让此心光明，充满敬慎，去除狐疑，专心致志，众志成城，也就渡过去了，可谓修整团队再出发，但要时刻把握自居的分寸。

[Illuminating Intentionality]

Hexagram Weiji (Unfinished) has the meaning both of success and starting a new cycle, and of failure. The name of the Weiji hexagram mainly refers to the fact that the river has not been crossed yet, with the meaning of unfinished and as yet unsuccessful. The little fox is about to cross the water, but it has not yet swam out of the water, and its tail has been wetted by the water, which is dangerous. Of course, such a dangerous sign will not be without some benefits. The reason may be that the little fox has too little strength, and will be in danger of not being able to swim to the end, so is likely to fail.

The intentionality of internal danger is that it requires external light to shine over it, so that the heart can be bright and full of respect, eliminate doubts, concentrate on one thing, and unite as one to overcome it. It can be said that the team is reorganized and sets off again, but must always grasp a sense of proportion.

初六：濡其尾，吝。

《象》曰："濡其尾"，亦不知极也。

【明译】

初六：小狐狸渡河尾巴沾了水，会有麻烦。

《象传》说：小狐狸渡河尾巴沾了水，说明不知道自己能够承受的极限。

Six (*yin*/soft line) in the first place: If the little fox crosses the river and gets its tail wet, it will be in trouble.

The *Image Commentary* (*Xiang Zhuan*) says: The little fox crossed the river and got water on its tail, indicating that it did not know the limits of what it could bear.

【明意】

从人的角度看，人的意能是有限的，功业再大也是有限的，所以建功立业都只能是未济的。以这样的心态警示自己，无论功业多大，都是未完成的状态，不可过度执着，不宜过度在意，《周易》最后要人们保持平易的意境，用轻松的心态，去积极成事。

虽然未济卦可谓成功之后最困难的状态，因为一爻都有相应者，所以可以理解为事情在最难的时候，都会有转机。

[Illuminating Intentionality]

From a human point of view, human intentional energy is limited, and no matter how great one's achievements are, they are also limited, so any achievements can only be incomplete. Using this mentality, one can warn oneself that no matter how great one's achievements are, they are still in an unfinished state, so one should not be overly persistent or concerned. The *Book of Changes* finally requires people to maintain a peaceful mood and use a relaxed attitude to actively accomplish things.

Although Hexagram Weiji (Unfinished) can be said to be the most difficult state after success, because every line has a counterpart, it can be understood that things will always turn around at the most difficult time.

九二：曳其轮，贞吉。

《象》曰：九二"贞吉"，中以行正也。

【明译】

九二：拖住车轮，不让它快进，持守正道可以吉祥。

《象传》说：九二持守正道可以吉祥，因为九二在卦变中一直在中位，行走得光明正直。

Nine (*yang*/strong line) in the second place: Hold the wheel to prevent it from advancing quickly. Staying on the upright *dao* can bring good fortune.

The *Image Commentary* (*Xiang Zhuan*) says: The Nine (*yang*/strong line) in the second place can be auspicious by adhering to the upright *dao*, because the Nine (*yang*/strong line) in the second place has always been in a central position during the hexagram-changes and walks brightly and uprightly.

【明意】

车子难行，有意向而无法去伸展，中道给了保持原意向的转机。意向发动被阻止拖拽是正常的现象，而且意念实化之后，又会有他意来牵扯，不让实化的过程圆满，所以未济除了本身一直处于未完成的状态之外，也有情境迫使自己的意念处于未完成的途中之意。对自我意念实化的阶段性来说，意念可以暂时达到既济的完成状态，但情境永远是未完成的，也会影响意念本身处于未完成的状态。

[Illuminating Intentionality]

The carriage is difficult to move, and there is an intention but cannot be extended. The central *dao* gives a chance to maintain the original intention. It is a normal phenomenon for the initiation of an intention to be blocked or dragged, and after the intention is realized, there will be other intentions involved, preventing the concretization process from being completed. Therefore, in addition to being in an unfinished state, Hexagram Weiji (Unfinished) also has situations that force one's own intentions into an unfinished state. In the stage of concretizing of self-intention, the intention can temporarily reach a complete state of success, but the situation is always unfinished, which will also affect the intention itself to be in an unfinished state.

六三：未济，征凶。利涉大川。

《象》曰："未济，征凶"，位不当也。

【明译】

六三：还没成功，继续征进有凶险，有利于渡过大河险阻。

《象传》说：还没成功，继续征进有凶险，因为位置不当。

Six (*yin*/soft line) in the third place: It has not yet succeeded, but there are dangers in continuing to march. It will be helpful for crossing a great river.

The *Image Commentary* (*Xiang Zhuan*) says: It has not been successful yet. It is dangerous to continue the expedition because the position is inappropriate.

【明意】

事情做多了，最后重新开始，步步都难。虽然未完成，但因为有正应，所以有呼应的力量，阴意得到阳意的指引，可以预计将来最终能够完成大事。可见未济的计划受外在情境和呼应力量的影响，如果呼应的力量有力，自然可能实化意向，达到目标，也就是有了比较合理的意识方向。

[Illuminating Intentionality]

After going too far, starting over again becomes difficult every step of the way. Although it is not yet completed, it has the power to respond because it has a positive response. *Yin* intentionality is guided by *yang*, and it can be expected that great things will be completed in the future. It can be seen that Hexagram Weiji (Unfinished)'s plan is affected by the external situation and the force of response. If the force of response is strong, it will naturally be possible to realize the intention and achieve the goal, that is, there will be a more reasonable direction of consciousness.

九四：贞吉，悔亡。震用伐鬼方，三年，有赏于大国。

《象》曰："贞吉悔亡"，志行也。

【明译】

九四：坚守正道就可以吉祥，没有什么值得后悔的。如雷震而起征伐遥远的鬼方，三年成功并得到大国的赏赐。

《象传》说：坚守正道就可以吉祥，没有什么值得后悔的，因为九四的心志得到了实现。

Nine (*yang*/strong line) in the fourth place: If one sticks to the upright *dao*, one will be fortunate, and there is nothing to regret. Like thunder, he rose up to conquer distant Kingdom Guifang. He succeeded in three years and was rewarded by the empire.

The *Image Commentary* (*Xiang Zhuan*) says: If one sticks to the upright *dao*, one will be fortunate. There is nothing to regret, because the aspirations of the Nine (*yang*/strong line) in the fourth place have been realized.

【明意】

意向可行，即心志可以实化，但未定的意向在尚未展开的境遇当中是如何可能的呢？此爻意向指向鬼方，指代只要坚守正道就可以努力实化自己意念的状态，如果发动意念去征伐他国，应该最后能够成功，表示纵然在未济这种尚未完成的状态，也并不是不可以计划，而是只要根据自己的实力让意念发动行于中道，仍然可以成就大事。

关键在于是否推行自己的心志，只要推行了，坚持正道去做，忧悔自然消亡，这是行动哲学，是行高于知，行先于知的哲学，只要努力践行，知识的多寡和情感的纠结，都可以在变动的时空当中慢慢改换，在延伸当中修正，展开并得以实化。

[Illuminating Intentionality]

Intentions are feasible, that is, intentions can be concretized, but how is an undecided intention possible in a situation that has not unfolded? The intention of this line points to the Kingdom Guifang, referring to the state in which, as long as one sticks to the upright *dao*, one can work hard to concretize one's intentions. If one launches one's intentions to conquer other countries, one should be able to succeed in the end. It means that even in the unfinished state of Hexagram Weiji (Unfinished), it is not unfulfilled. One can plan, but as long as one lets one's intentions move on the middle *dao* according to one's own strength, one can still accomplish great things.

The key is whether to implement one's own aspiration. As long as one implements it, sticks to the upright *dao* and acts, regrets will disappear naturally. This is a philosophy of action, the philosophy that action is higher than knowledge, and action precedes knowledge. As long as one practices hard, the degree of knowledge and emotional entanglements will be different, and can be slowly changed in a changing time and space, modified in the process of extension, expanded and concretized.

六五：贞吉，无悔。君子之光，有孚，吉。

《象》曰："君子之光"，其辉"吉"也。

【明译】

六五：坚守正道可以获吉，没有忧悔。君子的光辉在于取信于人，自然是吉祥的。

《象传》说：君子的光辉，是在他的光辉照耀之下获得了吉祥。

Six (*yin*/soft line) in the fifth place: If one sticks to the upright *dao*, one will gain good fortune and have no regrets. The brilliance of an exemplary person lies in winning the trust of others, which is naturally auspicious.

The *Image Commentary* (*Xiang Zhuan*) says: The brilliance of an exemplary person is auspicious under the illumination of his brilliance.

【明意】

君子心意发动即有光辉，其意向光明所以光辉显要。光辉都是吉祥的，能带给人们好运。这是心意虽然未定，但状态很好，意向的潜质实化的过程好像内心的光辉自然映照其境。君子的心意之光在于诚于人天之意。心意真诚至极，即使在未完成的事业当中，也时刻散发着仁天之意的光辉。

这一爻是本《周易》修心制意境界的顶峰，意向光辉而吉祥，这是心意发动的最高境界。

[Illuminating Intentionality]

When an exemplary person's intentionality is initiated, there is brilliance, and one's intentionality is bright, so one is radiant and conspicuous. The brilliance is auspicious and can bring people good fortune. This is a situation where, although the intentionality is undecided, it is in a good state, and the potential of the intentionality is concretized, as if the inner radiance is naturally reflected in it. The light of an exemplary person's intentionality lies in being sincere to the cosmological intentionality of humanity and heaven. The heart-mind is extremely sincere, and even in unfinished business, it always exudes the brilliance of benevolent heaven's intentionality.

This line is the pinnacle of the state in cultivating the heart-mind and regulating intentionality in the *Book of Changes*, and the intention is glorious and auspicious. This is the highest state of intentionality initiation.

上九：有孚于饮酒，无咎。濡其首，有孚失是。

《象》曰："饮酒濡首"，亦不知节也。

【明译】

上九：饮酒的时候，很有诚信，没有问题。但如果喝多了，自己拿酒浇湿了头，那么即使有诚信也会功败垂成。

《象传》说：酗酒到自己拿酒浇湿头部的地步，说明上九也太不知道节制了。

Nine (*yang*/strong line) in the top place: When drinking wine, one is very sincere and has no problems. But if one drinks too much and wets one's head with wine, even with sincerity, one's success will end in failure.

The *Image Commentary* (*Xiang Zhuan*) says: One drank too much to the point of pouring wine on one's head, which shows that the Nine (*yang*/strong line) in the top place did not know how to control oneself.

【明意】

这一爻是饮酒作乐不知节制，放纵自己，功败垂成，非常遗憾。象辞强调太不知节制了，好比饮酒时把头都淹湿了，说明纵欲酗酒到了相当过分的程度。一解像小狐狸那样头都浸到水里面去了。

　　过分沉浸在不能成功中，反而有潜在的危险，事情做不成，意向没法实现，只能重新来过。心意到了极端的情况就过了，会迷失自己，好像喝酒太多，最后意识都不清醒了。那就从自明的未济到了无明的未济了。当意念不发动的时候，就跟昏厥与死去都差不多，那时意念已经没有合适的方向了。如果到了最后，功败垂成，那就太过遗憾和可惜了。《周易》之教，要求人的心意不可到达上亢之境，因为那样过度失去节制就失去《周易》修心修意之教的意义。

[Illuminating Intentionality]

This line is about drinking and having fun without restraint, indulging oneself, and failing on the brink of success, which is very regrettable. The *Image Commentary* (*Xiang Zhuan*) emphasizes that it is being too out of control, like getting one's head wet when drinking, indicating that one has indulged in excessive amounts of wine. It is explained as a little fox with its head immersed in the water.

Being too immersed in what cannot succeed will lead to potential dangers. Things will not be done, intentions will not be concretized, and one can only start over. When one's intentionality reaches an extreme level, one will lose oneself, as if one drank too much, and eventually one will lose consciousness. Then it moves from the self-evidence of incompletion to the ignorance of incompletion. When intentions are not initiated, it is almost in a state like fainting or dying. At that time, intentions have no suitable direction. It would be a great pity if one fails right before the success. The teachings of the *Book of Changes* require that people's heart-minds should not reach a state of overexertion, because if they lose too much control, they will lose the meaning of the teachings of the *Book of Changes* on cultivating intentionality and the heart-mind.-